Other Kaplan Books on Law School Admissions:

Law School Admissions Adviser
Two Real LSATs Explained
LSAT 180

LSAT*
2004

By the Staff of Kaplan, Inc.

Simon & Schuster

New York · London · Sydney · Toronto

*LSAT is a registered trademark of Law School Admission Council, which is not affiliated with this product.

Kaplan Publishing
Published by Simon & Schuster
1230 Avenue of the Americas
New York, NY 10020

"The Kaplan Advantage™ Stress Management System" by Dr. Ed Newman and Bob Verini, Copyright © 1996, Kaplan, Inc.

"Hazardous Waste and Environmental Liability: An Historical Perspective," by Martin V. Melosi, *Houston Law Review*, Volume 25: 741, 1988. Reprinted by permission of the *Houston Law Review*.

"Pool Coverage, Press Access, and Presidential Debates: What's Wrong with This Picture?" by Wendy S. Zeligson, *Cardozo Law Review,* Vol. 9, 1988. Reprinted by permission of *Cardozo Law Review*.

"The Profit Motive in Medicine," by Dan W. Brock and Allen E. Buchanan. *Journal of Medicine and Philosophy,* Vol. 12, 1987. Reprinted by permission of *Journal of Medicine and Philosophy*.

"The Republic Reborn by Steven Watts," by Fred Anderson, *American Historical Review*, vol. 94, no. 2 (April 1989), p. 516. Reprinted with permission of *American Historical Review*.

"Equal Pay for Jobs of Comparable Worth: An Analysis of the Rhetoric," by Judith Olans Brown, Phyllis Tropper Baumann, and Elaine Miller Melnick, *Harvard Civil Rights & Civil Liberties Review*, No. 1, Winter 1986. Copied with permission; copyright 1988 by the President and Fellows of Harvard College.

Project Editor: Charli Engelhorn
Contributing Editors: Albert Chen and Justin Serrano
Production Editor: Maude Spekes
Interior Production: Renée Mitchell
Production Manager: Michael Shevlin
Managing Editor: Déa Alessandro
Executive Editor: Del Franz

Special thanks to: Nicole Shiu-Horowitz, Eileen Mager, Ingrid Multhopp, Grace Begany, Hugh Haggerty, Jan Gladish, Larissa Shmailo, Dave Chipps, Ben Paris, and Matthew Dunne.

Manufactured in the United States of America
Published simultaneously in Canada

June 2003
10 9 8 7 6 5 4 3 2

ISBN 0-7432-4144-4

CONTENTS

www.kaptest.com/booksonline

Want more help preparing for the LSAT? Log on to **www.kaptest.com/booksonline** to access a wide selection of additional practice questions. Prepare for all parts of the LSAT online, or focus on those sections where you feel weakest.

Access to this selection of Kaplan's online LSAT practice questions is free of charge to purchasers of this book. When you log on, you'll be asked to input the ISBN number of the book you purchased (see the bar code on the back cover). And you'll be asked for a specific password derived from a passage in this book, so have your book handy when you log on.

www.kaptest.com/publishing

The material in this book is up-to-date at the time of publication. However, the Educational Testing Service (ETS) may have instituted changes in the test or test registration process after this book was published. Be sure to carefully read the materials you receive when you register for the test.

If there are any important late-breaking developments—or any changes or corrections to the Kaplan test preparation materials in this book—we will post that information online at **www.kaptest.com/publishing**. Check to see if there is any information posted there for readers of this book.

READER'S COMMENTS

Here's what some of our readers have to say about previous editions of Kaplan's *LSAT*:

"The practice test questions were exactly like those on the real test. Thanks, you guys, for putting together such a top-quality study guide."
—*Michelle Petrone, Birmingham, Alabama*

"An excellent aid to ace the LSAT; it significantly improves test-taking skills, helps identify and eliminate weaknesses, and is easy to read."
—*Dinara Tuychiera, Houston, Texas*

"I found this book user-friendly, comforting, and insightful. It was of great assistance to me. Thank you!"
—*Francis Wey III, Altamont, New York*

"This is the second book I've used, and it was much clearer and more useful than the first book I used. My LSAT score proved I had chosen the right book."
—*Patrick Geile, Denver, Colorado*

"'When to Apply,' 'Where to Apply,' and 'How to Apply' sections are all full of essential info for the first-time applicant. Timetables are great."
—*Andrea Monk, Fort Worth, Texas*

"Even though I'm studying for a Canadian law school, this book was excellent! There was such clarity in the explanations—it made studying fun!"
—*Sarah Dawn Adams, Ontario, Canada*

HOW TO USE THIS BOOK

We're confident that Kaplan's *LSAT* and the accompanying CD-ROM will serve as indispensable resources for you in your quest to master the LSAT exam. For technical information on how to use the CD-ROM, turn to the "CD-ROM Installation and Technical Support" section at the back of this book. What follows are some suggestions on how to most effectively use the various components of the book and software in your test preparation:

STEP ONE: Familiarize Yourself with the LSAT

Kaplan's live LSAT course has set the industry standard for decades. We've distilled the main techniques and approaches from our course in a clear, easy-to-grasp format. We'll introduce you to the mysteries of the LSAT and show you how to take control of the test-taking experience on all levels. In addition, at the beginning of each chapter, you'll find a Highlights box containing the most important concepts in the chapter. You can use these Highlights as a guidepost for study and a review before the test.

- **LSAT Diagnostic Test.** Before you embark upon our LSAT training, try your hand at the diagnostic test on the CD-ROM. This test will give you a taste of what to expect on the LSAT and will help you to identify areas in which you need more practice.
- **LSAT Test Content.** Our CD-ROM offers a wide array of question-type tutorials and practice lessons to hone the skills you'll need to ace the LSAT. In the book, turn to the four chapters devoted to the content of the LSAT—"Logical Reasoning," "Logic Games," "Reading Comprehension," and "The Writing Sample"—for specific methods, strategies, and practice problems for every kind of LSAT question you're likely to see.
- **Taking Control of the Test.** The peculiarities of a standardized test can sometimes be used to your advantage; we can teach you how. This chapter will also provide you with the proper test attitude for executing all you've learned. And don't forget to check out the "Secrets of the LSAT" section of the CD-ROM.

You'll also find the most important points regarding the LSAT and invaluable Kaplan teacher advice in easy-to-read sidebars throughout the book.

STEP TWO: Take a Kaplan LSAT Practice Test

Your next step is to use one of the full-length Practice Tests—a timed, simulated LSAT—as a test run for the real thing. We suggest Final Test One on the CD-ROM to take advantage of our advanced diagnostics.

Kaplan's software allows you to take this Practice Test, termed "Final Test," under enforced time conditions. The computer will record and analyze your timing, confidence level, use of elimination strategies, and answer-changing habits.

The software will also analyze your overall performance by question type and content area, provide concise explanations for each question, and give you a score for the exam.

STEP THREE: Use the Strategic Explanations

These explanations for every test question, found both in the book and on the CD-ROM, will enable you to understand your mistakes so that you don't make them again on the test. Try not to confine yourself to the explanations of the questions you've answered incorrectly. Instead, read all of the explanations—to reinforce good habits and to sharpen your skills so that you can get the right answer even faster and more reliably next time.

STEP FOUR: Review to Shore up Weak Points

Go back to the test content chapters and CD-ROM question-type tutorials to review the areas in which your performance was weak. Also, for access to a wide selection of additional preparation and practice questions, log on to *www.kaptest.com/booksonline*. You will need to have your book handy.

STEP FIVE: Repeat the Process with the Other Practice Tests

Once you've gone through the steps outlined above with Practice Test One, repeat the steps with Practice Tests Two and Three in the book, and then try your hand at a second full-length CD-ROM test, termed "Final Test 2." After you've completed all the practice tests and done all you can to master the concepts with which you continue to have difficulty, reread the "Taking Control of the Test" chapter to make sure you're in top shape for the test.

Follow these five steps, and you can be confident that your application to law school will be as strong as it can be.

Special Bonus: "Getting into Law School" Section

Sure, your LSAT performance is a very important criterion in your application, so the bulk of this book is devoted to test prep. But law schools base their admissions decisions on far more than just the LSAT. In fact, a host of other parts of your application can make or break your candidacy. So, to give you the very best odds, we provide expert advice to lead you through the parts of the application process before and beyond the LSAT. We'll give you an overview of the application process, drawing from our years of helping law school candidates, and outline a plan to make your application as strong as it can be. We've also included checklists and schedules to keep you on track.

A Special Note for International Students

In recent years, U.S. law schools have experienced an increase in inquiries from non-U.S. citizens, some of whom are already practicing lawyers in their own countries. This surge of interest in the U.S. legal system has been attributed to the spread of the global economy. When business people from outside the United States do business with Americans, they often find themselves doing business under the American legal system. Gaining insight into how the American legal system works is of great interest around the world.

This new international interest in the U.S. legal system is having an effect on law schools. Many schools have developed special programs to accommodate the needs of this special population of lawyers and students from around the globe. If you are an international student or lawyer interested in learning more about the American legal system, or if you are considering attending law school in the United States, Kaplan can help you explore your options.

Getting into a U.S. law school can be especially challenging for students from other countries. If you are not from the United States, but are considering attending law school in the United States, here is what you'll need to get started.

- If English is not your first language, you'll probably need to take the TOEFL (Test of English as a Foreign Language), or provide some other evidence that you are proficient in English. Most law schools require a minimum computer TOEFL score of 250 (600 on the paper-based TOEFL) or better.

- Depending on the program to which you are applying, you may also need to take the LSAT (Law School Admissions Test). All law schools in the United States require the LSAT for their J.D. programs. LL.M. programs usually do not require the LSAT. Kaplan will help you determine if you need to take the LSAT. If you must take the LSAT, Kaplan can help you prepare for it.

- Since admission to law school is quite competitive, you may want to select three or four programs and complete applications for each school.

- You should begin the process of applying to law schools or special legal studies programs at least eighteen months before the fall of the year you plan to start your studies. Most programs will have only September start dates.

- In addition, you will need to obtain an I-20 Certificate of Eligibility from the school you plan to attend if you intend to apply for an F-1 Student Visa to study in the United States.

- For an overview of the law school admissions process, see the Getting into Law School section of this book.

General Intensive English

Kaplan's General Intensive English classes are designed to help you improve your skills in all areas of English and to increase your fluency in spoken and written English. Classes are available for beginning to advanced students, and the average class size is 12 students.

General English Self-Study

For students needing a flexible schedule, this course helps improve general fluency skills. Kaplan's General English Self-Study course employs the communicative approach and focuses on vocabulary building, reading and writing. You will receive books, audio and video materials as well as three hours of instructor contact per week.

TOEFL and Academic English

This course provides you with the skills you need to improve your TOEFL score and succeed in an American university or graduate program. It includes advanced reading, writing, listening, grammar and conversational English, plus university admissions counseling. You will also receive training for the TOEFL using Kaplan's exclusive computer-based practice materials.

TOEFL Test Preparation Course

Kaplan's TOEFL course can help you learn test taking skills and strategies to raise your TOEFL score. This course is for intermediate to advanced English learners with a TOEFL score of at least 517 (187 computer).

LSAT Test Preparation Course

The LSAT is a crucial admission criterion for law schools in the United States. A high score can help you stand out from other applicants. This course includes the skills you need to succeed on each section of the LSAT, as well as access to Kaplan's exclusive practice materials.

Other Kaplan Programs

Since 1938, more than 3 million students have come to Kaplan to advance their studies, prepare for entry to American universities, and further their careers. In addition to the above programs, Kaplan offers courses to prepare for the SAT, GMAT, GRE, MCAT, DAT, USMLE, NCLEX, and other standardized exams at locations throughout the United States.

Applying to Kaplan International Programs

To get more information, or to apply for admission to any of Kaplan's programs for international students and professionals, contact us at:

Kaplan International Programs
700 South Flower, Suite 2900
Los Angeles, CA 90017, USA
Phone (if calling from within the United States): 800-818-9128
Phone (if calling from outside the United States): 213-452-5800
Fax: 213-892-1364
Website: www.kaplaninternational.com
Email: world@kaplan.com

Kaplan is authorized under federal law to enroll nonimmigrant alien students.
Kaplan is accredited by ACCET (Accrediting Council for Continuing Education and Training).
Test names are registered trademarks of their respective owners.

MASTERING THE LSAT

CHAPTER ONE

An Introduction to the LSAT

The LSAT is unlike any other test you've ever taken in your academic career. Most of the tests you've encountered in high school and college have probably been content-based tests, that is, tests requiring you to recall and be conversant with a certain body of facts, formulas, theorems, or other acquired knowledge. The LSAT, on the other hand, is a skills-based test. It doesn't ask you to spit back memorized facts. It doesn't ask you to apply learned formulas to specific problems. In fact, all you'll be asked to do on the LSAT is think—thoroughly, quickly, and strategically. There's literally no content to study!

Sound too good to be true? Well, before you get the idea that you can waltz into the most important test of your life stone cold, let's clarify the very important distinction between study and preparation.

If you were taking the National Medical Boards, you would need to study things like anatomy beforehand, to make sure you were up-to-date on all of the required knowledge in that area. But the LSAT isn't designed to evaluate your grasp of this kind of field-specific knowledge. Instead, it's designed to test only the critical reading and analytical thinking skills that have been deemed necessary (by the governing body of law schools themselves) for success in the first year of law school. These are skills that you

Kaplan Tip

The LSAT should be viewed just like any other part of your application—as an opportunity to show the law schools who you are and what you can do. If you can take control of your LSAT experience, you can take the fullest advantage of that opportunity.

Resources

If you plan to take the LSAT, you will need to obtain a copy of the *LSAT/LSDAS Registration & Information Book*. This book will provide you with the most up-to-date information on how to register for and take the LSAT and how to subscribe to the Law School Data Assembly Service. Call (215) 968-1001 or visit the LSAC website at www.lsac.org to order a copy.

already possess to some extent; you've acquired them gradually over the decade-and-a-half (or more) of your education. But what you probably haven't yet acquired is the know-how to use these skills to your best advantage in the rarified atmosphere of a standardized skills-based test.

And that's where test preparation—and this section of this book—comes in. In this section, we'll teach you to tailor your existing skills to the very specific and idiosyncratic tasks required by the LSAT. For example, you already know how to read, but we'll show you how to take your critical reading skills and use them most effectively to unlock the dense but highly structured arguments and passages on the LSAT. Similarly, while you've probably developed plenty of sound, logical ways of analyzing problems in everyday life, we'll teach you how to apply those natural deductive and analytical skills to the unusual demands of the Logic Games and Logical Reasoning sections of the LSAT.

So, while you can't technically study for a standardized skills-based test like the LSAT, you can and must prepare for it. And in the section that follows, we'll show you just how to do that.

Before launching into strategies, though, you need to know exactly what you're dealing with on the LSAT.

What Is the LSAT?

Let's start with the basics. The LSAT is, among other things, an endurance test. It consists of 175 minutes of multiple-choice testing, plus a 30 minute writing sample. Add in the administrative details at both ends of the testing experience, plus a break of 10 to 15 minutes midway through, and you can count on being in the test room for at least four-and-a-half to five hours.

It's a grueling experience, to say the least. And if you can't approach it with confidence and rigor, you'll quickly lose your composure. That's why it's so important that you take control of the test, just as you've been taking control of the rest of your application process.

The LSAT consists of five multiple-choice sections—two Logical Reasoning sections (Logical Reasoning), one Logic Games section (Logic Games), one Reading Comprehension section (Reading Comprehension), and one unscored "Experimental" section, which will look exactly like one of the other multiple-choice sections. In addition to these five sections, there will be a Writing Sample section in which you'll have to write a short essay.

Here's how the sections break down:

Section	Number of Questions	Minutes
Logical Reasoning	24–26	35
Logical Reasoning	24–26	35
Logic Games	23–24	35
Reading Comprehension	26–28	35
"Experimental"	24–28	35
Writing Sample	n/a	30

Some important things to note:

- The five multiple-choice sections can appear in any order, but the Writing Sample invariably comes last.
- The 10- to 15-minute break will come between the third and fourth sections of the test.
- The unscored "Experimental" section will look just like any other multiple-choice section, but it won't contribute to your score. (No, the test makers don't throw in the experimental section just to make you crazy; they do it to test out questions for use on future tests.)

We'll talk more about each of these question types in later chapters. But the big thing to take note of right now is this: You'll be answering roughly 125 multiple-choice questions (101 of which are scored) over the course of three intensive hours. That's just a little over a minute per question, not counting the time required to read passages and set up games. Clearly, you're going to have to move fast. But you can't let yourself get careless. Taking control of the LSAT means increasing the speed of your work without sacrificing accuracy!

Kaplan Tip

Many people could probably ace the LSAT if they had unlimited time. But they don't. To succeed on the LSAT, you've got to think smart and fast.

How Is the LSAT Scored?

You'll receive one and only one score for the LSAT (no separate scores for Logical Reasoning, Logic Games, and Reading Comprehension, in other words). That one score will fall in a range of 120 to 180. Here's how they'll calculate it.

There are roughly 101 scored multiple-choice questions on each exam:

- About 50 from the two Logical Reasoning sections
- About 24 from the Logic Games section
- About 27 from the Reading Comprehension section

Definition

The percentile figure tells you how many other test takers scored at or below your level. In other words, a percentile figure of 80 means that 80 percent did as well as or worse than you did and that only 20 percent did better.

Kaplan Rules

There's no penalty for a wrong answer on the LSAT, so never leave any questions blank, even if you have time for only a wild guess.

(Remember, the Writing Sample doesn't receive a numerical score, and the Experimental section, no matter what question type it contains, doesn't count.)

The number of these 101 questions that you answer correctly is your "raw score." Your raw score will then be multiplied by a complicated scoring formula (which is different for each test, to accommodate differences in difficulty level) to yield the "scaled score"—the one that will fall somewhere in that 120–180 range. This scaled score is what is reported to the schools as your LSAT score.

Because the test is graded on a largely preset curve, the scaled score will always correspond to a certain percentile, which will also be given on your score report. A score of 160, for instance, corresponds roughly to the 80th percentile, meaning that 80 percent of test takers scored at or below your level. The percentile figure is important because it allows law schools to get a sense quickly of where you fall in the pool of applicants.

All questions (again, except those on the Experimental section) are worth the same amount—one raw point—and there's no penalty for guessing. That means that you should always fill in an answer for every question, whether you get to that question or not! Never let time run out on any section without filling in an answer for every question.

What's a "Good" LSAT Score?

Of course, what you consider a good LSAT score depends on your own expectations and goals, but here are a few interesting statistics:

If you got about half of all of the scored questions right (a raw score of roughly 50), you would earn a scaled score of roughly 147, putting you in about the 30th percentile—not a great performance. But on the LSAT, a little improvement goes a long way. In fact, getting only one additional question right every ten minutes would give you a raw score of about 64, pushing you into the 60th percentile—a huge improvement. That's why it's important to maximize your performance on every question. Just a few questions one way or the other can make a big difference in your score.

By the same token, however, you don't have to be perfect to do well. On most LSATs, you can get as many as 28 wrong and still remain in the 80th percentile or as many as 21 wrong and still remain in the 90th percentile. Even students who receive perfect scaled scores of 180 usually get a handful of questions wrong.

SOME SAMPLE PERCENTILES		
Percentile	Approx. Scaled Score (Range 120–180)	Approx. Raw Score
99th percentile	172	~91 correct out of 101
95th percentile	167	~84 correct out of 101
90th percentile	164	~80 correct out of 101
80th percentile	160	~73 correct out of 101
75th percentile	158	~69 correct out of 101
50th percentile	152	~59 correct out of 101

Note: Exact percentile-to-scaled-score relationships vary from test to test.

Teacher Tip

"When explaining to students why they should put down an answer for every question, I liken the test to a lottery where the tickets are free, and you have a one in five chance to win (one in four or three if you can eliminate some wrong answers). How could you not take the chance?"
—Jaelithe Russ
Kaplan Teacher
Akron, OH

Although many factors play a role in admissions decisions, the LSAT score is usually one of the most important. And—generally speaking—being average just won't cut it. Whereas the median LSAT score is somewhere around 152, you need a score of at least 163 to be considered competitive by most law schools. And if you're aiming for the top, you've got to do even better. According to *Careers 2000* (published by Kaplan/*Newsweek*), the median LSAT scores of the best law schools in the country, such as Yale, Stanford, and Columbia, range from the high 160s to the low 170s. That translates to a percentile figure of 95 and up.

What Kinds of Questions Are on the LSAT?

Now let's take a quick look at each question type you'll encounter on the test. We'll get into strategies and techniques later. For now, just familiarize yourself with the kinds of questions asked on each section.

Logical Reasoning

What It Is
Each of the two scored Logical Reasoning sections consists of 24 to 26 questions based on short passages we call "stimuli." Most stimuli take the form of an argument—i.e., a conclusion based on evidence. You need to

At a Glance

Logical Reasoning:
- Accounts for about 50 percent of your score
- Thirty-five minutes long
- Consists of two scored sections
- Usually consists of 24 to 26 questions each (common types: weakening, strengthening, assumption, main point, inference, parallel logic)
- Tests ability to understand, analyze, evaluate, and manipulate arguments. Each of these skills is essential during the first year of law school, where much of the work involves analyzing arguments embedded in legal cases
- Is so important that it's half the test

understand a stimulus argument to answer the one or two questions based on it. Some Logical Reasoning stimuli aren't arguments per se; they're a series of facts from which you must make logical deductions. Although you don't need to know the technical terms of formal logic, you do need the critical reasoning skills that enable you to analyze a stimulus and make judgments accordingly.

Why It's on the Test

The law schools want to see whether you can understand, analyze, evaluate, and manipulate arguments, and draw reliable conclusions—as every law student and attorney must. It's important to note that this question type makes up half of your LSAT score, so you know that the law schools value these skills.

What It's Like

Here are the directions to the section, along with a sample question:

Directions: This test is composed of questions that ask you to analyze the logic of statements or short paragraphs. You are to choose as the answer to each question the one choice you consider best on the basis of your common-sense evaluation of the statement and its assumptions. Although a question may seem to have more than one acceptable answer, there is only one best answer, and it is the one that does not entail making any illogical, extraneous, or conflicting assumptions about the question.

1. A study of twenty overweight men revealed that each man experienced significant weight loss after adding SlimDown, an artificial food supplement, to his daily diet. For three months, each man consumed one SlimDown portion every morning after exercising, and then followed his normal diet for the rest of the day. Clearly, anyone who consumes one portion of SlimDown every day for at least three months will lose weight and will look and feel his or her best.

   Which one of the following is an assumption on which the argument depends?

   (A) The men in the study will gain back the weight they lost if they discontinue the SlimDown program.
   (B) No other dietary supplement will have the same effect on overweight men.
   (C) The daily exercise regimen was not responsible for the effects noted in the study.

(D) Women will not experience similar weight reductions if they adhere to the SlimDown program for three months.

(E) Overweight men will achieve only partial weight loss if they do not remain on the SlimDown program for a full three months.

Choice (C) is correct. We'll show you how to approach Logical Reasoning questions like this in a later chapter.

Logic Games

What It Is
There are 23 to 24 questions in the Logic Games (a.k.a., Analytical Reasoning) section, and these are almost always based on four games, with five to seven questions each. They require an ability to reason clearly and deductively from a given set of rules or restrictions, all under strictly timed conditions.

Why It's on the Test
The section exists to test your command of detail, your formal deductive abilities, your understanding of how rules limit and order behavior (which is the very definition of law itself), and your ability to cope with many pieces of data simultaneously in the course of solving problems.

What It's Like
What follows are directions to the Logic Games section as well as a shortened sample game and questions:

Directions: Each group of questions is based on a set of conditions. You may wish to draw a rough sketch to help you answer some of the questions. Choose the best answer for each question and fill in the corresponding space on your answer sheet.

Questions 1–2
Five workers—Mona, Patrick, Renatta, Saffie, and Will—are scheduled to clean apartments on five days of a single week, Monday to Friday. There are three cleaning shifts available each day—a morning shift, an afternoon shift, and an evening shift. No more than one worker cleans on any given shift. Each worker works exactly two cleaning shifts during the week, but no one works more than one cleaning shift in a single day.

Exactly two workers clean on each day of the week.
Mona and Will clean on the same days of the week.

At a Glance

Logic Games:
* Thirty-five minutes long
* Accounts for just under 25 percent of your score
* Consists of 23 to 24 questions
* Four games (common types: sequencing, grouping, matching)
* Tests how rules create systems of order and limit possible outcomes
* Attention to detail is key, as is the ability to maintain awareness of multiple facts simultaneously
* Basic logic is important: *if* versus *only if*; the logical meaning of *or*; the contrapositive
* Often the most intimidating section initially
* Often shows rapid improvement with practice

Patrick does not clean on any afternoon or evening shifts during the week.

Will does not clean on any morning or afternoon shifts during the week.

Mona cleans on two consecutive days of the week.

Saffie's second cleaning shift of the week occurs on an earlier day of the week than Mona's first cleaning shift

1. Which one of the following must be true?

   (A) Saffie cleans on Tuesday afternoon.
   (B) Patrick cleans on Monday morning.
   (C) Will cleans on Thursday evening.
   (D) Renatta cleans on Friday afternoon.
   (E) Mona cleans on Tuesday morning.

2. If Will does not clean on Friday, which one of the following could be false?

   (A) Renatta cleans on Friday.
   (B) Saffie cleans on Tuesday.
   (C) Mona cleans on Wednesday.
   (D) Saffie cleans on Monday.
   (E) Patrick cleans on Tuesday.

(Note that there are only two questions accompanying this game; a typical logic game will have five to seven questions.)

For Question 1, the answer is (C); for 2 it's (E). You'll see an explanation for this game in the Logic Games chapter of this book. Games are highly amenable to systematic technique and the proper use of scratchwork, which we'll discuss in detail in the Logic Games chapter.

Reading Comprehension

What It Is
The Reading Comprehension section consists of four passages, each about 450 words long, with five to eight questions per passage. These long excerpts of scholarly passages are reminiscent of the kind of prose found in law texts. The topics are chosen from the areas of social sciences, humanities, natural sciences, and law.

Why It's on the Test

The purpose of the section is to see whether you can quickly get the gist of long, difficult prose—just as you'll have to do in law school.

What It's Like

Here are the directions and a sample passage. Note that the passage below is just an excerpt from a full-length passage; standard passages are generally longer.

Directions: Each selection in this test is followed by several questions. After reading the selection, choose the best response to each question and mark it on your answer sheet. Your replies are to be based on what is stated or implied in the selection.

It has been suggested that post–World War II concepts of environmental liability, as they pertain to hazardous waste, grew out of issues regarding municipal refuse collection and disposal and industrial waste disposal in the period 1880–1940. To a great degree, the remedies available to Americans for dealing with the burgeoning hazardous waste problem were characteristic of the judicial, legislative, and regulatory tools used to confront a whole range of problems in the industrial age. At the same time, these remedies were operating in an era in which the problem of hazardous waste had yet to be recognized. It is understandable that an assessment of liability was narrowly drawn and most often restricted to a clearly identified violator in a specific act of infringement of the property rights of someone else. Legislation, for the most part, focused narrowly on clear threats to the public health and dealt with problems of industrial pollution meekly if at all.

4. The author's primary purpose is to discuss

   (A) contrasts in the legislative approaches to environmental liability before and after World War II
   (B) legislative trends which have been instrumental in the reduction of environmental hazardous wastes
   (C) the historical and legislative context in which to view post–World War II hazardous waste problems
   (D) early patterns of industrial abuse and pollution of the American environment
   (E) the growth of an activist tradition in American jurisprudence

The answer: (C). We'll show you how to approach Reading Comp questions (including this passage and its questions) in the Reading Comprehension chapter of this book.

Kaplan Tip

The LSAT battlefield is littered with the bodies of those who've tried to outsmart the test by guessing (incorrectly) which section is experimental and then using that time to rest. Don't take the chance! Perform your best on every section.

At a Glance

The Writing Sample:
- Thirty minutes long
- Is unscored
- Consists of one essay
- Task is to choose between two alternatives and make a sound argument for your choice. The alternatives are intentionally chosen to be equally valid, such that the decision to take one side or the other will not give any advantage
- Tests ability to write a clear, persuasive argument
- Does not require outside knowledge
- Is photocopied and sent to schools along with your score report
- Is read and used to evaluate applications more frequently than is commonly thought
- Helps schools choose between relatively equal candidates, decide on borderline candidates

The Experimental Section

The experimental (unscored) section allows Law Services to test questions for use on future tests. This section will look just like one of the others—either Logical Reasoning, Logic Games, or Reading Comprehension—so don't try to figure out which section is experimental and then just cruise through that section. That's an extremely risky proposition. Just do as well as you can on every section, and you're covered.

The Writing Sample

What It Is
The Writing Sample comes at the end of your LSAT day. You'll be given a scenario followed by two options and two criteria for decision making. And you'll have 30 minutes to make a written case that one option is superior.

Why It's on the Test
The writing sample shows the law schools whether you can argue for a position while breaking down the argument of an opponent. This essay is ungraded but is sent to law schools along with your LSAT score.

What It's Like
Here's a sample topic for a Writing Sample:

> The *Daily Tribune*, a metropolitan newspaper, is considering two candidates for promotion to business editor. Write an argument for one candidate over the other with the following considerations in mind:
>
> • The editor must train new writers and assign stories.
> • The editor must be able to edit and rewrite stories under daily deadline pressure.

Laura received a B.A. in English from a large university. She was managing editor of her college newspaper and served as a summer intern at her hometown daily paper. Laura started working at the *Tribune* right out of college and spent three years at the city desk covering the city economy. Eight years ago the paper formed its business section and Laura became part of the new department. After several years covering state business, Laura began writing on the national economy. Three years ago, Laura was named senior business and finance editor on the national business staff; she is also responsible for supervising seven writers.

Palmer attended an elite private college where he earned both a B.S. in business administration and an M.A. in journalism. After receiving his journalism degree, Palmer worked for three years on a monthly business magazine. He won a prestigious national award for a series of articles on the impact of monetary policy on multinational corporations. Palmer came to the *Tribune* three years ago to fill the newly created position of international business writer. He was the only member of the international staff for two years and wrote on almost a daily basis. He now supervises a staff of four writers. Last year, Palmer developed a bi-monthly business supplement for the *Tribune* that has proved highly popular and has helped increase the paper's circulation.

Obviously, there can be no right or wrong "answer" to the Writing Sample topic, but there are good and bad responses. We'll show you one possible response to this topic later, in the Writing Sample chapter.

How Do You Take Control of the LSAT?

Now that you have an idea of what the LSAT is and how it's set up, let's talk a little about how to approach the test in a general way. As we'll see, knowing the specific strategies for each type of question is only part of your task. To really do your best on the LSAT, you have to approach the entire test in the proper spirit. That spirit—and the proactive, take-control kind of thinking it inspires—is something we call the LSAT Mindset.

The LSAT Mindset
The LSAT Mindset is what you want to bring to every question, passage, game, and section you encounter. Being in the LSAT Mindset means reshaping the test-taking experience so that you are in the driver's seat. It means:

- Answering questions *if* you want to (by guessing on the most difficult questions rather than wasting time on them).
- Answering questions *when* you want to (by saving tough but doable games, passages, and questions for later, coming back to them after racking up points on the easy ones).
- Answering questions *how* you want to (by using our shortcuts and strategies to get points quickly and confidently, even if those methods aren't exactly what the test makers had in mind).

Kaplan Tip

Knowing strategies for each question type is only the beginning. You also have to approach the test with the proper attitude— a proactive, take-control kind of thinking we call the LSAT Mindset.

The following are some overriding principles of the LSAT Mindset that will be covered in depth in the chapters to come:

- Read actively and critically.
- Translate prose into your own words.
- Prephrase answer choices so you know what to look for.
- Save the toughest questions, passages, and games for last.
- Know the test and each of its components inside and out.
- Allow your confidence to build on itself.
- Take a full-length practice test the week before the test to break down the mystique of the real experience.
- Learn from your mistakes—it's not how much you practice, it's how much you get out of the practice.
- Look at the LSAT as a challenge, the first step in your legal career, rather than as an arbitrary obstacle to it.

That's what the LSAT Mindset boils down to: taking control. Being proactive. Being on top of the test experience so that you can get as many points as you can as quickly and as easily as possible.

To take control in this way, though, you have to be in command on all levels of the test. You may be great at individual Logical Reasoning questions, for instance, but that expertise won't do you much good unless you also have a plan for the entire Logical Reasoning section so that you get a chance to use your expertise on as many Logical Reasoning questions in a section as possible. That's why we've developed a plan for integrating strategies and techniques on all levels of the test—from the microlevel of individual question strategies, to the midlevel of handling the mechanics of a whole section, to the macrolevel of bringing the right kind of thinking to the entire test as a whole. We call this plan "The Kaplan Master Plan for the LSAT."

The Kaplan Master Plan

Test Content

Here we'll talk about managing individual questions, games, and reading passages. For success on the LSAT, you'll need to understand how to work through the specifics of each section. What's the difference between assumption and inference questions? What are the best ways of handling each? What's a matching game, and how do I approach it? How should I read a Reading Comp passage, and what should I focus on? What essay formats are best for the Writing Sample? We'll provide you with all of the information, strategies, and techniques you'll need to lay the groundwork for your LSAT success.

Teacher Tip

"Students have to become aware of all the common mistakes that can be made on a question. If they do this, they will be more careful not to make these errors."
—Derek Veazey
  Kaplan Teacher
  Fort Worth, TX

Test Expertise and Test Mentality

Next, we'll move up the ladder from individual questions, passages, and games to discussing how to manage full sections within the specified time limit. We'll show you how to handle the test mechanics so that you have a framework in which to use the content strategies—and the time to use them. Then we'll show you how to pull it all together, marshalling the strategies and expertise with the right mindset, so that you're in control of the entire test. With good test mentality, you can have everything at your fingertips—from the contrapositive to gridding techniques and from sequencing game strategies to pacing methods. We'll outline all of the subtle attitudinal factors, often overlooked, that are nonetheless integral to tying together all of the disparate elements of your training, so that you can perform your absolute best on the test.

> ## Teacher Tip
>
> "I always tell my students that the best gift that Kaplan can give them is that we can help them avoid being tested by ambush—they will always know what is coming. Remember, *you* are in control of the test. You are not a victim of this test: You get to decide how to approach it and in what order. The test makers can dictate the questions themselves but not how you handle them."
> —Fran Longo
>   Kaplan Teacher
>   Boston, MA

LSAT CHECKLIST

Before the Test

❑ **Get the** *LSAT/LSDAS Registration and Information Book.*
It's available at most colleges and law schools and at all Kaplan Centers; you can also order it by phone from LSDAS (Law School Data Assembly Service). Keep in mind that the information in this book is up-to-date at the time of publication, but LSDAS may have instituted changes after this book was published.

❑ **Choose a test date.**
June is best, October second best.

❑ **Complete and send LSAT/LSDAS Registration Form.**
Parts A, B, and D apply to the LSAT.
Make sure you list a first- and second-choice test center.
Don't forget to sign the form and include payment!

❑ **Receive your LSAT admission ticket.**
Check it for accuracy.
Check out your test center.

❑ **Create a test-prep calendar to ensure that you're ready by the day of the test.**

The Day of the Test

❑ **Make sure you have your LSAT admission ticket.**

❑ **Make sure you have one form of acceptable ID.**

❑ **Make sure you have the "LSAT Survival Kit" described in chapter 6 of this book.**

Logical Reasoning

- Master the seven basic principles of Logical Reasoning

- Familiarize yourself with the nine Logical Reasoning question types and the strategies for each

- Learn the Kaplan Four-Step Method for Logical Reasoning

- Practice working with contrapositives, inferences, and common LSAT arguments

- Complete the Logical Reasoning Practice Set

The fact that Logical Reasoning comprises half of your LSAT score is actually good news because you already have most of the Logical Reasoning skills you need for the test. In fact, we all do. But as we pointed out earlier, the LSAT tests your ability to use those skills thoroughly, quickly, and strategically in the context of a strictly timed, multiple-choice test.

On the LSAT, in law school, and in your law career, you'll need the ability to see and understand complex reasoning. It's not enough to sense whether an argument is strong or weak; you'll need to analyze precisely why it is so. This involves an even more fundamental skill, one that's called on by nearly every Logical Reasoning question—the ability to isolate and identify the various components of any given argument. That brings us to the basic principles of Logical Reasoning.

Note

There's nothing bizarre or esoteric about the skills you need for Logical Reasoning. You just have to learn how to adapt those skills to the peculiar requirements of a timed, standardized test.

The Seven Basic Principles of Logical Reasoning

Here are the basic things you must do to succeed on the Logical Reasoning sections.

Understand the Structure of Arguments

Success in Logical Reasoning depends on knowing the structure of arguments so that you can break an argument down into its core components.

First of all, let's clarify what's meant by the word *argument*. We don't mean a conversation in which two or more people are shouting at one another. No, the word *argument* in Logical Reasoning means any piece of text where an author puts forth a set of ideas and a point of view and attempts to support it.

Every LSAT Logical Reasoning stimulus—that is, every argument—is made up of two basic parts:

- The conclusion (the point that the author is trying to make)
- The evidence (the support that the author offers for the conclusion)

Success on this section hinges on your ability to identify these parts of the argument. There is no general rule about where conclusion and evidence appear in the argument—the conclusion could be the first sentence, followed by the evidence, or else it could be the last sentence, with the evidence preceding it, or any sentence in between. Consider the following short stimulus.

> The Brookdale Public Library will require extensive physical rehabilitation to meet the new building codes passed by the town council. For one thing, the electrical system is inadequate, causing the lights to flicker sporadically. Furthermore, there are too few emergency exits, and even those are poorly marked and sometimes locked.

Let's suppose that the author of the argument above were allowed only one sentence to convey her meaning. Do you think that she would waste her lone opportunity on the statement: "The electrical system at the Brookdale Public Library is inadequate, causing the lights to flicker sporadically"? Would she walk away satisfied that she got her main point across? Probably not. Given a single opportunity, she would have to state the first sentence: "The Brookdale Public Library will require extensive physical rehabilitation. . . ." This is her conclusion. If you pressed her for her *reasons* for making this statement, she would then cite the electrical and structural problems with the building. This is the evidence for her conclusion.

Teacher Tip

"Students seem to struggle most with logic games, reading for arguments, and the concept of necessity versus sufficiency. I help my students to understand in the clearest possible way what the terms *only if* and *not unless* mean for the behavior of arguments on the test. Learning to identify the scope and main idea of arguments is paramount in LSAT training."
—Chris Skinner
  Kaplan Teacher
  Santa Barbara, CA

But does that mean that an evidence-statement such as, "The electrical system at the Brookdale Public Library is inadequate" can't be a conclusion? No; we're saying that it's not the conclusion for this particular argument. Every idea, every new statement, must be evaluated in the context of the stimulus it appears in. For the sake of argument (no pun intended), let's see what a stimulus would look like in which the statement above serves as the conclusion:

> The electrical wiring at the Brookdale Public Library was installed over forty years ago and appears to be corroded in some places *(evidence)*. An electrician, upon inspection of the system, found a few frayed wires as well as some blown fuses *(evidence)*. Clearly, the electrical system at the Brookdale Public Library is inadequate *(conclusion)*.

To succeed in Logical Reasoning, you have to be able to determine the precise function of every sentence in the stimulus. Use structural signals or keywords when attempting to isolate evidence and conclusion. Words in the stimulus such as *because, for,* and *since* usually indicate evidence is about to follow, while words such as *therefore, hence, thus,* and *consequently* usually signal a conclusion.

The explanations of the Practice Tests in the back of this book discuss the structure of all 50 Logical Reasoning arguments on the test, so read these carefully to shore up your understanding of this crucial aspect of Logical Reasoning.

Preview the Question Stem

Looking over the question stem before reading the stimulus tells you in advance what to focus on in your initial reading of the stimulus. In effect, it gives you a jump on the question. For example, let's say the question attached to the original library argument above asked the following:

> The author supports her point about the need for rehabilitation at the Brookdale Library by citing which of the following?

If you were to preview this question stem before reading the stimulus, you would know what to look for in advance—namely, evidence, the "support" provided for the conclusion. Similarly, if the question asked you to find an assumption that the author is relying on, this would tell you in advance that there was a crucial piece of the argument missing, and you could begin to think about it right off the bat.

Previewing the stem allows you to set the tone of your attack on each particular question and thus will help you save time in the long run. As you'll soon see, this technique will come in especially handy when we discuss approaches to the various question types.

Kaplan Rules

Certain clue words and phrases can help you isolate the conclusion and the evidence in a stimulus.

Clues that signal evidence include *because, since, for, as a result of,* and *due to.*

Clues that signal the conclusion include *consequently, hence, therefore, thus, clearly, so,* and *accordingly.*

Kaplan Tip

It's much easier to understand and remember an argument if you restate it simply, in your own words.

Paraphrase the Author's Point

After you read the stimulus, you'll want to paraphrase the author's main argument, i.e., restate the author's ideas in your own words. Frequently, the authors in Logical Reasoning (and in Reading Comprehension, as we'll see) say pretty simple things in complex ways. But if you mentally translate the verbiage into a simpler form, you'll find the whole thing more manageable.

In the library argument, for instance, you probably don't want to deal with the full complexity of the author's stated conclusion:

> The Brookdale Public Library will require extensive physical rehabilitation to meet the new building codes just passed by the town council.

Instead, you probably want to carry a much simpler form of the point in your mind, something like:

> The library will need fixing up to meet new codes.

Often, by the time you begin reading through answer choices, you run the risk of losing sight of the gist of the stimulus. After all, you can concentrate on a certain amount of information at one time. Restating the argument in your own words will not only help you get the author's point in the first place, but it'll also help you hold on to it until you've found the correct answer.

Judge the Argument's Persuasiveness

You must read actively, not passively, on the LSAT. Active readers are always thinking critically, forming reactions as they go along. They constantly question whether the author's argument seems valid or dubious. On a section where many of the questions deal with finding flaws in the author's reasoning, it's imperative to read with a very critical eye.

For instance, how persuasive is the argument in the library stimulus? Well, it's pretty strong, since the evidence certainly seems to indicate that certain aspects of the library's structure need repair. But without more evidence about what the new building codes are like, we can't say for sure that the conclusion of this argument is valid. So this is a strong argument, but not an airtight one.

Remember, part of what you're called on to do in this section is to evaluate arguments, so don't allow yourself to fall into the bad habits of the passive reader—reading solely for the purpose of getting through the stimulus. Those who read this way are clueless when it comes to answering the questions and invariably find themselves having to read the stimuli twice or even three times. Then they wonder why they run out time on the section. Read the stimuli right the first time—with a critical eye and an active mind.

Make Sure You Answer the Question Being Asked

It's disheartening when you fully understand the author's argument and then blow the point by supplying an answer to a question that wasn't asked. For example, when you're asked for an inference supported by the argument, it does you no good to jump on the choice that paraphrases the author's conclusion. Likewise, if you're asked for an assumption, don't be fooled into selecting a choice that looks vaguely like a piece of the author's evidence.

When asked why they chose a particular wrong choice, students sometimes respond by saying such things as, "Well, it's true, isn't it?" and "Look, it says so right there," pointing to the stimulus. Well, that's simply not good enough. The question stem doesn't ask, "Which one of the following looks vaguely familiar to you?" It asks for something very specific. It's your job to follow the test makers' line of reasoning to the credited response.

Also, be on the lookout for "reversers"—words such as *not* and *except.* These little words are easy to miss, but they change entirely what kind of statement you're looking for among the choices.

Try to Prephrase an Answer

This principle, which is really an extension of the last one, is crucial. You must try to approach the answer choices with at least a faint idea of what the answer should look like. This is not to say that you should ponder the question for minutes until you're able to write out your own answer—it's still a multiple-choice test, so the right answer is there on the page. Just try to get in the habit of instinctively framing an answer to each question in your own mind.

If you can come up with a hint of a possible answer, scan the choices. Sure, the correct answer will be worded correctly, will be grammatically correct, and will be more fleshed out than your little seed of an idea. But if it matches your thought, you'll know it in a second. And you'll find that there's no more satisfying feeling in Logical Reasoning than prephrasing correctly, allowing you to choose the correct answer quickly and confidently.

For instance, let's say a question for the library argument went like this:

> The author's argument depends on which of the following assumptions about the new building codes?

Kaplan Rules

You read the argument. You see a major weakness in it. You find an answer choice that points out this weakness. You choose that answer. And you miss the point. Why? Because the question stem was asking for a statement that strengthened the argument, not one that weakened it. Don't let this happen to you. Always double-check the question stem.

Having thought about the stimulus argument, an answer to this question may have sprung immediately to mind—namely, the assumption that the new codes apply to existing buildings as well as to new buildings under construction. After all, the library will have to be rehabilitated to meet the new codes, according to the author. Clearly, the assumption is that the codes apply to existing buildings, and that's the kind of statement you would look for among the choices.

By the way, don't be discouraged if not all questions are good candidates for prephrasing answers. Some questions just won't have an answer that jumps out at you. But if used correctly, prephrasing can work on many, many questions. It will really boost your confidence and increase your speed on the section when you can come up with a glimmer of what the right answer should look like and then have it jump right off the page at you.

Keep the Scope of the Argument in Mind

One of the most important Logical Reasoning skills, particularly when you're at the point of actually selecting one of the five choices, is the ability to focus in on the scope of the argument. The majority of wrong choices on this section are wrong because they are "outside the scope." In everyday language, that simply means that these choices contain elements that don't match the author's ideas or that simply go beyond the context of the stimulus.

Some common examples of scope problems are choices that are too narrow, too broad, or literally have nothing to do with the author's points. Also, watch for and eliminate choices that are too extreme to match the argument's scope; they're usually signaled by words such as *all*, *always*, *never*, *none*, and so on. Choices that are more qualified are often correct for arguments that are moderate in tone and contain words such as *usually*, *sometimes*, *probably*, etcetera.

To illustrate the scope principle, let's look again at the question mentioned above:

The author's argument depends on which of the following assumptions about the new building codes?

Let's say one of the choices reads as follows:

(A) The new building codes are far too stringent.

Knowing the scope of the argument would help you to eliminate this choice very quickly. You know that this argument is just a claim about what the new codes will require—that the library be rehabilitated. It's not an argument about whether the requirements of the new codes are good, or justifiable, or ridiculously strict. That kind of value judgment is outside the scope of this argument.

Recognizing scope problems is a great way of eliminating dozens of wrong answers quickly. Make sure to pay special attention to the scope issues discussed in the Practice Test explanations.

The Nine Crucial Logical Reasoning Question Types

Now that you're familiar with the basic principles of Logical Reasoning, let's look at the most common types of questions you'll be asked. As we said earlier, certain question types crop up again and again on the LSAT, and it pays to be familiar with them. Of the types discussed below, the first three predominate on most Logical Reasoning sections, but try to become familiar with the others as well.

Assumption Questions

An assumption bridges the gap between an argument's evidence and conclusion. It's a piece of support that isn't explicitly stated but that is required for the conclusion to remain valid. When a question asks you to find an author's assumption, it's asking you to find the statement without which the argument falls apart.

In order to test whether a statement is necessarily assumed by an author, therefore, we can employ the **Denial Test**. Here's how it works: simply deny or negate the statement and see if the argument falls apart. If it does, that choice is the correct assumption. If, on the other hand, the argument is unaffected, the choice is wrong. Consider, as an example, this simple stimulus:

> Allyson plays volleyball for Central High School. Therefore, Allyson must be more than 6 feet tall.

You should recognize the second sentence as the conclusion, and the first sentence as the evidence for it. But is the argument complete? Obviously not. The piece that's missing—the unstated link between the evidence and conclusion—is the assumption, and you could probably prephrase this one pretty easily:

> All volleyball players for Central High School are more than 6 feet tall.

To test whether this really is an assumption necessary to the argument, let's apply the Denial Test, by negating it. What if it's *not true* that all vol-

Teacher Tip

"Assumptions are the unstated evidence that glues evidence and conclusion together. An assumption is that which an author takes for granted as true in proceeding to his conclusion.

"Assumptions are neither bad nor good. They're simply risky, as the author is depending on them on faith. If an assumption is proven to be false, then a wedge has been created between evidence and conclusion, and the argument has been weakened."
—Bob Verini
    Kaplan Teacher
    Los Angeles, CA

leyball players for Central High School are more than 6 feet tall? Can we still logically conclude that Allyson *must be* taller than 6 feet? No, we can't. Sure, it's possible that she is, but just as possible that she's not. By denying the statement, then, the argument falls to pieces; it's simply no longer valid. And that's our conclusive proof that the statement above is a necessary assumption of this argument.

As we've just seen, you can often prephrase the answer to an Assumption question. By previewing the question stem, you'll know what to look for. And stimuli for Assumption questions just "feel" like they're missing something. Often, the answer will jump right out at you, as in this case. In more difficult Assumption questions, the answers may not be as obvious. But in either case, you can use the Denial Test to check quickly whichever choice seems correct.

Sample Stems
Here are some of the ways in which Assumption questions are worded:

- Which one of the following is assumed by the author?
- Upon which one of the following assumptions does the author rely?
- The argument depends on the assumption that . . .
- Which one of the following, if added to the passage, will make the conclusion logical?
- The validity of the argument depends on which one of the following?
- The argument presupposes which one of the following?

Strengthen and Weaken Questions

Determining an argument's necessary assumption, as we've just seen, is required to answer assumption questions. But it also is required for another common question type—Strengthen-the-Argument and Weaken-the-Argument questions.

One way to weaken an argument is to break down a central piece of evidence. Another way is to attack the validity of any assumptions the author may be making. The answer to many Weaken-the-Argument questions is the one that reveals an author's assumption to be unreasonable; conversely, the answer to many Strengthen-the-Argument questions provides additional support by affirming the truth of an assumption or by presenting more persuasive evidence.

Let's take the same stimulus we used before, but look at it in the context of these other question types:

Allyson plays volleyball for Central High School. Therefore, Allyson must be more than 6 feet tall.

Remember the assumption holding this argument together? It was that all volleyball players for Central High School are more than 6 feet tall. That's the assumption that makes or breaks the argument. So, if the question asked you to weaken the argument, you'd want to attack that assumption:

> Which one of the following, if true, would most weaken the argument?

> *Answer:* Not all volleyball players at Central High School are more than 6 feet tall.

We've called into doubt the author's basic assumption, thus damaging the argument.

But what about strengthening the argument? Again, the key is the necessary assumption:

> Which one of the following, if true, would most strengthen the argument?

> *Answer:* All volleyball players at Central High School are more than 6 feet tall.

Here, by making explicit the author's central assumption, we've in effect bolstered the argument.

Extra Tips

Weaken questions tend to be more common on the LSAT than Strengthen questions. But here are a few concepts that apply to both question types:

- Weakening an argument is not the same thing as disproving it, while strengthening is not the same as proving the conclusion to be true. A strengthener tips the scale towards believing in the validity of the conclusion, while a weakener tips the scale in the other direction, toward doubting the conclusion.
- The wording of these question types always takes the form "Which one of the following, if true, would most [weaken or strengthen] the argument?" The *if true* part means that you have to accept the truth of the choice right off the bat, no matter how unlikely it may sound to you.
- Don't be careless. Wrong answer choices in these questions often have exactly the opposite of the desired effect. That is, if you're asked to strengthen a stimulus argument, it's quite likely that one or more of the wrong choices will contain information that actually *weakens* the

At a Glance

Strengthen/Weaken
Questions:
- Weaken questions are very popular; strengthen questions are less so.
- They are related to assumption; strengtheners often shore up the central assumption, while weakeners often show the central assumption to be unreasonable.
- You must evaluate each choice as to the effect it would have on the argument if true.
- Correct choices don't prove or disprove argument, but simply tip the scale the most in the desired direction.

argument. By the same token, weaken questions may contain a choice that *strengthens* the argument. So once again, pay close attention to what the question stem asks.

Sample Stems
The stems associated with these two question types are usually self-explanatory. Here's a list of what you can expect to see on the test:

Weaken:
- Which one of the following, if true, would most weaken the argument above?
- Which one of the following, if true, would most seriously damage the argument above?
- Which one of the following, if true, casts the most doubt on the argument above?
- Which one of the following, if true, is the most serious criticism of the argument above?

Strengthen:
- Which one of the following, if true, would most strengthen the argument?
- Which one of the following, if true, would provide the most support for the conclusion in the argument above?
- The argument above would be more persuasive if which one of the following were found to be true?

Inference Questions

Another of the most common question types you'll encounter on the Logical Reasoning section is the Inference question. The process of inferring is a matter of considering one or more statements as evidence and then drawing a conclusion from them.

Sometimes the inference is very close to the author's overall main point. Other times, it deals with a less central point. A valid inference is something that must be true if the statements in the passage are true—an extension of the argument rather than a necessary part of it.

For instance, let's take a somewhat expanded version of the volleyball team argument:

Allyson plays volleyball for Central High School, despite the team's rule against participation by nonstudents. Therefore, Allyson must be over 6 feet tall.

Inference: Allyson is not a student at Central High School.

At a Glance

Inference Questions:
- They are one of the most popular LR question types.
- The answer must be true if statements in the stimulus are true.
- They often stick close to the author's main point.
- The question stems vary considerably in appearance.
- They can be checked by applying the Denial Test.

Clearly, if Allyson plays volleyball *despite* the team's rule against participation by nonstudents, she must not be a student. Otherwise, she wouldn't be playing *despite* the rule; she'd be playing in accordance with the rule. But note that this inference is not an essential assumption of the argument, since the conclusion about Allyson's height doesn't depend on it.

So be careful; unlike an assumption, an inference need not have anything to do with the author's conclusion—it may simply be a piece of information derived from one or more pieces of evidence. However, the Denial Test works for inferences as well as for assumptions: A valid inference always makes more sense than its opposite. If you deny or negate an answer choice, and it has little or no effect on the argument, chances are that choice is not inferable from the passage.

Sample Stems

Inference questions probably have the most varied wording of all the Logical Reasoning question stems. Some question stems denote inference fairly obviously. Others are more subtle, and still others may even look like other question types entirely. Here's a quick rundown of the various forms that Inference questions are likely to take on your test:

- Which one of the following is inferable from the argument above?
- Which one of the following is implied by the argument above?
- The author suggests that . . .
- If all the statements above are true, which one of the following must also be true on the basis of them?
- The author of the passage would most likely agree with which one of the following?
- The passage provides the most support for which one of the following?
- Which one of the following is probably the conclusion towards which the author is moving?

Flaw Questions

This question type—known also by the moniker of Critique the Logic—asks you to recognize what's wrong with an argument. There are two basic types.

In the *general type* of Flaw question, the correct choice will critique the reasoning by pointing out that it contains a classic fallacy (e.g., "The argument attacks the source of an opinion, rather than the opinion itself"). In this case, the flaw falls into a general, well-defined category.

In the *specific type* of Flaw question, the correct choice won't refer to a classic fallacy, but rather it will attack a specific piece of the argument's

Kaplan Rules

A good inference:

- Stays in line with the gist of the passage
- Stays in line with the author's tone
- Stays in line with the author's point of view
- Stays within the scope of the argument or the main idea
- Is neither denied by, nor irrelevant to, the argument or discussion
- Always makes more sense than its opposite

At a Glance

Flaw Questions:
- They ask: "What's wrong with this argument?"
- Some correspond to well-defined categories.
- Some are specific to individual arguments.
- Understanding structure of arguments is the key.

reasoning. An example of this would be: "It cannot be concluded that the number of male turtles has increased simply because the percentage of turtles that are male has increased."

Notice that the subject of the above statement isn't turtles; it's the author's faulty reasoning *about turtles.* Similar to many other question types, the required skill is the ability to identify the structure of the author's argument—specifically, where the argument goes wrong.

Method of Argument Questions

Method of Argument questions bear a similarity to Flaw questions. Once again, you'll be asked to demonstrate an understanding of how an author's argument is put together. However, unlike Flaw questions, Method of Argument questions don't always involve faulty logic. You're simply asked to pick the choice that describes how the author goes about presenting his or her case. The key skill—once again—involves being able to analyze the structure of an argument. If you can't identify the evidence and conclusion, you'll have difficulty describing how an argument works.

Also like Flaw questions, there are two distinct types of Method of Argument questions—one *general*, one *specific*. The first deals with classic arguments. These are the classic argumentative structures, such as, "arguing from a small sample to a larger group," or "inferring a causal relationship from a correlation." The other type of Method of Argument question gives you a description of the argument in much more specific terms. An example of this might read, "The author presents the case of his mother in order to show that not all astronauts are men."

Focus on the following: What is the evidence? What is the conclusion? How does the author link the evidence and conclusion together? These are the questions you have to ask yourself in order to determine the author's method of argument.

Parallel Reasoning Questions

Parallel Reasoning questions require you to identify the answer choice that contains the argument most similar, or parallel, to that in the stimulus in terms of the reasoning employed. To do this kind of question, you need to grasp the distinction between an argument's form and its content. "A causal relationship concluded from a correlation" is a form—a type—of reasoning. Any argument with this form can contain virtually any content. Your task is to abstract the stimulus argument's form, with as little content as possible, and then locate the answer choice that has the form most similar to that of the stimulus. Don't let yourself be drawn to a

At a Glance

Method of Argument Questions:
- They may or may not involve faulty logic.
- They are similar to Reading Comp questions that ask about author's intentions and passage structure.
- Understanding the structure of arguments is the key.

choice based on its subject matter. A stimulus about music may have an answer choice that also involves music, but that doesn't mean that the *reasoning* in the two arguments is similar.

A good approach to these questions is to see first if the argument can be symbolized algebraically, using X's and Y's. Take the following example:

All cows eat grass. This animal eats grass. Therefore, it must be a cow.

This (flawed) argument can be symbolized in the following way:

All X do Y. This does Y. Therefore, this must be an X.

If the stimulus can be symbolized this way, your job will be to search for the choice that can be symbolized in the same way. Your answer might look something like this:

Every politician *(all X)* tells lies *(does Y)*. Stegner is lying *(this does Y)*. So he must be a politician *(therefore, this must be an X)*.

Notice how the exact wording doesn't have to match ("all X" means "every X"), and notice that the subject matter doesn't have to match in the least. What's important is the parallel structure.

Sometimes, though, an argument's reasoning isn't amenable to symbolization. In such a case, see if you can put a label on the type of argument being used, such as "Arguing from a Part to a Whole," or "Circular Reasoning" (evidence and conclusion are identical). Naming the argument will often help eliminate two or three choices that don't even come close to this general form.

But whatever way you choose, as long as you can summarize the argument's form without including content, you're well on your way to finding the parallel argument among the choices.

Extra Tips
Here are a few more tips on parallel reasoning:

- *All* elements of the original argument must be present in its parallel. For example, if the original argument made a generalization to a specific case, a second argument, no matter how similar in structure otherwise, cannot be parallel unless it makes a comparable generalization.

At a Glance

Parallel Reasoning Questions:
- They must mimic structure or form, not content, of stimulus.
- They are sometimes amenable to algebraic symbolization.
- The key is to summarize argument's overall form and match it to that of the correct choice.

- Stay away from answer choices written about the same subject matter as the original. This is an old trick of the test makers, intended to catch those who mistakenly try to mimic the content rather than the structure of the stimulus.
- Statements that are logically parallel don't have to have all logical elements in the same sequence. Provided all elements of the first argument exist in the second, even in a different order, the two arguments are parallel.

Paradox Questions

A paradox exists when an argument contains two or more seemingly inconsistent statements. You'll know you're dealing with a paradoxical situation if the argument ends with what seems to be a bizarre contradiction. Another sure sign of a paradox is when the argument builds to a certain point, and then the exact opposite of what you would expect to happen happens.

In a typical Paradox question, you'll be asked either to find the choice that "explains the paradoxical result" or "resolves the apparent discrepancy." Basically, this will be the choice that reconciles the seemingly inconsistent statements that make up the argument while allowing them all to still be true.

Take the following question:

Fifty-seven percent of the registered voters in this district claimed to support the Democratic candidate, and yet the Republican candidate won the election with 55 percent of the vote.

Which of the following would resolve the apparent discrepancy above?

The stimulus seems paradoxical since the Republican won the election, even though more registered voters preferred the Democrat. But do all registered voters vote? No. So a correct answer for this question might read something like this:

Because of an intensive get-out-the-vote effort in traditionally Republican neighborhoods, a disproportionate number of registered Republicans actually voted in the election.

This statement reconciles the seemingly contradictory elements of the argument by showing that the group of registered voters is not identical to the group of people who actually voted in the election.

At a Glance

Paradox Questions:
- The correct choice will resolve apparent discrepancy or contradiction.
- The correct choice should have an intuitive "click."
- The correct choice will often involve realizing that two groups presented as identical are actually not.

KAPLAN

Extra Tips
Here are a few tips for handling this question type:

- Before attempting to resolve a paradox, make sure you have a good grasp of what the paradox is. If it doesn't hit you right off the bat, look hard for an unexpected result, or what seems to be a blatant contradiction between the author's evidence and conclusion.
- Resolving paradoxes is often a matter of recognizing that two things that are being compared aren't really the same thing. Read critically to note these subtle distinctions.
- In Paradox questions, avoid choices that merely amplify points already raised in the argument.

Principle Questions

Principle questions involve fitting a specific situation into a global generality (or, occasionally, vice versa). Usually, you'll be given an argument, and then asked to find the principle that seems to justify the author's reasoning. For example, suppose that an author's evidence leads to this conclusion in the final sentence of the stimulus:

> Therefore, Marvin should provide a home for his ailing grandmother until she gets back on her feet.

The question stem might read: "The author's position most closely conforms to which one of the following principles?" In other words, what principle best accounts for or justifies the author's position? The answer could sound like this:

> If a close relative is in need, one should always do his or her best to help that person, regardless of personal inconvenience.

On the other hand, the question stem might read: "Which one of the following principles would justify Marvin's refusal to follow the author's recommendation?" In this case, the answer may sound something like this:

> No person should be obligated to provide support for another person, even if that other person is a close relative.

Notice the general nature of both principles. Whereas they don't specifically mention Marvin or his grandmother, or the exact conditions of the stimulus *per se,* the general situation (helping a relative in need) is addressed in both.

At a Glance

Principle Questions:
- They're a relatively new question type.
- They are the closest question type to the actual workings of the law.
- The correct choices usually express author's key concepts and terms.

The correct answer to Principle questions is usually the one that expresses the key concepts and contains the key terms that the other choices leave out. Be extremely wary of choices that are outside the scope of the argument. Most of the wrong choices contain principles that sound very formal and look good on the page by themselves, but that don't address the author's main concern.

Formal Logic Questions

The manner in which formal logic is tested on the LSAT has evolved over the last few years. Gone (at least for now) are the days when the test makers would line up formal if/then and all/some/none statements and ask you what can, must, or cannot be true on the basis of them. Nowadays, the test makers bury formal statements in the context of a casual argument, asking for an inference that can be drawn from the passage. You may not easily recognize formal logic when you see it, and questions of this nature are fewer in number than in the past. But formal logic skills are tested in Logic Games as well, so it's best to get a solid handle on it now.

Let's look at an example:

> Ian will go to the movies only when his wife is out of town. He'll go to a matinee alone, but will see a movie at night only if accompanied by Ezra and Mabel.

This simple stimulus looks like any other casual argument in Logical Reasoning, but in fact, it's made up of a couple of formal logic statements, each fraught with its own implications. Formal logic statements resemble rules in Logic Games. Be on the lookout for Logical Reasoning stimuli that contain sentences that can be boiled down to such hard and fast rules. When you come across examples of these, you can apply the following principles of formal logic to help you arrive at the correct answer.

The Contrapositive

For any if/then statement—or a statement that can be translated into if/then form—the contrapositive of the statement will result in an equally valid second statement. This is a nice shortcut to employ when faced with formal logic on the test.

The contrapositive can be formed by reversing and negating the terms of any if/then statement. The general model goes like this:

> If X, then Y.

At a Glance

Formal Logic Questions:
- They have a direct bearing on Logic Games as well as Logical Reasoning.
- They are usually tested in the context of a casual argument.
- The formal statements can be boiled down to hard and fast rules.
- The contrapositive can be applied to any if/then statement.

The contrapositive of this statement is:

> If *not* Y, then *not* X.

The contrapositive of a valid if/then statement will always be valid itself.

Let's illustrate this with a simple example. Consider the following strict formal logic statement:

> If the building has vacancies, then the sales office will be open.

To form the contrapositive, reverse and negate the terms, like so:

> If the sales office is NOT open, then the building does NOT have vacancies.

This would be a valid inference based on the original statement. The contrapositive, while quite a fancy term, is nothing more than everyday common sense.

Now let's apply the contrapositive to the first sentence of the earlier example. Here's the original:

> Ian will go to the movies only when his wife is out of town.

This is a little trickier, because it's not stated in the form of a true if/then statement. But we can translate this statement into an if/then statement without changing its original meaning:

> *If* Ian goes to the movies, *then* his wife must be out of town.

If the statement above is true, which one of the following must be true on the basis of it? Why, the contrapositive of it, of course:

> If Ian's wife is *not* out of town, then Ian does *not* go to the movies.

Simple enough, right? One caveat: wrong answers often result from either forgetting to switch around the terms before negating them, or negating only one of the terms. For instance, from the above example, if Ian doesn't go to the movies, we can't infer anything about whether his wife is in or out of town. Similarly, if Ian's wife *is* out of town, we can't tell for sure whether Ian goes to the movies or not.

If one part of the formal logic statement contains a compound phrase, then both parts of the phrase must be taken into account. For example, let's take the other part of the stimulus above:

Note

The contrapositive is probably the most important rule of logic you need for LSAT success. It's essential that you learn what it is and how to use it.

Teacher Tip

"Make it mechanical! It's easy to get tangled up in thinking it through, but you can't go wrong taking it step by step. *Every* if/then statement can be simply switched and negated."
—Tiffany Sanders
 Kaplan Teacher
 Downers Grove, IL

Ian will see a movie at night only if accompanied by Ezra *and* Mabel.

Translation: If Ian sees a movie at night, then he's accompanied by Ezra *and* Mabel.

Contrapositive: If Ian is *not* with Ezra *and* Mabel, then he does *not* see a movie at night.

Correct Interpretation: If either Ezra or Mabel is missing, then Ian's out of luck. If he's with only one of them, or neither of them, then he can't go to a night movie.

Finally, if one part of a formal logic statement is already in the negative, the same rules that apply to math apply to forming the contrapositive: negating a negative yields a positive.

If the sun is shining, then Samantha does not wear green.

Contrapositive: If Samantha *is* wearing green (if she's *not not* wearing green), then the sun is *not* shining.

Necessary versus Sufficient Conditions

For success in formal logic, it's crucial that you distinguish clearly between necessary and sufficient conditions. Here are examples of each:

Sufficient: If I yell loudly at my cat Adrian, he will run away.
Necessary: The TV will work only if it is plugged in.

My yelling loudly is a sufficient condition for Adrian to run away. It's all I need to do to get the cat to run; it's sufficient. But it's not necessary. My cat will run if I throw water at him, even if I don't yell loudly.

The TV's being plugged in, on the other hand, is a necessary condition of its working. My TV won't work without it, so it's necessary. But it's not sufficient. Other conditions must apply for the TV to work (for example, the electricity to the house must be on).

You must be clear on what kinds of deductions you can and can't make from statements of necessary and sufficient conditions. For instance, sufficient conditions are usually signaled by an if/then statement, which means that the contrapositive can be used.

If I yell loudly at my cat Adrian, he will run away.

KAPLAN

Given that the above statement is true, which one of the following statements must also be true?

> **Not Valid:** If I don't yell loudly at my cat Adrian, he will not run away.
> **Not Valid:** If my cat Adrian has run away, then I yelled loudly at him.
> **Valid:** If my cat Adrian has not run away, then I did not yell loudly at him.

The third statement is the contrapositive, and is the only one of the three statements that's inferable from the original. My yelling loudly is sufficient to make Adrian run away, but it's not necessary; that is, it'll do the trick, but it's not the *only* possible thing that will make him head for the hills. If I squirt him with a water gun, he'll also run away. This is why the first two statements are not inferable from the original statement.

Necessary conditions, on the other hand, are usually signaled by the word *only*:

> The TV will work only if it is plugged in.

Given that the above statement is true, which one of the following statements must also be true?

> **Not Valid:** If my TV is plugged in, it will work.
> **Not Valid:** If my TV is not working, then it must not be plugged in.
> **Valid:** If my TV is working, then it must be plugged in.
> **Valid:** If my TV is not plugged in, then it won't work.

Plugging the TV in is necessary for the TV to work. To work, the TV needs to be plugged in. However, plugging in the TV is not sufficient to make the TV work. True, the TV won't work without plugging it in, but plugging it in is not a *guarantee* that the TV will work. What if other conditions interfere? Maybe the picture tube is broken. Maybe my electricity is out due to a hurricane. So the first two statements above are not inferable from the original statement, while the last two are.

The Kaplan Four-Step Method for Logical Reasoning

Now that you've learned the basic Logical Reasoning principles and have been exposed to the full range of question types, it's time to learn how to orchestrate all of that knowledge into a systematic approach to Logical

Note

It's necessary that you learn the difference between necessary and sufficient requirements, but knowing that is not sufficient in and of itself to get a great score.

Reasoning. We've developed a four-step approach that you can use to attack each and every question on the section.

Here are the four steps:

1. Preview the question stem.
2. Read the stimulus.
3. Try to prephrase an answer.
4. Choose an answer.

1. Preview the Question Stem

As we mentioned in the discussion of basic principles, previewing the stem is a great way to focus your reading of the stimulus, so that you know exactly what you're looking for.

2. Read the Stimulus

With the question stem in mind, read the stimulus, paraphrasing as you go. Remember to read actively and critically, pinpointing evidence and conclusion. Also get a sense for how strong or weak the argument is.

3. Try to Prephrase an Answer

Sometimes, if you've read the stimulus critically enough, you'll know the answer without even looking at the choices. It will be much easier to find it if you have a sense of what you're looking for among the choices.

4. Choose an Answer

If you were able to prephrase an answer, skim the choices looking for something that sounds like what you have in mind. If you couldn't think of anything, read and evaluate each choice, throwing out the ones that are outside the scope of the argument. After settling on an answer, you may wish to briefly double-check the question stem to make sure that you're indeed answering the question that was asked.

Using the Kaplan Four-Step Method for Logical Reasoning

Now let's try this approach on a genuine Logical Reasoning item:

A study of twenty overweight men revealed that each man experienced significant weight loss after adding SlimDown, an artificial food supplement, to his daily diet. For three months, each man consumed one SlimDown portion every morning after exercising, and then followed his normal diet for the rest of the day. Clearly, anyone who consumes one portion of SlimDown every day for at least three months will lose weight and will look and feel his or her best.

Which one of the following is an assumption on which the argument depends?

(A) The men in the study will gain back the weight they lost if they discontinue the SlimDown program.

(B) No other dietary supplement will have the same effect on overweight men.

(C) The daily exercise regimen was not responsible for the effects noted in the study.

(D) Women will not experience similar weight reductions if they adhere to the SlimDown program for three months.

(E) Overweight men will achieve only partial weight loss if they do not remain on the SlimDown program for a full three months.

1. Preview the Question Stem

We see, quite clearly, that we're dealing with an Assumption question. Good—immediately we can adopt an "assumption mindset," which basically means that, before even reading the first word of the stimulus, we know that the conclusion will be lacking an important piece of supporting evidence. We now turn to the stimulus, already on the lookout for this missing link.

2. Read the Stimulus

The first sentence introduces a study of twenty men using a food supplement product, resulting in weight loss for all twenty. The second sentence describes how they used it: once a day, for three months, after morning exercise. So far so good; it feels as if we're building up to something. The structural signal word *clearly* usually indicates that some sort of conclusion follows, and in fact it does: the author concludes in the third sentence that anyone who has one portion of the product daily for three months will lose weight, too.

You must read critically! Notice that the conclusion doesn't say that anyone who follows the *same routine* as the twenty men will have the same results; it says that anyone who simply *consumes the product* in the same way will have the same results. You should have begun to sense the inevitable lack of crucial information at this point. The evidence in the sec-

Teacher Tip

"Ordinary reading is too slow to find things and too fast to analyze text. Good test takers scan quickly to find what they need and then analyze intensely. Structural keywords and references from the stem are crucial. Looking for a conclusion? Scan for keywords and for words with heavy emotional content. If the stem asks for an assumption made by a researcher, scan for the word 'research' or 'researcher.' Then read up and down from that spot."
—Eirik Johnson
    Kaplan Teacher
    Chicago, IL

ond sentence describes a routine that includes taking the supplement after daily exercise, whereas the conclusion focuses primarily on the supplement and entirely ignores the part about the exercise. The conclusion, therefore, doesn't stem logically from the evidence in the first two sentences. This blends seamlessly into Step 3.

3. Try to Prephrase an Answer

As expected, the argument is beginning to look as if it has a serious shortcoming. Of course, we expected this because we previewed the question stem before reading the stimulus.

In really simplistic terms, the argument proceeds like so: "A bunch of guys did A and B for three months and had X result. If anyone does A for three months, that person will experience X result, too." Sound a little fishy? You bet. The author must be assuming that A (the product), not B (exercise), must be the crucial thing that leads to the result. If not (the Denial Test), the conclusion makes no sense.

So, you might prephrase the answer like this: "Something about the exercise thing needs to be cleared up." That's it. Did you think your prephrasing had to be something fancy and glamorous? Well, it doesn't. All you need is an inkling of what the question is looking for, and in this case, it just seems that if we don't shore up the exercise issue, the argument will remain invalid and incomplete. So, with our vague idea of a possible assumption, we can turn to Step 4, which is . . .

4. Choose an Answer

Since we were able to prephrase something, it's best to skim the choices looking for it. And, lo and behold, there's our idea, stated in a very LSAT-like manner, in choice (C). (C) clears up the exercise issue. Yes, this author must assume (C) to make the conclusion that eating SlimDown alone will cause anyone to lose weight.

At this point, if you're stuck for time, you simply choose (C) and move on. If you have more time, you may as well quickly check the remaining choices, to find (we hope) that none of them fits the bill.

Of course, once you grasp the structure of the argument and have located the author's central assumption, you should be able to answer any question they throw at you. This one takes the form of an Assumption question. But it could just as easily have been phrased as a Weaken-the-Argument question:

> Which one of the following, if true, casts the most doubt on the argument above?

Kaplan Tip

Your prephrasing of an answer need not be elaborate or terribly specific. Your goal is just to get an idea of what you're looking for, so the correct answer will jump out at you.

Answer: Daily exercise contributed significantly to the weight loss experienced by the men in the study.

And here's a Flaw question that could have been based on the same stimulus:

The author's reasoning is flawed because it . . .

Answer: . . . overlooks the possibility that the results noted in the study were caused by daily exercise rather than by the consumption of SlimDown.

So there you have it—a quick demonstration of how to use the strategies and techniques outlined in this chapter to work through the complete Logical Reasoning process. Try to apply these techniques as best you can on the following practice set and in the Logical Reasoning sections of the three full-length Practice Tests in this book. Pay careful attention to all of the written explanations, even those for the ones you got right.

After you work through the practice set, we'll move on to another major section of the test: Logic Games.

Logical Reasoning Practice Set

<u>Directions:</u> This test is composed of questions that ask you to analyze the logic of statements or short paragraphs. You are to choose as the answer to each question the one choice you consider correct on the basis of your common-sense evaluation of the statement and its assumptions. Although a question may seem to have more than one acceptable answer, there is only one answer, and it is the one that does not entail making any illogical, extraneous, or conflicting assumptions about the question. These questions do not presuppose any knowledge of formal logic on your part.

Question 1

In his long and epochal career, Beethoven was both synthesizer and innovator, the supreme classicist who startled the musical world of his time by his bold surges forward toward the chromaticism to come. But because his later music made so much use of unprecedented dissonance, a few cynical critics have suggested that the composer's progressively worsening deafness must have weakened his ability to imagine and produce consistently harmonious music. In other words, he was writing what he misheard, according to these critics. I maintain that, on the contrary, if the deaf Beethoven had been trying to create in a medium he had known intimately but could no longer manipulate successfully, he would have been all the more likely to _____.

Which one of the following best completes the passage above?

(A) depend heavily upon the rules of conventional harmony to produce predictable sounds
(B) compose dissonances from his inability to hear what he had written
(C) rely upon his own judgment in deciding what type of music to compose

(D) avoid cynical criticism by composing only consistently harmonious music
(E) suspect that his ear had become so untrustworthy that he should end his career before full maturation

Ⓐ Ⓑ Ⓒ Ⓓ Ⓔ

Question 2

Many factors affect the home-building industry, but the number of single-family homes under construction generally rises as interest rates decline. Contractors are able to plan their hiring schedules and order essential building materials in response to reliable predictors of the movement of prevailing interest rates.

It can be inferred from the passage above that

(A) the price of building materials rises when interest rates decline
(B) no factor affecting home building is as reliable a predictor as interest rates
(C) assessments of growth in the housing industry are sometimes based upon expected fluctuations of interest rates
(D) a contractor does not order building materials until a hiring schedule is set up
(E) most housing being built today is single-family housing

Ⓐ Ⓑ Ⓒ Ⓓ Ⓔ

Question 3

Critics of current commercial TV programming expect that Federal Communications Commission (FCC) rules restricting such popular items as children's adventure cartoons and sexually explicit motion pictures would result in more responsible programming, such as public affairs panel discussions, medical self-help series, and live productions of classic drama. But would they so fervently advocate government intrusion into broadcasting if they knew a little more about the real workings of the marketplace? Actually,

41

enforced restrictions on programming would result in milder but still mindless offerings: more situation comedies about bewildered housewives, more coverage of obscure sporting events in minor cities, and more talk shows devoted to the private lives of forgettable "instant celebrities."

The author of the above passage assumes that

(A) current commercial TV programming is not irresponsible

(B) FCC restrictions of commercial TV programming will not necessarily be easy to enforce

(C) those who wish to restrict certain popular TV programs will dislike their popular replacements

(D) the FCC should have no control over the broadcast industry, which is likely to serve the public better if it is not regulated

(E) the marketplace is the true test of whether or not a new program idea is worthwhile

Ⓐ Ⓑ Ⓒ Ⓓ Ⓔ

Question 4

The federal government currently interferes blatantly in the relationship between parent and child. The Internal Revenue Service provides a child-care or dependent's deduction on the annual income tax return. In effect, the government, by rewarding some providers of support, determines which taxpayers are to be considered worthy enough to care for dependents.

Which one of the following, if true, weakens the argument above?

(A) A taxpayer need only attach the appropriate schedule to the tax form to apply for the deduction.

(B) The deduction is likely to offer a proportionately greater benefit to the lower income taxpayer.

(C) A child must be living at home with the provider of support in order to qualify as a dependent.

(D) The deduction actually affects a fairly small percentage of taxpayers.

(E) The deduction is available to anyone who supplies the principal support of a dependent.

Ⓐ Ⓑ Ⓒ Ⓓ Ⓔ

Question 5

Detective-adventure series and other action programming on prime-time television have been criticized for inciting some viewers, male adolescents in particular, to commit acts of violence. The most carefully engineered studies have not, however, supported this assumption. Rather, it seems likely that someone who is frustrated and resentful, and therefore prone to violence, is drawn to the kind of programming that shows characters who release their frustrations in acts of violence.

Which one of the following would provide the most logical concluding sentence for the paragraph above?

(A) In fact, action programming probably helps a frustrated viewer release his hostility without resorting to violence.

(B) Moreover, there are studies that indicate that male adolescents are more likely than other viewers to believe that the world shown in action programming is realistic.

(C) In other words, an unusual interest in action programming may be an indication of a violence-prone personality rather than an incitement to violence.

(D) Be that as it may, action programming continues to grow in popularity with the American TV audience.

(E) Therefore, the reasonable observer of the American scene will conclude that action programming should be banned from prime-time viewing hours.

Ⓐ Ⓑ Ⓒ Ⓓ Ⓔ

Questions 6–7:

Although the legislative process in our democratic government is based on the proposition that Congress must represent the interests of the majority of its constituents, this principle that the majority rules is frequently contradicted by the efforts of lobbyists. Minority interests with the wherewithal to finance hard-sell lobbying campaigns can distort an elected official's sense of public opinion, thereby exercising a destructive influence over political decisions.

Question 6

The argument above depends upon the truth of which one of the following assumptions?

(A) The democratic process is a reflection of our capitalist economic system.

(B) The democratic process requires that minority interests be protected by constitutional amendment.

(C) Minority interests cannot be protected without spending large sums of money on lobbying activities.

(D) The democratic process cannot function properly unless the activities of big business are restrained.

(E) The democratic process depends on the ability of all members of society to have equal influence on the legislative process.

(A) (B) (C) (D) (E)

Question 7

Which one of the following, if true, would most weaken the argument above?

(A) The majority opinion on many political issues is ill-informed and unconsidered.

(B) Elected officials are rarely influenced by pressures of lobbying campaigns.

(C) Interest groups can accumulate large sums of money through fund-raising activities.

(D) All groups and interests are entitled to hire professional lobbyists to represent their cause.

(E) There is no clear-cut majority position on many political issue facing Congress.

(A) (B) (C) (D) (E)

Question 8

If we reduce the rate of income taxation, people will spend a larger portion of their gross incomes on consumer goods. This will stimulate economic growth and result in higher salaries and thus in higher government revenues, despite a lower rate of taxation.

Which one of the following arguments most closely resembles the reasoning in the statements above?

(A) If we reduce the amount of overtime our employees work, production costs will decline and our total income will thus increase.

(B) If we make it harder to participate in the school lunch program, people will have to pay for more of their food and the farm income will therefore increase.

(C) If a movie is classified as obscene, more people will want to see it and the morals of the general community will be corrupted more than they would be otherwise.

(D) If we give our employees more paid holidays, their efficiency while actually on the job will improve and our total productivity will thus increase.

(E) If we give our children more spending money, they will learn to manage their finances better and will thereby realize the virtue of thrift.

(A) (B) (C) (D) (E)

Question 9

If a judge is appointed for life, she will make courtroom decisions that reflect the accumulated wisdom inherent in this country's judicial history, relying upon the law and reason rather than upon trends in political thinking. If, on the other hand, the judge is appointed or elected for short terms in office, her decisions will be heavily influenced by the prevailing political climate. In sum, the outcome of many court cases will be determined by the method by which the presiding judge has been installed in her post.

Which one of the following, if true, does not support the argument in the passage above?

(A) Surveys indicate that judges enjoy their work and want to remain in office as long as possible.

(B) Judges appointed for life are just as informed about political matters as are judges who must run for re-election.

(C) The rulings of judges who must run for re-election are generally approved of by the voters who live in their elective districts.

(D) Most judges appointed for life hand down identical rulings on similar cases throughout their long careers.

(E) Only judges who are selected for short terms of office employ pollsters to read the mood of the electorate.

Ⓐ Ⓑ Ⓒ Ⓓ Ⓔ

Question 10

These so-called pacifists are either the victims or the propagators of a false logic. They claim that weapons reductions would result in a so-called climate of peace, thereby diminishing the likelihood of conflicts leading to war. But what are the facts? In the past ten years, during which time we have seen increased spending for such defense requirements as state-of-the-art weapons systems and augmented combat personnel, there have been fewer military actions involving our forces than in any previous decade in the twentieth century. Our own installations have not been attacked and our allies have rarely found it necessary to ask for our armed support. In other words, defense readiness is, in the real world, the most efficient peace-making tool.

Which of the following is an assumption underlying the conclusion of the passage above?

(A) Military actions involving our forces can be instigated by any of a number of different factors.

(B) Our buildup of weapons systems and combat personnel has prevented our adversaries from increasing their own spending on defense.

(C) The increased defense spending of the past ten years has lessened the need for significant military expenditure in future decades.

(D) At the present time, state-of-the-art weapons systems and the augmentation of combat personnel are equally important to a nation's resources.

(E) The number of military actions involving our forces would have been greater in the past decade if we had not increased our defense spending.

Ⓐ Ⓑ Ⓒ Ⓓ Ⓔ

Question 11

It is possible for a panhandler to collect a considerable amount of money from passersby if she can convince them that she is destitute and that begging is the only way for her to help herself. If, on the other hand, passersby get the impression that they are being conned or that the panhandler is just being lazy, they will not give her anything at all.

Which one of the following statements can be most reliably concluded from the passage above?

(A) Most panhandlers are unwilling to work.

(B) If someone begs when she does not need to, people will not give her any money.

(C) Most passersby would give a panhandler money if they thought that she was not conning them.

(D) Passersby often base their decision of whether or not to give money to a panhandler on their impressions of her and her honesty.

(E) People who give money to panhandlers are not influenced by how much change they have in their pockets when they decide the amount of money they will give.

Ⓐ Ⓑ Ⓒ Ⓓ Ⓔ

Answers and Explanations

Question 1

In Question 1, you have to fill in the blank. You'll want to get an idea of the direction in which the passage is going so that you can extrapolate to the most likely ending.

The passage begins by labeling Beethoven as two things. He was both an innovator—meaning he brought music forward, moving towards what the passage says was "the chromaticism to come" (whatever that is)—and a synthesizer, presumably not the Mogue variety but someone who "put it all together," that is, who also worked with classical forms. *But*—structural signal of contrast here—some critics have said that Beethoven's innovations (his work with dissonance) were *not* some kind of wonderful experimentation, but merely a manifestation of his increasing deafness—hence, they represent an unharmonious flaw in his later music.

The author doesn't hold with this interpretation. She does, after all, label them "cynical critics." And she says, "I maintain that, on the contrary . . . ," which is another signal of contrast announcing that the author is about to take issue. Her belief is that if Beethoven's deafness was (as is alleged) impairing his ability to handle his musical medium, then he would have been all the more likely to do . . . what? Well, she wants to finish with a statement of a contrary effect. Her argument is: If the cause the cynics describe were, in fact, the case (if deafness made Beethoven less competent), then there would be an opposite effect, an effect something like choice (A). A less competent Beethoven would have played it safe by producing conventional, traditional music.

Choice (B) directly echoes or parallels the opinion of the cynical critics—it doesn't stand in contrast to

it—so it's not an opinion that would be cited to bolster the author's own feelings about Beethoven. Jumping to choice (E)—by seeming to agree that Beethoven was losing his abilities towards the end of his career—you can see that choice (E), too, is more in line with the view of the cynical critics.

Choice (C)'s sentiment is somewhat in line with that of the author; it makes a bit of sense in that it suggests that Beethoven composed what he wanted to compose. But it doesn't act as a clear contrast to the notion that Beethoven composed dissonant music because his hearing was impaired and didn't know what sounds he was making, so it doesn't act in a satisfactory way to fill in the blank.

Finally, choice (D) brings up the issue of "harmonious music," which you want. But by assigning a motive to Beethoven—that he was trying to defuse critical response—choice (D) goes far afield. No such reference to motive has a place in the argument as written. Choice (A) best completes the paragraph in Question 1.

Question 2

Question 2's stimulus isn't much of an argument, is it? It's little more than a series of flat statements on a topic, and that topic is interest rates, one of the major factors affecting the housing industry. Interest rates are cited as having an inverse relationship with the building of single-family dwellings: as rates go down, construction goes up, literally. In line with that (says the second sentence), contractors order building materials based on predictions of which way interest rates will go. This should make sense. If the contractors believed that rates were about to decrease, they would be likely to order more supplies in expectation of a greater demand for single-family homes. Conversely, an expected rise in interest rates would prompt a cutback in supply orders, in expectation of less demand.

All of this is in line with choice (C). And remember, when you're asked what can be inferred from the passage, you really want something that must be true—something in line with the scope and point of view. Choice (C) is just a broader rephrasing of the relationship cited in the stimulus and is thus the best answer. (Note that the choice is rendered even more reasonable by its use of the qualifier *sometimes*. Because it's not an extreme statement with no exceptions possible, it's easy to sign on to choice (C) as a reflection of the author's equally moderate views.)

Choice (A) brings up the cost of building materials, but since the passage says nothing at all about the costs of home building—there isn't a single reference to costs—it goes beyond the scope and must therefore be rejected quickly. You can't infer that those who sell building materials raise their prices in response to the greater demand they expect from the lower interest rates.

Choice (B) distorts the paragraph. Interest rates are cited as *a* good predictor. But are they the best? Who knows? And anyway, they're cited only in terms of one type of home—the single-family dwelling. Choice (B) evokes the entire industry—again, going beyond the scope.

As for choice (D), just because the author mentions hiring schedules before mentioning orders for new materials does not mean that one of those things must come first on the builder's agenda.

And (E) is an unwarranted inference since the author's only concern is one type of dwelling, the single-family home. You cannot fairly extrapolate from this paragraph to any statement about the home-building industry in general.

Again, it was choice (C) for Question 2.

Question 3

The speaker in Question 3 doubts that stricter FCC regulations will result in better quality television. Some expect that greater restrictions on kid's shows and dirty movies will prompt TV programmers to give us more, shall we say, elevating fare. But the speaker feels that stronger FCC rules will do no such thing—that the networks will be able to conform to the rules while continuing to provide the same vapid programming choices that have always been popular (that's the refer-

ence to the marketplace). The networks (it is predicted) will simply switch from controversial themes—that is, from sex and violence—to milder but still mindless shows. In other words, the networks won't attempt (as the proregulators predict) to put on more educational shows. They will just shift to whatever dopey (yet popular) fare is not restricted by the FCC.

You're to find an assumption, and the credited choice—the thing the speaker must be taking for granted as true—is (C). The speaker is taking for granted that the people who dislike TV as it is now will also dislike the shows that will be broadcast after the rules are instituted. After all, the speaker is essentially saying to the proregulators, "You're wrong in wanting to institute those rules because you'll get no better programming than before." But the speaker ignores the possibility that those in favor of the FCC rules will gladly greet the new dumb sitcoms and sports shows as a welcome change from the sex and violence that the rules are designed to reduce.

Choice (A) says that current TV is not irresponsible. But the speaker doesn't argue that the proposed rules are superfluous because current TV programming is responsible. Rather, the speaker argues that the rules won't make TV any better. In fact, the whole passage indicates that the author believes the opposite of (A): that much programming is irresponsibly mindless.

Choice (B) is not a necessary assumption either, since the speaker is not concerned with the ease or difficulty of enforcement but rather with how effective or ineffective the rules would be when enforced.

Choice (D) isn't assumed because the author doesn't argue that unregulated TV will be better, but rather that regulated TV will not be any better. The thrust here is that, because of the marketplace, TV will always be a vast wasteland.

Finally, choice (E) suggests that the true test of programming worth is the marketplace. Well, the speaker does believe that it's the marketplace that determines what we see on TV. But what the public sees is, to the speaker, execrable: sexy, violent, dopey, and worthless. Choice (E)'s rather democratic sentiment is completely at odds with the author's argument, and so it's not something that is assumed or built into that argument. Again, choice (C) is correct for Question 3.

Question 4

Always watch for tone words! The charge in Question 4's stimulus that the government interferes "blatantly," wrongly using its bureaucratic power, alerts you immediately to the author's opinion.

It seems that the IRS gives a child-care deduction to certain people who provide support to a dependent. The complaint is that the government exercises unfair control in its choice of which people receive this deduction and which do not. The author believes that the government can have no justifiable basis on which to make this decision and is in effect deciding which people are worthy of caring for dependents and which are not.

The choice that most weakens this argument is (E). If the tax deduction is, as choice (E) says, available to anyone who is the principal supporter of a dependent, then that answers the implicit charge that the government has arbitrarily set itself up as an authority, with the right to decide people's personal worth. If the IRS, in other words, is using an appropriate criterion that is applied equitably to all, then the charge that the deduction is being selectively used to decide people's worth is rendered groundless. If you provide someone's principal support, then you get the deduction. If not, you don't. So (E) really damages the reasoning.

Choice (A) might have fooled you because it seems to be saying that anyone who wants the deduction can have it. But it really says that anyone who attaches the appropriate schedule may apply for the deduction; they won't necessarily get it. The fact that the IRS will consider anyone doesn't mean that it isn't (as the author alleges) making the final decision on inappropriate criteria, choosing people arbitrarily on the basis of what it deems to be their personal worth. So choice (A) is incorrect.

Choice (B) mentions the deduction but is otherwise beyond the argument's scope, going off on the interesting but irrelevant topic of the relative size of the deduction for lower-income taxpayers.

As for choice (C), even if it were true, the government might still be reaching its decision as to who gets the deduction based on improper criteria. All choice (C) gives us is one of those criteria—the requirement that a dependent be a co-resident. But perhaps the other criteria are just as objectionable as the author seems to feel they are.

Finally, choice (D)'s implication that only a few people will get the deduction is another "error in scope," because choice (D) has nothing to do with the main issue, which is the government's methods or motives. The "weakener" you need has to somehow demonstrate that the government—contrary to what the author believes—is awarding the deduction based on proper criteria. Only choice (E) does that, and that's why it's correct for Question 4.

Question 5

In Question 5, the author counters the view that violent TV shows incite people to commit violent acts. Apparently, a correlation has been noticed—and a correlation, of course, is an acknowledgment that two phenomena accompany each other, whether or not they're causally related—between watching TV violence and committing violent acts. Apparently, it's true that people who watch violent shows are more likely to commit violent crimes than those who don't watch those shows. And this finding might well suggest that the TV shows are causing the viewers to commit the crimes. But the author believes that the correlation is better explained in another way—that violence-prone people tend to watch violent shows because they feel an affinity to the violence-prone characters of the shows. So to the author, the critics cited in the first sentence are guilty of confusing cause and effect. The TV shows don't make the viewer violence prone; rather, it's frustration and resentment that make people violence prone and make these people watch violent TV programs.

The passage ends abruptly without a proper conclusion—for obvious reasons, since you're asked to come up with that yourself. The best answer is (C), which takes the author's argument to its logical conclusion: A person's addiction to action TV shows may reveal something about that person's tendency towards violence, but it doesn't indicate an inducement to commit violence.

Choice (A) goes too far. It states that the effect of action shows is salutary, by helping the violence-prone viewer vent his hostility in a nonthreatening way. But that doesn't at all follow from the argument, which merely contends that the crime-and-TV-show correlation can be explained in an alternative way. To say, as choice (A) does, that TV violence can act as a corrective goes far afield.

Choice (B) raises the issue of who finds the action programs realistic. This issue comes from left field. You're looking for a summation of the given argument. (B) introduces a new point, and you really can't say what effect this new point has on the passage. It's certainly not a good conclusion.

Choice (D) is irrelevant—you would never expect a paragraph about whether action TV leads to violence to end with a quick reference to action shows' general popularity.

And it's more likely that the author would disagree with choice (E) than end her discussion with it. In a way, her views are a defense of action programming against the charge of aiding and abetting violent crime. Therefore, choice (E)'s call for a ban on action shows is just plain uncalled for. In any case, the idea of a ban comes from left field and cannot provide a logical concluding sentence. Once again, it was choice (C) for Question 5.

Question 6 Question 6

In the stimulus for Questions 6 and 7, the conclusion is expressed in the main clause of the first sentence: Lobbyists have a negative effect on the principle of "the majority rules" as practiced in Congress. The reason for that conclusion—the evidence or support—comes in the second sentence: Wealthy minority interests can afford to finance lobbyists, who pressure elected officials. These lobbyists make the officials believe that the opinions of the lobby are held by the people

at large. So, the argument goes, some people (namely, the rich interest groups) have a greater influence on decision making than do others. And this, it's alleged, thwarts majority rule.

Thinking about a key assumption connecting this evidence to that conclusion—and that's what Question 6 is asking for—you should note that the author jumps from the idea that lobbyists distort Congress's sense of public opinion, to the conclusion that lobbyists undermine the majority-rule concept. To make this leap, the author must be assuming that all members of society have to have equal influence on legislation in order for majority-rule to work. All the evidence says is that lobbyists distort Congress's sense of public opinion—it doesn't claim that the opinion of the majority is completely silenced. The majority-rule principle (according to this passage) implies that Congress should represent the interests of the majority of its constituents. So, by asserting that the lobbyists muck things up, the author must be taking for granted that all members of society have to be heard from, have to have equal influence, in order for the concept of majority rule to work. That's what choice (E) is saying, and that's why choice (E) is correct for Question 6.

Of the incorrect choices, (A)'s reference to capitalism takes it way, way beyond the scope of the argument. The only connection between money and the argument's content is a more or less tangential one—the idea that money helps the lobbyists distort Congress's sense of public opinion. Choice (A) blows that out of proportion. Choice (B), meanwhile, is too specific. To say that minority interests have to be protected by constitutional amendment is to propose a specific solution to a problem floating around the argument, but the author need not be assuming or signing on to that solution as he reasons. Choice (C) is off the point because the argument is concerned with protecting majority interests—the concept of majority rule is what's allegedly in danger here. (This could be brought up as an objection to choice (B), as well.) Finally, choice (D) plays off your possible assumption that the minority interests in the passage are big-business fat cats, but as far as the passage goes, it may be the case that other minority interests, ones not connected with big business at all, engage in lobbying, too. Once again, choice (E) is correct for Question 6.

Question 7

Now there's another major assumption at work here—it's not among the answer choices for Question 6, but it's the key to Question 7. The author is assuming that Congress, bullied and influenced by the lobbyists, goes about the act of legislating under that influence. He's assuming (in short) that lobbyists' efforts are, by and large, successful. But if, as choice (B) says, it's a rare day when an elected official is at all moved by a lobbying campaign, then the lobbyists are not successful. If (B) is true, if Congress gives these minority interests a deaf ear, then that denies the allegation (in the last sentence) that the lobbyists have destructive influence over decisions. That in turn categorically defuses the author's concerns about the danger to majority rule. Thus, choice (B) is an excellent weakener and the correct answer for Question 7.

Choice (A) is no good because the argument isn't about the quality of the majority opinion; the author is only concerned with whether the majority's opinion is being sufficiently represented and doesn't care if that opinion is rather ignorant or foolish. Choice (C) supports the argument: If interest groups can (as it says) raise a lot of cash, they can then use the cash for lobbying purposes—the exact sort of situation that has the author all bent out of shape. So (C) lends fuel to the author's flame. As for choice (D), even if groups are entitled to employ lobbyists, it doesn't weaken the author's claim that the effect of lobbyists is dangerous. There are many things all of us are entitled or permitted to do that may not be good for us or for society. Finally, choice (E): there need not be any clear-cut majority position on any one issue in order for the argument to make sense. The point again is that lobbies obscure the majority position such that Congress can't even tell whether it is clear-cut, or even what it

is. Even if the majority position were not, as (E) says, one definite position but a mush of many, the author wants Congress to be able to have a clear view that that is the case. Despite choice (E), the lobbyists may still muddy Congress's view, as the author alleges. But if choice (B) is true, then the lobbyists do not muddy the view, and that's why it's the answer to Question 7.

Question 8

To look for an argument that "resembles" the stimulus is to find a parallel argument, one whose structure is as close as possible to that of the original. The stimulus says that if you lower taxes, people will buy more things. Doing so will stimulate economic growth, which in turn will raise salaries, which in turn will bring in more money for the government. Of course, you're not concerned here with whether this is a sound program or a bogus one but with how it's put together. And the bottom line is, what you have here is something of a paradox: begin by lowering taxes, which (you'd assume) would lower government revenues, and in the end, government revenues will increase. To abstract it further, it goes like so: engaging in a particular action will (in the end) give you a result that's the opposite of what you might have expected.

And that's what you get in correct choice (D). Though it would be reasonable to expect that more employee days off would reduce productivity (since they'd be spending less time on the job), in fact productivity will be greater, the exact opposite effect, because of the greater efficiency that (D) says will emerge. The chain of events described in the stimulus may be a little longer—it has more steps—than choice (D), but its overall shape is very similar.

Choice (A) presents no paradox at all. You would expect that reducing overtime would bring down costs and increase total income. Naturally it would. The course of action choice (A) outlines is predictable. But what you want in your answer is a surprising result from a course of action.

Choice (B) departs from the stimulus's pattern.

 KAPLAN 49

The original gives you the government reducing income taxes and getting more money back because of it. (B) has the government changing the rules about the school lunch program and the farmers—a third party—reaping a benefit. This is a bit underhanded, but it's certainly not a paradox; more importantly, the benefit to a third party is not at all what happens in the stimulus.

Choice (C)'s plan certainly carries a bit of irony in its assertion that rating a movie "X" ends up corrupting the morals of the community. But as in choice (B)—and *unlike* correct choice (D)—the agent who performs the first action here (the censor) is not the one who reaps the ultimate benefit or, indeed, is directly affected by the action. Choice (E), meanwhile, may be even less of a paradox than choice (A). It is not at all surprising that a kid given more practice managing money ends up learning the value of thrift. It is surprising that a company's giving employees more days off should make them better workers and bring the business more revenue, and that's why choice (D) is correct for Question 8.

Question 9

Four of the five answer choices in Question 9 support the logic, so you'll be looking for a statement that either weakens the logic or has no effect on it. The conclusion is that the way a judge came into his or her job, and thus how much job security he or she has, often determines how a case will come out—that judges decide differently depending on whether they were elected or appointed for life or only for a short term. How so? Short-term judges (it goes on to say) think about their cases in light of which way the political winds are blowing, whereas appointed-for-life judges don't care about political trends and rely solely on a long tradition of judicial theory. In the end, then, the author evidently believes that the wiser judge is the life-term judge.

Since the author provides nothing concrete to back up his claim that short-term judges keep looking back over their shoulders to politics, whereas life-term judges

don't, the answer choices have many opportunities to support the reasoning. Choice (A), for instance, supports the idea that the short-term judges are likely to be moved by the prevailing political climate. If, as (A) says, they really want to keep their jobs, they will be more likely to decide the way the voters want them to decide in order to improve their election chances. Likewise, choice (C) supports that connection between the approval of the voters (which is necessary for re-election, of course) and the voters' view of the judge's decisions, by showing that short-term judges "happen" to rule in a way the voters approve of. And if you jump ahead to choice (E), here you get perhaps the strongest support for the allegation that short-term judges have one eye on the scales of justice and the other on the mood of the voters—according to (E), they're the only judges who use pollsters, whose sole purpose is to track public opinion.

So choices (A), (C), and (E) lend greater credence to the allegations about short-term judges. Meanwhile, Choice (D) lends support to the other part of the argument—the view of lifelong judges—in its comment that appointed judges show great consistency in their thinking over the years. Choice (D) implies that those judges, as alleged by the author, do turn a blind eye to the vicissitudes of politics and decide based on fundamental, lasting principles.

You're left with choice (B), which may in fact weaken the argument. If (B) is right in its claim that long-term judges keep their ear to the political ground as much as short-term judges do, then that damages the distinction between judges raised in the argument. And when that distinction is hurt, so is the conclusion based on it. Even if long-term judges don't act on their political knowledge, choice (B) is simply irrelevant. You might have seen this directly—you might have picked (B) right from the start. But it was useful to go through this process and demonstrate how you could have answered it by process of elimination. Either way may be helpful for you on a given question on the LSAT. Certainly, either way gets you to choice (B) for Question 9.

Question 10

The author in Question 10 is refuting some "so-called pacifists" (that's his phrase) who, you learn by inference, have been calling for weapons reductions to create a climate of peace. The author, however, believes quite the opposite, that a "climate of peace" has been created by increased military spending on things like new weapons systems and more personnel. How does the author support this claim that a climate of peace exists and exists because of the greater military spending? He does so by pointing to the number of attacks on this country and its allies. Fewer attacks, it is said, have occurred since military spending began to rise, and thus the author sees a causal connection between the "defense readiness" maintained by greater spending and the low number of attacks.

Now the assumption underlying this causal connection is your goal in Question 10, and you find it in choice (E). It has to be true that had defense spending not gone up, the number of attacks on this country and its allies would have increased. Otherwise there would be no causal connection between the two phenomena, as the author claims. Remember the assertion is that high defense spending has caused fewer military engagements (and, in turn, a "climate of peace"). That assertion is true only if choice (E) is true, and that's what you need in a major assumption.

Choice (A), in its reference to the possible causes of military actions, is irrelevant. The author doesn't refer to what causes them but simply asserts that military readiness can prevent them irrespective of the cause. With regard to choice (B), the author doesn't tell you how and why more defense spending has prevented military actions, just that it has done so. The so-called "climate of peace," in the author's view, is based on the greater spending on defense this country has engaged in and is not necessarily attributable to any trends in defense spending on the part of this country's adversaries (which is choice (B)'s thrust). And the author makes no claim about the future of peace or of military spending, choice (C). The thrust of the argument is toward the past and what past spending has done to

peace in the past. Whether all this readiness can permit future cuts is a matter upon which the author doesn't speculate. Finally, choice (D)'s equation of weapons and personnel is silly, specious, and irrelevant. Both are mentioned as key elements of the current peace climate, and both have benefited from having more money available. But while the author might have an opinion as to which (weapons or personnel) are more valuable, he's keeping it to himself if he does. So you cannot ascribe choice (D)'s view to him. You can be sure he subscribes to choice (E), which makes it the best answer for Question 10.

Question 11

In Question 11, you're asked for a conclusion. The stimulus argument basically describes some conditions and factors that influence whether or not, and how much, passersby will give to panhandlers.

There are two conditions here. First, if passersby find a panhandler to be destitute and forced to beg, they may give her quite a bit of money. Second, and on the other hand, if passersby think they are being conned or that the panhandler is merely lazy, they won't give her anything at all.

So basically the passage is showing you how the perceptions that people have of panhandlers affect their reactions to them. Thus, the most reliable conclusion is choice (D). People decide whether to give to a panhandler based on how they perceive her—as sincere or lazy and dishonest. It's choice (D) for Question 11.

As soon as you realize that the passage is describing only how people's perceptions influence their reactions, you can eliminate a couple of wrong answers. The passage never tells you whether most panhandlers are lazy or not; it merely speaks of what happens if people perceive them as lazy. Thus, (A) is incorrect.

The same problem exists in (B). You don't know that some beggars can't fool passersby. The stimulus speaks of people's perceptions, not the reality underneath those perceptions.

As for (C), it's a misreading of the first condition. Appearing truly needy is necessary for getting money from passersby; yet it need not be sufficient. Furthermore, (C) speaks of most passersby, which needn't be true at all. Perhaps most people never give money to panhandlers.

And finally, (E) concludes that a completely new factor, the amount of change one has, doesn't influence the decision making of passersby. There are no grounds for concluding this. The stimulus presents some factors in the decision making, but it never says that these are the only factors. So (E) could well be false, and the correct answer for Question 11 remains choice (D).

Answer Key for Logical Reasoning Practice Set

1. A   5. C   9. B
2. C   6. E   10. E
3. C   7. B   11. D
4. E   8. D

CHAPTER THREE

Logic Games

HIGHLIGHTS

• Understand the four basic principles of Logic Games

• Improve your sequencing, grouping, and matching skills

• Use the Kaplan Five-Step Method for Logic Games

• Complete the Logic Games Practice Set

Nothing inspires more fear in the hearts of LSAT test takers than Analytical Reasoning, affectionately known as Logic Games. Why? In part because the skills tested on the section seem so unfamiliar—you need to turn a game's information to your advantage by organizing your thinking and spotting key deductions, and that's not easy to do.

Games tend to give most trouble to students who don't have a clearly defined method of attack. And that's where Kaplan's basic principles, game-specific strategies and techniques, and Five-Step Method for Logic Games will help most, streamlining your work so you can rack up points quickly and confidently.

The following are the major analytical skills that the Logic Games section is intended to measure:

• **Organization**—the ability to assimilate efficiently, both in your head and on the page, the formidable amount of data associated with each game

Note

Many LSAT takers live in fear of the Logic Games section. But Logic Games are definitely manageable —if you take control of the test as we recommend.

- **Mental agility**—the ability to keep track of multiple pieces of information simultaneously, and still maintain enough flexibility to shuffle the pieces around in different ways for each question
- **Memory**—the ability to retain the work done in the setup stage while focusing on the new information in each question stem
- **Concentration**—the ability to keep focused on the task at hand and not let your mind wander

Let's now take a look at the major principles that should guide your work on this section.

The Four Basic Principles of Logic Games

The rallying cry of the Logic Games–impaired is: "If only I had more time, I could do these!" Well, this is no consolation on the day of the test, when you simply won't have any extra time. You can spend as much time on a game as you like when you're sitting in your own living room, but when your proctor says, "You have 35 minutes . . . begin," he or she is not kidding around. Remember, the test makers aren't testing just to see who can answer the 23 to 24 Logic Games questions correctly, but also who can do so in 35 minutes.

Logic Games is perhaps the most speed-sensitive section of the test. The test makers know that if you (not to mention an intelligent ten-year-old) could spend hours methodically trying out every choice in every question, you'd probably get everything right. But what does that prove? Nothing. Who's going to get the sought-after legal position or win the important client—the person who can write the legal brief and prepare the court case in four days, or the person who can do the same job in four hours? It's all about efficiency, both on the test and in your future career.

And that brings us to the first, and somewhat paradoxical sounding, Logic Games principle:

To Go Faster, Slow Down

To gain time in Logic Games, you must spend a lot of time thinking through and analyzing the setup and the rules. This is not only the most important principle for Logic Games success, it's also the one that's most often ignored, probably because it just doesn't seem right intuitively; people having timing difficulties tend to speed up, not slow down. But by spending a little extra time up front thinking through the stimulus, the "action" of the game, and the rules, you'll be able to recognize the game's key issues and make important deductions that will actually save you time in the long run.

Teacher Tip

"Students often look quizzical when I reveal to them that I like Logic Games. I explain that when I first learned how to do them, my instructor treated them like games, instead of like problems. If you enjoy crosswords, card games, or puzzles, for example, you can enjoy Logic Games."
—Jaelithe Russ
Kaplan Teacher
Akron, OH

Kaplan Tip

We know it sounds paradoxical, but you really do save time in the long run by taking the time to think about a Logic Game's scenario before jumping into its questions.

Games are structured so that, in order to answer the questions quickly and correctly, you need to search out relevant pieces of information that combine to form valid new statements called *deductions*. Now, you can either do this once, up front, and then utilize the same deductions throughout the game, or you can choose to piece together the same basic deductions—essentially repeating the same work—for every single question.

For instance, let's say that two of the rules for a Logic Game go as follows:

If Bob is chosen for the team, then Eric is also chosen.
If Eric is chosen for the team, then Pat will not be chosen.

You can, as you read through the rules of the game, just treat those rules as two separate pieces of independent information. But there's a deduction to be made from them. Do you see it? If Bob is chosen, Eric is, too. If Eric is chosen, Pat is not. That means that, if Bob is chosen, Pat is not chosen. That's an important deduction—one that will undoubtedly be required from question to question. If you don't take the time to make it up front, when you're first considering the game, you'll have to make it over and over again, every time it's necessary to answer a question. But if you take the time to make this deduction up front, and build it into your entire conception of the game, you'll save that time later. You won't be doing the same work several times.

The choice is yours; we just find that the rush-to-the-questions method is inefficient, time-consuming, and stress-inducing.

So, always try to take the game scenario and the rules as far as you can before moving on to the questions. Look for common elements among the rules (like Eric in the rules above)—this will help you combine them and pull out major deductions. The stimulus creates a situation, and the rules place restrictions on what can and cannot happen within that situation. If you investigate the possible scenarios, and look for and find major deductions up front, you'll then be able to rack up points quickly and confidently.

Understand What a Rule Means, Not Just What It Says

If you're interested in demonstrating how well you can read a statement and then spit it back verbatim, you'd be better off training to be a legal secretary instead of a legal practitioner or scholar. That's why you'll never see this on the LSAT:

RULE: Arlene is not fifth in line.
QUESTION: Which one of the following people is not fifth in line?
ANSWER: Arlene.

Kaplan Rules

To fully grasp a rule in Logic Games, you must know more than just what it says. You've got to know what the rule means in the context of the game and in combination with other rules.

True, some Logic Games questions are easy—but not that easy. The LSAT, after all, measures critical thinking, and virtually every sentence in Logic Games has to be filtered through some sort of analytical process before it will be of any use. You may have to use the information about Arlene to help you eliminate a choice or lead you to the right answer, but even in the simplest of cases, this will involve the application, as opposed to the mere parroting, of the rule.

So, getting back to the principle, it's not enough just to copy a rule off the page (or shorthand it, as we'll discuss momentarily); it's imperative that you think through its exact meaning, including any implications it might have. And don't limit this behavior to the indented rules; statements in the games' introductions are very often rules in and of themselves, and warrant the same meticulous consideration.

For instance, let's say a game's introduction sets up a scenario in which you have three boxes, each containing at least two of the following three types of candy—chocolates, gumdrops, and mints. Then you get the following rule:

Box 2 does not contain any gumdrops.

What does that rule say? That there aren't any gumdrops in Box 2. But what does that rule *mean,* when you think about it in the context of the game? That Box 2 *does* contain chocolates and mints. Each box contains at least two of three things, remember. Once you eliminate one of the three things for any particular box, therefore, you know that the other two things *must* be in that box.

Part of understanding what a rule means, moreover, is grasping what the rule *doesn't* mean. For example, take the rule we mentioned earlier:

RULE: If Bob is chosen for the team, then Eric is also chosen.
MEANS: Whenever Bob is chosen, Eric is, too.
DOESN'T MEAN: Whenever Eric is chosen, Bob is, too.

Remember the discussion of formal logic in the Logical Reasoning chapter? If I yell loudly at my cat Adrian, he will run away. That does mean that whenever I yell at him loudly, he runs away. But it *doesn't* mean that whenever he runs away, I've yelled at him.

Use Scratchwork and Shorthand

The proper use of scratchwork can help you do your best on Logic Games. As you may recall, the directions state: "You may wish to draw a rough sketch to help answer some of the questions." Notice that they use the wording *rough sketch,* not *masterpiece, work of art,* or *classic picture for*

Kaplan Rules

You must know the rules of a Logic Game cold—what they mean, how they impact on other rules, and what implications they have in the context of the game scenario.

the ages. The LSAT is not a drawing contest; you get no points for creating beautiful diagrams on the page.

Although some games aren't amenable to scratchwork, for most games you'll find that it is helpful to create a master sketch, one that encapsulates all of the game's information in one easy-to-reference picture. Doing so will not only give your eye a place to gravitate towards when you need information, but it will also help to solidify in your mind the action of the game, the rules, and whatever deductions you come up with up front.

Remember to keep your scratchwork simple—the less time you spend drawing, the more time you'll have for thinking and answering questions. Pay careful attention to the scratchwork suggestions in the explanations to the four games on each of the Practice Tests in the back of this book.

Part of your scratchwork should involve jotting down on your page a quick and shortened form of most rules. *Shorthand* is a visual representation of a mental thought process, and is useful only if it reminds you at a glance of the rule's meaning. Whether you shorthand a rule or commit it to memory, you should never have to look back at the game itself once you get to the questions.

The goal of the entire scratchwork process is to condense a lot of information into manageable, user-friendly visual cues. It's much easier to remember rules written like so:

B → E
No G in 2

than ones written like so:

If Bob is chosen for the team, then Eric is also chosen.
Box 2 does not contain any gumdrops.

This is helpful as long as you know, for instance, what the arrow from B to E means, and you're consistent in using it. If you can develop a personal shorthand that's instantly understandable to you, you'll have a decided advantage on the day of the test.

Try to Set off Chains of Deduction

When hypothetical information is offered in a question stem, try to use it to set off a chain of deductions. Consider the following question. (Since this question is excerpted without the accompanying introduction and rules, ignore the specific logic of the discussion; it's just presented to make a point.)

If the speedboat is yellow, which one of the following must be true?

(A) The car is green.
(B) The airplane is red.
(C) The train is black.
(D) The car is yellow.
(E) The train is red.

The question stem contains a *hypothetical*, which is an if-clause offering information pertaining only to that particular question. The wrong approach is to acknowledge that the speedboat is yellow and then proceed to test out all of the choices. The muddled mental thought process accompanying this tragic approach might sound something like this:

> "All right, the speedboat's yellow, does the car have to be green? Well, let's see, if the speedboat's yellow, and the car is green, then the train would have to be yellow, but I can't tell what color the airplane is, and I guess this is okay, I don't know, I better try the next choice. Let's see what happens if the speedboat's yellow and the airplane is red. . . . "

Don't do this kind of dithering! Notice that the question doesn't ask: "What happens if, in addition to this, the car is green?" or "What happens if this is true and the airplane is red?" So why is the confused test taker above intent on answering all of these irrelevant questions? Never begin a question by trying out answer choices; that's going about it backwards. Only if you're entirely stuck, or are faced with a question stem that leaves you no choice, should you resort to trial and error.

Most Logic Games questions are amenable to a more efficient and systematic methodology. The correct approach is to incorporate the new piece of information into your view of the game, creating one quick sketch if you wish. How do you do this? Simple: Apply the rules and any previous deductions to the new information in order to set off a new chain of deductions. Then follow through until you've taken the new information as far as it can go. Just as you must take the game and rules as far as you can before moving on to the questions, you must carry the information in a question stem out as far as you can before moving on to the choices.

So make sure to stay out of answer-choice land until you have sufficiently mined the hypothetical. If the question stem contains a hypothetical, then your job is to get as much out of that piece of information as you can before even looking at the choices. This way, *you* dictate to the test, and not the other way around. You'll then be able to determine the answer and simply pick it off the page.

Kaplan Rules

Trial and error with the answer choices should be your last resort, not your first. It's much quicker to follow a chain of deduction until it leads you to the answer. In some cases, trial and error is necessary, but don't turn to it unless you have to.

KAPLAN

You'll have a chance to see these major Logic Games principles in action when you review the explanations to the games in the Practice Tests in the back of this book.

The Three Crucial Logic Games Skills

Although the Logic Games section can contain a wide variety of situations and scenarios, certain skills are required again and again. These are the most common:

Sequencing

Logic Games that require sequencing skills have long been a favorite of the test makers. No matter what the scenario in games of this type, the common denominator is that in some way, shape, or form, they all involve putting entities in order. In a typical sequencing game, you may be asked to arrange the cast of characters numerically from left to right, from top to bottom, in days of the week, in a circle, and so on. The sequence may be a sequence of degree—say, ranking the eight smartest test takers from one to eight. On the other hand, the sequence may be based on time, such as one that involves the order of shows broadcast on a radio station. In some cases, there are two or even three orderings to keep track of in a single game.

Fixed and Unfixed Sequences
There are generally two types of sequence games: the fixed, or standard sequence, and the unfixed, or "free floating" sequence. In a *fixed* sequence game, the placement of entities is very strictly defined. We may be told, for example, that "A is third," or that "X and Y are adjacent," and so on. These are definite, concrete pieces of information, and the game centers around placing as many people into definite spots as possible. In contrast to this, in an *unfixed* or "free floating" sequence game, our job is to rank the entities only in relation to one another. We're usually never asked to fully determine the ordering of the cast of characters. Instead, the relationships *between* the entities constitute the crux of the game.

Typical Sequence Game Issues
The following is a list of the key issues that underlie sequencing games. Each key issue is followed by a corresponding rule—in some cases, with several alternative ways of expressing the same rule. At the end, we'll use these rules to build a miniature Logic Game, so that you can see how rules work together to define and limit a game's "action." These rules all refer to a scenario in which eight events are to be sequenced from first to eighth:

At a Glance

Sequencing:
- It's historically the most popular game type.
- It involves putting entities in order.
- It comes in two varieties—fixed and unfixed ("free floating").
- Its orderings can be in time (the sequence of shows on a radio station), space (people standing next to one another in line), or degree (shortest to tallest, worst to best, etcetera).

• Which entities are concretely placed in the ordering?

> X is third.

• Which entities are forbidden from a specific position in the ordering?

> Y is not fourth.

• Which entities are next to, adjacent to, or are immediately preceding or following one another?

> X and Y are consecutive.
> *X is next to Y.*
> *No event comes between X and Y.*
> *X and Y are consecutive in the ordering.*

• Which entities *cannot be* next to, adjacent to, or immediately preceding or following one another?

> X does not immediately precede or follow Z.
> *X is not immediately before or after Z.*
> *At least one event comes between X and Z.*
> *X and Z are not consecutive in the sequence.*

• How far apart in the ordering are two particular entities?

> Exactly two events come between X and Q.

• What is the relative position of two entities in the ordering?
> Q comes before T in the sequence.
> *T comes after Q in the sequence.*

How a Sequence Game Works
Let's see how rules like those above might combine to create a simple Logic Game.

> Eight events—Q, R, S, T, W, X, Y, and Z—are being ordered from first to eighth.
> X is third.
> Y is not fourth.
> X and Y are consecutive.
> Exactly two events come between X and Q.
> Q occurs before T in the sequence.

How would you approach this simplified game? Remember our third basic principle: use scratchwork and shorthand. With eight events to sequence from first to eighth, you'd probably want to draw eight dashes in the margin of your test booklet, maybe in two groups of four (so you can easily determine which dash is which). Then take the rules in order of concreteness, starting with the most concrete of all—Rule 1—which tells you that X is third. Fill that into your sketch:

Jump to the next most concrete rule, Rule 4, which tells you that exactly two events come between X and Q. Well, since Q can't obey this rule coming before X, it must come after X—in the sixth space.

Rule 5 says that Q comes before T. Since Q is sixth, T must be either seventh or eighth. To indicate this, under the sketch, write T with two arrows pointing to the seventh and eighth dashes.

Meanwhile, Rule 3 says that X and Y are consecutive. X is third, so Y will be either second or fourth. Rule 2 clears up that matter. Y can't be fourth, says Rule 2, so it will have to be second:

$$\underline{} \quad \underline{Y} \quad \underline{X} \quad \underline{} \quad \quad \underline{} \quad \underline{Q} \quad \underline{} \quad \underline{}$$
$$\kern{9em}\nwarrow T \nearrow$$

And this is how the rules work together to build a sequence game. The questions might then present hypothetical information that would set off the "chain of deduction" we mentioned in the basic principles section. You'll see how this works in the sequencing games on the Practice Tests. Those are full-strength sequencing games, so make sure to pay careful attention to the written explanations.

Grouping

All games begin with a set of entities. What sets grouping apart is the "action" of the game, or specifically, what you're asked to do with the entities. In a pure grouping game, unlike sequencing, there's no call for putting the entities in order. Instead, you'll usually be required to "select" a smaller group from the initial group, or "distribute" the entities in some fashion into more than one subgroup. As a distinct skill, grouping differs from sequencing in that you're not really concerned with what order the entities are in, but rather how they're grouped—who's in, who's out, and who can and cannot be with whom in various subgroups.

Grouping:
- It's a very popular game type.
- It comes in two varieties—selection and distribution.
- The number element is often crucial (how many chosen, how many in each group, etcetera).
- Its action involves deciding if each entity is in or out; if it is in, you may then need to determine where (in distribution games).

Grouping Games of Selection and Distribution

In "selection" games, you'll be given the cast of characters and told to select from them a smaller group, based, of course, on a set of rules. For example, a game may include eight musical cassettes, from which you must choose four. Sometimes the test makers specify an exact number for the smaller group, and other times they don't. A small variation of this type occurs when the initial group of entities is itself broken up in groups to begin the game. An example would be a farmer choosing three animals from a group of three cows and five horses.

In "distribution" games, we're more concerned with who goes where than we are with who's chosen and who isn't (who's in and who's out, in other words). Sometimes, every entity will end up in a group—an example is placing or distributing eight marbles into two jars, four to a jar. On the other hand, it's perfectly viable for a game to mandate the placement of three marbles in each jar, leaving two marbles out in the cold.

It's important for you to be aware of the numbers that govern each particular grouping game, because although all grouping games rely on the same general skills, you have to adapt these skills to the specific situations of each. Still, all grouping games revolve around the same basic questions. Is this entity in? Is it out? If it's not in this group, is it in that one?

Like sequencing games, grouping games have a language all their own, and it's up to you to speak that language fluently when you come across games that require this particular skill on your test.

Typical Issues—Grouping Games of Selection

The following is a list of the key issues that underlie grouping games of selection. Each key issue is followed by a corresponding rule—in some cases, with several alternative ways of expressing the same rule. At the end, again, we'll use these rules to build a miniature Logic Game.

These rules all refer to a scenario in which you are to select a subgroup of four from a group of eight entities—Q, R, S, T, W, X, Y, and Z:
- Which entities are definitely chosen?

    Q is selected.

- Which entities rely on a different entity's selection in order to be chosen?

    If X is selected, then Y is selected.
    X will be selected only if Y is selected.
    X will not be selected unless Y is selected.

Note: A common misconception surrounds the rule, "If X is selected, then Y is selected." This works only in one direction; if X is chosen, Y must be, but if Y is chosen, X may or may not be. Remember the discussion of the second principle above—understand what a rule means, but also what it doesn't mean!

• Which entities must be chosen together, or not at all?

> If Y is selected, then Z is selected, and and if Z is selected, then Y is selected.
> *Y will not be selected unless Z is selected, and vice versa.*

• Which entities cannot both be chosen?

> If R is selected, then Z is not selected.
> *If Z is selected, then R is not selected.*
> *R and Z won't both be selected.*

How Grouping Games of Selection Work
We can combine these rules to create a rudimentary grouping game of selection:

> A professor must choose a group of four books for her next seminar. She must choose from a pool of eight books—Q, R, S, T, W, X, Y, and Z.
>> Q is selected.
>> If X is selected then Y is selected.
>> If Y is selected, Z is selected, and if Z is selected, then Y is selected.
>> If R is selected, Z is not selected.

One good way of dealing with this kind of game is to write out the eight letters—four on top, four on the bottom—and then circle the ones that are definitely selected while crossing out the ones that are definitely not selected. Thus, Rule 1 would allow you to circle the Q:

The other rules can't be built into the sketch just yet, since they describe eventualities (what happens if something else happens). Here's where you'd want to use shorthand:

- Rule 2 translates as, "If X, then Y" or "X ——> Y."
- Rule 3 might be rendered as, "YZ together" (as a reminder to choose them together, if at all).
- Rule 4 could be shorthanded as, "Never RZ" (since R and Z are mutually exclusive).

The rules would then be poised to take effect whenever a question would add new hypothetical information, setting off a chain of deduction. For instance, let's say a question reads like so:

If R is selected, which of the following must be true?

This new information would put the rules into motion. R's inclusion would set off Rule 4—"Never RZ"—so we'd have to circle R and cross out Z:

This would in turn set off Rule 3—"YZ together." Since Z is out, Y is out, because they must be chosen together or not at all:

Now Rule 2 comes into play. "X ———> Y" means that if Y is not chosen, X can't be either (since X's inclusion would require Y's). So we can take the chain of deduction one step further:

A correct answer to this question, then, might be "X is not selected." And that, in a nutshell, is how a (simplified) grouping game of selection works.

Typical Issues—Grouping Games of Distribution
Here are the issues involved in the other kind of grouping game—grouping games of distribution—along with the rules that govern them. These rules, by the way, refer to a scenario in which the members of our old favorite group of eight entities—Q, R, S, T, W, X, Y, Z—have to be distributed into three different classes:

- Which entities are concretely placed in a particular subgroup?

    X is placed in Class 3.

- Which entities are barred from a particular subgroup?

    Y is not placed in Class 2.

- Which entities must be placed in the same subgroup?

    X is placed in the same class as Z.
    Z is placed in the same class as X.
    X and Z are placed in the same class.

- Which entities cannot be placed in the same subgroup?

    X is not placed in the same class as Y.
    Y is not placed in the same class as X.
    X and Y are not placed in the same class.

- Which entity's placement depends on the placement of a different entity?

    If Y is placed in Class 1, then Q is placed in Class 2.

How Grouping Games of Distribution Work

The above rules, neatly enough, also can combine to form a miniature grouping game of distribution.

> Eight students—Q, R, S, T, W, X, Y, and Z—must be subdivided into three different classes—Classes 1, 2, and 3.
>
> X is placed in Class 3.
> Y is not placed in Class 2.
> X is placed in the same class as Z.
> X is not placed in the same class as Y.
> If Y is placed in Class 1, then Q is placed in Class 2.

A good scratchwork scheme for games of this type would be to draw three circles in your booklet, one for each of the three classes. Then put the eight entities in the appropriate circles as that information becomes known.

Here again, start with the most concrete rule first, which is Rule 1, which definitively places X in Class 3. Rule 2 just as definitively precludes Y from Class 2, so build that into the scratchwork, too:

Rule 3 requires Z to join X in Class 3:

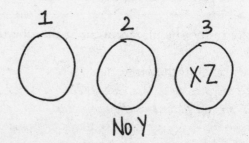

Rule 4, prohibiting Y from being in the same class as X, means that Y can't be in Class 3. But we already know that Y can't be in Class 2. We can deduce, therefore, that Y must go in Class 1. That in turn puts Rule 5 into play: if Y is in Class 1 (as it is here), Q is in Class 2:

No Y

And that is the dynamic of most grouping games of distribution (though, again, in much simplified form). For more complex distribution games, check out the Practice Tests and Answers in the back of this book.

Matching

The third skill we need to discuss is matching. Matching games have haunted LSAT test takers since they came into favor some years ago. As the name implies, matching games ask you to match up various characteristics about a group of entities. They often require you to distribute many characteristics at once. A game may involve three animals, each assigned a name, a color, and a particular size. It's no wonder test takers get bogged down in these types—there's often a lot to keep track of.

Some people dislike matching games because they feel as if they're being bombarded with information, and they don't know where to start. Organization, as in any game, is crucial for matching games. A table or grid can be helpful, but for some games you need to rely on your instincts to organize the information efficiently based on the particulars of the game. If you do use a sketch, and this goes for any game, remember that *thinking must always precede writing*. A visual representation of a mental thought process can be invaluable, whereas scribbling thoughtlessly for the sake of getting something down on the page is useless, and even detrimental.

One matching hint is to try to center the game around the most important characteristic—the one with the most information attached to it. Going back to the example above, don't necessarily assume that you should organize your thinking, or a sketch, around the animals—there may be a better attribute, one that you know more about, that should take center stage. An efficient test taker spends less time panicking and being intimidated by all of the information in a matching game, and more time visualizing the action and creating a mental picture or a sketch on the page that places the elements into a logical order. If you think through the scenarios and don't get scared off by their seeming complexity, you should find matching games accessible and even fun.

At a Glance

Matching:
- It's a very popular game type.
- It's often the most complicated game type.
- It usually has many characteristics and relationships to keep track of.
- It may include if/then rules, which can be handled by applying the contrapositive.
- A table or grid will often help keep track of the information.

Typical Matching Game Issues

The following is a list of the key issues that underlie matching games. Each key issue is followed by a corresponding rule or set of rules. All of these rules refer to a situation in which we have three animals—a dog, a cat, and a goat. Each animal has a name (Bimpy, Hank, and Sujin), a color (brown, black, or white), and a size (large or small):

• Which entities are matched up?

>   The dog is brown.
>   The black animal is small.

• Which entities are not matched up?

>   Bimpy is not white.
>   The goat is not large.

Kaplan Rules

Use the contrapositive on all if/then rules in Logic Games. It will almost always yield an important deduction.

• Which entity's matchups depend on the matchups of other entities?

>   If the cat is large, then Hank is brown.
>   If the white animal is small, then Sujin is not the dog.

Notice that these last rules take the form of if/then statements, which, based on our discussion of Logical Reasoning in the previous chapter, means that the contrapositive can be employed. Whenever rules take this form, you should always work out the contrapositive and then add the result, as a valid deduction, to your view of the game. Remember, the contrapositive can be formed by reversing and negating the terms of an if/then statement. For the first, we get:

>   If Hank is NOT brown, then the cat is NOT large.

Taking the contrapositive of the second rule results in this statement:

>   If Sujin IS the dog, then the white animal is NOT small.

Both of these new pieces of information are just as powerful as any of the indented rules given in the game's introduction.

How Matching Games Work

You know the drill by now. Let's take some of the rules above and form them into a minilogic game:

A rancher owns three animals—a dog, a cat, and a goat. The animals are named Bimpy, Hank, and Sujin, though not necessarily in that order. One of the animals is brown, one is black, and one is white. Two of the animals are large and one is small.

The dog is brown.
The black animal is small.
Bimpy is not white.
The goat is not large.
If the cat is large, then Hank is brown.

A good way to approach this game would be to set up a grid or chart to keep track of all of the attributes to be matched up:

(animal)	Dog	Cat	Goat
(name) BHS			
(size) LLS			
(color) br bl wh			

Notice that Rules 1 and 4—the most concrete rules—can be built into the sketch immediately.

(animal)	Dog	Cat	Goat
(name) BHS			
(size) LLS			not L
(color) ~~br~~ bl wh	br		

Kaplan Tip

Like math questions, Logic Games questions have definite right and wrong answers. Once you find the answer that works, pick it and move on. There's no need to check out the other choices.

But remember, think about what Rule 4 means, not just what it says. There are only two sizes here—small and large. If the goat is not large, it must be small, and since there are two large and only one small animal, we can deduce the size of the other two as well:

(animal)	Dog	Cat	Goat
(name) BHS			
(size) ~~L~~ ~~S~~	L	L	S not L
(color) ~~br~~ bl wh			

Once we know that the cat is large, moreover, Rule 5 kicks in, telling us that Hank is brown. And since we've already deduced that the brown animal is the large dog, we know that Hank is the large brown dog.

And that's how a simple matching game works. The third game of the Logic Games section on the Practice Tests is a typical matching game for you to work on. Pay careful attention to the way in which it's set up, as outlined in the written explanations.

More Logic Game Tips

Here are some other points to keep in mind on the Logic Games section:

Hybrid Games

Many games are what you might call "hybrid games," requiring you to combine sequencing, grouping, and/or matching skills (we'll have a look at one later on when we talk about the five-step method). Keep in mind that while we try to recognize games as a particular type, it's not necessary to attach a strict name to every game you encounter. For example, it really doesn't matter if you categorize a game as a sequencing game with a grouping element or as a grouping game with a sequencing element, as long as you're comfortable with both sets of skills.

No "Best" Choice

Unlike the answer choices in Logical Reasoning and Reading Comprehension, in which the correct answer is the "best" choice, the answers in Logic Games are objectively correct or incorrect. Therefore, when you find an answer that's definitely right, have the confidence to circle it and move on, without wasting time to check the other choices. This is one way to improve your timing on the section.

Common Elements and Deductions

Rules that contain common elements are often the ones that lead to deductions. Consider the following three rules:

> If Sybil goes to the party, then Edna will go to the party.
> If Jacqui goes to the party, then Sherry will not go to the party.
> If Edna goes to the party, then Dale will go to the party.

Rules 1 and 2 have no entities in common, which is a sure sign that we can't deduce anything from combining them. The same goes for Rules 2 and 3. But since Rules 1 and 3 have Edna in common, a deduction is possible (although not guaranteed). In this case, combining Rules 1 and 3 would allow us to deduce another rule: if Sybil goes to the party, then Dale will go also.

Focus on the Important Rules

Not all rules are equal—some are inherently more important than others. Try to focus first on the concrete ones and the ones that have the greatest impact on the situation, specifically the ones that involve the greatest number of the entities. These are also the rules to turn to first whenever you're stuck on a question and don't know how to set off the chain of deduction.

Know the Forms of Question Stems

You must have a solid command of the various forms of Logic Games question stems. When you take a few seconds to think through what kind of statements would be the right and wrong answers to a particular question, your work becomes more time efficient. You're also less likely to slip up at the last minute and pick the wrong thing. The following should clear up any misconceptions you may have regarding what the choices should look like for each of the major types of questions:

- If the question reads: Which one of the following statements *could be true?*—the right answer will be a statement that could be true, and the four wrong choices will be statements that definitely cannot be true (that is, statements that must be false).

Teacher Tip

"Don't overcorrect yourself, and don't think that just because the answer comes easily, it's got to be wrong. Stay confident!"
—Marilyn Engle
   Kaplan Teacher
   Encino, CA

Kaplan Tip

If you find you can't make a single important deduction by combining rules, you're probably missing something. Check the game introduction and rules again to make sure you're not misinterpreting something.

- If the question reads: Which one of the following statements *cannot be true?*—the right answer will be a statement that cannot be true, and the four wrong choices will be statements that either must be true or merely could be true.

- If the question reads: Which one of the following statements *must be true?*—the right answer will be a statement that must be true, and the four wrong choices will be statements that either cannot be true or merely could be true.

- If the question reads: All of the following statements *could be true EXCEPT . . .* , the right answer will be a statement that cannot be true, and the four wrong choices will be statements that either could be true or even must be true.

- If the question reads: All of the following statements *must be true EXCEPT . . .* , the right answer will be a statement that either cannot be true, or merely could be true, and the four wrong choices will be statements that must be true.

- If the question reads: Which one of the following statements *could be false?*—the right answer will be a statement that cannot be true or could be true or false, and the four wrong choices will be statements that must be true.

- If the question reads: Which one of the following statements *must be false?*—the right answer will be a statement that cannot be true, and the four wrong choices will be statements that either must be true or merely could be true.

KAPLAN

The Kaplan Five-Step Method for Logic Games

Now that you have some Logic Games background, it's time to see how you can marshall that knowledge into a systematic approach to games. The five steps of the Kaplan Method are as follows.

1. Get an Overview

Carefully read the game's introduction and rules to establish the "cast of characters," the "action," and the number limits governing the game.

2. Visualize and Map Out the Game

Make a mental picture of the situation, and let it guide you as you create a sketch, or some other kind of scratchwork, if necessary, to help you keep track of the rules and handle new information.

3. Consider the Rules Individually

As you think through the meaning and implications of each rule, you have three choices. You can:

- Build it directly into your sketch of the game situation
- Jot down the rule in shorthand form to help you remember it
- Underline or circle rules that don't lend themselves to the first two techniques

4. Combine the Rules

Look for common elements among the rules; that's what will lead you to make deductions. Treat these deductions as additional rules, good for the whole game.

5. Work on the Questions Systematically

Read the question stems carefully! Take special notice of words such as *must, could, cannot, not, impossible,* and *except.* As always, use the hypothetical information offered in *if*-clauses to set off a chain of deduction.

Using the Kaplan Five-Step Method for Logic Games

Here's how the approach can work with an actual Logic Game:

Questions 1–2

Five workers—Mona, Patrick, Renatta, Saffie, and Will—are scheduled to clean apartments on five days of a single week, Monday–Friday. There are three cleaning shifts available each day—a morning shift, an afternoon shift, and an evening shift. No more than one worker cleans in any given shift. Each worker cleans exactly two shifts during the week, but no one works more than one cleaning shift in a single day.

Exactly two workers clean on each day of the week.
Mona and Will clean on the same days of the week.
Patrick doesn't clean on any afternoon or evening shifts during the week.
Will doesn't clean on any morning or afternoon shifts during the week.
Mona cleans on two consecutive days of the week.
Saffie's second cleaning shift of the week occurs on an earlier day of the week than Mona's first cleaning shift.

1. Which one of the following must be true?

   (A) Saffie cleans on Tuesday afternoon.
   (B) Patrick cleans on Monday morning.
   (C) Will cleans on Thursday evening.
   (D) Renatta cleans on Friday afternoon.
   (E) Mona cleans on Tuesday morning.

2. If Will does not clean on Friday, which one of the following could be false?

   (A) Renatta cleans on Friday.
   (B) Saffie cleans on Tuesday.
   (C) Mona cleans on Wednesday.
   (D) Saffie cleans on Monday.
   (E) Patrick cleans on Tuesday.

(Note that there are only two questions accompanying this game; a typical logic game will have five to seven questions.)

1. Get an Overview

We need to schedule five workers, abbreviated M, P, R, S, and W, in a particular order during a five-day calendar week, Monday to Friday. The ordering element tells us we're dealing with a sequencing task, though there is a slight grouping element involved in that a couple of the rules deal with grouping issues—namely, which people can or cannot clean on the same day of the week as each other. That makes this a "hybrid" game—but remember, it doesn't matter what you call it, as long as you can do it.

Be very careful about the numbers governing this game; they go a long way in defining how the game works. There are to be exactly two workers per day (never cleaning on the same shift). Each worker must clean exactly two shifts, and since workers are forbidden to take two shifts in the same day, this means that each worker will clean on exactly two days. So, in effect, ten out of the 15 available shifts will be taken, and five will be left untouched.

2. Visualize and Map Out the Game

Go with whatever you feel is the most efficient way to keep track of the situation. Most people would settle on a sketch of the five days, each broken up into three shifts, like so:

Into this sketch—one letter per box—each entity will have to go twice (each worker does two shifts, remember). So your pool of entities to place would be: MMPPRRSSWW. You might want to include five X's (or Ø's) for the five shifts that won't be taken by anyone.

3. Consider the Rules Individually

We've already dealt with some of the number-related rules hidden in the game's introduction. Now let's consider this statement from the intro:

No more than one worker cleans in any given shift.

Kaplan Rules

Remember, you get no points for categorizing a game; you get points for answering questions correctly. Don't worry about what to call a game. Just decide what skills it will require.

Make sure you interpret rules like this correctly. You may have to paraphrase, in your own words, its exact meaning. In this case: two workers per shift is no good, three is out of the question, etcetera. But it doesn't mean that any given shift *must* have a worker. If the test makers meant to imply that, they would have written, "Exactly one worker cleans on every given shift." Notice the difference in wording. It's subtle, but it has a huge impact on the game.

Let's consider the other rules:

1) We've already handled Rule 1. You may wish to jot down "2 a day," or something like that, to remind you of this important information.

2) Mona and Will clean on the same days, and that holds for both of the days they clean. Shorthand this any way that seems fitting (one suggestion is to draw MW with a circle around it on your page).

3) and 4) We can handle these two rules together because they're so similar. You can shorthand these rules as they are, but you'd be doing yourself a great disservice. Instead, first work out their implications, which is actually a pretty simple matter. If Patrick doesn't clean afternoons or evenings, he *must* clean mornings. If Will doesn't clean mornings or afternoons, he *must* clean evenings. Always take the rules as far as you can, and *then* jot down their implications on your page for reference.

5) This one is pretty self-explanatory; Mona's shifts must be on consecutive days, such as Thursday and Friday. MM might be a good way to shorthand this.

6) Here's another sequencing rule—you must place both S's for Saffie on earlier days of the week than the two M's, for Mona. That means that Saffie and Mona can't clean on the same day (although we already knew that from Rule 2), and that Mona's shifts can't come before Saffie's. Try shorthanding this as (S . . . S . . . MM).

4. Combine the Rules

This is the crucial stage for most games. Here, notice that Mona appears in three of the six indented rules; that's a good indication that combining these rules should lead somewhere useful. Combining Rule 2 and Rule 5 gives us two Mona/Will days in a row: Will must be scheduled for evening shifts (remember, we turned Rule 4 into this positive statement). That means that Mona would take the morning or afternoon shift on these consecutive days.

Rule 6 concerns Mona as well: two Saffies before the two Monas. How is this possible? We need two S's on different days to come before the two consecutive M's. If Saffie's cleaning shifts are as early in the week as possible, she'll clean on Monday and Tuesday. That means that the earliest day that Mona can clean (and Will as well, thanks to Rule 2) is Wednesday. There's our first really key deduction:

> Mona and Will cannot clean on Monday and Tuesday;
> they must clean Wednesday, Thursday, or Friday.

Do we stop there? No, of course not. The difference between the Logic Games expert and the Logic Games novice is that the expert knows how to press on when further deductive possibilities exist. If you relate this deduction back to Rule 5, it becomes clear that Mona and Will must clean on Wednesday and Thursday, *or* on Thursday and Friday. This brings us to another big deduction:

> Either way, Mona and Will must clean on Thursday. Thanks to Rule 4, we can slot in Will for Thursday evening. Mona will then take Thursday morning *or* afternoon. The other Mona/Will day must be either Wednesday or Friday, to remain consecutive.

The following sketch shows what your completed sketch may look like, with as many of the rules built into it as possible.

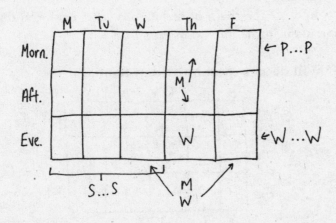

Now that we've combined the rules and have even uncovered a few big deductions, it's time to move on to the questions.

5. Work on the Questions Systematically

Now you'll see how all the work we did up front pays off. Question 1 offers no hypothetical information; it simply asks what must be true. And since we've already deduced a few things that must be true, we can scan the choices for one that matches any one of our newly discovered pieces of information. It doesn't take long to spot choice (C)—it's our big deduction staring us right in the face. You shouldn't even waste time checking the other choices. Instead, have the confidence that you've done the right work the right way, and circle (C) and move on. (Just for the record, for those of you who are curious, (A), (B), and (D) could be true, but need not be, while (E), as we discovered earlier, is an impossibility.)

Question 2 contains a hypothetical: no Will on Friday. One glance at our sketch tells us that the second Mona/Will cluster must therefore be placed on Wednesday, next to the Thursday Mona/Will group. Saffie must then clean on Monday and Tuesday, in order to satisfy Rule 6 (although we don't yet know the exact shifts she takes during those days).

That brings us to the two questions that test takers ask all too infrequently: "Who's left?" and more importantly, "Where can they go?" Two P's and two R's are left to place, with one spot on Monday, one spot on Tuesday, and two spots on Friday open to place them. How can this be done? Friday can't get both P's or both R's (from the last sentence in the introduction), so it will have to get one of each, with P in the morning and R in either the afternoon or evening. The other P and the other R will join S on Monday or Tuesday, in either order. Of course, whichever day P is on, he must be in the morning, whereas the exact shifts for R and S are ambiguous.

Look at how far the chain of deductions takes us, beginning with the simple statement in the question stem:

If Will doesn't clean on Friday, then . . .

With all of this information at our disposal, there's not a question in the world we can't answer correctly. This one asks for a statement that could be false—which means that the four wrong choices will all be things that must be true. And in fact, choices (A) through (D) match the situation in this question perfectly, while (E) merely could be true: Patrick's first cleaning shift of the week *could be* on Tuesday, but it just as easily *could be* on Monday as well. (His second shift must be on Friday, of course.) (E) is therefore the only choice that could be false.

Conclusion

This concludes our general discussion of the Logic Games section. Try to use the Five-Step Method, and all of the techniques mentioned in this chapter, when you work through the following set of practice questions and the games in the Practice Tests.

Logic Games Practice Set

<u>Directions:</u> Each group of questions is based on a passage or a set of conditions. You may wish to draw a diagram to answer some of the questions. Choose the <u>best</u> answer for each question.

Questions 1–5: Six people—Matt, Ned, Qi Li, Stanley, Tonga, and Vladimir—are sitting around a rectangular table with six seats, one at the head of the table, one at the foot, and two on each long side of the table. The chairs are numbered 1 through 6 in a clockwise fashion, beginning with the chair at the head of the table, such that Chairs 1 and 4, 2 and 6, and 3 and 5 are directly across the table from each other.

Consecutively numbered chairs are considered adjacent. Chairs 1 and 6 are also considered adjacent.

Ned is sitting in chair 1 or chair 4.

Stanley and Tonga are sitting in adjacent chairs on one long side of the table.

Qi Li and Stanley are not sitting in adjacent chairs.

Question 1

Which one of the following could be the seating arrangement of the six people in Chairs 1 through 6, respectively?

(A) Ned, Vladimir, Tonga, Stanley, Matt, Qi Li
(B) Vladimir, Stanley, Tonga, Ned, Matt, Qi Li
(C) Qi Li, Matt, Ned, Stanley, Tonga, Vladimir
(D) Ned, Tonga, Qi Li, Vladimir, Stanley, Matt
(E) Qi Li, Vladimir, Matt, Ned, Tonga, Stanley

Ⓐ Ⓑ Ⓒ Ⓓ Ⓔ

Question 2

If Vladimir is sitting in Chair 4, then which one of the following pairs must be sitting in adjacent seats?

(A) Matt and Ned
(B) Matt and Qi Li
(C) Ned and Qi Li
(D) Ned and Stanley
(E) Stanley and Vladimir

Ⓐ Ⓑ Ⓒ Ⓓ Ⓔ

Question 3

If Qi Li is sitting in Chair 1, then which one of the following must be sitting adjacent to her?

(A) Ned
(B) Matt
(C) Stanley
(D) Tonga
(E) Vladimir

Ⓐ Ⓑ Ⓒ Ⓓ Ⓔ

Question 4

If Stanley and Vladimir are sitting in adjacent chairs, then Matt could be sitting in any of the following EXCEPT:

(A) Chair 1
(B) Chair 2
(C) Chair 3
(D) Chair 5
(E) Chair 6

Ⓐ Ⓑ Ⓒ Ⓓ Ⓔ

Question 5

If Stanley is sitting in Chair 3 and Matt is sitting in Chair 6, then which one of the following pairs CANNOT sit directly across the table from each other?

(A) Ned and Qi Li
(B) Ned and Vladimir
(C) Qi Li and Stanley
(D) Qi Li and Vladimir
(E) Stanley and Vladimir

Ⓐ Ⓑ Ⓒ Ⓓ Ⓔ

Questions 6–11: A history teacher has administered two different tests—one on ancient history and one on modern history—to the five students in his honors class. The five students are Ken, Lea, Marc, Nell, and Otis. The ten exams were graded on the descending scale of A, B, C, D, and F, with A being the highest grade and F the lowest.

No student who received a B on the ancient history exam received lower than a C on the modern history exam.

Marc and exactly one other student each received an A on the modern history exam.

Exactly two students received F's on the ancient history exam.

Ken and Otis each received a higher grade on the modern history exam than on the ancient history exam.

Lea received a B on her ancient history exam.

Question 6

If Nell and Marc each received an A on the ancient history exam, then which one of the following must be Ken's grade in the ancient history exam?

(A) A
(B) B
(C) C
(D) D
(E) F

Ⓐ Ⓑ Ⓒ Ⓓ Ⓔ

Question 7

Which one the following students could possibly have received an F on the modern history exam?

(A) Ken
(B) Lea
(C) Marc
(D) Nell
(E) Otis

Ⓐ Ⓑ Ⓒ Ⓓ Ⓔ

Question 8

If exactly three of the students each received a D on the modern history exam, then all of the following must be true EXCEPT:

(A) Ken received an F on the ancient history exam.
(B) Lea received an A on the modern history exam.
(C) Marc received a B on the ancient history exam.
(D) Nell received a D on the modern history exam.
(E) Otis received an F on the ancient history exam.

Ⓐ Ⓑ Ⓒ Ⓓ Ⓔ

Question 9

If Ken and Otis each received a C on the ancient history exam, and if Nell received an A on the modern history exam, then what is the maximum total number of B's that could have been received by the five students?

(A) 3
(B) 4
(C) 5
(D) 6
(E) 7

Ⓐ Ⓑ Ⓒ Ⓓ Ⓔ

Question 10

Assume that each student was awarded 4 points for each A, 3 for each B, 2 for each C, 1 for each D, and no points for each F. If Otis received a total of 6 points for his two exams, then what is the maximum total number of points Ken could have received for his?

(A) 4
(B) 5
(C) 6
(D) 7
(E) 8

Ⓐ Ⓑ Ⓒ Ⓓ Ⓔ

Question 11

Assume that each student was awarded 4 points for each A, 3 for each B, 2 for each C, 1 for each D, and no points for each F. If Lea and Marc received the same total number of points for the two exams, and if Nell received an A on both exams, then what is the maximum number of points Otis could have received for his two exams?

(A) 3
(B) 4
(C) 5
(D) 6
(E) 7

Ⓐ Ⓑ Ⓒ Ⓓ Ⓔ

Answers and Explanations

Question 1

This game involves placing people around a table, and it's pretty straightforward. The table is clearly described, maybe even too clearly. It's awfully wordy for all it has to say.

There is a rectangle in which Chairs 1 and 4 are at opposite ends, the head and foot, with Chairs 2 and 3 adjacent to each other on one side, and Chairs 5 and 6 adjacent on the other. You go clockwise around the table, the rules tell you, and, although you might have figured it out for yourself, you're even told exactly which chairs are opposite which. So this all turns out to be pretty simple to sketch.

Rule 2 says Ned is in Chair 1 or 4. Of course, that means he is either at the head or foot of the table. You could have written a note to yourself at the top of the page: "N head or foot." And, as a result, each time you drew the table to answer a question, you would have seen that note and remembered right away to put Ned at the bottom or the top of the rectangular table.

Same thing for the other rules. You could have written in big letters "ST" at the top of the page to remind yourself that those two characters, Stanley and Tonga, have to be next to each other along one of the table's two long edges. Alternatively, you might have written "ST = 2 and 3 or 5 and 6." That's just another way of noting the relevant information. And there's no need to do much more with Rule 4 than write something like "Q not = S," a reminder always to separate Qi Li and Stanley.

Armed with all that information, you should be able to make short work of Question 1, which asks for the one and only one acceptable sequence. Ned has to be in Chair 1 or 4. That means that choice (C) is unacceptable since (C) puts him in Chair 3. Cross out (C); there's no point in ever looking at it again. Next, remember that Stanley and Tonga have to be adjacent, and that eliminates choice (D), which puts two people between S and T in either direction. Moreover, they have to be adjacent along a long side of the table, that is, in Chairs 2 and 3 or 5 and 6. This eliminates choice (A), in which they are next to each other but Stanley is sitting in Chair 4, that is, at the foot of the table.

Nothing seems to have violated Rule 4 yet, but dollars to doughnuts, one choice will. And it turns out to be choice (E). You can't have Q in 1 and S in 6 because that, according to the first rule, counts as adjacency. You're left with choice (B), which must be okay since the other four choices violate rules. (B) is correct, although you needn't bother to check it at this point as long as you're sure the others are wrong. Just choose (B) and move on.

Question 2

A quick sketch for Question 2 puts V in Chair 4, and should immediately put Ned in Chair 1. Ned has to be in one or the other, and since someone else is in 4, he has to be in Chair 1. On one side of the table, as always, you put Stanley and Tonga. You don't know which side right now. That leaves two people, Qi Li and Matt, and they, too, will be along one long side of the table. That's all that's left. So, when Question 2 asks who has to be next to each other, you should look for Qi Li and Matt, and you'll find them in correct choice (B). All of the other pairs *could* be adjacent but needn't be. So it's choice (B), and you're done with that one almost as quickly as you started.

Question 3

Question 3 can be done very quickly, too. Putting Qi Li in Chair 1, as you're told to do, means that Ned goes to

Chair 4 this time. That leaves Stanley and Tonga, once again, along one of the long sides. But remember Rule 4: you have to separate Qi Li and Stanley. Therefore, Q, who will have to sit next to either S or T, since she's at the head, will be next to Tonga for sure, choice (D). Ned, choice (A), is opposite Qi Li. Stanley, choice (C), can't be next to her. And, certainly, either Matt, choice (B), or Vladimir, choice (E), will have to be next to Qi Li, too, although you cannot choose between them. So it's Tonga, choice (D), for Question 3.

Question 4

Question 4 asks, "Where could Matt *not* be?" The rules tell you very little about Matt, so build on the concrete information you're given about the other characters and see where that leaves Matt at the end.

Stanley and Vladimir are next to each other, you're told to assume. Stanley and Tonga are likewise next to each other, right? So, both V and T will flank S at the table. However, you specifically know that Stanley and Tonga take up one long side of the table. This means that Vladimir will have to end up at one end of the table or the other, either the head or the foot. Well, the other end, the head or the foot, is reserved for Ned. So if you look at the answer choices with the head and the foot going to Vladimir and Ned, there's no way that Matt or anyone else, besides those two, could occupy Chair 1 or Chair 4. The former has been chosen as the correct answer, choice (A). As for the others, Matt could take any of those. He and Qi Li will occupy 2 and 3 or 5 and 6, but more than that you don't know. So it's choice (A) for Question 4.

Question 5

Question 5, in its exploration of who can or cannot sit across from whom, explicitly places two people in chairs and allows you to do likewise with a third. Specifically, if Stanley is in Chair 3, Tonga (who again has to be next to Stanley along a long side of the table) has to take the other chair along that side,

Chair 2. Stanley in 3, Tonga in 2, and Matt in 6. Now, at this point, a lot depends on the placement of Ned. Both Chair 1, the head, and Chair 4, the foot, are available to him. If Ned is in Chair 1, the head, that is between Tonga on his left and Matt on his right, that leaves two chairs, 4 and 5, available to Qi Li and Vladimir. But Qi Li can't take Chair 4 while Stanley is in Chair 3. Rule 4 forbids it. So you would have to have Vladimir in 4 and Qi Li in 5. Under those circumstances, you would see choice (C), Qi Li and Stanley opposite each other in Chairs 5 and 3 respectively, and also choice (B), Ned and Vladimir opposite each other at the ends of the table.

But suppose Ned's in Chair 4 at the foot. With Matt in 6, Ned in 4, Stanley in 3, and Tonga in 2, the possibilities are slightly more numerous. Chairs 1 and 5 remain for Qi Li and Vladimir, with no restrictions as to which one is in which. Under those circumstances, you could certainly have Ned in 4 opposite Qi Li in 1, leaving Vladimir in 5 opposite Stanley in 3. And thus A and E must be rejected. Either is a possibility. But under no circumstances will you ever see Qi Li and Vladimir opposite each other (as it turns out, in none of these scenarios did you see that), and that makes choice (D) correct for Question 5.

Question 6

In this game, you have to wade through some manipulations of two parallel grading scales. This is a grouping game of distribution. Five students each take two tests and receive a grade of A, B, C, D, or F on each test. You have to distribute the grades, and you're given five indented rules to help you figure out who got what grade.

The first rule can be best understood as a simple if/then statement. If a student got a B in ancient history, then that student got no lower than a C in modern history. Put another way, if a student got a B in ancient history, then that student got an A, B, or C in modern history. You could very well have written it that way at the top of the page. That way every time

in the course of the game you saw that someone got a B in ancient history, you could have referred to the note to see what follows.

Next you get a rule about someone's specific grade. You can keep track of that data as well as everything else you've learned about people's specific grades in a very simple way. Draw two columns, one labeled *ancient history* and the other *modern history*, and label them with the names of the five students. You can enter Marc's A under the modern history column, and at the bottom of that column you can note *one more A*, or something like that. In the same way, at the bottom of the ancient history column, you can note two F's, and thus incorporate the information provided by Rule 3. You can also, skipping ahead to Rule 5, note Lea's B in ancient history. The point of jotting all this down, remember, is so that you can easily refer to it and access it in the course of the questions.

The remaining rule, the fourth one, is a little tougher to jot down. You could write *better grade* in the modern history column next to Ken's name, and do the same thing next to Otis's name in the same column. If you were to note for Ken and Otis that the better grade would fall in the modern history column, you would probably be able to remember that their ancient history grades are lower, and proceed accordingly. But again, it doesn't matter how you deal with a rule, whether you jot it down or write it in shorthand on the page, provided that you get the rule right, and that you are able to remember it during the course of the game.

By the way, you might have stopped at some point to note that, since Ken and Otis did better on the modern exam than the ancient, neither of them could have gotten an F in modern history. Right? You can't do worse than an F. This may not seem very significant as a deduction, but it is deducible, and it does prove to be a key element in a question coming up, as you'll see in a few minutes.

Okay, there's at least one more major thing you should realize. Lea is affected by Rule 1. Based on that rule, you can jot down A, B, or C next to Lea in the modern history column, because Lea must have received one of those three grades on that exam. Can you deduce anything else here? Not really. Anyone—Ken, Lea, Nell, or Otis—could get the remaining A in modern history. Any two of Ken, Marc, Nell, and Otis could get the two F's in ancient history. And you have no idea of how anything else falls out. So it's time to move on to the questions.

Question 6 starts out very concretely by telling you to assume that Nell and Marc got A's on the ancient history test. This works out pretty simply. You know from Rule 3 that there were exactly 2 F's on that test. And you know already that Lea didn't get an F because she got a B. With Nell and Marc also eliminated from contention for those F's, it has to follow that the only two people who remain, Ken and Otis, got the F's. So not only did Ken get an F, choice (E), but so did Otis.

This sort of process of elimination is very important in Logic Games. Here, you have to keep thinking of the fact that once you've identified the grades of one or more students, the restrictions given in the rules may allow you to figure out some more grades. And in this game there are only five students involved, which also has an impact. Anyway, (E) is correct for Question 6.

Question 7

Question 7 involves a little more thinking, but it's still pretty easy if you keep your cool. Who could have received an F in modern history? You should see immediately that it's impossible for Lea to get an F on a modern history exam, because she received a B on the ancient history exam, so, according to Rule 1, she must get at least a C on the modern history exam. Marc couldn't have received an F on the exam, either, because Rule 2 tells you that he got an A. So Marc is out. What about the remaining folks, Ken, Otis, and Nell? This was covered back in the discussion of Rule 4. Ken and Otis did worse on ancient history than on modern history, but if one of them had received an F on modern history, where could he go from there? If a student got an F in modern history there would be no

room to do worse on ancient history, as the rule requires. Therefore, Ken and Otis did better than an F on modern history. This leaves you with Nell, choice (D), the correct answer to Question 7. Maybe no one got an F on that test, but only Nell *could* have done so.

Question 8

Question 8 is one of those in which you're given four true statements and you have to find the one bad apple. The best way to approach this is to take the information you're given, plug it in, and see what happens. Do that first before you worry about eliminating all the answer choices. In this case, if three students got D's on the modern history exam, then you have all the grades mapped out. Why? Because after those three D's there are only two students unaccounted for, and you already know that Marc and one other student got A's. Furthermore, you know that Lea must be the one who got the A with Marc because, having received a B on the ancient history exam, she can't get less than a C on the modern exam. Therefore, Ken, Otis, and Nell must be the three students who, according to the stem, have received D's on the modern exam. This means you've ruled out choices (B) and (D). You know that both of those choices must be true. What else can you conclude? Rule 4 comes in handy here. Ken's and Otis's D's on the modern test mean that both of them got F's on ancient history. Right? Their ancient history grade has to be lower than their modern history grade, and only F is lower than D. So choices (A) and (D) are also true. Ken and Otis must have received F's. That leaves choice (C), which certainly may be true, but doesn't have to be. Marc might have received an ancient history B, but not necessarily, so it's choice (C) for Question 8.

Question 9

Question 9 begins more concretely than any of the previous questions. You start by resketching your columns off to the side, a sketch that includes what you've learned from the rules and then puts in what you're told for this question: Ken's and Otis's ancient history C's, and Nell's modern history A. The question: "What's the maximum number of B's all around?"

Start with ancient history. You have to factor in the need for two F's in the ancient history column, and with Ken, Lea, and Otis now variously getting B's or C's in ancient history, Marc and Nell have to bite the bullet and take those F's. So only one B will come out of ancient history, the one bestowed on Lea by the original rule.

Look at the B grade in modern history. The A's are set. According to this question and Rule 2, Marc and Nell get those A's. Ken and Otis, according to Rule 4, have to improve on their ancient history C's, and there are no A's left. Therefore, Ken and Otis definitely get B's here. Lea could get a modern history B, too. Rule 1 doesn't forbid it. So you have three definite B's and one potential B for a total of four. There could be as many as four B's here, so (B) is the correct choice for Question 9.

Question 10

Question 10 tells you to understand and make use of a 0–4 grading point system, one that (happily enough) you are probably familiar with from everyday life. You're also told that Otis received a total of 6 points between his two exams. Given the system—4 points for an A, 3 for a B, 2 for a C, 1 for a D, and 0 for an F—without too much trouble you can figure out exactly what Otis's two grades were. Why? Because there's only one combination of grades that can give Otis 6 points while abiding by Rule 4. He must have received a C on the ancient history exam and an A on the modern—2 plus 4. Of course, 3 plus 3 is impossible, because one of the grades has to be better than the other. Now, the big impact of all this is determining that you're out of A's to give in modern history. The only A's go to Marc and someone else, and in this question you've just deduced that the other A belongs to Otis. Therefore, the best grade Ken can

possibly get in modern history is a B for 3 points. And since his ancient history grade has to be inferior to his modern history grade, the best he can possibly do in ancient history is a C for 2 points. His points add up to 5, so that's the best possible point total Ken can get. And 5 points is correct—choice (B) for Question 10.

Question 11

This same point system is in effect for Question 11. The length of Questions 10 and 11 might have seemed a little daunting at first until you realized that both of them make use of the same familiar, logical point system. Anyway, your goal is a decision about Otis's maximum score.

Nell gets two A's. The net effect of that is, once again, all the available modern history A's have been given. As noted several times, only Marc and one other person get A's on the test. Here, that other person is Nell. You're to assume that Lea, with 3 points for her B in ancient history, and Marc with 4 points for his A in modern history, end up with the same point total. You should investigate what that total is or could be and remember, thanks to Rule 1, the only possibilities for Lea's modern history grade are A, B, and C.

But wait a minute. A grade of A is out—there are no modern history A's left. So Lea's total is either 6 based on receiving two B's or 5 points for a B in ancient history and a C in modern. Marc, too, will have a total of 5 or 6, and since he already has 4 points from modern history, it follows that in ancient history Marc got either a C for 2 points or a D for 1 point.

Now think a little more about ancient history. You need 2 F's there. They don't belong to Lea, Marc, or Nell, so it's Ken and Otis who get F's or 0 points. And that makes Otis's best possible total 3, choice (A). With an F in ancient history and no more A's available in modern history, the best Otis can hope for is a 3-point B in modern history, so it's choice (A) for Question 11.

Answer Key for Logic Games Practice Set

1. B   5. D   9. B
2. B   6. E   10. B
3. D   7. D   11. A
4. A   8. C

CHAPTER FOUR

Reading Comprehension

- Learn the seven basic principles of Reading Comprehension
- Practice reading critically
- Review strategies for Global questions, Inference questions, and Explicit Test questions
- Study the Kaplan Three-Step Method for Reading Comprehension
- Complete the Reading Comprehension Practice Set

Reading Comprehension is the only question type that appears on all major standardized tests, and the reason isn't too surprising: no matter what academic area you pursue, you have to make sense of dense, unfamiliar prose. Law, of course, is no exception. The topics for LSAT Reading Comp passages are taken from four areas:

- Social sciences
- Natural sciences
- Humanities
- Law

These passages tend to be long, densely worded, and difficult—not unlike at least some of the material you'll face in law school. So right now is a good time to start shoring up your reading skills, both for the test and for your future study and practice of law.

A Word About Outside Knowledge

On the LSAT, no outside knowledge on your part is presupposed, and that holds for the Reading Comp section, too. It's not necessary to know anything about the topics covered in the passages; everything you'll need to answer every question is included in the passages themselves. However, the passages are always logical, and always reflect ideas that you have heard about and can understand. Don't read in a vacuum—relate what you read to your world, and recognize the common sense of the text. One warning, though: The questions test your understanding of the author's points, not your previous understanding or personal point of view on the topic.

So use your own knowledge to help you understand the passages, but be careful not to let it interfere with answering questions correctly.

The Seven Basic Principles of Reading Comprehension

Improvement at Reading Comprehension requires practice and patience. You may not see dramatic improvement after taking only one section. But with ongoing practice, the principles below will help to increase your skill and confidence on this section by the day of the test.

Read the First Third of the Passage Carefully

The first third of any passage usually introduces the topic and scope, the author's main idea/primary purpose, and the author's tone, and it almost always hints at the structure that the passage will follow. Let's take a closer look at these crucial elements of a Reading Comp passage.

Topic, Scope, and Purpose
Topic and *scope* are both objective terms, meaning they include no specific reference to the author's point of view. The difference between them is that the topic is broader; the scope narrows the topic. Scope is particularly important because the (many) answer choices that depart from it will always be wrong. The broad topic of "The Battle of Gettysburg" would be a lot to cover in 450 words. We should ask, "What *aspect* of the battle does the author take up?"—and, because of length limitations, it's likely to be a pretty small chunk. Whatever that "chunk" is—the prebattle scouting, how the battle was fought, or the effects of the battle on the U.S. political scene—will be the passage's scope. Answer choices that deal with anything outside of this narrowly defined chunk will be wrong.

Kaplan Tip

Reading the first third of the passage is a zooming-in process. First, you get a sense of the general topic. Then you pin down the more specific scope of the passage. Finally, you glean the author's purpose in writing the passage—and the main idea that he or she is trying to get across about that particular subject.

The topic/scope distinction ties into the all-important author's purpose. The author deliberately chooses to narrow the scope by including certain aspects of the broader topic and excluding others. Why the author makes those choices has to do with why the passage is being written in the first place. We can say that the topic is broadly stated and objective (for instance, a passage's topic might be "solving world hunger"). Scope is also objective but narrower (a new technology for solving world hunger) and leads rather quickly to the author's subjective purpose (the author is writing in order to describe a new technology and its promising uses). And this is what turns into the author's main idea, which will be discussed at greater length in the next principle.

All this leads to a clear point of attack. Don't just "read" the passage; instead, try to do the following three things: identify the topic; narrow it down to the precise scope that the author includes; and make a hypothesis about why the author is writing and where he or she is going with it. A clear conception of these three things translates directly into points.

Structure and Tone

In a quest to master the content side of the passages—namely, *what* the author says—test takers are notorious for ignoring the less glamorous, but just as important, structural side—namely, *how* the author says it. One of the keys to success on this section is to understand not only the purpose, but also the structure of each passage. Why? Simply because the questions ask both what the author says and how he or she says it. The following is a list of the classic LSAT passage structures:

- Passages based on a strong opinion
- Passages based on a serious problem or situation
- Passages based on differing opinions
- Passages based on significant new findings (often science passages)

Many LSAT passages have been based on one of these classic structures or a variation thereof. You've most likely seen these structures at work in passages before, even if unconsciously. Your task is to seek them out actively as you begin to read a passage—usually, the structure is announced within the first third of the passage. Let these classic structures act as a "jump start" in your search for the passage's "big picture" and purpose.

As for how the author makes his or her point, try to note the author's position within these structures, usually indicated by the author's tone. For example, in the third structure, the author may simply relate the two sides of the story, or may at some point jump in and take a side, or even reject the conflicting opinions in favor of his or her own. In the first structure, the opinion could be the author's, in which case the author's tone may be opinionated, argumentative, heated, or passionate. On the other hand, the author could simply be describing the strongly held opinions of someone else. This author's writing style would be more descriptive, factual, and even-handed. His or her method may involve mere storytelling or the simple relaying of information, which is altogether different from the former case.

Notice the difference in tone between the two types of authors. Correct answer choices for a primary purpose question in the former case would use terms like *argue for, propose,* and *demonstrate,* whereas correct choices for the same type of question in the latter case would use terms like *describe* and *discuss.* Correct answers are always consistent with the author's tone, so noting the author's tone is a good way to score points.

Focus on the Main Idea

Almost every passage boils down to one big idea. We discussed above how topic leads to scope and then, in turn, to the author's purpose in writing the passage. An author's primary purpose and main idea are forever intertwined. Take, for example, the hypothetical passage stated above, in which the author had the following purpose.

> The author is writing in order to describe a new technology and its promising uses.

The main idea is simply a restatement of this without the active verb structure:

> Biochemical engineering (or whatever new technology is discussed) can help solve world hunger.

Your job is to cut past the fancy wording and focus on this big idea. Most often, the main idea will be presented in the first third of the passage. But occasionally the author will build up to it gradually, in which case you may not have a solidified conception of the author's purpose or big idea until the very end.

In any case, the main idea must appear somewhere in the passage, and when it does, you must take conscious note of it. For one thing, the purpose of everything else in the passage will be to support this idea. Furthermore, many of the questions—not only "main idea" or "primary purpose" questions, but all kinds of questions—are easier to handle when you have the main idea in the forefront of your mind. Always look for choices that sound consistent with the main idea. Wrong choices often sound inconsistent with it.

Kaplan Tip

You should always keep the main idea in mind, even when answering questions that don't explicitly ask for it. Correct answers on even the detail questions tend to echo the main idea in one way or another.

Get the Gist of Each Paragraph

The paragraph is the main structural unit of any passage. After you've read the first third of the passage carefully, you need only find the gist, or general purpose, of each succeeding paragraph, and then attempt to relate each paragraph back to the passage as a whole. To find the gist of each paragraph, ask yourself:

- Why did the author include this paragraph?
- What shift did the author have in mind when moving on to this paragraph?
- What bearing does this paragraph have on the author's main idea?

This process allows you to create a mental roadmap of the passage, which ties in strongly with the structure and main idea. When questions arise that require you to look back into the passage, having a roadmap will help you locate the place in the text that contains the answer. For example, it's helpful to know that, say, the author's critique of a recommendation is in paragraph three. Doing so will allow you to zero in on the relevant information quickly. The art of *not* trying to understand every little thing in the passage brings us to our next principle.

Don't Obsess over Details

There are differences between the reading skills required in an academic environment and those useful on standardized tests. In school, you probably read to memorize information for an exam. This kind of reading most likely includes taking note of and memorizing details as well.

But this is not the type of reading that's good for getting points on LSAT Reading Comprehension. On the test, you'll need to read for short-term, as opposed to long-term, retention. When you finish the questions on a certain passage, that passage is over, gone, done with. You're free to promptly forget everything about it.

What's more, there's certainly no need to memorize details—it's an open-book test, after all. You always have the option to relocate details if a particular question requires you to do so. If you have a good sense of a passage's structure and paragraph topics and your mental road map is clear in your mind, then you should have no problem navigating back through the text when the need arises.

Attack, Don't Just Read, the Passages

Always remember that you get no points for just "getting through" the passage. Don't be the kind of test taker who views reaching the end of a passage as a moral victory—this type of victory is short-lived when you find you can't answer any questions.

Kaplan Tip

Try labeling each paragraph so you know what's covered in each and how it fits into the overall structure of the passage. This will help you get a fix on the passage as a whole, and it will help you locate specific details later.

No, you must *attack*—not simply read—the passages. The former embodies the winning mindset: you're entering the passage for the sole purpose of picking up the author's key ideas that will enable you to rack up points. By thinking in terms of attack, you're less likely to be diverted from this mission or to let the densely worded prose distract you.

Attacking a passage involves the application of all of the strategies mentioned in the previously stated principles. It also means reading actively. Active readers keep their minds working at all times, while trying to anticipate where the author's points are leading. Typically when we read—say a newspaper—we start with the first sentence and read the article straight through. The words wash over us and are the only things we hear in our minds. This is typical of the passive approach to reading.

Active reading, on the other hand, involves doing more than just reading the words on the page—it means thinking about what you're reading as you read it. It means paraphrasing the complicated-sounding ideas and jargon. It means asking yourself questions as you read:

- What's the author's main point here?
- What's the purpose of this paragraph? of this sentence?

When you read actively, there's a running commentary going on in your mind as you read. You may want to jot down notes or underline. When you read actively, you don't absorb the passage, you attack it!

Beware of Classic Wrong Answers

Knowing the most common types of wrong answer can help you eliminate wrong choices quickly, winning you extra time. Of course, ideally, you want to have prephrased an answer choice in your mind before looking at the choices. But in cases where that technique doesn't apply, you'll have to go to the choices and eliminate the bad ones to find the correct one. In such cases, you should always be on the lookout for:

- Choices that go beyond the author's scope
- Choices that are "half-right, half-wrong"
- Choices that use the wrong verb
- Choices that distort the passage's ideas
- Choices that say the exact opposite of what you are looking for
- Choices that use extreme language

Being sensitive to these classic wrong choices will make it that much easier to zero in on the correct choice quickly and efficiently.

Teacher Tip

"Mark up the passages! Have a system worked out where you use different symbols to mean different things. For example, circle names, box numbers and dates, underline key sentences, and draw arrows to lists of details. Once you know your system, you can find the facts you are looking for faster."
—Laura Cunnington
 Kaplan Teacher
 Reno, NV

Read Critically

The single most important factor in Reading Comp success is the basic skill that underlies each of the preceding principles as well as the rest of the test: critical reading.

Critical reading involves perspective—the ability to step back from a piece of prose and carefully evaluate it. On the Reading Comp section, critical reading echoes all of the principles we've been talking about, including:

- **Reading for purpose and idea**
  Why is the author writing? What's his or her point of view or main idea?

- **Reading for structure**
  How is the passage put together?

- **Reading between the lines**
  What is implied by the text?

The following are ways in which you can improve the specific critical reading skills necessary for success on Reading Comprehension:

- **Get a handle on the "spirit" of the passage.**
  Is it passionate? Neutral? Is it academic, conversational, or poetic in tone? What does the author favor? Disapprove of?

- **Keep paraphrasing key ideas.**
  Make sure you can put the author's most important concepts into your own words.

- **Keep anticipating where the author is going.**
  Each step of the way, ask yourself: "What could or must follow?"

- **Don't let complex-sounding words and sentences scare you.**
  Most passages consist of pretty simple ideas written to sound impressive.

- **Connect abstract ideas to your own experience.**
  Visualize the subject matter if you can.

- **Read carefully for the gist or main point.**
  Read loosely for everything else—details, etcetera.

Teacher Tip

"Read for the moment, not for memory. Unlike in a school class, you're not going to be tested on details two weeks from now. Don't try to remember them, pronounce them, even totally understand them. If there's a question about a particular detail, then you'll go back and figure it out. If there's no question, forget it!"
—Marilyn Engle
 Kaplan Teacher
 Encino, CA

Review

Remember the discussion of keywords from the Logical Reasoning section? They're very useful in Reading Comp as well. Keywords are invaluable guides to the structure of the passage.

• **Remember that authors are repetitious.**
Not every sentence they write adds a new idea.

• **Use keywords.**
Like Logical Reasoning arguments, Reading Comprehension passages are full of structural signals—words or phrases whose main function is to help the author string ideas together logically. They allow you to infer a great deal about content, even if that content is obscure or difficult. Conclusion signals *(therefore, consequently, thus)* and evidence signals *(because, since)* are extremely helpful, as are contrast signals *(but, however, although, by contrast)*, which indicate an opposition or shift in ideas.

The Three Crucial Reading Comprehension Question Types

While it might be convenient to break down the Reading Comprehension section into the types of *passages* that typically appear on it, Kaplan feels that that's not the best way to master the section. In Logic Games, categorizing the games is helpful because Sequencing games and Matching games, for instance, have their own sets of peculiarities, making a distinction between them useful. However, the same types of differences don't separate a humanities passage from a social science one, or even a natural science passage from a law passage. Their topics differ, but we read them in the same way, employing the same critical reading techniques for each.

For that reason, we find it more efficient to break the section down into the three main question types that accompany each passage: Global, Explicit Text, and Inference. Let's look at each of these more closely.

Global Questions

A Global question asks us to sum up the author's overall intentions, ideas, or passage structure. It's basically a question whose scope is the entire passage. Global questions account for 25 to 30 percent of all Reading Comp questions.

In general, any Global question choice that grabs onto a small detail—or zeros in on the content of only one paragraph—will be wrong. Often, scanning the verbs in the Global question choices is a good way to take a first cut at the question. The verbs must agree with the author's tone and way in which he or she structures the passage, so scanning the verbs can narrow down the options quickly. The correct answer must be consistent with the overall tone and structure of the passage, whereas the wrong choices will go beyond the scope or focus on a detail or be inconsistent with the author's tone. You'll often find Global questions at the beginning of question sets, and often one of the wrong choices will play on some side issue discussed at the tail end of the passage.

Main Idea and Primary Purpose Questions
The two main types of Global questions are main idea and primary purpose questions. We discussed these types a little earlier, noting that main idea and purpose are inextricably linked because the author's purpose is to convey his or her main idea. The formats for these question types are pretty self-evident:

- Which one of following best expresses the main idea of the passage?
- The author's primary purpose is to . . .

Title Questions
A very similar form of Global question is one that's looking for a title that best fits the passage. (This question type disappeared for a while from the LSAT but has started to make a comeback.) A title, in effect, is the main idea summed up in a brief, catchy way. This question may look like this: "Which of the following titles best describes the content of the passage as a whole?"

Be sure not to go with a choice that aptly describes only the latter half of the passage; a valid title, like a main idea and primary purpose, must cover the entire passage.

Structure Questions
Another type of Global question is one that asks you to recognize a passage's overall structure. Here's what this type of question might sound like: "Which of the following best describes the organization of the passage?"

Answer choices to this kind of Global question are usually worded very generally; they force you to recognize the broad layout of the passage as opposed to the specific content. For example, here are a few possible ways that a passage could be organized:

- A hypothesis is stated and then analyzed.
- A proposal is evaluated, and alternatives are explored.
- A viewpoint is set forth and then subsequently defended.

When choosing among these choices, literally ask yourself: "Was there a hypothesis here? Was there an evaluation of a proposal or a defense of a viewpoint?" These terms may all sound similar, but in fact, they're very

At a Glance

Global Questions:
- They represent 25–30 percent of Reading Comp questions.
- They sum up author's overall intentions or passage structure.
- Nouns and verbs must be consistent with the author's tone and the passage's scope.
- Types of Global questions: main idea, primary purpose, title, structure, logic, and tone.

different things. Learn to recognize the difference between a proposal, a viewpoint, and so on. Try to keep an eye on what the author is doing as well as what the author is saying, and you'll have an easier time with this type of question.

Logic Questions

Logic questions are those that ask why the author does something—cite a source, bring up a detail, put one paragraph before another, etcetera. Choices that discuss the content or a detail will be wrong for these questions.

Tone Questions

The last type of Global question is the tone question, which asks you to evaluate the style of the writing or how the author sounds. Is the author passionate, fiery, neutral, angry, hostile, opinionated, low-key? Here's an example: "The author's tone in the passage can best be characterized as . . . ."

Make sure you don't confuse the nature of the content with the tone in which the author presents the ideas—a social science passage based on trends in this century's grisliest murders may be presented in a cool, detached, and strictly informative way. Once again, it's up to you to separate what the author says from how he or she says it.

Inference Questions

Inference questions make up 55 to 60 percent of the Reading Comprehension section and are very similar to those found in Logical Reasoning. An *inference* is something that is almost certainly true, based on the passage, but that is contained "between the lines." The answer is something that the author strongly implies or hints at but does not state directly. Furthermore, the Denial Test, which was introduced earlier for Logical Reasoning assumption and inference questions, works for inference questions on Reading Comp as well. The right answer, if denied, will contradict or significantly weaken the passage. So in those two respects, Logical Reasoning and Reading Comp inferences are similar. The differences?

- Reading Comprehension Inference questions can be on major points or small, whereas Logical Reasoning Inference questions tend to focus on major elements of the stimulus.
- In Reading Comprehension, we can't always be sure where in the passage to look for the answer to an Inference question.
- Reading Comprehension text is tougher to get through than Logical Reasoning prose, which is much briefer, so Reading Comprehension

Inference questions are tougher.

The same rules that apply to inferences in Logical Reasoning also apply to inferences in Reading Comp. A good inference:
- Stays in line with the gist of the passage
- Stays in line with the author's tone
- Stays in line with the author's point of view
- Stays within the scope of the passage and its main idea
- Is neither denied by, nor irrelevant to, the ideas stated in the passage
- Always makes more sense than its opposite

Extracting valid inferences from Reading Comp passages requires the ability to recognize that information in the passage can be expressed in different ways. The ability to bridge the gap between the way information is presented in the passage and the way it's presented in the correct answer choice is vital. In fact, Inference questions often boil down to an exercise in translation.

Standard Inference Questions
The most common type of Inference question simply asks what can be inferred from the passage, but does so in a variety of different ways:

- It can be inferred from the passage that . . .
- The passage/author suggests that . . .
- The passage/author implies that . . .
- The passage supports which one of the following statements . . .

Usually, some specific information will complete these question introductions, so you'll almost always have a clue as to which idea or set of ideas from the passage is the key to the answer. When evaluating the answer choices, keep the relevant ideas firmly in mind. The farther you stray from them to endorse a choice, the more likely it is that this choice will be wrong. Occasionally, the stem won't contain specific information, in which case you simply have to work your way through the choices until you find the one that's most consistent with the passage.

Agreement Questions
Another common form of Inference question is one that asks you to find a statement that the author (or some character or group mentioned in the passage) would agree with. Once again, the question stem will usually provide a hint as to in which part of the passage the answer can be found.

At a Glance

Inference Questions:
- They represent 55–60 percent of Reading Comp questions.
- They are similar to Logical Reasoning inferences.
- They test ability to read between the lines.
- The Denial Test works to test choices.
- They often boil down to translating the author's points.
- The Inference question stem usually provides a clue as to where in the passage the answer will be found.
- They will ask either for something that can be inferred from a specific part of the passage or for something with which the author would agree.

Explicit Test Questions

The third major category of Reading Comprehension questions is the Explicit Test question. As the name implies, an Explicit Test question is one whose answer can be directly pinpointed and found in the text. This type makes up roughly 10 to 20 percent of the questions on the section. It's fairly simple to identify an Explicit Text question from its stem:

- According to the passage/author . . .
- The author states that . . .
- The author mentions which one of the following as . . .

Often, these questions provide very direct clues as to where an answer may be found, such as a line reference or some text that links up with the passage structure. (Just be careful with line references—they'll bring you to the right area, but usually the actual answer will be found in the lines immediately before or after the referenced line.) Detail questions are usually related to the main idea, and correct choices tend to be related to major points.

You may recall that we advised you to skim over details in Reading Comp passages in favor of focusing on the big idea, topic, and scope. So what do you do with a question type that's specifically concerned with details? The fact is, most of the details that appear in a passage aren't tested in the questions. With the few that are, you'll do one of the following:

- Remember them from your reading
- Be given a line reference to bring you right to them
- Simply have to find them on your own in order to track down the answer

If that's the case—if your mental roadmap and understanding of the purpose of each paragraph are both in the forefront of your mind—it shouldn't take long to locate the relevant detail and then choose an answer. And if even that fails, as a last resort, you have the option of putting that question aside and returning to it later, if and when you have the time to search through the passage. The point is, even with the existence of this question type, the winning strategy is still to note the purpose of details in each paragraph's argument, but not to attempt to memorize the details themselves.

Most students find Explicit Test questions to be the easiest type of Reading Comp question, since they're the most concrete. Unlike inferences, which hide somewhere between the lines, explicit details reside in the lines themselves. For this reason, we suggest placing Explicit Test

At a Glance

Explicit Test Questions:
- They represent 10–20 percent of Reading Comp questions.
- The answers can always be found in the text.
- They sometimes include line references to help you locate the relevant material.
- They are concrete, and therefore the easiest RC question type for most people to answer.

questions high on your list of priorities, above Inference questions but below Global questions, when choosing the order in which you tackle the questions.

And speaking of setting priorities, this brings us to our next major topic, which should help bring all of these principles and strategies together.

The Kaplan Three-Step Method for Reading Comprehension

Now that you have the basics of LSAT Reading Comp under your belt, you'll want to learn our three-step method that allows you to orchestrate them all into a single modus operandi for Reading Comprehension questions:

1. Attack the first third of the passage.
2. Read the rest of the passage.
3. Do the questions in an efficient order.

1. Attack the First Third of the Passage

As outlined in the Basic Principles section, read the first part of the passage with care in order to determine the main idea and purpose (via the zooming-in process we talked about earlier). Keep in mind two caveats, however. First, in some passages, the author's main idea doesn't become clear until the end of the passage. Second, occasionally a passage won't include a main idea, which in itself is a strong hint that the passage is more of a descriptive, storytelling type of passage, with an even-handed tone and no strong opinions. Bottom line: Don't panic if you can't immediately pin down the author's main idea and purpose. Read on.

2. Read the Rest of the Passage

Do so as we described in the Basic Principles section, making sure to take note of paragraph topics, location of details, etcetera.

3. Do the Questions in an Efficient Order

Quickly scan the question stems for Global questions, specifically main idea or primary purpose questions. Doing these questions first will often help you solidify your conception of the author's main idea and purpose, and you're more likely to answer them correctly while the passage is still fresh in your mind.

If there are any other global types, such as questions regarding the author's overall tone or the organization of the passage, you may benefit from seeking out and handling those next. Explicit Text questions, espe-

Teacher Tip

"Once you've finished reading a passage and its questions, put it out of your mind. There's no connection at all between passages, so don't carry your stress or doubt to the next one. Approach each passage as if it were the only one. Stay active and confident!"
—Marilyn Engle
   Kaplan Teacher
   Encino, CA

cially those with line references, are good candidates to tackle after that. Many test takers benefit from leaving the more difficult Inference questions for last.

This, of course, is only a rough order based on question type. You may want to revise this order to account for the difficulty level of each individual question. For example, on any given passage, some Inference questions may be easier than some Explicit Text questions. So, for each question, quickly ask yourself: "Can I answer this question quickly?" Shop around—tackle the questions that you think will get you quick points first, and leave the others for later. This reinforces the all-important LSAT mindset—your conscious decision to take control of the test.

Using the Kaplan Three-Step Method for Reading Comprehension

Now let's try the three-step method on an actual LSAT-strength Reading Comprehension passage. For the time being, we've just included the question stems of the questions attached to this passage, since you don't want to get into individual choices until later.

It has been suggested that post–World War II concepts of environmental liability, as they pertain to hazardous waste, grew out of issues regarding municipal refuse collection and disposal and industrial waste disposal in the period 1880–1940. To a great
(5)   degree, the remedies available to Americans for dealing with the burgeoning hazardous waste problem were characteristic of the judicial, legislative, and regulatory tools used to confront a whole range of problems in the industrial age. At the same time, these remedies were operating in an era in which the problem of haz-
(10)   ardous waste had yet to be recognized. It is understandable that an assessment of liability was narrowly drawn and most often restricted to a clearly identified violator in a specific act of infringement of the property rights of someone else. Legislation, for the most part, focused narrowly on clear threats to the public
(15)   health and dealt with problems of industrial pollution meekly if at all.

Nevertheless, it would be grossly inaccurate to assume that the actions of American politicians, technologists, health officials, judges, and legislators in the period 1880–1940 have had little
(20)   impact on the attempts to define environmental liability and to confront the consequences of hazardous waste. Taken as a whole, the precedents of the late nineteenth through the mid-twentieth century have established a framework in which the problem of hazardous waste is understood and confronted today. Efforts at
(25)   refuse reform gradually identified the immutable connection between waste and disease, turning eyesores into nuisances and nuisances into health hazards. Confronting the refuse problem and other forms of municipal pollution forced cities to define public responsibility and accountability with respect to the envi-
(30)   ronment. A commitment to municipal services in the development of sewers and collection and disposal systems shifted the burden of responsibility for eliminating wastes from the individual to the community. In some way, the courts' efforts to clarify and broaden the definition of public nuisance were dependent on
(35)   the cities' efforts to define community responsibility themselves.

The courts retained their role as arbiter of what constituted private and public nuisances. Indeed, fear that the courts would transform individual decisions into national precedents often contributed to the search for other remedies. Nonetheless, the
(40)   courts remained an active agent in cases on the local, state, and national level, making it quite clear that they were not going to be left out of the process of defining environmental liability in the United States. In the case of hazardous waste, precedents for

behavior and remedial action were well developed by 1940. Even
(45)   though the concept of *hazardous waste* is essentially a post–World
War II notion, the problem was not foreign to earlier generations.
The observation that the administrative, technical, and legal
problems of water pollution in the 1920s were intertwined is
equally applicable to today's hazardous waste problem.

1. According to the author, the efforts by cities to define public responsibility for the environment resulted in which of the following?

2. Which of the following, if substituted for the word *immutable* (line 25), would LEAST alter the author's meaning?

3. With which one of the following statements would the author be most likely to agree?

4. The author's primary purpose is to discuss . . .

5. The tone of the author's discussion of early attempts to deal with waste and pollution problems could best be described as . . .

6. According to the passage, judicial assessments of liability in waste disposal disputes prior to World War II were usually based on . . .

7. The passage suggests that responses to environmental problems between 1880 and 1940 were relatively limited in part because of . . .

1. Attack the First Third of the Passage Carefully

The first few sentences introduce the topic: hazardous waste. The scope, as you recall, is the specific angle the author takes on the topic, and this seems to be the post–World War II concept of environmental liability associated with hazardous waste. The author points out that it's been suggested that this concept of liability has some connection to issues from the time period 1880–1940; latter-day remedies for hazardous waste are "characteristic of the judicial, legislative, and regulatory tools used to confront a whole range of problems in the industrial age." Since hazardous waste liability concepts of the postwar era had their roots in an era that predated the recognition of hazardous waste problems, the author finds it understandable that liability assessment and the ensuing legislation regarding hazardous waste were both "narrowly drawn."

All of this comes out of the first paragraph. In some cases, this would be enough to cover the "first third of the passage" reading. However, the keyword *nevertheless* at the beginning of the next paragraph indicates that it may be helpful to include this sentence in your initial reading as well. This sentence harks back to and solidifies the connection between the actions and policies from the period 1880–1940 and the concept of environmental liability associated with hazardous waste. This connection is the author's main idea.

2. Read the Rest of the Passage

The sentence from lines 21 to 24—"Taken as a whole . . . confronted today."—is simply another restatement of the main idea. It's followed by a description of the gradual recognition of the hazardous waste problem and some of the repercussions of the cities' and courts' efforts to define the problem and to assign responsibility for it. Note that there's some talk in the paragraph about individual versus community responsibility and the role of cities, but don't fuss over the specifics. If there's a question on these issues, you'll know where to look.

The first part of the last paragraph deals mainly with the courts' role in defining environmental liability. The last three sentences of the passage reinforce the main idea; namely, that there's a historical context for the ways in which hazardous waste problems are viewed today.

3. Do the Questions in an Efficient Order

Let's look again at the seven question stems attached to this passage:

1. According to the author, the efforts by cities to define public responsibility for the environment resulted in which of the following?

2. Which of the following, if substituted for the word *immutable* (line 25), would LEAST alter the author's meaning?

3. With which one of the following statements would the author be most likely to agree?

4. The author's primary purpose is to discuss . . .

5. The tone of the author's discussion of early attempts to deal with waste and pollution problems could best be described as . . .

6. According to the passage, judicial assessments of liability in waste disposal disputes prior to World War II were usually based on . . .

7. The passage suggests that responses to environmental problems between 1880 and 1940 were relatively limited in part because of . . .

Global Questions

Quickly scan the question stems for Global questions, specifically main idea or primary purpose. Upon inspection, if you come across the following question, you should attempt it at this point while the author's big idea is fresh in your mind:

4. The author's primary purpose is to discuss

(A) contrasts in the legislative approaches to environmental liability before and after World War II

(B) legislative trends which have been instrumental in the reduction of environmental hazardous wastes

(C) the historical and legislative context in which to view post–World War II hazardous waste problems

(D) early patterns of industrial abuse and pollution of the American environment

(E) the growth of an activist tradition in American jurisprudence

Choice (C) has the elements of a right answer: the connection (denoted by "the historical and legislative context . . . to view . . . waste problems") that represents the author's main idea, and the correct topic and scope—hazardous waste, post–World War II.

Choice (B) is tempting; legislative trends were discussed, but not in enough depth to constitute the author's primary purpose. More damaging to (B) is the fact that the discussion hinges on defining liability for hazardous wastes and doesn't specifically discuss any factor "instrumental in the *reduction of environmental wastes*."

Meanwhile, (A) misinterprets the passage structure—there is no such contrast presented, and (D) and (E) both violate the topic and scope of the passage (notice that neither one even mentions the topic of hazardous wastes).

Question 5, focusing on tone, is another Global question that you may wish to answer early on. Continuing to scan the question stems, the one with the line reference, question 2, may have caught your eye. This type simply tests your understanding of a certain word in a particular context, and since it tells us exactly where in the passage the word is, you'd be justified in trying this one next. Questions 1 and 6 are clearly Explicit Text questions, so you should do those next, beginning with the one that seems the most familiar. Questions 3 and 7, the Inference questions, are good candidates to be saved for last.

We've already discussed one of the Global questions, question 4, so let's now conclude this discussion with a brief look at one Explicit Text question and one Inference question:

Explicit Text Question

Here's the complete form (with answer choices) of question 6:

6. According to the passage, judicial assessments of liability in waste disposal disputes prior to World War II were usually based on

(A) excessively broad definitions of legal responsibility
(B) the presence of a clear threat to the public health
(C) precedents derived from well-known cases of large-scale industrial polluters
(D) restricted interpretations of property rights infringements
(E) trivial issues such as littering, eyesores, and other public nuisances

Pre–World War II judicial assessments of liability should ring a bell—they were discussed in the first paragraph. The correct answer, choice (D), is a direct paraphrase of the passage: " . . . an assessment of liability was narrowly drawn and most often restricted to a clearly identified violator in a specific act of *infringement of the property rights* of someone else."

Choice (E) is a common type of wrong answer; it consists of wording taken straight from the passage, but unfortunately, the wrong *part* of the passage. Don't choose an answer simply because you recognize some of the words or phrases in it; this is a common trap that snags many careless test takers.

Choice (B) is another classic wrong answer—the *au contraire* choice. This choice actually represents the *opposite* of what's stated or implied in the passage. According to the author, pre–World War II was "an era in which the problem of hazardous waste had yet to be recognized."

Inference Question

Finally, let's take a quick look at question 3, a complete Inference question:

3. With which one of the following statements would the author be most likely to agree?

(A) The growth of community responsibility for waste control exemplifies the tendency of government power to expand at the expense of individual rights.
(B) Although important legal precedents for waste control were established between 1880 and 1940, today's problems will require radically new approaches.
(C) While early court decisions established important precedents involving environmental abuses by industry, such equally pressing matters as disposal of municipal garbage were neglected.

Kaplan Tip

Same-wording and *au contraire* wrong choices are common. Recognize them and avoid them.

(D) Because environmental legislation between 1880 and 1940 was in advance of its time it failed to affect society's awareness of environmental problems.

(E) The historical role of U.S. courts in defining problems of hazardous waste and environmental liability provides valuable traditions for courts today.

Remember the basic rule for inferences: An inference must stay in line with the author's tone as well as the passage's topic and scope. The author's tone in this passage—factual, evenhanded—doesn't seem to fit with choices (A) and (B).

Choice (A) offers a judgment taken from the community/individual responsibility issue, something the author never does; he or she simply says that the burden shifted from one to the other.

There's no reason to believe that the author would agree with (B), either. While he or she would certainly agree with the first part, there's nothing that indicates that the author would advocate radical new approaches for today's problems. Both of these choices fail to match the author's tone and are slightly outside the scope of the passage as well.

Notice how correct choice (E) sounds like an offshoot of the author's main idea. The first sentence of the second paragraph says that it would be wrong to assume that the actions of judges and legislators, among others, had little impact on defining liability and confronting the issue of hazardous waste. This implies that the courts had a positive impact, which is bolstered by lines 39 to 43. Combine that with the statement in lines 21 to 24: "Taken as a whole, the precedents of the late nineteenth through the mid-twentieth century have established a framework in which the problem of hazardous waste is understood and confronted today." All of this points towards (E) as a statement that the author would agree with, and therefore, it is the answer to this Inference question.

After you work through the following set of Reading Comp practice questions, we'll address the last section of the LSAT: the Writing Sample.

KAPLAN

Reading Comprehension Practice Set

<u>Directions:</u> Each passage in this test is followed by several questions. After reading the passage, choose the best answer to each question. Your replies are to be based on what is *stated* or *implied* in the selection.

Passage for Questions 1–7:

Various factors influence voter preference in United States presidential elections, but perhaps none is so persuasive as a candidate's performance on nationally televised debates just prior to the
(5) election. Newspapers and television news programs generally attempt to provide thorough coverage of the debates, further augmenting the effect of good or bad candidate performances. In this way, the news media fulfill the traditional
(10) role of educating the public and enabling voters to make better informed decisions about elected officials. However, the same media that bring live debates into millions of living rooms across the nation also limit the availability of debate cover-
(15) age by use of "pool" coverage, the sharing of news coverage with other news organizations. When typical pool situations arise, one of the major networks covers the event, and a "feed" is created so other broadcasters may have access to the same
(20) coverage. Individual broadcasters are unable to convey a unique account to their viewers. The pool system limits the news-gathering ability of television news organizations and denies viewers an opportunity to gain maximum insight from
(25) the debate. The First Amendment freedoms afforded the press exist largely to ensure that the public benefits from the free flow of information. Some commentators suggest that the purpose of a free press is to inform citizens about matters of
(30) public concern. Others, however, believe that the value of free press lies in its ability to foster a marketplace of ideas in which the best options prevail. Presidential debates embody all these consid-

erations. Not only do candidates provide infor-
(35) mation about matters of utmost interest, they also offer diverse views on how to approach the major issues. Given television's ability to further informational and marketplace-of-ideas goals of the First Amendment, debate coverage should be
(40) diverse as possible.

What difference does it make whether viewers saw a "tight shot" of one candidate or a "two-shot" of both candidates at a given time? The answer depends on what happens, when it
(45) happens, and whether the pool director anticipated it or was fortunate enough to have captured it anyway. It may be argued that none of this matters. The important thing, the argument goes, is that viewers will know generally what happened.
(50) According to this line of reasoning, the number of news organizations covering an event—and even which ones—would be irrelevant. But courts have held differently: "It is impossible to treat two news services as interchangeable, and it
(55) is only by cross lights from varying directions that full illumination can be secured." Undoubtedly, there are some circumstances in which pool coverage is the only way to cover an event. But these few situations must not foster a casual acceptance
(60) of pool implementation in other situations.

Question 1

It can be inferred that the author's primary objection to the pool system of covering presidential debates is that it

(A) restricts the public's access to a diversity of ideas and information
(B) limits the number of people who have access to debates on television
(C) undermines candidates' ability to persuade voters
(D) dissuades voters from exercising their right to choose between candidates
(E) contributes to an overreliance by the public on televised accounts of political issues

Ⓐ Ⓑ Ⓒ Ⓓ Ⓔ

Question 2

The author would probably assert that the opinion of the court presented in the second paragraph is

(A) useful but biased
(B) reflective of an unfortunate trend
(C) overly permissive
(D) substantially correct
(E) commendable but ineffective

Ⓐ Ⓑ Ⓒ Ⓓ Ⓔ

Question 3

In the first paragraph, the author cites two opinions concerning the benefits provided to society by a free press primarily in order to

(A) suggest the range of benefits that potentially would be provided by competitive coverage of presidential debates
(B) indicate that some of the defenses of pool coverage contradict one another
(C) criticize the assumptions held by some commentators on journalism

(D) contend that First Amendment freedoms do not apply to presidential debates
(E) reconcile different points of view in an effort to reach a more acceptable definition of press freedom

Ⓐ Ⓑ Ⓒ Ⓓ Ⓔ

Question 4

It can be inferred from the passage that a proponent of the pool system of debate coverage would be most likely to defend her viewpoint with which of the following remarks?

(A) Broadcasters rarely betray their political preferences in debate coverage.
(B) Although imperfect, pool coverage is the only practical means of reporting most political events.
(C) Presidential debates are too complex to be covered thoroughly by any one broadcaster.
(D) Broadcasters are prevented by public opinion from presenting biased coverage.
(E) Small differences in style of coverage do not significantly affect the amount of information conveyed to viewers.

Ⓐ Ⓑ Ⓒ Ⓓ Ⓔ

Question 5

The author warns that the use of pool coverage in situations in which it may be needed may lead to other situations in which

(A) public events covered by the media are subjected to undue analytical scrutiny
(B) broadcasters accept further limitation of their First Amendment freedoms
(C) the informational content of news events is diminished
(D) pool coverage is relied upon when it is in fact undesirable

KAPLAN

(E) broadcasters suffer increasing erosion of their capacity for news gathering

Ⓐ Ⓑ Ⓒ Ⓓ Ⓔ

Question 6

The author's argument that the pool system "denies viewers an opportunity to gain maximum insight from the debate" (lines 23–25) would be most WEAK-ENED if it could be shown that

(A) candidates' debate performances rarely make a difference of more than a few percent in voting results

(B) most debate viewers form their opinions primarily on the basis of post-debate commentary presented separately by each network

(C) candidates' posture and mannerisms during debates are as important in forming voter opinion as their actual words

(D) few viewers of televised debates bother to read follow-up commentary in newspapers and magazines

(E) competitive coverage would provide viewers with a wider variety of interpretations on which to base their opinions

Ⓐ Ⓑ Ⓒ Ⓓ Ⓔ

Question 7

Which of the following titles best describes the content of the passage?

(A) Debate Coverage: How It Changes Voters' Opinions

(B) The "Pool" System: A Limitation on Public Access to Information

(C) The "Pool" System: Its Benefits Versus Its Impracticalities

(D) First Amendment Press Rights: How They Conflict with Presidential Politics

(E) Televised Debates: Their Role in Presidential Politics

Ⓐ Ⓑ Ⓒ Ⓓ Ⓔ

Passage for Questions 8–10:

It is crucial to question the assumption that for-profit health care institutions have special obligations to help subsidize care for the needy over and above their general obligation as taxpayers. As the
(5) for-profits are quick to point out, supermarkets are not expected to provide free food to the hungry poor, and real estate developers are not expected to let the poor live rent free in their housing. Yet food and housing, like health care,
(10) are basic necessities for even minimal subsistence. If there are basic human rights to some adequate level of health care, it is reasonable to think there are such rights to food and shelter as well.

Whose obligation is it, then, to secure some
(15) basic health care for those unable to secure it for themselves? Assuming that private markets and charity leave some without access to whatever amount of health care that justice requires be available to all, there are several reasons to believe
(20) that the obligation ultimately rests with the federal government. First, the obligation to secure a just or fair overall distribution of benefits and burdens across society is usually understood to be a general societal obligation. Second, the federal
(25) government is the institution society commonly employs to meet society-wide distributive requirements. With its taxing power, it has the revenue-raising capacities to finance what would be a massively expensive program for an adequate
(30) level of health care to be guaranteed to all. This taxing power also allows the burden of financing health care for the poor to be spread fairly across all members of society and not to depend on the vagaries of how wealthy or poor a state or local
(35) area happens to be. The federal government also has the power to coordinate programs guaranteeing access to health care for the poor across local and state boundaries. This is necessary both for reducing inefficiencies that allow
(40) substantial numbers of the poor to fall between the cracks of the patchwork of local and state

programs, and for ensuring that there are not great differences in the minimum of health care guaranteed to all in different locales within our (45) country.

If we are one society, a *United* States, then the level of health care required by justice for all citizens should not vary greatly in different locales because of political and economic contingencies. (50) It is worth noting that food stamp programs and housing subsidies, also aimed at basic necessities, similarly are largely a federal responsibility. These are reasons for the federal government having the obligation to guarantee access to health care for (55) those unable to secure it for themselves. It might do this by directly providing the care itself or by providing vouchers to be used by the poor in the health care marketplace. *How* access should be guaranteed and secured—and in particular, to (60) what extent market mechanisms ought to be utilized—is a separate question.

Question 8

The author's primary concern in the passage is to discuss

(A) the level of expenditures required to ensure equitable access to health care for all

(B) measures that might be enacted to carry out a program of subsidized health care

(C) differences among states and localities in the provision of basic social services

(D) whether a national commitment to health care can be reconciled with the federal structure of the United States

(E) which institutions bear the obligation for assuring adequate health services for the poor

Ⓐ Ⓑ Ⓒ Ⓓ Ⓔ

Question 9

The author mentions federal "food stamp programs and housing subsidies" (lines 50–51) primarily in order to

(A) modify a previous point in response to new information

(B) support his argument by mentioning a comparable situation

(C) argue that these programs should be modified

(D) make a concession to a contrasting opinion

(E) acknowledge that not all programs would benefit from the approach he favors

Ⓐ Ⓑ Ⓒ Ⓓ Ⓔ

Question 10

According to the passage, the federal government possesses all the following powers in regard to health care EXCEPT the power to

(A) raise the revenue to finance health care expenditures

(B) distribute the costs of health care equitably among different sectors of the country

(C) ensure that the poor have access to health care regardless of state and local boundaries

(D) compel private businesses and charities to assume greater responsibility for financing health care for the needy

(E) set comparable standards for the minimum level of health care in different areas

Ⓐ Ⓑ Ⓒ Ⓓ Ⓔ

Answers and Explanations

Passage for Questions 1–7:

Question 1

The first passage is pretty straightforward. It revolves around the author's argument that "pool" coverage of presidential debates stifles the news media's ability to gather and present news. Why does the author find such a limitation on the media so alarming? She feels that it denies viewers an opportunity to gain maximum insight from presidential debates—that is, it sets limits on the amount and variety of information that the public receives. That's the passage's main point. Be aware that the author is talking about the actual "shooting" of a news event—the visual image broadcast to the viewer. She feels that a diversity of images is needed to fully illuminate an event. Although she concedes at the end of the passage that pool coverage may be the only way to cover *some* events, she cautions against the indiscriminate use of such coverage.

Question 1 asks for the author's primary objection to pool coverage of presidential debates. As noted, the author is primarily concerned with the way pool coverage limits the public's exposure to a variety of viewpoints and information. Choice (A) says exactly that and is the correct answer. The author never charges the pool coverage system with limiting the *number* of people who have access to televised debates. Her point is that it limits the number of *versions* of a debate being offered to people, so choice (B) is wrong. The author discusses the impact of a candidate's debate performance in the first paragraph. But when examining the effects of pool coverage, the author clearly is thinking of the effect on the public's ability to judge, not on the candidates' ability to persuade, so choice (C) is out. Choice (D) involves a similar distortion of the passage's contents. The author claims that pool coverage, by limiting the information viewers receive, hinders the public's ability to choose between candi-

dates, not its right to choose. As for choice (E), the author salutes TV's ability to bring live debates into millions of living rooms across the country. She sees this as an important factor in enabling voters to make better informed decisions about candidates. Her argument doesn't include a discussion of the dangers of an "overreliance" by the public on television, as choice (E) incorrectly suggests. Again, it's (A) for Question 1.

Question 2

Take a look at the second paragraph and see what motivates the author's reference to court opinion. The author begins the paragraph by anticipating a possible counterargument—that it doesn't matter what specific images people see as long as they know generally what happened. This argument would lead a proponent of pool coverage to say that the number of news organizations covering an event is irrelevant. At the end of the paragraph, the author attacks this counterargument by quoting a court decision. That is, she's using the words of the court to defend her own views. If you realize this, you don't even have to look at the quote to infer the author's opinion of the court's findings. She must agree with them to a large extent, right? The only answer choice that reflects this level of agreement is choice (D)—"substantially correct." Choices (B) and (C) are way too negative, and choices (A) and (E) are not positive enough. So choice (D) is the answer for Question 2.

Question 3

To answer Question 3, you need to take a close look at the second half of the first paragraph. The two benefits of a free press cited there are (1), its ability "to inform citizens about matters of public concern," and (2), its ability "to foster a marketplace of ideas in which the best options prevail." The author presents these not as contradictory benefits but as complementary ones. Both benefits are involved when television airs a presidential debate, and the author argues that diversity of coverage would maximize these benefits.

Choice (A) paraphrases this argument and is the correct choice. The author doesn't mention these benefits as proposed "defenses" of pool coverage, and they certainly don't contradict each other, so choice (B) is off the mark. (C) is wrong—you more or less know this as soon as you see the verb *criticize*—it just doesn't fit what the author is doing in the first paragraph. The author is in no way critical of the benefits of a free press or of the commentators who have suggested them. The same goes for (E); the author does not "reconcile" anything here. In fact, there's no need to—the different views on free press benefits are presented here as being complementary. Finally, choice (D) is dead wrong—the point of this paragraph is that First Amendment freedoms have a whole lot to do with presidential debates. Once again, it was (A) for Question 3.

Question 4

Question 4 asks how a proponent of the pool system would defend her viewpoint. Since the author argues that pool coverage limits the information provided to viewers, you need a choice that would challenge the author's point of view. Choice (A) doesn't address this position. So what if broadcasters only rarely betray their political preferences in debate coverage? Pool coverage still limits viewers to coverage by only one of these broadcasters. (B) could be tempting, too, but it also doesn't attack the author's main argument. The author already concedes that pool coverage may be the only way to cover some events. But the drawbacks of such coverage still exist for nonpolitical events—and you might have to forgo "practicality" at some point in deference to larger issues. Choice (C) only serves to strengthen the author's argument. If presidential debates are so complex that one broadcaster cannot cover them properly, pool coverage should be eliminated, allowing coverage by a number of broadcasters. Choice (D) is similar to choice (A) and is wrong for the same reason. (By the way, when you see that two or more answer choices on the LSAT are very similar, it's a strong signal that these choices are wrong. After all,

there should be only one "right" answer to a given question.) Choice (E) is your last chance—and it's the correct answer. If small differences in style of coverage don't affect the amount of information conveyed to viewers, then the premise to the author's argument is blown out of the water. (E) would be the best remark for a proponent of pool coverage to make in its defense.

Question 5

Question 5 is a detail question. The authorial warning occurs in the last paragraph. There the author expresses the hope that the few situations in which pool coverage is necessary will not "foster a casual acceptance of pool implementation in other situations." Unnecessary pool coverage translates to undesirable pool coverage for the author—so choice (D) is your answer. (A) comes out of left field—the author never mentions the dangers of analysis-crazed media. (Who knows, she might even welcome such a situation. It would provide the public with a lot of information, wouldn't it?) (B) calls attention to the author's fleeting reference—back in the first paragraph—to the First Amendment freedoms afforded the press. But in her discussion of these freedoms, the author never makes the specific argument that pool coverage violates them. So expanded use of pool coverage couldn't be referred to as a "further limitation."

Choice (C) could have been tempting if you made things difficult for yourself. If you thought, "Well, gee, the author thinks pool coverage limits the informational content of presidential debates, so she probably would claim that expanded use of pool coverage would reduce the informational content of other news events, too." But such logical gymnastics shouldn't be necessary on the LSAT. And remember, this is a specific-detail question—you've got to stick to what the author is doing in the last paragraph, where her warning occurs. The same thing goes for (E). The author does think pool coverage limits news gathering, but this point never arises in her final warning to you. Once again, it was (D) for Question 5.

KAPLAN

Question 6

Question 6 calls your attention to a specific part of the passage, namely lines 23–25, but you're actually dealing once again with the author's overall argument. The author feels that the pool system "denies viewers an opportunity to gain maximum insight from the debate" because the sharing of news coverage means that viewers are receiving only one set of images—only one version of the debate—not a wide variety representing various viewpoints. According to the author, this prevents individual broadcasters from conveying a unique account of the debate to their viewers. The question asks you to find an answer choice that would weaken the author's contention that this limitation adversely affects viewers' ability to make voting decisions.

Choice (A) might be tempting at first. If debate performances don't sway many voters one way or another, what difference does it make what version of the debate they saw? But choice (A) doesn't address the author's specific argument concerning the effects of the pool system on voter insight. It doesn't matter if a debate doesn't have a major impact on the outcome of an election. What matters—to the author at least—is that the public has access to as much information as possible when deciding how to vote. So (A) wouldn't weaken the author's argument. Choice (B) reveals a way to alleviate—if not make irrelevant—the limits that the pool system places on the public's access to a variety of ideas. If networks were to wrap up a debate with their own follow-up commentary, providing the public with a diversity of ideas that they then use as a basis for making voting decisions, then the author's objections to the pool system would be weakened. So (B) looks pretty good, but go on to the other choices. (C), (D), and (E) would all strengthen, not weaken, the author's argument. If (C) is correct, then the author's objections to pool coverage are right on the mark—no amount of post-debate coverage could make up for viewers' having access to only one visual version of a debate. If (D) is correct, the importance of televised coverage—and a variety of it—is empha-

sized all the more. Finally, (E) just restates the author's argument. "Competitive coverage" means the same thing as elimination of pool coverage. So it was choice (B) for Question 6.

Question 7

Question 7 asks for the title that best describes the content of the passage. Wrong answer choices in such questions usually involve titles that are either too general or too specific—or those that are totally outside the passage's scope. Take choice (A), for example. The author doesn't discuss how debate coverage changes voters' opinions, does she? Throw it out! The author also doesn't discuss the benefits or impracticalities of the pool system. Throw (C) out! Does the author discuss how First Amendment press rights conflict with presidential politics? Nope—forget (D). How about (E)? In the first paragraph, the author does touch on the influence exercised by televised presidential debates. But the brunt of the passage involves the pool system and the limitations it imposes on public access to information. That's (B), your answer—the only choice that accurately reflects the author's main concerns.

Passage for Questions 8–10:

Question 8

The main topic of this passage isn't immediately apparent. The first paragraph leaves you expecting the author to examine the obligations of for-profit health care or the basic human rights to food and shelter. The author's real topic becomes clear only when you reach the second paragraph and its introductory question—"Whose obligation is it to secure basic health care for those unable to secure it for themselves?" According to the author, it's the federal government's obligation; the rest of the passage serves to back up this claim. The second paragraph outlines the powers that enable the federal government to guarantee access to health care for all those who need it.

Finally, the third paragraph reiterates the basic right to an adequate level of health care and the government's responsibility to provide it. The author ends by introducing the problem of how the federal government should guarantee access to health care.

Question 8 is a main idea question that takes you back to the beginning of the second paragraph. Remember, that's where the author first introduces his main topic—the question of whose obligation it is to secure basic health care for those unable to secure it for themselves. That's this passage's big idea, and choice (E), the correct choice, captures it well. Turning now to the wrong answers, choice (A) is way too specific. The author mentions in the second paragraph that the government's taxing power enables it to raise the money required for health care expenditures, but he doesn't delve into specifics, like the exact level of expenditures that would be required. The same goes for choices (B) and (C). In the last paragraph, the author only fleetingly discusses the how of his argument, choice (B). He also mentions that differences among various states and localities in the provision of basic social services could arise, choice (C), but these differences aren't specifically described, and they don't take up the bulk of the discussion. As for choice (D), the author's argument presupposes that a national commitment to health care can be reconciled with the federal structure of the United States. Indeed, the author's whole argument is that the federal structure is ideal for assuring access to health care. Again, the correct answer is choice (E).

Question 9

Look at lines 50–51, where the author mentions federal food stamp programs and housing subsidies. Why are these mentioned? The author notes that the food stamp programs and housing subsidies, both of which are aimed at basic necessities, are largely a federal responsibility. He mentions these two already established federal programs in order to support his argument that the federal government should start a *similar* program involving access to health care—another

basic necessity. Now, keeping that in mind, you probably could have picked the correct answer, choice (B), by looking solely at the verbs of the answer choices.

But take a closer look at the wrong answers. As for (A), the author certainly doesn't modify a previous point—in fact, he reiterates his main argument wholesale. And he doesn't argue for the modification of the aforementioned programs, either. He just wishes that a federal health care program would join them, so (C) gets eliminated. The author's reference to food stamp programs and housing subsidies does not involve a "contrasting opinion." As you know, the author sees the existence of these programs as support for his own argument. Since no contrasting opinion is presented, no "concession" can be made to it, and choice (D) is wrong. The "approach" favored by the author is federal support of programs involving basic human necessities. Food stamps and housing subsidies are examples of programs that have already benefited from this approach, so (E) doesn't make sense. Again, choice (B) is the answer.

Question 10

This is a detail question, and the second paragraph provides you with all the information you need. It is there that the author lists the federal government's powers regarding health care. If you managed to remember the nature of these powers, it might have been fairly easy for you to run down through the choices and pick out the one that looked suspicious. Assuming you didn't, compare each choice with the information in the second paragraph. Choice (A) corresponds to the first power cited—the federal government's ability to tax. This power enables it to raise the revenue needed to finance health care expenditures. Choice (B), conveniently enough, corresponds to the second power cited. The government's taxing power ensures that the burden of financing health care would be spread equitably across all members of society. Choice (C) corresponds nicely to the third power— the power to coordinate programs guaranteeing access to health care for the poor across local and state boundaries. The ability to ensure that there are not great differences in the minimum of health care guaranteed to all is the last power cited and one that is paraphrased in choice (E). This leaves you with choice (D). Nowhere does the author mention a state power that can compel private businesses and charities to assume greater responsibility for financing health care for the needy. By virtue of being wrong, choice (D) is the answer to Question 10.

Answer Key for Reading Comprehension Practice Set

1. A	6. B
2. D	7. B
3. A	8. E
4. E	9. B
5. D	10. D

CHAPTER FIVE

The Writing Sample

HIGHLIGHTS

- Learn the eight basic principles of Writing Sample success
- Familiarize yourself with sample essay topics

The Writing Sample comes at the end of your LSAT day. Typically, it consists of a scenario followed by two possible courses of action. You'll have 30 minutes to make a written case that one of the two courses of action is superior.

This section tests your ability to write a clear, concise, and persuasive argument. No outside knowledge whatsoever is required.

You will need to have a pencil to write the essay, as well as scrap paper to plan out your response before you actually write it. Your essay must be confined to the space provided, which is roughly the equivalent of one sheet of standard lined paper. You won't be given additional paper, so you'll have to keep your argument concise. Usually, two or three paragraphs will be enough. Note that there's really no time or space to change your mind or radically alter your essay once you've begun writing, so *plan your argument out carefully before beginning to write*. Make sure to write as legibly as you can.

The Writing Sample is ungraded, but it is sent to law schools along with your LSAT score. Many law schools use the Writing Sample to help make decisions on borderline cases or to decide between applicants with otherwise comparable credentials. Granted, it may not carry the same

Note

The Writing Sample may not matter in some admissions decisions, but in others, it will be crucial. Therefore, if you take it seriously, you'll be covered either way.

weight as the scored sections of the test, but since it can impact on your admission chances, your best bet is to take it seriously.

Sample Topic

The structure of every Writing Sample topic is the same: a brief introduction first outlines the choice to be made. That's followed by two bullet-pointed criteria that should guide your decision. Finally, the two alternatives that you're to choose from are described in a paragraph each.

The following is an example of a Writing Sample topic:

> The *Daily Tribune*, a metropolitan newspaper, is considering two candidates for promotion to business editor. Write an argument for one candidate over the other with the following considerations in mind:
>
> - The editor must train new writers and assign stories.
> - The editor must be able to edit and rewrite stories under daily deadline pressure.
>
> Laura received a B.A. in English from a large university. She was managing editor of her college newspaper and served as a summer intern at her hometown daily paper. Laura started working at the *Tribune* right out of college and spent three years at the city desk covering the city economy. Eight years ago, the paper formed its business section, and Laura became part of the new department. After several years covering state business, Laura began writing on the national economy. Three years ago, Laura was named senior business and finance editor on the national business staff; she is also responsible for supervising seven writers.
>
> Palmer attended an elite private college where he earned both a B.S. in business administration and an M.A. in journalism. After receiving his journalism degree, Palmer worked for three years on a monthly business magazine. He won a prestigious national award for a series of articles on the impact of monetary policy on multinational corporations. Palmer came to the *Tribune* three years ago to fill the newly created position of international business writer. He was the only member of the international staff for two years and wrote on almost a daily basis. He now supervises a staff of four writers. Last year, Palmer developed a bimonthly business supplement for the *Tribune* that has proved highly popular and has helped increase the paper's circulation.

Kaplan Rules

The admissions officers don't care what you think here; they care *how* you think. Make your choice of alternative quickly and then stick with it.

Teacher Tip

"You may have a gut reaction as to which alternative is preferable. Note it, but don't act on it. You might be able to write a better, easier essay for the one your gut doesn't at first favor."
—Bob Verini
Kaplan Teacher
Los Angeles, CA

The Eight Basic Principles of Writing Sample Success

Here are the most important rules of thumb to remember when attacking the Writing Sample:

Use Scrap Paper to Plan Your Essay

The proctors give you scrap paper for a reason. Use it! Make yourself a rudimentary outline, listing the points you want to make in each paragraph. Ideally, you should know what you want to say and how you want to say it before putting pen to paper.

Don't Obsess over Making Your Choice of Alternative

Nobody really cares which choice you make (for example, whether you choose to support Laura or Palmer in the sample above). What's important is how well you support the choice you make. Generally, the alternatives are written to be pretty evenly matched, so there's no right or wrong answer, just a well-supported or ill-supported position.

Get Right to the Point

The first sentence should immediately offer a solid endorsement of one choice over the other. Assume that the reader is already familiar with the situation; there's no need to waste time describing the scenario and the alternatives.

Use a Clear, Simple Essay Format

Since all the essay topics have the same structure, you can decide in advance how you will structure your response. One possibility is the "winner/loser" format, in which the first paragraph begins with a statement of choice and then discusses the reason why your choice (the winner) is superior. The next paragraph focuses on why the other alternative (the loser) is not as good and should end with a concluding sentence reaffirming your decision. Another possibility is the "according to the criteria" format, in which the first paragraph would discuss both the winner and the loser in light of the first criterion, and the second paragraph would discuss them both in light of the second criterion.

Whether you adopt one of these formats or use one of your own, the most important thing is that your essay be coherent in its reasoning. The more organized your essay is, the more persuasive it will be.

Teacher Tip

"When trial lawyers recognize a weakness in their case, they usually try to bring it up under favorable conditions during direct examination rather than allow their opponents to bring it up under cross examination. You can use this same concept effectively when analyzing an issue. In other words, forthrightly admit (but downplay the significance of) weaknesses in your case or strengths of the opposing side. In this way, you can not be accused of having ignored something. Instead, you have considered it but found it to be relatively less important."
—Vince LoCascio
Kaplan Teacher
New Brunswick, NJ

Mention, but Downplay, the Loser's Strengths and the Winner's Weaknesses

Use sentence structures that allow you to do this, such as, "Even though Palmer won a prestigious national award . . . " and then attempt to demonstrate why this is really no big deal. This is an example of mentioning yet downplaying one of the loser's strengths. Try to do the same thing for at least one of the winner's obvious weaknesses. Doing so demonstrates that you see the full picture. Recognizing and dealing with possible objections makes your argument that much stronger.

Don't Simply Repeat Facts About the Candidates

Try instead to offer an *interpretation of the facts in light of the stated criteria*. If you're arguing for Laura in the topic above, you can't state simply that "Laura was named senior business and finance editor on the national business staff" and expect the reader to infer that that's a good thing. For all we know, being in that position may be a detriment when it comes to the criteria—training new writers and working under daily deadline pressure. It's up to you to indicate why certain facts about the winner are positive factors in light of the criteria, and vice versa for facts about the loser. Merely parroting what's written in the topic won't win you any points with the law schools.

Write Well

It sounds obvious, of course, but you should try to make your prose as clean and flawless as you can. Some people get so entangled in content that they neglect the mechanics of essay writing. But spelling, grammar, and writing mechanics are important. Use structural signals to keep your writing fluid and clear, and use transitions between paragraphs to keep the entire essay unified. Above all, write legibly. Nothing annoys essay readers more than an illegible essay.

Budget Your Time Wisely

We suggest spending roughly five to seven minutes reading the topic, making a decision, and planning out your essay. As we suggested, use the scrap paper provided to jot down a quick outline of the points you intend to make. Then spend about twenty minutes writing the essay. This should be plenty of time; remember, we're only looking at two or three paragraphs at the most. This schedule will leave about three to five minutes at the end to proofread your essay for spelling and grammar.

Sample Essay

At this point, you'll probably want to try your hand at writing an essay on the above-mentioned topic. Please do so (observing the thirty-minute time limit, of course). Then check your essay, making sure it observes the basic principles outlined above.

The following is a sample response to the essay topic above:

> Both candidates are obviously qualified, but Laura is the better choice. For one thing, Laura has been working at the *Tribune* for eleven years, and has therefore had plenty of opportunity to learn the workings of the paper. For another, her experience has been in national rather than international business, and national business will certainly be the focus of the *Tribune*'s financial coverage. In her current capacity, she is responsible for writing and editing articles while simultaneously overseeing the work of a staff of seven. Clearly, then, Laura can work under deadline pressure and manage a staff, a capability she demonstrated at an early age as the managing director of her college newspaper. Although Laura's academic credentials may not measure up to Palmer's, her background in English, her history of steady promotions, and her work as senior national business writer—combined with a solid business knowledge and obvious drive for accomplishment—will certainly spur the department to journalistic excellence.
>
> Palmer's résumé is admirable but is nonetheless inferior to Laura's. True, Palmer has evidently done a fine job managing the international section, but his staff numbers only four, and the scope of the venture is smaller than Laura's. True, Palmer's articles on the impact of monetary policy did win an award in the past, but since he has been working for the *Tribune,* no such honors have been forthcoming. Not only does Palmer lack the English literature background that Laura has, but he also lacks her long experience at the *Tribune.* Furthermore, Palmer's editing experience seems slight, considering the length of his current tenure and the size of his staff, and while he demonstrates competence in the area of international business, he has little experience in the national business area.
>
> In light of these circumstances, the newspaper would meet its stated objectives best by promoting Laura to the position of business editor.

This generally well-reasoned and well-written essay would be an asset to any applicant's law school admissions file. The writer states his or her choice in the first sentence and then substantiates this choice in a para-

Teacher Tip

"Neither alternative will meet the decision maker's criteria 100 percent—each will have strengths and weaknesses. Your job is to make a clear-cut choice and defend it. Choose your 'winner' and explain why it will do the job despite any weaknesses. And keep it simple!"
—Bob Verini
  Kaplan Teacher
  Los Angeles, CA

graph on the winner and a paragraph on the loser. Notice the way this writer acknowledges, yet rebuts, the winner's flaws and the loser's strengths. Whether or not one agrees with the choice of Laura over Palmer, the essay definitely makes a strong, well-reasoned case for the choice—and that, after all, is what the law schools will be looking for.

A Note on Finishing

Before leaving the topic of the Writing Sample, we want to make one more important point—make sure you finish your essay. Some students find that time is called while they're still writing. Bad move. Not only does that leave you with an incomplete essay, it also hints to the admissions officers that your organization and time-management skills aren't stellar.

So don't make this classic error. Give yourself plenty of time to finish the essay.

CHAPTER SIX

Taking Control of the Test

HIGHLIGHTS

- Learn how to tackle the structure, organization, and timing of each LSAT section

- Master the answer grid

- Improve your test mentality with awareness, stamina, confidence, and the right attitude

- Find out what to do in the time before, during, and after the test

- Learn how to manage stress

The first year of law school is a frenzied experience for most law students. In order to meet the requirements of a rigorous work schedule, they either learn to prioritize and budget their time or else fall hopelessly behind. It's no surprise, then, that the LSAT, the test specifically designed to predict success in the first year of law school, is a time-intensive test, demanding excellent time-management skills as well as that *sine qua non* of the successful lawyer—grace under pressure.

As we saw, it's one thing to answer a Logical Reasoning question correctly; it's quite another to answer 25 of them correctly in 35 minutes. And the same goes for Reading Comp and Logic Games—it's a whole new ballgame once you move from doing an individual game or passage at your leisure to handling a full Logic Games or Reading Comp section under actual timed conditions. In fact, the only section of the test that's

Kaplan Rules

For complete LSAT success, you've got to get as many correct answers as possible in the time you're given. Knowing the strategies is not enough. You've got to perfect your time management skills so that you get a chance to use those strategies on as many questions as possible.

not very time intensive is the Writing Sample; most test takers find they have ample time to write the essay. But when it comes to the scored sections, time pressure is a factor that affects virtually every test taker.

So when you're comfortable with the content of the test, namely, the type of material discussed in the previous chapters, your next challenge will be to learn how to manage the all-important time element of the test.

Test Expertise

On most of the tests you take in school, you wouldn't dream of not taking at least a try at every single one of the questions. If a question seems particularly difficult, you spend significantly more time on it, since you'll probably be given more points for correctly answering a hard question. Not so on the LSAT. Remember, every LSAT question, no matter how hard, is worth a single point. And since there are so many questions to do in so little time, you'd be a fool to spend three minutes getting a point for a hard question and then not have time to get a couple of quick points from two easy questions later in the section.

Given this combination—limited time, all questions equal in weight— you've got to develop a way of handling the test sections to make sure you get as many points as you can as quickly and easily as you can. Here are the principles that will help you do that:

Attack the Questions in Any Order that Strikes You as Logical

One of the most valuable strategies to help you finish the sections in time is to learn to recognize and deal first with the questions, games, and passages that are easier and more familiar to you. That means temporarily skipping those that promise to be difficult and time consuming. You can always come back to these at the end, and if you run out of time, you're much better off not getting to questions you may have had difficulty with, rather than missing potentially doable material. Of course, since there's no wrong-answer penalty, always fill in an answer to every question on the test, whether you get to it or not.

Learn to Recognize and Seek Out Questions You're Good At

Another thing to remember about managing the sections is that LSAT questions, games, and passages, unlike items on the SAT and other standardized tests, are not presented in order of difficulty. There's no rule that says that you have to work through the sections in any particular order; in fact, the test makers scatter the easy and difficult questions throughout the section, in effect rewarding those who actually get to the end. Don't

Kaplan Rules

In order to meet the stringent time requirements of the LSAT, you've got to cultivate the following elements of test expertise:

- A sense of timing
- An ability to skip around without getting mixed up
- An ability to assess the difficulty level of a question or passage or game
- A cool head

lose sight of what you're being tested for along with your reading and thinking skills—efficiency and cleverness. If you find sequencing games particularly easy, for example, seek out the sequencing game on the Logic Games section and do it first. Similarly, if you just love formal logic questions, head straight for such questions when you first turn to the Logical Reasoning sections.

Know That the Test Questions Are Written at Different Levels of Difficulty

It's imperative that you remain calm and composed while working through a section. You can't allow yourself to be rattled by one hard logic game or reading passage, so that it throws off your performance on the rest of the section. Expect to find at least one difficult passage or game on every section, but remember, you won't be the only one to have trouble with it. The test is curved to take the tough material into account. Having trouble with a difficult logic game isn't going to ruin your score, but getting upset about it and letting it throw you off-track will. When you understand that part of the test maker's goal is to reward those who keep their composure, you'll recognize the importance of not panicking when you run into challenging material.

Control Time Instead of Letting Time Control You

Of course, the last thing you want to happen is to have time called on a particular section before you've gotten to half the questions. It's essential, therefore, that you pace yourself, keeping in mind the general guidelines for how long to spend on any individual question, passage, or game (we'll give you those guidelines below). No one is saying that you should spend, for instance, exactly one and a quarter minutes on every Logical Reasoning question. But you should have a sense of how long you have to do each question, so you know when you're exceeding the limit and should start to move faster.

Keeping track of time is also important for guessing. Remember, there's no penalty for a wrong answer on the LSAT! So it pays to leave a little time at the end to guess on the questions you couldn't answer. For instance, let's say you never get a chance to do the last logic game on an Logic Games section. If you just leave the grids for those questions blank, you're going to get no points for that entire game. If, on the other hand, you give yourself a little time at the end to fill in a guess for each of those questions, you'll have a very good chance of getting lucky on at least one or two questions. That would up your raw score by one or two points— which translates into a higher scaled score.

So, when working on a section, always remember to keep track of time.

Don't spend a wildly disproportionate amount of time on any one question or group of questions. Also, give yourself 30 seconds or so at the end of each section to fill in answers for any questions you didn't get to. After all, a correct guess is worth just as much as any other correct answer.

Section-Specific Strategies

Let's now look at the section-specific timing requirements and some tips for meeting them.

Logical Reasoning

Time Per Question

Tackling 24 to 26 questions in 35 minutes works out to roughly a minute and a quarter per question. Keep in mind that this is only an average; there are bound to be some questions that take less time and some that take more. It's okay if the occasional question takes you two minutes, if you're able to balance it out with a question that takes 45 seconds. Remember, too, that every question is worth the same, so don't get hung up on any one question. No single point on this section is worth three minutes of your valuable time, that's for sure. And think about it—if a question is so hard that it takes you that long to answer it, chances are you may get it wrong anyway. In that case, you'd have nothing to show for your extra time but a lower score.

Managing the Section

What kind of Logical Reasoning questions should you skip? Certainly questions containing stimuli that are indecipherable to you after a quick reading. Questions containing extra-long stimulus arguments may be good to skip initially as well, especially if you're running behind on time. But don't automatically be intimidated by the sheer length of a stimulus; often, the long ones are uncomplicated and easy to understand.

If you adhere to our strategy of reading the question stem first, you may be able to single out questions to postpone based solely on question type. This is a matter of recognizing your own strengths and weaknesses. For example, if a question involves finding a principle that lends credence to an argument, and you know historically that principle questions are a problem for you, then that's a good question to postpone.

A good stimulus is one that comes with two questions attached. There are usually anywhere from two to four double-question stimuli on each Logical Reasoning section. Working through these, as opposed to single question arguments, saves a little time, as you can potentially rack up two points for reading only one stimulus.

Logic Games

Time Per Game

There are four games to get through in 35 minutes, which works out to roughly eight and a half minutes per game. Remember, just as in Logical Reasoning, this is an average—some games may take a little more time, while some may take a little less.

Managing the Section

There are definitely some things to keep in mind when it comes to working through an entire Logic Games section. First, and most important, is the necessity of previewing the section. By this, we mean that you should literally flip through the pages, having a glance at each game in order to decide which games look the easiest and most familiar to you. Previewing, of course, is not foolproof; a game that looks fairly straightforward at first glance could easily turn out to be a killer. But it works more often than not.

The ideal goal is to tackle the games in order of difficulty, from easiest to hardest. But if you achieve nothing more than saving the hardest game for last, then the strategy is a winner.

So how do you tell which games may be difficult? The best way is to know the game types discussed in the Logic Games section cold and to have a feeling for which types you're strong in and which ones you should avoid like the plague (until the end, of course). A game that doesn't look familiar at all could simply be an oddball game—a good candidate to postpone. And don't necessarily be scared off by games with a lot of rules; sometimes, this works to your advantage. The more rules they give you, the more definite and concrete the game situation is, and the easier it will be to answer the questions. It's the games with few rules that often turn out to be tough because they're inherently ambiguous.

If you have several Logic Games to practice on, you may wish to build gradually to the point where you're ready to take full-length sections. Begin by attempting one game in eight or nine minutes. Next, try two games in 17 minutes. When you're ready to move on, try three games in about 26 to 27 minutes, until finally you can handle a full four-game section in 35 minutes.

Finally, remember what we said about the way the test makers test efficiency. They're crafty—they'll sometimes throw an intentionally time-consuming question at the end of a game, possibly one involving a rule change that requires you to backtrack and set the game up all over again. Bear in mind that when this happens, they may not be testing who's smart enough to get the right answer, rather who's clever enough to skip the killer question in order to devote their precious time to the next game, with a possible payoff of six or seven new points.

Review

Here's how best to manage your time on the LG section:

- Spend about eight and a half minutes per game.
- Preview the section so you know what you're up against.
- Do the easiest game first; save the toughest for last.
- Skip rule-change questions and others that promise to be especially time consuming.

If you apply the principles regarding making deductions and working through questions discussed earlier, and combine that with these tips on how to approach a full Logic Games section, you'll be well on your way to an excellent Logic Games performance on the day of the test.

Reading Comprehension

Time per Passage

The Reading Comp section format is similar to that of the Logic Games section: four passages in 35 minutes, which means about eight and a half minutes per passage. The Reading Comp strategies and techniques in the previous chapter should help you to get through each passage as quickly as possible, but here are a few additional points about tackling a full section.

Managing the Section

It's a little more difficult to preview the Reading Comp section than it is to preview a Logic Games section, but it is possible to know that it's time to move on if the first third of a passage is extraordinarily confusing or simply really boring to the point of distraction. Concentration is a major key in Reading Comp, and if you simply can't "lock into" the ideas in a particular passage, then it's time to put that one aside and look for friendlier territory. As in Logic Games, the goal is to save the most difficult stuff for last.

Quite often, you'll encounter Reading Comprehension passages that contain a preponderance of technical details or difficult concepts, only to find that few if any questions deal with the part of the passage that's so dense. Just as in the Logic Games example above, the test makers aren't necessarily testing to see who's smart enough to understand that section of the passage; they may be looking to see who's clever enough to skim past those details and focus on the more important aspects of the passage instead. If you keep this in mind, you'll be less likely to get mired in extraneous details.

Answer Grid Expertise

An important part of LSAT test expertise is knowing how to handle the answer grid. After all, you not only have to pick the right answers; you also have to mark those right answers on the answer grid in an efficient and accurate way. It sounds simple, but it's extremely important: *Don't make mistakes filling out your answer grid!* When time is short, it's easy to get confused going back and forth between your test book and your grid.

If you know the answer, but misgrid, you won't get the points. Here are a few methods of avoiding mistakes on the answer grid.

Always Circle Questions You Skip

Put a big circle in your test book around the number of any question you skip (you may even want to circle the whole question itself). When you go back, such questions will then be easy to locate. Also, if you accidentally skip a box on the grid, you can more easily check your grid against your book to see where you went wrong.

Always Circle Answers You Choose

Circle the correct answers in your test booklet, but don't transfer the answers to the grid right away. That wastes too much time, especially if you're doing a lot of skipping around. Circling your answers in the test book will also make it easier to check your grid against your book.

Grid Five or More Answers at Once

As we said, don't transfer your answers to the grid after every question. Transfer your answers after every five questions, or at the end of each Reading Comp passage or Logic Game (find the method that works best for you). That way, you won't keep breaking your concentration to mark the grid. You'll save time and improve accuracy. Just make sure you're not left at the end of the section with ungridded answers!

Save Time at the End for a Final Grid Check

Make sure you have enough time at the end of every section to make a quick check of your grid, to make sure you've got an oval filled in for each question in the section. Remember, a blank grid has no chance of earning a point, but a guess does.

Now let's turn our attention to test mentality, and put the finishing touches on your comprehensive LSAT approach.

Test Mentality

We've already armed you with the weapons you need to do well on the LSAT. But you must wield those weapons with the right frame of mind and in the right spirit. This involves taking a certain stance towards the entire test. Here's what's involved:

Review

What makes for good test mentality? We're glad you asked. The important elements are:

- Test awareness
- Stamina
- Confidence
- The right attitude

1. Test Awareness

To do your best on the LSAT, you must always keep in mind that the test is like no other test you've taken before, both in terms of content and in terms of scoring system. If you took a test in high school or college and got a quarter of the questions wrong, you'd probably receive a pretty lousy grade. But on the LSAT, you can get a quarter of the questions wrong (about 25) and still score higher than the 80th percentile! The test is geared so that only the very best test takers are able to finish every section. But even these people rarely get every question right. As mentioned earlier, you can get a "perfect" score of 180 and still get a handful of questions wrong.

What does this mean for you? Well, just as you shouldn't let one bad game or passage ruin an entire section, you shouldn't let what you consider to be a below par performance on one section ruin your performance on the entire test. A lousy performance on one single section will not by itself spoil your score (unless you miss almost every question). However, if you allow that poor section to rattle you, it can have a cumulative negative effect, setting in motion a downward spiral. It's the kind of thing that could potentially do serious damage to your score. Losing a few extra points won't do you in, but losing your head will.

Remember, if you feel you've done poorly on a section, don't sweat it. Who knows, it could be the experimental. And even if it's not, chances are it's just a difficult section—a factor that will already be figured into the scoring curve anyway. The point is, you must remain calm and collected. Simply do your best on each section, and once a section is over, forget about it and move on.

While we're on the topic of the experimental section, we'd like to reiterate an important point: never, ever try to figure out which section is unscored. This practice has caused trouble for countless test takers. They somehow convince themselves that a certain section is the one that doesn't count, and then don't take it seriously. And they're pretty upset when they find out they guessed wrong. You can't know which section is the experimental section, so handle each section as if it counts. That way, you're covered no matter what. If a section you had trouble with turns out to be experimental, it's gravy. If it turns out to be scored—well, think how much worse you'd have done if you blew it off entirely.

2. Stamina

The LSAT is a fairly grueling experience, and some test takers simply run out of gas before it's over. To avoid this, take as many full-length practice tests as possible in the week or two before the test. That way, five sections plus a writing sample will seem like a breeze (well, maybe not a breeze, but at least not a hurricane).

One option is to buy PrepTests, which are the actual released exams published by Law Services. The available PrepTests are listed in the *LSAT Registration and Information Book*, which is available at most colleges and law schools, as well as on the Law Services website at www.lsac.org. Or you can call Law Services at (215) 968-1001 for information. (Try to send away for them early, since they can take two to three weeks for delivery.) You can also download a single free PrepTest from the Law Services website.

Another option, if you have some time, would be to take the full Kaplan course. We'll give you access to every released test plus loads of additional material, so you can really build up your LSAT stamina. As a bonus, you'll also have the benefit of our expert live instruction in every aspect of the LSAT. If you decide to go this route, call (800) KAP-TEST for the Kaplan Center location near you.

3. Confidence

Confidence feeds on itself, and unfortunately, so does self-doubt. Confidence in your ability leads to quick, sure answers and a sense of well-being that translates into more points. If you lack confidence, you end up reading sentences and answer choices two, three, or four times, to the point at which you confuse yourself and get off-track. This leads to timing difficulties, which only perpetuate the downward spiral, causing anxiety and a tendency to rush in order to finish sections.

If you subscribe to the LSAT mentality we've described, however, you'll gear all of your practice towards the major goal of taking control of the test. When you've achieved that goal—armed with the principles, techniques, strategies, and methods set forth in this book—you'll be ready to face the LSAT with supreme confidence. And that's the one sure way to score your best on the day of the test.

4. The Right Attitude

Those who approach the LSAT as an obstacle and who rail against the necessity of taking it, usually don't fare as well as those who see the LSAT as an opportunity to show off the reading and reasoning skills that the law schools are looking for. Those who look forward to doing battle with the LSAT—or, at least, who enjoy the opportunity to distinguish themselves from the rest of the applicant pack—tend to score better than do those who resent or dread it.

It may sound a little dubious, but take our word for it: attitude adjustment is a proven test-taking technique. Here are a few steps you can take to make sure you develop the right LSAT attitude:

Kaplan Tip

Losing a few extra points here and there won't do serious damage to your score, but losing your head will. Keeping your composure is an important test-taking skill.

Note

You wouldn't run a marathon without working on your stamina well in advance of the race, would you? The same goes for taking the LSAT.

Kaplan Rules

It sounds New Age, we know. But your attitude towards the test really does affect your performance. We're not asking you to "think nice thoughts about the LSAT," but we are recommending that you change your mental stance towards the test.

- Look at the LSAT as a challenge, but try not to obsess over it; you certainly don't want to psyche yourself out of the game.
- Remember that, yes, the LSAT is obviously important, but this one test will not single-handedly determine the outcome of your life.
- Try to have fun with the test. Learning how to match your wits against the test makers can be a very satisfying experience, and the reading and thinking skills you'll acquire will benefit you in law school as well as in your future legal career.
- Remember that you're more prepared than most people. You've trained with Kaplan. You have the tools you need, plus the know-how to use those tools.

Global Principles

Let's conclude with a recap of some of the most important global principles and strategies for success on the LSAT:

- The test questions are not necessarily presented in order of difficulty. Answer the questions in any order that seems effective.
- There is no penalty for wrong answers on the LSAT. *Always guess if you can't answer a question*, or if you can't get to it! Never leave a question blank.
- All questions are worth the same amount, so don't spend an excessive amount of time on any one question.
- You are rewarded for correctly identifying the "credited answer." Learn to think like the test maker—follow the test maker's reasoning to that credited answer.

For access to additional preparation and practice questions, log on to www.kaptest.com/booksonline. You will need to have your book handy.

Tips for the Final Week

Is it starting to feel like your whole life is a buildup to the LSAT? You've known about it for years, worried about it for months, and now spent at least a few weeks in solid preparation for it. As the test gets closer, you may find your anxiety is on the rise. You shouldn't worry. After the preparation you've received from this book, you're in good shape for the test.

To calm any pretest jitters you may have, though, let's go over a few strategies for the days before the test.

The Week Before the Test

In the week or so leading up to the test, you should do the following:

- Recheck your admission ticket for accuracy; call Law Services if corrections are necessary.
- Visit the testing center if you can. Sometimes seeing the actual room where your test will be administered and taking notice of little things—like the kind of desk you'll be working on, whether the room is likely to be hot or cold, etcetera—may help to calm your nerves. And if you've never been to the campus or building where your test will take place, this is a good way to ensure that you don't get lost on the day of the test. Remember, you must be on time—the proctors won't wait for you.
- Practice getting up early and working on test material, preferably a full-length test, as if it were the real day of the test.
- Time yourself accurately, with the same device and in the same manner in which you plan to keep track of time on the test.
- Evaluate thoroughly where you stand. Use the time remaining before the test to shore up your weak points, rereading the appropriate sections of this book. But don't neglect your strong areas; after all, this is where you'll rack up most of your points.

The Day Before the Test

Try to avoid doing intensive studying the day before the test. There's little you can do to help yourself at this late date, and you may just wind up exhausting yourself and burning out. Our advice is to review a few key concepts, get together everything you'll need for test day, and then take the night off entirely. Go to see a movie or watch some TV. Try not to think too much about the test.

The Day of the Test

Get up early, leaving yourself plenty of time. Read something to warm up your brain—you don't want the LSAT to be the first written material your brain tries to assimilate that day.

Dress in layers for maximum comfort. That way, you'll be able to adjust to the testing room's temperature.

In traveling to the test center, leave yourself enough time for traffic and mass transit delays.

Be ready for a long day. Total testing time, remember, is three hours and 25 minutes. When you add the administrative paperwork before and after, and the 10- to 15-minute break in the middle, you're looking at an experience of four and a half to six hours.

Teacher Tip

"Everybody wants to know the easiest way to a higher score. I say, practice, practice, practice."
—Suzanne Riskin
  Kaplan Teacher
  Miami, FL

Kaplan Tip

On the night before the test, get together an "LSAT survival kit" containing the following items:

- A watch
- A few No. 2 pencils (pencils with slightly dull points fill the ovals better)
- Erasers
- Photo ID card
- Your admission ticket
- A snack—there's a break and you'll probably get hungry

Don't get flustered when they fingerprint you as you enter the testing room—this is standard operating procedure and is not intended for your FBI file. The test administrators do this because occasionally they have reason to believe that some test takers are not exactly who they say they are. If you're on the up and up, you'll have nothing to worry about.

After the test booklets are handed out, and you've filled out all of the required information, the test will begin. Your proctor should write the starting and ending time of each section on a blackboard in front of the room, and will usually announce the time remaining at specified intervals, such as when there's ten minutes remaining, five minutes remaining, and one minute remaining.

Most test centers have a clock on the wall that the proctor will use to time the test, but don't take anything for granted—your test center may not (stranger things have been known to happen). You should definitely bring along your own timing device, such as a watch or a stopwatch, so long as it doesn't make any noise (devices that beep on the hour or sound an alarm at specified times are prohibited from the testing site).

It's also best to practice using a timing routine that you'll follow during the real test. For example, some students find it helpful to set their watches at 25 past the hour for the scored sections, often 11:25. This way, they know that the section will end exactly when their watch says 12:00. Others reset their watches exactly on the hour at the beginning of each section, and know that every section will end at thirty-five minutes after the hour (except for the Writing Sample, of course, which will end on the half-hour). Still others synchronize their watches with the room clock and follow the proctor's timing guidelines. It doesn't matter which one of the these procedures you adopt, or even if you come up with one of your own that you're comfortable with, just as long as you use it consistently, so that keeping track of time during test is second nature.

Here are some other last-minute reminders to help guide your work on the test:

- Read each question stem carefully, and reread it before making your final selection. Also, to make sure your answer sheet is gridded accurately, say the question number and choice to yourself (silently, of course) as you grid.
- Give all five choices a fair shot in Logical Reasoning and Reading Comp, time permitting. For Logic Games, go with the objectively correct answer as soon as you find it and blow off the rest.
- Don't get bogged down in the middle of any section. At the end of *every* section are questions that may be really easy and manageable. Make sure that you get to them! Conversely, don't be alarmed if you run across extra-tough questions at the beginning, especially in Logical Reasoning.

It happens. Skip past tough ones and come back to them later, making sure to circle them in the test booklet so you can find them fast.

- Preview the Logic Games and Reading Comprehension sections before you launch into them. The third or fourth game or reading passage could be the easiest one. Take a brief look at all four before you decide where to begin.

- Don't bother trying to figure out which section is unscored. It can't help you, and you might very well be wrong. Instead, just determine to do your best on every section.

- Confidence is key. *Accentuate the positives, and don't dwell on the negatives!* Your attitude and outlook are crucial to your performance on test day.

- During the exam, try not to think about how you're scoring. It's like a baseball player who's thinking about the crowd's cheers and the sportswriters and his contract as he steps up to the plate. There's no surer way to strike out. Instead, focus on the question-by-question task of picking (A), (B), (C), (D), or (E). The correct answer is there. You don't have to come up with it; it's sitting right there in front of you! Concentrate on each question, each passage, each game—on the mechanics, in other words—and you'll be much more likely to hit a home run.

Test Rhythm

Between sections 1 and 2, 2 and 3, and 4 and 5, the proctor will say only: "Time's up on this section. Go on to the next section." Notice that there's no break here—you must go immediately from one section to the next. Also, if you finish a section early, you're not allowed to move on to another section. They're pretty strict about this one, so watch your step. If you have extra time, spend it looking back over your work on that section alone.

After section 3, you'll be instructed to close your test booklets and take a ten- to 15-minute break. Pay no attention to people's nervous chatter during the break. Some will say it's the hardest test since the dawn of time; others will say it's so easy they can't believe it. Either kind of comment can rattle you. Instead, bring a Walkman, headphones, and some tunes that'll pump you up and some that'll relax you, to use as needed.

After the break, you'll return to the testing room for the remaining sections. Then, after section 5, your test materials will be collected, and the Writing Sample materials will be handed out.

After the Writing Sample is collected, the test ends and you're free to get on with your life. For most of you, this means getting back to the rest of the application and admission process we will talk about in the

Note

Don't rely on proctors. Hey, they're usually nice people, but nobody's perfect. Be your own timer.

Kaplan Tip

During the break, there will undoubtedly be those who want to talk about the test—how hard or easy it is, which section is "definitely experimental," etcetera. Don't listen to these people. They will probably be wrong, for one thing. And their comments will just hurt your concentration on the rest of the test.

Note

The key question to ask yourself when deciding whether to cancel is this, "Will I really do significantly better next time?"

Resources

While we hope you won't find it necessary to cancel your LSAT score, here are a few points to keep in mind:

- Scores can be canceled on the spot or within five working days after the test date.
- To avoid anxiety, use a mailgram, telegram, fax, or overnight letter.
- A form is provided at the test site, or write your own letter with name, address, social security number, signature, test date, test center name, test center code number.
- Send to: Law Services Score Cancellation, Box 2000-T, 661 Penn Street, Newtown, PA 18940-0995, or fax to (215) 968-1277.
- Scores can now be canceled at the site of the test. But we recommend that you not do so except in extreme cases of performance disaster. Better to sleep on it and cancel later if necessary.

section titled, "Getting into Law School." In the short term, however, this signals the beginning of a well-deserved night out to unwind.

After the Test

Cancellation and Multiple Scores Policy

Unlike many things in life, the LSAT allows you a second chance. If you walk out of the test feeling that you've really not done as well as you could have, you have the option of canceling your score—as long as you notify Law Services within five business days after the day of the test. Canceling a test means that it won't be scored. It will just appear on your score report as a cancelled test. No one will know how well or poorly you really did—not even you.

There's been a recent change in the LSAT cancellation policy. Previously, in order to cancel a test, you had no option except to mail or fax the signed cancellation form to Law Services within five business days. While you still have that option, it's now possible to cancel your score immediately after the test, right at the test center. However, we strongly advise against this. When deciding whether to cancel your score, a good rule of thumb is to make an honest assessment of whether you'll do better on the next test. Wishful thinking doesn't count; you need to have a valid reason to believe that the next time would be different. Remember, no test experience is going to be perfect. If you were distracted by the proctor's hacking cough this time around, next time you may be even more distracted by construction noise, or a cold, or the hideous lime-green sweater of the person sitting in front of you.

Two legitimate reasons to cancel your test are illness and personal circumstances that cause you to perform poorly on that particular day. Also, if you feel that you didn't prepare sufficiently, then it may be advisable to cancel your score and approach your test preparation a little more seriously the next time.

But keep in mind that test takers historically underestimate their performance, especially immediately following the test. They tend to forget about all of the things that went right and focus on everything that went wrong. So unless your performance is terribly marred by unforeseen circumstances, don't cancel your test immediately—at least sleep on the decision for one or two nights, and if you still feel you want to do it again, then send in the form. Just remember, cancellations are permanent. Once the form is sent, you can't change your mind.

What the Schools Will See

If you do cancel your test and then take it again for a score, your score report will indicate that you've canceled a previous score. Since it won't be scored, you don't have to worry about this score showing up on any subsequent score report. If you take more than one test without canceling, then all the scores will show up on each score report, so the law schools will see them all. Most law schools average LSAT scores, although there are a few exceptions. Check with individual schools for their policy on multiple scores.

Post-LSAT Festivities

After all the hard work you've done preparing for and taking the LSAT, you want to make sure you take time to celebrate afterwards. Plan to get together with friends the evening after the test. Relax, have fun, let loose. After all, you've got a lot to celebrate. You prepared for the test ahead of time. You did your best. You're going to get a good score.

So start thinking about all of the great parties you'll be attending at the law school of your choice.

Managing Stress

The countdown has begun. Your date with the test is looming on the horizon. Anxiety is on the rise. The butterflies in your stomach have gone ballistic and your thinking is getting cloudy. Maybe you think you won't be ready. Maybe you already know your stuff, but you're going into panic mode anyway. Don't freak! It is possible to tame that anxiety and stress—*before* and *during* the test.

Remember, some stress is normal and good. Anxiety is a motivation to study. The adrenaline that gets pumped into your bloodstream when you're stressed helps you stay alert and think more clearly. But if you feel that the tension is so great that it's preventing you from using your study time effectively, here are some things you can do to get it under control.

Take Control

Lack of control is a prime cause of stress. Research shows that if you don't have a sense of control over what's happening in your life, you can easily end up feeling helpless and hopeless. Try to identify the sources of the stress you feel. Which of these can you do something about? Can you find ways to reduce the stress you're feeling about any of these sources?

Focus on Your Strengths

Make a list of areas of strength you have that will help you do well on the test. We all have strengths, and recognizing your own is like having reserves of solid gold at Fort Knox. You'll be able to draw on your reserves as you need them, helping you solve difficult questions, maintain confidence,

Kaplan Tip

Create a set of positive, but brief affirmations and mentally repeat them to yourself just before you fall asleep at night. (That's when your mind is very open to suggestion.) You'll find yourself feeling a lot more positive in the morning. Periodically repeating your affirmations during the day makes them even more effective.

Teacher Tip

"Take care of yourself. Sounds simple, no? Sleep well, eat well, be nice to others and drive safely before you take the test. Sick and injured people don't do well on exams!"
—Tayna Kormeili
   Kaplan Teacher
   Los Angeles, CA

and keep test stress and anxiety at a distance. And every time you recognize a new area of strength, solve a challenging problem, or score well on a practice test, you'll increase your reserves.

Imagine Yourself Succeeding

Close your eyes and imagine yourself in a relaxing situation. Breathe easily and naturally. Now, think of a real-life situation in which you scored well on a test or did well on an assignment. Focus on this success. Now turn your thoughts to the LSAT, and keep your thoughts and feelings in line with that successful experience. Don't make comparisons between them; just imagine yourself taking the upcoming test with the same feelings of confidence and relaxed control.

Set Realistic Goals

Facing your problem areas give you some distinct advantages. What do you want to accomplish in the time remaining? Make a list of realistic goals. You can't help feeling more confident when you know you're actively improving your chances of earning a higher test score.

Exercise Your Frustrations Away

Whether it is jogging, biking, pushups, or a pickup basketball game, physical exercise will stimulate your mind and body and improve your ability to think and concentrate. A surprising number of students fall out of the habit of regular exercise, ironically because they're spending so much time prepping for exams. A little physical exertion will help to keep your mind and body in sync and sleep better at night.

Avoid Drugs

Using drugs (prescription or recreational) specifically to prepare for and take a big test is definitely self-defeating. (And if they're illegal drugs, you may end up with a bigger problem than the LSAT on your hands.) Mild stimulants, such as coffee or cola, can sometimes help as you study because they keep you alert. On the down side, too much of these can also lead to agitation, restlessness, and insomnia. It all depends on your tolerance for caffeine.

Eat Well

Good nutrition will help you focus and think clearly. Eat plenty of fruits and vegetables, low-fat protein such as fish, skinless poultry, beans, and legumes, and whole grains such as brown rice, whole wheat bread, and pastas. Don't eat a lot of sugar, high-fat snacks, or salty foods.

Keep Breathing

Conscious attention to breathing is an excellent way of managing stress while you're taking the test. Most of the people who get into trouble during tests take shallow breaths: They breathe using only their upper chests and shoulder muscles and may even hold their breath for long periods of time. Conversely, those test takers who breathe deeply in a slow, relaxed manner are likely to be in better control during the session.

Stretch

If you find yourself getting spaced out or burned out as you're studying for or taking the test, stop for a brief moment and stretch. Even though you'll be pausing for a moment, it's a moment well spent. Stretching will help to refresh you and refocus your thoughts.

"Managing Stress" adapted from "The Kaplan Advantage Stress Management System" by Dr. Ed Newman and Bob Verini, copyright 1996 by Kaplan, Inc.

Kaplan Tip

When you're in the middle of studying and hit a wall, take a short, brisk walk. Breathe deeply and swing your arms as you walk. Clear your mind. (And don't forget to look for flowers that grow in the cracks of the sidewalk.)

PRACTICE TESTS
AND ANSWERS

HOW TO TAKE THE PRACTICE TESTS

Before taking each test, find a quiet place where you can work uninterrupted for about two and a half hours. Make sure you have a comfortable desk and several No. 2 pencils.

Each Practice Test includes four scored multiple-choice sections. Keep in mind that on the actual LSAT, there will be an additional multiple-choice section—the experimental section—that will not contribute to your score, plus an unscored Writing Sample.

Use the grids immediately preceding each test to record your answers for Practice Tests One, Two, and Three.

Once you start a Practice Test, don't stop until you've gone through all four sections. Remember, you can review any questions within a section, but you may not go back or forward a section.

You'll find answer keys and explanations following each test. Use the score converter on the following pages to calculate your score for each Practice Test.

Good luck!

HOW TO CALCULATE YOUR SCORE

Step 1

Add together your total number correct for all four sections.
This is your raw score.

Section 1 _____
(# correct)

Section 2 _____
(# correct)

Section 3 _____
(# correct)

Section 4 _____
(# correct)

_____

Total Correct _____
(raw score)

Step 2

Find your raw score on the table below and read across
to find your scaled score and your percentile.

Raw Score	Scaled Score	Percentile Rank	Raw Score	Scaled Score	Percentile Rank
0	120	0	19	129	1
1	120	0	20	130	2
2	120	0	21	130	2
3	120	0	22	130	2
4	120	0	23	131	2
5	120	0	24	132	3
6	120	0	25	133	3
7	120	0	26	133	3
8	121	0	27	133	3
9	122	0	28	134	4
10	122	0	29	135	5
11	123	0	30	136	6
12	124	0	31	136	6
13	124	0	32	137	8
14	125	0	33	137	8
15	126	1	34	138	9
16	126	1	35	138	9
17	127	1	36	139	10
18	128	1	37	140	13

Raw Score	Scaled Score	Percentile Rank	Raw Score	Scaled Score	Percentile Rank
38	140	13	70	157	74
39	140	13	71	158	77
40	141	15	72	158	77
41	142	17	73	159	80
42	142	17	74	159	80
43	143	20	75	160	83
44	144	23	76	160	83
45	144	23	77	161	86
46	144	23	78	162	88
47	145	26	79	162	88
48	146	29	80	162	88
49	146	29	81	163	90
50	147	33	82	164	92
51	147	33	83	164	92
52	148	37	84	165	93
53	148	37	85	166	95
54	149	41	86	166	95
55	150	45	87	167	96
56	150	45	88	167	96
57	150	45	89	168	97
58	151	50	90	169	97
59	151	50	91	170	98
60	152	54	92	170	98
61	153	58	93	171	98
62	153	58	94	172	99
63	153	58	95	173	99
64	154	62	96	174	99
65	155	66	97	175	99
66	155	66	98	176	99
67	156	70	99	177	99
68	156	70	100	179	99
69	156	70	101	180	99

PRACTICE TEST ONE

Remove or photocopy this answer sheet and use it to complete Practice Test One.
See the answer key immediately following the test to correct your answers when you're finished.
Then use the score converter on pages 145 and 146 to calculate your score and percentile rank.

Start with number 1 for each new section. If a section has fewer questions than answer spaces, leave the extra spaces blank.

SECTION 1	SECTION 2	SECTION 3	SECTION 4
1 Ⓐ Ⓑ Ⓒ Ⓓ Ⓔ	1 Ⓐ Ⓑ Ⓒ Ⓓ Ⓔ	1 Ⓐ Ⓑ Ⓒ Ⓓ Ⓔ	1 Ⓐ Ⓑ Ⓒ Ⓓ Ⓔ
2 Ⓐ Ⓑ Ⓒ Ⓓ Ⓔ	2 Ⓐ Ⓑ Ⓒ Ⓓ Ⓔ	2 Ⓐ Ⓑ Ⓒ Ⓓ Ⓔ	2 Ⓐ Ⓑ Ⓒ Ⓓ Ⓔ
3 Ⓐ Ⓑ Ⓒ Ⓓ Ⓔ	3 Ⓐ Ⓑ Ⓒ Ⓓ Ⓔ	3 Ⓐ Ⓑ Ⓒ Ⓓ Ⓔ	3 Ⓐ Ⓑ Ⓒ Ⓓ Ⓔ
4 Ⓐ Ⓑ Ⓒ Ⓓ Ⓔ	4 Ⓐ Ⓑ Ⓒ Ⓓ Ⓔ	4 Ⓐ Ⓑ Ⓒ Ⓓ Ⓔ	4 Ⓐ Ⓑ Ⓒ Ⓓ Ⓔ
5 Ⓐ Ⓑ Ⓒ Ⓓ Ⓔ	5 Ⓐ Ⓑ Ⓒ Ⓓ Ⓔ	5 Ⓐ Ⓑ Ⓒ Ⓓ Ⓔ	5 Ⓐ Ⓑ Ⓒ Ⓓ Ⓔ
6 Ⓐ Ⓑ Ⓒ Ⓓ Ⓔ	6 Ⓐ Ⓑ Ⓒ Ⓓ Ⓔ	6 Ⓐ Ⓑ Ⓒ Ⓓ Ⓔ	6 Ⓐ Ⓑ Ⓒ Ⓓ Ⓔ
7 Ⓐ Ⓑ Ⓒ Ⓓ Ⓔ	7 Ⓐ Ⓑ Ⓒ Ⓓ Ⓔ	7 Ⓐ Ⓑ Ⓒ Ⓓ Ⓔ	7 Ⓐ Ⓑ Ⓒ Ⓓ Ⓔ
8 Ⓐ Ⓑ Ⓒ Ⓓ Ⓔ	8 Ⓐ Ⓑ Ⓒ Ⓓ Ⓔ	8 Ⓐ Ⓑ Ⓒ Ⓓ Ⓔ	8 Ⓐ Ⓑ Ⓒ Ⓓ Ⓔ
9 Ⓐ Ⓑ Ⓒ Ⓓ Ⓔ	9 Ⓐ Ⓑ Ⓒ Ⓓ Ⓔ	9 Ⓐ Ⓑ Ⓒ Ⓓ Ⓔ	9 Ⓐ Ⓑ Ⓒ Ⓓ Ⓔ
10 Ⓐ Ⓑ Ⓒ Ⓓ Ⓔ	10 Ⓐ Ⓑ Ⓒ Ⓓ Ⓔ	10 Ⓐ Ⓑ Ⓒ Ⓓ Ⓔ	10 Ⓐ Ⓑ Ⓒ Ⓓ Ⓔ
11 Ⓐ Ⓑ Ⓒ Ⓓ Ⓔ	11 Ⓐ Ⓑ Ⓒ Ⓓ Ⓔ	11 Ⓐ Ⓑ Ⓒ Ⓓ Ⓔ	11 Ⓐ Ⓑ Ⓒ Ⓓ Ⓔ
12 Ⓐ Ⓑ Ⓒ Ⓓ Ⓔ	12 Ⓐ Ⓑ Ⓒ Ⓓ Ⓔ	12 Ⓐ Ⓑ Ⓒ Ⓓ Ⓔ	12 Ⓐ Ⓑ Ⓒ Ⓓ Ⓔ
13 Ⓐ Ⓑ Ⓒ Ⓓ Ⓔ	13 Ⓐ Ⓑ Ⓒ Ⓓ Ⓔ	13 Ⓐ Ⓑ Ⓒ Ⓓ Ⓔ	13 Ⓐ Ⓑ Ⓒ Ⓓ Ⓔ
14 Ⓐ Ⓑ Ⓒ Ⓓ Ⓔ	14 Ⓐ Ⓑ Ⓒ Ⓓ Ⓔ	14 Ⓐ Ⓑ Ⓒ Ⓓ Ⓔ	14 Ⓐ Ⓑ Ⓒ Ⓓ Ⓔ
15 Ⓐ Ⓑ Ⓒ Ⓓ Ⓔ	15 Ⓐ Ⓑ Ⓒ Ⓓ Ⓔ	15 Ⓐ Ⓑ Ⓒ Ⓓ Ⓔ	15 Ⓐ Ⓑ Ⓒ Ⓓ Ⓔ
16 Ⓐ Ⓑ Ⓒ Ⓓ Ⓔ	16 Ⓐ Ⓑ Ⓒ Ⓓ Ⓔ	16 Ⓐ Ⓑ Ⓒ Ⓓ Ⓔ	16 Ⓐ Ⓑ Ⓒ Ⓓ Ⓔ
17 Ⓐ Ⓑ Ⓒ Ⓓ Ⓔ	17 Ⓐ Ⓑ Ⓒ Ⓓ Ⓔ	17 Ⓐ Ⓑ Ⓒ Ⓓ Ⓔ	17 Ⓐ Ⓑ Ⓒ Ⓓ Ⓔ
18 Ⓐ Ⓑ Ⓒ Ⓓ Ⓔ	18 Ⓐ Ⓑ Ⓒ Ⓓ Ⓔ	18 Ⓐ Ⓑ Ⓒ Ⓓ Ⓔ	18 Ⓐ Ⓑ Ⓒ Ⓓ Ⓔ
19 Ⓐ Ⓑ Ⓒ Ⓓ Ⓔ	19 Ⓐ Ⓑ Ⓒ Ⓓ Ⓔ	19 Ⓐ Ⓑ Ⓒ Ⓓ Ⓔ	19 Ⓐ Ⓑ Ⓒ Ⓓ Ⓔ
20 Ⓐ Ⓑ Ⓒ Ⓓ Ⓔ	20 Ⓐ Ⓑ Ⓒ Ⓓ Ⓔ	20 Ⓐ Ⓑ Ⓒ Ⓓ Ⓔ	20 Ⓐ Ⓑ Ⓒ Ⓓ Ⓔ
21 Ⓐ Ⓑ Ⓒ Ⓓ Ⓔ	21 Ⓐ Ⓑ Ⓒ Ⓓ Ⓔ	21 Ⓐ Ⓑ Ⓒ Ⓓ Ⓔ	21 Ⓐ Ⓑ Ⓒ Ⓓ Ⓔ
22 Ⓐ Ⓑ Ⓒ Ⓓ Ⓔ	22 Ⓐ Ⓑ Ⓒ Ⓓ Ⓔ	22 Ⓐ Ⓑ Ⓒ Ⓓ Ⓔ	22 Ⓐ Ⓑ Ⓒ Ⓓ Ⓔ
23 Ⓐ Ⓑ Ⓒ Ⓓ Ⓔ	23 Ⓐ Ⓑ Ⓒ Ⓓ Ⓔ	23 Ⓐ Ⓑ Ⓒ Ⓓ Ⓔ	23 Ⓐ Ⓑ Ⓒ Ⓓ Ⓔ
24 Ⓐ Ⓑ Ⓒ Ⓓ Ⓔ	24 Ⓐ Ⓑ Ⓒ Ⓓ Ⓔ	24 Ⓐ Ⓑ Ⓒ Ⓓ Ⓔ	24 Ⓐ Ⓑ Ⓒ Ⓓ Ⓔ
25 Ⓐ Ⓑ Ⓒ Ⓓ Ⓔ	25 Ⓐ Ⓑ Ⓒ Ⓓ Ⓔ	25 Ⓐ Ⓑ Ⓒ Ⓓ Ⓔ	25 Ⓐ Ⓑ Ⓒ Ⓓ Ⓔ
26 Ⓐ Ⓑ Ⓒ Ⓓ Ⓔ	26 Ⓐ Ⓑ Ⓒ Ⓓ Ⓔ	26 Ⓐ Ⓑ Ⓒ Ⓓ Ⓔ	26 Ⓐ Ⓑ Ⓒ Ⓓ Ⓔ
27 Ⓐ Ⓑ Ⓒ Ⓓ Ⓔ	27 Ⓐ Ⓑ Ⓒ Ⓓ Ⓔ	27 Ⓐ Ⓑ Ⓒ Ⓓ Ⓔ	27 Ⓐ Ⓑ Ⓒ Ⓓ Ⓔ
28 Ⓐ Ⓑ Ⓒ Ⓓ Ⓔ	28 Ⓐ Ⓑ Ⓒ Ⓓ Ⓔ	28 Ⓐ Ⓑ Ⓒ Ⓓ Ⓔ	28 Ⓐ Ⓑ Ⓒ Ⓓ Ⓔ
29 Ⓐ Ⓑ Ⓒ Ⓓ Ⓔ	29 Ⓐ Ⓑ Ⓒ Ⓓ Ⓔ	29 Ⓐ Ⓑ Ⓒ Ⓓ Ⓔ	29 Ⓐ Ⓑ Ⓒ Ⓓ Ⓔ
30 Ⓐ Ⓑ Ⓒ Ⓓ Ⓔ	30 Ⓐ Ⓑ Ⓒ Ⓓ Ⓔ	30 Ⓐ Ⓑ Ⓒ Ⓓ Ⓔ	30 Ⓐ Ⓑ Ⓒ Ⓓ Ⓔ

PRACTICE TEST ONE
Time—35 minutes
26 questions

Directions: This test consists of questions that ask you to analyze the logic of statements or short paragraphs. For each question, choose the answer you consider best on the basis of your common-sense evaluation of the statement and its underlying assumptions. Although a question may seem to have more than one acceptable answer, there is only one best answer, and that is the one that does not entail making any illogical, extraneous, or conflicting assumptions about the question.

1. "Litigiousness" is the habit of unnecessarily taking to court matters that could probably be settled fairly by other means. According to judicial experts, the United States is rapidly becoming the most litigious country in the world. Disputes that could easily have been settled out of court in any number of ways, including binding arbitration, now clog the average court calendar in all parts of the nation.

   Which one of the following statements, if true, best supports the argument?

   (A) An increasing number of court cases involve employee-employer disputes, which can be handled by government administrative boards.
   (B) The greater the number of unnecessary court cases in a society, the larger the number of trial lawyers who are gainfully employed.
   (C) Litigiousness is not necessarily a socially negative trait, since it may encourage shy individuals to defend their own rights.
   (D) Studies of litigiousness may not have taken into account the average American's lack of sophistication about courtroom procedure.
   (E) The litigiousness of urban dwellers can be explained by their feelings of isolation in a forbidding, hostile environment.

2. From the eighth through the nineteenth century, the Japanese imperial power underwent a period of steady decline. This is often wrongly attributed to a fundamental bias in Japanese society ensuring that clan loyalty was always more important than loyalty to any emperor. A close look at the evidence, however, reveals that even as late as the Kamakura period in the thirteenth and fourteenth centuries, military dictators with the title "shogun" ruled in the name of the emperor and exercised a strong, centralized power.

   Which one of the following, if true, would most seriously weaken the argument?

   (A) Many Japanese followed the shogun because they feared his power and not because they were loyal.
   (B) The Kamakura shogunate collapsed in 1333, and Japan experienced 200 years of civil war.
   (C) The shoguns came from independent clans and ruled without concern for the emperor.
   (D) During the earlier Heian period, from the years 794 to 1185, the power of the shoguns was far less than that of the emperor.
   (E) Many historians believe that geography and the system of taxation were more crucial than clan loyalty in undermining imperial power.

GO ON TO THE NEXT PAGE.

3. Factories that want to increase productivity should pay their workers piecemeal, according to how much they produce rather than on an hourly wage system. Workers who receive a flat rate of, say, two dollars per item will have more incentive to produce as many items as possible than will workers who know that they will receive the same salary regardless of how hard they work.

The argument assumes which one of the following?

(A) Most factories pay their workers in hourly wages.

(B) Most factories want to increase their output whenever possible.

(C) Economic reward is the only incentive that can increase productivity.

(D) A worker who works hard will produce more items than one who does not.

(E) Workers would prefer their pay to be based on the number of items they produce.

4. Advocates of foreign language study have reacted with uncritical enthusiasm to recent surveys showing increased enrollment in college-level foreign language classes. Most of the classes in question, however, employ conversational methods rather than the traditional exercises in grammar and rigorous analysis of literary texts. Unfortunately, by providing an easier way of meeting language requirements for the bachelor's degree, these classes will actually have the pernicious effect of decreasing the numbers of graduates who are capable of appreciating the subtleties of another culture's means of expression.

Which one of the following beliefs is necessary for the author's conclusion to be reasonable?

(A) Abolishing the foreign language requirement for the bachelor's degree would allow the abandonment of most conversational language classes.

(B) A conversation course typically attracts more students than a literature course when a choice exists.

(C) Foreign language courses taught conversationally lack the cultural insights provided by traditional courses oriented to grammar and literature.

(D) Continued emphasis on conversation courses will eventually reduce the pool of qualified foreign language instructors.

(E) Most college graduates today have a reading knowledge of at least one foreign language.

GO ON TO THE NEXT PAGE.

Questions 5–6

The socioeconomic status of its family has often been cynically proposed as the determining factor of a child's later intellectual prowess. To test the validity of this belief, infants from underprivileged families were removed from their homes and placed in special schools, where they were taught relatively advanced subjects from the time they were only three months old. These children had an average IQ of 110 by the time they reached school age. It would seem then, that it is the degree of pre-kindergarten education the child has received, rather than the socioeconomic level of its parents, that determines future intelligence.

5. The author's method of argument is to

    (A)   present an alternative conclusion that explains the same evidence
    (B)   argue that children from poorer backgrounds are actually more intelligent than those from richer backgrounds
    (C)   cite specific evidence that supports her own conclusion
    (D)   disprove the statistics presented by opponents
    (E)   suggest that the cause-and-effect relationship presented by her opponents is actually reversed

6. Which one of the following, if true, would provide the best foundation for a rebuttal of the argument above?

    (A)   The degree of pre-kindergarten education that a child receives is related to its family's socioeconomic status.
    (B)   Children from wealthy families who were placed in the same special schools had an average IQ of 110 when they reached school age.
    (C)   Families in lower income brackets often have more children and thus cannot give as much attention to each one.
    (D)   Children learn more readily between the ages of five and ten than they do between the ages of one and five.
    (E)   Few parents at any socioeconomic level attempt to teach their children before the children reach the age of five.

GO ON TO THE NEXT PAGE.

7. In our society, personality is considered an expression of individuality. We like to see ourselves as self-created, distinct from the influences of the past, bent upon our own development as self. Effects upon us are viewed as intrusions. But in the tribal society of the Bambara peoples, personality is the sum of many parts—less an individual phenomenon than a reflection of the family, less a single unit than an integer of a larger, sustaining tribal identity. Personality is richer because it is not self-centered, maturer because it benefits from diversity, and stronger because it draws its strength from the clan.

The argument has been designed to emphasize the supposed interrelationship between

(A) richness of personality and integration in a society
(B) individuality of expression and development of the self
(C) diversity of personality and self-centeredness
(D) a sustaining tribal identity and the strength of the clan
(E) development of the self and the intrusion of outside effects

8. Experts on the American political process have long agreed that voters like a certain amount of combativeness, even aggressiveness, in a presidential candidate. A poll just after the 1988 election, however, showed that many people had been annoyed or disgusted with the campaign and had not even bothered to vote. In addition, many voters felt that most candidates were "non-presidential." Campaigns that feature combativeness have therefore become counterproductive by causing voters to lose respect for the combative candidate.

Which one of the following, if true, most seriously weakens the argument?

(A) Many presidential campaigns have been memorable because they were full of surprises.
(B) The poll cited does not specifically show that combative campaigning was responsible for voter disaffection.
(C) Even before 1988, many voters were skeptical about politicians, particularly candidates for President.
(D) What seems to be aggressiveness is really assertiveness, a necessary quality for keeping one's name in the public eye.
(E) Political campaigning is a means of giving the voter essential information on which he must base his decision.

GO ON TO THE NEXT PAGE.

Questions 9-10

It is healthier to eat frozen vegetables than fresh ones, not because of any beneficial property of freezing (which actually robs food of some nutrients) but because of the common practice of harvesting crops before they are ripe. Vegetables are at their most nutritious when they are allowed to ripen in the field. Vegetables picked when ripe would be overripe or even rotten by the time they reached the consumer, so they must be picked early and allowed to ripen in transit. These crops never achieve their full nutritive value. However, the ripening process of vegetables destined for freezing can be stopped soon after harvest. As a result, frozen vegetables are generally more nutritious than the fresh vegetables we buy at the local grocery store.

9. The above argument is based on which one of the following assumptions?

    (A) Frozen food companies freeze only the most nutritious varieties of vegetables.
    (B) Nutritional loss from freezing is less than that from premature harvesting.
    (C) Fresh vegetables are never sold immediately, but rather sit on shelves for long periods.
    (D) People never freeze the vegetables they buy at the grocery store.
    (E) All kinds of vegetables ripen at approximately the same rate in the same amount of time.

10. Which one of the following, if true, would most seriously undermine the argument in the passage?

    (A) Overripe vegetables are more nutritious than underripe ones.
    (B) Vegetables destined for freezing and those destined for the grocery store are harvested at the same time.
    (C) Fresh vegetables are refrigerated during transport to prevent excessive spoilage.
    (D) Many consumers who live near farms can purchase vegetables directly from growers.
    (E) Tests have shown that fresh vegetables taste substantially better than frozen vegetables.

11. Recent cuts in the state budget have impaired the data-collection capabilities of the State Archival Statistics Center, but it is unclear to what extent. Because of the budget cuts, the information necessary to compare current processing levels with those in earlier years is no longer being gathered.

    Which one of the following situations is LEAST similar to that described above?

    (A) The earthquake that devastated the village a century ago altered the path of the nearby stream, but we'll never know exactly how; the same earthquake also destroyed the only existing surveyors' records.
    (B) My sturdy old car survived a bad collision, and I've driven it many miles since then. The odometer stopped working after the accident, though, so I don't know just how many miles.
    (C) The satellite link failed temporarily while our London correspondent's story was being transmitted to New York. Since there's no way to tell whether any text was lost, we'll have to have the whole story transmitted again.
    (D) Setting the thermostat too high was what caused the fire, but we don't know the temperature at which it was set—the thermostat itself was destroyed.
    (E) Having more than a certain number of beers made me forgetful, and it also made me forget how many beers I drank.

12. The state legislature has before it a bill outlawing capital punishment, and certain lawmakers are doing everything in their power to see that it does not get passed. To these lawmakers I say, go to death row and it will become obvious that even convicted murderers are people worthy of our mercy.

    Which one of the following best describes the author's method of argument?

    (A) She makes an appeal to her opponents' emotions.
    (B) She argues from a general principle to a particular conclusion.
    (C) She uses irony to mock her opponents' position.
    (D) She attacks the way in which her opponents have presented their view.
    (E) She overlooks a distinction that is essential to her opponents' case.

GO ON TO THE NEXT PAGE.

13. Lest charity become confused with self-interest, it is well to remember that we can hope to rehabilitate a convicted felon without demanding that he or she be remade in our own image. To insist that the former pusher become a social worker, or the former burglar a bank clerk, is to deny the very individuality of expression that true rehabilitative programs should develop.

Which one of the following sentences best completes the statement of the position put forth in the passage above?

(A) For proper rehabilitation, however, the convicted felon must follow the advice of professionals in choosing a career.

(B) Moreover, forcing an unsuitable career upon the subject for rehabilitation might pressure him or her to return to the criminal life out of frustration.

(C) In particular, it is unlikely that any individual will find self-expression in work that involves reporting daily to an institution.

(D) Furthermore, many a social worker has less knowledge of the motivations behind criminal acts than a felon who has actually committed a crime.

(E) In addition, society has the right to demand that rehabilitated felons take jobs that benefit the society as a whole.

14. State revenues from the corporate income tax are seriously threatened by the new trend towards decentralization of corporate headquarters. Many of the companies leaving the city, with its extensive public transportation system, are finding it necessary to import costly executive helicopters to transport personnel to and from isolated locations in the suburbs. Because money spent on these helicopters is deductible from gross corporate income as an expense of doing business, such companies will thus pay lower taxes to the state. We must apply appropriate economic sanctions to avoid the loss of these much-needed tax revenues.

Which one of the following identifies the main weakness in the reasoning behind the argument?

(A) The writer fails to suggest alternative modes of transportation less costly than helicopters.

(B) The writer fails to demonstrate that higher personnel transport costs are not offset by other economies at the new corporate headquarters.

(C) The writer fails to consider the increased taxes paid by the helicopter manufacturers as a result of booming business.

(D) The writer fails to consider the higher productivity achieved through rapid helicopter travel.

(E) The writer fails to specify other economic difficulties caused by the corporations' flight from the city.

GO ON TO THE NEXT PAGE.

15. A student at any college within the Metropolitan Consortium for Higher Education is permitted and encouraged to take classes at other member colleges when these complement the offerings of his home institution. Please note, however, that the final determination of credits earned and degree requirements satisfied will remain the prerogative of the student's own academic dean, regardless of any conflicting policies at other institutions. The rules governing a student's course of study depend solely on the institution in which he is officially enrolled, that is, not on his physical presence in a given classroom.

The above policy statement of the Metropolitan Consortium for Higher Education implies that

(A) any student admitted to a college within the Consortium will be allowed to transfer his enrollment to another member college

(B) a college may exclude a student enrolled in the Consortium from its non-academic programs.

(C) each college's Admissions Office is the sole judge of eligibility to attend its classes

(D) students are not required to follow rules of conduct established by colleges at which they are not enrolled

(E) a student's academic dean can refuse to accept course credits awarded by another college within the Consortium

16. Early in this century, the doctor was a comforter, expected to predict the progress of a disease or to help the patient cope with a struggle or an imminent defeat, but not to work miracles. This situation changed with the coming of such drugs as penicillin, insulin, and antibiotics. Add the rapid technological developments of contemporary medicine, and we find the medical professional under pressure to defeat every disease, correct every physical defect, and maximize the patient's quality of life. Society no longer is satisfied with the dedicated efforts of human beings; it now demands perfect performance of technicians as foolproof as the most sophisticated machines.

Which one of the following can be most reasonably inferred from the passage?

(A) Today's physician does not view comforting the patient as part of his or her job.

(B) The patient today expects results rather than sympathy from his or her physician.

(C) Medical incompetence is more widespread today than it was in the early twentieth century.

(D) As medical technology has advanced, health-care workers have become less sensitive to the feelings of their patients.

(E) Because doctors cannot meet the often unrealistic expectations of their patients, they are subjected to an ever-increasing number of malpractice suits.

GO ON TO THE NEXT PAGE.

17. Those who oppose psychological testing of school-children, alleging that teachers will unconsciously "write off" pupils labeled as slow, overlook the fact that a self-fulfilling prophecy is necessarily also a true one. Information about a student's probable development can only help his or her teacher to arrange an appropriate remedial program.

Which one of the following arguments is most similar in logical structure to that above?

(A) Opponents of long-term testing of newly developed drugs maintain that intensive short-term testing is sufficient to identify possibly dangerous side effects. This ignores the possibility that some side effects may become evident only after decades of use.

(B) There are risks involved in the arms limitation talks, but they are risks worth taking. We should always err on the side of survival, rather than on the side of patriotically-inspired self destruction.

(C) Claims that hospital diets are often unbalanced and even harmful, because of their high sodium and starch content, are beside the point, since hospitals hire trained nutritionists to design their menus.

(D) The majority of contact lens wearers agree that the benefits of improved vision and physical appearance outweigh the admitted inconveniences of the lenses in comparison to traditional eyeglasses.

(E) Whether the possibility of contagion through door handles and water faucets touched by many people is real or imagined, installation of swinging doors and pedal-controlled wash basins in public restrooms is an easy way to allay such fears.

18. Housing statistics for other cities conclusively disprove the frequently advanced claims that New York City's rent control laws caused the widespread abandonment of apartment houses that the city has suffered in recent decades. Some cities with strict controls on rentals have experienced little abandonment, while in others without controls of any kind, landlords walked away from entire neighborhoods.

The author of the argument is assuming which one of the following?

(A) Since rent control laws restrict landlords' profits, a landlord's decision to abandon his property must be motivated solely by financial considerations.

(B) Since rent control was not the cause of housing abandonment in every case, it was not the cause in the case of New York City.

(C) Since rent control did not lead to housing abandonment in New York City, its net impact on the city has been beneficial.

(D) New York City's rent control laws fostered widespread abandonment of property because they were insufficiently strict.

(E) Despite rent control laws, New York City has experienced only negligible abandonment of rental properties in recent decades.

19. The unexpected plummet of the stock market in September badly shook the economy. For this past holiday season, retail sales comprised a lower percentage of total annual sales than it has in any of the previous twenty years. Retailers and legislators are worried. New rules that govern trading on the stock exchange may be put into effect.

The main point of the passage is that

(A) the stock exchange wishes to enlist the aid of the government

(B) legislators typically do not become concerned until a real market effect is felt

(C) new rules governing the trading of stocks will increase the volume of retail sales

(D) the decline in the percentage of retail sales was due to the September stock market fall

(E) in September the stock market fell to its lowest point in twenty years

GO ON TO THE NEXT PAGE.

20. It is barbarous in the extreme to equate murder with simple acquiescence in the choice of a pain-wracked, dying friend to find self-deliverance from an onerous life. To assist a friend in suicide is to give solace, to respect the individual's free choice; to murder, of course, is to perform the ultimate act of disrespect for individual civil rights. Both our legislators and our justices must be urged to use reason rather than to respond as they have with traditional prejudice.

    It can be inferred from the passage that

    (A) the concept of murder in any given society is related to that society's interpretation of the idea of individual rights
    (B) terminally-ill patients frequently contemplate suicide
    (C) our legislators and our justices do not agree with the author of the passage that assisting a suicide is not an act of murder
    (D) suicide should always be considered an act of self-deliverance, just as murder should be considered an act of disrespect for individual civil rights
    (E) whether or not suicide can be considered a legal act depends upon whether or not the suicide victim is suffering great pain

21. All candidates for the master's degree who enrolled after 1977 take a seminar on Heidegger, and all candidates for the master's degree who enrolled after 1981 take a seminar on Wittgenstein.

    If a student took a seminar on Heidegger but did not take a seminar on Wittgenstein, which one of the following must be true?

    (A) The student enrolled prior to 1982.
    (B) The student enrolled after 1977 and prior to 1982.
    (C) If the student was a candidate for the master's degree, then the student enrolled prior to 1982.
    (D) If the student was a candidate for the master's degree, then the student enrolled prior to 1978.
    (E) If the student was a candidate for the master's degree, then the student enrolled after 1977 and prior to 1982.

22. The proposal to reduce grain prices by mandating a government-controlled price level would _____. Artificially stabilized pricing drains the economy while it encourages inefficient production and discourages individual initiative. To let the forces of the free market operate would be to give efficient producers the advantage they earn.

    Which one of the following most logically fills the blank in the passage above?

    (A) reward producers who are not responding adequately to market forces
    (B) actually have the contrary effect of increasing grain prices
    (C) strike a necessary balance between government intervention and a free market economy
    (D) make grain available to those who cannot now afford to eat well
    (E) allow individual efforts to influence the operation of the free market

23. Samuel Taylor Coleridge must have found the inspiration for "The Rime of the Ancient Mariner" in Hakluyt's 1600 edition of the real-life sea narrative, *The Southern Voyage of John Davis*. Although the poet did not mention the 200-year-old work in his notes, both "Mariner" and *Southern Voyage* prominently feature a tale of misfortune resulting from the murder of a bird, a rotting ship drifting out of control in the tropics, and a scene of a dying man cursing his fate. Furthermore, Wordsworth, Coleridge's good friend and occasional collaborator, had an interest in books about actual historical sea voyages and may have owned a copy of Davis' story.

    The author of the passage makes his point primarily by

    (A) drawing an analogy between literature and seafaring
    (B) reinterpreting a classic literary work
    (C) paralleling an author's work with the events of the author's life
    (D) supporting a claim with circumstantial evidence
    (E) documenting a controversial claim of literary influence

GO ON TO THE NEXT PAGE.

24. Society still wastes incalculable human potential when men and women are denied career advancement because of false but unthinkingly perpetuated age stereotypes. To combat this situation, now and in the future, the mature job applicant should do everything possible to seem young, competent, and energetic—and, once hired, should conceal his or her true age to ensure unbiased treatment from co-workers.

    Which one of the following, if true, is most damaging to the argument above?

    (A) Harmful age stereotypes can only be destroyed if capable older people reveal their true age.

    (B) Neurological studies have found certain changes in brain function to be widespread in those over sixty-five.

    (C) Increasing numbers of older people are already finding employment in clerical and food service jobs.

    (D) Legislation forbidding age-based discrimination for workers between forty and seventy has wide popular support.

    (E) Improved nutrition can prevent, and to a lesser degree reverse, many of the physical changes traditionally associated with aging.

25. On the desert island off the coast of Long Beach, goats had multiplied in the wild, denuding the hills of ground foliage essential to prevent erosion and drastically reducing their own food supply. It was thought that the introduction of a predator like the coyote, which had overpopulated the Mojave Desert and dangerously thinned its own sources of prey, would naturally stabilize the island ecology.

    Which one of the following, if true, is most damaging to the argument?

    (A) Neither the coyote nor any of its close relatives has ever been found living naturally on any of the offshore islands along the coast in question.

    (B) The goats on the island are all descended from a small herd of domesticated goats and have never experienced the threat of a predator.

    (C) As the ground foliage disappears, a prickly cactus native to the island will spread, effectively stopping soil erosion.

    (D) The coyote, an effective hunter and rapid breeder, would soon overpower the goats, exhaust its food supply, and experience starvation in great numbers.

    (E) In suburban areas at the edge of the Mojave Desert, residents are frightened because coyotes kill household pets.

GO ON TO THE NEXT PAGE.

26. Recent purchases by the Social Documentation Division of the university library have made this collection one of the best in the nation, with a complete and up-to-date range of statistical reference tools, census studies, and the like. All new acquisition funds should therefore be shifted away from the now extensive Social Documentation collection and towards other departments, such as Latin literature and Renaissance art, where the library's deficiencies are most notable.

Which one of the following if true, provides the best criticism of the argument?

(A) Today's emphasis on technology makes such essentially unquantifiable subjects as literature and art less important within the university curriculum.

(B) Despite the completeness of the Social Documentation collection, new computerized study devices are still being developed, and funds should be allotted for their purchase.

(C) Social documentation by its very nature is an ongoing process, and the library must continue to purchase new materials to keep its collection current.

(D) Increased student enrollment in sociology courses may necessitate additional copies of works already in the library's holdings.

(E) In order to encourage greater library use by students, funds could be shifted not towards additional book acquisition but towards remodeling and enhancing existing lounge areas.

S T O P
**IF YOU FINISH BEFORE TIME IS CALLED, YOU MAY CHECK YOUR WORK ON THIS SECTION ONLY.
DO NOT WORK ON ANY OTHER SECTION IN THE TEST.**

SECTION II
Time—35 minutes
27 questions

Directions: Each selection in this test is followed by several questions. After reading the selection, choose the *best* response to each question, and mark it on your answer sheet. Your replies are to be based on what is *stated* or *implied* in the selection.

Traditional justifications of the free speech principle originate in the belief that speech is entitled to greater tolerance than other kinds of activity. A review of the traditional justifications reveals two distinct models of
(5) explanation: the "classical model" and the "fortress model." Although both these models link the need to protect speech to its inherent value, they agree on little else.

According to the classical model, freedom of speech serves an indispensable function in democratic self-
(10) government. Meiklejohn uses the traditional New England town meeting as the paradigmatic setting for a self-governing society. From this perspective, the free speech principle need only protect political speech—the facts, theories, and opinions relating to any issue on which the citizens must
(15) vote. Meiklejohn insists that even extremist views cannot be concealed from voting citizens if these views bear on any public issue before them. Protection of free speech, including extremist political speech, serves the collective interests of a self-governing society made up of all rational, equal, and
(20) fully participating citizens. This theory is predicated on the belief that speech itself is valuable and thus ascribes positive value to a very broad range of speech, including that which may be offensive to many people.

In contrast to the serene and optimistic outlook of the
(25) classical model, the fortress model is built on a foundation of pessimism, individualism, relativism, and self-doubt. Whereas this model considers freedom of speech necessary to the discovery of truth, it assumes that any belief held by an individual is likely to ultimately prove false. In this frame,
(30) speech represents not so much a free marketplace of ideas as a kind of counsel of despair. From Holmes' perspective, the government and a majority of the people pose a great danger of intolerance. Despite the high probability that any individual's beliefs will eventually prove to be false, people
(35) nonetheless tend to feel certain about them and, consequently, feel justified in requiring others to conform. The fortress model's prescription for combating the tendency to censor nonconforming views is to overprotect speech. This strategy provides a broad "buffer zone" that
(40) encompasses extremist speech because its protection substantially diminishes the probability that inherently valuable speech will be suppressed. Even if these views are so

extreme that they cannot seriously be considered to contribute to the discovery of truth—like the most extreme
(45) views propounded by the Nazis—they still ought not to be censored, because once unleashed, censorship cannot be reasonably expected to remain confined to worthless views.

Bollinger, rejecting both the classical and the fortress models as inadequate, furnishes a new model designed to
(50) account for the changes in the function of speech attributable to the emergence of a society marked by stability and widespread consensus on essential values. This new model referred to as the *self-restraint* model casts new light on the free-speech principle. Although continuing staunchly
(55) to support free speech, the *self-restraint* model inverts the relationship between speech and tolerance. Under the traditional models, the value of tolerance is subordinated to the value of speech. However, the self-restraint model often subordinates the value of speech to that of tolerance because
(60) in a stable, consensual society, the pursuit of self-control, self-discipline, and self-restraint becomes of paramount importance.

1. The author is primarily concerned with discussing

   (A) arguments for and against free speech
   (B) different theoretical justifications for supporting free speech
   (C) Bollinger's criticisms of the right of extremist speech
   (D) Meiklejohn's and Holmes' understanding of free speech principles
   (E) a new approach to the problem of constitutionally limiting extremist speech

GO ON TO THE NEXT PAGE.

2. Which of the following is most probably an assumption made by Meiklejohn?

(A) In order to make rational decisions, members of a democratic society need to consider all views, even extremist ones.
(B) Most members of a democratic society would embrace extremist views if exposed to them.
(C) Many views that are unpopular when first expressed are eventually accepted by the majority.
(D) Useful social reforms are often originally proposed by extremist groups.
(E) Protection of free speech is useful only in a small self-governing community where all can join in decision-making.

3. It can be inferred that Meiklejohn's model of free speech would NOT necessarily extend protection to

(A) speech expressing extremist political viewpoints
(B) extremist speech that is not political
(C) views that reject the basis of democratic government
(D) opinions that the majority of citizens find offensive
(E) speech that represents the beliefs of individuals, rather than the community

4. It can be inferred that Holmes would agree with all of the following statements EXCEPT:

(A) In order to protect useful speech, it is necessary to protect extremist speech.
(B) Views that have little value to society may nevertheless deserve protection.
(C) Censors cannot be trusted to distinguish reliably between worthwhile and worthless views.
(D) It is potentially less harmful to censor valuable speech than to tolerate extremist speech.
(E) Censorship of extremist views makes it more likely that nonextremist views will also be censored.

5. It can be inferred that all of the following are true of Bollinger's model EXCEPT that it

(A) assumes that tolerance is inherently valuable in a stable society
(B) conceives the relationship between speech and tolerance differently than do the classical and fortress models
(C) does not protect speech as fully as the classical and fortress models
(D) applies to a society that shares agreement on fundamental values
(E) assumes that the justification for protecting free speech may change as society evolves

6. Which of the following best describes the organization of the first three paragraphs of the passage?

(A) The author describes two theories and links each to the historical situation in which it was proposed.
(B) The author refers to a traditional way of viewing a question and examines two contrasting approaches that spring from that view.
(C) The author establishes contrasts between two approaches to a question and then explores their points of agreement.
(D) The author discusses two theories and the opposed conclusions that follow from them.
(E) The author summarizes two views of a controversial issue, mentions two questions they cannot answer, and calls for a synthesis.

7. The author indicates that Meiklejohn's and Holmes' understanding of free speech is similar in that both

(A) believe that free speech ultimately leads to the discovery of truth
(B) favor extending the right of speech to those who express extremist doctrines
(C) consider that censorship involves the suppression of valuable speech
(D) justify free speech by referring to the citizen's right to be informed of all views relevant to public issues
(E) argue that protecting free speech is important mainly because it promotes tolerance as a social value

GO ON TO THE NEXT PAGE.

Although research in molecular biology has yet to have a major impact on the prevention and treatment of disease, a backlash already seems to be developing. Lay critics as well as members of the profession have argued that molecular
(5) biologists should focus on certain areas, like fertility mechanisms, whereas other areas, like genetics or aging, are possibly dangerous and not worthy of public financial support. These critics believe that they can channel contemporary biology to fit their own conception of
(10) appropriate research. However, the traditional pact between society and scientist, in which the scientist is given responsibility for determining the direction of research, is necessary if basic science is to be effective. This does not mean that society is at the mercy of science, but rather that
(15) society, who must determine the pace of scientific innovation, should not attempt to prescribe its directions.

It is partly the successes of molecular biology that have brought on this questioning. One advance has been the development of the process called recombinant DNA
(20) research. Because the method allows genes from any species to be put into a common type of bacterium, there is a theoretical possibility of hazard. But if safety were the most important consideration about recombinant DNA, then we might expect the debate to focus on the hazards of
(25) recombinant DNA experiments. Instead, many discussions soon turn to a consideration of genetic engineering.

One type of genetic engineering involves altering some body cells so that they can perform needed functions. A second type, involving replacement of genes in germ cells
(30) that transmit their genes to our offspring, presents more of a dilemma because it could change the human gene pool. Both forms, but especially the latter, present perplexing problems: who is to decide, and how shall they decide what genes are malfunctional? These are moral decisions and
(35) therefore highly subjective. Although genetic engineering is not the same as recombinant DNA research, the two are rightly linked because recombinant DNA work is hastening the day when genetic engineering will be a feasible process for use on certain diseases. Because recombinant DNA work
(40) is bringing closer the discovery of new medical treatments and is likely to bring other new capabilities, why is there so much focus on genetic engineering? I believe that genetic engineering has become a symbol to many people of the frightening potential of modern technology.

(45) Rather than seeing in molecular biology the same complex mixtures of appropriate and inappropriate applications that characterize all powerful sciences, many people have allowed a negative catch phrase, "genetic engineering," to dominate discussions. People worry that if
(50) the possibility of curing a genetic defect by gene therapy should ever become a reality, the inevitable result would be

"people made to order." It is being too hastily argued that unless we block recombinant DNA research now, we will never have another chance to control our fate.

8. The passage as a whole can be characterized as an attempt to answer which of the following questions?

(A) What are the likely dangers to society of research in recombinant DNA?
(B) Should limits be placed on biological research because of the risks that new knowledge can carry for society?
(C) Does society have valid concerns about the safety of genetic engineering?
(D) How has public criticism of recombinant DNA research affected the pace of scientific innovation?
(E) Do hazardous research techniques primarily pose moral or practical problems for biologists?

9. The author suggests which of the following about research into "fertility mechanisms" (line 5–6)?

(A) It is the most promising area of study in molecular biology.
(B) It has attracted both lay and scientific criticism.
(C) It is an area within which too few scientists are interested in working.
(D) It is a focus of dissension among various groups in society.
(E) It is viewed as a relatively uncontroversial area of study.

10. In the argument, the author acknowledges that society should exercise control over which of the following?

(A) direction of scientific work
(B) application of new medical treatments
(C) specific priorities of scientists
(D) expenditure of allocated funds
(E) rate of scientific advance

GO ON TO THE NEXT PAGE.

11. The passage does NOT provide an answer to which of the following questions?

(A) Why has molecular biology so far failed to produce many tangible benefits?
(B) What is the traditional role played by scientists engaged in scientific study?
(C) Do critics consider some areas of study in molecular biology more acceptable than others?
(D) Has work in molecular biology raised legitimate questions of moral concern?
(E) Why have questions concerning recombinant DNA often tended to turn to a discussion of genetic engineering?

12. It can be inferred that the author is most likely to agree with which of the following statements about science and society?

(A) Public constraint of scientific inquiry is one of the social costs of democracy.
(B) Excessive interference by society can threaten the intellectual freedom and activity upon which all scientific innovation depends.
(C) As scientists increase their ability to prevent disease, society will gradually lose interest in monitoring scientific research.
(D) Scientists have a right to block public discussion as a way of keeping society from participating in decisions which do not concern it.
(E) The current conflict between scientific researchers and their social critics will never be satisfactorily resolved.

13. The author suggests that the debate over genetic engineering has

(A) failed to examine many of the risks involved in the research
(B) fully documented the potential dangers of the research
(C) shed light on a related discussion of recombinant DNA research
(D) been used to exaggerate the dangers of recombinant DNA research
(E) helped to stimulate the development of new medical treatments

14. The author implies that the probability of "inappropriate applications" (lines 46–47) of new technologies by molecular biologists is

(A) somewhat more likely than in other fields of research
(B) unlikely because most molecular biologists are trained in ethics
(C) no more likely than in other fields of scientific research
(D) much less likely than in other fields of research
(E) unlikely because most researchers work as part of a team

15. The content and style of the passage suggest the passage was most probably taken from

(A) a speech given to medical students on the importance of ethics in contemporary medicine
(B) a government report outlining the likely impact of contemporary research on society
(C) an introduction to current theoretical and practical research in molecular biology
(D) a review assessing the progress of molecular biology in the areas of disease prevention and treatment
(E) a paper delivered at a seminar devoted to examining the costs and benefits of limiting scientific inquiry

GO ON TO THE NEXT PAGE.

KAPLAN

Within the family law setting, a tension exists between the state's primary goal of ordering family relationships and the state's adversarial divorce process that dissolves those relationships. The adversarial divorce process, involving a
(5) lawyer guided by adversarial ethics, frustrates the ability of divorcing spouses to fulfill their family legal obligations mandated by the state. Consequently, the mediated divorce has evolved as an alternative mechanism that promises to be more consistent with the state's primary goals for the family.

(10) The adversarial nature of the divorce process does not lend itself to achieving the fulfillment of post-divorce obligations. Divorce wreaks havoc in the lives of the individuals involved, and the adversarial divorce process intensifies this turmoil. The couple whose united love
(15) resulted in the birth of children now fight with dogged determination to obtain "possession" of their offspring. Liberalized property distribution schemes provide additional incentives to battle. The spoils of this legal battle are obtained at great emotional and psychological cost to the
(20) participants. The adversarial lawyer zealously strives to capture the better position for his client in the realms of property division, child custody, and support monies. It is impermissible for a lawyer to advocate a generous, equitable settlement offer if the best interests of the client require
(25) seeking a less costly result, even though it would be less fair to the former spouse. Victories count more than seeking peaceful coexistence.

Fortunately, recent changes in the practice of divorce law suggest that solutions are being found. For couples facing
(30) divorce, mediation of the dissolution by a trained mediator is an increasingly popular choice. Divorce mediation is less expensive, limits the amount of legal bloodshed, and better promotes an amicable split. Instead of frustrating the fulfillment of family obligations, mediation allows couples to
(35) craft their own solutions defining their own responsibilities. The goal of the family attorney in mediation should be to assist the client in achieving the most amicable divorce possible. In mediation, the attorney is an instrument of peace trained to avoid litigation. As a result, the legal
(40) counselor influences and facilitates choice in the law office and not in court. The attorney is also an adviser, trained to advise, plan, conciliate, and negotiate the social goals of the individuals in the family unit. The chosen course of conduct should be the most beneficial to the individual client as well
(45) as other interested parties (e.g., grandparents and children) and society. In divorce mediation, counselors, social workers, psychologists, and clergy can assist the parties in dealing with emotional problems. By contrast, lawyers in the adversarial divorce process typically use emotions to fight for
(50) their clients. However, only if the fear, anger, and resentment can be dissipated can the parties better come to terms with

the drastic changes in their lifestyles. If the emotional problems can be resolved in the counselor's office where supportive help is available, they can be kept out of the legal
(55) proceedings. Through mediation, the divorce process then becomes one of reconciliation. The participants strive to heal the wounds of individuals "rent asunder" and the wounds inflicted on society by the breakup of society's fundamental unit. The participants in mediation leave the marital
(55) relationship empowered to fulfill the primary legal obligations imposed by the state.

16. Which of the following titles best describes the content of the passage?

   (A) Divorce and the State's Goals for the Family
   (B) The Drawbacks of the Adversarial Divorce Process
   (C) Mediation: An Alternative to the Adversarial Divorce Process
   (D) Equitable Divorce Settlements Through Mediation
   (E) The Rising Popularity of Divorce Mediation

17. According to the passage, a lawyer cannot advocate an equitable settlement while involved in the adversarial divorce process if

   (A) property division, child custody, and support monies are involved
   (B) the result includes any provisions beneficial to the other party
   (C) the result would be economically disadvantageous to the client
   (D) the settlement discourages the fulfillment of the client's primary legal obligations as imposed by the state
   (E) the settlement will be to the client's advantage

GO ON TO THE NEXT PAGE.

18. Which of the following statements best describes the organization of the passage?

    (A)   The author calls for a change in methods, outlines the virtues of an alternative approach, and defends it against an anticipated criticism.

    (B)   The author outlines a situation, presents the drawbacks of a procedure, and then discusses an alternative procedure and its benefits.

    (C)   The author makes a general statement about a situation, discusses two methods of resolving it, and then proposes a solution that combines the best of both methods.

    (D)   The author offers a historical account of how different approaches to a problem have developed and supplanted one another.

    (E)   The author condemns the practitioners of one procedure while extolling the virtues of those using the alternative procedure.

19. The author's attitude toward the assertion that the adversarial divorce process facilitates the ability of divorcing spouses to fulfill their family legal obligations would most likely be one of

    (A)   strong disagreement
    (B)   moral outrage
    (C)   ironic amusement
    (D)   lack of interest
    (E)   cautious disapproval

20. Which of the following, if true, would most WEAKEN the author's claims about divorce mediation?

    (A)   Most couples who try mediation find that they must eventually resort to litigation in order to resolve their conflicts.

    (B)   Even those couples who use mediation go through a period of conflict during the divorce process.

    (C)   The adversarial process does not lend itself to settling divorces equitably.

    (D)   Many lawyers choose not to try mediation when they are divorcing their own spouses.

    (E)   Most divorces are negotiated by means of the adversarial process.

21. The passage was most likely written by

    (A)   a sociologist interested in the impact of divorce on the family

    (B)   a lawyer who advocates the use of mediation in divorce

    (C)   a legislator who is advocating a change in the state's divorce laws

    (D)   the editor of a newsletter published by a support group for those going through the divorce process

    (E)   a psychologist who specializes in counseling families involved in the divorce process

GO ON TO THE NEXT PAGE.

It is interesting to note that the circle and square, not arrows and bullets, saved the Plains Indians from total annihilation. Their survival was encoded and transmitted through the Medicine Wheel, which integrated the tribe to
(5)   the cosmos, to each other, and to the Self within— requirements for any community that seeks to flourish and persist.

The Medicine Wheel integrated the tribe to the cosmos and to the recurring cycles of the sun, moon, and stars.
(10) Stones were arranged in circles, around which key points were marked. Carefully arranged piles of rock, for example, would mark the sunrise and sunset of the Summer solstice, the rise of important constellations, and the rise of significant, bright stars. Divided into 28 segments, these
(15) circles symbolically represented the 28 houses or "mansions" of the moon, which revolved around the centerpoint, the house of the Sun. The Medicine Wheel, then, was a solar and stellar observatory. It was the basis of the Plains Indians' calendar, by which time, the seasons and the rhythm of
(20) tribal life were calculated—agriculture, migration, festivals, and war.

Although the Medicine Wheel functioned in a cosmic manner, orienting the tribe to time through the movements of the heavenly bodies, it had an equally important mental
(25) or psychological function as well. It integrated the members of the tribe to each other and to humanity at large. Tribal lore stated that all members of the community began their life at a particular point on the Medicine Wheel, the Great Circle of Life. Because all perspectives pointed toward the
(30) Center, there was no advantage or disadvantage to any particular point. Yet, although each point on the Circle was considered unique, major personality types were recognized. The Medicine Wheel was divided into four cardinal directions, a quaternity that represented four psychological
(35) powers. Thus, the Medicine Wheel taught diversity within unity. For example, a tribal member might have her or his Beginning Place in the South, in the Power of Innocence or Trust. Such a person would then be taught to recognize the other Powers of the Medicine Wheel—North, West, and
(40) East—by observing and then imitating the qualities of those who possessed Wisdom, Introspection, or Illumination, respectively, as their dominant trait.

Thus, tolerance for the four different Powers was taught—an important element for any community that
(45) wishes to survive. However, tribal members were taught more than tolerance. Each member of the tribe was actually encouraged to cultivate the recessive or undeveloped traits of her personality in order to grow as a whole person. Plains Indian training thus raised the passive virtue of tolerance to
(50) the active and passive virtue of tolerance to the active and higher virtue of integration.

22. According to the information in the passage, each of the following is an accurate statement about the Medicine Wheel EXCEPT that

(A)   it was integral to the survival of the Plains Indians

(B)   it measured both astronomical cycles and the change of seasons

(C)   its psychological function was more valuable than its cosmic function

(D)   it symbolized the individual as well as the community

(E)   it celebrated the diversity of personality types

23. The passage provides information most useful in answering which of the following questions?

(A)   Which forces jeopardized the survival of the Plains Indians?

(B)   Which personality traits did the Plains Indians consider to be dominant?

(C)   Why were certain constellations considered important in Plains Indian cosmology?

(D)   How did the Plains Indians calculate agricultural rhythms and seasonal changes?

(E)   Why did the Plains Indians value tolerance and integration?

GO ON TO THE NEXT PAGE.

24. The primary purpose of this passage is to

   (A) detail the spiritual beliefs of the Plains Indians
   (B) illustrate how Native Americans overcame adversity through tolerance and integration
   (C) describe both the cosmological and the psychological functions of the Medicine Wheel to the Plains Indians
   (D) suggest that the social value of the Medicine Wheel surpassed its natural value
   (E) analyze the personality traits recognized and valued by the Plains Indians

25. The passage implies that the primary psychological function of the Medicine Wheel was to

   (A) establish a hierarchy of personality traits
   (B) teach individuals to recognize their own personality types as well as those of other tribal members
   (C) encourage tribal members to develop those traits essential to the tribe's survival
   (D) orient tribal members to recurring cosmological and natural cycles
   (E) emphasize the value of passivity and tolerance to the community

26. Which of the following provides the best title for the passage?

   (A) Plains Indian Culture: A Proud Heritage
   (B) Visionary Power and Cultural Survival
   (C) The Medicine Wheel and Ancient Astronomy
   (D) The Medicine Wheel: Instrument of Survival
   (E) The Medicine Wheel: Mirror of Native American Psychology

27. Of the following, the author of the passage is most probably

   (A) an anthropologist
   (B) an astronomer
   (C) a social psychologist
   (D) a theologian
   (E) an archaeologist

S T O P
IF YOU FINISH BEFORE TIME IS CALLED, YOU MAY CHECK YOUR WORK ON THIS SECTION ONLY.
DO NOT WORK ON ANY OTHER SECTION IN THE TEST.

SECTION III
Time—35 minutes
24 questions

<u>Directions</u>: Each group of questions is based on a set of conditions. You may wish to draw a rough sketch to help you answer some of the questions. Choose the *best* answer for each question and fill in the corresponding space on your answer sheet.

Questions 1–6

A salesperson will display nine cheeses in three groups of three cheeses each. The groups are labeled A, B, and C. Four of the cheeses—F, G, H, and J—are domestic cheeses, and five—P, Q, R, S, and T—are imported cheeses. Each cheese will be displayed in exactly one of the three groups. The display must meet the following conditions:

At least one cheese in each group must be a domestic cheese.
F must be displayed with two imported cheeses.
Q must be displayed in Group C.
S must be displayed in Group A.
Neither F nor J nor R can be displayed in the same group as Q.

1. If both P and T are displayed in Group B, then which one of the following must be true?

   (A)　F is displayed in Group A.
   (B)　G is displayed in Group A.
   (C)　H is displayed in Group A.
   (D)　J is displayed in Group A.
   (E)　R is displayed in Group A.

2. Which one of the following statements must be true?

   (A)　If F and R are displayed together, they are displayed in the same group as S.
   (B)　If G and H are displayed together, they are displayed in the same group as Q.
   (C)　If G and T are displayed together, they are displayed in the same group as F.
   (D)　If H and J are displayed together, they are displayed in the same group as P.
   (E)　If R and S are displayed together, they are displayed in the same group as J.

3. All of the following are groups of three cheeses that can be displayed together in Group B EXCEPT:

   (A)　F, P, and R
   (B)　G, H, and T
   (C)　G, J, and R
   (D)　J, P, and T
   (E)　J, R, and T

4. If G is displayed in Group A, then which one of the following could be true?

   (A)　H is displayed in Group A.
   (B)　J is displayed in Group B.
   (C)　P is displayed in Group A.
   (D)　R is displayed in Group A.
   (E)　T is displayed in Group C.

5. If both H and P are displayed in Group B, then which one of the following must be the cheeses displayed in Group A?

   (A)　F, J, S
   (B)　F, R, S
   (C)　F, S, T
   (D)　J, S, R
   (E)　J, S, T

6. If J is displayed in Group B, then which one of the following CANNOT be true?

   (A)　F and R are displayed in the same group.
   (B)　G and R are displayed in the same group.
   (C)　H and S are displayed in the same group.
   (D)　R and S are displayed in the same group.
   (E)　S and T are displayed in the same group.

GO ON TO THE NEXT PAGE.

<u>Questions 7–12</u>

Fred's Fish Salon serves a special Friday night seafood banquet consisting of seven courses—flounder, grouper, haddock, jumbo shrimp, kingfish, lobster, and mackerel. Diners are free to select the order of the seven courses, according to the following conditions:

The kingfish is served some time after the jumbo shrimp.
The grouper is served exactly two courses before the haddock.
The lobster is served some time before the grouper.
The kingfish is served either fifth or sixth.
The flounder is served second.

7. Which one of the following sequences would make for an acceptable banquet?

    (A) jumbo shrimp, flounder, lobster, mackerel, grouper, kingfish, haddock
    (B) jumbo shrimp, flounder, mackerel, grouper, kingfish, haddock, lobster
    (C) lobster, flounder, grouper, jumbo shrimp, kingfish, haddock, mackerel
    (D) lobster, flounder, jumbo shrimp, kingfish, grouper, mackerel, haddock
    (E) lobster, grouper, jumbo shrimp, haddock, kingfish, flounder, mackerel

8. Which one of the following is a complete and accurate list of the courses in which haddock can be served?

    (A) fifth, sixth
    (B) fourth, fifth, sixth
    (C) fifth, sixth, seventh
    (D) third, fifth, sixth, seventh
    (E) third, fourth, fifth, sixth, seventh

9. If kingfish is the fifth course served, then which one of the following must be true?

    (A) Grouper is the third course served.
    (B) Haddock is the fourth course served.
    (C) Jumbo shrimp is the third course served.
    (D) Lobster is the first course served.
    (E) Mackerel is the seventh course served.

10. Which one of the following would make it possible to determine the exact ordering of the courses?

    (A) Grouper is the fourth course served.
    (B) Haddock is the fifth course served.
    (C) Kingfish is the sixth course served.
    (D) Lobster is the first course served.
    (E) Mackerel is the seventh course served.

11. If kingfish is the sixth course served, then which one of the following CANNOT be true?

    (A) Grouper is the fifth course served.
    (B) Haddock is the seventh course served.
    (C) Jumbo shrimp is the fifth course served.
    (D) Lobster is the third course served.
    (E) Mackerel is the first course served.

12. If mackerel is the third course served, which one of the following must be true?

    (A) Grouper is the fourth course served.
    (B) Haddock is the seventh course served.
    (C) Jumbo shrimp is the first course served.
    (D) Kingfish is the fifth course served.
    (E) Lobster is the fourth course served.

GO ON TO THE NEXT PAGE.

Questions 13–18

There are five tin cans in a row, labeled one through five, from left to right. The five cans together contain a total of 10 marbles—four red, two green, two blue, one orange, and one yellow. Each can contains at least one marble.

The can containing the yellow marble is adjacent to the can containing the orange marble.
The fourth can contains exactly three marbles, of which, exactly two are red.
The third can contains exactly two marbles.
Exactly one of the blue marbles is in the second can.
The first can contains no blue marbles.

13. If both green marbles are in the second can, how many marbles does the fifth can contain?

(A) one
(B) two
(C) three
(D) four
(E) five

14. If the fifth can contains the orange marble and nothing else, which one of the following can possibly be a complete and accurate list of the marbles in the third can?

(A) two red marbles
(B) one green marble and one red marble
(C) one blue marble and one green marble
(D) one blue marble, one green marble, and one red marble
(E) one blue marble and two red marbles

15. If the first can contains three marbles, which one of the following CANNOT be true?

(A) The first can contains a green marble.
(B) The first can contains a yellow marble.
(C) The first can contains a red marble.
(D) The last can contains a yellow marble.
(E) The last can contains an orange marble.

16. If the fifth can contains exactly two red marbles and one green marble, which one of the following is a complete and accurate list of the marbles in the first can?

(A) one orange marble
(B) one green marble
(C) one yellow marble and one blue marble
(D) one green marble and one yellow marble
(E) one green marble and one orange marble

17. If the orange marble is in the third can and a green marble is in the fourth can, which one of the following must be true?

(A) The first can contains a green marble.
(B) The fifth can contains a green marble.
(C) If the third can contains a green marble, then the fifth can contains a blue marble.
(D) If the fifth can contains a blue marble, then the third can contains a green marble.
(E) If the fifth can contains a green marble, then the third can contains a blue marble.

18. If the orange marble must be in the same can as two green marbles, which one of the following pairs of cans contains no red marbles?

(A) the first and second
(B) the first and third
(C) the first and fifth
(D) the second and third
(E) the second and fifth

GO ON TO THE NEXT PAGE.

Questions 19–24

Four children—Peter, Rita, Sam, and Thelma—are in art class. Each child will work alone or in a pair. Each child or pair of children will create a project based on the following guidelines:

If Peter works with either Sam or Thelma, the pair will create a clay figure. If Peter works by himself, he will create a clay figure.

If Rita works with Peter, the pair will create a watercolor painting. If Rita works by herself, she will create a mobile.

If Sam works with either Rita or Thelma, the pair will create a mobile. If Sam works by himself, he will create a watercolor painting.

If Thelma works with Rita, the pair will create a papier mache ball. If Thelma works by herself, she will create a papier mache ball.

19. All of the following could be complete lists of all of the projects created by the children EXCEPT:

(A)   clay figure, papier mache ball
(B)   mobile, watercolor painting
(C)   mobile, mobile, clay figure
(D)   clay figure, clay figure, watercolor painting
(E)   clay figure, mobile, papier mache ball, watercolor painting

20. If no clay figures are created by the children, which one of the following pairs of children must work together?

(A)   Peter and Rita
(B)   Peter and Sam
(C)   Rita and Sam
(D)   Rita and Thelma
(E)   Sam and Thelma

21. If exactly two children work together and that pair creates a mobile, which one of the following could be the projects created by the children who work on their own?

(A)   clay figure, mobile
(B)   clay figure, watercolor painting
(C)   mobile, papier mache ball
(D)   mobile, watercolor painting
(E)   papier mache ball, watercolor painting

22. If all of the children pair up and exactly one mobile is created, which one of the following pairs of children cannot work together?

(A)   Peter and Rita
(B)   Peter and Thelma
(C)   Rita and Sam
(D)   Rita and Thelma
(E)   Sam and Thelma

23. If all of the children pair up and none of the pairs creates a project that the individual children making up that pair would have created if each worked alone, then which one of the following must be the projects created by the children?

(A)   clay figure, mobile
(B)   clay figure, watercolor painting
(C)   mobile, papier mache ball
(D)   mobile, watercolor painting
(E)   papier mache ball, watercolor painting

24. Which one of the following CANNOT be true?

(A)   Peter works alone, and exactly one papier mache ball is created by the children.
(B)   Rita works alone, and exactly one clay figure is created by the children.
(C)   Sam works alone, and exactly two watercolor paintings are created by the children.
(D)   Exactly two mobiles are created by the children.
(E)   Exactly two papier mache balls are created by the children.

STOP
**IF YOU FINISH BEFORE TIME IS CALLED, YOU MAY CHECK YOUR WORK ON THIS SECTION ONLY.
DO NOT WORK ON ANY OTHER SECTION IN THE TEST.**

SECTION IV
Time—35 minutes
25 questions

<u>Directions</u>: This test is composed of questions that ask you to analyze the logic of statements or short paragraphs. You are to choose as the answer to each question the one choice you consider *best* on the basis of your common-sense evaluation of the statement and its assumptions. Although a question may seem to have more than one acceptable answer, there is only one *best* answer, and it is the one that does not entail making any illogical, extraneous, or conflicting assumptions about the question. These questions do not presuppose any knowledge of formal logic on your part.

1. The mural in the executive dining room was painted more than 40 years ago, and its subsequent exposure to extremes of heat and humidity has caused some of the once-vivid colors to fade. Fortunately, the muralist's preliminary studies included precise instructions for mixing pigments. Using these instructions and his left-over paints, skilled preservationists will be able to restore the mural to its original hues.

   Which one of the following is an assumption on which the conclusion logically depends?

   (A)   The preservationists will be able to duplicate the muralist's technique.
   (B)   The wide fluctuations in temperature and humidity typical of food-service areas make the executive dining room a poor location for a mural.
   (C)   The artist foresaw that the colors would fade with time.
   (D)   The paints left over from the mural's creation have not themselves changed color.
   (E)   Temperature- and humidity-control technology was insufficient at the time of the mural's painting to prevent its subsequent fading.

2. As today's agribusiness concerns standardize cultivation, older plant varieties are often dropped, and many are no longer available in seed form. For the plant breeder, the potential extinction of even ill-tasting and ugly varieties is cause for alarm. Such plants, scorned by backyard gardeners, may well contain desirable traits such as disease resistance and quick maturation.

   Which one of the following can be inferred from the passage?

   (A)   Plant breeders seek to develop new varieties of cultivated plants without concern for their taste or appearance.
   (B)   In the future, backyard gardeners will be able to choose from a greater variety of plants.
   (C)   Individual traits from many plant varieties can be combined into a future hybrid.
   (D)   Agribusiness concerns are seeking the extinction of many plant varieties.
   (E)   The typical backyard gardener is not concerned with the maturation period of the plants he cultivates.

GO ON TO THE NEXT PAGE.

3. Many undeveloped areas of the world suffer from air pollution, even though there are no factories or combustion engines in use. Evidently, the connection between industrialization and air pollution has yet to be proved to the dispassionate observer.

Which one of the following most closely parallels the reasoning in the argument above?

(A) A few of his analyses of our capitalization program were overly optimistic. I think we can agree that he does not have the steadiness necessary to manage our banking division.

(B) When the new diet drink was tested at the shopping mall, some people detested the taste. It is safe to assume that most people will like it very much.

(C) Many people who rarely eat red meat have developed cardiac problems. We may conclude, therefore, that a diet including much red meat is not demonstrably harmful to the heart.

(D) Even if more students sign up for gymnastics, the school will still be buying the same amount of equipment for the sport. We must urge our gymnasts to scout out alternative sites for practice.

(E) At first, we hired a famous violinist to teach the music class, but few students really improved dramatically. We should have just hired someone who knew only fundamentals.

4. The form of the Petrarchan sonnet fosters a more exquisite literary experience than does the form of the detective novel. We can be assured of this truth by the fact that the best critics, those with delicate sensibilities, inevitably prefer the Petrarchan sonnet to the detective novel. And we know these critics to be superior by their preference for the Petrarchan sonnet.

A proper critique of the logic expressed in the argument above would most likely point out that the author

(A) fails to cite specific critical authorities
(B) assumes the point he wishes to establish
(C) generalizes from a specific example to a general rule
(D) does not provide evidence in support of his conclusion
(E) fails to provide exceptions to the classification he outlines

5. When we returned home after our six month vacation abroad, we found several drinking glasses shattered in place on the kitchen shelf—something that can only happen during a sonic boom or when there is an earth tremor. This must have been the loud noise that we heard not long after we drove off to the airport our last night in this country. Since there was no report on the car radio that night about tremors in the area, which always receive great attention, the glasses must have been shattered by a sonic boom, an occurrence so common that it is never reported.

The speaker's conclusion about the "loud noise" assumes which one of the following?

(A) It is easy to tell the difference between glass shattered by an earth tremor and that shattered by a sonic boom.
(B) A sonic boom always causes more damage in the house than does an earth tremor.
(C) No earth tremor has occurred since the night the family left on their vacation.
(D) The drinking glasses on the shelf were shattered because they were not securely protected.
(E) Every time there is an earth tremor in the area, some of the kitchen glassware will be shattered.

GO ON TO THE NEXT PAGE.

Questions 6–7

The moral condemnation, voiced by some segments of the public, of the students arrested recently while demonstrating at City Hall is an error. We should keep in mind that, more than 200 years ago, our forefathers dumped tea in Boston Harbor in defiance of the British.

6. Which one of the following would be the most effective response for the author's opponents in disputing his argument?

   (A) It is unpatriotic to demonstrate in front of a City Hall.
   (B) Students are too inexperienced to understand the consequences of demonstrations.
   (C) In today's world, one's beliefs and conscience are rarely the motivation behind one's actions.
   (D) The American patriots who threw tea into Boston Harbor had some public support for their cause.
   (E) Simply because some past demonstrations by citizens are considered justified does not mean all such acts are justified.

7. Which one of the following best describes the author's method of argument?

   (A) He attacks the public for its manifest hypocrisy.
   (B) He argues from a general principle of rebellion to a specific instance of that rebellion.
   (C) He argues from a specific instance of rebellion to a general principle concerning the justification of all rebellion.
   (D) He draws an analogy between the students' actions and the actions of patriots now deemed justified.
   (E) He argues from the lack of sufficient evidence concerning the students' actions to a conclusion supporting the students' actions.

8. Educators have too eagerly embraced the rise, after a decade of decline, in median SAT scores. Unfortunately, this encouraging statistic is actually yet another indictment of our educational system. The scores have risen because fewer students take the tests. In particular, students with disadvantaged backgrounds have become discouraged and have given up their hopes for attending colleges that require the tests. In other words, the low scorers have dropped out of competition, and today's higher median scores reflect an increasingly homogeneous test-taking population of privileged students.

The author argues primarily by

   (A) denying the accuracy of his opponents' figures
   (B) finding an alternative explanation for his opponents' evidence
   (C) refining an existing argument
   (D) defending an argument against the claims of his opponents
   (E) suggesting that his opponents may be unduly influenced by self-interest

9. Recent studies have indicated that a certain type of freshwater cod has more tumors than other species of fish in the Hudson. Long before this phenomenon was recognized, significant strides had been made in clearing the river of chemical and other kinds of industrial pollution thought to promote tumorous growth.

Which one of the following conclusions can most reliably be drawn from the statements above?

   (A) There is no causal link between chemical pollution and the tumors on the freshwater cod.
   (B) A sudden change in the river environment has had a drastic effect on the freshwater cod.
   (C) Efforts to clear the Hudson of chemical and other kinds of industrial pollution have not been vigorous enough.
   (D) No other fish but the freshwater cod is susceptible to the effects of chemical and other kinds of industrial pollution.
   (E) The mentioned studies provide no evidence that the number of tumors in the freshwater cod is related to the level of industrial pollution in the river.

GO ON TO THE NEXT PAGE.

10. Politics is the art of the possible; ideology, the articulation of the desirable. The ideologue will demand free lunch for all, and never alter his cry, but the like-minded politician will accept the offer of half-price lunch tickets or even a partial subsidy of dessert, waiting for another day to press the issue yet again.

In distinguishing between the politician and the ideologue, the author of the passage argues that

(A) the politician, unlike the ideologue, is willing to change his views to suit the occasion

(B) the ideologue demands everything at once, but the politician sees the practical virtue of gaining a little bit at a time

(C) a politician will accept whatever is possible, no matter what his announced ideology may be

(D) the ideologue is more capable of addressing the desires of man, while the politician sees to such practical concerns as food and housing

(E) neither the politician nor the ideologue is likely to be what he or she pretends to be

Questions 11–12

The people behind this movement to impeach me charge that I drastically exacerbated our state's unemployment problems. By raising corporate taxes, they claim, I single-handedly forced many labor-intensive industries to move out of the state. What they fail to realize, however, is that my purpose in increasing the corporate income tax was to raise revenues to fund a statewide jobs program. The remarks I made two years ago before the legislature would bear me out, if my detractors would read the Legislative Record. But no, they prefer to persecute me for wanting to create jobs and ease our state's economic woes.

11. Which one of the following is most similar in logical features to the response the author makes above?

(A) Emperor Hirohito's claim that, though he was opposed to Japan's invasion of Manchuria, he was powerless to restrain the military from launching it

(B) Benedict Arnold's declaration that, while he did not originally intend to betray the revolutionary army, the injustices he suffered had forced him to do so

(C) Galileo's assertion that he had renounced his true beliefs before the Inquisition because failure to do so would have resulted in his conviction as a heretic

(D) Alfred Nobel's contention that he had invented dynamite to be used as a tool of peacetime technology rather than as the destructive weapon it later became

(E) Charles I's pronouncement on the scaffold that his duty had been to care for his subjects as a loving father, and that he had done so to the best of his ability

GO ON TO THE NEXT PAGE.

12. Which one of the following points out the principal flaw in the reasoning of the argument?

   (A) There is no guarantee that a statewide jobs program would be effective in eliminating unemployment.
   (B) The number of jobs created by a statewide jobs program would not necessarily offset the number of jobs lost as a result of the tax increase.
   (C) The author's constituents want to impeach him because of the effects of his tax increase, and not because of the intent of his tax increase.
   (D) The author's claim concerning the intent of his tax increase is impossible to verify.
   (E) Raising taxes is not an effective method of creating jobs in industry.

13. When I was in high school, the teachers were always warning us against ever using drugs. Yet many of the students freely admitted in later years that they had used drugs regularly in high school. I can only draw the unfortunate conclusion from this that my teachers' warnings were in vain.

   Which one of the following claims, if true, would be most useful in refuting the argument of the passage above?

   (A) Many of the students who used drugs were aware of the dangers involved because of the teachers' warnings.
   (B) Some students use drugs for legitimate reasons.
   (C) The school had to compel teachers to warn their students against drug use.
   (D) Some of the author's fellow students were persuaded not to use drugs by their teachers' warnings.
   (E) Drug use invariably results in bad study habits and poor class attendance.

14. No matter what their early education, some students seem to have more aptitude for mathematics than do others. Students with a facility for numbers usually learn musical theory more quickly than do equally intelligent students whose gifts are not primarily mathematical in nature. College students concentrating in the sciences, or in any other fields that tend to attract math-adept students, typically have less difficulty grasping the logic of compositions of so-called "new music" than do students majoring in the humanities.

   Given the accuracy of the statements in the passage above, which one of the following draws the most well-founded conclusion from the passage?

   (A) Students who major in the humanities have rarely taken courses in mathematics during the early years of their education.
   (B) Students with a facility for numbers are generally more intellectually gifted than are students who major in the humanities.
   (C) There is a direct correlation between musical talent and one's aptitude for mathematics.
   (D) Students majoring in the humanities are likely to learn musical theory less quickly than are students concentrating in the sciences.
   (E) Students who have an aptitude for mathematics do not choose to concentrate in the humanities at the college level.

GO ON TO THE NEXT PAGE.

Questions 15–16

Government support for the arts cannot help but interfere with the free flow of the creative process. Monies, inevitably channeled at the dictates of the politically powerful, will accumulate around the established institutions when a certain philosophy prevails, or just as swiftly revert to the more experimental groups when the political pendulum swings. Individual creators will swerve willy-nilly, pursuing the funds at the expense of their own sure and inner-directed development.

15. The author's logic in the argument would be most weakened if it were argued that

(A) approximately the same number of individual creative artists are associated with so-called established institutions as with the more experimental groups

(B) in assigning monies to the arts, politicians in power heed the advice of committees composed of artists who are well known in their fields

(C) while it can be argued that political ideas swing in and out of fashion, it is equally arguable that trends in the arts are often short-lived

(D) individual artists who produce lasting works of art do not typically tailor their efforts to attract monies, either private or public

(E) many people who would not otherwise experience the arts have had the opportunity to do so because of increased government funding over the past few years

16. Which one of the following conclusions to a final sentence beginning, "As a result, the creative process in this country. . ." would be most appropriate, given the logic of the rest of the paragraph?

(A) would be continually diverted, distracted, and otherwise degraded by the intrusion of governmental decisions into the world of art

(B) would become the plaything of the politically powerful, inevitably and irretrievably captured by the established institutions

(C) would dry up entirely in those regions where political representation is weakest and thrive wholesomely in areas dominated by aggressive, successful political leaders

(D) would be seen at its most exuberant when the political pendulum swings toward support of the experimental groups, and at its most moribund when the reverse is true

(E) might become, at last, the expression of the individual's own inner-directed development rather than a pale reflection of the prevailing political philosophy

17. The advantages of a college education are too precious to be squandered upon students who are not seriously dedicated to learning. Administrators should strenuously enforce the philosophy that enrollment in college is a privilege that must be earned, and earned again. When a student fails a course, he should be dismissed at once, so that more deserving applicants can take his place.

Which one of the following is the best rebuttal of the argument advanced above?

(A) A student should not be expected to fulfill university requirements at the expense of choosing the electives needed for his individual course of study.

(B) The university may not have made the student fully aware of the demands of its curriculum and the intensity of study required.

(C) To dismiss a student who fails a course is to place achievement over the individual's right to education.

(D) Scholarship is only one of the possible contributions that a student might make to the university community.

(E) Personal and other circumstances unrelated to a student's dedication may have interfered with his studies and caused his grades to suffer.

GO ON TO THE NEXT PAGE.

18. The problem with arms reduction is that it is an illusory concept benefiting none. Even though designated stockpiles are being reduced, the weapons race continues, as the destructive power of new technologies and remaining arsenals is enhanced in order to maintain the pre-existing firepower. Thus, although it fosters an illusion of progress, arms reduction does nothing to curtail the proliferation of weaponry, and all must continue to live under the constant threat of annihilation.

Which one of the following, if true, would most strengthen the author's argument?

(A) Arms reduction allows steady maintenance of the existing balance of power.
(B) No arms limitation proposals have aimed at completely eliminating a nation's armament stockpile.
(C) The five largest military powers have increased funding for new weapons in each of the last ten years.
(D) The distinction between offensive and defensive weapon systems is often merely a matter of interpretation.
(E) Arms limitation treaties have only accounted for the elimination of fifteen percent of the total firepower possessed by the five largest military powers.

19. The summer heat wave and drought in the Midwest threaten to cut the 1988 corn harvest by more than one-third. Such a shortfall will undoubtedly lead to higher meat and other food prices in 1989, rises that could be as high as 18.6% in 1989 and 20.8% in 1990. Either we can ignore this problem, or else spend a comparatively small amount now to irrigate some of the major corn fields. Those who believe that we should not spend this money forget that if we do not, we face an imminent food shortage and economic disaster.

The argument is valid only if

(A) the government can afford the cost of irrigation now
(B) irrigation is the only way that the crop yield can be significantly increased
(C) the heat wave and drought will persist through 1990
(D) irrigation will insure that corn harvests reach expected yields
(E) other agricultural areas are also not expected to meet their anticipated corn yields in 1988

20. Those who condemn the Governor for being unsympathetic to the plight of the automobile industry are just using that allegation as a smokescreen for their own partisan politics. The naive citizen who believes their charges fails to realize that a politician may sometimes appear to be lacking compassion for a special interest group when, in reality, he is just trying to implement a public policy that is beneficial to great numbers of people representing diverse interests.

Which one of the following, if true, provides the strongest support for the assertion made in the first sentence of the passage?

(A) Sometimes it is difficult to distinguish between insensitivity to special interest groups and public-spirited devotion to broader concerns.
(B) The Governor's harshest critics are members of automobile workers' unions and politicians with strong ties to the automotive industry.
(C) Many people who accuse the Governor of being unsympathetic to the plight of the automobile industry voted for him in the last election.
(D) The Governor is not a politician who makes a clear distinction between partisan politics and civic responsibility.
(E) Sometimes a politician believes he is acting in the community's best interest, when, in reality, he is just being insensitive to the concerns of a minority group.

GO ON TO THE NEXT PAGE.

21. Without the profound structural changes in the Irish agricultural economy that began with the first grudging acceptance of the potato into the human diet, the great Potato Famine of the 1840s would never have been the disaster it was. Although other staples continued to be cultivated, primarily for export to England, the total dependence of much of the Irish population on potatoes turned the blight-induced failure of several potato crops in the latter part of the decade into a sweeping sentence of death or emigration.

Which one of the following conclusions can most reliably be drawn from the statements in the passage?

(A) The adoption of the potato as the staple of the Irish diet represented a nationalistic rejection of English social patterns.

(B) Other staples are less susceptible to crop failure than is the potato.

(C) Reliance on a single crop made Ireland a fertile ground for revolutionary activity when that crop failed.

(D) Absence of alternative sources of food left much of the Irish population with nothing to eat when the potato crop failed.

(E) Those who resisted the potato when it was introduced into Ireland did so to forestall the potential dangers of a restructured agricultural system.

22. Imagine that upon entering your living room I find that you are reading a book I consider morally repugnant; imagine that in my indignation I steal the volume and burn it or simply rip out the offending pages; and imagine that when you file a complaint you find that my behavior is condoned by the police and the courts. This may seem absurd, but if you replace me in this scenario with certain moralistic individuals, and if you replace your living room with your children's schools and our municipal libraries, the result is a description of a situation that is eating away at the very roots of our constitutional system—the banning of so-called "offensive" books from our library collections.

Which one of the following describes the principal weakness in the author's analogy?

(A) Burning a book is not the same as banning a book.

(B) The police and the courts do not condone the theft of personal property.

(C) Schools and municipal libraries, unlike the reader's living room, are public institutions.

(D) Books that may be suitable for adults may not be suitable for children.

(E) The Constitution does not clearly define what makes a book "offensive" in the eyes of the law.

GO ON TO THE NEXT PAGE.

23. During exam periods, cookie sales in the college cafeteria are high. Cookies are selling well in the cafeteria today, so it must be exam time.

Which one of the following is logically most similar to the argument above?

(A) Proficiency at logical thinking is enough to ensure success in the computer programming field. But there are no computer programmers among my friends, so they must all be illogical.

(B) Someone who thinks logically can become a computer programmer. David thinks very logically, so he can become an excellent programmer.

(C) Skill in thinking logically is one guarantee of success at computer programming; a degree from a prestigious computer-science department is another.

(D) A computer programmer must be able to think logically. Rob is a very logical person, so he must be a programmer.

(E) Computer programmers are always able to solve logic problems. None of the students can solve logic problems, so none of them are computer programmers.

24. Deviations from social norms, particularly in such emotionally charged areas as eating, are usually accompanied by defensiveness, self-justification, and attempts at proselytizing others. That meat-eating is still fundamental to mainstream American culture can be seen from the fact that most vegetarians, regardless of the specific motivation underlying their diet, express strong feelings about the rightness of their eating pattern and its potential benefits for others.

A logical critique of the argument above would most likely emphasize which one of the following?

(A) the difference between proselytizing and educating others

(B) the failure to consider that not all proselytizers are deviants

(C) the failure to define "mainstream American culture"

(D) the author's evident prejudice against vegetarians

(E) the actual number of vegetarians in America today

GO ON TO THE NEXT PAGE.

25. Each and every one of the typists who works at the Ace Employment Agency works overtime. Jonathan Simson works overtime at the Ace Employment Agency. Therefore, Jonathan Simson must be a typist.

Which one of the following is most similar in structure to the above argument?

(A) All rabbits eat carrots. My pet Scamper eats carrots, so he must be a rabbit.

(B) All members of the Eastside Racquetball Club purchase raffle tickets. Suzanne Child is a member of the Eastside Racquetball Club. Therefore, she must purchase raffle tickets.

(C) Every woman who chooses to take this drug must be aware of the risks involved. Joanne doesn't like to take risks. Therefore, she will not choose to take this drug.

(D) Every performer who sings at the nightclub is served a free meal. Therefore, if you are hungry, you should arrange to sing at the nightclub.

(E) None of the construction workers at this site belong to a union. Jack Krone is not a construction worker at this site. Therefore, he belongs to a union.

S T O P
IF YOU FINISH BEFORE TIME IS CALLED, YOU MAY CHECK YOUR WORK ON THIS SECTION ONLY. DO NOT WORK ON ANY OTHER SECTION IN THE TEST.

ANSWER KEY ON FOLLOWING PAGE

PRACTICE TEST ONE ANSWER KEY

Section 1 Logical Reasoning	Section 2 Reading Comprehension	Section 3 Logic Games	Section 4 Logical Reasoning
1. A	1. B	1. E	1. D
2. C	2. A	2. B	2. C
3. D	3. B	3. B	3. C
4. C	4. D	4. E	4. B
5. C	5. C	5. B	5. C
6. A	6. B	6. C	6. E
7. A	7. B	7. A	7. D
8. B	8. B	8. C	8. B
9. B	9. E	9. E	9. E
10. B	10. E	10. B	10. B
11. C	11. A	11. C	11. D
12. A	12. B	12. B	12. C
13. B	13. D	13. A	13. D
14. B	14. C	14. C	14. D
15. E	15. E	15. B	15. D
16. B	16. C	16. B	16. A
17. B	17. C	17. C	17. E
18. B	18. B	18. E	18. C
19. D	19. A	19. D	19. B
20. C	20. A	20. A	20. B
21. C	21. B	21. A	21. D
22. A	22. C	22. D	22. C
23. D	23. D	23. D	23. D
24. A	24. C	24. E	24. B
25. D	25. B		25. A
26. C	26. D		
	27. A		

PRACTICE TEST ONE EXPLANATIONS

Section I: Logical Reasoning Explanations

1. A

The author's conclusion is that our nation's courts are currently clogged with disputes that could be solved by other means. The passage contains no real evidence for this, oddly enough; the author merely defines litigiousness and claims that the American judicial system suffers from an excess of it—citing only the opinion of judicial experts, but no real facts. So the answer choice which best supports the passage will be the one that does provide examples or other significant evidence to support the author's claim. Only choice (A) gives us the needed examples: an increasing number of court cases involving labor/management disputes that could be settled by government boards.

(B) fails to support the conclusion; it merely indicates an effect of litigiousness—low-unemployment among lawyers.

(C) tries to justify litigiousness on the grounds that it has redeeming social value, "since it may encourage shy individuals to defend their own rights." But whether litigiousness per se is a bad thing is not the issue here; the issue is whether or not our legal system suffers from an excess of litigiousness.

(D) would have us doubt the validity of studies of litigiousness, but the passage never mentions any such studies.

(E) attempts to explain the litigiousness of urban dwellers. But the author has not claimed that the courts are backed up by unnecessary lawsuits brought by greedy city dwellers; his or her claim is that the courts everywhere are besieged by unnecessary lawsuits.

2. C

The author's argument is that the decline the Japanese imperial power underwent was not due to a fundamental bias favoring clan loyalty over loyalty to the emperor. The evidence supporting this claim is that, for hundreds of years during this period of decline, centralized power was held by shoguns, who ruled in the name of the emperor. The assumption here is that the rule of the shoguns was in fact imperial rule rather than clan-based rule. In the passage, we're given little information about this. Choice (C) claims that, in fact, the shoguns were representative of the different clans and ruled with little regard for the emperor. This denies the assumption, and makes the example of the shoguns a piece of evidence for the author's opponents.

(A) does not weaken the argument because we're essentially concerned with *who* held power, rather than *why* they held power. It does deny that there was loyalty involved, but that doesn't greatly weaken the claim made.

(B) gives us a piece of history that implies nothing about the type of rule the shoguns exercised, nor about the object of people's loyalty and obedience.

(D) reduces the power of the shoguns during the early part of the period we're discussing, and gives it to the *emperor*. Since the author mentions the shoguns as an example of the reach of imperial power, this would tend to *strengthen* his case by showing that loyalty and obedience were given to the emperor, and that the explanation proposed by the author's opponents is off-base.

(E), too, provides another reason for the decline of the imperial power and so would strengthen the author's case, not weaken it.

3. D

The argument concludes that factories that want to increase productivity should pay workers on a piecemeal scale, rather than an hourly wage. In other words, they should pay based on the number of finished products, rather than on the time spent working. The evidence provided is that paying on a piecemeal scale will maximize worker incentive; workers will work harder. But does a harder-working factory worker necessarily produce more items? We don't know. Suppose the factory is heavily mechanized or short on raw materials. Suppose, that is, that the amount of items a worker can produce is not determined by how hard the worker works but by some other factors. In that case, such a proposal will motivate workers, yet not increase productivity. So, the author must be assuming choice (D), that workers who work harder will produce more items than those who do not. This assumption is necessary to link the evidence concerning motivation to the conclusion concerning productivity.

(A) is not assumed because it's not necessary that most factories pay an hourly wage, but merely that some do so.

(B) is also wrong because it speaks of most factories. Determine the scope of logical reasoning arguments carefully.

(C) is too strong to be a necessary assumption. The author argues that piecemeal pay is incentive to increase productivity, but not that piecemeal pay is the only incentive that can increase productivity.

(E), concerning workers' preferences, is clearly outside the argument's scope. What the workers prefer is of no concern to this argument.

4. C

The conclusion of this argument is that the recent surge in popularity of college-level foreign language classes will decrease the number of graduates who are capable of appreciating the subtleties of another culture's means of expression. The evidence is that most of these newly popular classes employ conversational methods. The assumption that links evidence and conclusion is that conversational methods (as distinct from the traditional format of grammar exercises and rigorous analysis of literary texts) will not teach students cultural subtleties. In other words, the author assumes that if you've been trained in the conversational method, you'll be unable to appreciate the subtleties of that foreign culture's means of expression. Choice (C) articulates this assumption and is therefore correct.

(A) brings in the extraneous idea of abolishing the foreign language requirement in order to get rid of the conversation classes. But the author's argument isn't about saving or abandoning the requirement; it's about the effects of different kinds of language classes, so (A) is not assumed.

(B) plays on the assertions made in the first two sentences of the passage: first, that attendance in college-level foreign language classes is up, and second, that most of these classes are conversational in format. However, the author is not assuming that, given a choice, students prefer conversation classes to the more traditional format. This may be the case, but the question of student choice is simply not an issue here.

KAPLAN

(D) is plausible: it sounds like a possible long-term effect of what the author considers a surfeit of second-rate classes producing second-rate students. However, (D) is not an assumption of the argument. (D) would probably function better as a further conclusion to the author's argument, but it doesn't link the author's evidence with his actual conclusion.

(E) simply contradicts the entire thrust of the passage, which is that newfangled teaching methods are producing students with inadequate foreign language skills. If the author assumes that most students have a reading knowledge of a foreign language, why would he complain about the new format? Furthermore, if a student has gained this reading knowledge from the now popular conversation classes, the author's argument would be weakened; (E) therefore cannot be an assumption of the argument.

5. C

The author of the argument disagrees with the "cynical" claim that a child's socioeconomic background is the factor that determines his or her later intellectual capacity. She then presents the results of a study, which show (she claims) that it's the level of pre-kindergarten education, not socioeconomic background, that actually determines subsequent intellectual prowess. Thus the best description of the argument is (C).

(A) is wrong because the evidence the author provides is not the same as that on which the "cynical" conclusion was originally based; the study is new evidence that she's come up with.

(B) is contrary to the author's point that socioeconomic background does not determine intelligence.

(D) can't be right, because as far as we know the author's opponents have not presented any statistics at all.

(E) seems to say that the author has shown that high intelligence causes a high socioeconomic background, which, aside from making no sense, contradicts the author's stated opinion that the two things (socioeconomic background and intelligence) do not correlate.

6. A

The author believes that, by demonstrating that the level of pre-kindergarten education correlates with future intelligence, she has shown that future intelligence is not a result of socioeconomic background. If it is true, as (A) states, that the level of pre-kindergarten education correlates with socioeconomic background, then all three things correlate, and it becomes likely that future intelligence and pre-kindergarten education are effects of socioeconomic background.

(B) would actually help the author's argument by showing that socioeconomic background has no effect on the children's later intelligence.

(C) doesn't tell us enough to be a good answer; what is the relationship between amount of attention and amount of pre-kindergarten education?

(D) fails because it sheds no light on the issue of what, if anything, accounts for high intelligence—socioeconomic background or pre-kindergarten education.

(E) can have no effect on the author's argument, which does not concern how many children receive pre-kindergarten education, but rather what that pre-kindergarten education means for later intelligence.

7. A

This passage sets up a distinction between two apparently different concepts of "personality," as the author views them: our current idea of self-created individuality, and the traditional Bambara notion of the individual as part of a larger whole.

After contrasting the concepts, he argues that the latter is preferable; the personality that is "the sum of many parts" will be the richer type. In other words, as stated in choice (A), the author believes that richness of personality has a relationship with the degree to which one is integrated with a society; the former follows from the latter.

(B) describes two related aspects of our society's idea of personality. These are similar ideas, however, and are not presented in a relationship that is central to making the main argument of the passage.

(C), on the other hand, an inaccurate relationship is described. Far from arguing that diversity of personality and self-centeredness are in any way related, the author explicitly states that the reverse is true.

(D) The relationship in choice (D) is not discussed by the author; furthermore, it cannot be reasonably inferred from the passage that he would agree that such a relationship exists.

(E) suggests that the development of the self, according to the concepts described in the first part of the passage, might be affected by the kind of intrusions mentioned, but such a relationship is not presented directly, much less used for purposes of argument.

8. B

The argument of the passage is not closely reasoned, as you may have noticed in the use of "however" in the second sentence. The adverb implies that what follows is a refutation of the first sentence. In fact, there is no such clear, logical relationship: there need not be a conflict between the notion that American voters prefer a combative Presidential candidate and the poll showing voter disaffection in 1988. Because the writer assumes the connection, he concludes that the disaffection, added to the feeling of many voters that the candidates were not "presidential," proves that aggressive

candidates are not gaining voter respect. As we have seen, the logical error occurs in the writer's assumption that "people had been annoyed" by the "combativeness, even aggressiveness" of candidates, and not by something else. His argument is seriously weakened, therefore, if, as stated in (B), the poll did not reveal that voters were annoyed by combativeness in the campaign. Furthermore, there is no indication that any of the candidates actually were combative or aggressive.

(A), meanwhile, is completely off the point. The issue is not whether the 1988 campaign was "memorable," but whether it revealed a certain change in voter attitudes concerning combativeness.

(C) refers to a general attitude on the part of many voters, but the passage is confined to an argument about specific attitudes that the author feels were created by specific events of the 1988 election. A prior climate of public skepticism would not damage the argument unless we knew that combativeness did not play a role in those earlier elections.

(D) An attempt is made to soften the charge of aggressiveness by redefining it as a somewhat more admirable and arguably essential quality for a politician. Even if this were true, however, the passage is concerned with public perceptions rather than with a discussion of the merits of what looks like combativeness.

(E) is an interpretation of events which, however legitimate in itself, has no effect on the basic argument of the passage. This choice addresses a general concept, not the specific 1988 campaign and the specific topic of the effectiveness of combative campaigning styles.

9. B

The argument concludes that frozen vegetables are healthier than fresh vegetables. The evidence for this claim is the fact that vegetables are most nutritious when allowed to ripen on the vine. This fact must be applied to the farmer's situation. Because of the time necessary to ship fresh produce, fresh produce must be harvested before it's ripe. Thus, fresh produce loses some of its nutritive value. Frozen vegetables, on the other hand, can be allowed to ripen on the vine prior to freezing. Thus, although freezing produce robs it of some nutrients, the fact that it can be vine-ripened adds nutrients. The author's conclusion, that frozen produce is healthier, is only true, however, if the nutritional loss entailed by freezing is less than the loss entailed by premature harvesting. Thus, the argument assumes choice (B).

(A) and (E) The author speaks of vegetables in general, not specific vegetables, so (A) is not assumed. Likewise for (E); the contrast is not between different vegetables, but rather between different ways of harvesting and distributing vegetables.

(C) is not assumed. Even if the fresh produce doesn't sit on the shelf, the author can still argue that it is less nutritious.

(D) is irrelevant. The author is concerned with the nutritional value of the produce prior to any freezing by the consumer.

10. B

Because the author has described a possible farming scenario in which frozen vegetables are healthier than fresh vegetables, and because the author has concluded that this scenario has real consequences for our diets, the author must be assuming that farms do operate as described. The argument, therefore, will be severely weakened by choice (B), which claims that farmers do not operate according to the author's model. If all vegetables are harvested at the same time (which would have to be prematurely), then the frozen vegetables aren't vine-ripened, and the author's evidence falls apart.

(A) The relative nutritional content of overripe and underripe vegetables, choice (A), is irrelevant because the author is speaking only of ripe vegetables. The author's point rests on how these ripe vegetables came to be ripe.

(C) speaks of refrigeration, which is not the same as freezing, and therefore has no direct impact on the argument.

(D) speaks of the few consumers who can buy directly from the farm. Yet the author is speaking about the vast majority of consumers who must buy their produce from middlemen.

(E) concerns the taste of the two types of vegetables. The author, though, is concerned solely with nutritional content; nothing about taste will weaken the argument.

11. C

Here, you are less concerned with specific information than with the structure of the situation that uses that information. The passage has as its subject the effect of budget cuts upon a state center's data-collection capabilities. To answer the question, however, you must recognize the lack of similarity between the situation and one of the situations given in the answer choices; you are looking for the most dissimilar choice. In the passage an event occurs (the budget cuts) that cannot be assessed (the extent of impairment is unclear) because a necessary factor (the information) is not available because of the event. In choice (C), a failure of a system (the satellite link) results in a possible error (a partially lost text); to ensure success (transmission of the complete text), the process will be repeated. Here the lost information, if there is such, can be regained. It is difficult to see any similarity between the situation in (C) and that in the paragraph, but we should look at the other answer choices to see whether they are similar to the passage.

(A) turns out to be quite similar: an event (the earthquake) cannot be accurately assessed because the information in the surveyors' records has been destroyed; like the information on data processing levels, it is not available as a result of the event in question.

(B) In choice (B) as well, there is a lack of information (the number of miles driven since the accident) because of a failed odometer; consequently, the true survivability of the damaged auto cannot be accurately assessed.

(D) also includes the essential components of the situation in the paragraph—because there can be no information from the destroyed thermostat, the cause of the fire (i.e., the high setting) cannot be precisely determined.

(E) Forgetfulness caused by inebriation is the type of information loss that makes assessment of a situation impossible.

12. A

The author argues that the bill outlawing capital punishment should be passed. Her reasoning is that if the opponents of the bill actually visit those who stand to be executed, they will see that these criminals deserve our mercy. The author, then, is not presenting any logical evidence to support her view on the bill; she is appealing to her opponents' emotions—mercy, in particular. Thus (A) is correct.

(B) is incorrect because aside from incorrectly using emotion as a logical principle, she states no other principle.

(C) is incorrect because there's no reason to believe that her speech is ironic or mocking.

(D) fails because she attacks only the fact that her opponents have not visited death row and felt the appropriate amount of mercy. We're never given a clue as to how they presented their opposing view.

(E) is incorrect because she hasn't overlooked some distinction relevant to her opponents' case. She's overlooked their entire case itself, concentrating instead on provoking their tears. While you may have tried to force (E) onto her irrelevant emotional appeal, it's that appeal that is her actual argument, and choice (A) best describes it.

13. B

The author warns us not to confuse charity with self-interest by preventing a convict from exercising free will in the choice of a new career. To do this would be "to deny the very individuality that true rehabilitative programs should develop." We can thus expect a concluding statement that completes this theme—that convicts must be permitted free choice in determining their new careers. Only choice (B) takes this approach. If we try to rehabilitate convicts in careers of our choosing, we may frustrate them to the point that they return to a life of crime.

(A) and (E) both contradict the author's message by arguing that someone else should have the power to determine a convict's new career: either professional advisors, (A), or society as a whole, (E).

(C) Even choice (C) is sneakily repressive: would the author take such a stand with a convict who wanted a new career in an institutional setting? Moreover, (C) is a broad generalization that comes from left field.

(D) Finally, the motivation behind the criminal act, choice (D), is irrelevant to the issue of whether a convict should be allowed to choose his or her new career.

14. B

The author recommends a course of action, the application of economic sanctions, because, in his view, the relocation of companies from city to isolated suburbs has decreased the contribution made to state revenues by the corporate income tax. How? The new locations require expensive helicopter transportation for personnel; this expense is deductible from corporate tax payments. The assumption here, evidently, is that the corporate moves have not also had the contrary effect upon a company's total deductible business expenses. In other words, as suggested in choice (B), the paragraph takes for granted that "other economies" have not accompanied the move to the suburban locations, thus offsetting the effect of the increased transportation costs and sustaining or possibly raising the total amounts paid in corporate income taxes.

(A) is not a useful criticism of the author's reasoning since it is a given of the situation that helicopter transportation has been found "necessary." The use of the term indicates that reasonable alternatives do not exist.

(C) is based on at least two unwarranted assumptions: that the helicopters are manufactured in the state whose finances are being discussed, and that even in that event the taxes generated would be at least as great as the amount lost from the taxes of the companies using the helicopters. There is no justification for assuming either of these to be the case. In fact, the helicopters are described as "imported," indicating that they were manufactured elsewhere.

(D) In (D), there is a similar reliance upon unjustified assumptions. While it is possible that helicopter travel in the suburbs might have the effect of increasing productivity above levels in the city (with its mass transit), it is not very likely. Nor do we know that this supposed rise in taxes would be great enough to offset the loss which the author of the passage now deplores.

(E) The author is not required to demonstrate any difficulties other than those mentioned in the passage. As long as helicopter use reduces tax income, the argument stands.

15. E

The Consortium's policy statement tells us that, although a student at any of its colleges may enroll in certain classes at any other member college, the student's own academic dean has final say on whether these courses may be taken for credit, or used to satisfy degree requirements. If the academic dean has final say in this matter, then the implication is that he or she can refuse to accept credits awarded by other member colleges for these courses. Thus, choice (E) is the correct answer.

(A) would have you believe that the policy statement was about transferring enrollment from one member college to another, and not about the transferring of credits, which is actually the case.

(B) and (D) bring in irrelevant issues never touched upon by the author and not implied by the policy statement; this passage has nothing to do with either non-academic programs, choice (B), or codes of conduct, choice (D).

(C) directly contradicts the first sentence of the passage, in which the author tells us that students are "permitted and encouraged" to attend classes at any other member college.

16. B

This passage is a brief history of society's changing view of physicians from the beginning of the 20th century to the present. In sum, we are told that the great strides in combating disease have led patients nowadays to expect that medical professionals, once less able to heal than to give comfort, should always deliver technically proficient service rather than, as (B) would have it, "sympathy." In effect, (B) is a condensed version of the idea expressed in the last sentence of the paragraph.

(A) We are not told how the physician views his or her job; the emphasis is on the expectations patients may have of medical professionals.

(C) cannot be inferred, for it is the author's main contention that the rapid increase in medical successes has led patients to expect "perfect performance." Even if one were to interpret the phrase "medical incompetence" somewhat differently, as referring to individual failures within the profession, (C) is simply not addressed in the passage; no comparison is made between the competence of physicians in the past and that of today's medical professionals.

(D) goes too far. There is no suggestion here that health-care workers have become less sensitive; again, the emphasis is on the patients' expectations.

(E) is beyond the scope, as malpractice suits are never mentioned at all in the passage.

17. B

As in two earlier questions, the point here is to grasp the essential structure of the argument in the passage, then compare it with the logical structure of each of the answer choices. Here, you are asked to select the answer choice with a structure most similar to that of the passage given, in which the author argues that the possible danger of psychological testing of schoolchildren is outweighed by the likelihood that the results of such testing will benefit students. In other words, an activity should be pursued if the good effects will probably be greater than the possible bad effects. Similarly, (B) states that arms limitation talks should be pursued because increased chances of survival outweigh the possible risks involved. The subjects of the two arguments are different, but the logical structures are similar.

(A) does not argue in favor of pursuing a certain activity (intensive short-term testing of drugs) but attacks it, bringing up an objection which, to the author, affirms the need for the alternative program of long-term testing.

(C) The claim being discussed—that hospitals serve high-sodium, high-starch diets—is merely dismissed with the counterclaim that hospital menus are designed by trained nutritionists (the assumption being that trained nutritionists would not design harmful meals).

(D) The structure of (D) at first seems roughly similar to that of the passage. The good results (improved vision, improved appearance) are contrasted with the bad effects, the inconveniences as compared with eyeglasses. But "inconveniences" do not weaken the possible good of wearing lenses; this is a side effect, not something detrimental to the essential aim of improved vision. In addition, the argument, unlike that of the paragraph, includes a comparison between two alternatives, rather than merely discussing the merits and possible drawbacks of only one.

(E) is an argument for adding devices (swinging doors, pedal-controlled wash basins) to make another device (the public restroom) appear less dangerous, or contagious, than people think it is. Rather than weigh a greater good against a possible lesser evil, this argument contends that the public should be distracted from concern over a perceived, but possibly nonexistent, evil.

18. B

There is no connection between rent control laws in New York and abandonment of apartment houses there, this passage argues, because no such connection can consistently be found in all other cities. We read that some cities without the laws have experienced widespread abandonment, while some cities with the laws have not. In other words, the logic here is aptly summed up in answer choice (B): The rent control laws of New York could not be responsible for abandonment because cities exist where similar laws did not have a similar effect.

(A) The assumption in (A), even if true, would not help explain the apparently conflicting data; after all, it is the author's point of view that the rent control laws do not cause abandonment, but the assumption of (A) would in fact strengthen the likelihood of such a causal connection.

(C) is completely unwarranted; we have no indication that the author believes the laws to be beneficial simply because she argues that they are not responsible for one problem—the abandonment of apartment houses.

(D) is incorrect because it contradicts the author's contention that New York's rent control laws did not foster widespread abandonment of property.

(E) also contradicts the author, who would not use "despite" to refer to laws which she feels have no effect upon abandonment. In addition, she has made abundantly clear that she accepts as a given that abandonment in New York has indeed been "widespread" rather than "only negligible."

19. D

The question asks for the main point of the passage. We're told that the September stock market fall shook the economy. Then we're told that retail sales during the holiday season were lower, when compared to the total annual sales, than in any of the previous twenty years. This is followed with the statement that retailers and lawmakers are worried, and that they may institute new rules concerning stock trading. Well, what inference leaps out at us? The inference that the stock market plummet is responsible for the fall in retail sales. If the stock market fall weren't responsible, then, as far as the passage is concerned, there would be no reason for the worries of retailers or the proposal of new rules governing trading. As a result, (D) is inferable as the point being made.

(A), and the stock market's wishes, are outside the scope of the passage. Although the legislature is considering rules, we have no indication that the market desires such rules, or any other "aid."

(B) Similarly, the typical habits of legislators, in choice (B), are also outside the argument's scope. This argument concerns only the recent market plummet.

(C) All that can be inferred from this piece of journalism is that the new rules might protect the market and retail sales, not that they will increase the volume of retail sales.

(E) is not the main point because no indication of the seriousness of previous market falls is given. It was the holiday season retail sales that hit a twenty year low.

20. C

This author argues that an individual ought to be allowed to help a "pain-wracked, dying friend" to commit suicide. To do so would not be an act of murder, according to the author, but a giving of solace and a mark of respect for an individual's free choice. The correct inference can be drawn from the final sentence of the passage, where the author concludes that lawmakers and judges must treat such cases reasonably, instead of responding "as they have with traditional prejudice." We can infer, then, that lawmakers and judges disagree with the author (otherwise, the author would not be trying to win them over to his side). Choice (C) is thus the correct answer: lawmakers and judges, according to the author, feel that assistance of suicide is murder, and the author wishes to change their minds.

(A) is sensible but cannot be inferred from the passage. A logical inference must be provable, or at least likely, solely on the basis of the given information. The author never discusses his idea in the context of other societies, so we cannot infer a universal application for it.

(B) is far off the mark. The passage tells us nothing about the thoughts and feelings of the terminally ill; perhaps very few contemplate suicide.

(D) goes too far. The author very carefully describes exactly the type of assistance of suicide he thinks is justified, and never implies that the act of suicide is always an act of self-deliverance.

(E) also tries to cover too much ground. The author's case for the legality of suicide assistance rests on the free choice of the victim, not on the amount of pain the victim is suffering.

21. C

The stimulus tells us about courses taken by master's degree candidates. If a master's degree candidate enrolled during or after 1977, then he or she takes a Heidegger seminar. This, of course, does not mean that candidates enrolled during or prior to 1977 do not take a Heidegger seminar. We don't know anything about those people. Furthermore, if a master's degree candidate enrolled after 1981, then he or she takes a Wittgenstein seminar. We're given information about a specific student—that he or she took a Heidegger seminar but not a Wittgenstein seminar—and asked for an inference about the student. We can infer nothing unless the student is a master's degree candidate because all our information is limited to this type of student. Thus, choices (A) and (B) need not be true. If the student is a master's degree candidate, then we know that his or her not taking a Wittgenstein seminar means that he or she could not have enrolled after 1981. Thus, as correct choice (C) has it, if the student is a master's degree candidate, he or she must have enrolled prior to 1982. To have enrolled after 1981 and not taken a Wittgenstein seminar would deny the second stimulus statement. As for when prior to 1982 the student enrolled, we haven't a clue. It could have been after 1977, as choice (E) says, which would explain the Heidegger seminar. Yet it could also have been before 1978, as (D) has it. Remember, the stimulus does not say that only those enrolled after 1977 take a Heidegger seminar.

22. A

To fill in the blank correctly, we must understand the basic argument of the paragraph, which links government-stabilized pricing with increased inefficiency and decreased individual initiative. Mirroring this concept is the author's conclusion

that the reverse policy would have the reverse effect; efficiency would increase in a free market as efficient producers gain deserved economic rewards. The topic sentence, therefore, must convey the notion that government control of prices would not result in such deserved rewards. On the contrary, as stated in correct answer choice (A), undeserving producers who have been inefficient in a free market would be rewarded.

(B) is nonsensical. The mandated pricing might have any number of economic repercussions, but the price level itself would be lower because the policy would so ordain. Whether the lower prices would reflect economic reality is another matter.

(C) The author has made clear in the passage that she is in sharp disagreement with the proposal to control grain prices. This answer choice incorrectly suggests that the idea represents some sort of happy medium rather than, as the author believes, a wrong-headed policy.

(D) Whereas (D) is a possible effect of the proposal, it is not a topic explored by the author in the rest of the passage and would not logically be raise

(E) is based on a misreading of the author's economic assumptions. She believes that government should not intervene in what to her is the natural functioning of the free market. She does not suggest that individuals should or could have an effect upon the forces of the market; rather, she praises individuals who know how to exploit those forces efficiently.

23. D

To prove that a particular sea narrative was partial inspiration for a Coleridge poem, the author of the passage first lists several concrete characteristics that the two works have in common. In addition, he notes that the poet's good friend Wordsworth might have owned a copy of the narrative; the implication is that he shared it with Coleridge.

Similar qualities have appeared in works written two centuries apart, and the earlier work could have been available to the author of the more recent work; however, no connection between events has actually been documented in the passage. In other words, the argument relies entirely upon the citation of evidence that is circumstantial, as stated in correct answer choice (D).

(A) is incorrect because the author doesn't create an analogy between seafaring and literature; the author is comparing two literary works about seafaring.

(B) introduces an element that is not found at all in the paragraph. The author has not attempted to reinterpret the poem, but merely to explain its genesis; no attention is paid to the meaning of the work.

(C) is incorrect because the parallels adduced in the passage are between two works rather than between one work, "The Rime of the Ancient Mariner," and the life of its creator, Coleridge. The reference to his real-life friendship with Wordsworth is not presented as a parallel to any aspect of the poem, although the author implies that the relationship could have had an effect upon the work.

(E) As we have seen, precisely what the argument in the passage lacks is concrete documentation for this new claim about literary influence; answer choice (E) is therefore incorrect.

24. A

The argument here is that older workers, in order to combat societal bias against them, should pretend to be younger, both when applying for work and after being hired. Is this a reasonable strategy? It would not be if, as suggested by answer choice (A), there is the possibility that older workers can effectively combat bias by confronting society with the truth—that maturity in itself does not diminish or destroy the capabilities of all workers. In this case,

older people would not only achieve the short-term goal of gaining employment, but also attain the long-term goal of making employment more available to their peers.

(B) would tend to reinforce the argument of the passage, since the statement tends to suggest that older men and women are subject to changes that might diminish their capabilities as workers.

(C) At first glance, choice (C) might seem to indicate that the original contention about the waste of human potential has been overstated, but it is possible that these "increasing numbers of older people" have found jobs because they have followed the advice of the author of the passage. Also, it is possible that these jobs, clerical and food service, do not fully utilize the potential of older workers, and represent, in fact, the problem stated by the author.

(D) suggests a solution, reinforcing the idea that a problem currently exists. Since the solution has not yet been implemented, the answer choice does not refute the author's argument that deception is necessary at the moment.

(E) might be considered a case of too little, too late. If the basic problem is the need for mature workers to find employment now in the face of age bias, it is not very helpful to learn that they could have avoided, and might indeed be able to reverse, certain problems associated with age. According to the author, older workers are already often capable. False stereotypes, not actual deficiencies, have become a bar to their employment.

25. D

The suggestion here is that the introduction of a highly successful predator into a closed environment will stabilize the ecology. How? By reducing overpopulation of a basically defenseless animal that has caused, and will continue to cause, environmental damage. We are asked to determine which of the answer choices offers information that would show this plan to be misguided. If (D) were true, one ecological problem would be supplanted by another; the goats, now in danger of starving, would be replaced by ravenous coyotes, who would eventually bring themselves to starvation. This would hardly constitute "stabilization" of the ecology. Choice (D) is correct because it gives a very good reason for not acting upon the argument in the passage. On the other hand, choice (A) is not to the point, since it is possible that the island environment would be congenial to coyotes; this answer choice does not rule out the coyotes' adaptation to the island environment. Nor does choice (B) rebut the argument of the passage, for the point is to reduce the number of goats, not to give them a fair shake in terms of dealing with predators. Only one of the two problems cited in the passage is addressed by choice (C). Even if soil erosion were stopped, the loss of ground foliage would still lead to the distressing result of a whole population of goats starving to death. We have no reason to believe that they can gain sustenance from the native cactus.

(E) is completely irrelevant, since (so far as we know) there are no household pets to be endangered by transplanted coyotes on the wild desert island.

26. C

The proposal in the passage seems straightforward enough. Now that one division of the university library is superior, why not use incoming monies to upgrade those divisions that are still inferior? What this argument ignores, however, is the possibility that different kinds of effort may be necessary to ensure that different divisions remain "complete and up-to-date." Specifically, the Social Documentation Division, relying as it must upon such materials as census studies and statistics, prob-

ably needs to keep making substantial purchases of new materials in order to "keep its collection current." Or, as described in correct answer choice (C), the division must have access to continued funding because it is concerned with the documentation of "an ongoing process."

(A) is not an effective criticism of the argument in the passage. Even assuming that social documentation as a study is more important to the university community than other disciplines, that is no reason to leave these other areas without adequate funding if there is no further need for monies in the Social Documentation Division. Literature and art may be less important, but they have not been abandoned.

(B) places undue importance on an inessential factor. The new computerized devices do not yet exist; it is not clear what kind of improvement they could bring when perfected.

(C) is a better answer than (B) because (C) points to an inherent quality of social documentation that necessitates further funding.

(D) is a weak argument since it is not definitely known that additional copies will indeed be needed. Rather than hold back money for a possible need, the university would logically address needs that already exist. Furthermore, there is no reason to place a priority on the convenience of sociology students when other areas of the library may be lacking basic resource materials.

(E) shows a misplacement of emphasis. Since the library has deficiencies, the author would respond, the principal effort should be to improve the collection, rather than encourage greater use of a flawed collection.

Section II: Reading Comprehension Explanations

PASSAGE 1—Free Speech Passage

Topic and Scope

Free speech; specifically, three theories about speech.

Purpose and Main Idea

The author wants to show the different sides surrounding the argument of free speech.

Paragraph Structure

Paragraph 1 mentions two traditional justifications of the free speech principle, the classical and fortress models. This paragraph is mainly introduction, but read carefully and make note of what you're told: traditional justifications protect speech more than other actions; the two models agree that speech has an inherent value, and otherwise, they disagree. Paragraphs 2 and 3 explore the two models in detail, associating them with Meiklejohn and Holmes, respectively. The major *difference* between the two models is that Meiklejohn sees the right of free speech in a positive light, as something that helps democratic government, whereas Holmes sees it more negatively, as a safeguard against intolerance. As is often in Reading Comp, this distinction becomes clearer when you get to the questions. Don't worry about pinning it down exactly as you read. Finally, paragraph 4 briefly presents Bollinger's model.

The Big Picture

The questions deal with the three theories, and it's sometimes hard to keep clear whose theory says what. But, in compensation, the questions do a lot of work for you. After a primary concern question, questions 2–5 go through the three theorists in the same order as the passage does; in each, it's easy to relocate the relevant material. There's one logic question and one comparing Holmes and Meiklejohn. Moreover, all the questions deal with major points about the various theorists, not with tiny details. Make use of this; knock these questions down in a row.

The Questions

1. **B**

The first question is a straightforward main idea question; look for a choice that covers the whole passage and gets the author's focus or point of view right. (B) works best because the three views presented in the passage are all theoretical justifications for free speech (as the very first sentence indicates).

(A) misses the author's point of view; no arguments against free speech are considered. The focus, rather, is on how one justifies the decision to support broad rights of free speech—this is why (B) works better.

(C) and (D) are both too narrow, making the views of one or two theoreticians the author's primary concern, whereas the author is equally concerned with all three; in addition, (C) distorts the discussion of Bollinger, which mentions no criticisms of the right of extremist speech.

(E) is wrong, first, because the author does not claim that his approach is "new" (although Bollinger's may be), and second, because neither Bollinger nor the author discusses "constitutionally limiting extremist speech"—in fact, the Constitution is never mentioned.

2. **A**

Questions 2 and 3 deal with Meiklejohn—paragraph 2. This one asks for an assumption Meiklejohn would make. (A) deals with Meiklejohn's basic argument on "extremist speech" contained in the last three sentences of the paragraph: extremist views cannot be concealed from citizens who must vote on public issues. (A) is a necessary assumption because, if it were not true, citizens could make rational decisions without the opportunity to consider extremist views, and Meiklejohn's justification for free speech would fall apart.

(B) is, if anything, an argument against free speech (assuming that Meiklejohn himself is not an extremist)—at any rate, all Meiklejohn says is that one needs to consider extremist views, not embrace them.

(C) and (D) are very similar. They are both something that often happens. Both offer secondary arguments in favor of free speech, but neither one is logically necessary to Meiklejohn's justification. Apply the same test as with (A): assume that (C) isn't true, that no unpopular views have ever been accepted eventually. Meiklejohn would just say, "Even so, people still need to *consider them in order* to make a choice." So (C) is not an assumption he makes, and the same with (D).

(E) Finally, (E) takes Meiklejohn's use of the New England town meeting as a "paradigm" (or model) for free speech and twists it into an idea that's never suggested, that free speech matters only in a community that's like a New England town meeting.

3. B

More Meiklejohn; you're asked what kind of speech Meiklejohn would NOT necessarily favor extending protection to. Once again, paragraph 2 has the correct answer; we're told in midparagraph that from Meiklejohn's perspective, the free speech principle need only protect *political* speech. So nonpolitical speech is not necessarily protected—choice (B).

(A) and (C) are out because we're told that Meiklejohn *would* favor protecting extremist speech so long as it had relevance to political issues.

(D) Similarly, we're told at the end of the paragraph that Meiklejohn sees a value in preserving a broad range of speech, including that which many people find offensive, (D).

(E), finally, is a detail from paragraph 3; it's Holmes, not Meiklejohn, who regards speech as the expression of individual beliefs.

4. D

On to Holmes (paragraph 3). The easiest way to understand (D) is to realize that if it were true, a lot of extremist speech and some "valuable" (nonextremist) speech would be censored—exactly what Holmes is not for. More specifically, sentences 6 and 7 of paragraph 3 say that the fortress model "overprotect[s] speech," protecting extremist speech to "diminish the probability that inherently valuable speech will be suppressed." So to Holmes, censoring valuable speech is more harmful than allowing extremist speech—not less (D).

(A) states exactly the opposite of this, exactly what Holmes does believe.

(B) Holmes' idea of protecting "extremist" speech to ensure protection of "valuable" speech implies that extremist speech is not very valuable and therefore supports (B).

(C) follows from the idea of a "buffer zone" and the statement at the end of the paragraph that "once unleashed, censorship cannot be reasonably expected to remain confined to worthless views."

(E) is another way of stating this same idea; it also repeats (in the negative) the earlier idea that protecting extremist speech accomplishes the protection of "valuable" speech too.

5. C

On to Bollinger (paragraph 4). Bollinger's is the "self-restraint model," and sentence 3 of this paragraph tells us that "although continuing staunchly to support free speech, the self-restraint model inverts the relationship between speech and tolerance." So it does "staunchly support" free speech, and (C) is not true, or at least, we have no reason to think it is true. This same sentence supports (B), which paraphrases "inverts the relationship" as "conceives the relationship . . . differently."

(A) paraphrases the last sentence—tolerance is part and parcel of the "self-control, self-discipline, and self-restraint" this sentence refers to as valuable in a stable society.

(D) is based on the first sentence of paragraph 4: Bollinger is referring to a society marked by "consensus on essential values."

(E) The same sentence says that Bollinger's model accounts for "changes in the function of speech attributable to the emergence" of such a society—in other words, free speech has a different function in such a society than in earlier societies, (E).

6. **B**

This is a variant on the standard "organization of the passage" question—you're asked about the first three paragraphs only: in other words, the introduction, Meiklejohn, and Holmes. The "traditional way of viewing a question" in (B) is referred to in sentence 1; it specifies greater tolerance for speech than action and finds inherent value in speech (sentence 3). The "two contrasting approaches" in (B) are, of course, the classical model (Meiklejohn) and the fortress model (Holmes).

So, this choice precisely describes paragraphs 1, 2, and 3.

(A) starts well (although it doesn't refer to paragraph 1) but then goes off the track—the author never discusses the historical background for either theory.

(C) is exactly backwards: the author first refers to points of agreement (and they are precious few)

and then spends two paragraphs on the disagreements.

(D) However, the conclusions are largely the same, not opposed (D)—both theories support extremist speech, although with different reasoning.

(E) starts well, like (A), but the author never mentions unanswerable questions or calls for a synthesis. (Bollinger's view is not a synthesis, but a third distinct model, and anyway, the author does not endorse it.)

7. **B**

What should stick in your mind is that Meiklejohn and Holmes both defend the right of free speech for extremist views, choice (B).

(A) is not a similarity; we're told in paragraph 3 that the belief that free speech leads to the discovery of truth is specific to Holmes' theory.

(C) The idea that censorship entails suppression of valuable speech (C) is also listed as one of Holmes' views.

(D) the need to keep the public abreast of all relevant issues—is something Meiklejohn stands for (paragraph 2), not Holmes.

(E) Finally, the promotion of tolerance as a social value is something that neither thinker stands for—it's described in paragraph 4 as a principle of Bollinger's.

PASSAGE 2—Limiting Science Passage

Topic and Scope

Science and society; who should control the direction of scientific research.

Purpose and Main Idea

The author argues that scientists should dictate the path of scientific research.

Paragraph Structure

The gist of this opinionated science passage, the issue, and the author's own view, is clear in paragraph 1. Paragraph 2 brings up recombinant DNA research, a possibly hazardous area of research; the paragraph ends by saying that debate inevitably turns to a more volatile issue, genetic engineering. Paragraph 3 explains why genetic engineering is so controversial and allows that recombinant DNA research is related to it. Paragraph 4 is a summary. The author reminds us of the benefits to be derived from recombinant DNA research and suggests that people are overreacting—they're letting a knee-jerk response to genetic engineering determine their thinking on it and recombinant DNA.

The Big Picture

Paragraphs 2, 3, and 4 go into particulars, and the best way to handle them is to scan them (with care and confidence), making a fast mental note of what each is *basically* about. That'll give you the information you'll need: the big idea, plus a simple road map of paragraph topics.

The Questions

8. B

This type of main idea question, with the choices worded as questions, occurs fairly regularly. Your strategy is the same—you want the choice that conveys the big idea and covers the whole passage.

(B) is best here; it sums up the big issue in one sentence. The wrong choices are typical of those in all main idea questions.

(A) and (C) are too narrow; they pick up on details. The danger of recombinant DNA research is mentioned in paragraph 2—and it's never explained (A). As for (C), the author admits in paragraph 3 that there are valid concerns about genetic engineering, but that, too, is subsidiary.

(D) and (E) never happen: there's no discussion of either the effect of criticism on the pace of research, (D), or the moral versus practical problems of hazardous research, (E).

9. E

A simple detail question. According to the passage, a lot of people, scientists and lay critics alike, agree that "fertility mechanisms" are appropriate areas of biological research in contrast to more dangerous areas like genetics and aging. The clear suggestion is that "fertility mechanisms" are pretty uncontroversial.

(A) and (C) There's no actual indication of either (A), which was probably meant to tempt, or (C). Be sure to reread with care.

(B) and (D) both contradict the suggested idea.

10. E

This refers to another point in paragraph 1. It comes up in the last sentence. The author, arguing that the *direction* of research should not be regulated, grants that society "must determine the pace of innovation." (E) gives a simple paraphrase.

(A) turns the idea around.

(B), application of new treatments, is never mentioned.

(C) and (D) seem confusing, which should have aroused suspicion. Setting specific priorities (C), and controlling fund expenditures (D), could affect either the rate or the direction of research. In any case, neither is mentioned.

(E) Correct choice (E) is mentioned—it's the clear choice.

11. A

The idea in (A) comes up at the start of the passage: we're told that molecular biology hasn't yet had a major impact in medical treatment. But we're never told why.

(B) The answer to (B) is given in the middle of paragraph 1: scientists have traditionally had responsibility for determining the direction of research.

(C), we saw with question 9, is answered near the beginning: studies of fertility mechanisms are more acceptable than studies of genetics and aging.

(D) We saw the answer to (D) with question 8: the author admits in paragraph 3 that there are real moral questions.

(E) is answered indirectly in paragraph 4: people's anxieties lead them to substitute a high-pitched polemic against genetic engineering for a reasonable consideration of recombinant DNA research.

12. **B**

The stem hints strongly that this is a disguised main idea question—you're being asked for a statement about *science* and *society* that the author would agree with. So you're looking for the statement that's consistent with the author's big idea. The right choice is (B). This is clearly an idea underlying the author's viewpoint.

(A) would weaken that viewpoint.

(C) As for (C), the author never suggests that society is about to start losing interest in regulating science. Quite the contrary.

(D) sounds too extreme. There's no advocacy by the author of desperate acts by scientists.

(E) is simply not suggested. In fact, the author clearly thinks it can be settled.

13. **D**

This gets back to the idea of genetic engineering being a symbol to people of the "frightening potential of modern science" (paragraph 4). The author's point is that some people want to abandon recombinant DNA research because of supposed dangers of genetic engineering. (D) gets to the same basic point. There's simply no suggestion of either (A) or (B).

(C) contradicts the real idea.

(E) gets things twisted; it's recombinant DNA research, not a public debate about genetic engineering, that may yield medical treatments.

14. **C**

The clear-cut suggestion in the relevant sentence is that all powerful sciences can be abused. The potential for abuse in molecular biology is no more or less than in any other science.

(A) and (D) simply miss the point.

(B) and (E) sound like nonsense; they're never suggested.

15. **E**

This is an application question. Note that the stem asks you to extrapolate from both the content and style of the passage. Well, the passage essentially represents an opinion, doesn't it? You can easily imagine somebody else writing a passage that comes down on the other side of the same big issue: society has a right to oversee dangerous research. The choice that's most consistent with the passage's content and style is (E). The passage could easily be one of several papers given at this type of seminar. The other choices are too neutral-sounding. Some of them have other problems, too.

(A) is out because the level of information in the passage is wrong for medical students, and the thrust isn't ethics.

(B) is out because a government report would sound unopinionated.

(C) and (D) misrepresent the passage. It's neither a broad outline of current work, (C), nor a look at progress in disease prevention/treatment, (D).

PASSAGE 3—Divorce Mediation Passage

Topic and Scope

Adversarial versus Mediated Divorce

Purpose and Main Idea

The author argues that mediated divorces are better for sustaining family relations.

Paragraph Structure

There's a clearcut structure: paragraph 1 introduces the problem, paragraph 2 criticizes the adversarial process, and paragraph 3 presents the alternative.

The Big Picture

There's one big idea in this passage, and it's a simple one: the adversarial process in divorce is bad, and mediation would be better. Nearly all the questions revolve around this. Keeping this simple structure in mind helps locate the material you need for questions.

The Questions

16. C

In paragraph 1, the author sets up the comparison between the adversarial process and mediation, referring to mediation as an "alternative mechanism." This structure is mirrored in the rest of the passage: paragraph 2 details some of the pitfalls of the adversarial process, and paragraph 3 outlines mediation as the preferred alternative. Choice (C) thus sums up the author's focus.

(A) The "state's goals" for the family are only fleetingly mentioned throughout the passage, and what these goals actually are is never clarified, (A).

(B), (D), and (E) are all too specific. (B) would only be appropriate if the author limited the discussion to the material covered in paragraph 2, and both (D) and (E) focus on points from paragraph 3 that are only parts of the author's main argument. (D) is most tempting, but it leaves out the adversarial process.

17. C

The correct choice rephrases the statement near the end of paragraph 2: "It is impermissible for a lawyer to advocate a generous, equitable settlement offer if the best interests of the client require seeking a less costly result."

(A) The adversarial lawyer may strive to do well for his client in the matters of property division, child custody, and support monies, (A), but nothing is said about whether this prohibits the lawyer from accepting an equitable settlement on behalf of his client.

(B) A settlement could be in the best interests of one client while still having some benefit to the other, so (B) is wrong.

(D) doesn't stand up to scrutiny either: in paragraph 1, the author states that the adversarial divorce process itself frustrates the fulfillment of a divorcing couple's legal obligations mandated by the state, and yet settlements are made using this process all the time.

(E) Finally, negotiating a settlement that will be to her client's advantage, (E), is presumably the goal of any adversarial divorce lawyer.

18. B

The author begins by outlining the situation he will discuss: the adversarial divorce process with all its attendant evils versus the preferable alternative of divorce by mediation. He proceeds to elaborate on the drawbacks of the adversarial process and finishes by singing the praises of the mediation process. (B) quite clearly fits the bill here. In the wrong choices, try to *quickly* focus on one or two words that make each one wrong.

(A) In (A), the author describes a change that is taking place in the practice of divorce law; he never directly "calls" for it, and no anticipated criticism is suggested.

(C) can be thrown out when you read "proposes a solution that combines the best of both methods." The author has nothing good to say about the adversarial method, and the "solution" that is offered is the mediation process itself.

(D) and (E) In the same way, (D) can be eliminated as soon as you hit the bit about a "historical account," and (E) should be dumped as soon as you realize that it focuses on the practitioners of the two methods rather than on the methods themselves.

19. A

Some attitude questions, like this one, focus on the author's attitude not to the topic as a whole but rather one narrow aspect of it. Be sure you answer the specific question asked, which is about the author's attitude toward the adversarial process in regard to family legal obligations and not in general— this is the key to picking correct choice (A) over (E). Looking at the passage, we see two places where the author mentions the effects of the adversarial process on the ability of divorcing couples to fulfill their family legal obligations. In both cases, the author states that the adversarial process frustrates this ability. Although the author is clearly against the adversarial process, he never becomes highly emotional about the issue, so "moral outrage" is too extreme, (B).

(D) We can exclude (D) right away.

(C) would be totally out of place here.

(E) tries to find a note of caution, when the author's disagreement is clear and definite. This choice might possibly describe the author's attitude towards adversarial divorce in general, but, as noted above, this question asks for something more specific.

20. A

The author has stated that, in divorce mediation, the attorney is "an instrument of peace trained to avoid litigation," litigation being what occurs in the adversarial divorce process. So, if most of the couples who initially try mediation have to resort to litigation in the end anyway, mediation doesn't come out looking too attractive.

(B) Although the author does claim that mediation reduces the stress of divorce, it is never claimed that mediation eliminates conflict altogether, (B).

(C) would strengthen the author's claims about mediation rather than weaken them.

(D) and (E) What the "experts" do, (D), and what most people do, (E), are typical irrelevancies that you'll meet over and over again in the Logical Reasoning portion of the test. Neither one answers the author because they involve what people do, and people don't necessarily act in the most rational way.

21. B

The answer choices for this question involve both style and content; the second part of each choice stakes out different territory, and your choice should be consistent with your answer to the best title question. This passage was clearly written by someone who favors the use of mediation in divorce, and he focuses mainly on legal aspects of the divorce process, the lawyer-client relationship, etcetera. (B) jumps out at us as the most likely answer. The style is appropriate for a lawyer.

A) The style could also fit a sociologist, (A). However, whereas the impact of divorce proceedings on the family is referred to in a general way throughout the passage, the main focus is the adversarial versus mediation question, (A).

(C) The need for a change in the state's divorce laws, (C), is never mentioned, only the need for a change in the practice of divorce law (paragraph 3).

(D) and (E) The style of this passage is not something you'd find in a newsletter for lay people, (D), and the legalistic content is a bit out of a psychologist's realm, (E). One more note: (E), like (A), is conceivable, but you have to do some pulling and stretching to make the case. This is nearly always a sure sign of a wrong choice.

PASSAGE 4—Medicine Wheel Passage

Topic and Scope
Medicine Wheel of the Plains Indians; specifically, its two primary functions.

Purpose and Main Idea
The author asserts that the Medicine Wheel had cosmic and psychological roles in Plains Indians' survival.

Paragraph Structure
Paragraph 1 describes the Medicine Wheel as important to the survival of the Plains people. Paragraph 2 sketches the Medicine Wheel's role in marking the movements of the heavens and describes its function as a calendar. Paragraph 3 concerns the Medicine Wheel's psychological and social functions and describes that through it the Plains Indians recognized diverse personality types, each of which was regarded with respect. Finally, in paragraph 4, the author suggests that the Medicine Wheel conveyed the values of tolerance and integration, values, the author asserts, that are essential to a community's survival.

The Questions

22. C

This is a straight detail question in the all–EXCEPT format. These can be time-consuming, so scan the choices to see if any pop out as being wrong. Choice (C) contradicts the idea that the cosmic and psychological functions of the Medicine Wheel were equally valuable (see the first sentence of paragraph 3).

(A) is true; the importance of the Medicine Wheel in the Plains' survival is emphasized in paragraph 1.

(B) is supported by the last two sentences of paragraph 2.

(D) and (E) are both true because paragraph 3 describes the "unity within diversity" that the Medicine Wheel taught.

23. D

Here we have another detail question. Information in the passage won't help you answer the question posed in choice (A); whereas paragraph 1 suggests that the survival of the Plains was threatened, we're not told *which* forces jeopardized their survival.

(B) Although paragraph 3 talks about different personality traits that the Plains recognized, no particular type was seen as dominant, so (B) is incorrect.

(C) is wrong too: although paragraph 2 mentions important constellations, we haven't a clue about which those important constellations were.

(D) However, the passage can help us with the question in (D)—the last sentence of the second paragraph says that the Plains calculated agricultural rhythms and seasonal changes through the Medicine Wheel.

(E) There isn't an answer for choice (E) in this passage; yes, the Plains valued tolerance and integration, as paragraph 4 states. Why? We're never told.

24. C

This question asks for the passage's primary purpose or main idea. The passage discusses the two equally important functions of the Medicine Wheel and suggests that it played an integral role in the survival of the Plains Indians. Consequently, choice (C) correctly reflects the passage's gist.

(A) Because the passage never explicitly discusses the spiritual beliefs of the Plains Indians, and certainly doesn't concern the much broader topic of Native American spirituality, choice (A) is incorrect.

(B) is also too broad—this passage concerns one Native American nation; it doesn't concern Native Americans in general or their fight against adversity.

(D) is incorrect because the social or psychological value of the Medicine Wheel equalled its cosmic or natural function: neither was of greater value.

(E) You can eliminate (E) because although personality traits are discussed in paragraph 3 in relation to the psychological function of the Medicine Wheel, you could hardly say that the passage's primary purpose is to analyze these traits.

25. B

The psychological function of the Medicine Wheel is discussed in paragraph 3, and the gist of this paragraph is that through the Medicine Wheel, the Plains Indians recognized major personality types and taught tribal members to recognize, respect, and imitate the qualities of other tribal members with other, equally valuable strengths. Choice (B) captures this.

(A) is wrong because the Medicine Wheel taught equality; it certainly didn't set up any hierarchy of personalities.

(C) is a distortion: tribal members were encouraged to imitate the traits of people possessing strengths other than their own so that each member would become a richer, more balanced person. The author never suggests that they were encouraged to develop traits that were particularly important to the tribe's survival.

(D) The primary psychological function of the Medicine Wheel had to do with the development of each individual's personality and respect for all tribal members, as described in paragraphs 3 and 4. Orienting members to cosmological and natural cycles was the Medicine Wheel's primary *cosmological* function, as

described in paragraph 2.

(E) is wrong because the passage doesn't suggest that the Medicine Wheel taught passivity; it taught tolerance and integration, as paragraph 4 says.

26. D

Best title questions test your knowledge of the passage's main idea. As we described before, this passage concerns the cosmological and psychological functions of the Medicine Wheel and its essential role in the survival of the Plains Indians. Considering that, choice (D) represents a reasonable title for the passage.

(A) misses the passage's focus on the Medicine Wheel.

(B) is way too broad.

(C) comes close to capturing the Medicine Wheel's cosmic function but never mentions its psychological function or role in the Plains' survival.

(E) is out for a similar reason: it neglects to mention the Medicine Wheel's cosmological function and besides, it's too broad in its general focus on Native American psychology.

27. A

Application questions like this one require you to consider the passage's focus as well as its tone. Considering that this passage concerns an artifact of cosmic, psychological, and spiritual value to a culture, its author is most likely an anthropologist, choice (A). It is unlikely that an astronomer, choice (B), would have devoted three of the four paragraphs discussing topics totally unrelated to astronomy. A social psychologist, (C), probably would have focused more on the thoughts and feelings of the individual members as they relate to the group and less on rituals and beliefs important to a culture's survival. It's likely that a theologian, (D), would have written more explicitly about the religious or spiritual aspects of the Medicine Wheel.

You can eliminate choice (E) because an archaeologist probably would have concentrated more on the Medicine Wheel as an artifact, object, or relic: this passage describes the function of the Medicine Wheel and its role in the survival of the Plains Indians, but it hardly goes beyond describing the Medicine Wheel as an arrangement of stones.

Section III: Logic Games Explanations

GAME 1—Cheese Display

The Action

After previewing the setup and rules, you see that this game asks you to distribute nine cheeses into three groups of three cheeses each—a Grouping game of Distribution. There are four domestic cheeses—F, G, H, and J—and five imported cheeses—p, q, r, s, and t (it can help to keep the entities separate if you use CAPS for one group and lower case letters for the other). The three groups are A, B, and C. The Key Issues will be:

1) What cheese is in what group?

2) What cheeses can, must, or cannot be selected with what other cheeses?

The Initial Setup

You've got three groups of three each. Set this up like you might in real life. Just list the three groups with three dashes under each. Be sure you also list the two types of cheeses:

The Rules

1) It's best to build a rule directly into the master sketch whenever you can. One of the cheeses in each group must be domestic. Make a note of this in the sketch; placing a "D" under one of the dashes in each group should suffice.

2) You don't know which group F is in, but F must always be accompanied by two imports—no domestics allowed in a group with F.

3) q, an imported cheese, goes in Group C. Build this right into the sketch.

4) s goes in Group A. That's another imported cheese definitely set.

5) Whew. Three rules in one. Be careful when you unpack this rule. Take it one step at a time. First of all, F can't be in the same group as q. Secondly, J can't go in the same group as q, and finally, r can't go with q either. Your mind is probably jumping ahead and combining this rule with Rule 3, and that's a good thing. It means that you're getting used to looking for deductions.

Key Deductions

Time to take a closer look at Rule 5 (and Rule 3). Don't just write "No F q." Ask yourself "What does that mean?"—q is in Group C, so F must be in either A or B. J, too, can't go with q. Again, this means that J must go in either Group A or Group B. Finally, r can't go with q, so r must also go in A or B.

Keep going. There's more to be deduced here. F and J and r each must go in either Group A or Group B. Can these entities go in the same group? Rule 2 told you that F must go in a Group with two imports. r is an import, so F and r could go in the same group, but J is a domestic. No way could F and J go in the same group. So, F must go in Group A or B, and J must go in the other.

As with all games, take a moment to work through the numbers aspect of the game. Here that means looking at Rule 1. Each group must have at least one domestic cheese. Rule 5 said that F and J (two domestics) can't go with q in Group C, but Group C must have at least one domestic. What domestic cheeses are left? G and H are the only other domestics. One of this pair must ALWAYS go in Group C. You can bet that one or two answer choices will try to put them both elsewhere. Now you're thinking like the test makers.

Finally, it's a good idea to identify the "floaters" in each game. These are those entities that don't appear in any rules or deductions. They will serve to fill in the remaining slots after you've placed all the other entities. Here, the "floaters" are p and t, two imported cheeses.

The Final Visualization

Here's what you have going into the questions:

DOMESTIC	imported
F G H J	p q r s t

A	B	C
_ s _	_ _ _	G/H q _
D	D	D i
F + 2 imp.	F + 2 imp.	No F
J	J	No J
r	r	No r
F ≠ J	F ≠ J	

The Big Picture

- When you have two or more types of entities, it's vital that you can easily tell them apart. One way is to put one group all in CAPS and the other in lower case letters. You can use your own way (circles and squares, underlining, etcetera) as long as it's quick, neat, and effective.

- The setup is the time to think, above all. The drawing is secondary. Consider the implications of each rule, and if you can build a rule directly into your master sketch instead of rewriting it (as in Rule 1), then great, do it.

- Don't be in a hurry to get to the questions. There are a number of things that you must do before answering a single question: Slow down during the setup, make sure you understand the game's action, and translate the setup, rules, and deductions into a neat, readily accessible sketch.

- It's very useful to identify the "floaters" in each game. These entities not explicitly tied to any rule or deduction will fill out the spaces in a game. In a "could be true" question, the flexibility of floaters make them likely answer choices. Conversely, a "must be true" question is more heavily based on restrictions, in which case floaters are not as likely to be part of the correct answer.

The Questions

1. E

You know that each group must have at least one domestic cheese. Because p and t (both imports) are in Group B, the remaining cheese must be domestic. We deduced in Rule 5 that r, an import, must be in Group A or B. The last cheese in B must be domestic, so r must go in Group A, choice (E).

(A) No, F could go in group B with p and t.

(B) No, G could be in Group C.

(C) No, H could be in Group C.

(D) No, J could go in Group B with p and t.

Remember:

- When you're given new information, get it down in the test booklet. Then ask yourself, "What entities does this new information affect?" Go back to your master sketch and the rules.

2. B

A "must be true" question with no new information often signals that the test makers are asking for a key deduction. However, you can tell that that's probably not the case here because of the complex answer choices. Each choice is like a question in itself. You can count on spending a good deal of time here. This question is a candidate for skipping the first time around if you need to preserve time because there's not much to do except try out each choice.

(A) Could F and r be together and not be in the group with s (that's Group A)? Sure they could. Here are the complete groupings that show choice (A) needn't be true: A—J s t, B—F p r, C—G H q.

(B) Could G and H be together and not be in the group with q? No way. We saw up front that J and F can't be with q (Rule 5), and because each group needs at least one domestic, either G or H must be with q. (B) must be true and is the answer. On test day you'd stop right here and go on to the next question. For the record, here are groupings that show the remaining choices needn't be true (you may have come up with other acceptable groupings to dispose of these choices):

(C) and (D) A—J H s , B—F p r, C—G q t

(E) A—F s r, B—J G r, C—H p q

Remember:

- To prove that a choice in a "must be true" question is wrong, find an exception to the choice, an acceptable situation that shows that the choice could be false.

3. B

This takes a slightly different form than most acceptability questions, but it's still an acceptability question. You're asked to find the one unacceptable Group B among the choices. What do we know about Group B? We deduced that either F or J must always go in Group B (see Key Deductions for a reminder of how we deduced that). Every acceptable Group B must therefore contain either F or J. Scan the choices. Choice (B) doesn't include F or J, and it tries to place both G and H in Group B—wrong on both counts. Remember, one of G or H must always go in Group C.

Remember:

- Always keep in mind exactly what the question is asking. If you had mistakenly thought that this question was asking for the one acceptable choice instead of the one unacceptable one, you would have been very confused.

4. E

G is in Group A. In what rules or deductions are you used to dealing with G? Questions 2 and 3 both were answered by realizing that either G or H must go in Group C. Here G is in A, so H must go in Group C. What else do you know about G? G is a domestic cheese, so F, which must be grouped with two imports, can't be in A. The only other choice for F is Group B. F and J can't be in the same group, so J must go in Group A. So far we have G, J and s in Group A, F and r in Group B, and H and q in Group C. Who's left? p and t will fill in the slots: one in Group B and the other in Group C. Don't hesitate to redraw your master sketch whenever needed. Here's what this question's sketch would look like:

A	B	C
G s J	F r p/t	H q p/t

Scan the choices; t could indeed be in Group C. (E) could be true and is the answer.

(A) No, H is in Group C.

(B) No, J is in Group A.

(C) No, p is in Group B or C.

(D) No, r is in Group B.

Remember:

- Work with any new information that you're given. Keep asking yourself, "In what rules and deductions have I seen this entity before?" and "What do I know about this entity?"

5. B

H is a domestic cheese, so F can't join H and p in Group B (Rule 2). Because F can't, J must be the one to fill out Group B. F's only other choice is Group A. r must go in Group A because B is now full. We're looking for Group A, and now we have it: F, r, and s, choice (B).

Remember:

- Only do the work required to answer the question. You could have taken the deductions further and filled out Group C, but there's no need to. The question is asking about Group A, so that's the only group you're interested in.

6. C

hat does it mean for J to be in Group B? It means that F must be in Group A—by now, splitting these two entities up between Groups A and B should be instinctual. Other than that, there's not much else to deduce: r, as usual, can go in either A or B, and our perpetual floaters p and t can pretty much go anywhere. What leads to the answer here is the situation of G and H. These two domestic cheeses can both join q in C or they can split up between B and C. The one thing neither of them can do is end up in Group A because that's where F is in this ques-

tion, and F's companion cheeses are always both imports. (C) is therefore impossible—for H to be displayed with s (in Group A) would mean placing H in the same group as F, which is a no-no.

(A) and (D) No problem here—r can go in Group A with F and s while the remaining entities fill out Groups B and C in any one of a number of different ways.

(B) G and r can join J in Group B as long as H joins q in Group C. Then p and t can fill in the remaining slots in Groups A and C.

(E) The situation just described in (B) above works for this one; just put t in Group A along with F and s and p in Group C along with H and q.

Remember:

- This question is a powerful argument for managing your time well. Just because a question is the last one on a game doesn't mean that it's the most difficult. Many, many games on the LSAT have manageable and even easy questions towards the end. If you allow yourself to get caught up in early, difficult questions, you may never get to these later, easier questions.

GAME 2—Fish Salon

In this Sequencing game, you're asked to put seven courses in order. The natural way to picture this is to simply write 1 through 7 across the page. As you work with each rule, try to find a way to build each rule into the sketch. As it turns out, you can put many of these rules directly into the sketch. K must be served after J. G is served two courses before H. L must be served before G. K is served either fifth or sixth, and F is served second:

$$1 \quad 2 \quad 3 \quad 4 \quad 5 \quad 6 \quad 7$$
$$F \quad (J) \ldots K \ or \ K$$
$$L \ldots G \_ H$$

You have quite a few restrictions on the entities, so it's worth the time to consider the implications of these restrictions. F is set at second, K is fifth or sixth, J is served some time before K, G can't be sixth or seventh, and L must be before G. Therefore, there are only two entities left that can be served seventh: H or M. Also recognize that because L must come before G, the earliest that G can be served is third.

Even though it looks like there aren't any Big Deductions here, you are given a lot of information. As long as you've taken the time to thoroughly think through the important implications, you should be all set to rack up some points.

The Questions

7. A

Here's an acceptability question, so grab each rule and see which choices violate that rule. The answer will be the one choice that violates no rules. Rule 1, placing J before K, doesn't eliminate any choices. However, rule 2, which places G two courses before H, eliminates (C). According to rule 3, L is served before G, which kills (B). Rule 4 places K fifth or sixth, eliminating (D); and rule 5 places F second, so (E) must be wrong. You're left with (A), the correct answer.

8. C

It's never too early to start benefiting from your previous work. You're asked for the courses in which haddock could be served. Well, in question 1, you saw haddock served seventh. It could be true then, so it can be true now. Eliminate any choice that doesn't include seventh. Good-bye choice (A). We saw up front that the earliest G can be served is third. Because G is two places to the left of H, the earliest H can be is fifth. Cross off any choice that has H in an earlier course than fifth. Good-bye (B), (D), and (E), which leaves us with (C), the answer.

9. E

If K is fifth, G can't be third because that would require H to be fifth. G can't be sixth or seventh (nowhere for H to go), so G must be fourth. Rule 2 then forces us to place H sixth. We deduced up front that H or M must always be seventh, so here M must be seventh. Choice (E) must be true and is the answer.

If you *didn't* make the up-front deduction that either M or H must be seventh, then you had a longer road ahead of you. You still knew that F is second, G is fourth and H is sixth. In this scenario, K must be fifth because it isn't sixth, and we're left with this arrangement:

1	2	3	4	5	6	7
_	F	_	G	K	H	_

J must be served before K, and L must be served before G. So between them, J and L must occupy the first and the third positions, although we don't know their order. Regardless, there's only one space left for M, and that's seventh, which again, is choice (E).

10. B

Again, use your previous work. In question 3, G was fourth and M was seventh, but the ordering was not determined (we didn't know exactly when J or L were served). Therefore, you can eliminate choices (A) and (E). From there, you have to try out each choice. If H is fifth, G must be third (rule 2) and K must be sixth (rule 4). We deduced up front that either H or M must be seventh, so here M must be seventh. L must be before G, and the only open spot before G is 1. J is left to fill in the remaining fourth spot. Everything is determined, so (B) is the answer. Choices (C) and (D) both lead to more than one possible ordering.

11. C

Where have you seen K in the sixth slot before? In the right answers to questions 1 and 4, K was sixth, so look at the setups and eliminate choices that mirror either of those choices. If it could be true then, it can be true now. In question 1, G was fifth with K sixth, so cross off (A). In that choice, H was seventh, so eliminate (B). That choice also had L third, so good-bye (D). Could M be first? Sure. Here is the ordering that allows us to kill (E): 1—M, 2—F, 3—L, 4—J, 5—G, 6—K, 7—H. We are left with the answer, choice (C). If J were fifth, there would be no place for the "G _ H" block.

12. B

The last question of a game isn't always the most difficult or even difficult at all. We deduced up front that the only two entities that could be seventh are M and H. Here M is third, so H must be seventh, choice (B).

If you missed that deduction, you had a longer route to the same answer. If M is third, then where could the G _ H block go? G cannot be third, because M is third, so how about fourth? If G is fourth, then H is sixth, and therefore K is fifth (rule 4). But J must precede K and L must precede G. However, there is only one available space before K and G, so this scenario is impossible, which means that G cannot be fourth. The only space left for G is fifth. So G must be fifth, which makes H seventh, and we're left with the same answer, choice (B).

GAME 3—Marbles in Cans

One of the most common reasons students run out of time in Logic Games is that they've wasted time rereading the rules over and over again. We see this syndrome most often when, as in this game, there are many variables and many rules. To avoid this problem, you should do two things:

First, take a few extra seconds with each rule. Don't just read it—ponder it. Identify some of its logical implications the first time through. If you've understood a rule thoroughly the first time around, there will be less need to go back to it later.

Second, when putting together a master grid, take pains to incorporate into it as much of the data as you can. Having put the data in one place in an easy-to-read-and-recall format, you won't have to go back to the original rules out of desperation: The data will have become part and parcel of your understanding of the entire game and will always be convenient for reference.

Here's how a master grid for this game might have evolved, starting with a basic setup and roster:

Remember, you can attack the rules in any order you want as long as you remember to get them all. In an effort to start filling in spaces, let's translate the second and third indented rules for starters:

A dash indicates a marble we know is present, but whose color is as yet uncertain. (Note the way the sketch has been drawn: This student will never, ever be tempted to add any more than 2 marbles for Can 3 and 3 marbles for Can 4! Let's incorporate the last two rules—

(Notice the comma in Can 2—the student's reminder to himself that more than one marble may go there.)

We've left the first indented rule till last, simply because it's not directly relevant at this moment to the job of filling in the cans. To incorporate it into the work, how about making the roster look like this, eliminating the deadwood while we're at it:

Remember, though, that for a complicated rule, symbolization is not enough! If you take a few seconds to fix the information in your mind— "Wherever the O goes, the Y is in an adjacent can"—chances are you won't forget about it later on.

There is actually one more thing we could add to our master grid, and you may see it if you wonder what we know about Cans 1 and 5. Because no can is empty, we can actually set it up like this:

—which accounts for eight of the ten marbles!

The Questions

13. A

If (as the stem says) Can 2 gets two green marbles, it will have a total of three—and, adding from left to right, 1 + 3 + 2 + 3 + 1 = the full complement of 10. Thus, Can 5 will have only its minimum of one marble, and (A) is correct.

14. C

Your first step should have been to notice that the hypothetical is about Can 5 and that the question asks about Can 3. Doing so helps you organize your work thereafter; it also helps you throw out choices (D) and (E) immediately because each mentions three marbles even though the third rule clearly states there can only be two marbles in Can 3. Next, you could have realized that if the orange marble is in Can 5, the yellow marble must be adjacent in Can 4. Thus far, things are pretty routine. We next turn our attention to the marbles yet to be placed: R R G G B. That "B" must go into Can 3, because neither Can 1 nor Can 2 will accept it, means that choices (A) and (B), neither of which names a blue marble, must also be eliminated. That leaves (C) as the correct answer, and in fact, Can 3 will contain either B and G, as (C) states, or B and R, as it might have stated.

15. B

If Can 1 gets three marbles, then once again all ten marbles have been accounted for (adding from left to right, 3 + 1 + 2 + 3 + 1 = 10). Because Can 2 can only have one marble and already has a blue one, the O/Y group cannot go in Cans 1 and 2. Can 1 can contain neither the O nor the Y; the answer to what cannot be true, therefore, is choice (B), a yellow marble in Can 1, because this would require the orange to be in Can 2, an impossibility in this question. A red or green marble in Can 1 violates no rules, so (A) and (C) can be true, and because the O/Y group could show up in Cans 4 and 5, it is possible for the last can to contain either a yellow or orange marble, eliminating (D) and (E).

16. B

This is perhaps the first question in the game more or less requiring a full, new grid of its own. After entering the stem info, we're left with:

—and once again, all ten marbles are accounted for! The question asks for the possibilities for Can 1, which cannot contain B. Nor can O or Y be included (Can 2 is full here, so we'd have to violate the O/Y rule). That leaves only G—and "one green marble," choice (B), must be correct.

17. C

If the orange marble is in Can 3, then the Y will have to be in adjacent Can 2 or Can 4. But Can 4, according to the stem, is full: It will take a G along with its original two R's for its total of three. Therefore, the Y goes into Can 2:

There's still a lot up in the air—four marbles, and we only know where three of them go. That may be a hint that it's one of the "if/then" choices that will be correct, the "if" clause acting as more information to narrow down the options a bit. In any event, (C) turns out to be the answer: If, as (C) says, the remaining G goes into Can 3, there would still be a B left, forbidden to Can 1 and Can 2 and thus destined for Can 5. (A) and (B) can be quickly eliminated because the remaining G could just as easily go into Can 3 as into Can 1 or 5. As for (D) and (E), neither one's "if" clause leads inevitably to its "then" clause: Whether Can 5 takes a blue marble, choice (D), or a green marble, choice (E), Can 3 could contain a red marble rather than blue or green.

18. E

Your intuition was working well if, after seeing the requirement that "G, G, O" go together, your immediate reaction was to ask "In which can?" Can 3 is surely out because it's only permitted two marbles; beyond that, "G, G, O" have to be the only marbles in a can (otherwise we can't give each can its minimum of one). That rules out Cans 2 and 4. Now, If "G, G, O" were in Can 1, putting the Y into adjacent Can 2 wouldn't leave enough marbles for the other cans. By process of elimination, then, "G, G, O" must go into Can 5.

The Y then goes into Can 4; one B is left to be placed and must go into Can 3 (because Cans 4 and 5 are filled and Cans 1 and 2 can take no more Bs). One of the remaining two marbles (both Rs) must go into Can 1 and the other Can 3. In the end, it's Cans 2 and 5 that contain no red marbles—choice (E).

GAME 4—Art Class

The Action

This game is an example of one of the newest types of game on the LSAT, games that aren't particularly amenable to diagramming. However, this game is just as susceptible to Kaplan's Five-Step Method as any other type. Work systematically and you'll find that there are quite a few makeable points here. There are four children—Peter, Rita, Sam, and

Thelma—in art class. The "action" of the game involves the kids pairing off or working alone, and each child or pair of children creating some project. The Key Issues will be:

1) When two children pair up, what project will they make?

2) When a child works alone, what project will he or she make?

3) When given a project or set of projects created, what individuals or pairings could or must have accounted for such a result?

The Initial Setup

There's not much to draw here. Make a list of the kids and possible items, and be ready to deal with the rules.

The Rules

Take your time when you unpack the information in all of these rules. One mistake in a game like this, and you're in for a long, unproductive ordeal.

1) If Peter and Sam pair up, they'll create a clay figure. If Peter pairs up with Thelma, they'll also create a clay figure. If Peter works on his own, he'll create a clay figure. Carefully make a note of this, something like "Peter and Sam = clay" and "Peter and Thelma = clay" and "Peter alone = clay."

2) Again we have information about what the children make. This time it's Rita. If Rita and Peter team up, they'll create a watercolor painting. If Rita works alone, she'll create a mobile. Make a note of this in the master sketch.

3) Now it's Sam's turn. If Sam and Rita team up, they'll create a mobile. If Sam and Thelma team up, they'll also create a mobile. If Sam works on his own, he'll create a watercolor painting. Make a note of this.

4) Finally, here's Thelma. If Thelma teams up with Rita, they'll create a papier mache ball. If Thelma works by herself, she'll also create a papier mache ball. Again, mark this information down where you can easily access it.

Key Deductions

There are no real deductions, but you must be able to understand how the entities work within the situation. On games such as this one that aren't amenable to diagramming, the key to success is accurately working with the rules. If you need the extra help, you can go through various scenarios of what happens when the different children pair up. For instance, if Peter and Sam team up, they make a clay figure. If the other two children work alone, they make a mobile (Rita) and a papier mache ball (Thelma). Going through these "what ifs" can help you get a grasp of the game's workings if you're confused. However, don't spend all day going through countless possibilities.

The Final Visualization

Here's the master sketch. We've divided it up by child to keep it clear even though this meant including some pieces of information twice:

Peter and Rita = watercolor	Sam and Peter = clay
Peter and Sam = clay	Sam and Rita = mobile
Peter and Thelma = clay	Sam and Thelma = mobile
Peter alone = clay	Sam alone = watercolor

Rita and Peter = watercolor	Thelma and Peter = clay
Rita and Sam = mobile	Thelma and Rita = ball
Rita and Thelma = ball	Thelma and Sam = mobile
Rita alone = mobile	Thelma alone = ball

The Big Picture

- This game shows why it's so important to depend on thinking rather than drawing for your Logic Games success. If you approach this type of game trying to "draw to win," you'll be very disappointed with the results. In fact, while you didn't have to draw at all to be successful on this game, you DID have to fully understand the action.

- Accuracy is vital in all logic games, but especially so in games that aren't amenable to diagramming. If you misread a rule, you're sunk.

- If you see a game like this on your section and it throws you for a loop, skip it. Go for the easier, more accessible points, confident that you're using your time in the best possible way. A game like this would most likely come last in the section (based on previous LSATs), but remember, on your LSAT, this type of game could come earlier, and you don't have to do the games in the order they're presented.

- Just because a game is unfamiliar doesn't necessarily mean that it's hard. There are some very doable questions here—look for them.

The Questions

19. D

Here we have a "reverse" acceptability question—four of the choices work, and only one has a problem. Check each choice to see if there's a way for the children to create the projects in each.

(A) Peter and Sam pair up to create a clay figure. Rita and Thelma create a papier mache ball. (A) works, so it isn't the answer.

(B) Sam and Thelma can create a mobile, whereas Peter and Rita make a watercolor painting. (B) is possible and therefore isn't the answer either.

(C) Sam and Thelma can pair up to create a mobile. Rita, working alone, can also create a mobile. This leaves Peter to work alone and create a clay figure. (C) can work and isn't the answer.

(D) There are only three ways for the children to make a clay figure: Peter and Sam, Peter and Thelma, and Peter alone. If Peter teams up with Sam or Thelma, he obviously can't also

work alone. Therefore, it's not possible for the children to make two clay figures, which means that (D) is the answer.

(E) There's nothing in the rules that says any of the children must team up. If they all work alone, they would make the items listed in this choice. (E) is possible, which means that it isn't the answer.

Remember:

- Acceptability questions are valuable for many reasons. They provide an opportunity to see exactly how the entities interact within the given situation. A normal acceptability question (which one of the following works?) gives you one valid situation, the "acceptable" answer, which you can use for later reference. A "reverse" acceptability question like this one is even more valuable because it gives you four, count 'em four, examples of situations that work.

20. A

We don't want any clay figures made. In the last question, we saw that clay figures are created in three situations: Peter and Sam, Peter and Thelma, and Peter alone. If no clay figures are to be created, Peter can't work alone or in any combination that results in the creation of a clay project. Peter must therefore team up with the only child left—Rita. Peter and Rita team up and make a watercolor. Choice (A) is correct.

(B), (C), and (D) are all impossible, based on the fact that we just saw that Peter must pair up with Rita in order to avoid the creation of a clay project.

(E) is possible: If Peter and Rita work together, the remaining children, Sam and Thelma, could also work together to create a mobile, which is fine in this situation. However, Sam and

KAPLAN

Thelma could just as easily work on their own. The pair in choice (A) is the only one that's absolutely necessary to satisfy the requirement of the question stem.

Remember:

- Have a goal in mind—think systematically: "The children can't make any clay figures, so what does that rule out? O.K., what's left?"

21. A

This stem gives us two pieces of information. Exactly two of the children pair up (which means the other two work alone), and the pair creates a mobile. What pairings can create a mobile? Rita and Sam can create a mobile, and Sam and Thelma can create a mobile. We're looking for the projects that the two solo children create. Well, simply try out the two possibilities:

If Rita and Sam pair up, that means that Peter and Thelma work on their own. Peter working alone would create a clay figure, and Thelma working alone would create a papier mache ball. Unfortunately, clay figure and papier mache ball isn't an answer choice, so on to the second possibility.

If Sam and Thelma team up, that means that Peter and Rita work on their own. Peter working alone would create a clay figure, and Rita working alone would create a mobile. Clay figure and mobile is choice (A), the correct answer.

Remember:

- When you have actively pursued the answer and found it, don't waste time checking the other choices. Trust your work. You want to have time to at least look at every question on the section.

22. D

In this one, no one flies solo, so the children must form two teams, exactly one of which we're told will create a mobile. As we just saw in the previous question, the only pairs that can create a mobile are Rita and Sam or Sam and Thelma. In the first case, the two pairs will be Rita/Sam and Peter/Thelma. In the second case, we'd have Sam/Thelma and Rita/Peter. Choices (A) and (E) conform to the second set of pairings, whereas (B) and (C) conform to the first. The only pairing that's impossible is the one found in (D): Rita and Thelma together would leave Sam and Peter for the other pair, in which case we wouldn't get the requisite mobile—we'd get a papier mache ball and a clay figure, and who needs that? (At least for the sake of this question.) Choice (D) is the pair that can't team up.

Remember:

- Use your work from previous questions—half the thinking that went into this one was done already in question 21—both questions involve the similar aspect of having one pair create a mobile.

23. D

Read this stem very carefully. The first part is easy enough: The children form two teams. Now for the tougher part. No team creates anything that the individual members of that team would create on their own. Let's start at the top with Peter. Peter working alone would create a clay figure. Who can Peter team up with that wouldn't result in a pair creating a clay figure? Rita is the only one. So Peter and Rita must team up to make a watercolor. Rita working alone wouldn't make a watercolor, so we're fine so far. That leaves only Sam and Thelma, who paired up will create a mobile. Neither Sam working alone nor Thelma working alone create a mobile, so this works out. The children's projects must be a watercolor and a mobile, choice (D).

Remember:

- Break up complex question stems and take the information one part at a time. If you find a stem confusing, try putting it in your own words.

24. E

Here's a "cannot be true" question with no new information. Not much to do except try each choice. If you can find a situation in which a choice works, it can be true and isn't the answer.

(A) If all four children work alone, Thelma would create the only papier mache ball. (A) can be true and isn't the answer.

(B) If all four children work alone, Peter would create the only clay figure. (B) can be true and isn't the answer.

(C) Sam working alone creates a watercolor painting. Peter and Rita can pair up and create another watercolor painting. That leaves Thelma working alone to create a papier mache ball. (C) can be true and isn't the answer.

(D) Rita working alone creates a mobile. Sam and Thelma can pair up and create a mobile. That leaves Peter working alone to create a clay figure. (D) can be true and isn't the answer.

(E) There are only two ways to get a papier mache ball—Thelma and Rita or Thelma working alone. Because Thelma can't work with Rita and work alone (obviously), the children can't make two papier mache balls. (E) cannot be true and is the answer.

Remember:

- Pick easy situations when you attempt to disprove choices in a "cannot be true" question. There's no need to get overly elaborate. In this case, a simple situation is all four children working alone, creating four different projects. This simple and familiar scenario quickly eliminates the first two choices.

Section IV: Logical Reasoning Explanations

1. D

In this passage we read that a 40-year-old mural has faded because of exposure. It is thought that the vividness of the original colors can be restored by using the muralist's leftover paints and mixing them according to his surviving instructions. Can this ploy work? Only if the leftover paints have not themselves deteriorated or otherwise altered over the years; otherwise, the mixing instructions, however precise, would result in colors unlike the original. Therefore, choice (D) is an assumption that is critical to the preservationists' plans.

(A), on the other hand, is a sweeping assumption. The point is to restore color, not to try to emulate the muralist's personal technique of painting; the latter goal is not the focus of the argument of the passage.

(B) takes the unwarranted line that the executive dining room must have suffered "extremes of heat and humidity" because of side effects from the serving of food. However, the cause of the exposure is not an essential part of the argument, so (B) is not assumed.

(C) In (C), we are invited to assume that the muralist left his original paints and instructions for the use of later generations, but the "precise instructions" may actually have been for his own use, and we have no indication that the paints were set aside for future restoration.

(E) may be true, but is not necessarily so, on the basis of the passage. Perhaps technology was sufficient to prevent fading, but the company did not invest in any form of temperature and humidity control.

2. C

To select the best inference drawn from the passage, you have to read between the lines. In the paragraph we are explicitly told that the potential extinction of certain ill-tasting or ugly plant varieties is alarming because these plants might also be disease-resistant or have the ability to mature quickly. Why would these desirable traits of unwanted plants appeal to the breeder? It must be that the traits can be passed on to more attractive varieties; specifically, as expressed in choice (C), an attractive plant hybrid can be produced that will include desirable characteristics from two or more different species—good taste from one, disease resistance from another. That explains how a generally undesirable plant can nonetheless be desirable—for one of its traits.

(A), on the other hand, goes against the passage. As the second sentence implies, many plants may face extinction because of undesirable taste or appearance; breeders want to save these plants not because taste and appearance are unimportant, but because the plants have other traits that are desirable.

(B) cannot be inferred from the facts given us. We know that many plant varieties have already disappeared; more will disappear in the future.

(D) confuses unintended consequence with basic intent. As the first sentence of the passage explains, the extinction of plant varieties occurs along with the tendency toward standardized cultivation. The goal of the agribusiness concerns is to standardize; it would be unwarranted to say that extinction per se is part of that goal.

(E) In (E), another unwarranted inference has been drawn. As we have read, the typical backyard gardener may indeed scorn certain varieties that nonetheless have a desirable maturation period. The latter is only a secondary characteristic when the aim is, as suggested, to produce plants that taste good or look attractive. It is quite possible, however, that the gardener could be concerned with the maturation period if it were the only difference between two otherwise equally attractive plants.

3. **C**

In this question you are being asked to select an argument that resembles in logic the argument about air pollution. Note the logical shape of this argument. According to the writer, we cannot (if dispassionate) make a connection between industrialization and air pollution if the latter occurs without the presence of the former. In other words, we cannot say that a specific cause (X) has a specific effect (Y) unless that specific cause (X) is always associated with that specific effect (Y). Without evaluating the logic of this kind of argument, you will note that it resembles the argument of correct choice (C). In this case, the contention is that we cannot say that eating red meat (the specific cause X) leads to cardiac problems (the specific effect Y) because some people who have cardiac problems (Y) do not eat red meat (X).

(A) The logical structure is quite different. Someone is described as giving occasional evidence of a certain characteristic (unwarranted optimism); this evidence is interpreted or redefined as another quality (lack of requisite steadiness).

(B) The argument of (B) can be broken down this way: If a small portion of a sampling responds one way (e.g., detests the diet drink), the larger portion will have a completely opposite reaction (like it very much). Remember, it is not the quality of logic that concerns us here, but the shape of the argument being advanced in each case; in that regard, (B) does not resemble the original argument.

(D) argues that if more gym students have the same amount of practice equipment available, some will have to go elsewhere to practice. In other words, if there is more demand for a constant supply of a resource, the demand will require other sources of the resource.

(E) Equally dissimilar in structure to the stimulus is (E), in which the cause (a famous violinist) has little effect, so it is argued that a lesser cause (the teacher schooled only in fundamentals) would have a greater effect.

4. **B**

The author concludes that a more exquisite literary experience is to be had from a Petrarchan sonnet than from a detective novel. The evidence used to support this claim is that the best critics agree with it; the critics with the most delicate sensibilities (whom the author takes to be the best critics) prefer the Petrarchan sonnet to the detective novel. And how do we know that these critics are the best critics? Why, because they prefer the sonnets. Thus, the conclusion (the superiority of the sonnets) is presupposed in the evidence (in the identification of who are the best critics). This is circular reasoning. In order for this argument to work, some other criterion would be needed to determine the qualifications of the critics. As it now stands, it is logically flawed; and this flaw is described by choice (B). The author assumes the point he wishes to argue.

(A) does a little damage, as the author has never named one of the critical authorities. Yet that's not the main flaw here; the main flaw is the criterion he used in deciding who the best authorities are.

(C) is incorrect for the simple reason that no specific example is given.

(D) is incorrect because the author does provide evidence—the best critics' opinions; the problem resides in the fact that the evidence is inappropriate.

(E) is incorrect because the author need not provide exceptions; he may not believe that there are any exceptions.

5. C

This passage makes clear that the phenomenon of the shattered glasses could only have been caused by either a sonic boom or an earth tremor. The speaker heard a loud noise just as he was leaving for a vacation abroad, but he did not turn back to investigate. The car radio carried no mention of earth tremors, which are always reported in the area; the speaker assumes that the noise was therefore a sonic boom, which would not have gained broadcast attention. In other words, it is assumed that the noise heard was connected with the shattering of the glassware. This assumption ignores the possibility that the glasses were broken some time later, either by another sonic boom or by an earth tremor, while the speaker was in another country and unlikely to hear a report about such a local phenomenon. Choice (C) states this assumption.

(A) proposes a distinction which is not necessary for the argument to work. In fact, if it were possible to tell the difference as suggested in this answer choice, there would be no need for the speculation of the speaker's concluding sentence.

(B) also suggests a distinction which is not an assumption of the speaker's; on the contrary, the extent of the damage is not seen as a clue to its cause, which (on that basis alone) could be either an earth tremor or a sonic boom.

(D) It is of course possible that more secure protection might have prevented the shattering of the glasses, as suggested in (D), but we have no indication that the speaker assumes so.

(E) The assumption in (E) is not essential to the speaker's conclusion, which designates a sonic boom rather than an earth tremor as the cause of the shattering. In any event, the speaker states that the breaking of glassware is "something that can only happen during a sonic boom or when there is an earth tremor"—not something that inevitably must happen.

6. E

The author's conclusion is that the public is in error in its condemnation of the students who were arrested. The evidence is an analogy drawn between the students' actions (which in all likelihood broke the law) and the actions of the patriots in Boston, who dumped tea into the harbor. The implied conclusion here is that since history has justified the violent actions of the patriots, it will probably do the same for the students' actions. The best response to this line of reasoning is to point out that merely because one such incident of rebellion (the Boston Tea Party) has proved justified, is no reason to assume that any such incident is, or will later appear, justified. That's correct choice (E).

(A) fails because it just begs the question. The author is arguing that it may in fact be patriotic, or at least justified, to demonstrate in front of City Hall. So (A) just ignores his argument.

(B) points out that students are too inexperienced to understand the consequences of their demonstration. But is this a reason to condemn their demonstration? Their demonstration could be the morally correct act, yet not be fully understood in all its consequences. So (B) is dealing with a different issue.

(C) is a general, cynical statement, but has no obvious bearing on the argument. Perhaps the students' act was one of those few which are based on beliefs and conscience.

(D) says only that the patriots had some support. Yet we don't know for sure that the students haven't had some support. Secondly, (D) speaks of support for the patriots' cause, whereas it's their actions that the author is using in his analogy.

7. D

As we saw in question 3, the author uses a case of justified rebellion as an analogy to argue that the students' actions may very well have been justified. That's choice (D).

(A) goes too far. He accuses the public of not keeping the patriots in mind, not of purposely ignoring the Boston Tea Party.

(B) and (C) There really is no general principle of rebellion here, as the author compares only two particular instances of rebellion, so (B) and (C) are incorrect.

(E) is incorrect because the author never says that we don't have sufficient evidence to condemn the students. His point is that we're overlooking an important and relevant precedent.

8. B

For this passage you are asked to describe the type of argument used by the author. First, it is important to understand the intent of the passage, which concerns the nationwide rise in median SAT scores. The trend has gratified educators, we read, but the author contends that an accurate interpretation reveals a disturbing truth: Scores have not risen because all students have improved as test-takers, but because an increasing number of potentially low scorers no longer take the tests, leaving the field to the more privileged students. In other words, the author accepts the basic evidence of optimistic educators—the rise in test scores—but offers a contrasting explanation. The correct answer is therefore choice (B).

(A) Self-evidently, (A) is incorrect, because it is essential to the author's argument that he accept "the accuracy of his opponents' figures."

C) would suggest that the author has clarified an explanation of the statistic; in fact, he offers an original explanation that flies in the face of the educators' optimistic reading of the test results.

(D) Because his argument is original, (D) cannot apply in this case, for he is articulating a new idea rather than defending one previously stated.

(E) One should not be misled by the author's somewhat facetious reference to the educators' all too eager embrace. Although he has adopted a dry tone toward his opponents and hints that they may have been hasty in their judgment, he in no way suggests that self-interest has clouded their ability to interpret the rise in median SAT scores (remember that the question asks for the author's "primary" method of argument).

9. E

There are only two sentences in this brief paragraph. Assuming that one logically follows from the other, what conclusion can reasonably be drawn? First, we are told that one Hudson River fish, a cod, suffers more from tumors than do other fish in the river. Second, we learn that pollution thought to cause such growths was being cleaned out of the river long before the cod tumors were discovered. What relationship does the second fact have to the first? The correct choice is (E); that is to say, there is no evident relationship at all between the two facts, at least as far as we can tell from the study. There is certainly no proof of a connection between cod tumors and Hudson River pollution; the former were discovered after the latter began to abate. This is not to say that there isn't a relationship, merely that we have no evidence of a relationship. The other answer choices offer unwarranted conclusions.

(A) The lack of evidence is taken to an illogical extreme; i.e., since there is no evidence that pollution causes the tumors, there must be no connection. But a lack of evidence for one possibility does not prove that its opposite is true.

(B) is not only an unjustified conclusion but also plays fast and loose with the facts. There was no "sudden change" in the river, so far as we know; rather, the passage suggests, if anything, an impressive but gradual change in the amount of pollution. More to the point, sudden or not,

KAPLAN

the change cannot be linked to the appearance of the tumors, simply on the basis of the information in the passage. The tumors may have existed long before they were discovered, or may have been undetectable in their early stages.

(C) There is no indication that choice (C) is a reasonable conclusion; on the contrary, the author cites the "significant strides" made. It is always possible that the efforts could be more vigorously pursued, but we have no reason to suspect that to be the case.

(D) rides roughshod over logic in two ways—by making the assumption that the Hudson River pollution causes the cod tumors, and by assuming that the alleged causal relationship would only affect the freshwater cod. The latter error, presumably, would result from a misreading of the statement that one type of cod has more tumors than other fish swimming the same waters.

10. B

On the one hand, according to the author, the ideologue will "never alter his cry," which is defined as an expression of what is most desired; on the other, the politician is said to accept a partial victory, if only because it is the one possible at the moment, while planning to gain more ground in the future. As stated in correct choice (B), the author's distinction could be interpreted to mean that the former cannot accept a partial victory but demands immediate and complete satisfaction, while the latter believes it sensible to accept the piecemeal nature of progress in the actual world. This is not to say, however, as choice (A) incorrectly states, that the politician's pragmatism involves shifting views to suit the occasion; he or she may accept a certain reality, as the author would have it, and tailor actions accordingly, but not alter any beliefs that are held. The sweeping statement in choice (C) is not justified by the passage. The author does not claim that the typ-

ical politician will accept any or all things that are possible; the politician is described as accepting what is possible within his views. The distinction made in choice (D) is also not suggested by the passage, which leaves open the possibility that either politician or ideologue can equally well address either practical concerns or abstract concepts.

(E) is not implied by the passage; so far as the author is concerned, neither politician nor ideologue, despite their use of characteristically different strategies, is necessarily deceitful.

11. D

The author (who is obviously a politician) is defending himself against a call for his impeachment. The call for his impeachment is a response to the author's having raised corporate taxes, thereby forcing many industries out of the state. The resulting loss of jobs has exacerbated the state's unemployment problems. The author's defense consists not of disputing the alleged effects of his corporate tax increase, but of pointing out his intentions in raising the tax. He responds to the impeachment call with the reason behind his tax increase. So the form of the reasoning is something like this: "Regardless of the effects of my actions, I had good intentions behind them." Choice (D) mirrors this reasoning: Alfred Nobel created dynamite, which has led to much death and suffering, but he originally intended it to be used in peaceful pursuits.

(A) describes an example in which someone (Hirohito) claims not to be responsible for some wrong-headed undertaking. This is different from the stimulus plea because the politician never denies responsibility for the tax increase.

(B) has Benedict Arnold changing his intentions. This is not the same as having good intentions that go unfulfilled in practice.

(C) just provides a sensible reason for Galileo's renunciation. There's no idea here of a distinction between effects and original intentions, so (C) cannot be correct.

(E) is incorrect because Charles I is not making a plea to escape responsibility. His intention had presumably been to carry out his duty, and he claimed to have done so as well as he could. There is no hint here of a plea to ignore the effects of his policies in favor of his original intent.

12. C

The principal flaw in the author's reasoning is his unreasonable assumption that his constituents want to impeach him because of his original intentions. This is very unlikely. What has angered his constituents is the effect of the author's policy. Thus (C) is correct; the issue here is the effects of the tax increase, and not the purpose behind it.

(A) and (B) are attacks upon the strategy of increasing the corporate tax rate. Yet the author did not imply that this was guaranteed, choice (A), to eliminate unemployment. He merely thought it likely to reduce unemployment. (B) points out that the plan could fail, and the state could wind up with higher unemployment. Well, this doesn't weaken the author's argument because he is not arguing that the plan was foolproof, merely that it was well-intentioned.

(D) is both false and irrelevant. The author tells us that the Legislative Record can verify his claim, and even if it couldn't, the real problem is the nature of his claim—that his intentions are what is important—and not its verifiability.

(E) is incorrect because the author does not believe that raising taxes itself will create jobs. The author's idea was that raising taxes will provide revenues, and that these revenues could fund a statewide jobs program. Furthermore, (E) ignores the author's principle mistake—the mistake of thinking that his intentions are more important to the issue than his competence.

13. D

The writer has concluded that the teachers' warnings about drug abuse must have been useless, since many of their students regularly used drugs while attending the school. The key word here is "many;" not all students became drug users. What about those who did not? It is possible, as choice (D) correctly suggests, that some of the non-users chose to avoid drugs as a result of the faculty's warnings; this answer choice does refute the argument that the warnings were "in vain." On the other hand, choice (A) does not. If the intent of a warning is to prevent an act, the teachers' efforts were certainly "in vain," no matter how much educational information was passed along. If, as suggested in (B), some students had defensible reasons for using drugs, we can assume that the teachers' warnings were not directed toward them. Yet the other students did not have such reasons, and their actions would prove that, for them at least, the warnings had been in vain. Thus, choice (B) does not refute the main argument of the passage. The statement in choice (C) is not relevant to the discussion: administration pressure on the teachers could have affected the sincerity of their delivery of warnings, perhaps, but the passage is about the supposed inefficacy of the warnings, not about the possible causes of this lack of effect. Similarly, answer choice (E) introduces information that is off the main point. The passage does not discuss the bad effects of drugs, although we can assume that the teachers did so in their warnings against drug use.

14. D

The author of this passage claims that there is a correlation between aptitude for mathematics and the ability to learn music theory; in a similar vein, she sees a relationship between a student's attraction to math-related courses and his or her ability to comprehend the composition of contemporary music. From these linked ideas, we can conclude that students in courses not related to math—that is to say, students unlikely to have math aptitude as their principal intellectual gift—would not have as great an ability to learn musical theory as students majoring in subjects that require math aptitude. In slightly different form, this conclusion is expressed in correct answer choice (D).

(A) We have no reason to conclude, as stated in choice (A), that humanities majors have not studied math as younger students. Even if likely to be less gifted in math than others, they could have been required or could have chosen to enroll in math or math-related courses. There is no reason to suspect otherwise.

(B) states a relationship that is not at all suggested by the paragraph. In fact, the second sentence makes clear that the author is comparing two types of intelligence that are of equal intellectual luster; the difference is in kind, not intensity.

(C) At first glance, answer choice (C) might seem to be a logical conclusion, but the phrase "musical talent" is a misstatement of the author's terms of comparison. She sees a correlation between math aptitude and the ability to understand musical theory and new forms of musical composition. This latter ability is not synonymous with musical talent, which would include the ability to perform or compose or otherwise creatively engage in the musical art.

(E) is an unwarranted conclusion. The author believes that students gifted in math are more likely to major in math-related courses than in the humanities; she cites this tendency. She does not go so far, however, as to imply that no student with mathematical aptitude would ever choose to major in the humanities.

15. D

With some force, the author of the passage criticizes government funding of the arts on two counts. First, it will be distributed according to the views of those temporarily in power; second, as a necessary consequence, artists will produce according to the changing political realities. In other words, government agencies will not support the best artists, but those whose ideas are most acceptable at any given moment; artists will not produce truly individual works, but those which are currently acceptable. The logic of this argument would be seriously weakened if most important artists tended to ignore the lure of government funds, or, as in choice (D), the influence of either private or public monies. This answer choice leaves open the possibility that lesser artists will be influenced as the author predicts, but weakens the contention that, overall, "the free flow of the creative process" will be interfered with.

(A) The information in (A) would put equal numbers of working artists at each extreme of the political spectrum but does not address their motives. Without more information, then, choice (A) cannot qualify as a refutation of the argument in the passage.

(B) The artists who are "well known in their fields" might well share the political philosophies of the "politicians in power." The participation of the advisory committees would, in that case, exacerbate the problem outlined by the author; politicians and artists of a certain stripe might tend to channel monies to artists or groups of the same stripe.

(C) does not weaken the argument of the passage; it is simply not directly relevant. Interesting as it may be that both politics and the arts may be characterized by rapid shifts in fashion, that fact would not change the relationship described in the passage between government money and interference with individual creativity.

(E) changes the focus by referring to another aspect of government arts funding; the effect upon audience rather than the effect upon artists.

The author has not addressed this issue. While audiences may have increased, they could have been experiencing only those performances or exhibits which had found political favor or had been created, as the author fears, to appeal to the tastes of those disbursing government funds.

16. A

For this question, you are being asked to choose a comprehensive summation of the passage about government funding's possibly harmful effect on the arts. The topic sentence which opens the paragraph lays down the basic charge that such support interferes with creativity. The author, as we have seen, expands upon the point by describing how it can or will do so. As stated in choice (A), a logical conclusion of the argument is that this type of interference with the creative process will be diverting, distracting, and otherwise degrading. These rather overheated terms are in keeping with the polemical tone of the writing; they follow logically from the author's picture of "willy-nilly" pursuit of government funds. The first half of (B) seems to follow logically, both in tone and in substance; the author suggests that politicians would adopt such a condescendingly proprietary attitude toward the arts. The second half of (B), however, misses an important point; rather than be "inevitably and irretrievably captured" by one type of institution, the arts would, in the author's view, become the plaything of whichever group held power at a particular moment in a continually shifting process.

(C), at first glance, seems logical enough. The author does believe that "the politically powerful" can control arts funding; it would seem likely that the most powerful leaders would divert funds to their own legislative districts. But we must remember that the author does not believe that increased arts funding always correlates with "wholesomely thriving" art. The passage makes clear that, to the author, arts funding is likely to produce debased or insincere art.

(D) There is a misreading of the second sentence of the passage. Experimental groups and established institutions are apparently equal, from the author's point of view; neither is more likely than the other to encourage the individual artist to pursue his or her own path.

(E) directly contradicts the intent of the passage. This answer choice describes the state of affairs that the author would like to see occur, but is the reverse of the supposed effect of government funding of the arts as denounced in the passage.

17. E

According to the argument of this passage, college students who fail a course should be expelled because their failure indicates a lack of serious dedication to learning. But is that necessarily true in every case? It is possible that even the most dedicated student might encounter an obstacle outside his or her control, as expressed in correct answer choice (E). In that event, it could be the obstacle (e.g., serious illness), not the student's attitude, that leads to failure; thus hindered, the student would be no less "deserving" than others, solely from the evidence of his or her performance in the course, and the argument of the passage would be refuted.

(A) raises an issue that is irrelevant. The author of the passage condemns a student for failing any course. To imply, as choice (A) does, that some courses are more difficult to pass than others does not tackle the main issue.

(B) Equally, the statement in (B) strays from the point. The author would surely argue that, fully informed or not, the student who fails is squandering university resources; the lack of awareness is not extenuating just as, traditionally, ignorance of the law is no excuse.

(C) The author would probably agree with (C), but find the statement an affirmation rather than a rebuttal. Clearly, the passage argues resoundingly that academic achievement is the only criterion for continued enrollment in college, and admits no such "right" to education.

(D) Similarly, although somewhat differently framed, (D) suggests that factors other than scholarship should be considered. Contributions to the community, however, are secondary to the topic being discussed—the college education itself and the means by which one earns the privilege of participating in it. As outlined by the author, the argument of the passage is not rebutted by the secondary considerations introduced in (D).

18. C

The author concludes that the benefits of arms reduction are merely illusory. The evidence presented is that even though some weapons are reduced, other weapons not covered by the treaty are increased to account for those that are reduced. In other words, if the superpowers agree to cut their tank forces in half, they will also double their navies, or some other arsenal not covered by the reduction treaty. This argument is most strengthened by choice (C). Choice (C) tells us that the five largest military powers have increased funding for new weapons in each of the last ten years. This supports the author's assertion that whatever firepower is reduced by the arms limitation treaties is reacquired through new weapons.

(A) says that the balance of power remains in spite of arms control. However, the balance of power is a proportion, and even though it is unchanged, the amount of firepower might well be reduced.

(B) doesn't strengthen the argument because although no proposals have called for the elimination of weapons, they might still account for a reduction in the number of weapons.

(D) comes from left field, introducing irrelevant outside knowledge. The author lumps all arms together, so this distinction is irrelevant to the argument as given.

(E) actually contradicts the author's claim by stating that fifteen percent of the firepower possessed by the largest military powers really has been cut. Even if this is not a great reduction, it contradicts the author's argument, which is that no reduction has been achieved through arms limitation.

19. B

The conclusion of this argument is that we must irrigate our corn fields now to prevent a food shortage and economic disaster later. The argument cites some evidence to prove that a disaster is on its way, but then it jumps to the conclusion that irrigation is what's needed to prevent this disaster. That conclusion is dependent on the claim that irrigation is the only thing that can do the job, choice (B). If there is some other measure that will prevent the disaster, then the conclusion is no longer valid, and irrigation may not be necessary.

(A) addresses the issue of the feasibility of irrigation, whereas the argument discusses only the necessity of irrigation.

(C) is irrelevant since the argument seems to imply that a cut in the 1988 harvest alone could produce price increases in 1989 and 1990. We don't need to know anything about the weather in 1989 and 1990, since it's the 1988 drought that threatens to cause the 1989 and 1990 economic disasters.

(D) is too strong. Irrigation does not have to produce harvests of expected yields in order for the conclusion to be valid; it need only improve the situation significantly, enough to prevent disaster.

(E) introduces the issue of other areas' agricultural yields, an issue that is not addressed by this conclusion.

20. **B**

This question focuses on the first sentence of the passage, which accuses the Governor's critics of partisanship. The two groups cited in answer choice (B) would be partisan, by definition, in regard to any "plight of the automobile industry;" therefore, if the statement were true, it would strongly support the idea that the state's chief executive is being attacked by people whose motives are not disinterested.

(A) The general observation in choice (A) may or may not have much merit as an abstract statement; in any case, however, it does not strengthen or weaken the force of the assertion made in the first sentence. There, the motives of the Governor's critics are being assessed; (A) addresses a concept brought up later in the passage—the assessment of the motives of a political figure like the Governor who is under attack.

(C) is irrelevant. Either the sincere critic or the disingenuously partisan critic might have voted for the Governor in the past when the current problems of the automobile industry might not have been an issue.

(D) focuses on the character of the Governor, but as we have seen, the assertion being discussed in this question has to do with a specific segment of the public. Furthermore, if (D) is true, the Governor is likely to merit honest criticism. This would weaken the author's assertion.

(E) takes the wrong focus. Whether or not it accurately reflects the author's point of view (and, logically speaking, we have no evidence either way), it does not directly speak to the assertion made in the first sentence—about the true nature of those who now condemn the Governor.

21. **D**

The author argues that, since much of the Irish population had become totally dependent on the potato for the bulk of its diet, successive failures of the yearly potato crop resulted in a national famine. The question asks for the most logical conclusion of this argument. (D) is the best conclusion, because if much of the population was totally dependent on the potato for its diet, then it follows that much of the population was left without alternative food sources when the potato crops continued to fail.

(A) and (B) There's no reason to conclude that the adoption of the potato as a staple of the Irish diet represented a rejection of English social patterns, choice (A), because the author never discusses either nationalism or social patterns. Similarly, the passage tells us nothing about the relative susceptibility of various staples to crop failure, choice (B). All the author tells us about other crops is that they continued to be cultivated, but "primarily for export to England."

(C) is also unwarranted; the author never implies that the great Potato Famine caused any revolutionary activity. Instead, the disastrous consequence of the Potato Famine, according to the author, was "a sweeping sentence of death or emigration."

(E) cannot be concluded because although the author asserts that the potato was grudgingly accepted as a staple of the Irish diet, the passage tells us nothing of those who resisted the potato, or their motivation in doing so.

22. **C**

The author is creating an analogy between the public's banning of books from schools and municipal libraries and the rather absurd hypothetical situation of the author's barging into my living room and taking away the book I am reading. The author hopes we will find the former situation just as absurd as the latter. The comparison on which the analogy is based, however, is weak, and (C) points to the principal weakness. While it is absurd to suggest that the author should have a say in what I read in my own living room, it may not be so absurd to say that certain representatives of the public should have a say in what can be read in public institutions like schools and municipal libraries. My living room belongs to me, not to the author; schools and libraries, on the other hand, belong to every member of the public.

(A) hinges on an irrelevant issue. Whether the book is burned or just banned is not important; what is important here is the parallel between living room and library, and the question of whether people can be forbidden to own and read certain types of books.

(B) is not a weakness in the analogy, since it only points to a lack of reality in the author's hypothetical situation, a lack of reality that the author intends in order to heighten the situation's absurdity. The author, after all, enjoins us to imagine that the courts condone this behavior.

(D) might weaken the analogy between the reader's living room and children's schools, but the analogy between the reader's living room and municipal libraries would remain untouched; thus, (D) is not as strong an answer as (C) is.

(E) may raise an interesting problem to be considered in any discussion of censorship, but since it has nothing to do with this particular analogy (remember your question stem!), it can hardly be our correct answer.

23. D

First, a statement is made about a relationship—during exam periods (whenever X), a rise in cookie sales occurs (then Y). Second, the argument assumes that neither factor in the relationship can occur separately from the other; that is, a rise in cookie sales must always signal an exam period, just as an exam period, as stated, is always accompanied by increased cookie sales (since Y, therefore X). The logical structure of the argument in (D) is very similar. Because a computer programmer must necessarily have the ability to think logically, it follows, according to this argument, that any logical person (Rob, in this example) must necessarily be a computer programmer. In other words, (D) says: "whenever X (computer programmer), then Y (logical thinker); since Y (logical thinker), therefore X (computer programmer)."

(A) Note that (A) has a very different structure. One factor, "proficiency at logical thinking," leads to another factor, "success in the computer-programming field." But the non-existence of this second factor among a group of friends is then said to imply the non-existence of the first. Put another way, the argument contends that, "whenever X, then Y; since not-Y, therefore not-X."

(B) In (B), one factor, a person's ability to think logically, is described as possibly leading to a job as a programmer; further, a specific person's ability to think very logically may possibly make him a very good programmer. Structurally, then, the argument says: "whenever X, possibly Y; since X, therefore Y."

(C) also differs in structure from the original argument. Here, one factor is presented as having a specific consequence; then a second factor is described as having the same consequence. In this case, we can say: "whenever X, then Y; but Z will also cause Y."

(E) The structure of (E) slightly resembles that of choice (A). One type of element, computer programmers as a class, is associated with a quality; if students do not possess this quality—the ability to solve logical problems—they cannot be computer programmers. In other words: "whenever X, then Y; since not-Y, then not-X."

24. B

In effect, this question asks you to determine what is illogical about the passage. The author begins by claiming that the attempt to proselytize or convert others is, among other characteristics, a likely trait of people whose behavior may not be strictly normal. As an example, he cites the case of vegetarians, who are, in his view, mostly proselytizers. This very tendency, he says, proves that vegetarianism is a deviation from the American social norm of meat-eating. What logical objection can be raised to this argument? As expressed in answer choice (B), the author has neglected the possibility that, while social deviation may indeed create proselytizers, it is not therefore true that all proselytizers have been created by a deviation from the social norm. Social deviation may be one cause, but not the only cause, of the urge to proselytize.

(A) The objection cited in choice (A) is less damaging, since it merely offers a less pejorative expression than "proselytizing" without addressing the question of whether or not the activity of "expressing strong feelings," however termed, is always associated with social deviation. Softening the term "proselytizing" does not change the form of the author's reasoning.

(C) In (C), there is the suggestion that an important term in the author's argument is too vague. In context, however, what he means by "mainstream American culture" is perfectly clear, since it is, by definition, that part of society that follows the social norms.

(D) brings an unwarranted charge. Although the author might seem to feel that social deviants in general have some unattractive qualities, as set forth in the first sentence, he does not reveal a prejudice against vegetarians per se. There is no evidence that his characterization of the behavior of vegetarians is unfair.

(E) seems an attractive choice because, if statistics showed that more than half of all Americans no longer eat meat, the author's conclusion would indeed be mistaken; vegetarianism would be a mainstream activity. This objection cannot be raised, however, if the figures are otherwise. Since we do not know which is the case, we cannot be certain that "the actual number" would weaken the author's main argument. (E) is therefore not as useful a critique as (B), which attacks the logic of the argument.

25. A

This is a parallel reasoning question that can be diagrammed with relative ease. The original diagram translates into: All X (typists at Ace) do Y (work overtime); since Y, therefore X. (A) is parallel: All X (rabbits) do Y (eat carrots); since Y, therefore X. (B) becomes: All X (Eastside members) do Y (purchase tickets); since X, therefore Y. (C) becomes: All X (drugtakers) do Y (become conscious of the risks); since Z (doesn't like risks), therefore not X. (D) becomes: All X (nightclub singers) do Y (get served free meal); if Z (hungry), then become X. If we translate (E)'s first sentence into "All construction workers at this site do not belong to a union," it becomes: All X (workers at site) do Y (eschew union membership); since not X, therefore not Y. So (E)'s "none" construction isn't parallel to begin with, and can't even be made parallel.

KAPLAN

PRACTICE TEST TWO

Remove or photocopy this answer sheet and use it to complete Practice Test Two.
See the answer key immediately following the test to correct your answers when you're finished.
Then use the score converter on pages 145 and 146 to calculate your score and percentile rank.

Start with number 1 for each new section. If a section has fewer questions than answer spaces, leave the extra spaces blank.

SECTION 1	SECTION 2	SECTION 3	SECTION 4
1 (A)(B)(C)(D)(E)	1 (A)(B)(C)(D)(E)	1 (A)(B)(C)(D)(E)	1 (A)(B)(C)(D)(E)
2 (A)(B)(C)(D)(E)	2 (A)(B)(C)(D)(E)	2 (A)(B)(C)(D)(E)	2 (A)(B)(C)(D)(E)
3 (A)(B)(C)(D)(E)	3 (A)(B)(C)(D)(E)	3 (A)(B)(C)(D)(E)	3 (A)(B)(C)(D)(E)
4 (A)(B)(C)(D)(E)	4 (A)(B)(C)(D)(E)	4 (A)(B)(C)(D)(E)	4 (A)(B)(C)(D)(E)
5 (A)(B)(C)(D)(E)	5 (A)(B)(C)(D)(E)	5 (A)(B)(C)(D)(E)	5 (A)(B)(C)(D)(E)
6 (A)(B)(C)(D)(E)	6 (A)(B)(C)(D)(E)	6 (A)(B)(C)(D)(E)	6 (A)(B)(C)(D)(E)
7 (A)(B)(C)(D)(E)	7 (A)(B)(C)(D)(E)	7 (A)(B)(C)(D)(E)	7 (A)(B)(C)(D)(E)
8 (A)(B)(C)(D)(E)	8 (A)(B)(C)(D)(E)	8 (A)(B)(C)(D)(E)	8 (A)(B)(C)(D)(E)
9 (A)(B)(C)(D)(E)	9 (A)(B)(C)(D)(E)	9 (A)(B)(C)(D)(E)	9 (A)(B)(C)(D)(E)
10 (A)(B)(C)(D)(E)	10 (A)(B)(C)(D)(E)	10 (A)(B)(C)(D)(E)	10 (A)(B)(C)(D)(E)
11 (A)(B)(C)(D)(E)	11 (A)(B)(C)(D)(E)	11 (A)(B)(C)(D)(E)	11 (A)(B)(C)(D)(E)
12 (A)(B)(C)(D)(E)	12 (A)(B)(C)(D)(E)	12 (A)(B)(C)(D)(E)	12 (A)(B)(C)(D)(E)
13 (A)(B)(C)(D)(E)	13 (A)(B)(C)(D)(E)	13 (A)(B)(C)(D)(E)	13 (A)(B)(C)(D)(E)
14 (A)(B)(C)(D)(E)	14 (A)(B)(C)(D)(E)	14 (A)(B)(C)(D)(E)	14 (A)(B)(C)(D)(E)
15 (A)(B)(C)(D)(E)	15 (A)(B)(C)(D)(E)	15 (A)(B)(C)(D)(E)	15 (A)(B)(C)(D)(E)
16 (A)(B)(C)(D)(E)	16 (A)(B)(C)(D)(E)	16 (A)(B)(C)(D)(E)	16 (A)(B)(C)(D)(E)
17 (A)(B)(C)(D)(E)	17 (A)(B)(C)(D)(E)	17 (A)(B)(C)(D)(E)	17 (A)(B)(C)(D)(E)
18 (A)(B)(C)(D)(E)	18 (A)(B)(C)(D)(E)	18 (A)(B)(C)(D)(E)	18 (A)(B)(C)(D)(E)
19 (A)(B)(C)(D)(E)	19 (A)(B)(C)(D)(E)	19 (A)(B)(C)(D)(E)	19 (A)(B)(C)(D)(E)
20 (A)(B)(C)(D)(E)	20 (A)(B)(C)(D)(E)	20 (A)(B)(C)(D)(E)	20 (A)(B)(C)(D)(E)
21 (A)(B)(C)(D)(E)	21 (A)(B)(C)(D)(E)	21 (A)(B)(C)(D)(E)	21 (A)(B)(C)(D)(E)
22 (A)(B)(C)(D)(E)	22 (A)(B)(C)(D)(E)	22 (A)(B)(C)(D)(E)	22 (A)(B)(C)(D)(E)
23 (A)(B)(C)(D)(E)	23 (A)(B)(C)(D)(E)	23 (A)(B)(C)(D)(E)	23 (A)(B)(C)(D)(E)
24 (A)(B)(C)(D)(E)	24 (A)(B)(C)(D)(E)	24 (A)(B)(C)(D)(E)	24 (A)(B)(C)(D)(E)
25 (A)(B)(C)(D)(E)	25 (A)(B)(C)(D)(E)	25 (A)(B)(C)(D)(E)	25 (A)(B)(C)(D)(E)
26 (A)(B)(C)(D)(E)	26 (A)(B)(C)(D)(E)	26 (A)(B)(C)(D)(E)	26 (A)(B)(C)(D)(E)
27 (A)(B)(C)(D)(E)	27 (A)(B)(C)(D)(E)	27 (A)(B)(C)(D)(E)	27 (A)(B)(C)(D)(E)
28 (A)(B)(C)(D)(E)	28 (A)(B)(C)(D)(E)	28 (A)(B)(C)(D)(E)	28 (A)(B)(C)(D)(E)
29 (A)(B)(C)(D)(E)	29 (A)(B)(C)(D)(E)	29 (A)(B)(C)(D)(E)	29 (A)(B)(C)(D)(E)
30 (A)(B)(C)(D)(E)	30 (A)(B)(C)(D)(E)	30 (A)(B)(C)(D)(E)	30 (A)(B)(C)(D)(E)

PRACTICE TEST TWO
SECTION I
Time—35 minutes
24 questions

<u>Directions</u>: Each group of questions is based on a set of conditions. You may wish to draw a rough sketch to help you answer some of the questions. Choose the *best* answer for each question, and fill in the corresponding space on your answer sheet.

<u>Questions 1–5</u>

A designer will select exactly two appliance designs and exactly two cabinet designs for the renovation of a house. The available appliance designs are H, J, K, L, and M, and the available cabinet designs are T, V, and W. The selections of appliances and cabinets must be made in accordance with the following conditions:

H is selected only if J and W are selected.
M cannot be selected unless J is selected.
If V is selected, then H is selected.

1. If V is selected, which one of the following must be selected?

   (A) K
   (B) L
   (C) M
   (D) T
   (E) W

2. Which one of the following pairs of designs cannot be selected together?

   (A) H and J
   (B) H and M
   (C) J and K
   (D) J and L
   (E) J and M

3. If J is not selected, which one of the following must be true?

   (A) H and T are selected.
   (B) K and L are selected.
   (C) K and M are selected.
   (D) L and V are not selected.
   (E) M and W are not selected.

4. If L is selected, how many distinct combinations of designs can be selected?

   (A) 1
   (B) 2
   (C) 3
   (D) 4
   (E) 6

5. If the conditions are altered such that H can be selected without selecting J, but all of the other conditions remain in effect, then which one of the following is a pair of designs that may be selected together?

   (A) H and M
   (B) K and M
   (C) K and V
   (D) M and V
   (E) T and V

GO ON TO THE NEXT PAGE.

Questions 6–12

For a family portrait, seven members of the Ellis family—Feisal, Gillian, Helen, Ian, Jeremy, Khalia, and Laura—stand in positions numbered one through seven from left to right, according to the following conditions:

Feisal and Gillian do not stand next to each other.
Exactly two people stand between Helen and Feisal.
Ian and Feisal stand next to each other.
Khalia and Gillian do not stand next to each other.
Helen's position is exactly two places to the left of Gillian's position.

6. Which one of the following is an acceptable arrangement of family members from left to right?

    (A) Feisal, Ian, Helen, Jeremy, Gillian, Laura, Khalia
    (B) Feisal, Ian, Khalia, Helen, Jeremy, Gillian, Laura
    (C) Feisal, Khalia, Ian, Gillian, Jeremy, Helen, Laura
    (D) Jeremy, Feisal, Ian, Laura, Helen, Khalia, Gillian
    (E) Khalia, Jeremy, Ian, Feisal, Gillian, Laura, Helen

7. If Laura stands in position one, then Jeremy must stand

    (A) between Gillian and Helen
    (B) between Ian and Laura
    (C) next to Feisal
    (D) next to Khalia
    (E) in position seven

8. If Laura stands next to Feisal, which one of the following CANNOT be true?

    (A) Gillian stands in position seven.
    (B) Ian stands in position one.
    (C) Ian stands between Feisal and Khalia.
    (D) Jeremy stands between Helen and Ian.
    (E) Laura stands between Feisal and Khalia.

9. If Jeremy stands in position seven, how many people stand between Jeremy and Laura?

    (A) none
    (B) one
    (C) two
    (D) four
    (E) five

10. If Ian and Jeremy stand next to each other, how many people stand between Laura and Khalia?

    (A) none
    (B) one
    (C) two
    (D) four
    (E) six

11. If Laura stands next to Khalia, how many people stand between Gillian and Jeremy?

    (A) none
    (B) one
    (C) two
    (D) three
    (E) four

12. Which one of the following CANNOT be true?

    (A) Feisal stands next to both Ian and Laura.
    (B) Gillian stands next to both Jeremy and Laura.
    (C) Jeremy stands next to both Gillian and Helen.
    (D) Khalia stands next to both Feisal and Laura.
    (E) Laura stands next to both Feisal and Jeremy.

GO ON TO THE NEXT PAGE.

Questions 13–17

Five sled dogs—Gakido, Hira, Jinook, Kini, and Leinheit—occupy five positions on a racing team. The positions are numbered one through five, and exactly one sled dog occupies each position. The sled dogs are hitched to harnesses as shown below:

The assignment of sled dogs to positions is subject to the following conditions:

> Each harness connects exactly two sled dogs, and sled dogs connected by harnesses are considered adjacent to one another.
> Exactly two sled dogs are experienced and exactly three sled dogs are inexperienced.
> An experienced sled dog must occupy the first position.
> Jinook is an experienced sled dog.
> Gakido is an inexperienced sled dog.
> The experienced sled dogs cannot be adjacent to one another.
> Kini is not adjacent to Leinheit.

13. Which one of the following is an acceptable list of the positions in a single team that could be occupied by inexperienced sled dogs?

(A) first, second, fifth
(B) first, third, fourth
(C) second, third, fourth
(D) second, fourth, fifth
(E) third, fourth, fifth

14. If Jinook occupies the fifth position, which one of the following must be true?

(A) Gakido occupies the second position.
(B) Hira occupies the third position.
(C) Leinheit occupies the fourth position.
(D) The sled dog occupying the third position is experienced.
(E) The sled dog occupying the fourth position is inexperienced.

15. If Leinheit and Hira occupy the fourth and fifth positions, respectively, then which one of the following must be false?

(A) Gakido is adjacent to Jinook.
(B) Gakido is adjacent to Kini.
(C) Gakido is adjacent to Leinheit.
(D) Gakido is adjacent to Hira.
(E) Jinook is adjacent to Kini.

16. If Kini occupies the fifth position, which one of the following would guarantee that an experienced sled dog occupies the fourth position?

(A) Gakido occupies the second position.
(B) Gakido occupies the third position.
(C) Hira occupies the third position.
(D) Jinook occupies the first position.
(E) Leinheit occupies the second position.

17. If Jinook is adjacent to both Kini and Leinheit, then Hira must be

(A) adjacent to Gakido
(B) adjacent to Jinook
(C) adjacent to Kini
(D) adjacent to Leinheit
(E) adjacent to either Jinook or Leinheit

GO ON TO THE NEXT PAGE.

Questions 18–24

A veterinarian has scheduled seven animals—Porter, Quint, Rocky, Slacker, Tammy, Venus, and Willoughby—to be examined on a single day, from first to seventh. Each animal will be examined exactly once during the day, and no two animals will be examined at the same time. The order of examinations must conform to the following restrictions:

Porter is examined immediately before Tammy is examined.
If Quint is examined fifth, Venus is examined sixth.
If Slacker is examined second, Porter is examined third.
Willoughby is examined either fourth or sixth.
Venus is not examined first or fifth.

18. Which one of the following is an acceptable ordering of animal examinations?

(A) Quint, Slacker, Porter, Tammy, Venus, Willoughby, Rocky
(B) Quint, Venus, Slacker, Willoughby, Porter, Tammy, Rocky
(C) Rocky, Slacker, Venus, Willoughby, Porter, Tammy, Quint
(D) Slacker, Porter, Tammy, Quint, Willoughby, Rocky, Venus
(E) Slacker, Rocky, Porter, Tammy, Quint, Willoughby, Venus

19. If Slacker is examined second, which one of the following animals must be examined fifth?

(A) Porter
(B) Quint
(C) Rocky
(D) Tammy
(E) Willoughby

20. If Quint is examined fifth and Rocky is examined before Willoughby is examined, then which one of the following must be true?

(A) Porter is examined first.
(B) Rocky is examined third.
(C) Slacker is examined seventh.
(D) Tammy is examined second.
(E) Willoughby is examined sixth.

21. If Porter is examined third, which one of the following is a complete and accurate list of animals who can be examined fifth?

(A) Quint
(B) Slacker
(C) Quint, Slacker
(D) Rocky, Slacker
(E) Quint, Rocky, Slacker

22. If Willoughby is examined immediately after Quint is examined, and Slacker is examined immediately after Venus is examined, then Rocky must be examined

(A) third.
(B) fourth.
(C) fifth.
(D) sixth.
(E) seventh.

23. If Tammy and Venus are both examined sometime after Willoughby is examined, then the number of possible orderings of animal examinations is

(A) 1
(B) 2
(C) 3
(D) 4
(E) 5

24. If Rocky is examined fourth, which one of the following could be true?

(A) Porter is examined third.
(B) Quint is examined first.
(C) Slacker is examined second.
(D) Slacker is examined seventh.
(E) Tammy is examined seventh.

S T O P
**IF YOU FINISH BEFORE TIME IS CALLED, YOU MAY CHECK YOUR WORK ON THIS SECTION ONLY.
DO NOT WORK ON ANY OTHER SECTION IN THE TEST.**

SECTION II
Time—35 minutes
25 questions

Directions: This test is composed of questions that ask you to analyze the logic of statements or short paragraphs. You are to choose as the answer to each question the one choice you consider *best* on the basis of your common-sense evaluation of the statement and its assumptions. Although a question may seem to have more than one acceptable answer, there is only one *best* answer, and it is the one that does not entail making any illogical, extraneous, or conflicting assumptions about the question. These questions do not presuppose any knowledge of formal logic on your part.

1. Researchers in the harbor town of Osceola have determined that the channeling of recycled wastewater into the harbor is endangering the health of the town's residents. A sharp increase in cases of the intestinal illness giardia has been directly attributed to bacteria that began to appear in drinking water supplies immediately following the implementation of the wastewater recycling program. The researchers have proposed adding the synthetic enzyme tripticase to the water during recycling. The addition of this enzyme would solve the health problem by eliminating the bacteria that causes giardia.

    Which one of the following statements, if true, most weakens the researchers' argument?

    (A) The tripticase enzyme also acts to break down bacteria causing intestinal conditions other than giardia.

    (B) Giardia is one of the least common and the least severe of all known illnesses related to the consumption of contaminated drinking water.

    (C) No other illnesses aside from giardia have increased significantly in Osceola since the wastewater recycling program began.

    (D) Giardia may be caused by the ingestion of contaminated food as well as contaminated drinking water.

    (E) The tripticase enzyme also breaks down chlorine that is essential to maintaining a safe drinking water supply.

2. Toy Manufacturer: This rubber ball is costly to make. We should switch to a less costly brand of rubber for this product.

    Marketing Analyst: But the ball sells so well because of its superior bouncing properties. No other material performs as well. We should stick with what we know we can sell.

    The speakers above disagree over which one of the following issues?

    (A) Whether the rubber used for this ball is more expensive than other available materials.

    (B) Whether this product regularly meets its sales quotas.

    (C) Whether the company should make the rubber ball from a different brand of rubber.

    (D) Whether customer priorities should factor into product d evelopment decisions.

    (E) Whether other rubber materials perform as well as the material currently used.

GO ON TO THE NEXT PAGE.

Questions 3–4

Salesman: The revolutionary new Shepherd's Gate Protection System represents the latest in sheep-tending technology. The built-in sensors recognize the scent of predators from miles around. When your flock is in danger of attack, the electronic gates surrounding the flock will quickly slam shut, keeping any unwanted animals away and your flock safer than ever. Sure, the system is prone to false alarms, but you know what they say: "Better safe than sorry."

3. Which one of the following, if true, most strengthens the salesman's argument?

(A) Sheep cannot be injured by the electronic gates when they quickly slam shut.

(B) Similar electronic protection systems are currently used to protect cattle from attack from predators.

(C) Roughly half of the incidents in which the gates are activated are triggered by false alarms.

(D) Some sheep predators have been hunted almost to extinction.

(E) Flocks of sheep are rarely attacked by predators.

4. The phrase "better safe than sorry" plays which one of the following roles in the argument above?

(A) It illustrates how a supposedly problematic aspect of the Gate Protection System is actually beneficial.

(B) It provides additional evidence of the mechanical efficacy of the Gate Protection System.

(C) It reinforces the notion that false alarms from the Gate Protection System are relatively rare.

(D) It attempts to diminish the magnitude of a deficiency of the Gate Protection System.

(E) It introduces a further reason for the need for sheep-tending technology.

5. Administrator: Sandra would not make an effective teacher. She is too lenient to fail students and too critical to reward any students with high marks.

An assumption central to the argument above is that

(A) effective teachers fail a certain percentage of their students and reward the rest with high marks

(B) a teacher must be capable of either rewarding students with high marks or failing students in order to be an effective teacher

(C) in order to fail or reward her students, Sandra must be an effective teacher

(D) it is impossible to fail a student and then later reward the same student with high marks

(E) if Sandra were less critical, she would reward students with high marks

GO ON TO THE NEXT PAGE.

6. The financial burden imposed by job-related costs is greatest for individuals who make a salary of $30,000 to $40,000 per year, and less for those who make much lower or much higher salaries. The reason for this is that individuals in low-paying entry-level positions making far less than $30,000 per year generally have fewer costs associated with maintaining their jobs, such as wardrobe costs, dry-cleaning, and medical bills due to work-related stress. The burden of these costs increases as one is promoted to higher-ranking positions, but lessens as the salary levels commensurate with further promotions become more than adequate to offset such costs. Jenny, who now makes $40,000 per year as an administrative director, will therefore be less financially burdened over the coming years by costs related to this job.

The argument above depends on which one of the following assumptions?

(A) Jenny will be promoted in the years to come.
(B) Over the next several years, Jenny's employer will provide benefits that help reduce stress-related medical costs.
(C) $40,000 is not considered an entry-level salary for Jenny's position.
(D) None of Jenny's co-workers who earn the same salary as Jenny is as burdened as she is by job-related costs.
(E) The costs related to Jenny's previous job were not as high as the costs related to her current position.

7. An individual may become more personally appealing as he or she becomes more physically beautiful. At the same time, however, the positive attention brought on by greater beauty may make the person vain or arrogant, which may decrease his or her personal appeal.

Which one of the following statements is best illustrated by the situation described above?

(A) The link between beauty and personal appeal is entirely superficial.
(B) Traits that appear positive are usually negative.
(C) A characteristic may be both enhanced and reduced by a single factor.
(D) Negative traits can only be balanced by positive traits of equal importance.
(E) Beauty is in the eye of the beholder.

8. Educational consultant: Most school districts today do not provide adequate educations for their students. Teachers do not receive quality training. Moreover, after-school academic programs are limited by tight budgets, and parental involvement in the classroom is at an all-time low. The Prentice school district, however, is looking up; parents and community volunteers are spending more time assisting in classrooms than in previous years.

Which one of the following statements below is best supported by the education consultant's argument if the information in that argument is accurate?

(A) The education provided by the Prentice school district displays at least one component of adequate education more so than it has in the past.
(B) The education provided by the Prentice school district can be considered adequate.
(C) The Prentice school district surpasses others in terms of the quality of education that its students receive.
(D) Many schools currently offer fewer after-school academic programs than do the schools in the Prentice school district.
(E) There is less parental involvement in other school districts than there is in the Prentice school district.

GO ON TO THE NEXT PAGE.

Questions 9–10

A consumer survey of independent feature films revealed that the percentage of action films that received the survey's highest rating was greater than the percentage of romance films that received the highest rating. Yet, the survey organizers were probably erroneous in their conclusion that subject matter determines a feature film's popular appeal, since the action films were all directed by filmmakers with at least one hit film to their credit, while the romance films were directed by newer filmmakers, many of whom had not produced a previous film.

9. The statements above, if true, support which one of the following inferences?

(A) Fewer romance films than action films received the survey's highest rating.

(B) There is no relationship between the popular appeal of the feature films evaluated in the survey and any previous successes of the directors of those films.

(C) If consumers were surveyed regarding their impressions of big-budget mainstream films, the percentage of romance films that would receive the survey's highest rating would be lower than the percentage of action films that would receive the highest rating.

(D) Experienced filmmakers are more likely to produce hit films than are new filmmakers.

(E) Among directors with the same number of hit films to their credit, differences in the subject matter of their feature films may not affect the way the films are popularly rated.

10. Each of the following, if true, supports the author's contention that the organizers misinterpreted the survey data EXCEPT:

(A) The fact that one has directed a previous hit film is a positive indicator of that director's filmmaking talent.

(B) Consumer ratings of a new film are influenced by the previous history of success of the film's director.

(C) Action films generally require larger budgets than romance films and are thus prohibitive for many first-time film directors.

(D) It is rare for the films of first-time directors to attain the popular appeal of films directed by filmmakers with at least one hit film to their credit.

(E) Directors who have produced a previous hit film generally obtain the largest budgets and attract the most talented and well-known actors for their subsequent films.

11. Candidate: I am worried about the effects that the recent media coverage of my personal life will have on my chances of gaining office. Even though the reports are untrue, some voters interviewed on television, in response to these reports, have already expressed doubts regarding my ability to lead.

Campaign manager: Your concern is unfounded. Of 1,000 people in this city randomly surveyed by e-mail, only 25 have responded that their perception of your ability to lead has been negatively impacted by the recent media coverage.

The campaign manager's argument is most vulnerable to criticism on the ground that it fails to acknowledge the possibility that

(A) future media reports that follow up on the story of the candidate's personal life will further damage the public's perception of the candidate's ability to lead

(B) the candidate's main opponent will use the opportunity created by the recent media coverage to conduct her own survey to assess the damage done to her opponent's credibility

(C) the voting public would understand that its reaction to the recent media coverage of the candidate's personal life was the intended primary focus of the survey

(D) opinions expressed in television interviews are not always the most reliable indicator of how interviewees are likely to act in given situations

(E) many of those surveyed who are skeptical of the candidate's ability to lead due to the recent reports did not actually respond to the survey

GO ON TO THE NEXT PAGE.

12. Sarah's Principal: Sarah's teacher should spend more individual time with Sarah instead of generating more vocabulary charts for her to memorize. Sarah makes a large number of usage mistakes when she writes and does not seem to have a grasp of basic phonetics. She has yet to memorize one of the vocabulary charts entirely, and she continues to misuse in her writing words she has already learned. Research shows that individual attention is more effective in helping students learn than is rote memorization, so Sarah's teacher is not displaying good judgment in continuing to rely on vocabulary charts to improve Sarah's writing.

Which one of the following statements best describes the function served by the principal's proposal that Sarah's teacher should personally provide Sarah with additional help?

(A) It represents a central assumption of the argument.
(B) It is a claim that is supported by evidence in the passage, while at the same time it also supports another conclusion in the passage.
(C) It is a hypothesis that is not supported by evidence in the passage.
(D) It is the conclusion that the rest of the argument upholds.
(E) It is a piece of evidence designed to support the ultimate conclusion of the argument.

13. If too much pressure is exerted on the bottom shelf of a bookcase, the entire bookcase will collapse. Sherry's bookcase has collapsed. Therefore, too much pressure must have been exerted on its bottom shelf.

Which one of the following criticisms best describes a weakness in the argument above?

(A) It supports its conclusion with irrelevant evidence.
(B) It contains a shift in the meaning of the word "collapse" from "partial collapse" to "full collapse."
(C) It concludes that an outcome has been caused by a particular factor that may be only one possible cause of the outcome in question.
(D) It overlooks the possibility that some bookshelves have only one shelf.
(E) It draws an overly broad conclusion from contradictory evidence.

14. College Dean: Parker College provides a great deal of financial aid to its students. This year, every registered student is receiving either a student loan or a scholarship.

Financial Aid Officer: Then all of our registered students have loans this year, because every student who received a scholarship this year also received a student loan.

In which one of the following dialogues below does the pattern of reasoning most closely parallel the reasoning presented in the dialogue above?

(A) Florist: We are pleased with the mixed bouquets that your company delivered. Every bouquet that was delivered this week contained either beautiful orchids or vibrant red roses.
Flower Wholesaler: Then most of the bouquets delivered also contained a silver rose, because most of the bouquets delivered containing orchids this week also contained a silver rose.
(B) Grandmother: I am so proud of this family! Every member of our immediate family has attended either Branston College, the school you attend, or Browning College.
Grandson: Then I may be the first to attend both, because I am thinking of transferring to Browning.
(C) Psychiatrist: The patients on Ward A are generally improving. Each patient now receives either an antidepressant drug or an anti-schizophrenic drug.
Nurse: Then patients on Ward B must also be improving, because those patients also receive either an antidepressant or anti-schizophrenic drug.
(D) Margaret: The hospital is encouraging all patients to eat more vegetables. Tonight every patient ordered either brussel sprouts or corn.
Cafeteria Worker: Every patient who ordered corn tonight also ordered brussel sprouts. So every patient in the hospital ordered brussel sprouts tonight.
(E) Contractor: The architect's design calls for ornate crown moldings to be added to either the West wing or East wing, but not both.
Foreman: The moldings will be more obtrusive on the smaller West wing, so we will have to add them to the East wing.

GO ON TO THE NEXT PAGE.

15. A passenger vehicle is defined as any fully enclosed four-wheeled vehicle with room to transport at least one other passenger in addition to the driver. A semi truck, though it may have enclosed room to transport one non-driving passenger, always has more than four wheels. A jeep, though it may have four wheels and room to carry a driver and additional passengers, is rarely fully enclosed. A postal van, though it may be enclosed and have four wheels, usually does not have room to transport passengers other than the driver.

If the statements in the passage above are true, which one of the following must also be true?

(A) If an automobile is neither a semi truck, nor a jeep, nor a postal van, then it is not a fully enclosed four-wheeled vehicle.

(B) If an automobile is not a semi truck, or a jeep, or a postal van, then it is a passenger vehicle.

(C) If a jeep is fully enclosed with four wheels and room to carry non-driving passengers, then it is both a jeep and a passenger vehicle.

(D) Postal vans are more like passenger vehicles than are semi trucks.

(E) Some postal vans may be considered to be jeeps.

16. Superintendent: Teachers in our district must refrain from intervening in student conflicts in order to encourage students to hone their social interaction skills, except for cases in which physical violence is involved.

Which one of the following is an application of the Superintendent's principle of teacher intervention?

(A) A gym teacher watches while students break up a fistfight between the players of two teams that was ignited over a disputed call.

(B) An English teacher takes the side of one student in an argument concerning a school locker, and sends the other student to the principal's office.

(C) A parent instructs her child who is having difficulty getting along with certain schoolmates to work it out on his own.

(D) A philosophy teacher instigates a heated debate between students holding radically different opinions on a controversial topic.

(E) A math teacher allows a group of students to tease another student about her new haircut.

17. Over the past seven years, private college tuition rates have increased, resulting in a large decrease in private college attendance across the country. Private college revenues, however, have progressively increased in each of the seven years during this period, and researchers predict further increases in the years to come.

Which one of the following, if true, offers the best explanation for the situation described above?

(A) Most private colleges increase tuition rates approximately once every two years.

(B) Attendance at vocational schools generally exceeds attendance at private colleges in most cities.

(C) The increase in tuition rates at private colleges has influenced many prospective students to seek a state scholarship to attend a public university.

(D) The decrease in students attending private colleges over the last seven years has been more than offset by the increases in tuition.

(E) Private colleges gain a larger percentage of their revenue from alumni contributions than do public universities.

GO ON TO THE NEXT PAGE.

18. Children never develop strong self-esteem if they are guided by critical adults. Therefore, if children are guided by uncritical adults, they will develop strong self-esteem.

The flawed pattern of reasoning in which one of the following arguments is most similar to that in the argument above?

(A) Even though Hannah studies hard, she does not make good grades. Therefore, Hannah should not try to make good grades by studying hard.

(B) Telephone solicitors who have bad phone manners do not sell any products. Therefore, telephone solicitors with low sales records must have bad phone manners.

(C) Using the store's new knitting machine, the knitting store owner made twice as many sweaters yesterday as she did the day before. Therefore, if she uses the knitting machine again tomorrow, she will make twice as many sweaters as she did today.

(D) Puppies who are not well-socialized with humans do not interact comfortably with a large group of people. Therefore, the more a puppy is socialized with humans, the more comfortably the puppy will interact with a large group of people.

(E) Individuals who take calcium supplements do not increase their risk of heart disease. Therefore, it stands to reason that individuals who do not take calcium supplements will increase their risk of heart disease.

19. Some sports historians claim that professional tennis players develop unique playing styles that result from a combination of the peculiarities of each player's physical attributes and the influence of coaches during their early adaptation to the game. But when the increase in strength and endurance of modern players is discounted, it becomes readily apparent that the playing styles of the current crop of professional tennis players are no different from the styles of players from previous generations. Clearly, there is a universally efficient tennis style to which all professional tennis players conform.

The argument above is most weakened by which one of the following statements?

(A) The differences in physical attributes among tennis players are even more pronounced than the sports historians believe.

(B) Few current professional tennis players are familiar with the professional tennis players of fifty years ago.

(C) The increased strength of current tennis players contributes more to the development of individual playing styles than does increased endurance.

(D) All of the early coaches of today's professional tennis players were professional tennis players themselves earlier in their lives.

(E) Weight training and greater attention to diet are the primary factors in the increased strength and stamina of the current generation of professional tennis players.

GO ON TO THE NEXT PAGE.

20. Recently, the research and development departments at major pharmaceutical companies have been experimenting with new injections that provide the boost in iron that anemic children need to reverse their condition. These companies have expressed confidence that children who are suffering from anemia will be cured relatively simply through the use of such biochemical supplements.

    In concluding that the biochemical remedy being developed will have its desired effect, the pharmaceutical companies assume that

    (A) major pharmaceutical companies have the primary responsibility to cure childhood anemia

    (B) a low iron level in the body is the major factor influencing the incidence of anemia in children

    (C) a diet rich in iron cannot improve the conditions of children suffering from anemia to the point that biochemical supplements would become unnecessary

    (D) children afflicted with anemia will find out about and submit to injections that can reverse their conditions

    (E) the use of biochemical supplements is the safest way to cure anemia in children

21. When choosing pilots to participate in outer space missions, mission commanders subject applicants to challenging isolation tests. Commanders argue for the necessity of these tests by pointing out that performance on an isolation test may well indicate how safely a pilot could operate a craft during a long voyage home in the event that his or her crewmates were killed during a mission. But an individual's ability to withstand isolation may also arise from an antisocial personality disorder. Therefore, mission commanders should not use this test in selecting pilots.

    The argument above is flawed because it fails to consider each of the following possibilities EXCEPT:

    (A) Isolation tests may give applicants a more realistic idea of the dangers of an actual space mission, prompting some to reevaluate their decision to apply.

    (B) Mission commanders may select more qualified pilots if the pilot tests are not subject to specific limitations.

    (C) An applicant's ability to withstand isolation may indicate a capacity to cope with pressure.

    (D) Good performance in isolation testing may indicate a high level of stamina and endurance in an applicant.

    (E) Applicants who may not perform well under actual isolation conditions may nonetheless perform well in a simulated isolation test.

GO ON TO THE NEXT PAGE.

22. When Harry expressed frustration over the disarray of his baseball card collection, his older brother suggested that he organize the cards in a display album containing special pages to showcase his most valuable cards. After investigating albums available on the market, Harry concluded that his brother's suggestion would not help organize his collection because none of the albums with the special showcase pages were big enough to hold all of his cards.

Which one of the following assumptions is central to the reasoning behind Harry's dismissal of his brother's recommendation?

(A) Larger showcase display albums produced in the past were big enough to hold all of Harry's cards.

(B) Albums without showcase pages are never as effective for organizing baseball cards as are albums containing such pages.

(C) Any album large enough to hold all of Harry's cards would contain enough special showcase pages to display all of his most valuable cards.

(D) Harry's baseball card collection would not be well-organized if displayed in several showcase albums.

(E) Harry's baseball card collection is in disarray because he has more cards in his collection than he did last year.

23. A free press always informs the public of all aspects of a country's current military operations except for cases in which the safety of troops or the success of a mission would be jeopardized by the public's right to know.

Which one of the following adheres most closely to the principle set forth above?

(A) A free press would publish editorials supporting a current military campaign, but could repress dissenting opinions regarding the campaign.

(B) An unfree press would release information on the country's prisoners of war taken during a current military campaign, unless such information would hamper efforts to secure the prisoners' release.

(C) A free press would accurately report the number of casualties suffered on both sides of a battle, but could withhold information regarding the possible targets for a future military strike.

(D) An unfree press would print inflammatory accounts of an international event in order to garner public support for an unpopular war.

(E) A free press would reveal any new information regarding the country's past involvement in secret military operations as soon as that information became available.

GO ON TO THE NEXT PAGE.

24. Lillian has expressed concern about maintaining cohesion in her drug addiction recovery group that she leads at her youth center. She has worked to develop cohesion by encouraging group members to share their experiences openly with the group. But some of the group members take advantage of this opportunity for openness by sharing long violent stories primarily intended to shock the others. Aversion to these stories has caused some members to quit the group. These violent lengthy stories also take time away from other members, preventing them from sharing their experiences. To ensure cohesion in the group, then, Lillian should delineate a specific time slot for each member to speak during each session.

Which one of the following best describes the logical flaw in the argument above?

(A) Two actions that merely occur simultaneously are presented as actions that are causally related.

(B) A hypothesis is presented that runs counter to a proposal related to that hypothesis.

(C) A course of action is proposed to resolve a problem that would in actuality address only one cause of the problem.

(D) A conclusion is based on evidence that is unrelated to the issue at hand.

(E) A conclusion is supported by evidence that contradicts the conclusion.

25. The kuva weave fabric, produced by American Synthetics, Inc., was once thought to be a miraculous invention due to its properties of strength and durability. However, industrial accidents over the past three years have proven that the material is extremely flammable. This discovery dealt a large blow to manufacturers who use the fabric in their products, as the fabric provided an excellent alternative to weaker textiles implicated in many product failures. Since the kuva weave fabric can no longer be used, manufacturers must eliminate all American Synthetics materials from their inventories.

The argument's conclusion is best justified if which one of the following statements is assumed?

(A) Early trial runs that testified to the safety of the kuva weave fabric have subsequently been shown to be incomplete.

(B) All materials produced by American Synthetics contain some form of the kuva weave fabric.

(C) The incidence of industrial fires in manufacturing plants that use the kuva weave fabric is relatively high compared to plants that do not use the fabric.

(D) Kuva weave fabrics are not as durable as originally believed.

(E) Manufacturers are likely to incur product liability lawsuits stemming from accidents caused by flammable products containing the kuva weave fabric.

STOP
IF YOU FINISH BEFORE TIME IS CALLED, YOU MAY CHECK YOUR WORK ON THIS SECTION ONLY. DO NOT WORK ON ANY OTHER SECTION IN THE TEST.

SECTION III
Time—35 minutes
25 questions

<u>Directions:</u> This test is composed of questions that ask you to analyze the logic of statements or short paragraphs. You are to choose as the answer to each question the one choice you consider *best* on the basis of your common-sense evaluation of the statement and its assumptions. Although a question may seem to have more than one acceptable answer, there is only one *best* answer, and it is the one that does not entail making any illogical, extraneous, or conflicting assumptions about the question. These questions do not presuppose any knowledge of formal logic on your part.

1. John's Father: John has complained frequently that his psychoanalysis sessions are not helpful. But John has no knowledge of psychology, and he cannot accurately judge his analyst's techniques. His dissatisfaction in no way indicates that his analyst's methods are unsound and is therefore no reason for him to discontinue his counseling sessions.

    John's Mother: But the purpose of his therapy is to help him adjust to our divorce. While it is true that John is not qualified to assess the analyst's methods, the only way to know if John is being helped by the therapy is through his evaluations of his own progress. If he believes that the sessions are a waste of time, he should stop seeing the analyst.

    Which one of the following is an assumption upon which John's mother's argument depends?

    (A) John's father is correct in concluding that John is unhappy with his counseling sessions.
    (B) Involvement in the therapeutic process does not hamper John's ability to perceive the value of his counseling sessions.
    (C) Psychoanalysts do not need to have extensive qualifications in order to be helpful to their clients.
    (D) If a psychoanalyst employs a sound method, then his or her clients will perceive the counseling sessions as helpful.
    (E) John is entitled to act on any belief concerning his own well-being, regardless of the origin or merits of that belief.

2. Harriet's husband: My wife Harriet has long desired to vacation in a region that is culturally rich. According to this travel brochure, income from the manufacture of industrial documentaries makes Sunshine Valley the second wealthiest region in the state. I have therefore decided to surprise Harriet with accommodations for a two-week trip to Sunshine Valley.

    Which one of the following best characterizes a flaw in Harriet's husband's method of reaching his decision?

    (A) He displays circular reasoning in his attempt to justify his decision.
    (B) He equivocates with respect to a key factor in his decision.
    (C) He uses unreliable and potentially biased evidence as support for his decision.
    (D) He makes a major decision without consulting each party that the decision will affect.
    (E) He fails to demonstrate that his decision is economically feasible.

GO ON TO THE NEXT PAGE.

3. Chocolate is derived from the beans of the tropical New World tree *Theobroma cacao*. When chocolate arrived in Europe around 1500, it was consumed only as a hot drink. In the mid-1800s, however, the Swiss invented the first method for producing it in a solid edible form. Today, millions more pounds of chocolate are produced for eating than for drinking.

Which one of the following can be inferred from the statements above?

(A) Today, Theobroma cacao is grown only in the tropical New World.

(B) When chocolate was introduced to Europe, it was most commonly used in a solid form.

(C) The number of pounds of chocolate made for eating today is greater than the number of pounds of chocolate that were made for drinking during the 1800s.

(D) Chocolate was not consumed in a solid form in the New World during the 1500s.

(E) If the Swiss had not invented a method for producing chocolate in a solid edible form, chocolate would not have become as popular as it is today.

4. Nuclear physicist: *The Fairmarch Times* should make an effort to include the protestors' views in their stories on the nuclear reactor controversy. The *Times* has covered the controversy for a week now, but so far they have presented only the industry side of the issue. No effort has been made to cover the protestors' side. Stories regarding that perspective are completely lacking.

Plant engineer: The protestors' views do not need to be included. The *Times* coverage is fine as is.

Which one of the following statements, if true, most effectively counters the plant engineer's position?

(A) Newspaper reporting must present the views of both sides of a controversy in order to be truly effective.

(B) The *Times* is well known for the quality of its reporting and has presented a number of stories on controversies similar to the nuclear reactor controversy.

(C) Newspaper accounts of the nuclear reactor controversy are read by industry representatives as well as by members of the protest movement.

(D) One of the *Times* reporters covering the nuclear reactor controversy is a former member of the group that has organized protests against the reactor.

(E) Industry groups typically receive more media coverage than do protest organizations.

5. Botanists once claimed that plants of the Faura species required a balanced fertilizer comprised of the following elements to grow: nitrogen, boron, copper, and iron. This approach, however, inhibited Faura propagation.

The conclusion above is supported by each of the following EXCEPT:

(A) Advocating that Faura plants required a balanced composition of the four elements gave the impression that these elements would be sufficient for plant growth, but the plants cannot grow without an appropriate percentage of soluble potash as well.

(B) The omission of zinc from the list of necessary elements conveys the false impression that zinc is less essential to Faura plant growth than are the other four elements.

(C) The emphasis on balance between the four fertilizer elements suggests that the elements should be present in the same amounts, but nitrogen and iron are more essential to Faura plant growth and thus should be present in larger quantities.

(D) The recommendation that the growth-promoting fertilizer should contain copper overlooks the fact that in order for the copper to function effectively, Faura plants must also be fertilized with extremely small amounts of molybdenum.

(E) The inclusion of the element boron in the list served to remind botanists to include this less well-known element in their fertilizer treatment for Faura plants.

GO ON TO THE NEXT PAGE.

6. Three years ago, Ron and Crystal agreed that they would open a restaurant only when they both were prepared to put in the necessary long hours. At the beginning of this year, Ron assumed that Crystal was prepared to make this time commitment, but this erroneous belief was most likely the product of wishful thinking: Crystal just took on a new year-long project at her current job that requires a great deal of travel and takes up most of her focus and energy.

    The argument above is structured to lead to which one of the following conclusions?

    (A) Ron was mistaken when he assumed that Crystal was ready for the time commitment required to open the restaurant.
    (B) Opening a restaurant requires a great deal of personal focus and energy.
    (C) Opening the restaurant would involve even longer hours than Crystal's current job.
    (D) Crystal was never truly interested in opening a restaurant with Ron.
    (E) Ron and Crystal will not open their restaurant this year.

Questions 7–8

Center director: The number of volunteer applications for our elderly care center has doubled over the past five years. This clearly shows that community members are taking a greater interest in working with their aging parents.

Nurse: Unfortunately, my research indicates that just the opposite is true. If you look closely at our records, applications from patients' family members have decreased by 20 percent over the past five years. This would indicate that, contrary to your conclusion, community members' interest in working with their elderly parents has actually decreased.

7. If the statistics cited by both the center director and the nurse are correct, which one of the following must be true?

    (A) The center has had a decline in its patient population over the past five years.
    (B) The quality of care provided to patients at the facility has improved over the past five years.
    (C) The center has received volunteer applications from individuals who are not related to patients at the center.
    (D) The cost of maintaining adequate staff to care for the center's patients has risen enough to warrant the need for additional volunteers.
    (E) Only a small percentage of all the people who apply to volunteer at the center actually assume volunteer positions.

8. Which one of the following, if true, would most seriously weaken the nurse's argument?

    (A) Many community members living near the center have moved into newly constructed housing developments on the outskirts of town.
    (B) Over the past five years, center funding for family-oriented activities has decreased significantly.
    (C) Volunteering in elderly care facilities requires training for which most individuals do not have the time.
    (D) Due to a recent change in policy, many family members who volunteer at the elderly care center do not fill out formal applications.
    (E) The time commitment required by volunteers at elderly care centers is relatively modest compared to other volunteer opportunities in the region.

9. Angie: If Bernard decides to allow his dog Pepe to sleep at the foot of his bed, Pepe will become spoiled, and his current disciplinary problems will worsen.

    Theresa: On the contrary, the dog's behavior would improve. Julian's dog used to chew his furniture at night just like Bernard's dog does now. When Julian followed a trainer's advice and allowed the dog to sleep in his bedroom, at the foot of his bed, his dog calmed down and stopped destroying the furniture within weeks. Similarly, if Bernard allowed his dog to sleep near his bed, the dog's destructive chewing would soon stop.

    In her argument, Theresa does which one of the following?

    (A) She provides a reinterpretation of evidence against a plan by pointing out how that evidence supports the plan.
    (B) She offers a general recommendation to resolve a specific problem.
    (C) She gives a rationale for why following a particular plan would cause difficulties for those who adhere to it.
    (D) She claims that the results of one course of action would be similar to the results of a different course of action.
    (E) She forecasts the results of following a plan in one instance by comparing that situation to a similar situation from the past.

GO ON TO THE NEXT PAGE.

10. A study sponsored by the Association of Educational Consultants has found that students learn and retain 20 percent of material they hear in class, 30 percent of material from written assignments, and 90 percent of material they teach to others. Based on these findings, the principal of Clarkstown Elementary School, interested in enhancing her students' learning and retention of typical grade-school material, has proposed the creation of a new curriculum in which the students conduct all of the teaching.

Which one of the following best characterizes the flaw in the principal's proposal above?

(A) It fails to take into account the fact that under the new curriculum students would still be required to listen in class much of the time.

(B) It mistakenly assumes that written assignments are as valuable a teaching aid as hearing material discussed in the classroom.

(C) It fails to demonstrate how the new curriculum would directly lead to higher test scores.

(D) It overlooks the possibility that the study's findings may be motivated in part by the self-interest of the sponsoring association.

(E) It ignores the fact that most elementary school children are limited in the number of typical grade-school subjects they are qualified to teach.

11. Most students at Carmine University feel overwhelmed by the elective choices available to them in their course offering handbook. This could be because the elective courses are not properly categorized or because the descriptions of the elective courses are too extensive. A review of the lengths of typical elective course descriptions shows that each description is far less lengthy than the length that most students can absorb in any given reading. So it must be that the elective courses are not properly categorized.

Which one of the following is an assumption upon which the argument above depends?

(A) Improper categorization of elective course offerings makes it impossible to choose between those courses.

(B) Some students are overwhelmed by the length of the course descriptions.

(C) Some students find that the coursebook is not well-organized.

(D) The number of elective course offerings provided in the handbook is not the reason the students are overwhelmed.

(E) Most students can absorb rather lengthy course descriptions.

12. Due to a rash of behavioral problems among a particular group of high school students, the principal has canceled all school extracurricular activities for the next month. The organizers of a pep rally scheduled to take place during this period have made the case that this event should be allowed because the increase in school spirit brought about by the pep rally will bond the participants together, which in turn will result in a decrease in aberrant behavior among the students in the long run.

The organizers of the pep rally assume which one of the following in making their argument?

(A) The principal did not intend to include the pep rally among the group of extracurricular activities canceled for the next month.

(B) The students exhibiting behavioral problems will take part in the pep rally.

(C) No other extracurricular activities besides the pep rally should be allowed to take place during the next month unless it can be determined that such activities would bond the students together.

(D) A pep rally is the most effective type of extracurricular activity to deal with the problem of aberrant school behavior.

(E) The principal will allow other canceled events to take place once she sees the beneficial effect that the pep rally has on the students.

GO ON TO THE NEXT PAGE.

13. Some individuals believe that attending cooking school in Southern France teaches one all there is to know about French cooking. All branches of La Terrelle Cooking Academy are located in Southern France. Yet, a recent graduate of La Terrelle did not know how to make bechamel sauce, a sauce widely used in French gourmet cooking.

If the statements above are true, which one of the following must also be true?

(A) Attending cooking school in Southern France does not always teach one all there is to know about French cooking.

(B) No graduate of La Terrelle Cooking Academy has learned all there is to know about French gourmet cooking.

(C) At least one branch of La Terrelle Cooking Academy is located outside of Southern France.

(D) La Terrelle Cooking Academy does not provide an effective education in French gourmet cooking.

(E) Cooking schools located in Southern France teach their students less about French gourmet cooking than do schools located in other parts of the country.

14. Tsumi bats are a rare breed of omnivorous bat found only in highly temperate climates. Most Tsumi bats living in captivity develop endocrine imbalances from their normal zoo diets, which consist mostly of fruits and berries. The healthiest way to feed the bats, therefore, is to provide them primarily with nuts, grubs, and vegetables, and only minimal amounts of fruits and berries.

Which one of the statements below does NOT reflect an assumption upon which the argument depends?

(A) Tsumi bats living in captivity will consume diets that consist of nuts, grubs, and vegetables, but no fruits or berries.

(B) Tsumi bats living in captivity will not be malnourished on diets that contain minimal fruits and berries.

(C) Those who care for Tsumi bats in captivity should avoid feeding them diets that produce endocrine imbalances.

(D) Tsumi bats living in captivity will be adequately nourished on a diet that consists primarily of nuts, grubs, and vegetables.

(E) For Tsumi bats living in captivity, no health problem stemming from diets consisting mostly of nuts, grubs, and vegetables would surpass in severity the health problems associated with endocrine imbalances.

15. Before the advent of writing, each of the isolated clans of the Comaquogue tribe contained master storytellers whose function was to orally transmit the tradition of each clan from one generation to the next. When writing was developed within certain clans of the tribe, the master storytellers of these clans disappeared within a few generations. This stands to reason, considering that the availability of written records obviated the need for masterful oral communicators to keep the tradition of literate clans alive. What has puzzled anthropologists, however, is the total lack of masterful storytellers in modern illiterate Comaquogue clans.

Which one of the following, if true, best helps to explain the puzzling situation mentioned above?

(A) Modern illiterate Comaquogue clan members display personality characteristics that resemble their ancestors more closely than they resemble the characteristics of modern literate Comaquogue clan members.

(B) Modern illiterate Comaquogue clans participate in more ritual gatherings than most modern literate Comaquogue clans do, but they participate in fewer ritual gatherings than did their common ancestors.

(C) Modern illiterate Comaquogue clans are recently descended from long-time literate clans that failed to pass on the skills of reading and writing due to a devastating 75-year war.

(D) The celebrations of modern illiterate Comaquogue clans involve a great deal of singing and dancing, and children are taught clan songs and dances from a very young age.

(E) The traditions of modern illiterate Comaquogue clans are an amalgamation of the cumulative experiences of previous generations plus innovations to the heritage added by the current generation of clan members.

GO ON TO THE NEXT PAGE.

16. Playing in a rock band during college has caused Matthew's grades to suffer, which in turn has decreased his chances of being accepted to a prestigious graduate program. But being active in extracurricular activities such as music can in some cases compensate for bad grades and help a candidate's chances for admission to graduate school by demonstrating that one is a well-rounded individual with varied interests. However, the dean of Wentworth Business School refuses to allow Matthew's participation in the band to positively impact his acceptance chances.

Which one of the following principles best justifies the dean's position?

(A) The consequences of an action can only be evaluated with respect to the possible consequences of an opposing alternative action.

(B) Nothing that causes a condition can be used to compensate for the consequences of that condition.

(C) The overall value of an activity must not be overridden by a negative result of a single aspect of that activity.

(D) A decision that affects the future of an individual must not discount any factor relevant to that decision.

(E) A factor that eliminates a candidate from consideration in one instance should not be used to eliminate that candidate from consideration in a dissimilar situation.

17. Computer scientists have discovered two particularly insidious computer viruses known as the alphatron and b-scan viruses. These viruses typically infiltrate a computer's systems files and prevent files from being stored properly, namely by storing them in incorrect locations. Fortunately, at present there is no evidence to prove that the alphatron and b-scan viruses erase computer files entirely, so computer users who detect one or both of the viruses can rest assured that their files will not be erased.

The argument above is flawed because it

(A) fails to consider the fact that causal relationships that cannot be proven may nonetheless influence people who assume that these relationships exist

(B) fails to consider the possibility that a cause-and-effect relationship may exist even where it has not been demonstrated to exist

(C) neglects to explain the technical mechanisms by which computer files may be erased by viruses

(D) equivocates with respect to a key term

(E) supports its conclusion with evidence that merely restates the conclusion

18. If foods that require refrigeration are not kept at the proper temperature, they can become fertile environments for the growth of bacteria that invariably cause food poisoning in those who ingest it. Since the number of customers stricken with food poisoning at the Panhandler Restaurant rose significantly last month, the Panhandler must have served food that was not stored at the proper temperature.

Which one of the arguments below contains flawed reasoning similar to that in the argument above?

(A) Men over 65 with high blood pressure are at high risk for heart disease. Men over 65 from the Tonare tribe do not have high blood pressure, so they must not be at high risk for heart disease.

(B) Magelli is the only cabinet maker who could have crafted a cabinet similar to this one. But the records show that Magelli died 15 years ago. This cabinet must therefore be a copy.

(C) PaintAll paint is sold at Decorator Outlet stores. PaintAll paint is very popular among housepainters because of its brilliant pigment and its stain-resistant finish. Therefore, Decorator Outlets must sell more cans of PaintAll than any other kind of paint.

(D) Relief-O! is a new pain reliever that has been known to cause blurred vision in some people who take it. When Molly took a pain reliever last week to relieve a migraine headache, she experienced a bout of blurred vision. So the pain reliever Molly took last week must have been Relief-O!

(E) If tigermint is allowed to grow out of control in a garden, it can overrun other plants and kill them. Sally recently noticed that a number of plants in her garden looked better than ever. Clearly, her tigermint problem must be under control.

GO ON TO THE NEXT PAGE.

19. The paintings of French painter Trianne Déjère sold best in the period following the production of *La Triumph*, now Déjère's most famous piece. In the 12-month period preceding the unveiling of this piece, Déjère sold 57 percent of the works she produced in this period, a far greater percentage than in previous years. In the 12-month period following a glowing review of *La Triumph* in a popular magazine, however, Déjère sold 85 percent of the paintings she produced. Interestingly, Déjère's revenue from painting sales was roughly the same in both periods, since she sold the same number of paintings in the 12 months before presenting *La Triumph* as she did in the 12 months following the favorable review.

Which one of the following statements can be properly concluded from the passage, if the information above is true?

(A) Due to the positive review, Déjère was able to charge substantially more for the works produced after *La Triumph* than the works produced before it.

(B) Déjère was more concerned with positive reviews than with increasing the prices of her paintings.

(C) The positive review of *La Triumph* brought Déjère's work to the attention of more art collectors than were previously aware of her work.

(D) Déjère painted fewer works in the 12-month period following the review of *La Triumph* than she had in the 12-month period preceding its unveiling.

(E) Déjère paid more attention to marketing her paintings after *La Triumph* received such a positive reception.

20. Most of the time, Doug has no stomach problems whatsoever when he eats dairy products. So it is unreasonable to claim that he has an allergy to dairy foods solely based on the fact that he has had stomachaches after eating dairy products on several occasions.

The argument above is most similar in reasoning to which one of the arguments below?

(A) A significant number of artists who take this fine arts program are later selected for fellowships to pursue their art. It is therefore unreasonable to believe that there is no connection between taking the program and receiving an art fellowship, even though many artists who attend the program never receive such fellowships.

(B) In some cases, dogs will display anxiety in the moments before an earthquake strikes. But it is unreasonable to conclude on this basis that dogs have the ability to sense earthquakes before they strike. In the vast majority of cases in which dogs display anxiety, no earthquake follows.

(C) Many people who try this diet show no long-term weight loss. So it is unreasonable to believe that this diet is effective for weight loss, even though many people have lost weight on the diet.

(D) Most theories must apply to a large number of cases before they are considered valid theories. It is therefore unreasonable to believe that a theory is valid when it has been applied to only a few cases, even if it has been applied successfully to those cases.

(E) Even though many businesses with decentralized operational structures earn a profit, it is unreasonable to believe the success of these businesses is solely attributable to their choice of operational structure. Only businesses with extensive capital resources can adopt a decentralized operational structure.

GO ON TO THE NEXT PAGE.

21. Membership in the Theta Delta Psi fraternity is easily obtained by those who have previously had strong social connections with existing fraternity members before college. However, one must have attended high school with one or more of the members in order to forge such strong social connections. People who lack these social connections because they have not attended high school with one or more current fraternity members will therefore find it difficult to join the fraternity.

This argument displays flawed reasoning because it neglects to consider the possibility that

(A) many of those who went to high school with Theta Delta Psi fraternity members did not themselves become members of the fraternity

(B) it is more important in the long run to socialize with non-fraternity members than to develop strong connections with fraternity members

(C) it is more difficult to forge social connections with fraternity members than with non-fraternity members

(D) one may easily obtain membership in the fraternity through means other than having strong social connections with existing fraternity members

(E) some current members of the fraternity did not go to high school with other members

22. The advantages of the new farm subsidy laws enacted last year do not warrant their continued enforcement. While these laws have enabled farmers to maintain their incomes despite overproduction and have at the same time stabilized the agricultural market, they will inevitably have negative long-term results stemming from the fact that they will encourage the production of surplus goods and lessen the need for competitive developments in agricultural technology.

In the argument above, the statement about the negative results of the farm subsidy laws plays which one of the following roles?

(A) It is used to disprove evidence cited in support of the laws.

(B) It is used to imply that the laws may not have actually stabilized the agricultural market to the degree previously believed.

(C) It is used to offset plausible reasons for supporting the laws.

(D) It is used to prove that in the absence of the laws the development of agricultural technology will remain a high priority.

(E) It is used as evidence for the claim that market stabilization is less important to the agricultural industry than the development of competitive technology.

GO ON TO THE NEXT PAGE.

23. Participants in Smallville's Annual Easter Egg Hunt search for special plastic Easter eggs containing valuable prizes. The top prize in the contest is an egg containing a three-carat diamond ring. The only way to locate the hidden eggs is by using clues provided to participants by the contest organizers. If every participant receives a complete list of clues for locating the eggs, then no participant will have any more information than any other participant about the whereabouts of the eggs. If no participant has any more information than any other participant, then no participant has a better chance of finding the diamond ring. However, the contest organizers did not provide a complete list of clues for locating the eggs to every participant. Therefore, some participant has a better chance of finding the diamond than all of the other participants.

Which one of the following statements is consistent with the facts of the above argument in such a manner that it points to a flaw in the argument's reasoning?

(A) Even if one participant received a more extensive clue list than all of the other participants, that participant might not necessarily find the diamond ring.

(B) None of the participants received a complete list of clues.

(C) Some participants may share a particular clue with other participants who did not receive that clue.

(D) All of the participants received identical clue lists.

(E) Some participants who did not receive a complete list of clues will nonetheless be able to locate the egg containing the diamond ring.

24. Judges in the Fair Valley Children's Essay Contest disqualified an entry by student Samuel Carter on the grounds that Samuel's entry broke one of the contest rules. The rules specified that entrants should place their names only on the cover page of their essays, and not on any other page, to allow for unbiased judging. Samuel's name was included on each page of his essay. In contesting the judges' decision, Samuel's teacher argued that Samuel's essay should be allowed to qualify because Samuel had recently undergone the traumatic and difficult experience of his parents' divorce.

Samuel's teacher's argument presents a flawed response to the judges' decision because it

(A) presents a conclusion without providing supporting evidence

(B) treats a factor that may cause a certain outcome as if that factor always causes that particular outcome

(C) focuses only on a trivial aspect of the judges' argument

(D) misrepresents evidence presented in the judges' argument

(E) appeals to the judges' emotions instead of addressing their reason for disqualifying Samuel

GO ON TO THE NEXT PAGE.

25. For healthy individuals who wish to improve their overall fitness, cross-training in several sports is more beneficial than training with a single activity. Cross-training develops a wide range of muscle groups, while single-sport training tends to isolate a select few muscles. Single-sport activities, especially those that target slow-twitch muscles, tend to increase the tonic muscle fibers in the body. Cross-training works instead to increase the body's phasic muscle fibers, which burn more calories than tonic muscle fibers.

Which one of the following, if true, best supports the argument above?

(A) In healthy persons, overall fitness increases in proportion to the number of calories burned by the body.

(B) Overall fitness is most effectively improved through athletic training.

(C) Tonic muscle fibers are of greater value to overall fitness than are phasic muscle fibers.

(D) Strenuous physical exertion on a single sport is not recommended for those recovering from a serious illness.

(E) Some slow-twitch muscles contain many phasic muscle fibers.

STOP
**IF YOU FINISH BEFORE TIME IS CALLED, YOU MAY CHECK YOUR WORK ON THIS SECTION ONLY.
DO NOT WORK ON ANY OTHER SECTION IN THE TEST.**

SECTION IV
Time—35 minutes
27 questions

Directions: Each selection in this test is followed by several questions. After reading the selection, choose the *best* response to each question and mark it on your answer sheet. Your replies are to be based on what is *stated* or *implied* in the selection.

The Frankenstein monster is the most recognizable character in the horror genre, if not in all of fiction. Beneath the endless Hollywood adaptations and campy TV shows lies one of the great philosophical and prophetic works of

(5) the nineteenth century. While present generations associate the name Frankenstein with the image of Boris Karloff's movie portrayal of the monster, Mary Shelley's story of the mad doctor Victor Frankenstein is best known to serious readers as a cautionary tale of the danger of man's scientific

(10) hubris.

> I saw—with shut eyes, but acute mental vision—I saw the pale student of unhallowed arts kneeling beside the thing he had put together. I saw the hideous phantasm of a man stretched out, and
> (15) then, on the working of some powerful engine, show signs of life, and stir with an uneasy, half-vital motion. Frightful must it be; for supremely frightful would be the effect of any human endeavor to mock the stupendous mechanism of
> (20) the Creator of the world.

From this horrifying dream during the summer of 1816, Shelley conceived the story in which Victor Frankenstein creates a man from body parts gathered from the dead. The clear clash of science and nature ensues. The book is

(25) structured to refute science and technology's attack on nature, and the most eloquent arguments come from the mouth of the monster himself. For seven brilliant and captivating chapters he tells his story and pleads his case for a companion. His point is clear: man should not create that

(30) for which he is not ready to take responsibility. The mad doctor ultimately refuses to create a mate for the monster, and Shelley portrays the horrifying consequences of man's abdication of responsibility and of arrogantly overstepping the bounds of nature.

(35) How a 19th century young woman crafted the timeless tale that has resonated through every successive generation is still a great mystery. For many years the book was published anonymously, as society could not yet cope with the fact that such a ghastly story was the work of a young woman.

(40) Yet if *Frankenstein* were merely the story of a monster run amok, we likely wouldn't know of it today. Its enduring appeal can best be attributed to the relevance of the themes infused throughout the narrative: alienation of the outcast; the role of visual appearance in society; science versus

(45) nature; and technology as man's salvation. These themes have only grown in importance since the novel's publication in 1818. The seriousness and complexity of these issues, so magically and prophetically synthesized in Shelley's tale of terror, account for the inability to capture in cinematic form

(50) the deep philosophical richness of the book. It can only be hoped that the visual adaptations will not entirely eclipse in the public's mind the genius of the original masterpiece.

1. The passage suggests that the author would most likely agree with which one of the following statements?

    (A) No artistic work can be successfully adapted from one medium into another.

    (B) An artistic work that is likely to shock the sensibilities of its original audience should be presented anonymously.

    (C) An artistic work that does not gain critical acclaim during its period of origin cannot appeal to successive generations.

    (D) The resonance of thematic elements can contribute to the current relevance of an artistic work.

    (E) The complexity and seriousness of an artistic work is directly related to its prophetic capabilities.

GO ON TO THE NEXT PAGE.

2. According to the author, "The clear clash of science and nature" (lines 23–24)

(A) is one of the major elements of *Frankenstein* that is mainly responsible for the current popularity of the cinematic adaptations of that work

(B) is one of the major elements of *Frankenstein* that is absent from the cinematic adaptations of that work

(C) is one of the major elements of *Frankenstein* that forced its author to publish that work anonymously

(D) is one of the major elements of *Frankenstein* that is less relevant today than it was at the time that work was first published

(E) is one of the major elements of *Frankenstein* that has contributed to the enduring appeal of that work

3. The passage implies that each of the following are relevant aspects of the current era EXCEPT:

(A) the belief in the power of technology to aid the human condition

(B) the appreciation of artistic seriousness and complexity

(C) the opposition between science and nature

(D) the physical appearance of societal members

(E) the isolation of individuals from society

4. The author views the cinematic adaptations of Mary Shelley's *Frankenstein* with

(A) unbounded appreciation for their artistic merit

(B) biting derision regarding the motivations of their producers

(C) concern for the effect they may have on the appreciation of their literary precedent

(D) guarded optimism as to the likelihood that they will spawn future efforts that will approach the philosophical richness of the original book

(E) unreserved condescension towards the public's demand for such unsophisticated reworkings of literary masterpieces

5. The author's mention of "Hollywood adaptations" in the first paragraph serves which one of the following functions in the passage as a whole?

(A) It provides a contrast that will resurface later as the basis of the author's central concern.

(B) It introduces the background of a debate that the author will attempt to settle.

(C) It reflects the main criticism of a work of art that the author will seek to deflect.

(D) It offers an example of a form of art that the author will argue is the inevitable successor to literature.

(E) It forms the basis of an artistic movement that the author will argue can never embody the seriousness and complexity of rich philosophical themes.

6. The passage is primarily concerned with

(A) praising a work of art and voicing concern over its possible obsolescence

(B) describing the process by which works of art are degraded when adapted to different forms

(C) outlining the origin of a masterpiece of world literature

(D) arguing that the human race will face serious consequences for arrogantly overstepping the bounds of nature

(E) paying tribute to an art form that has been overshadowed by a more recent art form

GO ON TO THE NEXT PAGE.

Max Weber's work is traditionally viewed as supporting a strictly objective, or value-neutral, approach to investigating social science issues. In many respects, Weber does uphold the notion of scientific objectivity throughout his writings. If
(5) we look at both his writings and his academic philosophies more carefully, however, it becomes clear that Weber's perspective on objectivity is more complicated than the traditional interpretation would have us believe.

The term "objectivity" is used to denote that which lies
(10) outside the framework of subjective perception or bias. It is traditionally defined as that which "exists as an object or fact, independent of the mind." Indeed, Weber does appear to believe in the concept of strict objectivity concerning questions of reality and truth. Weber postulates that there
(15) exists a true reality that is independent of individuals' viewpoints. This position is illustrated through his use of the concept of "ideal types." Ideal types are theoretical constructions that can be used to help the social scientist analyze, investigate, and uncover reality. If ideal types can
(20) help the scientist uncover true reality, then it stands to reason that "true reality" must itself exist.

In discussing our ability to investigate objective reality, however, Weber moves away from the notion of strict objectivity. While he postulates that an objective reality
(25) exists, he seems to believe that our knowledge of this reality cannot be totally objective. According to Weber, individuals can only know truths insofar as we share communal presuppositions about particular realms of knowledge. Our methods of investigating truths are limited to, and
(30) necessarily conditioned by, the value frameworks through which we approach issues. Thus individuals who investigate issues can generate only knowledge that is based upon assumptions and perspectives shared by the community of scholars within which they work. Knowledge may not be
(35) purely subjective or influenced by individual bias, but it is only "objective" insofar as the scientific community upholds its presuppositions.

Weber goes even further afield from the traditional interpretation when discussing how individuals should use
(40) scientific knowledge to guide their actions. On this issue, Weber's stance approaches the purely subjective. He tells us clearly that each person should be free to choose how he or she acts upon the reality discovered by science. This position is put forth in his essay "Science as a Vocation," in which
(45) Weber argues that teachers must avoid personally imposing their own stances on their students, and must rather help students to account for the ultimate meaning of their own conduct. In Weber's view, a professor must sit back and allow his students to reach their own conclusions. When it
(50) comes to action, Weber believes that individuals must make their own decisions and that not even a teacher can assert the truth for another person.

7. Which one of the following best expresses the main idea of the passage?

(A) Weber's theory on the topic of objectivity is more complicated than most other theories of objectivity.

(B) Weber's views on objectivity are useful in supporting arguments against the notion of absolute truth.

(C) Weber never clearly lays out his views on objectivity in his works.

(D) Weber's views on the topic of objectivity are not as straightforward as is typically supposed.

(E) Weber's views on objectivity are inconsistent and therefore cannot provide a reliable foundation for a belief in objective reality.

8. Based on the information in the passage, which one of the following statements would Weber most likely support?

(A) Scientific knowledge about reality can never be completely free of subjective perceptions or biases.

(B) The use of ideal types enables the scientist to perceive his or her own subjective biases concerning reality.

(C) Teachers should refrain from imposing their personal views on students unless students are incapable of reaching their own conclusions.

(D) The concept of objective reality is misleading because reality cannot exist apart from the value frameworks through which reality is perceived.

(E) Ideal types are the only reliable method for investigating objective reality.

9. The primary purpose of the passage is to

(A) resolve a debate over an author's theory
(B) summarize the complexities of an author's view
(C) reconcile two differing views of an author's works
(D) argue against an author's perspective
(E) present and test an author's hypothesis

GO ON TO THE NEXT PAGE.

10. According to the passage, which one of the following is true about Weber's views on how individuals should use scientific knowledge to guide their actions?

    (A)   Individuals may choose their own courses of action freely unless they are unable to account for the ultimate meaning of their own conduct.

    (B)   Individuals should distrust scientific knowledge when making decisions that will determine their personal actions.

    (C)   Individuals should be encouraged to determine their own courses of action based upon discovered scientific truth.

    (D)   If a teacher determines that a particular course of action would be most beneficial for a given student, he or she should direct the student towards this course of action.

    (E)   Teachers should follow their students' leads in determining the most appropriate course of action for themselves.

11. Which one of the following best describes the organization of the passage?

    (A)   An explanation is put forth and then rejected in favor of a second explanation.

    (B)   An author's viewpoint is first criticized and then reclaimed for its redeeming values.

    (C)   An argument is put forth and then negated by the presentation of conflicting evidence.

    (D)   A hypothesis is advanced and then strengthened through empirical testing.

    (E)   An interpretation of a view is presented and support for this interpretation is provided.

12. Which one of the following is mentioned in the passage as evidence for the assertion that knowledge of reality cannot be totally objective?

    (A)   Scientific methods of investigation are always influenced by the subjective biases of the community of scholars within which the scientist operates.

    (B)   Scientific methods of investigation are not legitimate unless they can be proven to be strictly objective.

    (C)   Scientific investigations use ideal types, which at best help to approximate reality.

    (D)   In order for truth to be objective, it must be independent of the mind of the investigating scientist.

    (E)   The concept of objective reality is illusory.

13. The author presents the traditional interpretation of Weber's view of objectivity in the first paragraph primarily in order to

    (A)   dismiss the relevance of all previous scholarship on Weber that does not accord with the author's line of reasoning

    (B)   argue that the concept of objective reality has been historically misunderstood by social scientists

    (C)   provide background for a contrasting interpretation of Weber's beliefs central to the argument that follows

    (D)   show how critics think that Weber's value-neutral approach to the notion of objectivity is more complicated than is traditionally believed

    (E)   illustrate the gist of a notion under attack that the author will subsequently attempt to vindicate

GO ON TO THE NEXT PAGE.

KAPLAN

If one always ought to act so as to produce the best possible circumstances, then morality is extremely demanding, perhaps overly so. No one could plausibly claim that at every moment of their lives they have acted with
(5) maximum efficiency to improve the condition of the world. Since it would seem strange to punish those intending to do good by sentencing them to an impossible task, some ethical philosophers have concluded that morality has an "overdemandingness" problem.

(10)   From an analytic perspective, the potential extreme demands of morality are not a "problem." A theory of morality is no less valid simply because it asks great sacrifices. In fact, it is difficult to imagine what kind of constraints could be put on our ethical projects. Shouldn't
(15) we reflect on our base prejudices, and not allow them to provide boundaries for our moral reasoning? Thus, it is tempting to simply dismiss the "overdemandingness" objection. However, in *Demands of Morality*, Liam Murphy takes this objection seriously.

(20)   Murphy does not tell us what set of "firm beliefs" we ought to have. Rather, he speaks to an audience of well-intentioned but unorganized moral agents, and tries to give them principles that represent their considered moral judgments. Murphy starts with an initial sense of right and
(25) wrong, but recognizes that it needs to be supplemented by reason where our intuitions are confused or conflicting. Perhaps Murphy is looking for the best interpretation of our convictions, the same way certain legal scholars try to find the best interpretation of the U.S. Constitution.

(30)   This approach has disadvantages. Primarily, Murphy's arguments, even if successful, do not provide the kind of motivating force for which moral philosophy has traditionally searched. His work assumes and argues in terms of an inner sense of morality, and his project seeks to deepen
(35) that sense. Of course, it is quite possible that the moral viewpoints of humans will not converge, and that some humans have no moral sense at all. Thus, it is very easy for the moral skeptic to point out a lack of justification and ignore the entire work.

(40)   On the other hand, Murphy's choice of a starting point avoids many of the problems of moral philosophy. Justifying the content of moral principles and granting a motivating force to those principles is an extraordinary task. It would be unrealistic to expect all discussions of moral philosophy to
(45) derive such justifications. Projects that attempt such a derivation have value, but they are hard pressed to produce logical consequences for everyday life. In the end, Murphy's strategy may have more practical effect than its more traditional counterparts, which do not seem any more likely
(50) to convince those that would reject Murphy's premises.

14. The passage is primarily concerned with

(A) highlighting the disadvantages in adopting a philosophical approach
(B) illustrating a philosophical debate by comparing two current theories
(C) reconciling the differences between two schools of philosophical thought
(D) reviewing scholarly opinions of an ethical problem and proposing a new solution
(E) evaluating the merits of a model of ethical inquiry

15. The author suggests which one of the following regarding Murphy's philosophy?

(A) The application of Murphy's philosophy to the situations of two different groups would help to solve the problems of one group but not of the other.
(B) The application of Murphy's philosophy to the situations of two different groups could result in the derivation of two radically different moral principles.
(C) The application of Murphy's philosophy to the situations of two different groups would be contingent on the two groups sharing the same fundamental beliefs.
(D) The application of Murphy's philosophy to the situations of two different groups could reconcile any differences between the two groups.
(E) The application of Murphy's philosophy to the situations of two different groups would not provide definitive recommendations for either group.

16. The passage implies that a moral principle derived from applying Murphy's philosophy to a particular group would be applicable to another group if

(A) the first group recommended the principle to the second group
(B) the moral viewpoints of the two groups do not converge
(C) the members of the second group have no firmly held beliefs
(D) the second group shares the same fundamental beliefs as the first group
(E) either group has no moral beliefs at all

GO ON TO THE NEXT PAGE.

17. According to the passage, the existence of individuals who entirely lack a moral sense has which one of the following consequences?

    (A) It confirms the notion that moral principles should be derived from the considered judgments of individuals.
    (B) It suggests a potential disadvantage of Murphy's philosophical approach.
    (C) It supports Murphy's belief that reason is necessary in cases in which intuitions are conflicting or confused.
    (D) It proves that more traditional approaches to ethical theorizing will have no more influence over the behavior of individuals than will Murphy's philosophical approach.
    (E) It is a necessary consequence of the "overdemandingness" problem.

18. The passage suggests that Murphy would agree that the application of reason is necessary for forming moral principles when

    (A) the beliefs of one group supersede the beliefs of another
    (B) people's firmly held beliefs are conflicting or confused
    (C) the belief system of a group conflicts with an overriding ethical principle
    (D) individuals have no moral sense at all
    (E) the demands of morality seem too extreme

19. A school board is debating whether or not to institute a dress code for the school's students. According to Murphy, which one of the following actions would constitute the best way to come to an ethical decision regarding the matter?

    (A) consulting the fundamental beliefs of the board members
    (B) analyzing the results of dress codes instituted at other schools
    (C) surveying the students as to whether or not they would prefer a dress code
    (D) determining whether or not a dress code has ever been instituted in the school's history
    (E) determining the best interpretation of the guarantees found in the U.S. Constitution

20. The primary purpose of the last paragraph of the passage is to

    (A) describe the method of determining the best interpretation of an individual's firmly held beliefs
    (B) explain the origin of the "overdemandingness" objection
    (C) identify advantages associated with Murphy's approach to ethics
    (D) reconcile two opposing schools of philosophical thought
    (E) characterize Murphy's response to the "overdemandingness" objection

21. The passage suggests that the author would be most likely to agree with which one of the following statements?

    (A) Arguing from a set of firmly held beliefs is an important element of traditional moral philosophy.
    (B) Philosophical works that attempt to discover a motivating force behind moral principles have no value.
    (C) No one who lacks a moral sense can make a significant contribution to an ethical debate.
    (D) Those who are not well-intentioned are unlikely to be influenced by traditional approaches to moral philosophy.
    (E) The "overdemandingness" objection does not represent a serious problem for traditional moral philosophy.

GO ON TO THE NEXT PAGE.

One of the many remarkable properties of water is the unwillingness of bodies of water of substantially different temperature to mix together. This property is responsible for the formation in freshwater lakes of a phenomenon known

(5) as the thermocline, a phenomenon that can play an important role in a lake's summertime ecology. Consider the annual temperature fluctuations in a typical deep-water impoundment in the southern United States. In late winter, usually sometime in February or March, whatever ice may

(10) have previously formed at the surface of the lake melts, and the water temperature measures a uniform 38–42 degrees. Wave action stirs oxygen into the water at the lake's surface, and the temperature uniformity allows distribution of this dissolved oxygen to all depths. With oxygen plentiful, many

(15) of the reservoir's fish species, both predator and forage, are found throughout the water column.

The windy, sunny days of early spring quickly warm the lake's surface. As the surface temperature increases, that water expands. Because 50-degree water is lighter than 40-

(20) degree water, a layer of warmer water builds at the surface of the lake, resting like a pillow on the mass of colder water below. The pillow of warm surface water slowly increases in thickness, as heat is transferred into the depths by the limited stirring of wave action.

(25) By early summer, a remarkable stratification has occurred. A sharp boundary separates two independent bodies of water within the lake. The boundary is a temperature gradient called the thermocline, and it acts as a barricade to prevent any further mixing of oxygen into the

(30) chilly depths. The depth of the thermocline fluctuates with air temperatures and the prevailing winds. On July 1, the water temperature might be 86 degrees at the surface, 84 degrees at 10 feet, and 82 degrees at 20 feet—but at 24 feet, the temperature has plunged to 65 degrees. When winter

(35) ended, the depths were well-oxygenated and populated with fish. But as the thermocline set up in late spring, the supply of oxygen to the depths was abruptly shut off. In summer, the temperature barrier prevents oxygen from circulating downward from the surface to replace the oxygen consumed

(40) by fish and dying zooplankton. In order to survive, fish are forced upward into the relatively narrow zone between the thermocline and the surface.

The cold nights of autumn reverse the trend, as the surface cools to the point that it is heavier than the water

(45) below the thermocline. This initiates a process known as the turnover: A current of richly oxygenated water plunges to the bottom of the reservoir, forcing stagnant water back to the surface. The lake reaches equilibrium by early winter and remains there until the process repeats itself the following

(50) spring.

22. The passage suggests that which one of the following can be inferred about dissolved oxygen in a lake?

(A) The colder the water, the less dissolved oxygen it can hold.

(B) There is always more dissolved oxygen within six feet of the surface than at 60 feet beneath the surface.

(C) The formation of ice can completely block the supply of dissolved oxygen.

(D) Dissolved oxygen is not necessary for organisms other than fish and zooplankton.

(E) Wave action at the surface is a significant source of dissolved oxygen.

23. Which one of the following most accurately describes the organization of the passage?

(A) A problem is described, its potential effects are summarized, and a possible solution is critiqued.

(B) A property is introduced, a process resulting from the property is described, and an effect is explored.

(C) A process is outlined and then described in greater detail, and its benefits are explained.

(D) A problem is defined, and its implications are considered and generalized.

(E) A chronology is described, various events are fit into the chronology, and predictions are made.

24. The author states in the second paragraph that 50-degree water is lighter than 40-degree water primarily in order to

(A) refute a commonly held theory regarding the effects of temperature increases in the water near lake surfaces

(B) explain why warmer water tends to sink below layers of colder water in lakes of the southern United States

(C) prove that the number of fish occupying different water levels in freshwater lakes is directly related to the formation of the thermocline

(D) show how the decreased oxygen level in the depths of freshwater lakes during certain seasons could lead to the death of zooplankton

(E) supply background information relevant to an explanation of a step in the lake stratification process

GO ON TO THE NEXT PAGE.

25. The passage suggests that the effects of temperature stratification

(A)   would be relevant to the interests of fisheries managers
(B)   cannot be predicted on an individual lake
(C)   represent the most important factor influencing a lake's ecology
(D)   become more pronounced as a lake gets older
(E)   are most severe in the lakes of the southern United States

26. Which one of the following is not mentioned in the passage as a step in the yearly lake stratification process?

(A)   Fish congregate in the water layer above the thermocline in the summer.
(B)   Water temperatures achieve a general uniformity by late winter.
(C)   The thermocline reaches its maximum depth by early summer.
(D)   Oxygen levels decline in the layer beneath the thermocline.
(E)   The fall turnover replaces stagnant water in the depths with oxygen-rich water.

27. The author is primarily interested in discussing

(A)   the effect of fish and other aquatic organisms on a phenomenon known as the thermocline
(B)   the relationship between a lake's ecology and water purity
(C)   the contribution of the thermocline to overfishing in southern lakes
(D)   an effect of the seasonal warming and cooling of water in freshwater lakes
(E)   the changes in a lake's water temperature caused by fluctuating oxygen levels

STOP
**IF YOU FINISH BEFORE TIME IS CALLED, YOU MAY CHECK YOUR WORK ON THIS SECTION ONLY.
DO NOT WORK ON ANY OTHER SECTION IN THE TEST.**

ANSWER KEY ON FOLLOWING PAGE

PRACTICE TEST TWO ANSWER KEY

Section I Logic Games	Section II Logical Reasoning	Section III Logical Reasoning	Section IV Reading Comprehension
1. E	1. E	1. B	1. D
2. B	2. C	2. B	2. E
3. B	3. A	3. D	3. B
4. B	4. D	4. A	4. C
5. C	5. B	5. E	5. A
6. B	6. A	6. E	6. A
7. A	7. C	7. C	7. D
8. D	8. A	8. D	8. A
9. B	9. E	9. E	9. B
10. D	10. C	10. E	10. C
11. A	11. E	11. D	11. E
12. E	12. D	12. B	12. A
13. C	13. C	13. A	13. C
14. E	14. D	14. A	14. E
15. D	15. C	15. C	15. B
16. A	16. E	16. B	16. D
17. A	17. D	17. B	17. B
18. B	18. E	18. D	18. B
19. C	19. D	19. D	19. A
20. C	20. D	20. B	20. C
21. D	21. E	21. D	21. D
22. C	22. D	22. C	22. E
23. D	23. C	23. D	23. B
24. B	24. C	24. E	24. E
	25. B	25. A	25. A
			26. C
			27. D

KAPLAN

PRACTICE TEST TWO EXPLANATIONS

Section I: Logic Games Explanations

GAME 1—Design Selections

The Action

A designer picks two out of five appliance designs and two out of three cabinet designs. So this a Grouping game of selection, with the minor wrinkle that we'll have to keep track of appliances and cabinets, too. The *Key Issues* are:

* Which appliance designs can, must, and cannot be selected?
* Which cabinet designs can, must, and cannot be selected?
* Which designs can, must, and cannot be selected with which other designs?

The Initial Setup

A list of entities with two columns—one for those that are selected and one for those that aren't—will do just fine. We can distinguish appliance from cabinet designs by writing the former in ALL CAPS.

H J K L M		t v w
pick 2		pick 2
IN		OUT

The Rules

1) Be careful when you see "only if." When translated into a standard "if-then," the term that follows "only if" will follow the "then." So Rule 1 means that if H is selected, then both J and w must be selected. Taking the contrapositive, if either J or w is absent, we cannot have H.

2) "M cannot be selected unless J is selected" means that if M is selected, then J is selected. So if J isn't selected, then M isn't selected, either.

3) Rule 3 is a little easier: v implies H, and not H implies not v.

Key Deductions

There really isn't much we can deduce for sure. All the rules are hypothetical, so this isn't a great game to plumb the depths looking for deductions. We can combine Rules 1 and 3 to deduce that if v is selected, the selected designs must be v, H, J, and w. But this isn't such a big deal. Having done some investigation, we can hit the questions, keeping in mind that we're picking two of each design type.

The Final Visualization

H J K L M		t v w
pick 2		pick 2
IN		OUT

H → J and w
no w or no J → no H
M → J
no J → no M
V → H, J, w
no w or no J or no H → no V

The Big Picture

- The first game in a section isn't always the easiest, but as it happens, this was a good place to start. A straightforward grouping game can help you gain some quick points and boost your confidence.

- Never forget about the numbers governing a grouping game. This game seems wide open until you remember that the initial paragraph specifies that the designer selects exactly two of each type.

- Know how to interpret and manipulate formal logic statements! "X cannot be selected unless Y is selected" simply means that X —> Y. The contrapositive of Rule 1 offered another challenge. Remember that the negation of "A and B" is "not A or not B." In other words, if it isn't the case that they are both selected, then it must be the case that one or the other (or both) is not selected.

The Questions

1. E

First up is a straightforward hypothetical. Combining Rules 1 and 3, as we did in the Key Deductions, we see that if v is selected, then the complete group is v, H, J, and w. So choice (E) is correct. The others are impossible.

Remember:

- If you can handle formal logic statements, questions like this one are easy. But if you can't, Logic Games will be impossible. Make sure you have the basics under control before test day.
- Always save your work. The correct answer to a

hypothetical question is a scenario that could be true. So we know now that v, H, J, and w can be selected together. Having an acceptable scenario on hand often helps to eliminate wrong choices later on.

2. B

There's not much to do here except hit the choices one by one. But there's no need to handle this question second. Chances are, if we hit it last, we'll be able to eliminate most of the wrong choices by using our previous work. But, if you attacked this question right away, you might have done something like this:

Choice (A) could be true and thus must be wrong, since we saw H and J together in the last question. (B), however, is impossible. If we have H and M, then we can select no more appliance designs. But Rule 1 says that when we select H we need to select J. So (B) doesn't work and must be correct. For the record, (C), (D), and (E) are out, because if we select t and w as our cabinet designs, we can select any of these choices without violating any rules.

Remember:

- It's always worth seeing if your previous work can help you knock off a few choices.
- You don't have to answer the questions in the order in which they appear on the page! Here, the question wasn't too brutal, anyway. But in another game, this strategy could be a real time-saver.

3. B

Without J, we can't have either H or M (contrapositives of Rules 1 and 2). Having eliminated three of the five appliance designs, we must select the remaining two. So K and L must be selected. Since we've rejected H, we must also reject v (contrapositive of Rule 3). Now we must select the only two cabinet designs left: t and w. That's the entire set.

(B) must be true, while the other choices are impossible.

Remember:

- Always work out the contrapositive of if/then rules, and then use those contrapositives to help you answer the questions quickly.

4. B

If L is selected, then we can select only one more appliance design. But if we select H, we must select J. And if we select M, we must select J. Either way, we'd select three appliance designs, so we can select neither H nor M. Having rejected H, we must also reject v, which in turn means we must select both t and w. So there are two possibilities: LKtw and LJtw. (B) has it right.

Remember:

- As you go through a game's questions, you should become familiar with the way the rules work. By now, you should be used to selecting t and w when you reject H, since that's what happened in the previous question.

5. C

For this one question, part of Rule 1 doesn't apply. Selecting H still requires us to select w, but now we can have H without J. Let's look at the choices.

(A) and (B) have the same problem. If we select M, we must select J, and so these two choices force us to select three appliance designs. (C), however, is possible. Selecting v means we must select H and therefore w. Now that we can select H without selecting J, HKvw is an acceptable arrangement, and so (C) is correct.

For the record, (D) is out, since selecting v means we must select H, selecting M means we must select J, and we have three appliance designs again. Selecting v means we must select H, which means

we must select w, and now we have three cabinet designs, and so (E) doesn't work, either.

Remember:

- Questions that change a rule should be handled last, if at all. You wouldn't want your work on this question to pollute your thinking on the other questions.

GAME 2—Family Portrait

Rules and Deductions

This game is perhaps not as difficult (or as open-ended) as it may first appear if you realize the implications of the second rule, the one about the placement of Helen. We know that there must be exactly two people between Helen and Feisal which means either —

$$\underline{H} \_ \_ \underline{F} \text{ or } \underline{F} \_ \_ \underline{H}$$

and Helen is two places to the left of Gillian, or

$$\underline{H} \_ \underline{G}$$

When you combine these two, the first combination proves impossible:

$$\underline{H} \_ \underline{G} \underline{F} \text{ No good!}$$

—since we're told that Feisal cannot stand next to Gillian (Rule 1). The only combination that will work is:

$$\underline{F} \_ \_ \underline{H} \_ \underline{G}$$

—which is therefore a constant for every question! The only thing up in the air is where the remaining space goes, but it can only be at either end of what we've got so far. If you see this, you have only to note the conditions in the other rules:

no KG or GK   always IF or FI

—and you are ready to go.

 269

The Questions

6. B

Use the Kaplan strategy for acceptability questions. Take each rule and test it against each choice. In this case, the requirement that Feisal and Gillian do not stand next to each other (Rule 1) eliminates (E). Exactly two people must stand between Helen and Feisal (Rule 2), and so (A) and (C) must be wrong. Khalia and Gillian do not stand next to each other (Rule 4), which kills (D), and we're left with (B), the correct answer.

7. A

Being told that Laura is in position one solves the problem of the remaining space. The arrangement must be:

L F _ _ H _ G

Since Ian stands next to Feisal (Rule 3), we can fill in:

L F I _ H _ G

—and since Gillian and Khalia do not stand next to each other, the only space for Khalia is between Ian and Helen, leaving only one spot remaining for Jeremy:

L F I K H J G

Jeremy is between Gillian and Helen, and the answer is (A).

8. D

You have to be extra cautious when two questions in a game—especially two back-to-back—seem somewhat similar, even identical. Don't automatically assume that there's no further work that can be done. At first glance it looks like the operational arrangement here is identical to that in question 2, and indeed the only way to put Laura next to Feisal is to add the remaining space on the far left. However, the final arrangement of people that we developed for the previous question is not the only

one that works here. Ian could also fulfill rule 3 by being in position one, giving us these two options:

L F I K H J G

or

I F L K H J G

Looking at these two options, what cannot be true? Jeremy is not between Helen and Ian in either scenario, and so (D) is impossible. As for the others, Gillian must be in position seven, which kills (A), and the other three are possibly true.

9. B

Once you've added Jeremy to the far right—

F _ _ H _ G J

—solving the problem is really a matter of three steps: Ian must be second, because of Rule 3; Khalia must be third, because of Rule 4; and Laura must be fifth, because that's the only space left. There is one person between Jeremy and Laura: Choice (B).

10. D

To put Ian and Jeremy next to each other, we of course need two adjacent spaces. Whichever end the remaining space is placed on, we won't get two adjacent spaces that way, so forget about that space for the moment. The only possible places for Ian and Jeremy are between Feisal and Helen, and since Ian stands next to Feisal:

F I J H _ G

Now we can deal with the seventh space. If it goes on the far right, we have to place Khalia next to Gillian, which is forbidden. Therefore the seventh space (and Khalia, for that matter) must go on the far left, leaving Laura to go between Helen and Gillian. There are four people between Laura and Khalia: Choice (D).

11. A

Once again, the only possible locations for the adjacent Laura and Khalia are between Feisal and Helen, though this time we don't know which one goes to Feisal's right. But Laura and Khalia are in there. Now we've got to get Ian next to Feisal—on Feisal's left, in other words—leaving the space between Gillian and Helen for Jeremy. There is no one between Gillian and Jeremy: Choice (A).

12. E

Use your previous work. You'll have to tackle this question choice-by-choice, but that process will go much faster if you don't repeat the work you did for previous questions. We're asked for the choice that cannot be true, and so the possible scenarios we worked out in previous questions can help us eliminate choices. The correct answer to the "acceptability" question gives us one of those possible scenarios. From question 1, we know the following scenario is possible:

$$\underline{F}\,\underline{I}\,\underline{K}\,\underline{H}\,\underline{J}\,\underline{G}\,\underline{L}$$

Does this help? Sure. We now know that Gillian can stand next to both Jeremy and Laura, which eliminates (B). We also know that Jeremy can stand next to Gillian and Helen, and so (C) is possible.

Choice (A) asks if it's possible for Feisal to stand next to Ian and Laura. Back in question 2, we worked out this scenario, which shows that (A) is possible:

$$\underline{L}\,\underline{F}\,\underline{I}\,\underline{K}\,\underline{H}\,\underline{J}\,\underline{G}$$

(D) asks us whether Khalia can stand next to both Feisal and Laura. Khalia and Laura cannot be on Feisal's left, since that would force Gillian into a non-existent eighth position:

$$\underline{L}\,\underline{K}\,\underline{F}\,\underline{I}\,\_\,\underline{H}\,\_\,\mathit{G}?$$

$$\underline{\mathit{no\ good}}$$

So, if (D) is possible at all, then Khalia must be on Feisal's right. After placing Ian and Khalia, there's only one spot open for Jeremy, and we're left with this possible scenario:

$$\underline{I}\,\underline{F}\,\underline{K}\,\underline{L}\,\underline{H}\,\underline{J}\,\underline{G}$$

Since (A) through (D) are possible, (E) must be the right answer, and on Test Day, you would just select it. In case you're interested in why Laura cannot stand next to both Feisal and Jeremy, here it goes: We know from working out (D) that Laura and Jeremy cannot stand on Feisal's right, since this would force Gillian into an eighth position. So, if (E) is possible at all, then Laura must be on Feisal's right. After placing Ian and Khalia, we're left with this scenario:

$$\underline{I}\,\underline{F}\,\underline{L}\,\underline{J}\,\underline{H}\,\_\,\mathit{G}$$

There's only one space left for Khalia, and unfortunately, that space is next to Gillian. Since Khalia cannot stand next to Gillian, (E) is impossible.

GAME 3—Sled Dogs

The Action

Five sled dogs are hitched together as the diagram indicates. We have to keep track of the positions of the sled dogs, so this game isn't too different from a Sequence game; it's just that the entities are arranged in an odd formation instead of in a line. If we had to assign a game type here, we'd call this a spatial Sequence game, but that's not important. What is important is that you identify the *Key Issues*:

• Which sled dogs can, must, and cannot occupy which positions?

• Which sled dogs can, must, and cannot be adjacent to which other sled dogs?

The Initial Setup

When the test maker gives you a picture, use it! The picture provided is a good framework for organizing your work. Add a list of entities, and you're set.

G H J K L

The Rules

1) This rule just defines "adjacency." This is pretty intuitive: sled dogs that are connected to the same harness are adjacent.

2) Rule 2 brings in a new distinction: experienced and inexperienced. So now the game has become a bit more complicated. We can keep track of the experienced/inexperienced distinction by making a note under our list of entities. "2 XP, 3 non-XP" is one way to do this.

3) Here's one we can build in directly. We can fill in an "XP" to remind us that the dog in position 1 is experienced.

4) and 5) These rules can also be built in directly, by adding an "XP" to J and a "non-XP" to G.

6) Rule 6 is straightforward enough. The two experienced dogs cannot be adjacent. "No XP adjacent" is one way to represent this.

7) Rule 7 is similar to Rule 6: K and L aren't adjacent. "No KL adjacent" will do.

Key Deductions

Since the experienced dogs aren't adjacent, and since an experienced dog is in position 1, positions 2 and 3 are occupied by inexperienced dogs. Therefore, J's assignment is limited. J is experienced, and so J can't be in either 2 or 3, and so J must be in 1, 4, or 5. Also, we know that since G is inexperienced, G can't be in position 1. That's plenty heading into the questions.

The Final Visualization

G(non-XP) H J(XP) K L

2 XP, 3 non-XP
No XP adjacent
No KL adjacent

The Big Picture

- This wasn't an easy game, but it was easier than the previous game. This game was probably best handled third, after games 1 and 4.

- Games that require you to arrange characters in an odd formation aren't common on the LSAT, but they have appeared from time to time. Expect that your sequencing skills will help you with such games. You're still putting things in order, even though the order may not be a straight line.

- When the entities themselves are broken up into different categories, make sure you recognize the distinction. You can bet that most of these questions will require you to recognize who must be experienced.

- To find deductions, you must translate the rules to find out what they mean in the context of the game. If the experienced dogs aren't adjacent, and we know that an experienced dog is in 1, what must be true? This is the kind of active thinking that leads to points.

The Questions

13. C

This question is a quick battle if you've done good work up front. We can't have an inexperienced dog in position 1, so (A) and (B) are wrong. Positions 2 and 3 must be occupied by inexperienced dogs, so (D), which omits the third position, and (E), which omits the second position, must be wrong. (C) is the only choice that remains, and yes, positions 2, 3, and 4 could all have inexperienced dogs.

Remember:

- Don't do more work than necessary! If you can eliminate four choices, pick the next one without further delay.

14. E

With J in 5, we have the experienced/inexperienced breakdown set. J is experienced, and position 1 has an experienced dog, and so positions 2, 3, and 4 must all have inexperienced dogs. The rest of the setup is pretty wide open, but (E) is inferable. Position 4 has an inexperienced dog, and so (E) is correct.

(A), (B), and (C) are all eliminated by this scenario:

(D) is impossible. As we deduced above, position 3 is always occupied by an inexperienced dog.

Remember:

- As long as the deductions are coming to you, keep making them. But as soon as you're stuck, consult the choices. You may have deduced the correct answer.

15. D

With L and H in 4th and 5th, J is forced into position 1, since otherwise J would be adjacent to an experienced dog in 1. That leaves G and K to be placed, but we know that K and L can't be adjacent, and so K must be in 3 and G must be in 2.

So all the choices must be true except (D). G and H aren't adjacent.

Remember:

- To make deductions, think about which rules and entities might be relevant. With slots 4 and 5 taken, you should think about where you can place J. With G and K yet to be placed, you should remember Rule 7, which states that K and L are not adjacent. Knowing where to look is often half the battle.

16. A

If K is in 5, what would guarantee that an experienced dog is in 4? From here, trying the choices is just as fast as anything else, and luckily, we don't have far to search. We have to separate K and L, so if G were in 2, then L would have to go in 1. That means J must go in 4, and so (A), if true, would guarantee that an experienced dog (i.e., Jinook) would be in 4.

(B), (C), (D), and (E) If J were first, L were second, and either G or H were third, then the other of the G/H pair must be fourth. Either way, K could be an experienced dog, and since we have only 2 experienced dogs (and one is first), all these choices fail to guarantee that the dog in position 4 is experienced.

Remember:

- Don't be afraid to postpone work on a tough question. Sometimes, a game that isn't that tough contains a killer question or two.

17. A

If J is next to K and L, where could J be? J can't be first, since that would place K and L in 2 and 3, next to each other. So J must be in either 4 or 5. If J is in 4, then K and L occupy the only positions adjacent to J: positions 2 and 5. That leaves G and H to place. G can't be in 1 (Rules 3 and 5), so G would go in 3, and H would go in 1. If J is in 5, we get much the same story: K and L split positions 3

and 4, G still can't go in 1 and so must go in 2, and H again goes in 1. So either way, Hira is adjacent to G, and choice (A) is correct.

(B) is impossible, since H is in 1 and J is in either 4 or 5.

(C) and (D) both could be true but need not be true—both K and L could be in either 4 or 5.

(E) also need not be true, since J and L could occupy positions 4 and 5.

Remember:

- Sometimes, you can't make any solid deductions, but you can break down a question into two distinct scenarios. That's okay. Work out those scenarios and you'll know what must, could, and cannot be true.

GAME 4—Animal Examinations

The Action

We have seven animals being examined, one at a time. Sounds like another basic sequence game. The familiar *Key Issues* are:

- What is the order of the examinations?
- Which animals could, must, and cannot be examined before and after which other animals?

The Initial Setup

Seven slots representing the seven exams, plus a list of entities, will do just fine:

P Q R S T V W

___ ___ ___ ___ ___ ___ ___
 1   2   3   4   5   6   7

The Rules

1) P is right before T. "PT" will do.

2) and 3) These rules are in if/then form, which means that we should determine their contrapositives, too. Since having Q 5th means that V is 6th, we also know that if V isn't 6th, Q cannot be 5th. Similarly, since having S 2nd means that P is 3rd, we also know that if P isn't 3rd, then S isn't 2nd.

4) This is easy enough to build in directly, with arrows pointing to both the 4th and 6th positions.

5) Rule 5 can also be built in directly. "No V" in the 1st and 5th positions will do.

Key Deductions

This one stays pretty wide open. There aren't major blocks of entities, the rules aren't too concrete, and lots of stuff is possible. A little time spent here wasn't wasted, but in general, simple sequencing games tend not to have big deductions that fill in large chunks of the picture.

The Final Visualization

P Q R S T V W

No V				No V		
1	2	3	4	5	6	7

W

PT
If Q 5th then V 6th
If V not 6th then Q not 5th
If S 2nd then P 3rd
If P not 3rd then S not 2nd

The Big Picture

- Never rush through the rules. Take your time to avoid sloppy mistakes that can make the entire game impossible.

- Whenever you see an if/then rule, determine its contrapositive. Make sure you know what conditions would bring a rule into play. Here, for example, Rule 2 comes into play whenever Q is 5th, but Rule 2 also comes into play whenever V cannot be 6th.

- Don't worry if you can't find a deduction on a game that's relatively simple. Simple games are less likely to contain big deductions. Check the most likely candidates, but then move on.

The Questions

18. **B**

The question set begins with the usual acceptability question, so we can use the familiar Kaplan strategy of using the rules to eliminate choices. Rule 1 is violated by no choice, but Rule 2 is violated by (E) which has Q fifth without V sixth. Rule 3 kills (C), which has S second without P third. Rule 4 axes (D), which has W fifth. Finally, Rule 5 eliminates (A), which has V fifth. Choice (B) remains and is correct.

Remember:

- Acceptability questions give you a shot at an easy point and give you the opportunity to practice applying the rules. That practice with the game's mechanics often helps on harder questions.

19. **C**

If S is second, then P is third (Rule 3), and thus T must be fourth (Rule 1). Since W isn't fourth, W must be sixth (Rule 4). Now who could be fifth? V is never fifth (Rule 5), and since V cannot be sixth, Q cannot be fifth either. So R is the only animal that can be fifth, and therefore (C) is correct.

Remember:

- When the stem provides concrete information in an "if clause," build the new information into a little picture and see where the new information takes you. If you don't see where to go, use the choices to help you.

20. C

If Q is fifth then V is sixth (Rule 2). Since W isn't sixth, W must be fourth (Rule 4). Only slots 1, 2, 3, and 7 are open, and so the PT pair will have to go either first and second or second and third. Joining them in the first three slots is R (as the stem indicates), so the only entity that could be seventh is S. So (C) must be true.

(A), (B), and (D) could be true, but R could be first, placing P second and T third.

(E) is impossible. W is fourth here.

Remember:

- When you're able to definitely place a number of entities, ask yourself "who's left?"

21. D

If P is third, T is fourth (Rule 1), and so W is sixth. Since V isn't sixth, Q isn't fifth, and we can eliminate (A), (C), and (E). The only difference between (B) and (D) is that (D) includes R. Could R be fifth? Sure. SVPTRWQ is one such acceptable arrangement. So R belongs on our list, and (D) is correct.

Remember:

- Don't do more work than necessary! Use the choices to help you answer "complete and accurate" questions more efficiently. Look to eliminate several choices at once, and never check entities that appear in all the remaining choices.

22. C

If W is right after Q, where could they be? W cannot be sixth, since that would place Q fifth which in turn would force V to be sixth. So W must be fourth, and Q must be third. Now where can we place the VS pair mandated by the stem? Placing them first and second would violate Rule 3, and V can never be fifth (rule 5), so V and S must be sixth and seventh, respectively. Now the only place for the PT pair is first and second. So R, the only animal left, must be fifth, the only space left. (C) is correct.

Remember:

- When you're working with a block of entities, see where it could go. You may be surprised to see that it can go in only one place.

23. D

If P, T, and V all are examined after W, then W must be fourth and not sixth. V can never be fifth (Rule 5), and if we placed V sixth we'd have to break up the PT pair. So V is seventh and P and T are fifth and sixth, respectively. Now we have to work out the possibilities for the first three slots. The only restriction that applies comes via Rule 3. We know that S cannot be second because we know P cannot be third. If S is first, then the arrangement is either SQRWPTV or SRQWPTV. If S is third, the arrangement is either QRSWPTV or RQSWPTV. So four combinations are possible.

Remember:

- Straightforward sequencing games are usually quick and easy points, but not this time. The questions here were fairly complicated, so don't worry if you found them time-consuming. Just remember, an easy game can be made harder by asking tough questions. But sometimes the test makers make a hard game easier by including easier questions.

24. **B**

If R is fourth, then W is sixth, but not much follows immediately from there. On to the choices:

(A) P can't be third because that would force T into the fourth position, and the stem places R fourth. So (A) is impossible.

(B), however, could be true. If Q is first, we could place P and T second and third, respectively. S could be fifth and V seventh, and presto! QPTRSWV is an acceptable arrangement. So (B) could be true and is therefore correct.

(C) If S is second, we have no place for our PT pair.

(D) is nastier. If S is seventh, then who could be fifth? Not P or T, since they have to be together. Not Q, since V isn't sixth. Not V (Rule 5). So if S is seventh, then no one could be fifth, and so (D) is impossible. Technically, we could have deduced that S must be fifth before we consulted the choices, but that deduction was pretty subtle, so there's nothing wrong with discovering it here.

(E) is impossible since P immediately precedes T, and we already know that W is sixth.

Remember:

- If you don't see the next deduction, hit the choices. You may still be able to find the correct answer quickly.

Section II: Logical Reasoning Explanations

1. E

The problem: Channeling recycled wastewater into the harbor seems to have brought dangerous bacteria into this town's drinking water. The solution: Researchers recommend adding the enzyme tripticase to the water to eliminate those pestilent bacteria, which in turn will "solve the health problem." Since you're looking to weaken this argument, ask yourself if there could be a problem with this solution. It removes the bacteria, which will only solve the health problem if tripticase itself doesn't introduce any other problems. If, however, tripticase merely replaces one problem with another, as (E) has it, then the author's conclusion about its effectiveness as a solution is weakened.

(A) Okay, so tripticase is supereffective since it solves the giardia problem as well as others. This certainly doesn't weaken the author's argument that tripticase is an effective solution (even though other illnesses are technically outside the scope).

(B) The frequency and severity of giardia isn't the issue here. The author addresses the effectiveness of a solution for a particular health problem. The relative size of that problem has no impact on the effectiveness of the solution.

(C) Other illnesses are irrelevant to this consideration, as was mentioned above in (A).

(D) The author discusses water-induced cases of giardia, so cases that arise from other causes aren't within the argument's scope.

Remember:

- When you're asked to weaken or strengthen an argument, remember to evaluate the impact that each answer choice has on that argument without questioning the information you're given. Assume that the stimulus is true, and reconsider it in light of each answer choice. Does the new information make the conclusion more or less plausible? Don't question the information; just focus on its impact on the argument.

2. C

This is a Point at Issue question that basically asks, "What are they fighting about?" Look to see where they disagree. The marketing analyst only disputes the manufacturer's conclusion; each person presents completely different evidence. They can only disagree about something that they both discuss, and the only thing that meets that criterion in this dialogue is the conclusion. Therefore, they disagree about whether the company should switch to a less expensive brand of rubber, or (C).

(A) The manufacturer certainly assumes that other brands cost less, but the analyst in no way disputes this or even directly mentions it. Both seem to agree that other brands would cost less.

(B) is not addressed by either person. The analyst mentions sales but not sales *quotas*, and the manufacturer doesn't even get close to discussing sales.

(D), like (B), brings up an issue that neither person directly addresses. Even if you thought the analyst's comments might have some relevance to customer preferences, the analyst never addresses them directly, and the manufacturer never gets near this subject.

(E) is addressed by the analyst, but not by the manufacturer, whose argument deals only with cost.

Remember:

- Notice that all of the wrong answer choices mention issues that would be more relevant to the analyst's comments than the manufacturer's. Don't neglect the first argument; the right answer will have to be something discussed and discussed with different opinions by both people.

3. A

Before hunting for an answer choice that will strengthen this argument, look for assumptions in it. The salesman argues that the system will provide safety because it will keep predators out, but this argument assumes that predators are the only real threats to the flock's safety. Perhaps the system provides its own dangers; the electronic gate that would apparently toast any wayward predator certainly sounds capable of hurting the flock surrounded by it. By affirming the argument's assumption that the system itself cannot harm the animals, choice (A) strengthens the argument.

(B) So the system is being used for cattle. We don't know how effective it is, and in any case, this argument is about sheep, not cattle.

(C) picks up on and intensifies the potential drawback discussed in the last sentence. That sentence is tangential to the argument, which would nevertheless certainly not be strengthened by such information about how often this system errs.

(D) The argument concerns the efficacy of the contraption "when [the] flock is in danger of attack." The fact that some sheep predators are almost extinct does nothing to help the argument here; in fact, it makes the system seem, if anything, *less* necessary.

(E) is like (D) in that it would, if anything, weaken the argument. The system protects against predators, so if those predators don't provide a substantial threat, then it would be hard to sell this system as a splendid sheep protector. Again, the salesman might protest that he simply touts the system *in the event* of attacks, which is fair enough—but that would only make (D) and (E) irrelevant and certainly not strengtheners.

Remember:

- Always try to identify the argument's assumption when dealing with Strengthen or Weaken questions. Making that assumption explicit is a surefire and common way to strengthen an argument.

4. D

And now we get to that tangential sentence in the stimulus. What role does the cliché play? Well, the salesman mentions a potential drawback in the system and follows that with an important "but" that signals the shift in the second half of this sentence. While the system may not be perfect, the salesman clearly suggests through the well-known adage that the problem is not that serious. "Better safe than sorry" therefore functions in the argument to downplay an imperfection in the system.

(A) takes the shift too far. The salesman never suggests that the false alarms are actually a *good* part of the system; he merely suggests that they're not all that terrible.

(B) Again, the false alarms aren't one of the salesman's selling points. (What kind of sales pitch would *that* be? "And best of all, the darn thing often misfires!") He presents the false alarms as a flaw, but as a relatively unimportant one.

(C) does more to downplay the problem than the salesman does. The salesman only says that they happen, not that they happen rarely, and the statement in question can't play a role in the argument that *nothing* plays in the argument.

(E) entirely ignores the fact that "better safe than sorry" is said in relation to the false alarms flaw. It is uttered in reaction, not as *further* evidence for the need of such protection.

Remember:

- When you're dealing with a stimulus that has two questions, don't just rely on your memory when you get to the second question. A different question type means that you need to look for different things in the stimulus, so don't hesitate to do the necessary rereading before attacking the choices.

5. B

Next up is an Assumption question. The administrator concludes that Sandra would not be an effective teacher. Why not? She has two flaws: she's too lenient to fail students and too critical to reward any with high marks. But are failing students and rewarding high grades the only criteria for teacher effectiveness? Why can't she be effective even if she does neither of these things? The author doesn't say, and that omission is the basis of her assumption. In making her argument, the administrator assumes that to be effective, a teacher must be able to do one of these two things. This assumption is laid out for us in choice (B).

(A) is a distortion of the administrator's assumption. She doesn't assume that effective teachers have only two options: failing students or rewarding them with high marks. Instead, she assumes they must be capable of doing at least one thing or the other in order to be effective.

(C) gets the cause and effect of the argument mixed up by telling us what teachers must do in order to fail or reward students. We're interested in what teachers must do in order to be effective, so nothing regarding the reverse need be assumed here.

(D) and (E) fail to address the key issue at hand, which again concerns what it takes to be an effective teacher. Neither need be assumed here.

Remember:

- Straightforward Assumption questions lend themselves well to prephrasing. To determine the assumption, first isolate the conclusion and the evidence. Then ask, "What unstated yet necessary premise does the author rely on to draw her conclusion? What premise must she accept in order for the conclusion to follow logically from the evidence?" The assumption must bridge the gap between the conclusion and the evidence given.

6. A

Here we must choose an assumption upon which the argument in the stimulus depends. The conclusion is stated directly in the last sentence: In the coming years, Jenny will be less financially burdened by costs related to her job. The people most financially burdened by the costs associated with working are those making between $30,000 and $40,000 per year. Those who make less than $30,000 have lower job-related costs, so they generally are not as burdened—and folks who make more than $40,000 tend to make enough to compensate for their increased job costs, so they don't feel the burden as much either.

The author assumes that Jenny will move out of the $30,000–$40,000 income category in the coming years. Either she will start to make less than $30,000, or she will make more than $40,000 (for instance, if she receives a raise). If she stays in the same job, as the stimulus indicates, she's not likely to receive a pay cut, so the pay raise option is most feasible. Scanning the choices, we see that choice (A) captures this last possibility nicely. If Jenny is promoted, her salary will probably go up, and the burden of her job-related costs will decrease.

(B) Tempting, because it provides one avenue through which Jenny's job-related costs could be reduced. Yet it doesn't address the issue of salary that is central to the evidence. The evidence tells us that job costs are less burdensome if an individual's salary surpasses $40,000. If Jenny's salary doesn't increase, she may still feel the burden of her job-related costs even if they're lessened.

(C) provides irrelevant information. We might try the Denial Test to eliminate this one: Even if $40,000 was an entry-level salary for Jenny's job, the argument could still work as is.

(D) may also be eliminated with the Denial Test. If Jenny's co-workers *did* find their job costs as burdensome as she finds hers, how would this affect the argument? Not at all—therefore this choice cannot be a central assumption.

(E) Irrelevant. We are not interested in what Jenny made at her previous job; we are merely interested in her current salary, and how it and the financial burdens related to it are likely to change in the future.

Remember:

- Whenever possible, prephrase the answers to Assumption questions and scan quickly for your answer. If you can gain quick points through prephrasing here, you'll have more time to spend gaining points on more difficult questions later in the section.

7. C

This stimulus doesn't offer an argument with a conclusion, but rather discusses two different qualities of physical beauty. Physical beauty can increase one's physical appeal, but the attention that physical beauty generates can also make someone arrogant and decrease that appeal. Since this is an Inference question and the stimulus is missing a conclusion, odds are pretty good that the right answer will be a conclusion supported by the stimulus as it stands. If you were to prephrase a conclusion, it would probably look something like, "Therefore, physical beauty can both increase and decrease one's personal appeal." (C) is entirely consistent with the information that the stimulus provides and could easily serve as the conclusion towards which this author is moving.

(A) directly contradicts the stimulus, which creates two links between one's beauty and one's physical appeal.

(B) distorts the stimulus, which doesn't say whether beauty's impact on personal appeal is more positive than negative, or vice versa. The author merely mentions one positive effect and one negative; he doesn't rank them.

(D) Again, the author doesn't say whether the positive trait and the negative trait are of equal or of varying weights. We can't infer a statement that the author doesn't directly support.

(E) might be a nice cliché, but it's certainly not consistent with the stimulus. The stimulus discusses beauty as something that exists and has two contradictory impacts on appeal; the author doesn't discuss what determines beauty.

Remember:

- When looking for a choice that is "best illustrated" by the statements in a stimulus, the right answer must above all be consistent with the stimulus and must also in some fundamental way reflect the essence of it. If a choice is inconsistent with the passage, kill it. If it's consistent but tangential, kill it. Something that is "best illustrated" by the stimulus must be better related to it than that.

8. A

The educational consultant offers three reasons why school districts don't provide adequate educations: Teachers are inadequately trained; tight budgets limit opportunities for after-school academic programs; and parents aren't participating enough in the classroom. Those are the author's criteria for adequate education. The Prentice school district has experienced greater parental participation and is therefore "looking up" as a district. It is coming closer to meeting the third criterion and is therefore coming closer to providing an adequate education, according to the terms of the argument. You're looking to identify a valid inference, and it's not always easy to prephrase inferences in cases like this, so you're probably best off evaluating the choices one by one without spending much time trying to prephrase an answer of your own. In evaluating each choice, the key is to not read too much or too little into the Prentice school district's accomplishment.

(A) Sound reasonable? Yup. This school district, because of its increased parental participation, displays at least one component of adequate education to a greater degree than it had. This inference is perfectly in line with the claims made about Prentice and about adequate education—and it doesn't overstep the bounds of the argument as do some of the other choices.

(B) This is far more than we can infer. All we know is that Prentice is making some improvements in one of the three criteria that define an adequate education. With such limited information, we can't infer that the district's education is adequate.

(C), (D), and (E) We have no basis for comparing the Prentice school district to other districts, and all three remaining choices bite the dust on this account.

Remember:

- Often the key to answering Inference questions correctly is understanding the exact extent of the author's claims. Here, Prentice is improving in one particular category, but that allows us to infer nothing about its performance in terms of the other categories or about its educational system as a whole. Don't infer anything beyond what the argument specifically supports.

- Beware of common wrong answer choices, like (C) here, that offer to rank what the author never did.

9. E

Again we're presented with two opposing views presented in a single argument. A survey showed that, as a group, action films were rated higher than romance films. Viewpoint number one comes from the survey organizers, who concluded from this that subject matter of popular movies must determine their appeal. Seems reasonable, but the author, making use of the contrast keyword "yet," states that this conclusion is probably wrong and offers an alternative explanation. She notes that the producers of the action films were more experienced in successful film production. Notice that the author doesn't disagree that action films receive better ratings, but rather supports a different explanation for that superiority; the effect is the same in both viewpoints, but the causes differ. We're looking for an inference based on this argument, so once you have a firm grasp of the content, it's time to move to the answer choices.

(A) This answer choice confuses percentages and numbers. The survey is based on the percentage of films in each category to receive the highest rating, not on the actual number of films to receive the top rating. A lower percentage does not necessarily mean a lower number.

KAPLAN

(B) *Au contraire:* The author *does* suggest a relationship between previous directorial successes and the popular appeal of the survey films.

(C) The argument is about independent feature films. Based on that argument, we cannot infer anything about what a survey of big-budget mainstream films would show.

(D) distorts the information in the stimulus. Sure, of the filmmakers whose work is represented in this particular survey, some have a hit film to their credit, while some have never even made a movie before. Does that allow us to conclude who's "more likely" to produce a hit? For all we know, the folks with previous hits were new filmmakers themselves when they produced those hits.

(E)'s all that's left. The author suggests that having a previous hit film to the director's credit is more important than subject matter in determining ratings, so it logically follows that subject matter may not be a significant factor in the popular ratings of films made by directors with an equal number of previous hits. By positing another factor besides subject matter that accounts for the survey results, the author's argument certainly does allow for the possibility that subject matter *may* have no effect on the ratings.

Remember:

- Learn to recognize the kinds of wrong choices that appear again and again on the LSAT. Looking back over (A) through (E) here, you should notice some pretty common wrong answer types: confusing numbers and percentages (A); an "*au contraire*" choice that suggests the opposite of what's in the passage (B); a choice that strays outside the scope (C); and a classic distortion (D).

10. **C**

The second question based on this stimulus asks us to locate the one answer choice that doesn't strengthen the author's argument. We therefore want to eliminate the four choices that strengthen the connection between the popular appeal of a director's film and that director's having a past hit film, as well as those that strengthen the connection between lack of a hit film and lesser popular appeal.

(A) If previous hits indicate talent, then the author's theory of the link between previous hit films and popular appeal of the survey films seems more plausible, and we're more likely to believe that the organizers *are* wrong, as the author maintains, about the effects of subject matter.

(B), (D), and (E) all strengthen the argument by tying past experience of success to present cinematic successes. (B) links previous experience to ratings directly. (D) takes it from another angle and explains that the films of first-timers do not often achieve the same popular appeal as that attained by previous hit-makers. (E) links previous experience of success to the ability to obtain the best actors, offering another benefit that accrues to experienced directors and makes them more likely to produce hit films.

(C) *Why* many first-time directors don't make action films has no impact on this argument. The fact remains that of the films in this particular survey, the action films were made by more experienced directors while the romances were made by novices, and the author uses this fact to counter a previous conclusion. (C) gives us one possible explanation for this fact but has no effect on how this fact is *used* by the author, which, after all, constitutes the crux of her argument. This is the one choice that does not strengthen (or, for that matter, even affect) the author's argument.

Remember:

- Many question stems, like the one here, are not written in the clearest possible manner. Before proceeding to the answer choices, pause for a moment to consider what you're being asked and what type of answer choice you're looking for, even when you can't specifically prephrase an answer. Here we want a choice that doesn't support the author's causal link between previous directorial success and the popular appeal of that director's other films.

11. E

The question stem directs us to find a weakness in the manager's argument, and it lies in the survey. What if others who are skeptical about the candidate simply didn't respond to the survey? The fact that only 25 responded negatively does not necessarily mean that the other 975 are okay with the reports and have confidence in the candidate's ability to lead, although this is the interpretation the manager implies. (E) picks up on this problem in the manager's argument: If the skeptics were disinclined to respond to the survey, then the conclusion that the candidate need not worry may be unfounded, and the candidate's concern may be legit.

(A) is beyond the argument's temporal scope. The candidate and his manager only discuss the impact of the recent media coverage; the possible effects of future coverage don't play a relevant role in that discussion.

(B) identifies a possible use to which the candidate's opponent might put the media coverage, but that too is outside the scope. Maybe the opponent's survey won't show any residual concerns based on the survey, or maybe it will. By itself, (B) doesn't point out a weakness in the argument.

(C) There's no indication that the survey was intended to hide its main focus; presumably, those surveyed knew that the survey was intended to measure the fallout from the media coverage. So (C) need not be something that the campaign manager's argument fails to acknowledge.

(D) deals with television interviews, which show up in the candidate's argument but not in his campaign manager's. Therefore, (D) doesn't identify a problem with the manager's argument.

Remember:

- Be suspicious of surveys in Logical Reasoning stimuli. Whenever you see one, ask yourself if there are any problems with it. Particularly, ask yourself whether the supposed results accurately represent the views of the whole group surveyed. Here, the campaign manager fails to specify how the majority of the participants in the survey responded, if they responded at all.

12. D

We're asked to identify the role of the recommendation that shows up in the first sentence, and we can see that it constitutes the argument's conclusion based on the fact that the argument's evidence supports it. All of the information after sentence 1 answers the question "Why do you think Sarah's teacher should spend more time with her?" (If you were tempted to identify the last part of the last sentence as the conclusion, notice that it only pertains to that last sentence.) This confirms that the proposal in question is the conclusion, as choice (D) clearly states.

(A) is technically impossible since the recommendation is actually stated in the argument, and an assumption is never stated.

(B) would tempt those who saw the first sentence as setting the stage for the true conclusion in the last sentence. The fact that Sarah's teacher is not displaying good judgment is still subordinate to the overall proposal that she needs to spend more quality time with her.

(C) Remember that a hypothesis is not a synonym for a conclusion on the LSAT. A hypothesis is a working theory that has yet to be adequately proven, which is not how the author presents her recommendation. Further, (C) totally misrepresents the argument because the evidence in the argument *does* support the principal's proposal, whether or not we erroneously accept that proposal as a hypothesis.

(E) gets the pieces of the argument mixed up, putting "evidence" where "conclusion" should accurately be and vice versa.

Remember:

- Identify conclusion and evidence only in the context of the argument as a whole. The first sentence appears to be the conclusion at first glance, but you can only be sure of that by seeing how that sentence plays in to the rest of the argument. Withhold final judgment until all the information is in.

13. C

Did you see the formal logic in this question? The author begins with the classic if/then formula: *if* there's too much pressure on the bottom shelf, *then* the bookcase will collapse. Since the stem directs you to find a weakness, you can anticipate that the logic will exhibit an error in the rest of the stimulus. A valid conclusion would be the contrapositive of this statement: If the bookshelf has not collapsed, then there is not too much pressure on the bottom shelf. This, however, is not what we get. Instead, the author concludes by flipping the original terms: If the bookcase has collapsed, then there must have been too much pressure on the bottom shelf. The correct choice is (C)—the author assumes that

excessive pressure, because it's offered as one sure cause, is the *only possible* cause, even though there may be others.

(A) The evidence and the conclusion are both about the exact same issues, even though the conclusion misinterprets the evidence. The problem isn't that the evidence is irrelevant, but rather the way in which the conclusion distorts that evidence.

(B) The author never mentions or implies the concept of a "partial collapse." It's impossible, according to the author, for just the bottom shelf to collapse. The author talks about an "entire" collapse and never deviates from this conception. There's no discontinuity in the meaning of collapse.

(D) The author has no obligation to consider the existence of single-shelf bookcases. This argument is specifically about Sherry's bookcase, which has at least a bottom shelf, which implies it has at least one more. We can't tell whether the author has overlooked the possibility mentioned in (D), but even if she has, that has no bearing on the validity of her argument.

(E) The conclusion is certainly too extreme, but since it just deals with Sherry's bookcase, it would be hard to classify it as "broad." Also, the evidence doesn't contradict itself. As it stands, the evidence offers a perfectly valid formal logic statement; the problem comes in the conclusion drawn *from* this evidence.

Remember:

- This question offers a good example of the benefits of identifying the different parts of an argument. After isolating the evidence and the conclusion, look for the flaws. The evidence is fine, so (A) and (E) are out. That means the conclusion must be the problem, in and of itself, or because it rests on a weak assumption.

Of the remaining answer choices, only (C) deals with the conclusion specifically. Even if you aren't sure what the weakness is, you can go far by identifying where it must be.

14. D

To parallel a dialogue accurately, we'll want to understand the structure of each part individually. The first speaker in the right answer choice will explain that everyone within a certain group receives one of two items. The second part of the right answer will describe how, no matter which item is originally chosen, everyone in the group receives the same item. On its most basic general level, then, the right answer choice will start off with two options and will then narrow down to one of those options that's common to both choices. We can't quite predict how this is going to look, so let's evaluate the answer choices.

(A) starts off fine, but the second speaker concludes that "most" of the bouquets included silver roses while the original argument concludes that "all" kids have loans. "Most" will never parallel "all."

(B) proceeds from discussing a group to discussing an individual. The original argument makes a conclusion about the group, not one of its members.

(C) follows the pattern we've seen by starting off okay but making its error in the second part. The psychiatrist discusses Ward A, but the Nurse discusses an entirely different group residing in Ward B. The original argument deals with one and only one group.

(D) finally remains faithful throughout the second part of the argument. Margaret describes two options available to patients (corn or sprouts), and the cafeteria worker shows how the patients all share one of those options (sprouts) because anyone who chose one (corn) also chose the other (sprouts). Perfect.

(E) makes its error right away by describing the two choices as mutually exclusive. It can't parallel the original argument that combines the two options. You should have stopped reading this one at the phrase "but not both."

Remember:

- Be aware that many Parallel Reasoning questions can be cut down to size with strategic comparisons of the original to the choices. For example, (A)'s "most" and (E)'s "but not both" allowed us to chop through these choices rather quickly.

- When time's running out, you may wish to focus on paralleling only one part of the original argument (for example, its conclusion). That may help you at least improve your odds if you have to guess.

15. C

Oddly, this stimulus presents us with nothing more than a list of different transportation vehicles and their definitions. With so much rather disconnected information, be prepared to refer back to the stimulus as you comb the answer choices for a proper inference. Choice (C) is the right answer, since any jeep meeting such criteria would also fulfill all of the criteria listed in the definition of a passenger vehicle. The author never says that a vehicle can't belong to more than one category.

(A) No. If the automobile in question were a passenger vehicle, then it *would be* fully enclosed with four wheels.

(B) knocks out three of the four vehicles described in the passage and therefore chooses the fourth, but that's only valid if there aren't any other vehicle options. Perhaps there are; nowhere does the author say that these are the only four vehicles in existence.

(D) This makes an unsupported comparison among the vehicles. Even if the definitions of two of these vehicles are more similar, that doesn't suggest that the vehicles themselves are necessarily more *alike*. Too vague.

(E) may be true, but it may not. Since the stimulus doesn't discuss this possibility or provide any rules that would support it, we can't infer that the postal van and jeep categories overlap. It's possible that no postal vans are jeeps.

Remember:

- An inference is something that is well supported by the information and logically follows from it. Don't settle for choices that leave room for argument.

16. E

In order to apply a principle, the first step is to have a very strong grasp of the principle as the author originally presented it. The Superintendent provides a general rule and offers one definite exception to it. The argument also contains a justification of his hands-off policy: it hones student interaction skills. It's pretty much impossible to prephrase an answer to such a question, so once you have a solid grasp on the principle presented, proceed to the answer choices, looking for the one that best conforms.

(A) presents a hands-off gym teacher, but the teacher's noninvolvement contradicts the stimulus' principle by not intervening even though violence is involved. Since violence justifies intervention, the situation in (A) doesn't accord with the principle in the stimulus.

(B) presents a teacher intervening in a dispute that is not clearly defined as violent. We therefore can't tell whether it demonstrates the original principle or not.

(C) is outside of the author's scope, which specifically concerns *teachers'* intervention in student conflicts. Parents have no role in the principle as it is originally presented, so they can't be centrally present in a situation that applies that original principle.

(D) Generating debate in philosophy class seems like a fully justifiable teaching activity. This is not the type of student conflict toward which the principle is geared, especially when it is instigated by a teacher.

(E) While we may pity the student with the new 'do, this is the right choice because it precisely follows the rules of the Superintendent's principle. The teacher does not intervene in a clearly nonviolent (teasing doesn't suggest violence) student conflict situation. Perfect.

Remember:

- When applying a principle, look for the answer choice that the author of the original statement would most likely agree with. In this sense, Principle questions are often similar to Inference questions—in both types, the right answers are strictly consistent with the information in the original argument.

17. D

The first step in an Explanation question is to understand the situation described in the stimulus that needs explaining. Here, the author discusses two simultaneous trends that might seem to contradict one another. Tuition has increased at private universities, leading to a decrease in enrollment—so far that's logical. However, revenue at these universities has continued to increase despite the decreased enrollment. The correct answer must offer some source of revenue that more than compensates for the decrease in revenues created by the lower enrollment. That's where (D) fits in: If the tuition hikes have brought in more revenue than the loss of enrollment has taken away, then it's easy to see how both trends discussed in the stimulus can simultaneously coexist.

(A) The frequency with which private schools increase tuition doesn't begin to explain the revenue situation in the stimulus. The relevant fact is that tuitions are increasing, which triggers the rest of argument. In what specific manner they're increasing is irrelevant.

(B) offers an irrelevant distinction between vocational schools and private colleges that doesn't contribute any new information to the stimulus.

(C) tells us what happens to some students who can no longer afford private universities. Their fate, sorry to say, doesn't matter, and again it doesn't add any new information to the scenario. We already know that enrollment decreased; this choice just gives us a human-interest story when we really want to know how it's possible under these circumstances for revenues to actually increase.

(E) is similar to (B) in that it provides another irrelevant distinction. It compares the role of alumni contributions at public and private colleges, while the stimulus does not express any interest in public universities or in alumni contributions. Even if private colleges do get a larger percentage of money from alumni, decreasing enrollment shrinks the number of alumni and would, if anything, seem to decrease revenue even further, deepening the mystery but not explaining it.

Remember:

- In Explanation questions, the information provided in the stimulus remains true; your task is to reconcile, not to change, the presented facts. If you stay focused on that task, you'll see that only one answer choice will work. Understanding the seemingly unusual situation in the stimulus is key.

18. E

The stimulus begins with an absolute statement and takes us directly into formal logic territory. Thus, the first sentence can be restated: If children are guided by critical adults, then the children will not develop strong self-esteem. The question stem allows us to anticipate that the second sentence will offer an incorrect inference, as indeed it does. There the author concludes that if children are NOT guided by critical adults, then they WILL develop strong self-esteem. Expressing the stem algebraically, we can rewrite the first sentence as: if A then B. The second sentence alters the equation to: if NOT A, then NOT B. That's an invalid inference, so we'll look through the answer choices for another argument that makes the same mistake.

(A) doesn't give us any formal logic statements, so it can't parallel the stimulus. The recommendation in (A) has no parallel in the original, either, so you may have axed (A) on that count as well.

(B) can be restated. If a solicitor has bad manners, then that solicitor won't sell any products (if A then B). The second sentence concludes that if a solicitor has low sales (which, you'll note, is different from NO sales), then that solicitor has bad manners (if C then A). That's a flaw, but it's not the one we're looking for.

(C) contains a description of an event and a future prediction based on that event. Moreover, the first sentence contains no formal logic. Not parallel.

(D) restated says that if a puppy is not well-socialized, then it won't interact well with a group of people (if A then B). The second sentence describes a proportional increase between socialization and comfortable interaction, which isn't a formal logic statement and therefore can't complete the parallel.

(E) is all that's left, so it had better work. In fact, on test day, you shouldn't even spend time checking it if you're totally confident that the others are lousy. But for the record: If one takes calcium supplements, then one does NOT increase one's risk of heart disease (if A then B). In the next sentence, the author concludes that if one does NOT take calcium supplements, one WILL increase one's risk of heart disease (if NOT A then NOT B). That's a perfect parallel of the flawed stimulus.

Remember:

- Always restate formal logic statements in an if/then format. That'll enable you to interpret them, form their contrapositives (by reversing and negating the terms), and, if necessary, compare them to one another accurately.

- The logical opposite of a negative statement is a positive statement! Here, the opposite of "NOT increasing a risk" is "increasing a risk."

19. D

The author begins by describing the view of some sports historians who subscribe to a basic formula: physical attributes + a coach's influence = a player's "unique" tennis style. After dismissing the relevance of modern players' greater strength and endurance, however, the author argues that current styles are really no different from previous styles, implying that the historians' claim of the existence of "unique" tennis styles is bogus. And this implication is stated outright in the last sentence, where the author posits the existence of a universally successful tennis style shared by all professionals. In other words, the author uses the fact that tennis styles haven't changed over the years to argue that there's simply one best way to play tennis; in contrast to the historians' theory of uniqueness, the author proposes the theory of universality. But the author ignores the role of the tennis coach: If, as (D) has it, the early coaches of today's players were the profes-

sionals of yesteryear, then it becomes plausible that the style that the author considers "universal" may simply be the style (one possible one among many) that was handed down from one generation to the next. Perhaps if the current crop of tennis stars don't go on to teach the next generation, whole new styles will develop. If the current style is learned, then it may not be universally inherent to the game. If (D) is true, the author's claim of "universality" is weakened.

(A) This answer choice emphasizes the truth of the first part of the sports historians' view regarding the individuality of physical attributes. Since the author doesn't explicitly disagree that players do vary in terms of some attributes, this choice doesn't weaken the argument. It just emphasizes a point on which the two views (historians and author) don't clearly disagree.

(B) if anything, strengthens the argument: If most current players don't know of the players of previous generations, yet their styles are for the most part similar to that of those players, then we'd be more likely to believe that the author is on to something with the claim that a universally efficient style exists in the world of professional tennis. (B) is somewhat the converse of correct choice (D) in that it lowers the probability that current players have simply copied the successful styles of previous players.

(C) This choice makes an irrelevant distinction between strength and endurance. Saying that one has a greater impact than the other has no effect on the argument, which never even begins to rank those two factors.

(E) The factors that contribute to the greater strength and weight of today's players are beyond the scope of this argument.

Remember:

- When the author describes the view of some other people (in this case "some sports historians"), be ready to encounter a contrasting view. The author often mentions such groups to contrast their views to his or her own. At the first sign of conflict in a Logical Reasoning argument or Reading Comprehension passage, ask yourself where the views differ. The answer choices often test your ability to recognize the distinction.

- One way to get through the more difficult questions is to pay extra attention to wrong answer choice elimination strategies. Even if choice (D) doesn't seem great to you, (A), (B), (C), and (E) all commit common errors. There's nothing wrong with eliminating four choices for good reasons and going with what remains.

20. D

The author's conclusion is the companies' confidence that anemic children will be cured relatively simply with a new iron injection. The evidence presents itself in the first sentence: A new injection can apparently reverse children's anemia. Can you see any gaps between the conclusion and evidence? Notice that the evidence explains that something can be done, and the conclusion states that something will be done. Just because the cure is possible doesn't mean it will automatically be administered. The author assumes that children will receive the injection based on the fact that it exists. (D) expresses this more concretely: the author assumes that children are aware of and willing to receive this injection.

(A) The argument focuses on the availability, not the production of this cure, so (A) is not necessary (or even relevant) to this argument.

(B) gives us irrelevant background information about causes. The author states that iron shots

reverse children's anemia, regardless of the specific cause, so (B) may or may not be true without affecting the argument.

(C) basically states that a managed diet would not cure anemia. But the author doesn't state that the injection is the *only* cure for anemia, so the argument needn't assume that no other cure exists.

(E) The author only claims that the injection cures anemia "relatively simply." Safety never comes up as an issue—the injection could almost kill the kids and still not hurt the argument, which states only that the shot cures the condition, not that it does so safely.

Remember:

- Even though Logical Reasoning stimuli are shorter than Reading Comprehension passages, don't try to memorize the information in either situation.

- Push yourself beyond recognizing the conclusion to considering how it operates in the context of the argument. Instead of stopping once you've recognized that the author concludes that a drug will provide a cure, really think about how that relates to the evidence. That'll make it easier to see the gap between them.

21. E

The author concludes that mission commanders should not choose pilots based on the candidates' performance on the isolation test. For evidence, the author says that a candidate who passes the test may have an antisocial personality disorder. Thus, the author argues against a current system of assessment by noting one particular instance in which the results might not indicate what they're meant to indicate. This is certainly not the strongest of arguments, offering as it does one apparently small disadvantage of the test and using it to condemn the test entirely, which is why we'll see four of its flaws among the answer choices. Notice that the question stem informs us that the four wrong answers will offer information that the author fails to consider; they will describe errors of omission.

(A) describes one way in which the isolation tests might work to accurately screen applicants. It describes a possible benefit offered by the test. The argument is flawed for failing to consider and rebuff this possibility.

(B) operates in much the same way as (A). Here we're told that mission commanders may select pilots more accurately if the tests they administer aren't limited. Since the author argues that such tests should be limited (arguing that there should be one fewer test), her argument is flawed since it fails to consider and, again, rebuff this opposing argument.

(C) and (D) again indicate two possible advantages of the isolation test. The author doesn't mention or contest these advantages, which means that she makes her conclusion without addressing the relevant issues that they describe. That's certainly a flaw in the argument.

(E) Rather than highlight a benefit of the test, (E) goes the other way by suggesting that the test itself may be flawed. The fact that a pilot may do well on the test and yet not do well under actual isolation conditions is, if anything, consistent with the author's conclusion that the test should be scrapped.

Remember:

- Be aware of the variations in the question stems throughout the exam. The stem here informs us that the four wrong answer choices will describe things relevant to the argument that the author doesn't consider, which is a particular type of flaw. If you are aware of that, you can approach the choices knowing what to expect.

22. D

The heart of the argument is the last sentence of the stimulus: Harry concludes that his brother's suggestion wouldn't help to organize his collection based on the evidence that no single special album could hold all his cards. Harry's argument depends on the assumption that the collection of cards cannot be organized if they're not in one singular album. (D) expresses the same idea: Harry's dismissal of his brother's suggestion makes sense only if the collection cannot be organized in more than one album.

(A) Harry needn't assume that the showcase albums from the olden days would have served his purposes. His argument isn't based on a comparison of what's available now compared to what used to be available, so (A) addresses a possibility that doesn't impact Harry's argument.

(B) isn't entirely relevant to this argument, since other album types don't figure in to this argument. Moreover, we're concerned only with Harry's predicament.

(C) contradicts the stimulus, which explicitly states that no showcase album on the market is large enough to contain all of Harry's cards.

(E) The reason *why* Harry's collection is disorganized doesn't provide a link between the evidence and conclusion because neither part of the argument concerns this issue.

Remember:

- Even when you aren't able to prephrase an assumption, you can still go far with a knowledge of the issues involved in the argument. Here, those issues are organization and showcase albums. Only (B) and (D) actually mention both issues, and only (D) stays focused solely on them.

23. C

We're asked for a situation that conforms to a principle, so your best bet is to understand the principle thoroughly, and then test the choices against this understanding. The author offers an absolute truth with two restrictions. First the rule: A free press always reports all information about a country's military operations. There are two cases, and only two cases, in which this might not be true. First, if such information would jeopardize the safety of the troops. Second, if such information would jeopardize the success of a mission. With such clear rules, we'll be looking for the answer choice that follows them faithfully.

(A) To make this answer choice work, you'd have to assume that such dissenting opinions would jeopardize the troops and/or the success of the mission. This choice supports no such assumption, so based on the information that it alone provides, it is not consistent with the stimulus' principle.

(B) and (D) discuss unfree presses, and therefore fall outside the scope of the argument. The rules pertain only to a free press, and we can't infer how an unfree press would behave in regard to these issues.

(C) This answer choice succeeds where (A) fails because, while it doesn't directly state that the publication of future military targets would jeopardize the success of a mission, the link between the two is far clearer and more logical. According to the principle, a free press *could* withhold information that endangers the troops or mission, and it's reasonable to say that the info discussed in (C) could fall into that category.

(E) The principle deals with *current* military operations and therefore doesn't shed any light on what's appropriate behavior in regard to previous engagements. Clandestine past military operations are outside the scope.

Remember:

- No correct answer choice will require you to make a significant, unfounded assumption in order to make it work. The right answer choice will be correct on its own merit, without requiring you to introduce extra information.

24. C

Lillian's goal is simple: to create cohesion in her drug addiction recovery group. In order to achieve this goal, she has encouraged members of the group to share their personal experiences openly. The problem: Some members have begun telling long and violent stories to shock the others, causing some members to quit and leaving inadequate time for others to share. The conclusion: Lillian should limit the time available for each member to speak. The stem alerts us that there's a flaw in this argument, and that flaw becomes apparent in the conclusion. The problem that the conclusion seeks to resolve stems from two causes: members telling long and violent stories. The conclusion as it stands might prevent the stories from being long, but it doesn't prevent them from being violent. Therefore, the argument is flawed because its conclusion would only remedy one of two factors that create the problem it seeks to resolve, which is what (C) states.

(A) Apparently, "two actions" refers to the telling of long scandalous stories and members dropping out. (A) is most immediately wrong because the author does not suggest that these incidents occur simultaneously. On the contrary, the author presents them sequentially: According to the argument, the stories "cause" other members to quit.

(B) is perplexing because there is no hypothesis in this argument. Also, there is no contradiction within the elements of this argument. The conclusion is flawed because it's incomplete, not because it runs counter to anything.

(D) The evidence is all perfectly relevant to the conclusion. They are, after all, both focused on the same issues.

(E), like (B), suggests that the elements of the argument contradict one another, but that is not true in this case. Lil's evidence is consistent with the conclusion—the problem is that the recommendation in the conclusion simply doesn't go far enough.

Remember:

- The answer choices for Logical Flaw questions are particularly formulaic and repetitive, leaving you with similar answer choices for different flaw questions. Thus, given a stimulus with a causality problem, (A) would be your choice or, if there were a scope shift, (D) would be attractive. The good news is that the flaws in the arguments are equally repetitive. The bad news is that the answer choices will likely sound familiar, so it's important that you first prephrase the flaw in order that you not be lead astray.

25. B

This Assumption question picks up on the confusion in the argument between groups and subgroups. The author's conclusion addresses all of the materials produced by American Synthetics, Inc., but the evidence discusses only one particular material produced by the company: the kuva weave fabric. We're told that kuva weave, despite its impressive durability and strength, has an unfortunate tendency to burst into flames (a small drawback). Therefore, according to the author, manufacturers should eliminate ALL American Synthetics materials from their stocks. This would be a valid conclusion only if it were true that all of the materials produced by American Synthetics were equally likely to ignite. (B) states this assumption: If all of American Synthetics' materials contain kuva weave, then they're all flam-mable, and manufacturers should indeed get rid of their stocks. (B) makes the evidence about kuva weave relevant to the conclusion regarding all American Synthetics products—it connects the evidence to the conclusion and thus qualifies as the assumption we seek.

(A) Sure, they didn't catch that flammability problem, but we're not concerned with the accuracy of the trials or when the problem showed up. We're solely concerned with the flammability of the material and what that flammability means for the company's products as a whole.

(C) Plants that *don't* use the fabric may suffer from just as high or even a higher incidence of fires due to other reasons. In other words, the author need assume nothing about the type of comparison stated in (C) in order to make an argument about what should be done as a result of kuva weave's flammability. We can negate (C) and the argument does not fall apart, which confirms that (C) is not a statement that's needed here.

(D) Apparently they're not as durable as originally suspected if they're burning, but durability isn't the issue, flammability is. As we saw in (A), the early tests are irrelevant.

(E) The manufacturers' liability is far off scope. While (E) may offer an additional reason for manufacturers to expunge their stocks, we're not looking to strengthen this argument but to identify its assumption, and this answer choice doesn't link kuva weave to American Synthetics' products as a whole.

Remember:

- An assumption has a very specific definition on the LSAT; it is an unstated yet necessary link between the evidence and the conclusion. After identifying the evidence and conclusion, look to eliminate all of the answer choices that don't relate to both elements. Even when you can't prephrase the assumption, you can evaluate the answer choices with very specific criteria in mind and increase your chances of finding it correctly and quickly.

Section III: Logical Reasoning Explanations

1. B

In order for the mother to conclude from her evidence that the sessions should end, she needs to assume that John is capable of accurately analyzing the sessions' usefulness. If he's not, then his feelings on the matter may not be an accurate indicator of the value of the sessions, and it may not be a good idea to base any decisions on them. Basically, John's mother assumes that John is right in believing that the sessions aren't helping him, which is where answer choice (B) comes in. If she's assuming that John is right, then she must also assume that his judgment hasn't been impaired.

(A) is wrong because John's mother just discusses what should be done if John is unhappy with the sessions. Her conclusion does not depend on him being happy or unhappy.

(C) is far outside of the scope of the mother's argument. She never addresses the issue of the psychoanalyst's qualifications; she just discusses John's feelings and their indication of the sessions' value.

(D) Again, whether or not the analyst's methods are sound is not the issue for John's mother. For her, the central issue is John, and how his feelings determine the helpfulness of the sessions. Therefore, the validity of her conclusion does not rest on whether John's perceptions accurately indicate the soundness of the analyst's methods, but whether they indicate the value of the sessions in helping him to adjust to his parents' divorce.

(E) By stating that John should "act on *any* belief," choice (E) exceeds the argument's scope. The argument does not deal with anything so broad as whether John should always act on his beliefs. Rather, it addresses whether his beliefs should be acted upon in this particular situation.

Remember:

- You can often eliminate a number of choices right off the bat that are simply too broad in their scope to be necessary to the particular argument.

2. B

Harriet's husband concludes that he will plan a trip to Sunshine Valley for he and Harriet. His evidence: Harriet wants to vacation in a culturally rich area, and her husband has discovered that Sunshine Valley is financially rich. His error: He responds to her desire for cultural richness with a city steeped in financial richness. He therefore mistakes her definition of richness. (B) captures this. To *equivocate* is to deduce the wrong meaning through ambiguous language, which is precisely what Harriet's husband does when he equates cultural and financial wealth. Further, this richness certainly constitutes a key (even the key) factor in his decision.

(A) An argument is circular when its evidence and conclusion are basically the same (i.e., "I should go to the store because I should go to the store"). That's not the case here, where the conclusion and evidence are clearly different.

(C) All travel brochures are biased—they want to convince the reader to visit that area. Relying on such evidence to decide where to go isn't the basis of a logical flaw. Moreover, there's nothing here to indicate that the information in the brochure is unreliable. The problem here is how the husband *uses* the evidence to make his traveling decision.

(D) He certainly does this, but the fact that he doesn't consult Harriet doesn't constitute a flaw in the argumentation as it's presented. If anything, it's a subjective and personal, not a logical, flaw to make important decisions unilaterally.

 295

(E), like (D), is certainly true, but why does he need to demonstrate the economic feasibility of his decision? We have no way of knowing whether they can afford the trip or not, but that's a separate issue. We're concerned only with the husband's decision as related to the evidence for it.

Remember:

- Flaw questions are distinct from Weaken questions in a few ways. A flaw is a logical error in the reasoning of the argument or an objective mistake committed by the argument. You'll often encounter wrong answer choices for Flaw questions that would weaken the argument, but a flaw is an internal mistake in the argument, whereas anything that makes the conclusion less credible weakens the argument. You can sometimes weaken an argument by identifying its flaw, but remember that a choice that weakens an argument isn't its flaw unless it points out an internal, logical error in the argumentation as the stimulus presents it.

3. D

This stimulus just tells us a story. Once you've grasped the basic contents of the stimulus, proceed to the answer choices.

(A) The stimulus tells us that *Theobroma cacao* is a tropical New World tree, but that doesn't allow us to infer that this tree *only* grows in the tropical New World. The tree might very possibly exist in other countries.

(B) contradicts the stimulus, which tells us that chocolate was introduced to Europe as a liquid.

(C) makes an unsupported comparison. We do know that more pounds of chocolate today are produced for eating than drinking, but we have no idea how the amount of drinkable chocolate in the 1800s compares to the amount of solid edible chocolate produced today.

(D) is valid: If the Swiss invented the first way to produce solid edible chocolate in the 1800s, then solid edible chocolate wasn't consumed anywhere in the 1500s.

(E) is entirely unsupported by the stimulus. Just because the Swiss made chocolate into a solid, that doesn't necessarily mean that nobody else would have done so if the Swiss hadn't. Take the Swiss out of the picture, and chocolate might very well be just as popular today.

Remember:

- Every once in a while you'll get a stimulus that isn't an argument (i.e., it doesn't have a conclusion and evidence, just a bunch of facts). The question that's attached to them will usually be Inference, since it's difficult to ask anything relating to how the evidence reaches the conclusion when there really is no conclusion to speak of.

- Make sure you stay within the scope when looking for the choice that must be true.

4. A

The nuclear physicist argues that the *Times* should try harder to print the views of protesters in this particular controversy. She proceeds to state, three times and in three different ways, that such views are lacking. The engineer states that the protesters' views needn't be printed because the *Times'* coverage is fine. The engineer thus concedes that such views are not represented but does not believe that they need to be. The engineer doesn't give us any concrete evidence to support this position, so the right answer will contradict this one idea given by the engineer. As you look through the answer choices, ask yourself which one shows that the engineer is somehow wrong to be satisfied with the absence of the protesters' views. (A) fits the bill because, if effective reporting needs to represent both sides of a controversy, the *Times'* coverage is not adequate, and the engineer's position is clearly contradicted.

(B) is consistent with the engineer's opinion that the *Times'* coverage is fine as it is, so it certainly wouldn't counter the engineer's claim.

(C) deals with the paper's readership, about which the engineer never offers an opinion. It doesn't justify why this issue is relevant to the engineer's position, so it can't counter that position.

(D), like (C), has no clear connection to the engineer's statements. This choice would only look tempting if you added more information to it.

(E) The engineer is totally comfortable with the imbalance in media coverage, so this information explaining an imbalance wouldn't counter his position.

Remember:

- When presented with more than one view, always make sure that you stay focused on the appropriate one when proceeding to the answer choices. Previewing the question stem will usually tell you where to focus your attention.

5. E

The author of this rather skimpy argument only implies her conclusion that the botanists were wrong. Evidence? The botanists believed that the Faura plants required a certain fertilizer composed of four specific elements, but adopting this approach actually hindered the growth of those plants. There's a lot of space available for information that would strengthen the author's conclusion, but since we can't predict anything concrete, let's go through them individually, crossing off anything that supports the conclusion.

(A), (B), and (D) all describe one negative effect of the botanists' belief. More specifically, each discusses the botanists' omission of one key ingredient that these plants need to grow. (A) explains in further detail that the botanists'

advocacy of the fertilizer inhibited Faura species plant growth because it led to the omission of the valuable potash. (B) doesn't directly state that the omission of zinc caused the problems experienced by the Faura species plants, but it certainly implies it, calling zinc "essential" to the plants' growth and therefore suggesting that the lack of it harmed the plants. (D) directly states that the plants require a necessary ingredient that the botanists' fertilizer lacks. All three choices expand on the author's argument, more clearly defining *why* exactly the botanists' belief yielded such negative results. By adding to the evidence, all three choices strengthen the author's argument.

(C) doesn't identify a missing ingredient necessary for healthy plant growth but identifies a problem with the presentation of the list itself, as it fails to prioritize the most important elements. Despite this minor difference, (C) serves the same function as the aforementioned choices by explaining why the botanists' belief had negative results and thus strengthens the author's argument.

(E) is correct because it identifies one way in which the botanists' claim likely benefited the Faura species plants. The author is concerned with the negative effects of the belief, so this piece of information certainly doesn't strengthen her case.

Remember:

- Don't expect the right answer choice for these "all/except" questions to be 180 degrees different than the four others. The answer for this question doesn't need to weaken the argument; it only needs to NOT strengthen it. More often than not, the right answers for questions of this sort just have no real effect on the argument one way or the other.

6. E

Ron and Crystal will open a restaurant when they can both put in the required hours. Accordingly, the argument offers this one condition that must be met before the two open the restaurant. The remainder of the stimulus focuses on Ron's realization that Crystal's year-long project won't give her enough time to focus on the restaurant. The author suggests as much when he writes that Ron thought she would have enough time, but was wrong. Therefore, the condition required for the opening of the restaurant has not been met and clearly will not be met in the current year. It is therefore reasonable to conclude that they will not open the restaurant this year, answer choice (E). This could also be stated through formal logic: If the two open the restaurant, then that means they have enough time to dedicate to it. The contrapositive is that they don't have enough time (which the stimulus states), so therefore, they won't open the restaurant (the implied conclusion).

(A) is stated in the stimulus, so it isn't what the argument "is structured to lead to." This is part of the evidence, not the conclusion.

(B) We can infer that Ron and Crystal would believe (B) to be true, hence their pact that they would wait to open the restaurant until they were ready to devote their time and energy to it. However, this general statement, while certainly sounding consistent with the stimulus, is not the conclusion the argument is leading to. What about Ron? What about Crystal? What about their proposed restaurant? These things are the crux of the matter; the statement in (B) is too broad and general to be what the author is ultimately after here.

(C) might or might not be true; the stimulus certainly doesn't support or lead to this statement either way.

(D) might touch on some bigger problems in the relationship, but it doesn't get any support from the stimulus. Indeed, it contradicts the stimulus, which defines only one barrier to the opening of the restaurant, and that barrier is time, not any secretive agenda of deception on Crystal's part.

Remember:

- Be on the lookout for this very common argument structure in which only one or two explicitly stated conditions determine whether a certain course of action will be followed. Only those conditions will impact the course of action in the argument and in any correct answer choice that is supposed to be faithful to it. You can also often rephrase such arguments through the aid of formal logic.

7. C

This question asks us to determine what can be inferred from the statements in the passage. If the statistics cited by both of the speakers are true, which of the answer choices must also be true? A look at the statistics shows that over the past five years, the elderly care center has seen an increase in its applications from volunteers—the director says they've almost doubled. The nurse points out, however, that applications from patients' family members have actually decreased by 20 percent. If overall applications have increased, but family members' applications have gone down, what can we infer? (C) provides a logical deduction—that the center is receiving applications from volunteers who are not patients' family members. We can use the Kaplan Denial Test to check our accuracy here. If the clinic received no applications from persons who were not related to patients, then the statistics cited would not make sense.

(A) does not necessarily follow from the statistics in the passage. The statistics concern volunteer applications, not the size of the patient population. The data that we're given about the volunteer applications tells us nothing about the patient population one way or another.

(B) might be tempting, but does not provide us with the inference we need. Based on the statistics given, we cannot know whether patient care has improved or not. We're told that the number of volunteer applications has increased, but we don't know whether the number of accepted volunteers has grown—and we certainly don't know whether the volunteers are providing better care to the patients.

(D) Again, here, we cannot be sure that this statement is true simply based on the passage. We merely know that more people are interested in volunteering. This doesn't necessarily mean that the extra volunteers are *needed*, and it tells us nothing about *why* they might be needed if they are.

(E) is again beyond the limits of what we can infer here. We are told that the number of applications has increased and that the number of applications from family members has decreased. But that's all that we're given. This is not enough information to tell us anything about the selection process for volunteers—for all we know, every person who applies may actually become a volunteer.

Remember:

• If you're not sure after scanning the answers on a "must be true" Inference question, you can use the Kaplan Denial Test to eliminate choices effectively and to confirm the choice that most appeals to you. It works the same way as it does in Assumption questions: If you deny an answer choice and the denied statement

makes the passage appear illogical, you know you've found the correct answer.

8. D

Next we're asked to find a statement that weakens the nurse's argument. Before we can choose a weakener, we must first isolate the nurse's conclusion and evidence. The nurse concludes that the director's interpretation is wrong, and that community members are less interested in working with their parents than they were five years ago. She bases this conclusion on one piece of evidence: Applications from patients' family members have decreased over this time period. To weaken the argument, we might find another explanation for why volunteer applications from family members are down. (D) provides just such an alternative: If family members are no longer required to fill out formal applications, their applications will obviously not be on file, which could easily explain the 20 percent decrease. But they may continue to volunteer just the same.

(A) Irrelevant. This doesn't affect the nurse's argument one way or the other, because it refers to "community members" in general. We do not know if these community members are volunteer applicants or if they are related to the elderly at the center.

(B) touches on the issue of family activities, but it doesn't tell us anything about the center's volunteers.

(C) might be tempting, because it provides another reason, besides lack of interest, for why an individual might not volunteer. The problem with (C) is that it addresses individuals in general and makes no distinction between family members and non-family members. Even if (C) is true, the fact remains that family member applications are down, and (C) does nothing to damage the conclusion that the nurse bases on that fact.

(E) If anything, this choice might serve to strengthen the nurse's argument. If the volunteer commitment is relatively not extensive, this might reinforce the notion that relatives don't volunteer because they lack interest. Whether we see it as a slight strengthener or not, (E) contains nothing that weakens the argument.

Remember:

• Make the most of "double" questions that rely on one stimulus. Read both question stems before approaching the stimulus. That way you know what you're looking for and can read for two questions at once.

9. E

We know from the question stem that we're concerned with Theresa's method of argument, so when reading the dialogue between them, look specifically at how Theresa responds to Angie. Angie argues that if Bernard allows Pepe to sleep at the foot of his bed, Pepe's disciplinary problems will worsen. Theresa disagrees and believes that the same course of action will have the opposite outcome. Her evidence is Julian's dog: When Julian allowed his dog to sleep at the foot of his bed, the dog's disciplinary problems lessened. (E) accurately characterizes this method of argument: She indeed makes a prediction about Bernard's dog based on a similar situation with Julian's dog.

(A) If you identify what exists as evidence in the two statements, this one won't be tempting. Angie doesn't really provide any evidence, and Theresa's evidence about Julian is uniquely her own. There's no reinterpretation here.

(B) Theresa's recommendation is quite specific—let the dog sleep on the bed and he'll behave better.

(C) Angie might almost do this, but Theresa doesn't discuss the difficulties that might arise from a plan. She only discusses the benefits that would likely result given a certain course of action.

(D) Within Theresa's argument, the course of action (letting the dog sleep on the bed) remains the same. Her whole point is that the same course of action would likely have the same result, so (D) is wrong because it states that Theresa offered two different courses of action.

Remember:

• It's easiest to evaluate the difference between two statements in a dialogue stimulus by sticking to the basics: Identify each person's conclusion and evidence and you'll be able to see what the second person reacts to and how that person goes about it. The two views presented are always different, so be systematic in order to see where that difference lies.

10. E

Let's start by looking for the author's assumption. The study shows that students remember a good deal of the specific material that they teach, and the principal concludes that the students should teach everything, but that conclusion is only valid if the students are actually capable of teaching every subject. Notice that the evidence only discusses students teaching some material, while the conclusion advocates that students should teach everything. The assumption needs to fill this gap by allowing that the small scale model will work on the large scale. This is an inadequately supported assumption and is thus a flaw in the argument. (E) expresses this flaw, noting that the assumption may not be true and that small scale student teaching may not work on the large scale.

(A) isn't a flaw since the principal doesn't suggest that teaching is the only way to learn and will be the students' only occupation.

(B) This assumption is not part of the principal's proposal, which makes no mention of written assignments or learning through hearing. Not even the study itself, which does mention these forms of learning, suggests that the two are equally valuable.

(C) Well, the argument certainly doesn't discuss this, but since the argument has nothing to do with test scores, this consideration wouldn't be relevant to the argument, and thus, its omission isn't a flaw.

(D) doesn't state that the survey is wrong but that it's motivations might not be pure. Even if the survey were intensely self-interested, the principal is not concerned with its motivations but with its results. Her argument might be flawed if we knew she relied on results that were grossly inaccurate or results that she herself misinterpreted, but that's not what (D) says.

Remember:

- Flaw questions are so common and the different flaws they demonstrate are so varied that you should get a good sense of the possibilities before test day. The most common flaws are *unwarranted assumptions, ignored alternative possibilities,* and *scope shifts.* Use your practice to become familiar with each of these types of flaws.

11. D

The author supports one explanation for why the hardly pitiable students at Carmine University are overwhelmed by their elective course options. As the stimulus begins, he describes this scandalous problem and offers two possible explanations for it: improper categorization and overly extensive course descriptions. The author then concludes that, since each individual description isn't so long as to exceed the boundaries of what students can absorb (possibility #1), the problem must be with the categorization (possibility #2). Not so fast. Sure, each individual description isn't too long, but isn't it possible that all of the descriptions together are too long? (D) points out this missing step. If all the descriptions together are too much to absorb, then perhaps possibility #1 is the correct explanation after all.

(A) would certainly strengthen the argument, explaining as it does why students would be overwhelmed as a result of improper categorization, but it's not an assumption. The right answer choice needs to somehow address how the author selected his preferred explanation, and (A) does not.

(B) would weaken the argument because it offers an alternative explanation that certainly could be true given the argument, but this is also not our task. An assumption doesn't undermine the argument's conclusion.

(C) suggests that perhaps the handbook is not properly categorized, which makes it somewhat similar to (A). (C), if anything, would only strengthen the argument; it doesn't begin to make reference to the argument's evidence.

(E) Our argument deals with course descriptions, which are "far less lengthy" than that which students can absorb. This answer choice discusses "rather lengthy" descriptions, which aren't necessarily the same thing and therefore aren't necessarily relevant to the argument.

Remember:

- While filling in an assumption is one surefire way of strengthening an argument, something that strengthens an argument is not necessarily an assumption. Don't be tempted by choices like (A) and (C), which support the author's conclusion but don't support it by connecting it to the evidence, which any valid assumption must do.

12. B

The organizers claim only that the participants in the rally will bond and will therefore be less inclined to display aberrant behavior. They do not claim that the entire student body will be less inclined to act up. If the pep rally really will help to remedy the student behavior problem in the way in which its organizers say it will, then the students with behavior problems must attend the rally. (B) states this assumption quite directly: Only if the students creating the problem go to the pep rally can they receive the positive effects of that rally and be discouraged from their unpalatable behavior.

(A) If this were true, then the whole argument would be unnecessary. The argument proceeds from the assumption that the pep rally *is* included among the extracurricular activities to be canceled or else the coordinators wouldn't need to argue against its cancellation.

(C) is outside of the argument's scope. The pep rally organizers make no claims about the value of *other* extracurricular activities, and thus, they don't need to assume anything about those activities in order for their conclusion to be valid.

(D) Too extreme. The organizers conclude that the pep rally will help, but (D) represents a much stronger version of that conclusion (i.e., that the pep rally will help *more than anything else*).

(E) again brings in the consideration of other events and adds to that error by focusing on what the principal will do in the future. Nothing regarding what effect the rally will have on the principal's consideration of allowing *future* events is necessary for the argument to stand.

Remember:

• Choices that deviate from the specific scope of the argument in equstion in any major way cannot function as necessary assumptions for that argument. Neither the pep rally organizer's conclusion or evidence for that conclusion deal with any other canceled activities, so choices like (C) and (E) can be eliminated quickly.

13. A

We start off with a statement of what "some individuals" believe, so be ready for the author to explicitly or implicitly disagree with their opinion. These individuals believe that the cooking schools in Southern France teach all that there is to know about French cooking. Nevertheless, one recent graduate of a cooking school in Southern France did not know how to make the ever-popular bechamel sauce. The keyword *yet* clearly suggests the author's belief that this piece of evidence undermines the first stated conclusion. The question stem directs us to look for an inference, and at this point in the argument we can see that the author doesn't actually make her own conclusion. She provides evidence that would weaken the first conclusion, thereby implying her own conclusion that cooking schools in Southern France do not necessarily teach a student all that there is to know about French cooking. Since the author doesn't directly state her conclusion and this is an Inference question, the right answer choice will likely state that implied conclusion, as (A) indeed does. Since the author provides an exception to the first conclusion, then it must not always be true.

(B) Too extreme. All we know is that *one* graduate didn't know everything, so La Terrelle doesn't necessarily teach all that there is to know about French cooking. Still, some graduates could have learned everything.

(C) contradicts the stimulus that clearly states that all of La Terrelle's branches are in Southern France.

(D) Just because La Terrelle may not teach all that there is to know about French cooking to every student, it might still provide an effective education. Incomplete does not mean ineffective.

(E) Other schools outside the region lie beyond the scope of this argument.

Remember:

- If a question stem directs you to look for an inference and you read the stimulus and see that the author doesn't actually state his or her conclusion, prephrase the conclusion and seek it among the answer choices. Whenever you can prephrase an answer, you're much more likely to find the correct choice quickly and correctly, so always look out for possibilities to use that tool.

14. A

Four assumptions in the answer choices? Be prepared to see a pretty weak argument. The author concludes that, to achieve maximum healthiness, these bats should be fed certain nuts and veggies and a minimum amount of fruits and berries. The evidence comes in the second sentence: These bats, who are now fed mostly fruits and berries, develop endocrine imbalances. There's clearly a causality problem here. The author provides no evidence that the fruits and berries cause this endocrine imbalance, but the author must assume that that is the case in order to have a valid conclusion. It's not worth the effort to try to prephrase all the assumptions you might find, but if a few ideas jumped out at you, great. At the very least, proceed to the answer choices with a clear understanding of the evidence and conclusion.

(A) The conclusion states that the bats will be fed a minimal amount of fruits and berries, while this choice says that they will eat none. Must that be a necessary part of this argument? No, it's too extreme: The author says straight away that eating some fruits and berries is okay, so it need not be assumed that the bats are denied these foods altogether.

(B) and (D) are valid assumptions. If the proposed diet will make the bats "healthiest," then the argument assumes that it will adequately nourish them (D) and that it won't malnourish them (B). Negate these choices via the Kaplan Denial

Test, and the argument falls apart, confirming that these are necessary assumptions here.

(C) is also valid. The author suggests that the bat's endocrine imbalance is a problem and that a revised diet might fix that problem. Thus, the argument does assume that bats should not be fed endocrine imbalance-producing foods.

(E) focuses again on the author's claim that the recommended diet will make the bats healthiest. If that is true, then the author must assume that it won't create any health problems that are more detrimental to the bats' health than the endocrine imbalances that inspired the proposed diet in the first place.

Remember:

- Read the answer choices carefully! Reading the stimulus carefully and strategically will certainly get you on the right path, but you still need to be able to notice minor inaccuracies in the answer choices, like the difference between "no" fruits and berries and "minimal" fruits and berries.

15. C

The author clearly identifies the source of the confusion when he mentions what puzzles anthropologists. They're perplexed by two facts that seem inconsistent with each other. First, the advent of writing in certain Comaquogue clans seems to have caused the disappearance of the master storytellers within those tribes. Nevertheless, the second fact is that modern illiterate Comaquogue clans also lack master storytellers. The basic question is: Why do these modern illiterate clans lack storytellers when earlier clans lost their storytellers only after they learned how to read? Let's look to the answer choices and find one that specifically answers this question.

(A) does nothing to explain why the modern illiterate clans lack storytellers. Personality similarities don't have any clear relationship to literacy and storytellers.

(B) A comparison of the frequency of clan gatherings also does not in any way explain why the current illiterate tribes lack storytellers.

(C) would explain the discrepancy. If it were true, then the storytellers did disappear when the clans became literate, but they subsequently lost that literacy. Thus, the modern tribes could both be illiterate and lack storytellers, as is the case in the stimulus, and they could have lost their storytellers during an earlier literate period.

(D) again touches on the issue of modern Comaquogue rituals without referring to literacy and storytelling, the central elements of the argument's paradox.

(E) Too broad. It might give you the room to start making assumptions, but it doesn't specifically address the issues of literacy and storytelling.

Remember:

- Don't read too much into a choice in order to try to make it work. A choice has to be right without any help from you.

- In Paradox questions, rephrase the paradox as a question, and go through the answer choices trying to answer it. The temptation in these questions is to lose track of the paradox; hence, we have answer choices like (A), (B), (D), and (E). If you stay focused on the seeming discrepancy, you can avoid this trap.

16. B

The question stem tells us to focus on the dean's position, but the author gives us a good deal of background information before we hear about the dean. Apparently, Matthew's membership in a rock band has lowered his grades, which has hurt his chances of getting into a good business school.

Matthew might be able to rock on, however, because extracurricular activities like his could compensate for the lower grades. Finally, we get to the dean, who will not allow Matthew's musical hobby to better his chances of getting into Wentworth Business School. Focusing on this last piece of information, let's look to the answer choices to find one that generalizes the dean's position.

(A) sounds extremely official and says relatively nothing that relates to this situation. What action does (A) refer to? If it's Matthew's rock playing, then "consequences" probably would have to be his lower grades. If the action is the dean's refusal, the consequences for Matthew may be that he won't get in. Either way, there's no way to relate any of this to an evaluation of the action in light of "possible" consequences of an "opposing alternative action."

(B) is entirely consistent with the dean's position and would, if true, support its validity. We were told that participating in the band has hurt Matthew's chances for admission, so if something (like playing in a band) can't simultaneously hurt and help an applicant, then it makes sense that the dean sees no way for the rock band to increase Matthew's chances of getting into business school. (B) would therefore justify the dean's view that the band can have no positive effect. If you had trouble seeing this, match up the general terms in the choice with the specifics of the original: The "cause" is playing in the band; the "condition" is lower grades; the "consequence of that condition" is a lowered chance of admission. The dean simply refuses to allow Matthew's playing in the band to mitigate against the lower grades that resulted from his playing in the band.

(C) is inconsistent with the dean's position, since she is not stressing the positive value of Matthew's activities over their negative results. Rather, she sees no positive value in Matthew's musical activities.

(D) Irrelevant. Even if we argued that the dean's refusal is a decision that could affect Matthew's future, we have no idea how many factors go into admitting someone to business school, and whether this particular dean has considered them all or missed a few.

(E), like (D), is irrelevant, because the candidate is never eliminated from consideration. The dean won't give him credit for playing in the band, but that doesn't mean that she's tossed out his application.

Remember:

• For Principle questions, the answer will contain the elements of the relevant portion of the stimulus, rephrased and generalized, but otherwise not significantly altered. Stay away from choices that take you places that the stimulus never did.

17. B

The two viruses clearly cause one problem: They mess up the file storage system, usually by putting the files in the wrong places. The author concludes that computer users who detect one or both of these viruses needn't worry about the destruction of their files, based on the evidence that there is no proof that either virus erases files entirely. Do you see the flaw? The author's evidence is basically that there is no evidence to support a causal relationship. Nevertheless, just because there's no proof that either virus destroys files, that doesn't mean that the viruses don't destroy files. The absence of proof doesn't mean that no proof is possible, so this argument is flawed because it doesn't adequately prove that the viruses don't cause the destruction of files. (B) expresses this flaw; according to the argument, it is still entirely possible that the viruses destroy files, even though there is "at present" no evidence that they do.

(A) is outside the scope. The issue is whether the viruses pose a threat to files, and not whether people believe that they do.

(C) The author certainly doesn't discuss this, but that doesn't constitute a flaw in the argument. A discussion about the mechanism of file erasure wouldn't be relevant to the conclusion, so its omission is not a flaw.

(D) suggests that a keyword has more than one definition in the argument, which is not the case.

(E) describes a circular argument, which exists when the evidence and the conclusion are the same. In this argument, the two are clearly different, and the extent of their difference is part of the real flaw.

Remember:

• The three most common types of flaws are unwarranted assumptions, unconsidered alternative possibilities, and scope shifts. This question gives us an example of the second type. Be on the lookout for all three when tackling Logical Flaw questions.

18. D

This Parallel Reasoning question lends itself well to algebraic characterization. The question stem itself gives us some critical information: We're told that the argument in the stimulus is flawed and that we're looking for an answer choice that is flawed in a similar manner. If foods aren't stored properly, they can give people food poisoning (if X, then possibly Y). Since people at the Panhandler got food poisoning, the restaurant must have served food that wasn't properly stored (Y, therefore X). This argument makes the mistake of concluding that a "reverse cause and effect" relationship is operating: Because the consequence occurred, the cause must have been in effect also. We know from formal logic that we simply can't get from "if X then Y" to "if Y then X." So all we need to do is find the choice that commits the same error. There's of course no way to prephrase the specifics of the right choice, only its structure, so the best bet is to simply work through the choices:

(A) tells us that if a man over 65 has high blood pressure, he is at risk for heart disease (if X, then Y). That has the first part of the argument right. But the second sentence tells us that Tonare males over 65 do not have blood pressure, so they are not at risk for heart disease—which translates into not X, therefore not Y. This conclusion simply negates the terms without switching them as in the original.

(B) and (C) can both be eliminated because neither of them presents a "reverse cause and effect" argument; in fact, neither one contains anything that can be translated into a formal logic if/then statement. (B) contains a temporal flaw; for all we know, Magelli might have crafted the cabinet before he died. We would need information that the cabinet is less than fifteen years old before the conclusion would be valid. And (C)'s conclusion is certainly premature as well, but again does not contain the same formal logic structure as the original; there's nothing in there that can be translated into "if X, then Y."

(D) contains the kind of flaw we seek. This choice states that Relief-O! has been known to cause blurred vision in people who take it. We can translate that sentence as: "If people take Relief-O, they may experience blurred vision" (if X, then possibly Y). So far so good. The following sentences then tell us that Molly took a pain reliever and experienced blurred vision (Y), so she must have taken Relief-O! (therefore X). Perfect.

(E) This argument deals with cause and effect, but not in the same manner as in the stimulus. (E) lays out an initial cause: If tigermint grows out of control, it can kill other plants (if X, then Y). But its second sentence introduces a negative condition: Sally's plants did *not* get killed—in fact, they look better than ever. Therefore, the tigermint must not be out of control. This reduces to not Y, therefore not X—and not parallel.

19. D

When you see percents or ratios in a stimulus, you'll likely need to exercise your ability to distinguish between rates and numbers. This is an Inference question, as the stem makes clear, and you can prephrase an answer by considering what conclusion this evidence would support. If 57 percent equals the same number of paintings before the unveiling as 85 percent equals after the unveiling, then Déjère must have produced more paintings in the period before the unveiling—that's the only way that the numbers could work out. (D) states this from the other angle: Déjère must have painted fewer paintings after the unveiling.

(A) The author tells us that revenue from both periods is equal since Déjère sells the same number of paintings in both. Therefore, if she had charged more in the second period, she would have made more money than she had in the first, which would contradict the stimulus. Because this is inconsistent with the passage, it certainly can't be inferred from it.

(B) is outside of the scope because the author never mentions Déjère's motivations behind painting. Since there's no information about this, we can't reasonably concluding anything pertaining to it.

(C) If anything, this might suggest that Déjère sells more paintings in the second period, which the stimulus explicitly contradicts. Further, the stimulus provides no information about how art collectors might have responded to the review, giving us no basis to make a conclusion about those collectors.

(E) would also act to explain why her sales are higher in the second period, but the author says that the sales were not any greater. Also, marketing is never discussed.

Remember:

- Percentages show up often in Logical Reasoning sections; make sure you're comfortable analyzing such data. Sometimes the difference between percentages and raw numbers forms the basis of a logical flaw. Other times, as is the case here, you'll simply need to understand what the percentages represent in order to draw an inference from the data.

20. B

Considering then the structure of the argument, the author states that something (the consumption of dairy products) doesn't usually create a certain result (stomachaches) and then concludes that something that might explain a causal relationship between the two (allergies) doesn't exist. In other words, if a causal relationship isn't usually present, then it isn't present. Looking for another choice that demonstrates the same structure, we can hold on to (B): There the author states that dog anxiety does not usually indicate coming earthquakes and therefore argues against a necessary relationship between the two. It matches the original in all the major elements.

(A) is wrong because the conclusion argues *for* a correlation while the stimulus argues *against* a correlation between two occurrences.

(C) begins by saying that something sometimes doesn't create a certain result. Already it isn't parallel, since the evidence in the stimulus states that something doesn't *usually* create a certain result. "Many people" in (C) doesn't parallel the "most of the time" in the stimulus. Moreover, (C) argues about the efficacy of a program, whereas the original and correct choice (B) are concerned with the relation between two events.

(D) presents an entirely different argument, arguing that a claim isn't valid because there isn't enough evidence to support it. The original argument says that a claim isn't valid because two factors usually aren't related. The notion of "validity," like "efficacy" in (C), is one step removed from the gist of the terms in the original argument.

(E) argues against a causal relationship, but it doesn't parallel the original evidence because it mentions what "many" businesses do, not what "most" do. More centrally, the conclusion veers away from the evidence: The evidence suggests that decentralized operations often yield a profit, while the conclusion suggests that the two aren't directly related. In the original, both the evidence and conclusion argue against a causal relationship.

Remember:

- It's often difficult to remember several pieces of information in your head without getting them mixed up, especially while you're evaluating five new pieces of information. Don't hesitate to make notes if they'll help keep you on track.

21. D

The argument begins by offering one route through which a student can gain a coveted membership to the Theta Delta Psi fraternity. For those aspirants who attended high school with a current member of the house and developed a strong social connection with that member before college, entrance into the fraternity is easy. People who didn't attend high school with a current member can't easily attain membership through this route, but we were never told that this was the only way to easily get into the fraternity. The author concludes that the unconnected individuals will have difficulty joining the fraternity, but that's only valid if the route the author describes is the only possible easy route. But the author never says that. (D) thus gets at the major point the author fails to consider in issuing her hasty conclusion: the possibility that there might be other ways to easily get into the frat.

(A) First of all, those who attended high school with fraternity members are not necessarily the same people who have forged strong social connections with them. So the "many" referred to here may not even be relevant to the argument. Secondly, even assuming these guys *are* good high school buddies of the members, the author argues only about what conditions make for easy entry into the frat, and need not consider the possibility that many high school classmates of the members would choose not to join.

(B) Associations with non-fraternity members are not relevant to the argument and fall outside of its scope. Additionally, this choice discusses the long-term benefits of such connections; we only care about entrance into the fraternity, not about lifelong happiness.

(C) The relative difficulty of building these connections has nothing to do with their necessity for membership. This choice also shares with (B) an interest in non-fraternity members, whom the author never mentions.

(E) is perfectly consistent with the author's argument, as it totally avoids the issue of the ease with which these "current members" got in. This choice falls outside of the author's scope, which is about the possibility of getting into the fraternity with ease, and we therefore can't fault the author for neglecting the possibility raised here.

Remember:

- Pay attention to author's topic and scope. Notice that answer choice (D) is the only one to address the difficulties of obtaining membership; most of the others fell outside of that scope.

22. C

Again the stimulus begins with the author's conclusion, which basically opposes the continued enforcement of the new farm subsidy laws. The author stipulates the advantages of the laws, but nevertheless stresses their negative long-term results. The question stem directs you to determine the role of the second part of that second sentence, the part that discusses the negative effects of the laws. Before looking at the answer choices, it's possible to determine that this is evidence for the author's conclusion—it answers the question, "Why do you oppose the continuation of the laws?" Correct choice (C) goes one step further: It shows more specifically how the statement functions as evidence. The author discusses the negative effects in order to counter the positive effects, which enables him to support his conclusion that the laws should be ditched.

(A) Don't be thrown by the presence of the word "evidence" here. First, the author doesn't tell us that the positive effects of the laws have been used as evidence to support them. Second, the author doesn't use the negative effects to argue that the laws *haven't* enabled farmers to maintain their incomes or stabilized the market; he offers those as true but stresses that the negative effects outweigh those benefits.

(B) commits the same error as (A). It distorts the passage by suggesting that the author contradicts and discredits the benefits of the laws, but he acknowledges that they have stabilized the agricultural market. The author doesn't disagree with that statement but places it in the context of what he sees as the more serious negative effects.

(D) is way too strong: The author cannot "prove" that without the laws agricultural technology will remain a high priority simply by stating that the laws discourage the need for competitive advancements. At most, the author sug-

KAPLAN

gests that in the absence of the laws, the opportunities for tech advances may improve, but that's far from "proving" anything.

(E) is half right and half wrong. It starts off on very strong footing by defining the statement as evidence, but it quickly takes a nosedive by making an irrelevant distinction between market stabilization and the development of competitive technology. The author does suggest that the negative effects of the laws outweigh the positive effects, and the author does mention these issues, but the author doesn't specifically rank one against the other. He shows that both of the negative effects outweigh both of the positive effects; he doesn't compare them piece by piece.

Remember:

- Be very careful when perusing the answer choices. Here, choices (A) and (E) use the word *evidence*, a sure temptation for those test takers who don't examine the answer choices carefully. (C) doesn't use the term "evidence" but basically defines what evidence is in the context of the passage. Even when you have a prephrase, remember that you still need to look at the answer choices carefully and not jump at the first one containing a specific term you had in mind. The whole choice must pan out.

23. D

Just because the organizers didn't give a complete list to everybody, it doesn't follow that they gave more complete lists to some people than others. You can use your formal logic skills on this one: We were originally told that if people are fully informed, then nobody has an advantage. It doesn't follow that if people are not fully informed, then somebody does have an advantage. That's a common formal logic error, and since the author commits it, the right answer choice will likely identify this as the flaw in the argument. (D) accomplishes

this by stating what still could be true given the argument: everyone could have received the same incomplete list. In concluding categorically that some lucky participant has a leg up on the others, the author doesn't allow for the possibility stated in (D), and so (D) legitimately points to a flaw in the argument.

(A) and (E) Probably the easiest way to eliminate (A) is to recognize that the author discusses who has the best *chance* of finding the diamond ring. The author never suggests that having a better chance of finding the ring means actually finding the ring. If the author had made such a suggestion, it would be a flaw, but since the author never did, it isn't. (E) takes this issue from another angle by suggesting that people with incomplete lists might still find the ring. The author never suggests otherwise, since again the author solely discusses who has the best chance of finding the ring, not who will therefore actually find it. So while (A) and (E) are indeed consistent with the stimulus, they don't point to a logical flaw in the argument.

(B) is close, but not fully there. Even if nobody receives a complete list (which is possible), there still exists the possibility that some people receive more complete lists than others, a situation that wouldn't by itself expose a flaw in the argument.

(C) just states one possible consequence of handing out different lists. The scenario in (C) is consistent with the facts in the stimulus, so it's okay on that count; but like (B), (C) still allows for the possibility that some person has a better chance than others, as the author maintains.

Remember:

- Reading critically means noticing small shifts in scope between the information in the passage and the focus of the choices. The author here is concerned with the participants' relative chances of finding the diamond. Choices like (A) and (E) that center around actually locating the ring are one step removed from this focus, so they aren't likely to point out a flaw in the logic.

24. E

The stem tells us that the teacher will make some error in her response to the judges' decision, so we can read knowing that we'll see at least two arguments and that the teacher's will be flawed. The judges decided to disqualify Samuel's essay from the contest only because he broke one rule: He put his name on every page of the essay when the rules required that he put it only on the cover page. Samuel's teacher disagrees with the judges' conclusion, but in her argument she doesn't address the judges' reason for disqualifying him. She completely ignores the judges' evidence, and introduces a new issue as her evidence: She believes that the personal problems in Samuel's life entitle him to have his essay considered in the contest. Her argument is flawed because she neglects to discuss the judges' actual reasoning and thus doesn't really address the judges' argument. While the emotional appeal may work on *Oprah*, in the world of argumentation, it's a flaw to disagree with a conclusion without disputing the link between it and the evidence offered to justify it.

(A) The teacher *does* offer evidence when she explains that Samuel's essay deserves another chance because his parents got a divorce. Weak or irrelevant evidence is not the same as *no* evidence.

(B) The teacher doesn't make a causal argument. She thinks that personal considerations should override the judges' decision, but she isn't concerned with whether one thing causes another.

(C) is out because the teacher doesn't address *any part* of the judge's argument, which is the real flaw. She merely disputes their action on grounds entirely divorced (so to speak) from their argument in support of that action.

(D) again suggests that the teacher actually addresses the judges' evidence justifying their decision. She doesn't.

Remember:

- To see where two arguments differ, compare their conclusions and their evidence. Here, the conclusions were different, and the evidence was different in the two arguments, so right off the bat you could eliminate (A), (C), and (D). The more structured you are in the way in which you compare two arguments, the easier it'll be to see where one differs or goes awry.

25. A

The author begins by concluding that cross-training is more beneficial than single-sport training for those who wish to improve their overall fitness. The author presents two pieces of evidence to support this opinion: First, cross-training develops a wider range of muscle groups. Second, cross-training increases phasic muscle fibers, which burn more calories. Can you see any gaps, a.k.a., assumptions, between the conclusion and the evidence? The author assumes a link between developing a wide range of muscles/burning calories and overall fitness, so we can check to see if any answer choice strengthens the argument by asserting that assumption. We can stop at choice (A), since it establishes the connection between burning calories and overall fitness.

(B) The fact that athletic training *in general* is the best way to improve overall fitness doesn't strengthen an argument that one kind of athletic training (cross-training) is better for fitness than another (single-sport training).

(C) *Au contraire:* This would actually weaken the argument. Tonic muscle fibers are exercised by single-sport training, so increasing their value would weaken the author's argument in support of cross-training.

(D) falls outside the scope: The author solely addresses which type of training works better to improve overall fitness in *healthy* individuals, so the danger of one type of training for those recovering from serious illness cannot have any bearing on the argument.

(E) On one hand, it would appear that (E) might actually weaken the argument. Single-sport training targets slow-twitch muscle groups. If that exercise simultaneously exercises phasic muscle groups, then it provides one of the benefits of cross-training. Therefore, (E) would increase the value of single-sport training in achieving overall fitness, which would run counter to the conclusion. But the fact that slow-twitch muscles contain many phasic muscle fibers doesn't necessarily mean that single-sport training would *increase* these fibers; that's still up in the air. So the best thing to say about (E) is that it is too ambiguous to have any effect on the argument at hand.

Remember:

- Whenever you see a central term in the conclusion that is unique to the conclusion, you're one step closer to prephrasing an author's assumption. Here, the conclusion contains a phrase—*overall fitness*—that shows up nowhere else in the argument. Since an assumption connects the evidence to the conclusion, it will make the evidence relevant to the dangling term in the conclusion. Specifically, developing a wide range of muscles and burning calories must lead to increased overall fitness if this argument is going to stand. Look out for terms unique to the conclusion as you search for assumptions that will help you to strengthen or weaken arguments.

Section IV: Reading Comprehension Explanations

PASSAGE 1—*Frankenstein*

Topic and Scope

Mary Shelley's novel *Frankenstein*; specifically, the great philosophical import of the book as compared to subsequent visual adaptations of it.

Purpose and Main Idea

The author's purpose in writing this passage is to demonstrate the complexities of Mary Shelley's *Frankenstein* and to argue for an appreciation of the novel on its own terms, apart from film adaptations of it. The main idea is that cinematic versions of the story of *Frankenstein* are actually based on a complex and compelling novel, the richness of which cannot be fully captured on film but nonetheless should not be overlooked.

Paragraph Structure

The first paragraph immediately contrasts the aura that the Frankenstein monster has taken on in popular culture with the thematic purpose known to serious readers of the book: to caution readers against the dangers of scientific hubris.

Paragraph 2 explains that the idea for the story came from a dream that Shelley had. The story is intended to refute the attacks of science on nature. It shows the negative consequences of not using our society's scientific capabilities responsibly.

In paragraph 3, we're told that the current appeal of the book is based on the many timeless themes that it contains, themes that have "only grown in importance" since its first publication. The full essence of the book cannot be captured by cinema, and the author hopes that film adaptations will not make people forget the book's richness.

The Big Picture

- As you read through each passage, focus on grasping the author's main idea. Once you've determined the main idea, whether it comes in the beginning or towards the end of the passage, lay out in your road map how each paragraph works to support that main idea.

- Good critical readers pick up on particular phrases that provide clues to the author's attitude toward someone or something in the passage. Here, phrases like "one of the great philosophical and prophetic works," "timeless tale," and "genius of the original masterpiece" strongly suggest the author's great admiration for Shelley's novel, a notion that leads us directly toward the author's main idea.

The Questions

1. **D**

This is a broad Inference question that asks us to choose the statement with which the author would most likely agree. Such an open-ended question is too difficult to prephrase, so the best approach is to evaluate the choices. Choice (D) fits well with paragraph 3: The author tells us that the enduring appeal of Shelley's book is attributable to the relevance of themes that she raises. The author would thus likely agree that a work's relevance in general increases when its elements resonate with its current audience.

(A) This choice is an exaggeration of the author's claim that visual adaptations have thus far not adequately captured the richness of Shelley's book. He believes this about film adaptations of *Frankenstein* but doesn't apply his claim to every artistic work.

(B) This choice also misrepresents the author's argument. Shelley published her work anonymously because it was not acceptable at the time for women to write such "ghastly" stories. The author never suggests that *every* shocking work should be published anonymously.

(C) and (E) Both of these choices distort elements of the passage. As for (C), the author never addresses works that receive no critical acclaim when they are written. We're not sure, in fact, how Shelley's work was originally received; all we know is that it was too risqué at first to attach her name to it. Further, the author never draws a relationship between the seriousness of a work and its ability to predict the future. Just because Shelley's work was both serious and prophetic doesn't allow us to infer the blanket statement in (E).

Remember:

- Wrong answer choices to Inference questions follow predictable patterns. Two of those patterns are represented in this question: extreme choices and distortions. Pay attention to the types of wrong answer choices that appear repeatedly and be prepared to avoid them on test day.

2. E

This Explicit Text question is signaled by the words "according to the author," which lets us know that the answer will come straight from the text. A line reference is given to make our work easier. This question doesn't seem tricky, but it turns out that the science-nature clash is mentioned in another place after the notion is introduced in the second paragraph—namely, in paragraph 3. Here the author tells us that the science versus nature conflict increases the book's current relevance, an almost exact paraphrase of choice (E).

(A) This choice is half right, half wrong. The science-nature clash is one of the factors responsible for the current appeal of the book itself, not its film versions.

(B) This choice exaggerates the author's argument. The author merely suggests that movies are unable to portray the "science versus nature" theme in all its "seriousness and complexity." He never argues that the movie versions don't portray this central theme at all.

(C) Here the issue of Shelley's anonymous publishing is again raised, but again, in an inappropriate context. We saw in choice (B) of the previous question that she published the book anonymously because society wasn't ready to accept women writing "ghastly" works. The science-nature clash itself doesn't seem to be the problem; the way in which that clash is *developed* (via the "ghastly" horror story device) is the reason she went underground for awhile.

(D) *Au contraire*: Paragraph 3 tells us that the science-nature clash is one of the themes of the work that has "grown in importance" since Shelley's day.

Remember:

- Keep an open mind concerning line reference questions and avoid focusing too narrowly. The correct answer will likely involve reading beyond the referenced line and may often involve connecting the reference to other relevant parts of the text.

3. B

If we read the portion of paragraph 3 that discusses the currently relevant themes of the work, we see that all of the choices are listed except for choice (B). If this *Frankenstein* example is any indication, we'd have to say that the author's complaint suggests the opposite of (B), namely that appreciation for artistic seriousness and complexity is waning.

(A) is covered by the phrase "technology as man's salvation."

(C) The theme in (C) comes up many times through-out the passage. Most relevant to this question is its appearance in the final paragraph as "science versus nature."

(D) is raised with "the role of visual appearance in society."

(E) is captured in the phrase "alienation of the out-cast."

Remember:

- As always, watch the "EXCEPT" questions carefully. Be sure to choose the answer that is NOT implied or stated in the text. Sometimes the correct choice will simply be outside the scope. Other times, as is the case here, it may even go against the grain of the sentiments in the passage.

4. C

This question addresses the author's attitude. To answer it, we should first determine whether the author's views on this issue are positive or negative. The wording of paragraph 1 gives us a clue: "endless Hollywood adaptations . . . campy TV shows . . ." Sounds like the author's not so hot on the visual adaptations, right? This is confirmed of course by the phrase in the final paragraph, "inability to capture in cinematic form the deep philosophical richness of the book." So this negativity kills (A) and (D) immediately. But just how negative are his views? Somewhat negative, although not drastic enough to say he displays "biting derision" (B) or "unreserved condescension" (E). We're therefore left with the more moderate (C).

Remember:

- Use the Kaplan strategy to make "attitude/tone" questions easy to handle. Determine first whether the author's views are positive, negative, or neutral—then eliminate all of the choices that don't conform to the general category you choose. If you determine the views are somewhat negative, as is the case here, then look to cross off any choices that contain any positivity. Then weed out any exaggerations or choices that are too weak and you should be left with the correct answer.

5. A

This question tests whether you understand one part of the passage in the context of the overall argument. Why does the author mention Hollywood film adaptations early on in paragraph 1? As we see from paragraph 3, he will argue eventually that film versions can't capture the depth of Shelley's original work. Citing film versions in paragraph 1 is therefore a means of setting up what will be the main idea, or as (A) describes it, the "basis of the author's central concern." The author certainly does return to this concept when developing the main idea in paragraph 3, so that part of the choice is accurate. But does the whole choice work? Is the example of film adaptations provided as a "contrast" as choice (A) would have it? Yes—the "endless" Hollywood adaptations, along with the other pop culture manifestations, are meant to stand in contrast to the philosophical and prophetic cautionary tale that spawned them. This contrast will build in paragraph 3 when it indeed "resurfaces" as the basis of the author's concern that the visual forms may one day eclipse the genius of the original work.

(B) The author never raises a debate much less try to settle one.

(C) The author does support Shelley's work, but doesn't deal with criticisms of it. No such criticisms appear in the passage.

(D) *Au contraire.* The author would not see film adaptations as an "inevitable successor" to literature. In fact, he believes that in this particular case, film cannot portray the literary work effectively.

(E) This choice is both too general and exaggerated. The author doesn't describe Hollywood adaptations as part of a larger "artistic movement." Neither does he make the sweeping claim that film can *never* capture literary works well. He just doesn't believe that film versions of *Frankenstein* do justice to the original book.

Remember:

- Reading with a critical eye towards purpose and structure will always pay off on the Reading Comp section. When you encounter new characters or material, ask yourself, "Why are they here? What function do they serve?" When you come to a question like this one, hopefully you can prephrase an answer or at least eliminate a handful of wrong choices based on your initial understanding of the purpose of each element of the passage.

6. A

This question asks us for the author's purpose in writing the passage, so think back about what you've been focusing on all along. We've seen how the author's purpose is to lay out the complexities of Shelley's work and to argue that it should be appreciated on its own terms and that the film versions should not overshadow the original story. The closest we get to this prephrase is found in choice (A), which is a bit more general than our prephrase, but hits closest to the mark.

(B) and (E) Too broad. The problem with (B) is that the author does not discuss "works of art" in general, but rather one work in particular. Similarly, with (E), the author does not pay tribute to the "art form" of literature in general—instead, he is praising one specific work of literature. Moreover, according to the author, this work has not yet *been* overshadowed, but rather is *in danger* of being overshadowed by its visual adaptations.

(C) Too narrow. The author does discuss how Shelley's novel originated, but this is only a small part of what he does in the text.

(D) Be careful here: This is the argument that Shelley makes in her novel, not the argument made by the author in the passage as a whole.

Remember:

- Choices like (D) here reinforce why we must be careful to distinguish between the various views presented in a passage. Here we have an author of a passage presenting the views expressed by an author described in the passage. Make sure to keep the various views straight, and you won't be tricked up by a choice like (D) above.

- When answering Global LSAT Reading Comp questions, such as those pertaining to the author's purpose or main idea, be on the lookout for choices that are overly broad or too narrow. The correct answer to a Global question will match the author's scope in the passage and will reflect the point of the passage as a whole—not just one part of it.

PASSAGE 2—Weber and Objectivity

Topic and Scope

Max Weber's views on objectivity; specifically, the degree to which Weber upholds a strict concept of objectivity in his work.

Purpose and Main Idea

The author's purpose is to make an argument regarding how Weber views the concept of objectivity and employs it in his writing. The main idea is that Weber does not believe in strict objectivity across-the-board and that his views on objectivity are therefore more complex than they are traditionally portrayed.

Paragraph Structure

The first paragraph of this passage presents the "traditional" or conventional explanation of Weber's views: Scholars normally see him as upholding a strict concept of objectivity in his work. Whenever we're presented with a traditional view in the opening paragraph, it's a good bet that the author will counter or refute that view in what's to follow. This paragraph is no exception—sure enough, the author quickly counters the traditional interpretation by asserting that Weber's views are "more complicated" than the traditional view would have it.

Given this starting point, we might expect the following paragraphs to show us how and why Weber's views are complicated. This is exactly what happens. Paragraph 2 concedes that in certain respects, Weber does believe in the possibility of strict objectivity: We see it in his views on the nature of reality. When it comes to questions of truth, Weber does believe that a value-neutral reality exists.

In paragraph 3, however, the complexities of Weber's views are introduced. Here the author shows that Weber doesn't think our knowledge of reality can be totally objective. This is because knowledge is rooted in the assumptions and perspectives of those who investigate reality—thus, some subjective bias enters in.

Paragraph 4 shows that Weber deviates most from strict objectivity on questions concerning ethics. When people use knowledge to decide how to behave, Weber thinks they should make their decisions subjectively, according to their own personal biases. So as the passage progresses, so does Weber's deviation from the strict concept of objectivity "traditionally" ascribed to him.

The Big Picture

- LSAT Reading Comp passages very often begin with an accepted view and then present an opposing view. When a passage starts out with a "traditional" perspective, be on the lookout for an opposing argument to come.

- If a passage starts out with a traditional view and provides an opposing argument, it is likely that the rest of the passage will develop that opposing argument. As you read through this type of argumentative passage, look for specific evidence that the author uses to support his or her counterview.

The Questions

7. **D**

This question asks us for the main idea of the passage, and in this case, the author presents an argument against a traditional view. Her opposing argument, or main idea, is laid out at the end of the first paragraph, where she tells us that Weber's views on objectivity are "more complicated than the traditional interpretation would have us believe." Choice (D) sums this up nicely.

(A) This choice goes beyond the scope of the passage. Nowhere are other theories of objectivity discussed—the passage focuses only on Weber's views.

(B) This choice contradicts what is stated in the passage. Paragraph 2 shows us that Weber upholds a strictly objective view concerning the nature of reality; he believes in the existence of absolute truth. It is in our attempt to *investigate* objective reality that Weber believes subjectivity creeps in.

(C) and (E) Both of these choices are distortions of information in the passage. While the author argues that Weber's views on objectivity are complex, she never claims that these views are

KAPLAN

not clearly presented (C). Neither does she go so far as to claim that they are inconsistent (E).

Remember:

- If you focus on the author's purpose and main idea as you read, this type of question should be a snap. If you relate all of the content in the passage to the main idea as you read, you should be able to prephrase answers to questions like this one accurately.

8. A

It's difficult to prephrase an answer to such an open-ended Inference question as this, so we must proceed to the choices to see which view can be most readily ascribed to Weber. Luckily, we don't have to look far: (A) presents a good summary of Weber's views on scientific knowledge as presented in paragraph 3. Here we learn that Weber believes that knowledge cannot be totally objective because it is influenced by the assumptions and perspectives of the particular scientific community involved in the investigation of reality.

(B) and (E) misrepresent Weber's use of "ideal types." Ideal types are presented in paragraph 2 as constructs that Weber believes can help scientists investigate reality, not their own biases regarding reality (B). And (E) goes way too far: Just because Weber believes that ideal types can be used to help the scientist investigate objective reality, that's far from saying that he believes this is "the *only* reliable method" possible.

(C) In paragraph 4 we're told that Weber believes that teachers should refrain from imposing their views on students *period*—regardless of how capable those students are.

(D) The fact that Weber believes that the *perception* of objective reality must be tinged by subjectivity doesn't mean that Weber finds the notion of objective reality itself "misleading"—on the contrary, paragraph 2 tells us that Weber *does* believe in the existence of strict objective reality.

Remember:

- Inference questions are usually not easy to prephrase, so the best approach to these questions is to quickly evaluate each answer choice. A good road map can help you determine whether a given choice fits with the ideas in the passage.

9. B

This question would have been a good one to prephrase, particularly if you looked for the author's purpose and main idea as you read the passage. Since this passage focuses only on Weber, the correct answer will indicate that one author's views are discussed. (B) throws in the key main idea word "complexities," describing the author's purpose succinctly.

(A) and (C) It can be said that the author enters into a debate by countering the traditional view of Weber's scholarship, but that's not the same as "resolving" a debate. If (A) were the intended right answer, two independent views would have to be presented, with the author choosing one over the other. Similarly, she does not "reconcile" opposing perspectives (C)—she merely develops her own position regarding Weber's views.

(D) The author does not argue against Weber's perspective but rather describes it for the reader.

(E) The author presents Weber's views but does not *test* them. Furthermore, Weber's views represent his position on objectivity, but they do not take the form of a formal hypothesis.

Remember:

- Reading for topic, scope, and purpose has many benefits. Not only does it allow you to gain a better grasp of the passage overall—it can also lead to quick points if you're handed a straightforward Global question like this one.

10. C

The phrase "according to the passage" here clues us in that this is an Explicit Text question; we can thus expect the answer to draw on a specific detail from the passage. Which paragraph discusses how individuals should use knowledge to guide their actions? Exactly—paragraph 4. A good road map would have quickly led you to this part of the passage, and the phrase "free to choose how he or she acts upon the reality discovered by science" is the one that best captures the gist of Weber's position regarding the uses of scientific knowledge. Choice (C) stands out as the best paraphrase of this.

(A) distorts the author's meaning in the passage. Paragraph 4 tells us that teachers should help students account for the meaning of their own conduct. It does not tell us that students should be restricted from making decisions if they cannot account for the meaning of their conduct.

(B) According to paragraph 4, Weber believes that individuals should use scientific knowledge in making decisions about action, not that they should distrust it.

(D) *Au contraire.* We are told that Weber believed that teachers should not guide their students' actions but should allow students to make their own decisions.

(E) also goes against the grain of the passage. "Weber believes that individuals must make their own decisions . . ." suggests that teachers should *not* follow the lead of their students but should also act on knowledge independently when determining their own course of action.

Remember:

- Explicit Text questions can often be answered by referring back to the part of the passage that contains the detail in question. If you must quickly reread the relevant parts of the paragraph to make your selection, do so.

11. E

Next up we're asked for the passage structure, and hopefully your work on the passage so far will help you prephrase an answer or at least quickly eliminate choices that stray beyond your road map. We know from our answer to question 9 that only one author's views (Weber's) are presented here, and our road map tells us that different aspects of these views are described in each paragraph. This fits with the gist of choice (E): The "interpretation" expands on the traditional position regarding Weber's view of objectivity, and the author certainly does support this interpretation throughout the passage with specific references to Weber's views and teachings.

(A) and (B) The author spends her time in this passage developing Weber's views. She does not reject his views as (A) indicates; nor does she first criticize these views as (B) states.

(C) *Au contraire.* As we saw with choice (A), the author does not negate Weber's views. Instead, she supports them.

(D) This choice tries the same trick we saw in question 9. We know that no hypothesis is presented here and that no testing is accomplished, so we can reject this choice.

Remember:

- The choices in "passage structure" questions are often phrased in general terms. The wrong answer choices will contain terms such as "reject" and "criticize" that violate the spirit of the passage and others such as "hypothesis" and "empirical testing" that sound nice and official but don't apply to the passage at all. Put the choices through their paces before settling on the one you prefer.

12. **A**

Our road map can again come in handy here by helping us locate the assertion that "knowledge of reality cannot be totally objective." A quick review shows us that this point is raised in paragraph 3, where the author discusses scientific knowledge. This Explicit Text question asks for evidence specifically mentioned in the passage that supports the assertion in the stem, and again we return to the same idea that we've discussed previously: The interpretation of objective reality is biased by underlying assumptions.

(B) This choice reflects the opposite of what is stated in the passage. The author claims that Weber believes that methods of investigation can never be strictly objective by their very nature.

(C) and(D) These choices present ideas raised in the passage, but neither of these statements reflects evidence for the assertion in question. Ideal types are discussed in the passage but only in paragraph 2. We're looking for evidence given in paragraph 3. The definition of "objective truth" is also raised in paragraph 2 but not as evidence for the point that knowledge can't be objective.

(E) once again plays off the distinction between objective reality and the *knowledge* of objective reality. Weber *does* believe in the concept of strict objectivity, so to say that objective reality is "illusory" goes against the grain of the passage, not to mention trying to posit it as evidence for something else in the passage.

Remember:

• When asked about specific details from the text, make sure to locate the part of the text from which the relevant details will be drawn. Then stick strictly to the author's argument. If you're asked for evidence, choose only the choice that provides support for the point or conclusion in question. Avoid choices taken from other parts of the text.

13. **C**

Why would the author have given us the "traditional" interpretation of Weber's view? To let us know which view she was reacting against—to provide an introduction into her opposing interpretation of his views. Choice (C) describes this reason well.

(A) This choice is an exaggeration. Although the author rejects the traditional view, it would be going too far to say that she "dismiss[es] the relevance of all previous scholarship" on Weber.

(B) again distorts the author's purpose. She does not argue that objectivity has been historically misunderstood in general, but rather that Weber's views on objectivity have been misunderstood.

(D) and (E) These choices state the opposite of the author's reason for presenting the traditional view. She does not use it to develop critics' views of Weber, but rather her own interpretation. Neither does she attempt to vindicate the traditional view; on the contrary, she refutes it.

Remember:

• Questions that end with the words "in order to" require you to look for how something functions to support the author's overall argument or purpose in the passage. When you're asked why an author includes something, think about the entire passage. What role is played by the part in question? How does it contribute to the passage? Some parts of the text may provide support or evidence; others may lay out the author's conclusions. Still others may serve as introductions or as background information. Focus on how the part in question fits within the whole.

PASSAGE 3—Murphy's Law

Topic and Scope

Morality; specifically, the pros and cons of Liam Murphy's views on morality.

Purpose and Main Idea

The purpose of the passage is to assess the value of Murphy's view. The main idea is that Murphy's argument may lack motivating force for those who don't have an inner sense of morality, but it also avoids having to justify the content of particular moral principles and is more practical than traditional views.

Paragraph Structure

Paragraph 1 introduces us to the "overdemandingness" problem in moral philosophy. If we define morality as requiring us to always act to produce the best circumstances, then morality may seem to ask too much of people. Paragraph 2 tells us that some people reject the idea that morality is overdemanding. The philosopher Liam Murphy, however, takes the "overdemandingness" problem seriously.

In paragraph 3, Murphy's philosophy is described. Murphy doesn't give people a set of firm beliefs or particular moral principles. Instead, he argues that each person should make moral decisions based first upon his or her own inner sense of right and wrong. If a person's inner sense of right and wrong is confused, the person can then use his or her reason to make the final decision.

Paragraph 4 lists the disadvantages of Murphy's view. The main disadvantage is that people who have no moral foundation aren't likely to get one through his

approach. Paragraph 5 then gives the advantages of Murphy's perspective. Murphy's view starts with the individual's own inner sense of morality, so it doesn't have to go through the difficult task of justifying specific moral principles. This view ends up being more practical than traditional approaches.

The Big Picture

- Don't be intimidated by long, philosophical passages! They're best handled just like any other passage. Invest your time in building a clear road map and determining topic, scope, purpose, and main idea. Your time will pay off by increasing your grasp of the passage thus producing more points.

- Remember that in certain Reading Comp passages, some questions can actually help you answer other questions on the passage. Sometimes you'll research an answer for one question that will give you information for a later question. In addition, some questions actually test your knowledge of the same concepts. Use this to your advantage on longer passages.

The Questions

14. E

Here's a case where the first question of the set is a good question to answer first. This overall purpose question is a good one to prephrase based on your road map. The author's purpose, which we determined earlier, is "to assess the value of Murphy's view." This answer is summed up well in choice (E), since the author is evaluating the merits of Murphy's model of ethical inquiry.

(A) Too narrow. The author does discuss the disadvantages of Murphy's view but only in one paragraph of the passage. The answer to a primary purpose question must apply to the entire passage, not just one part.

(B) and (C)   Both of these choices are incorrect because they suggest that two views are addressed in the passage. Choice (B) suggests that two theories are discussed, whereas choice (C) suggests that two schools of thought are reviewed. In fact, only one view—Murphy's—is developed in the passage.

(D) The author does not pose a solution to an ethical problem.

Remember:

- Prephrasing is a good strategy for answering questions rapidly and correctly. If you can prephrase an answer, do so before looking at the answer choices. A quick scan of the choices will tell you whether your prephrase is on target.

15. B

Here we're asked to draw an inference, as is denoted by the word "suggests." This Inference question is too broad to prephrase, so it's best to evaluate each answer choice, eliminating obviously incorrect choices. Each answer choice describes what might happen if Murphy's philosophy is applied to the situations of two different groups. Which outcome is more likely, based on the passage? We're told in paragraph 3 that Murphy's view starts with individuals' innate sense of right and wrong. We're also told in paragraph 4 that people's moral viewpoints might not converge. Thus, answer choice (B) is the most likely outcome: It's possible that the two groups could start with entirely different innate senses of right and wrong and therefore come out with principles that radically differ. It's also possible that the groups could come out with principles that were relatively similar. This doesn't negate answer (B), however. Depending on how similar the groups' starting views are, their principles could either be alike or very different.

(A) If two groups were using the approach, it's possible that one group might come up with a resolution while the other did not—but there's no reason to believe that this necessarily would be the case.

(C) This choice misrepresents the author's argument. Murphy's view could be applied to two different groups regardless of what views those groups held. Its outcome in each case, however, would depend on the group's particular beliefs. It is true that the outcomes would be similar only if the groups held similar views. But the philosophy itself could be applied to any group, regardless of whether they shared the same beliefs.

(D) This choice is beyond the scope of the author's argument. The author never discusses using Murphy's view to reconcile difference between groups. He merely describes how the view can be used to help individuals determine moral behavior.

(E) is a bit tricky. As with choice (A) above, we must pay attention to the statement's wording. It's possible that Murphy's philosophy could be applied to two groups and that neither group would use the philosophy effectively to determine a course of action for their group. This would be the case if both groups had no moral sense to begin with. This type of outcome is only possible, however—it's not certain.

Remember:

- When choosing an answer about potential outcomes, be careful to scrutinize the verbs in each answer choice. In LSAT Reading Comp, there is a significant difference between stating that something would happen and stating that something could happen. Pay attention to the difference as you choose your answer.

16. **D**

This Inference question deals with the same issue as the previous question: What happens when you apply Murphy's philosophy to two different groups? We know from question 15 that Murphy's philosophy can be applied to different groups but that it would produce the same outcome for both only if both groups started with the same moral foundation. Another way of putting this is to say that two groups could apply Murphy's philosophy to their problems, but they would only come up with the same moral principles of action if they both started with the same beliefs. Therefore, a principle derived by one group would only apply to another group if the second group shared the same beliefs as the first.

(A) This choice is beyond the scope of the passage. Nowhere does the author discuss individuals sharing recommendations regarding Murphy's principles. The author tells us instead that principles are developed by first starting with individuals' own sense of right and wrong (as opposed to recommendations from others).

(B), (C), and (E) *Au contraire.* Each of these choices gives an answer that conflicts with the author's argument. If the moral viewpoints of the two groups did not converge, as (B) states, then the principle derived by one group might not apply to the other group at all. With (C), if the members of the second group had no firmly held beliefs, a principle developed using Murphy's view would be difficult to apply to them. Finally, if (E) were true, it would be difficult to even come up with the first group's principle—much less apply it to another group.

Remember:

• LSAT Reading Comp questions aren't always unique. Often one question will test the same concept as a another question in the set. When this occurs, use your previous work to help you answer the second question. This will save you time and increase your score.

17. **B**

Here we are given a question that starts out with the words "according to the passage." That lets us know that we're being asked for specific detail from the passage—a good bet for a question to answer early on in the set. Where does the passage mention individuals who have no moral sense? In paragraph 4, where it tells us that individuals without moral beliefs would have no justification for using Murphy's system. This point describes one disadvantage of Murphy's approach, as we're told with answer (B).

(A) *Au contraire.* The existence of individuals without moral beliefs provides one reason for refuting Murphy's views. These individuals might not follow Murphy's views at all.

(C) This choice misrepresents the author's argument. The author does tell us that reason is necessary when people's beliefs conflict. But he tells us this in paragraph 3, as he's describing Murphy's approach. The issue of individuals without moral beliefs is not raised until the following paragraph, in the discussion of the philosophy's disadvantages.

(D) Again, this choice misrepresents the author's argument. The author does mention that traditional approaches might not be any more influential for some people than Murphy's approach would be. But he states this in paragraph 5 when discussing the advantages of Murphy's view. He doesn't raise the issue of people without moral beliefs to prove this point.

(E) This choice is beyond the scope of the argument. The author never discusses the consequences of the "overdemandingness" problem. He merely describes this problem for us.

KAPLAN

Remember:

- Watch out for choices that slap together two separate parts of the passage, comparing them in a way that the author doesn't.
- Don't let the test dictate the order in which you'll do the questions. Scan the question set before you begin answering, and knock the easier questions out of the way first. This will help ensure that you score every point that you possibly can.

18. B

This question asks us for an inference regarding Murphy's views (as distinct from the author's views). We can look back to the text to help us with the answer. Where is the issue of "reason" discussed? In paragraph 3, we're told that a person can use reason to determine moral principles if his or her fundamental beliefs are conflicting or confused. This would be a good prephrase to approach the answer choices with. As it turns out, choice (B) reflects the prephrase exactly.

(A) and (C) The issue of some beliefs superseding others is not discussed in the passage. Neither is the issue of a belief system conflicting with an ethical principle.

(D) *Au contraire.* An individual who had no moral sense would not be able to apply Murphy's philosophy because he would lack an innate sense of right and wrong, which is Murphy's starting point.

(E) This answer choice explains the meaning of the overdemandingness problem, discussed in paragraphs 1 and 2. Murphy's philosophy responds to this problem in general—but the problem itself doesn't explain when reason should be used.

Remember:

- Prephrasing doesn't work with most Inference questions, but it can help with some. If an Inference question is phrased specifically and you can posit a reasonable prephrase, it's worth a scan of the answer choices to see if your prephrase shows up. If not, you can always rule out choices by elimination.

19. A

This Application question requires us to take information from the passage and apply it to a situation not presented in the passage. We know from paragraph 3 that the use of Murphy's philosophy requires two steps: first, the person or group starts with innate beliefs about right or wrong and then uses reason if necessary to derive moral principles. The first step for the school board, then, is reflected in (A): Members would have to determine their fundamental beliefs regarding the dress code issue.

(B) and (D) are irrelevant to the application of Murphy's philosophy. The author never states that analysis of other situations or historical precedents is necessary for determining moral principles with Murphy's view.

(C) Because the school board members are deciding the policy, according to Murphy, they would need to start with their own beliefs—not those of the students.

(E) This choice misrepresents the author's argument. In paragraph 3, the author is merely comparing Murphy to legal scholars who interpret the Constitution. He doesn't imply that people using Murphy's view must also consult the Constitution.

Remember:

- Application questions require you to apply ideas from the passage to alternative scenarios not raised in the passage. Make sure that the answer choice fits within the scope of the author's argument and can reasonably be deduced from the text.

20. C

A good road map can help us answer this efficiently. What does the author discuss in paragraph 5? We might prephrase here that he presents the pros of Murphy's view. A quick scan of the answer choices reveals the credited answer: (C) matches our prephrase almost exactly.

(A) This idea is not discussed in the passage. Murphy doesn't give us any means of determining the best interpretation of beliefs—at least not in what we're told here.

(B) The "overdemandingness" issue is discussed in paragraph 1.

(D) The author does not address two schools of thought. This point is raised in the explanations for question 14, answers (B) and (C).

(E) This idea is addressed in paragraph 3, where Murphy's views are summarized.

Remember:

- We can't emphasize section management too emphatically! This question again demonstrates why it's vital to choose your own order for answering the questions. Logic questions are good candidates for prephrasing, thanks to the power of the road map. They should be tackled early to boost your score.

21. D

Which one of the answer choices would Murphy be likely to agree with? There's no way to form a prephrase here, so on to the choices:

(A) *Au contraire.* People who argue *from* firmly held beliefs would be following Murphy's approach, not a traditional approach.

(B) Again, *au contraire.* Paragraph 5 tells us that these sorts of works have value—they just aren't as practical as Murphy's approach.

(C) This choice exaggerates the author's argument. In paragraph 4, we're only told that people who lack moral sense won't be able to apply the particular approach developed by Murphy. However, they might still have contributions to make to ethical debates. We can't be sure from the passage that they would not contribute anything.

(D) is the winner. In the last paragraph of the passage, the author tells us that people who reject Murphy's premises aren't likely to accept traditional views either. What kind of people would reject Murphy's views? Moral skeptics, or those who have no moral sense at all, according to paragraph 3. So (D) provides the best answer choice here.

(E) We cannot determine whether the author himself believes that "overdemandingness" is a serious problem for traditional philosophy. We're only told that some scholars think it's not a serious problem and that Murphy does take it seriously. The author's tone in the passage implies that he sides with Murphy—but we don't have enough information to be sure. So this statement is either definitely incorrect or too poorly supported to evaluate. Either way, it gets ruled out.

Remember:

- Know your strengths and weaknesses when answering Reading Comp questions. This will help you determine which questions to answer last in the set. If Inference questions are a weak point, you might have left this question until last or even skipped it altogether. Don't be afraid to skip questions that look like they'll take a long time. You're better off concentrating your efforts on the questions that are likely to gain you points.

Passage 4—Thermocline

Topic and Scope

Lake stratification; specifically, the process and effects of freshwater lake stratification.

Purpose and Main Idea

The author's purpose is to explore the cyclical process of lake stratification and its effects on lake ecology. The main idea is that seasonal temperature differences within lake water cause the cyclical formation of water layers of various temperatures separated by the thermocline, which prevents oxygen from reaching the colder, deeper lake waters and periodically causes redistribution of fish within the lake.

Paragraph Structure

Paragraph 1 introduces the thermocline phenomenon and describes its development using the example of freshwater lakes in the southern United States. The description of the cycle that the author will describe throughout the passage begins at the end of the paragraph with info about late winter, when lake water temperatures are uniform and fish species thrive at all depths of the lake.

Paragraph 2 describes the changes that occur in early spring: The water on the surface of the lake becomes warmer and lighter than the water below it. This warm water expands and forms a layer over the water below.

Paragraph 3 describes the development and results of the thermocline. In summer, the warm water on top of the lake becomes distinctly separated from the colder water below it by the thermocline, a tem-

perature gradient that acts as a boundary between the two parts of the lake. The thermocline boundary prevents oxygen from reaching the lower depths of the lake, and this causes fish to swim up to the warmer surface of the lake to survive.

The final paragraph describes the reversal of the cycle. In fall, the water at the surface above the thermocline cools and becomes heavier than the water below the thermocline. This allows oxygen to plunge to the depths of the lake, and the lake reaches equilibrium again by early winter.

The Big Picture

- Science passages often present large amounts of detail that can bog down the unsavvy test taker. Skip this detail until you're asked a specific question on it. Instead, concentrate on the author's purpose and main idea and on how the passage is structured. This will help you to know where to look in the passage should an Explicit Text question require you to do so.

- Don't spend time rereading the passage during your first run through. Focus on the most important points raised in each paragraph. This will help you create a good road map, which will be your best tool for navigating through the question set.

The Questions

22. **E**

This Inference question asks about the subject of dissolved oxygen, which is raised many times in the passage. It's not easy here to pinpoint exactly which part of the passage we should review to answer this question, so the best tactic is to evaluate the answer choices, returning to the passage for verification when necessary. We're told in paragraph 1 that wave action stirs oxygen into the water, making (E) the best inference in this set.

(A) We aren't given information relating water temperature to oxygen capacity. True, during certain months the thermocline prevents oxygen from reaching the cooler depths, but for all we know, cold water can hold just as much dissolved oxygen as warm water, given the chance.

(B) *Au contraire:* The passage tells us in paragraph 1 that during late winter, oxygen is found plentifully throughout all of a lake's water levels.

(C) The only thing we're told about ice formation is that ice melts in February and March, which is not nearly enough information to allow us to infer the statement in (C).

(D) This choice misrepresents the author's claim in paragraph 3. We're told that fish and zooplankton consume oxygen below the surface, but not that they're the *only* organisms that do so.

Remember:

- If you're not sure where to look back for information in the passage, move to the answer choices and allow them to guide you back to the relevant sections. If you can kill a choice on sight, fine, but it's usually worth quickly verifying that a choice is bogus, especially in such a detail-heavy passage like this one.

23. B

Next up is a Global question concerned with the organization of the passage. Hopefully, in creating your mental road map you took the time to focus on the passage's structure; if so, a prephrase was certainly in order. Even though the details may be a bit cumbersome, the overall structure isn't that complex, and (B) provides a good summary of this structure: A "remarkable property" (the unwillingness of different temperature water to mix) leads to a process (the formation of the thermocline), which has some effects (determining the supply of oxygen and forcing the species of lakes to behave in certain ways).

(A) and (D) can be ruled out quickly because the author describes a property and a related phenomenon, not a particular problem or solutions.

(C) sounds plausible at first but fails in the end. The "benefits" of the thermocline aren't related here.

(E) Events from winter, spring, summer, and fall are related in that order, so presumably it's okay to say that a "chronology is described," if only in the loose sense of the word. As in (C), the main problem comes at the end—no "predictions" are made. Describing results or effects of a process is not the same as making predictions.

Remember:

- Beware of half-right, half-wrong choices like (C)—and to a lesser extent, (E)—here. Some choices start off pretty well but go awry towards the end. This reinforces the necessity to read and pay careful attention to the entire answer choice.

24. E

This question ends with the words "in order to," which indicates a Logic question: How does the author's statement function in the context of the section in which it appears? In this case, why does the author mention that 50-degree water is lighter than 40-degree water? In general, he's attempting to explain the process of lake stratification—you might have prephrased this answer and scanned the choices for it. In fact, choice (E) comes pretty close: The author mentions the difference to help the reader better understand his explanation of a particular step in the lake stratification process—the step in which a layer of warmer water forms over a layer of cooler water.

If you weren't able to prephrase this answer, you needed to evaluate the answer choices to eliminate the ones that *don't* represent the purpose of this detail:

(A) can be ruled out quickly because the author isn't attempting to refute any theories.

(B) *Au contraire.* The author explains in paragraph 2 why warmer water forms layers *on top of* colder water.

(C) is tricky because the author certainly does suggest that the number of fish dispersed through different layers of lakes is related to the thermocline, but showing this is not the reason the author included the bit about the 50-degree and 40-degree water. The comparison between these water temperatures doesn't prove anything, and besides, the information about the thermocline's effect on fish placement comes later.

(D) Zooplankton appear even later than the issue raised in (C) and is even further removed from the purpose of the author's comparison between 50-degree and 40-degree water.

Remember:

- In Logic questions, you're asked to determine the function of a specific detail in the context of a paragraph, or sometimes the function of an entire paragraph in the context of the passage as a whole. In the former case, pay strict attention to the lines surrounding the detail, and be wary of choices that bring up points that appear in much more distant sections of the passage.

25. A

Here we have another Inference question, denoted by the word "suggests." What does the author suggest about the effects of temperature stratification? The most significant effect he discusses is how temperature stratification causes fishes to move to the top layer of lakes during the summer. This might be pertinent for fisheries, as choice (A) indicates.

(B) *Au contraire*, the passage shows that the effects of temperature stratification can be predicted to

some degree, at least in terms of the general effect on lake ecology. It also shows that the general timing of these effects can be predicted as well. (Note that this doesn't conflict with the explanations above to question 23, choice (E), in which we say that the author doesn't make predictions. Suggesting that because of a stable process, results can be predicted is not the same as saying, from a passage structure point of view, that the author *himself* makes predictions.)

(C) and (E) exaggerate the author's claims in the passage. Paragraph 1 states that the thermocline plays an "important role" in lake ecology, but we don't know if it is the *most* important factor (C). It is also clear that temperature stratification affects southern U.S. lakes, but these effects aren't compared to those of other lakes, so we can't determine the relative severity of the effects (E).

(D) is outside the scope of the argument. The age of lakes is never brought up in the author's discussion, nor is anything implied regarding the way lake age may affect the stratification process described.

Remember:

- Open-ended Inference questions like this one require that we evaluate the answer choices—there isn't enough information in the question stem to attempt a prephrase.

- Remember that deductions must be reasonably inferred from what the author has stated in the passage. The correct choice will stick closely to the scope of the author's argument and won't include exaggerated or extreme ideas.

26. C

This Explicit Text question requires us to look for something that was NOT mentioned in the passage—a bit harder than the traditional detail question. Fortunately, the wrong answers are all stated in the passage fairly clearly. (C) is the only choice that's not mentioned; in fact, it even tends to contradict the passage: Paragraph 3 tells us that the depth of the thermocline fluctuates with temperature and winds, so we can't be sure when the depth is at its maximum.

All of the other answer choices repeat information from the passage. Paragraph 3 tells us that fish move above the thermocline in the summer, so this eliminates (A). We're told in paragraph 1 that water temperatures are uniform in late winter, eliminating (B). Paragraph 3 helps us eliminate (D) because it states that the thermocline shuts off the supply of oxygen to the lower depths. Finally, choice (E) can be eliminated by paragraph 4, which describes how the turnover brings oxygen to deeper, stagnant water.

Remember:

- Don't get caught off guard by questions containing the word NOT. Be careful to look for that which is NOT stated in the text—don't make the mistake of falling for an incorrect choice that IS stated in the text.

27. **D**

This question is a basic Global question, albeit worded slightly differently than usual. The stem itself gives away the fact that the author's purpose is "to discuss" something, so there's no need to choose between various verbs (discuss, argue, refute, etcetera)—but what is he interested in discussing? The author's main concern should be firmly planted in your mind by now; he's simply interested in discussing the process and effects of lake stratification. Choice (D) comes very close to this prephrase, merely substituting "seasonal warming and cooling of water" for the process described.

(A) and (E) both reverse the direction of causality in the author's discussion. The author is interested in how the thermocline affects lake ecolo-

gy, not vice versa, as in (A). Similarly, he shows how changing water temperatures, by means of the thermocline, affect oxygen levels, not the other way around, as (E) would have it.

(B) and (C) go beyond the argument's scope. The author mentions "stagnant" water in paragraph 4 but does not focus on water purity throughout the passage. And the phenomenon of overfishing, if it exists, is not discussed.

Remember:

- Sometimes, as is the case here, wrong answer choices use the right terminology but describe erroneous cause-and-effect relationships. If you're the least bit unsure about a relationship between two elements mentioned in the text, by all means take a quick look back. But never simply pick a choice because its terms are familiar.

KAPLAN

PRACTICE TEST THREE

Remove or photocopy this answer sheet and use it to complete Practice Test Three.
See the answer key immediately following the test to correct your answers when you're finished.
Then use the score converter on pages 145 and 146 to calculate your score and percentile rank.

Start with number 1 for each new section. If a section has fewer questions than answer spaces, leave the extra spaces blank.

SECTION 1	SECTION 2	SECTION 3	SECTION 4
1 Ⓐ Ⓑ Ⓒ Ⓓ Ⓔ	1 Ⓐ Ⓑ Ⓒ Ⓓ Ⓔ	1 Ⓐ Ⓑ Ⓒ Ⓓ Ⓔ	1 Ⓐ Ⓑ Ⓒ Ⓓ Ⓔ
2 Ⓐ Ⓑ Ⓒ Ⓓ Ⓔ	2 Ⓐ Ⓑ Ⓒ Ⓓ Ⓔ	2 Ⓐ Ⓑ Ⓒ Ⓓ Ⓔ	2 Ⓐ Ⓑ Ⓒ Ⓓ Ⓔ
3 Ⓐ Ⓑ Ⓒ Ⓓ Ⓔ	3 Ⓐ Ⓑ Ⓒ Ⓓ Ⓔ	3 Ⓐ Ⓑ Ⓒ Ⓓ Ⓔ	3 Ⓐ Ⓑ Ⓒ Ⓓ Ⓔ
4 Ⓐ Ⓑ Ⓒ Ⓓ Ⓔ	4 Ⓐ Ⓑ Ⓒ Ⓓ Ⓔ	4 Ⓐ Ⓑ Ⓒ Ⓓ Ⓔ	4 Ⓐ Ⓑ Ⓒ Ⓓ Ⓔ
5 Ⓐ Ⓑ Ⓒ Ⓓ Ⓔ	5 Ⓐ Ⓑ Ⓒ Ⓓ Ⓔ	5 Ⓐ Ⓑ Ⓒ Ⓓ Ⓔ	5 Ⓐ Ⓑ Ⓒ Ⓓ Ⓔ
6 Ⓐ Ⓑ Ⓒ Ⓓ Ⓔ	6 Ⓐ Ⓑ Ⓒ Ⓓ Ⓔ	6 Ⓐ Ⓑ Ⓒ Ⓓ Ⓔ	6 Ⓐ Ⓑ Ⓒ Ⓓ Ⓔ
7 Ⓐ Ⓑ Ⓒ Ⓓ Ⓔ	7 Ⓐ Ⓑ Ⓒ Ⓓ Ⓔ	7 Ⓐ Ⓑ Ⓒ Ⓓ Ⓔ	7 Ⓐ Ⓑ Ⓒ Ⓓ Ⓔ
8 Ⓐ Ⓑ Ⓒ Ⓓ Ⓔ	8 Ⓐ Ⓑ Ⓒ Ⓓ Ⓔ	8 Ⓐ Ⓑ Ⓒ Ⓓ Ⓔ	8 Ⓐ Ⓑ Ⓒ Ⓓ Ⓔ
9 Ⓐ Ⓑ Ⓒ Ⓓ Ⓔ	9 Ⓐ Ⓑ Ⓒ Ⓓ Ⓔ	9 Ⓐ Ⓑ Ⓒ Ⓓ Ⓔ	9 Ⓐ Ⓑ Ⓒ Ⓓ Ⓔ
10 Ⓐ Ⓑ Ⓒ Ⓓ Ⓔ	10 Ⓐ Ⓑ Ⓒ Ⓓ Ⓔ	10 Ⓐ Ⓑ Ⓒ Ⓓ Ⓔ	10 Ⓐ Ⓑ Ⓒ Ⓓ Ⓔ
11 Ⓐ Ⓑ Ⓒ Ⓓ Ⓔ	11 Ⓐ Ⓑ Ⓒ Ⓓ Ⓔ	11 Ⓐ Ⓑ Ⓒ Ⓓ Ⓔ	11 Ⓐ Ⓑ Ⓒ Ⓓ Ⓔ
12 Ⓐ Ⓑ Ⓒ Ⓓ Ⓔ	12 Ⓐ Ⓑ Ⓒ Ⓓ Ⓔ	12 Ⓐ Ⓑ Ⓒ Ⓓ Ⓔ	12 Ⓐ Ⓑ Ⓒ Ⓓ Ⓔ
13 Ⓐ Ⓑ Ⓒ Ⓓ Ⓔ	13 Ⓐ Ⓑ Ⓒ Ⓓ Ⓔ	13 Ⓐ Ⓑ Ⓒ Ⓓ Ⓔ	13 Ⓐ Ⓑ Ⓒ Ⓓ Ⓔ
14 Ⓐ Ⓑ Ⓒ Ⓓ Ⓔ	14 Ⓐ Ⓑ Ⓒ Ⓓ Ⓔ	14 Ⓐ Ⓑ Ⓒ Ⓓ Ⓔ	14 Ⓐ Ⓑ Ⓒ Ⓓ Ⓔ
15 Ⓐ Ⓑ Ⓒ Ⓓ Ⓔ	15 Ⓐ Ⓑ Ⓒ Ⓓ Ⓔ	15 Ⓐ Ⓑ Ⓒ Ⓓ Ⓔ	15 Ⓐ Ⓑ Ⓒ Ⓓ Ⓔ
16 Ⓐ Ⓑ Ⓒ Ⓓ Ⓔ	16 Ⓐ Ⓑ Ⓒ Ⓓ Ⓔ	16 Ⓐ Ⓑ Ⓒ Ⓓ Ⓔ	16 Ⓐ Ⓑ Ⓒ Ⓓ Ⓔ
17 Ⓐ Ⓑ Ⓒ Ⓓ Ⓔ	17 Ⓐ Ⓑ Ⓒ Ⓓ Ⓔ	17 Ⓐ Ⓑ Ⓒ Ⓓ Ⓔ	17 Ⓐ Ⓑ Ⓒ Ⓓ Ⓔ
18 Ⓐ Ⓑ Ⓒ Ⓓ Ⓔ	18 Ⓐ Ⓑ Ⓒ Ⓓ Ⓔ	18 Ⓐ Ⓑ Ⓒ Ⓓ Ⓔ	18 Ⓐ Ⓑ Ⓒ Ⓓ Ⓔ
19 Ⓐ Ⓑ Ⓒ Ⓓ Ⓔ	19 Ⓐ Ⓑ Ⓒ Ⓓ Ⓔ	19 Ⓐ Ⓑ Ⓒ Ⓓ Ⓔ	19 Ⓐ Ⓑ Ⓒ Ⓓ Ⓔ
20 Ⓐ Ⓑ Ⓒ Ⓓ Ⓔ	20 Ⓐ Ⓑ Ⓒ Ⓓ Ⓔ	20 Ⓐ Ⓑ Ⓒ Ⓓ Ⓔ	20 Ⓐ Ⓑ Ⓒ Ⓓ Ⓔ
21 Ⓐ Ⓑ Ⓒ Ⓓ Ⓔ	21 Ⓐ Ⓑ Ⓒ Ⓓ Ⓔ	21 Ⓐ Ⓑ Ⓒ Ⓓ Ⓔ	21 Ⓐ Ⓑ Ⓒ Ⓓ Ⓔ
22 Ⓐ Ⓑ Ⓒ Ⓓ Ⓔ	22 Ⓐ Ⓑ Ⓒ Ⓓ Ⓔ	22 Ⓐ Ⓑ Ⓒ Ⓓ Ⓔ	22 Ⓐ Ⓑ Ⓒ Ⓓ Ⓔ
23 Ⓐ Ⓑ Ⓒ Ⓓ Ⓔ	23 Ⓐ Ⓑ Ⓒ Ⓓ Ⓔ	23 Ⓐ Ⓑ Ⓒ Ⓓ Ⓔ	23 Ⓐ Ⓑ Ⓒ Ⓓ Ⓔ
24 Ⓐ Ⓑ Ⓒ Ⓓ Ⓔ	24 Ⓐ Ⓑ Ⓒ Ⓓ Ⓔ	24 Ⓐ Ⓑ Ⓒ Ⓓ Ⓔ	24 Ⓐ Ⓑ Ⓒ Ⓓ Ⓔ
25 Ⓐ Ⓑ Ⓒ Ⓓ Ⓔ	25 Ⓐ Ⓑ Ⓒ Ⓓ Ⓔ	25 Ⓐ Ⓑ Ⓒ Ⓓ Ⓔ	25 Ⓐ Ⓑ Ⓒ Ⓓ Ⓔ
26 Ⓐ Ⓑ Ⓒ Ⓓ Ⓔ	26 Ⓐ Ⓑ Ⓒ Ⓓ Ⓔ	26 Ⓐ Ⓑ Ⓒ Ⓓ Ⓔ	26 Ⓐ Ⓑ Ⓒ Ⓓ Ⓔ
27 Ⓐ Ⓑ Ⓒ Ⓓ Ⓔ	27 Ⓐ Ⓑ Ⓒ Ⓓ Ⓔ	27 Ⓐ Ⓑ Ⓒ Ⓓ Ⓔ	27 Ⓐ Ⓑ Ⓒ Ⓓ Ⓔ
28 Ⓐ Ⓑ Ⓒ Ⓓ Ⓔ	28 Ⓐ Ⓑ Ⓒ Ⓓ Ⓔ	28 Ⓐ Ⓑ Ⓒ Ⓓ Ⓔ	28 Ⓐ Ⓑ Ⓒ Ⓓ Ⓔ
29 Ⓐ Ⓑ Ⓒ Ⓓ Ⓔ	29 Ⓐ Ⓑ Ⓒ Ⓓ Ⓔ	29 Ⓐ Ⓑ Ⓒ Ⓓ Ⓔ	29 Ⓐ Ⓑ Ⓒ Ⓓ Ⓔ
30 Ⓐ Ⓑ Ⓒ Ⓓ Ⓔ	30 Ⓐ Ⓑ Ⓒ Ⓓ Ⓔ	30 Ⓐ Ⓑ Ⓒ Ⓓ Ⓔ	30 Ⓐ Ⓑ Ⓒ Ⓓ Ⓔ

PRACTICE TEST THREE
SECTION I
Time—35 minutes
27 questions

<u>Directions</u>: Each selection in this test is followed by several questions. After reading the selection, choose the *best* response to each question and mark it on your answer sheet. Your replies are to be based on what is *stated* or *implied* in the selection.

Every day the mailboxes of America are filled with millions upon millions of solicitations provided by the direct marketing industry. Most often they are straightforward advertisements for goods and services, but they also include
(5) such things as fund-raising solicitations, sweepstakes entries, and free trial offers. America's response to this deluge has been strangely mixed. On the negative side, poorly executed direct marketing produces unwanted, annoying, and wasteful solicitations, also known as "junk mail." The deluge of these
(10) solicitations constitutes an imposition on each household, putting a condition on that household's use of the mail system. Even worse, aggressive direct marketing techniques represent a serious threat to informational privacy. Rapid increases in technology have allowed direct marketers to have
(15) access to the personal characteristics of virtually everyone. Further, sophisticated computer matching programs can produce intrusive personal profiles from information which, standing alone, does not threaten individual privacy. Direct mailers disseminate this personal information originally
(20) revealed with an expectation of privacy. This information is disclosed without the subject's consent, and the target is typically never notified of the transfer.

The 1991 Harris-Equifax Consumer Privacy Survey addressed popular attitudes towards direct mailing practices
(25) and their impact on informational privacy. When asked how they viewed direct mail offers in general, 46 percent said they were a "nuisance," 9 percent considered them to be "invasions of privacy," and only 6 percent said they were "useful." But if Americans have such a negative opinion of
(30) the direct marketing industry, they have a strange way of showing it. Direct marketing is an effective technique that has grown in influence. Direct mail advertising expenditures rose from $7.6 billion in 1980 to $23.4 billion in 1990. The laws of the market dictate that companies would not have
(35) made these efforts without prospects of success. Moreover, in the Equifax survey mentioned above, almost half of the citizens who considered direct mail offers to be "invasions of privacy" had themselves bought something in response to a direct mail ad in the past year. Why, then, did not more of
(40) them express more positive opinions of direct marketing offers?

Analysis of this seeming contradiction reveals the central problem of regulation in this industry: Everyone hates receiving "junk mail," and everyone ought to be concerned
(45) about informational privacy. Still, direct marketing offers real advantages over other means of shopping, and the industry as a whole probably offers something for everyone. Even those who believe that the direct mailing industry has a generally negative societal impact probably would prefer to
(50) remain on some mailing lists. We like shopping by mail, and we don't want to throw out the good with the bad.

1. Which one of the following best expresses the main idea of the passage?

    (A) Increases in technology have been the main catalyst for the direct marketing explosion during the 1980s.
    (B) Concerns over privacy issues as expressed in popular opinion polls have influenced the way direct marketers have targeted their audience.
    (C) The discrepancy between the public's stated views of unsolicited "junk mail" and individuals' actual reaction to direct marketing materials has fueled the recent boom in the direct marketing industry.
    (D) The mixed response of Americans towards direct marketing stems from aggressive marketing techniques that threaten individual privacy.
    (E) The success of the direct marketing industry in the face of apparent public opposition to its practices can be explained in the light of consumer tendencies.

2. Which one of the following, if true, would best strengthen the author's explanation of the "seeming contradiction" expressed in line 42?

    (A) Awareness of commercial infringements on the rights of citizens has never been higher.
    (B) The number of people on more than one mailing list has increased in direct proportion to the increase in direct marketing expenditures.
    (C) Consumers do not perceive a connection between their individual purchasing behavior and infringements on their personal rights.
    (D) Some people believe that the benefits associated with the recent success of the direct marketing industry will filter down to consumers over time.
    (E) Some opinion polls on other topics indicate a similar discrepancy between what people say about an issue and how they act in relation to that issue.

GO ON TO THE NEXT PAGE.

3. Which one of the following critiques most approximates the logic underlying the author's concern regarding the effects of the computer matching programs mentioned in lines 16–18?

(A) An ecologist who states that since each of three species individually would not damage an ecosystem, it is safe to introduce all three into the ecosystem overlooks the possibility that the dominance of one species may lead to the extinction of one or both of the other two species.

(B) An ecologist who states that since each of three species individually would not damage an ecosystem, it is safe to introduce all three into the ecosystem overlooks the possibility that the three species taken together may very well pose a serious threat to the ecosystem.

(C) An ecologist who states that since each of three species individually would not damage an ecosystem, it is safe to introduce all three into the ecosystem overlooks the possibility that the addition of the three species to the ecosystem may preclude the addition of any further species.

(D) An ecologist who states that since each of three species individually would not damage an ecosystem, it is safe to introduce all three into the ecosystem overlooks the possibility that the ecosystem may not be the optimal environment for the species in question.

(E) An ecologist who states that since each of three species individually would not damage an ecosystem, it is safe to introduce all three into the ecosystem overlooks the possibility that any one of the three species may have posed a risk to the previous ecosystem in which it lived.

4. Which one of the following can be inferred from the passage about direct mail advertising expenditures in the years between 1980 and 1990?

(A) The rise in expenditures during this period is suggestive of the expectations of companies engaged in direct marketing at the time.

(B) The profit derived from sales linked to these expenditures in 1990 was more than double the profit derived from such sales in 1980.

(C) The lowest yearly expenditure on direct mail advertising during this period occurred in 1980.

(D) Direct marketing companies expect the pattern of expenditures during this period to continue in the decades to come.

(E) The rise in expenditures during this period closely parallel the laws of the market.

5. According to the passage, the author believes that the American public's reaction to the direct mail phenomenon

(A) is in accordance with the true dangers posed by the enterprise

(B) demonstrates an unusual willingness of people to consistently act against their deeply held convictions

(C) stems primarily from its fear of the loss of privacy that results from direct mail practices

(D) is unusual at first glance but more understandable once the motivations of the public are considered

(E) signals that the direct mail industry will need to alter its practices to respect informational privacy

6. The opinions expressed in the Harris-Equifax Consumer Privacy Survey in lines 25–29 serve as

(A) a justification for the increase in direct mail advertising expenditures in the 1980s

(B) the basis for the solution to a seemingly paradoxical situation

(C) the primary evidence for the author's conclusion about computer matching programs

(D) a contrast to additional evidence derived from another part of the survey

(E) an indication that the boom in direct marketing is not likely to continue

7. The author would most likely agree with which one of the following statements?

(A) Despite its drawbacks, direct marketing has had an overall positive effect on American society.

(B) The attitudes revealed in opinion polls can provide insight into actual behavior.

(C) Regarding the effects of commercial enterprises, presenting a nuisance is a more serious offense to society than is invasion of privacy.

(D) Everyone who would prefer to remain on at least one mailing list thinks that direct marketing negatively affects society in some way.

(E) The growth in direct marketing would be even more significant in the future if the percentage of people who find direct mail offers to be a nuisance were to decrease.

GO ON TO THE NEXT PAGE.

For at least 300 years prior to the beginning of the 20th century, people had noticed that the bulge along the eastern edge of South America fits remarkably well into the bight of Africa. Indeed, Francis Bacon suggested in 1620 that the fit

(5) could not be accidental. Several 19th century scientists offered explanations for the fit, but when Alfred Wegener first published the continental-drift hypothesis in 1912, his novel explanation for why the continents seem to fit together like pieces of a jigsaw puzzle drew explosive criticism from

(10) many geologists. Wegener used gravity measurements and observations of the Earth's surfaces to deduce that the continents are composed of lighter rock than the basalt that lies beneath the ocean floors. The continents, he suggested, float on the denser layer of basalt like icebergs on water.

(15) Wegener's early critics excoriated him for not proposing a mechanism for propelling the continental "icebergs" through solid basalt, although now there is some theoretical basis for thinking that convection might drive the process.

Wegener did not live long enough to find the clear and

(20) convincing evidence his hypothesis required, but since his death in 1930, geologists have learned much that supports his revolutionary idea. For example, belts of complementary rock formations found along the African and South American shorelines of the Atlantic Ocean make a strong

(25) argument for continental drift. In one experiment, geochronologists determined the age of a distinctive layer of crystalline basement rock in Ghana, Africa, and then predicted where the same rock layer would be found at the edge of South America if the two continents had indeed

(30) once been contiguous. By sampling and dating rocks in northeastern Brazil, the scientists demonstrated that the layer does occur in its predicted location. Another belt of two-billion-year-old rock that abruptly ends at the edge of the West African continental mass and begins again at the

(35) expected location along the coast of South America adds additional proof that the two continents once formed part of a larger land mass.

The fossil record contains additional evidence that Africa and South America were once connected. Large bodies of

(40) water act as barriers to the migration of many types of animals, yet the fossils of identical animal species are found on both sides of the southern Atlantic Ocean. For example, the remains of Mesosaurus, a small reptile of the Permian that lived in shallow, brackish swamps, are found in only

(45) two locations—in the Early Permian Dwyka Formation in South Africa and in the Irarare Formation in Brazil. The rock formations are the same age, are similar in composition, and lie directly across the ocean from each other, thus enhancing the plausibility of Wegener's theory of continental

(50) drift.

8. Which one of the following best expresses the main point of the passage?

(A) Several 19th century scientists offered explanations for the apparent fit of the coastlines of South America and Africa but none as intriguing as the hypothesis proposed by Wegener.

(B) Fossil evidence and the dating of certain rocks in South America and Africa has recently undermined the continental drift hypothesis.

(C) Scientists have uncovered a growing body of evidence for continental drift since the death of the theory's original proponent.

(D) The study of fossils and rock formations is an important aspect of geochronology.

(E) Scientists cannot conclusively prove the validity of Wegener's continental-drift hypothesis until the mechanism that causes it is understood.

9. The author's conclusion about the two-billion-year-old rock formations in West Africa and South America implies which one of the following?

(A) The rock formations would not be in their current locations if the continents had never been connected.

(B) Similar rock formations must be present in at least one other continent.

(C) The rock formations were formed by the same geological process that separated the continents.

(D) The rock formations must contain fossils common to both Africa and South America.

(E) Although much older, the rock formations resemble the crystalline basement rock found in Ghana.

GO ON TO THE NEXT PAGE.

10. According to the passage, Wegener's continental-drift hypothesis was originally

    (A) a modification of an earlier 19th century hypothesis about the structure of continents
    (B) rejected by most geologists because it was inconsistent with Francis Bacon's suggestion regarding the apparent fit between Africa and South America
    (C) an attempt to explain why South America and Africa share common rock formations
    (D) formulated with the use of scientific observations but lacking in supporting evidence
    (E) used to explain why certain fossils are found on both sides of the South Atlantic

11. Which one of the following, if true, would most weaken Wegener's theory of continental drift?

    (A) Far more Mesosaurus reptile fossils were uncovered in the Early Permian Dwyka Formation in South Africa than in the Irarare Formation in Brazil.
    (B) A new mechanism has been discovered that could displace convection as the motive force behind continental drift.
    (C) Francis Bacon based his observation on the non-accidental nature of the structural fit between continents purely on speculation and not on scientific fact.
    (D) There are many rock formations around the world that are the same age but not of similar composition.
    (E) In many cases, continents that do not appear to have interlocking coastlines nonetheless share common rock formations and fossils of identical animal species.

12. It can be inferred that the author of the passage would most likely agree with which one of the following statements about fossil evidence?

    (A) Fossil evidence is less conclusive than rock formation evidence in substantiating Wegener's theory of continental drift.
    (B) Fossil evidence can contribute to the plausibility of a geological model.
    (C) No fossil evidence links the animal species of South America to those of Australia.
    (D) Fossil evidence proves that identical animal species once lived in widely separated locations.
    (E) Fossil evidence suggests that convection is the underlying mechanism responsible for continental drift.

13. The primary purpose of the passage is to

    (A) describe some of the evidence for a popular hypothesis
    (B) detail how belts of complimentary rock formations can be used to support geochronological hypotheses
    (C) argue that the continental-drift hypothesis has been conclusively proven
    (D) assess certain types of evidence relied upon by modern geochronologists
    (E) describe Wegener's evidence for continental drift

GO ON TO THE NEXT PAGE.

Sensing that government defined by the Articles of Confederation did not meet the needs of the newly born United States, the Congress of the Articles of Confederation authorized commissioners to "devise such further provisions
(5) as shall appear to them necessary to render the Constitution of the federal government adequate to the exigencies of the Union." These provisions were to be reported to Congress and confirmed by every state and were to consist of alterations to the Articles of Confederation. Having given
(10) these instructions, Congress was quite surprised by the terms of the Constitution as submitted, and even claimed that the commissioners did not have the legal authority to submit such a revolutionary constitution.

In the Federalist Papers, James Madison defended the
(15) commissioners by returning to the terms of their mandate. Given the goals expressed by Congress, and the principle that conflicts ought to be resolved in favor of more important goals, Madison argued that the degree to which the Constitution departs from the Articles cannot make the
(20) Constitution illegal. Where the goal of amending the Articles conflicts with the goal of creating good government, the Articles must yield, since the goal of good government is an overriding consideration. This same argument, however, does not apply to the commissioners' decision to allow the
(25) Constitution to be ratified by only three quarters of the states. Unanimous approval was a fundamental aspect of national government under the Articles. Requiring non-ratifying states to be bound by the new Constitution was thus a powerful diminishment of their sovereignty because
(30) the Constitution changed the national government from a weak union of independent states to a strong union in which the interests of the many states could outweigh the protests of the few. Although history has validated the wisdom of the change, the question of whether the change was legal is
(35) another matter.

In authorizing the commissioners, the independent states requested a proposal for the alteration of the national government but never intended to waive their veto power. So even if Madison is correct, and the commissioners could
(40) have proposed anything they deemed likely to fulfill the goal of good government, it does not follow that their proclamations should impinge upon the legal rights of the states. This does not, however, imply that the Constitution ratified by the states has no moral authority. No government
(45) ought to have the power to entrench itself against amendment, and so the fact that the government under the Articles of Confederation did not consent to the alteration of the ratification process does not establish the moral illegitimacy of the Constitution. The case for rebelling
(50) against the government under the Articles is further strengthened by the fact that the government itself admitted its unfitness for the exigencies of the Union.

14. It can be inferred that Congress's surprise over the radical nature of the Constitution submitted by the commissioners could be attributed in part to the fact that its members did not foresee

(A) the inevitability that the Constitution it requested would be adopted without the unanimous ratification of the states

(B) the possibility that the Constitution it requested would contain provisions that jeopardized the government's moral authority

(C) a conflict between the modification of the Articles of Confederation and the creation of a Constitution adequate to the needs of the nation

(D) the possibility that the Constitution it requested would differ from the Articles of Confederation

(E) the likelihood that one such as Madison would invoke a principle as part of an argument attempting to justify the legality of the Constitution submitted

15. Which one of the following views can be attributed to Madison?

(A) In the case of conflicting interests, priority should be given to the course of action that best promotes peace in the nation.

(B) Applications of conflict resolution principles can be used to determine the legality of an action.

(C) Unanimous approval is the most important objective in drafting a new Constitution.

(D) The Constitution drafted by the commissioners corresponded precisely to the expectations of the Congress of the Articles of Confederation.

(E) In drafting the new Constitution, the commissioners had a moral obligation to forge a strong nation out of the weak union of independent states.

GO ON TO THE NEXT PAGE.

16. If a government decrees that it is illegal to make any changes to the structure or practices of the state, the author would most likely view a group within the state that attempts to violate the decree

    (A) with skepticism regarding its motivations
    (B) with admiration, since any law passed by such a government has no moral authority
    (C) with concern regarding the government's reaction to the group's act of dissent
    (D) with disdain for its violation of the orders of the state
    (E) with approval regarding its moral right to disobey the decree

17. Which one of the following, if true, would most seriously weaken the argument put forth in defense of the legality of the Constitution submitted by the commissioners?

    (A) Nonunanimous ratification of such a new Constitution is incompatible with the goal of creating a good government.
    (B) Extensive debate among statesmen is necessary in order to create a fair and legal Constitution.
    (C) It is nearly impossible to create an effective Constitution out of the pieces of a previous Constitution.
    (D) No legal Constitution can include provisions to safeguard the power of the ruling elite that commissioned the document.
    (E) In regard to heated political issues, arguments presented orally are generally more persuasive than arguments presented in written form.

18. According to the passage, which one of the following provided justification for the revolutionary nature of the new Constitution?

    (A) the current government's admission of its inadequacy in national affairs
    (B) the right of any given state to refuse to ratify the new Constitution
    (C) the moral right of a new government to entrench itself against amendment
    (D) the recommendation that the new Constitution be created from alterations of the current Articles of Confederation
    (E) the analysis presented by Madison that showed that the new Constitution did not differ from the Articles of Confederation to the extent asserted by Congress

19. Which one of the following relationships between legal and moral authority is implied by the author?

    (A) The morality of a constitution is the primary determinant of its legality.
    (B) A principle lacking moral authority can still be legally binding.
    (C) The morality of an action can never be determined irrespective of the legality of that action.
    (D) A document lacking legal authority can still carry moral weight.
    (E) The moral justification for an action can be used by a court to override the illegality of that action.

20. The primary purpose of the passage is to

    (A) reconcile two opposing viewpoints
    (B) illustrate the argumentative power of a principle
    (C) argue for the reconsideration of an established doctrine
    (D) support the establishment of one form of government over another
    (E) assess the authority of a political event on two grounds

GO ON TO THE NEXT PAGE.

Both Alexander Gerschenkron and Jerry Hough view the former Soviet Union as an "anomalous" nation in certain fundamental respects. Gerschenkron focuses on the degree to which the Soviet Union deviated from the expected
(5) European pattern of industrialization, while Hough emphasizes how the Soviet Union differed from the standard type of bureaucratic organization. Despite this difference in orientation, both authors share a similar theoretical approach.
(10) First, both authors react in their works to specific explanations already existing in their fields. Gerschenkron responds to the prevailing belief that all countries pass through similar stages of industrialization that can be modeled after England's industrial growth. He also reacts to
(15) the accepted notion that states must possess certain specific prerequisites before they can industrialize. Hough as well develops his argument in reaction to an existing view, the notion that the only type of bureaucracy that can operate efficiently is one that embodies the conventional American
(20) image of the ideal organization. This American image, known as monism, sees efficiency as maximized when bureaucrats perform only those duties passed down to them from a central authority.
Second, both Gerschenkron and Hough also clearly
(25) attempt to use their work to supplement the existing explanations prevailing in their fields. Gerschenkron expands W.W. Rostow's industrialization model by defining a causal factor that he calls the "degree of economic backwardness." Specifically, he argues that backwardness impacts the speed,
(30) organizational structure, institutional instruments, and ideology of a country's industrialization. In a similar vein, Hough broadens the conventional explanation in his field, concluding from his findings that the centralized, monistic model of organization must be expanded if it is to enable
(35) efficient administration. He uses the Soviet experience to show that overlapping bureaucratic duties can actually promote organizational efficiency in certain cases.
While Gerschenkron and Hough differ sharply regarding the focus of their research in their works, both authors
(40) portray the Soviet Union as anomalous with respect to the phenomena of industrialization and bureaucratic organization that they study. Both authors also attempt to use the anomalies that they discover to enhance the explanatory value of the theories already existing in their
(45) fields. Ultimately, Gerschenkron and Hough succeed at their similar tasks, because they develop explanations for their anomalous cases that enable the existing theories to more accurately explain the issues under investigation. Not only do both authors provide enough evidence to document the
(50) anomalous nature of the cases they investigate, but they use their anomalous cases to increase the explanatory range of the existing theories without altering those theories beyond recognition.

21. The author's main point in the passage is reflected most accurately in which one of the following statements?

(A) Gerschenkron and Hough share a similar theoretical enterprise in their works, and both manage this enterprise successfully.
(B) In their research, both Gerschenkron and Hough react to prevailing theories within their fields.
(C) Gerschenkron and Hough both use evidence from the Soviet case to highlight the anomalous features of the former Soviet experience.
(D) The works of Gerschenkron and Hough are expansive because both authors attempt to refute existing theories within their fields and to replace these theories with better explanations.
(E) The works of Gerschenkron and Hough are similar with respect to the specific central tenets of their research.

22. According to the author, the works of Gerschenkron and Hough are similar in that they both

(A) provide evidence to show how the experiences of the former Soviet Union invalidate prevailing theories in their fields
(B) adhere to the standard interpretations of prevailing theories in their fields
(C) develop the explanatory power of existing theories through the investigation of anomalous cases
(D) address anomalies in the stages of industrialization experienced by the former Soviet Union
(E) portray the development of the former Soviet Union in a generally critical light

23. The passage states which one of the following about Hough's portrayal of the former Soviet bureaucratic system?

(A) The former Soviet bureaucratic system mirrors the monistic model of bureaucratic organization exemplified in the American bureaucratic system.
(B) The experiences of the former Soviet bureaucratic system support the notion that bureaucracies must be organized according to the monistic model if they are to run efficiently.
(C) Throughout its development, the former Soviet bureaucratic system underwent growth stages similar to that experienced by England during its industrial growth.
(D) The development of the former Soviet bureaucratic system was impeded by the system's degree of economic backwardness.
(E) The experiences of the former Soviet bureaucratic system demonstrate that bureaucratic efficiency can be enhanced through the overlapping of organizational functions.

GO ON TO THE NEXT PAGE.

24. Which one of the following best describes the function of the third paragraph in the context of the passage as a whole?

    (A) It demonstrates that despite similarities in their approaches, the two authors cited study fundamentally different subjects.

    (B) It suggests that the most effective method for comparing the works of Gerschenkron and Hough is to focus on their research concerning the former Soviet Union.

    (C) It illustrates the role of W.W. Rostow's industrialization model in influencing Gerschenkron's analysis of the former Soviet Union.

    (D) It provides additional support for the notion that Gerschenkron and Hough share similar theoretical goals in developing their works.

    (E) It serves to refute the contention that the works of Gerschenkron and Hough exhibit any fundamental similarity.

25. The passage suggests that both Gerschenkron and Hough would be most likely to agree with which one of the following statements?

    (A) Scientific studies of the former Soviet Union should be limited to an emphasis on industrialization patterns or methods of bureaucratic organization.

    (B) W.W. Rostow's industrialization model can be expanded by incorporating the variable of economic backwardness.

    (C) All countries pass through stages of industrialization similar to those experienced by England during its early growth.

    (D) Empirical research into anomalous cases can broaden the explanatory range of current theories.

    (E) Empirical research should focus on attempting to falsify theories through emphasis on disconfirming cases.

26. Which one of the following is explicitly cited as evidence to demonstrate a specific use to which Gerschenkron put his work?

    (A) Gerschenkron reacted to the accepted notion that industrialization does not require states to possess any prerequisite characteristics.

    (B) Gerschenkron and Hough differed regarding the specific orientation of their respective works.

    (C) Gerschenkron described the monistic image of bureaucratic organization in order to show how centralized authority helps to promote bureaucratic efficiency.

    (D) Gerschenkron demonstrated that the speed of a country's industrialization affects the country's degree of economic backwardness.

    (E) Gerschenkron incorporated a new factor into the model of industrialization put forth by a previous theorist.

27. The author refers to the concept of monism in the second paragraph in order to

    (A) support the claim that the former Soviet Union deviated in its development from the normal European pattern of industrialization

    (B) refute the notion that Hough provides an alternative conception of bureaucratic efficiency

    (C) demonstrate that Hough's work takes issue with the conventional view that efficient bureaucratic organization must conform to the American idealized image

    (D) support the claim that Hough portrays the former Soviet Union as similar to most industrialized nations in its bureaucratic structure

    (E) provide evidence for the conclusion that the former Soviet case displayed many elements of the idealized American model of bureaucratic organization

S T O P
IF YOU FINISH BEFORE TIME IS CALLED, YOU MAY CHECK YOUR WORK ON THIS SECTION ONLY. DO NOT WORK ON ANY OTHER SECTION IN THE TEST.

SECTION II
Time—35 minutes
25 questions

Directions: This test is composed of questions that ask you to analyze the logic of statements or short paragraphs. You are to choose as the answer to each question the one choice you consider *best* on the basis of your common-sense evaluation of the statement and its assumptions. Although a question may seem to have more than one acceptable answer, there is only one *best* answer, and it is the one that does not entail making any illogical, extraneous, or conflicting assumptions about the question. These questions do not presuppose any knowledge of formal logic on your part.

1. Cross-species studies of animal groups indicate that offspring who are separated from their mothers during the first months of life frequently develop aggression disorders. During group feedings, for example, separated offspring exert excessive force in the struggle over food, continuing to strike at other offspring long after the others have submitted. The best explanation for this observed behavior is the hypothesis that aggression disorders are caused by lack of proper parent-led socialization during the first stage of an offspring's development.

Which one of the following, if true, provides the most support for the hypothesis above?

(A) Some wildebeests who are not separated from their mothers during infancy display excessive aggression in conflicts that establish their place in the dominance hierarchy.

(B) Human babies adopted in the first three months of life often display aggressive behavior disorders during early childhood.

(C) Chimps raised in captivity in environments simulating traditional parent-led socialization display far less aggression in mating-related conflicts than do chimps raised without such social interaction.

(D) Many polar bears display more aggression in conflicts over food and social dominance than they do in mating-related conflicts.

(E) Elephants who are separated from their mothers during the first months of life do not display excessive aggression in food or social dominance struggles.

2. Sarrin monks practice the Pran meditation technique only when extremely damaging weather conditions confront the farming villages surrounding Sarrin monasteries. Pran meditation is a more highly disciplined form of the ritual meditation that the monks practice daily and involves unique practices such as isolation and fasting.

Which one of the statements below does NOT follow logically from the passage above?

(A) Some meditation practices are less disciplined than Pran meditation.

(B) Pran meditation among Sarrin monks does not take place according to a precisely regulated schedule.

(C) The ritual meditation that a typical Sarrin monk practices daily does not take place in an atmosphere of isolation.

(D) Monks practice some types of meditation in response to threats faced by the local population.

(E) The ritual meditation that Sarrin monks practice daily is largely undisciplined.

GO ON TO THE NEXT PAGE.

3. Movie pirating, the illegal videotaping of a new theater release and subsequent selling of the tape on the black market, is a major concern to the film studios that produce today's mainstream movies. When pirating sales are high, individual studios whose movies are being taped and sold illegally lose a large amount of revenue from black market viewers who would otherwise pay the full theater price. A low level of pirating sales during a specific period, however, is a fairly reliable indicator of an economic downturn in the movie industry as a whole during that period.

Which one of the following, if true, most helps to reconcile the discrepancy noted above?

(A) The film studios that produce today's mainstream movies occasionally serve as distribution outlets for smaller budget independent films that are also susceptible to pirating.

(B) Movie piraters exclusively target blockbuster hits, the existence of which is inextricably tied to the financial success of the movie industry during any given period.

(C) Most movie piraters use small, hand-held video cameras that are specially designed to record images in the darkened environment of a movie theater.

(D) The five largest film studios take in a disproportionate amount of movie revenue compared to hundreds of smaller and independent film studios, regardless of whether pirating activity during a specific period is high or low.

(E) A movie pirater who is highly active in selling movies on the black market can sometimes make a full living doing so, while a less active pirater will usually have to supplement the income generated from pirated movies.

4. Six months ago, a blight destroyed the cattle population in the town of Cebra, eradicating the town's beef supply. Since that time, the only meat available for consumption in Cebra has been poultry, lamb, and other nonbeef meats.

If the above statements are true, which one of the following must also be true on the basis of them?

(A) Villagers in the town of Cebra consume only beef raised by Cebra farmers.

(B) Cebra villagers prefer lamb and poultry to beef.

(C) The town of Cebra has not imported beef for consumption during the last six months.

(D) Most of the residents of Cebra are meat eaters.

(E) Before the blight occurred, Cebra villagers ate more beef than any other type of meat.

5. The food critic who writes for the magazine *Dining Today* was misguided in his review of Fabri's Restaurant. He criticized the cold strawberry soup because it contained cilantro and sun-dried tomatoes. But Fabri's roasted chicken dish contains cilantro and sun-dried tomatoes, and the same critic awarded that dish the highest rating possible. Clearly, such blatant inconsistency proves that the critic is unqualified.

The argument above is based upon which one of the following assumptions?

(A) Fabri's roasted chicken dish is disliked by some of Fabri's customers.

(B) The evaluation of Fabri's cold strawberry soup should not suffer on account of its inclusion of a few ingredients that the critic happens to dislike.

(C) As enhancing ingredients, cilantro and sun-dried tomatoes are less appropriate for appetizers than for main dishes.

(D) Cilantro and sun-dried tomatoes enhance roasted chicken and cold strawberry soup dishes in a comparable manner.

(E) Cilantro and sun-dried tomatoes are best used in chicken dishes that are not roasted.

GO ON TO THE NEXT PAGE.

6. Peter Dovak has stated that his soon-to-be-released new novel *From Bad to Worse* will exhibit the same literary form as his previous six novels. Each of these previous books was a "philosophy novel," also known as a "novel of ideas," in which characters and events represent various expressions of the author's deeply held philosophical convictions. Therefore, while the plot will surely be different from those of his previous books, any astute literary critic will know in advance what underlying issues will dominate Dovak's forthcoming book.

The argument above assumes which one of the following?

(A) Dovak is consistent in the philosophical convictions that he expresses through the characters and events of his books.

(B) The plot of *From Bad to Worse* will have nothing in common with the plots from any of Dovak's previous six books.

(C) Nothing written by Dovak prior to the publication of his previous six books took the form of the philosophy novel.

(D) One of the functions of literary critics is to predict what will be in an author's forthcoming book.

(E) The plot of *From Bad to Worse* is less important than the underlying philosophical convictions expressed through its characters and events.

7. Despite the threat of legal prosecution, many agencies gather personal data from phony telephone solicitations, often luring details from the respondent through the promise of nonexistent prizes. Such solicitors sell this data to individuals and agencies that are willing to pay for information on people's personal lives, buying habits, and political views. Politicians, however, have relied less on phony solicitors thanks to recent advances in public opinion polling, which generally supplies them with reliable information regarding voter attitudes on major issues. It is therefore likely that the phony solicitation industry will dwindle significantly in the years to come.

Which one of the following, if true, most seriously undermines the conclusion above?

(A) Public opinion polling is not only effective at discerning the political attitudes of individuals, but also at revealing their buying habits and details of their personal lives.

(B) Most people are unwilling to share personal information on their preferences and attitudes with strangers over the telephone.

(C) Large retailers are by far the largest consumers of pirated personal information and do not benefit from the information gathered in public opinion polls.

(D) Those politicians who rely on legal public opinion polls for information on voter attitudes are nonetheless hesitant to encourage the prosecution of the illegal data-gathering agencies.

(E) Due to the recent success of public opinion polling, the phony solicitors have begun to co-opt the public opinion agencies' techniques for getting people to disclose information on their personal lives.

GO ON TO THE NEXT PAGE.

Questions 8–9

Albert: The CEO's proposal to conduct free career seminars for high school students does not make business sense. Teenagers do not use our products, since they do not have the disposable income to purchase luxury items.

Bill: I disagree. Any activities that improve the company's image can enhance our profit margins in the long run. The positive publicity received from the seminars will boost the company's image in the public's eye. Image enhancement, it has been proven, increases sales significantly.

8. A point at issue between Albert and Bill concerns whether

   (A) the business has suffered from recent problems with its image
   (B) the CEO's plan to offer career seminars makes financial sense for the company
   (C) the publicity received from the seminars is likely to be highly positive
   (D) the advice given in the free career seminars would enable high school students to buy the company's products
   (E) teenagers would be more likely to buy the company's products if the company maintained a stronger public image

9. Bill responds to Albert by

   (A) broadening the scope for the determination of whether offering the career seminars will be financially beneficial for the company
   (B) comparing the values of short-term versus long-term business gains
   (C) providing examples that demonstrate that image is more important to a company's financial health than its profit margins
   (D) showing that Albert's argument relies on the erroneous presupposition that increased product sales are not the only route to financial growth
   (E) presenting evidence that clarifies the issue of whether teenagers have enough disposable income to purchase the company's products

10. Veterinary technician: I disagree with Dr. Markey's analysis concerning the medical problems of Wisecrack, the Smiths' horse. Dr. Markey recommends that Wisecrack undergo hoof surgery because his hoof problems are causing him great pain. But the Smiths cannot afford to pay for this procedure, much less the cost of Wisecrack's hospital stay.

The argument above is logically suspect because it

   (A) supports its conclusion on the basis of evidence that fails to take into account the emotional or financial costs of not treating Wisecrack's condition
   (B) fails to draw a conclusion that is in the best interest of the owners of the horse
   (C) resorts to attacking the personality of an individual involved in order to direct attention away from the relevant issue
   (D) uses evidence regarding the feasibility of acting on a recommendation as grounds for questioning the validity of the analysis supporting that recommendation
   (E) supports its main point with evidence that is derived from sources that cannot be independently verified

GO ON TO THE NEXT PAGE.

KAPLAN

11. Pharmaceutical scientist: Any bone marrow taken from lab rats after their primary growth phase is degenerative and will not function properly in transplants. All marrow in this shipment was extracted from laboratory rats provided by Chronin Labs. Chronin Labs has a policy of supplying only rats that are four months of age or older. Therefore, the marrow in this shipment is degenerative and should not be used.

Which one of the following, if true, most helps to justify the subsidiary conclusion that leads to the pharmaceutical scientist's recommendation?

(A) The degenerative quality of a particular bone marrow supply is not a valid reason for definitively ruling out its use in transplants.

(B) All rat bone marrow that displays degenerative properties comes from rats that are more than four months old.

(C) Some bone marrow extracted from laboratory rats during the rats' primary growth phase is degenerative.

(D) Laboratory rats go through their primary growth phase between birth and four months of age.

(E) In rare instances, Chronin Labs agrees to supply rats under four months of age to certain experiment sites containing appropriate environmental conditions.

12. Many Maids, a well-known commercial cleaning franchise, has always relied heavily on income from its major clients and would have been forced to close down this year if any of its major clients had closed their accounts. However, Many Maids has not only been able to continue its operation throughout the year, but it has also announced the grand opening of its second office.

The above statements, if true, support which one of the following conclusions?

(A) During this year, Many Maids' clients have placed a larger than usual number of special cleaning orders.

(B) Over the past few months, Many Maids developed many new small client accounts, which made the company less dependent on its major clients for income.

(C) None of Many Maids' major clients closed their account with the company this year.

(D) Corporate use of cleaning services like Many Maids has recently increased.

(E) Major clients were the source of more than half of Many Maids' income for the current year.

13. The Fines Museum has a totem pole that was too tall to be stored in the museum's temperature-controlled storage vault. Fortunately, the totem pole can now be stored in the temperature-controlled vault thanks to the efforts of restoration artists who have discovered a way to separate the pole into two parts for storage purposes while allowing it to be reassembled later without any noticeable change in the appearance of the artifact.

The argument above depends on which one of the following assumptions?

(A) Neither of the separated parts of the totem pole is too tall to fit into the vault.

(B) The totem pole can be separated into two equal-sized parts.

(C) The procedure for separating the parts of the totem pole will not cost more than it would cost to replace the totem pole if it deteriorated.

(D) Placing the two parts of the totem pole into the vault would not require removing other key artifacts from the vault.

(E) The optimal temperature required to preserve the totem pole can be attained in the temperature-controlled vault.

GO ON TO THE NEXT PAGE.

14. Psychologists who wish to have one of their book reviews nominated for the prestigious *Boatwright Psychology Review* award should not submit book review articles that review more than three books at a time. This is because editors for the *Boatwright Psychology Review* will not publish a book review article if it is too lengthy and cumbersome to read. In their submission guidelines, the editors explicitly state that review articles that cover more than three books at a time are considered too lengthy and cumbersome to read.

Which one of the following statements represents an assumption upon which the argument above depends?

(A) The book review article that covers the most books must be the lengthiest and most cumbersome article to read.

(B) If a book review article is published in the *Boatwright Psychology Review*, that article will receive the prestigious *Boatwright Psychology Review* award.

(C) All articles published in the *Boatwright Psychology Review* must be limited to a certain length specified by the editors.

(D) The *Boatwright Psychology Review* editors generally prefer book review articles that cover one book rather than two books.

(E) To be nominated for the *Boatwright Psychology Review* award, a psychologist's book review article must be published in the *Boatwright Psychology Review*.

15. The best-tasting premium ice cream requires milk from organically raised cows. When milk supplies are obtained from nonorganic sources, ice cream manufacturers are unable to ensure that their products are free of pesticide residues, and taste tests have shown that only those products that are free of pesticide residues meet the highest quality standards for taste.

Which one of the following roles is played in the argument by the claim that ice cream products can meet the highest quality taste standards only if they are free of pesticide residues?

(A) It serves as support for the argument's conclusion.

(B) It represents a logical consequence of the argument.

(C) It is an assumption upon which the argument depends.

(D) It is a statement that must be proven false in order to weaken an opposing viewpoint.

(E) It functions as the argument's conclusion.

Questions 16–17

The proliferation of colloquialisms is degrading the English language. A phrase such as "she was like, 'No way!', you know?"—a meaningless collection of English words just a few decades ago—is commonly understood by most today to mean "she was doubtful." No language can admit imprecise word usage on a large scale without a corresponding decrease in quality.

16. The argument relies on which one of the following assumptions?

(A) Colloquialisms always evolve out of a meaningless collection of words.

(B) The colloquialisms appearing in the English language introduce imprecision into the language on what would be considered a large scale.

(C) The Russian, French, and German languages cannot admit imprecise word usage on a large scale without an inevitable decrease in the quality of those languages.

(D) The English language would not be degraded if there did not exist an alternative informal way to express the sentiment "she was doubtful."

(E) The widespread use of colloquialisms represents the most serious form of language degradation.

17. Which one of the following, if true, most weakens the argument above?

(A) Linguists have shown that the use of imprecise language on a small scale does not generally impair understanding.

(B) Many colloquialisms that appeared in earlier forms of the English language disappeared over time as the people who used those particular phrasings were assimilated into larger groups with different language patterns.

(C) Dissemination of a new word or phrase by the mass media is an important factor in whether or not the new word or phrase will become a colloquialism.

(D) Colloquialisms are more likely to be coined by the youth in a culture than by any other segment of the population.

(E) Languages of the highest quality often evolve over time out of a collection of colloquial usages woven into the formal dialect of a given people.

GO ON TO THE NEXT PAGE.

18. In order to teach in the writing program at Brenton University, graduate student instructors must complete the writing program themselves. The course directors justify this policy by invoking the principle that those who teach must thoroughly understand the subject matter and point out that the best means of learning the course material is to take the course as a student. Without taking the course, potential instructors might under-emphasize certain key concepts in their preparation.

The principle relied upon in the argument above is most applicable to which one of the following situations?

(A)   Dog trainers should be required to obtain kennel licenses before they open their practices, since most dog trainers end up boarding their clients' dogs for a period of time during the dogs' schooling.

(B)   Youth probation officers should be required to take a psychological development class as part of their on-the-job training, because it is difficult to document which officers previously completed such a class before they applied for their jobs.

(C)   Paramedic trainers should be required to ride as patients in ambulances before they become certified trainers, since only by experiencing the plight of the patient first-hand can the paramedic trainer truly convey the patients' needs to paramedic students.

(D)   Vocal coaches should train their students extensively before allowing their students to compete in singing competitions because untrained singers often waste a good deal of judges' time in these competitions.

(E)   Zookeepers should be required to have in-depth training in the botanical sciences because serious illnesses can occur if animals are placed in environments containing plants that are poisonous to the animals' species.

19. Without a fund-raising specialist, foundations have trouble meeting their fund-raising targets. Research shows that fund-raising specialists help foundations raise the majority of their yearly funds. Financial planners serve a key organizing and advisory role, but financial planners raise only a small percentage of foundation funds, if they raise any funds at all. Therefore, _____

The argument above can be best completed by which one of the following?

(A)   a foundation interested in raising funds should entrust its fund-raising activities to fund-raising specialists rather than financial planners

(B)   no foundation that does not employ fund-raising specialists can raise the same amount of funds as a foundation that employs financial planners

(C)   fund-raising specialists lacking financial planning knowledge will provide less help to foundations than will financial planners with no fund-raising knowledge

(D)   foundations that employ fund-raising specialists meet their annual fundraising targets

(E)   foundations should not routinely engage the services of financial planners

GO ON TO THE NEXT PAGE.

20. It would be futile to ask any of the runners to move that boulder on the path. None of the runners individually could move the bolder, so it will not be possible for the runners to move the boulder as a group.

Which one of the following arguments contains reasoning that is flawed in a manner most similar to that in the argument above?

(A) Charlotte should not be appointed for the new position. She has not succeeded in her previous position, so there is no reason to think that she would perform well in the new position.

(B) Our Board of Trustees is incorrect in suggesting that a committee should be appointed to oversee Treasury matters. We would not trust any individual member with the responsibility of overseeing these matters, so we should have no more trust in a committee, which after all is merely a conglomerate of individuals.

(C) This code will remain unbroken. Detective Tally cannot break the code, so none of the other detectives will be able to break it either.

(D) Wearing fashionable clothing will not ensure that a person is considered stylish. Many styles go quickly in and out of fashion, so clothing that is considered stylish by one group may not be seen as stylish by all.

(E) It is useless to argue with Arthur. No one but Margaret can win an argument with him, so it will not be possible to win no matter how hard we try.

21. Leroy could not possibly have given the flu to his co-worker on Monday. In fact, Leroy's records lead to only one conclusion: that Leroy did not have the flu himself on Monday. It is true that Leroy spent the day on Sunday visiting a friend who had the flu, but there is no evidence to show that Leroy had the flu on Monday. His records show only that Leroy had the flu on Tuesday, the day he went to see his doctor.

The reasoning in the argument is flawed because the argument does which one of the following?

(A) It concludes that there is a lack of evidence for Leroy having the flu, based on evidence suggesting that Leroy did not have the flu.

(B) It fails to consider that Leroy's co-worker might have caught the flu from exposure to someone other than Leroy.

(C) It overlooks the possibility that Leroy's flu diagnosis on Tuesday serves as an indicator that Leroy had the flu on Monday.

(D) It assumes that an individual's association with an ill person is relevant to the question of whether he or she contracted an illness from that person.

(E) It raises the question of Leroy's professional ethics without providing evidence to document the relevance of his ethics to the issue at hand.

GO ON TO THE NEXT PAGE.

22. Until 1990, the results of the Reading Level Assessment Test given in junior high schools of school districts X and Y indicated that the reading ability of students in the two districts was nearly identical. Since 1990, however, the average score on the test has been markedly higher in district Y than in district X. The Superintendent of district Y theorizes that the difference is due to the reinstatement of the minimum reading level requirement in all junior high schools in his district, which mandates students reading below grade level to attend after-school reading workshops one day a week.

If the statements above are true, which one of the following must also be true?

(A) The average score on the Reading Level Assessment Test in district Y has increased minimum reading level requirement.

(B) There was a minimum reading level requirement in the junior high schools of district X at some point before 1990.

(C) There was no minimum reading level requirement in the junior high schools of district Y at some point before 1990.

(D) There was no minimum reading level requirement in the junior high schools of district X at some point after 1990.

(E) Since 1990, the Reading Level Assessment Test score of every student in district Y has been higher than the Reading Level Assessment Test score of every student in district X.

23. An economic or political crisis in a poor country can lead to a lack of faith in the country's leaders, which is often followed by violent behavior, dissent, and even revolt among specific segments of the population. In many cases, propaganda is immediately issued from media outlets that quells such reactions by downplaying the extent of the recent crisis, thereby helping to restore belief in the efficacy of the government. However, the habitual violence exhibited by certain groups of disaffected youths in such countries generally has nothing to do with a lack of faith in their leaders, but rather is the consequence of an endemic boredom and lack of any vision of a positive future for themselves.

Which one of the following statements follows most logically from the statements in the passage above?

(A) It is easier to quell periodic revolts in poor countries than it is to solve the habitual problem of youth violence.

(B) In all poor countries, propaganda alone cannot entirely diffuse dissent stemming from an economic or political crisis.

(C) Economic and political crises do not lead to any instances of youth violence in poor countries.

(D) The effect that propaganda has in putting down revolts in poor countries is primarily related to its ability to alter people's fundamental beliefs.

(E) To the extent that propaganda may help to decrease youth violence in a poor country, it is probably not the result of restoring the youths' faith in their country's leadership.

GO ON TO THE NEXT PAGE.

24. Derek won this year's school science fair and is a star on both the school's football and basketball teams. Outside of school, he runs his own successful business and is an accomplished musician. Obviously Derek is good at everything he does and thus will undoubtedly make an excellent Student Government President if elected.

The argument above is suspect because it overlooks the possibility that

(A) Derek participates in only those activities at which he knows he will excel

(B) presiding over the Student Government requires different skills than those necessary to becoming an accomplished musician

(C) school, athletics, music, and business are the only activities in which Derek is engaged

(D) there may be other students as qualified as Derek to preside over the Student Government

(E) Derek has no time in his schedule to devote to the Student Government

25. Pediatric nurses in Downs Valley have typically been willing to accept overtime emergency home-care cases on short notice, despite the fact that this work is stressful, difficult, and not well-compensated relative to the demands related to home-based pediatric care. Many accepted these voluntary assignments because of the professional and personal satisfaction that comes from personally helping a child and the child's family through a true time of need, especially after a relationship with the patient had been forged. Over the past six months, however, the cynicism pervading the Downs Valley medical establishment has clearly taken root among the pediatric nurses. They are now less willing to sacrifice for the well-being of their patients, as evidenced by the steep decline during this period in nursing assignments to home-care cases, despite an overall increase in available pediatric nurses.

Which one of the following, if true, best strengthens the argument above?

(A) Over the past six months, the total number of medical cases in Downs Valley requiring a nurse's care in a hospital setting has greatly increased.

(B) Despite certain advances in the treatment of childhood diseases, there has been no decrease in the last six months in the number of illnesses in Downs Valley requiring the service of an at-home pediatric nurse.

(C) Over the past six months, an increase in the paperwork required by insurance companies has obligated pediatric nurses to spend more time producing reports and less time with patients and their families.

(D) The financial compensation for home-care nursing assignments in Downs Valley is far greater than that in communities of neighboring states due to differences in state funding of pediatric home-care treatment.

(E) The cynicism pervading the Downs Valley medical establishment stems from disgruntled doctors who are furious over recent substantial increases in the cost of malpractice insurance.

STOP
IF YOU FINISH BEFORE TIME IS CALLED, YOU MAY CHECK YOUR WORK ON THIS SECTION ONLY.
DO NOT WORK ON ANY OTHER SECTION IN THE TEST.

SECTION III
Time—35 minutes
24 questions

Directions: Each group of questions is based on a set of conditions. You may wish to draw a rough sketch to help you answer some of the questions. Choose the *best* answer for each question and fill in the corresponding space on your answer sheet.

Questions 1–6

A stadium has two walls available for advertisements, one circling its upper deck and one circling its lower deck. Each of six companies places exactly one ad on one of the two walls. Three of the companies—F, G, and H—sell beverages, and the other three companies—M, N, and P—sell clothing. No other companies will advertise at the stadium. The ads will be placed according to the following conditions:

Each wall must contain at least one beverage ad and at least one clothing ad.
M will advertise on the lower wall only if the upper wall contains exactly four ads.
Neither F nor N will advertise on a wall containing exactly two ads.

1. If the upper wall contains exactly four ads, which one of the following companies must advertise on the upper wall?

   (A) G
   (B) H
   (C) M
   (D) N
   (E) P

2. If G is one of exactly two companies that advertise on the upper wall, all of the following companies must advertise on the lower wall EXCEPT:

   (A) F
   (B) H
   (C) M
   (D) N
   (E) P

3. Which one of the following could be a complete and accurate list of companies advertising on the upper wall?

   (A) F, G, M
   (B) G, H, N, P
   (C) G, N
   (D) H, N, P
   (E) M, P

4. If N and P advertise on the upper wall, which one of the following must be true?

   (A) F advertises on the upper wall.
   (B) G advertises on the upper wall.
   (C) H advertises on the lower wall.
   (D) H advertises on the same wall as M.
   (E) P advertises on a wall containing exactly three advertisements.

5. F cannot be the only beverage company to advertise on the lower wall UNLESS:

   (A) G advertises on the same wall as N.
   (B) H advertises on the lower wall.
   (C) M advertises on the lower wall.
   (D) M advertises on the same wall as P.
   (E) N advertises on the lower wall.

6. If one wall contains exactly two beverage ads and exactly two clothing ads, then which one of the following must be true?

   (A) F and H cannot advertise on the same wall.
   (B) G and H advertise on the same wall.
   (C) G and N advertise on the same wall.
   (D) M and N cannot advertise on the same wall.
   (E) M and P cannot advertise on the same wall.

GO ON TO THE NEXT PAGE.

Questions 7–12

Three divers—Xavier, Yulissa, and Zeke—perform exactly six dives, numbered one through six from first to last, as part of a theme park exhibition. Exactly one diver performs each dive. The following additional restrictions apply:

Xavier performs exactly three dives, but none consecutively.

Yulissa performs exactly two dives, at least one of which must be the first dive or the second dive.

Zeke does not perform a dive immediately before or immediately after Yulissa performs a dive.

7. Which one of the following could be an acceptable ordering, from first to sixth, of divers performing in the exhibition?

(A) Xavier, Yulissa, Xavier, Zeke, Yulissa, Xavier
(B) Yulissa, Xavier, Xavier, Zeke, Xavier, Yulissa
(C) Yulissa, Xavier, Yulissa, Xavier, Zeke, Xavier
(D) Yulissa, Xavier, Zeke, Xavier, Xavier, Yulissa
(E) Zeke, Xavier, Yulissa, Xavier, Yulissa, Xavier

8. If Zeke performs the fifth dive, which one of the following must be true?

(A) Xavier performs the first dive.
(B) Xavier performs the second dive.
(C) Xavier performs the third dive.
(D) Yulissa performs the first dive.
(E) Yulissa performs the third dive.

9. Which one of the following cannot be true?

(A) Xavier performs the first dive.
(B) Yulissa performs the fourth dive.
(C) Yulissa performs the sixth dive.
(D) Zeke performs the first dive.
(E) Zeke performs the sixth dive.

10. If Xavier performs the third dive, which one of the following must be false?

(A) Xavier performs the first dive.
(B) Xavier performs the sixth dive.
(C) Yulissa performs the second dive.
(D) Yulissa performs the fourth dive.
(E) Zeke performs the fourth dive.

11. If Yulissa performs two consecutive dives, then each of the following must be true EXCEPT:

(A) Xavier performs the first dive.
(B) Xavier performs the sixth dive.
(C) Yulissa performs the second dive.
(D) Yulissa performs the third dive.
(E) Zeke performs the fourth dive.

12. If the restriction that Xavier's performances must not be consecutive is changed to the requirement that Xavier's performances must be consecutive, but all other conditions remain the same, then the number of possible orderings of divers performing the six dives is

(A) 1
(B) 2
(C) 3
(D) 4
(E) 5

GO ON TO THE NEXT PAGE.

Questions 13–18

Seven instructors—J, K, L, M, N, P, and Q—teach adult education courses at a community college. Each instructor teaches during exactly one semester: the fall semester, the spring semester, or the winter semester. The following conditions apply:

> K teaches during the winter semester.
> L and M teach during the same semester.
> Q teaches during either the fall semester or the spring semester.
> Exactly twice as many instructors teach during the winter semester as teach during the fall semester.
> N and Q teach during different semesters.
> J and P teach during different semesters.

13. Which one of the following could be an accurate matching of instructors to semesters?

(A)   M: the fall semester; P: the spring semester; Q: the fall semester
(B)   J: the winter semester; L: the winter semester; P: the winter semester
(C)   L: the fall semester; N: the spring semester; P: the winter semester
(D)   J: the fall semester; M: the winter semester; N: the spring semester
(E)   K: the spring semester; L: the winter semester; P: the winter semester

14. Which one of the following cannot be true?

(A)   L teaches during the fall semester.
(B)   M teaches during the spring semester.
(C)   M teaches during the winter semester.
(D)   N teaches during the spring semester.
(E)   P teaches during the fall semester.

15. If exactly one instructor teaches during the spring semester, which one of the following must be true?

(A)   J teaches during the winter semester.
(B)   L teaches during the fall semester.
(C)   M teaches during the winter semester.
(D)   P teaches during the spring semester.
(E)   Q teaches during the fall semester.

16. Each of the following contains a list of instructors who can all teach during the same semester EXCEPT:

(A)   J, K, M
(B)   J, L, M
(C)   K, L, P
(D)   K, P, Q
(E)   L, M, P

17. Which one of the following could be a complete and accurate list of instructors who do not teach during the winter semester?

(A)   J, L, Q
(B)   J, Q
(C)   L, M, Q
(D)   N, P, Q
(E)   N, Q

18. If more instructors teach during the spring semester than teach during the fall semester, then which one of the following instructors must teach during the spring semester?

(A)   J
(B)   M
(C)   N
(D)   P
(E)   Q

GO ON TO THE NEXT PAGE.

Medland has exactly seven doctors—Alice, Barbara, Camille, Dianne, Ed, Fred and Gretchen—each of whom practices one of the following specialties—Neurology, Psychiatry, Radiology, Surgery or Urology—in one of five adjacent offices, numbered 1-5 from left to right. Each office has a different specialty and at least one doctor.

Offices 4 and 5 have the same number of doctors.
The number of radiologists equals the number of surgeons.
There are fewer psychiatrists than neurologists.
Barbara and Gretchen work in the same office.
Only Fred works in office 2.

19. Which one of the following must be true?

   (A)   There are more neurologists than urologists.
   (B)   There are as many psychiatrists as urologists.
   (C)   There are fewer psychiatrists than surgeons.
   (D)   There are more neurologists than radiologists.
   (E)   There are as many radiologists as urologists.

20. If Fred practices urology, then which one of the following must be false?

   (A)   Surgery is practiced in office 3.
   (B)   Radiology is practiced in office 1.
   (C)   Neurology is practiced in office 4.
   (D)   Psychiatry is practiced in office 5.
   (E)   Urology is practiced in office 2.

21. If Barbara practices urology in Office 1, then which one of the following must be true?

   (A)   Alice's office is next to urology.
   (B)   Fred's office is next to neurology.
   (C)   Camille's office is next to psychiatry.
   (D)   Dianne's office is next to radiology.
   (E)   Ed's office is next to surgery.

22. Which one of the following could be true?

   (A)   Barbara and Camille practice urology.
   (B)   Gretchen practices radiology.
   (C)   Alice and Ed practice neurology.
   (D)   Barbara practices surgery.
   (E)   Camille and Gretchen practice psychiatry.

23. If the neurology office is next to Barbara's, then all of the following could be true EXCEPT:

   (A)   Fred's office is next to Dianne's.
   (B)   Camille practices psychiatry.
   (C)   Alice shares an office with Camille.
   (D)   Fred's office is next to Gretchen's.
   (E)   Ed's office is next to Barbara's.

24. If Gretchen and Ed practice in the same office, then which one of the following would make it possible to precisely determine the office in which they practice?

   (A)   Urology is practiced in office 4.
   (B)   Surgery is practiced in office 2.
   (C)   Psychiatry is practiced in office 5.
   (D)   Urology is practiced in office 3.
   (E)   Radiology is practiced in office 2.

STOP
**IF YOU FINISH BEFORE TIME IS CALLED, YOU MAY CHECK YOUR WORK ON THIS SECTION ONLY.
DO NOT WORK ON ANY OTHER SECTION IN THE TEST.**

SECTION IV
Time—35 minutes
25 questions

<u>Directions:</u> This test is composed of questions that ask you to analyze the logic of statements or short paragraphs. You are to choose as the answer to each question the one choice you consider *best* on the basis of your common-sense evaluation of the statement and its assumptions. Although a question may seem to have more than one acceptable answer, there is only one *best* answer, and it is the one that does not entail making any illogical, extraneous, or conflicting assumptions about the question. These questions do not presuppose any knowledge of formal logic on your part.

1. Attention Deficit Disorder (ADD) is a condition characterized by an inability to focus on any topic for a prolonged period of time and is especially common among children 5–10 years old. A recent study has shown that 85 percent of seven-year-old children with ADD watch, on average, more than five hours of television a day. It is therefore very likely that Ed, age 7, has ADD, since he watches roughly six hours of television a day.

The argument above is flawed because it

(A) cites as a direct causal mechanism a factor that may only be a partial cause of the condition in question

(B) fails to indicate the chances of having ADD among seven-year-old children who watch more than five hours of television a day

(C) limits the description of the symptoms of ADD to an inability to focus for a prolonged period of time

(D) fails to consider the possibility that Ed may be among the 15 percent of children who do not watch more than five hours of television a day

(E) does not allow for other causes of ADD besides television watching

2. Industry analyst: Individuals typically buy Internet access accounts from American providers for about $19.95 a month, which includes email but no other services. Recently, however, foreign Internet providers have begun offering website design and management in addition to Internet access and email for the same fee of $19.95. Representatives of these foreign Internet providers have boldly predicted that their services will put the American providers out of the Internet access business in the next few years. But they have yet to demonstrate that their companies will provide quality, reliable customer service that is as good as or better than that currently offered by American Internet providers.

In the argument above, the industry analyst

(A) demonstrates that any concern on the part of certain companies regarding the threat of foreign competition is entirely unfounded

(B) suggests that the proponents of a view are basing their conclusion on erroneous information

(C) reconciles a prediction with analogous facts from a previous situation

(D) casts doubt on a contention by introducing an additional consideration

(E) proposes a way for one group of companies to ward off competition from another group of companies

GO ON TO THE NEXT PAGE.

Questions 3–4

The incidence of suicide in the country of Travonia has increased dramatically in recent years, as evidenced by the fact that since the introduction of several nonprescription brands of sleeping pills, the number of deaths from overdoses alone has nearly doubled. However, certain types of suicides have not increased in number during this period. It is true that elderly suicides have seen a greater than 70 percent increase, but teen suicides now account for only 30 percent of all suicides in the country. This is a significant decrease from 1985, when teen cases represented 65 percent of all country-wide suicides.

3. The argument above is most vulnerable to criticism on the grounds that it does which one of the following?

    (A)   It discounts the possibility of suicides occurring in groups other than the elderly and teenagers.
    (B)   It takes for granted that the introduction of nonprescription sleeping pills has had the same effect on two different demographic groups.
    (C)   It assumes that a decrease in the percentage of teen suicides necessarily signifies a decrease in the number of teen suicides.
    (D)   It overlooks the possibility that the total number of deaths in Travonia has increased since 1985.
    (E)   It relies on evidence that contradicts its conclusion.

4. The assertion that suicides are increasing in Travonia is most justified if which one of the following is assumed?

    (A)   The elderly suffered the greatest number of overdoses from the nonprescription sleeping pills.
    (B)   Overdosing on sleeping pills was not the most pervasive method of suicide in Travonia ten years ago.
    (C)   The number of deaths from natural causes in Travonia has decreased in recent years.
    (D)   The majority of deaths resulting from overdosing on nonprescription sleeping pills were not accidental.
    (E)   Travonia's suicide rate is higher than the worldwide average suicide rate.

5. The overall rate of emphysema has declined 15 percent over the last 15 years in region A. During that period, the total cost of care for emphysema sufferers in region A, after accounting for inflation, declined by two percent per year until eight years ago, at which time it began increasing by approximately two percent per year so that now the total health care cost for treating emphysema is approximately equal to what it was 15 years ago.

Which one of the following best resolves the apparent discrepancy between the incidence of emphysema in region A and the cost of caring for emphysema sufferers?

    (A)   The overall cost of health care in region A has increased by seven percent in the last 15 years, after accounting for inflation.
    (B)   Improvements in technology have significantly increased both the cost per patient and the success rate of emphysema care in the past 15 years.
    (C)   About seven years ago, the widespread switch to health maintenance organizations halted overall increases in health care costs in region A, after accounting for inflation.
    (D)   The money made available for research into the causes and cures of emphysema had been declining for many years until approximately eight years ago, since which time it has shown a modest increase.
    (E)   Beginning about nine years ago, the most expensive-to-treat advanced cases of emphysema have been decreasing in region A at a rate of about five percent per year.

GO ON TO THE NEXT PAGE.

6. City planner: The businesses along Maple Street are struggling, while the shops along the much broader Walnut and Crescent Streets have been prospering recently. Therefore, I propose to widen much of Maple Street, which will benefit the stores along the widened portion of the road by increasing vehicle traffic and bringing more shoppers to the stores.

Which one of the following, if true, best supports the city planner's recommendation?

(A) Widening Maple Street will make the sidewalks narrower, making it less appealing to pedestrian shoppers.

(B) The increased traffic on Maple Street will consist almost entirely of drivers using the widened street to get to distant destinations more quickly.

(C) Maple Street is farther from the densely populated city center than is Walnut Street, while Crescent Street is farther from the city center than is Maple Street.

(D) Walnut Street was once a thoroughfare and is now a pedestrian mall.

(E) Widening Maple Street will create room for many more parking spaces near the shops on the street.

7. In theory, establishing the democratic principle of respecting the basic rights of individuals is unambiguous, but in actual practice, it may involve some rather interesting scenarios. For example, recently in country Q, major reforms of the legal system were enacted to prevent the violation of the basic rights of its minorities. However, these reforms were only possible because country Q is led by a nonelected dictator who may act directly contrary to the popular will without fear of being voted out of office.

The argument relies on which one of the following assumptions?

(A) In a democracy, when a political figure acts directly contrary to the popular will, that figure will be voted out of office.

(B) Nonelected dictators who act directly contrary to the popular will have no reason to fear being removed from office.

(C) The principles of democratic government and of respect for basic individual rights are inconsistent.

(D) The popular will in country Q does not support the protection of the basic rights of minorities in the country.

(E) The rights of minorities in dictator-led countries such as country Q are more restricted than they are in democratic countries.

8. The city is required by federal environmental regulations to build a new water treatment plant. If this plant is built inside the city limits, it will disrupt the lives of many more citizens than if it is built on vacant land near the city. However, despite the availability of the vacant land, the plant should be built inside city limits because of the increased economic benefits its construction would provide to the city in the form of jobs.

Which one of the following, if true, most weakens the argument above?

(A) The available land outside of the city is privately owned, whereas there is an adequate site within the city that is city-owned.

(B) Regardless of the site location, most of the jobs created by the plant's construction will go to residents of the city.

(C) A municipal plant like the water treatment plant will pay no taxes to city government regardless of its location.

(D) Most citizens of the city will tolerate brief disruptions in their daily lives if such disruptions will secure better water quality in the future.

(E) The amount of taxes paid by workers depends both on where they work and where they live.

GO ON TO THE NEXT PAGE.

9. School Chancellor: Just one school in this school district has failed to meet newly enacted minimum achievement standards for the three years the standards have been in existence. An investigation has shown that at this school counterproductive work habits have become entrenched among most of the teachers and administrators so that simply firing a few "bad apples" will not solve the problem. Therefore, the best solution is to close the school and send the students to neighboring schools in order to improve the overall educational performance in the district as a whole.

    Each of the following, if true, weakens the argument above EXCEPT:

    (A) Nearby schools in the district do not have the resources to adequately accommodate the children from the closed school.
    (B) The school had failed to meet the recently imposed minimum standards for over 10 years but has recently shown significant improvement.
    (C) In other districts, a thorough retraining program has been successful in improving the work habits of most sub-par teachers and administrators.
    (D) Earlier in her career, the principal at the school had proven herself to be a competent administrator outside the district.
    (E) The children from the school are academically so far behind the children from the other schools in the district that teachers in neighboring schools will be forced to slow down and teach at the level of the new students thus disadvantaging the current students.

10. If ad pages in *Fission* magazine have increased in December, then either ad rates have decreased or circulation has increased for the month, but not both. If circulation has increased in December, then the editors will receive year-end bonuses. If ad pages have not increased in December, then the editors will not receive year-end bonuses.

    If all of the above statements are true, which one of the following can be concluded from the fact that the editors of *Fission* will not receive year-end bonuses?

    (A) Ad rates have not increased in December.
    (B) Ad pages have increased in December.
    (C) Ad pages have not increased in December.
    (D) Circulation has increased in December.
    (E) Circulation has not increased in December.

11. Historian #1: The *metis* were a distinct people within Canadian society, the offspring of Native Americans and Europeans. Rejected by both groups, they sought to forge an identity for themselves and made claims for land and political autonomy much like the Native Americans. Tragically, these requests were not granted, with the result that the *metis* have gradually lost a distinct identity to the great detriment of Canada's cultural diversity.

    Historian #2: I disagree that this denial of the *metis'* demands was tragic. The *metis* were an artificial creation who lacked long-standing cultural traditions of their own. They were not so much a separate cultural group as a name given to all those who were neither fully European nor fully Native American—a wide range forming a necessary continuum connecting the two cultural poles.

    A point of disagreement between the two historians is whether

    (A) the denial of a people's request for identity can be considered tragic
    (B) the *metis* were a distinct cultural entity within Canadian society
    (C) the *metis* were offspring of Native Americans and Europeans
    (D) the denial of a people's request for identity can diminish a country's cultural diversity
    (E) the *metis'* claims for land and autonomy resembled the claims of the Native Americans

GO ON TO THE NEXT PAGE.

12. Before it closed last year, Betty's Beauty Parlor had been in the same location for 25 years. Two years ago, Felix's Hair Salon opened one block away offering similar services. The opening of Felix's Hair Salon directly caused the demise of Betty's Beauty Parlor. This provides yet another example of the effects of competition in a free marketplace.

Which one of the following can be inferred from the statements in the passage above?

(A) Competition is ultimately destructive in a free marketplace.

(B) Betty's Beauty Parlor did not face competitive pressures other than from Felix's Hair Salon.

(C) Felix's Hair Salon served some of the same customers who would have gone to Betty's Beauty Parlor.

(D) Betty's Beauty Parlor would be open today if Felix's Hair Salon had not opened nearby.

(E) Two businesses that offer the same services cannot both survive for long in close proximity.

13. General: The commander of the Air Force has recommended that we deploy the G28 aircraft in the reconnaissance mission because the G28 can fly lower to the ground without being detected and could therefore retrieve the necessary information more efficiently than the currently stationed D12. But the D12 is already in the area and poised for takeoff and would have just enough time to accomplish the mission if deployed immediately, while the G28 would require four days just to arrive in the area and get outfitted for the mission. Since the mission's deadline is immovable, I am forced to overrule the commander's recommendation and order the deployment of the D12.

Which one of the following is assumed in the general's argument?

(A) The quality of information retrieved from the mission would be higher if the D12 were deployed than if the G28 were deployed.

(B) By the time the G28 arrived in the area and was outfitted for the mission, the D12 would have already completed the mission if deployed immediately.

(C) The ability of an aircraft to fly low to the ground is not a significant consideration when choosing aircraft for a reconnaissance mission.

(D) It would take longer for any aircraft not currently in the area besides the G28 to arrive in the area and get outfitted for the mission.

(E) Any time saved during the mission due to the operation of the more efficient G28 would not offset the additional time required to deploy the G28.

GO ON TO THE NEXT PAGE.

14. For exactly ten years, it has not been legal to bungee-jump in state A. All of the members of the Rubberband Club must live in state A and have bungee-jumped at least once in the last two years. The Rubberband Club is currently taking applications for new members.

Which one of the following necessarily follows from the information provided above?

(A) Every current member of the Rubberband Club has bungee-jumped outside of state A.

(B) No current applicant to the Rubberband Club has legally bungee-jumped in state A.

(C) The current members of the Rubberband Club have bungee-jumped illegally at least once.

(D) Current members of the Rubberband Club who have never bungee-jumped outside of state A have broken the law in state A.

(E) The Rubberband Club does not include members who have bungee-jumped legally in state A.

15. The influence of McTell's work on Waters' formulation of psychosocial theory has long been recognized in the academic community. McTell was Waters' mentor and main confidant during the 1950s, the time just before Waters published his revolutionary findings. There is ample evidence of communication during this time between the two regarding the core issues that would eventually coalesce in Waters' theory. However, a recently discovered letter dated 1947—years before Waters met McTell—indicates that Waters had already formulated the basic conceptions of his psychosocial theory. While McTell may certainly have helped Waters develop his theories, it is not possible that McTell influenced the formulation of Waters' scholarship in the manner originally believed.

The author of the argument above assumes that Waters

(A) did not know of and read McTell's work before he met him

(B) did not model his theory on the work of some scholar other than McTell

(C) did not have a mentor and confidant during the 1940s

(D) did not allow McTell to influence any aspect of his psychosocial theory

(E) did not benefit in any way from his association with McTell in the 1950s

16. Fewer geniuses have emerged from the present era than had emerged in previous eras. In the seventeenth century, there were only about one one-hundredth as many people as today, and yet in Europe alone, geniuses like Galileo, Descartes, Newton, and Shakespeare flourished. In the twentieth century, Einstein is the only accepted genius of that stature.

Which one of the following, if true, provides the most support to the argument above?

(A) Geniuses are widely recognized during their lives or soon after their deaths.

(B) There are many different kinds of geniuses, some of which are not easily comparable.

(C) The very idea of genius has been questioned and seriously criticized.

(D) The twentieth century has seen the spread of education to a much greater proportion of the population, reducing the extremes in educational attainment present in previous centuries.

(E) Scientific knowledge has been expanding at an ever-increasing rate for hundreds of years.

GO ON TO THE NEXT PAGE.

17. Sylvia: The public has a false perception that Banner clothes dryers are dangerous machines that frequently catch on fire. In fact, the number of Banner dryers that have actually caught on fire is quite small. Moreover, that number is minuscule compared to the number of major manufacturers' dryers that have caught on fire.

Alice: It is possible, however, that the percentage of Banner dryers that catch on fire is larger than the percentage of dryers from major manufacturers that do so. After all, the total number of dryers manufactured by the Banner company is relatively small compared to the extremely large numbers of dryers that major dryer companies have produced.

In responding to Sylvia's argument, Alice does which one of the following?

(A) She accepts Sylvia's conclusion but shows that different evidence may be used to reach that conclusion.

(B) She disproves Sylvia's conclusion by bringing up evidence that contradicts the evidence used by Sylvia to support her conclusion.

(C) She proves the irrelevance of Sylvia's evidence by pointing out that Sylvia is comparing two groups of items that cannot be compared.

(D) She refutes the evidence that Sylvia uses to support her conclusion.

(E) She demonstrates that Sylvia's conclusion is suspect because it is based on a faulty comparison involving total numbers instead of percentages.

18. A building that does not have adequate ventilation and natural light cannot be well-designed. A building with many windows will have adequate natural light, and so the presence of many windows in a building ensures that it is well-designed.

A reasoning error in the argument is that the argument fails to establish that

(A) adequate ventilation is only possible with many windows

(B) natural light ensures the presence of many windows

(C) the presence of many windows suffices to provide adequate ventilation

(D) some buildings without many windows are well-designed

(E) some buildings that have adequate ventilation and natural light may not be well-designed

19. It is not illegal to use hairspray, air conditioners, or vacuum-pressurized aerosol food containers, but it is well known that the use of such products damages the ozone layer, which may in turn have serious negative ecological consequences for future generations. It is therefore incumbent upon us to stop using these products so as to preserve the environment as best we can, even though we believe these products may enrich our lives and there are no legal sanctions against them.

Which one of the following principles is most consistent with the line of reasoning presented above?

(A) The legality of one's self-interested actions should be determined in light of the moral quality of that action.

(B) The morality of one's self-interested actions should be judged in light of the legal ramifications of performing those actions.

(C) The legality of one's self-interested actions should be determined based on the consequences such actions had on previous generations.

(D) The morality of one's self-interested actions should be judged in light of the consequences those actions may have for others.

(E) The severity of punishment for an illegal action should be determined based on the moral quality of that action.

GO ON TO THE NEXT PAGE.

20. Public service announcements attempt to persuade teenagers to follow useful advice but cause them to resent being preached to. Teenagers will follow advice only if they do not resent being preached to. Therefore, public service announcements are ineffective and should be discontinued.

Which one of the following exhibits reasoning most similar to the reasoning displayed in the argument above?

(A) Mandatory seat belt laws are directed at those who do not like to feel constricted when they drive. Freedom from unnecessary restrictions is one of the fundamental principles of this country. Thus, mandatory seat belt laws damage one of the fundamental principles of this country and should be repealed.

(B) Zoning restrictions prevent the development of neighborhoods that include both industrial and residential buildings. Including both industrial and residential buildings in the same neighborhood is dangerous and very harmful to residential property values. Therefore, including both of these types of buildings in the same neighborhood should be prevented.

(C) The estate tax applies to those who possess large estates when they die but encourages them to reduce their savings. Savings are needed to stimulate growth in the economy. Thus, the estate tax causes more economic harm than good and should be repealed.

(D) Conservation laws are intended to protect endangered wildlife, which induces their expansion into land presently occupied by people. People will not support conservation laws when their land is occupied by the animals under protection. Thus, the conservation laws are self-undermining and should be abandoned.

(E) The use of twelve-hour shifts at a company is intended to maximize production by employees but encourages them to work inefficiently. Employees must work efficiently in order for a company to maximize production. Therefore, the use of twelve-hour shifts fails to further the company's objective and should be abolished.

Questions 21–22

In addressing the region-wide recession, the comptroller of County X has asserted that the depressed economy of County X is indicative of the inevitable consequences of the recession for all counties in the region. But that must be false, considering that the economy of neighboring County Y is as robust as ever, despite the overall current financial difficulties of the region.

21. Which one of the following, if true, most helps to explain the fact that the economy of County X is suffering while the economy of County Y is not?

(A) The level of economic recession in the region is less severe than that of its neighboring regions.

(B) In overall revenue generated, the economy of County X surpasses that of County Y, even during recessionary periods.

(C) Unlike County Y, County X's economy relies almost entirely on tourism, which has been crippled by the region's recession.

(D) County Y relies on imports for most of its nonessential consumer items, most of which come from County X.

(E) When the recession struck, a few retail businesses relocated from County X to County Y.

22. The argument above does which one of the following?

(A) It counters a claim by providing evidence that directly conflicts with that claim.

(B) It contests the relevance of one piece of evidence on the grounds that it is categorically dissimilar from an opposing piece of evidence.

(C) It counters a claim by asserting the impossibility under the current circumstances of that which is claimed.

(D) It supports its conclusion by appealing to an authority.

(E) It provides evidence in the form of a generalization that counters the claim being opposed.

GO ON TO THE NEXT PAGE.

23. Researchers, perplexed by the development of measles immunity in children who were not given the measles vaccination, believe that they now understand this phenomenon. The children in question were all raised from birth on a baby formula produced by the manufacturer Dihydro. The Dihydro formula contains a synthetic chemical known as dihydron-X, which has been shown in lab tests to rapidly destroy cells infected with measles. Researchers have concluded that those children who ingest the Dihydro formula maintain dihydron-X in their bloodstreams indefinitely. When measles-infected cells proliferate in the child's body, the dihydron-X responds to the invasion by quickly killing off all infected cells thus arresting the progress of the disease so rapidly the child is perceived to have a measles immunity.

Which one of the following most accurately characterizes the role played in the passage by the unstated assumption that some children who receive measles vaccinations develop an immunity to measles?

(A) It is a point that, taken together with the fact that some children who do not receive the measles vaccine develop an immunity to measles, generates the problem that motivated the research described in the passage.

(B) It is a generalization assumed by the researchers to prove that the explanation of their puzzling case must involve a reference to the chemical composition of measles-resistant cells.

(C) It is a generalization that, if true, makes impossible the notion that some children who do not receive a measles vaccine develop an immunity to measles.

(D) It is a hypothesis that the researchers take to be proven conclusively by the findings put forth in the passage.

(E) It is a conclusion that is overturned by the researchers' discovery that some children who do not receive vaccines nonetheless develop a measles immunity.

24. The Chief of Personnel declared yesterday that no human resource employees were fired in the embezzlement scandal. However, the records show that some human resource employees were fired in March, and they also show that some of the employees who were fired in March were fired in the embezzlement scandal. It thus stands to reason that the Chief of Personnel made a false declaration.

Which one of the following arguments contains reasoning that is flawed in a manner most similar to the reasoning in the argument above?

(A) Candy must have extremely good manners. She is a member of the hospitality team at the summer lodge, and all hospitality team members at the lodge have extremely good manners.

(B) Some of the summer theater actors who starred in *Icarus* also starred in *Mrs. Jones*, and some of the actors who starred in *Mrs. Jones* were schooled at the Zeller Drama School. Therefore, some of the summer theater actors who starred in *Icarus* were schooled at the Zeller Drama School.

(C) Many of the Parkers' neighbors have young children. People with young children tend to stay home on weekend nights. So at least some of the Parkers' neighbors probably stay home on weekend nights.

(D) Some artificial Christmas trees have white branches. Other types of artificial Christmas trees have blue branches. Therefore, some artificial Christmas trees have both white and blue branches.

(E) This is Bradley's third year on the delivery crew for Arlene's Grocery. Arlene's Grocery is famous for its efficient delivery service, so Bradley must be a fast worker.

GO ON TO THE NEXT PAGE.

25. Principal: Excellence Learning Services offers reading and math programs for elementary school children. In its promotional literature distributed last year, the company argued that the deficiencies in the current educational system put children at risk of failing statewide math and reading tests. The literature further claimed that the company's programs will remedy these problems. Our school responded to this message by enrolling our children in Excellence Learning Services' programs. However, this year the percentage of our students that passed the statewide math and reading tests is the same as it was 20 years ago. Therefore, the claims in Excellence Learning Services' promotional literature were misleading.

The principal's reasoning is most vulnerable to criticism on which one of the following grounds?

(A)   It merely criticizes the math and reading programs without offering an alternative method of addressing the problems of the current educational system.

(B)   It assumes that the parents of the enrolled children were not capable of critically evaluating Excellence Learning Services' promotional literature.

(C)   It uses emotionally charged terms as a substitute for relevant evidence.

(D)   It does not demonstrate that the programs did not provide benefits in areas other than math and reading skills.

(E)   It fails to consider the possibility that the programs were effective in improving math and reading scores.

STOP

**IF YOU FINISH BEFORE TIME IS CALLED, YOU MAY CHECK YOUR WORK ON THIS SECTION ONLY.
DO NOT WORK ON ANY OTHER SECTION IN THE TEST.**

ANSWER KEY ON FOLLOWING PAGE

PRACTICE TEST THREE ANSWER KEY

Section I Reading Comprehension	Section II Logical Reasoning	Section III Logic Games	Section IV Logical Reasoning
1. E	1. C	1. D	1. B
2. C	2. E	2. C	2. D
3. B	3. B	3. A	3. C
4. A	4. C	4. A	4. D
5. D	5. D	5. E	5. B
6. D	6. A	6. E	6. E
7. B	7. C	7. C	7. D
8. C	8. B	8. E	8. B
9. A	9. A	9. D	9. D
10. D	10. D	10. B	10. E
11. E	11. D	11. E	11. B
12. B	12. C	12. A	12. C
13. A	13. A	13. D	13. E
14. C	14. E	14. A	14. D
15. B	15. A	15. C	15. A
16. E	16. B	16. D	16. A
17. A	17. E	17. D	17. E
18. A	18. C	18. B	18. C
19. D	19. A	19. D	19. D
20. E	20. B	20. C	20. E
21. A	21. C	21. B	21. C
22. C	22. C	22. C	22. A
23. E	23. E	23. D	23. A
24. D	24. A	24. D	24. B
25. D	25. B		25. E
26. E			
27. C			

PRACTICE TEST THREE EXPLANATIONS

Section I: Reading Comprehension Explanations

PASSAGE 1—Direct Marketing

Topic and Scope
Direct mail marketing; specifically, the discrepancy between Americans' attitudes towards direct mail and their behavior in response to it.

Purpose and Main Idea
The author's purpose is to explain why direct mail marketing has been so successful despite Americans' seemingly negative attitudes towards direct mail techniques. The main idea is that even though Americans dislike receiving "junk mail," they value the advantages of shopping by mail and continue to respond positively to direct mail marketing, increasing the industry's success.

Paragraph Structure
Paragraph 1 introduces us to the notion that Americans' response to direct mail marketing has been "strangely mixed." We get the "negative side" of the American response in the first paragraph when, the author explains why Americans view direct mail marketing as annoying and invasive.

Paragraph 2 then helps us to see why the American response can be considered "mixed." It starts out by providing evidence from an opinion survey that supports the author's claim that Americans view direct mail negatively. It then shows that despite their attitudes, Americans' behaviors in response to direct mail have been positive: Direct mail has become a highly successful marketing industry. Evidence from the same opinion survey cited earlier is given to show that Americans buy items through direct mail even though they dislike its techniques.

This "seeming contradiction" is explained in paragraph 3, where the author tells us that Americans shop by direct mail even though they dislike it because it is convenient and offers distinct advantages over other types of shopping. In essence, Americans like shopping by mail—so they put up with the drawbacks of direct mail techniques.

The Big Picture
- As you read through the first paragraph of an LSAT passage, be on the lookout for the main idea or at least a guiding framework for what is to come. In this passage, the statement that "America's response . . . has been strangely mixed" strongly suggests that the passage will discuss both sides of the issue. Stay alert as you read to make sure that that indeed is what is discussed.
- Often LSAT passages will not present the entire main idea in the first paragraph of the passage. We may have a sense of what will be presented, as with this passage, but by the end of the first paragraph, we may only get part of the story. If you don't think you have the main idea by the end of the first paragraph, keep reading and

focus especially on the final paragraph. There's a good chance that the main idea will be summed up there.

The Questions

1. E

First off is a standard Global question looking for the main idea of the passage. If you've properly developed your road map and put some thought into the author's purpose and main idea up front, this question should be a good one to prephrase. The author argues that direct mail has been successful, despite negative attitudes about it, because people like the advantages of shopping by mail. This point is nicely summarized in choice (E).

(A) distorts the technology issue presented in the passage. Increases in technology are seen as responsible for the fact that direct mail marketers now have access to individuals' private information, but technology is not cited as a reason for the success of direct marketing.

(B) We are never told that concerns over privacy issues have affected the targeting of direct mail audiences. In fact, the opposite may be true—direct marketers seem to ignore individuals' concerns over privacy.

(C) misrepresents the author's argument. The boom in direct mail marketing appears to be the result of individuals' actual reaction to the technique, not a result of the discrepancy between attitude and reaction.

(D) Too narrow. Part of America's "mixed response" does stem from the perceived threat to privacy caused by aggressive marketing techniques—but what about the other reasons for this mixed response, especially the positive reasons?

Remember:

- When choosing the answers to Global questions, be careful to avoid choices that are either too narrow or too broad. Choices that are too narrow focus only on part of the passage, while overly broad choices go beyond the passage's scope. The correct answer will cover the main gist of the entire passage while accurately reflecting the passage's scope.

2. C

This Strengthen question requires that we first understand how the author explains the "seeming contradiction" in paragraph 3. He argues that Americans respond to direct marketing because of its conveniences, even though Americans don't like the annoyance or the invasion of privacy. This evidence assumes that Americans are willing to maintain certain shopping habits despite the drawbacks associated with them. Choice (C) bolsters this assumption and therefore strengthens the argument.

(A) and (B) These choices focus on one portion of the author's argument but do not help strengthen it as a whole. In (A), the fact that awareness of infringement is high would strengthen only one part of the author's claim—that people don't like direct mail. It doesn't bolster the full argument that direct mail marketing is successful *despite* these infringements because of the fact that Americans like to shop by mail. Similarly, with (B), the increased number of people on multiple mailing lists does not necessarily strengthen the argument that people use direct mail despite its drawbacks because they like its conveniences. These individuals may be on multiple lists simply because their names were sold to direct mail companies.

(D) contradicts the author's explanation of why direct mail marketing is successful. (D) states that direct marketing may eventually benefit consumers—its success will filter down to consumers over time. But the author tells us that people respond to direct mail marketing because they like its advantages—in other words, they benefit from it now, as they are using it. That's why they put up with its annoyance and invasion of privacy. If (D) is true, perhaps there's more to the story than the author perceives.

(E) The only thing that (E) may strengthen (and it's tenuous at best) is the notion that the "seeming contradiction" that the author describes exists.

Remember:

- The answer to any Strengthen/Weaken question will always be linked to the author's argument concerning the issue at hand in the question. To find a strengthener, first determine the components of the author's argument in that portion of the passage. Once you've isolated the evidence and conclusion, you'll be in a better position to look for the author's assumptions. As in the Logical Reasoning sections of the LSAT, strengtheners and weakeners in Reading Comp often work by bolstering or damaging the assumptions in an author's argument.

3. B

This question asks us to identify the criticism that most closely approximates the logic of the author's concern over the use of computer matching programs. Well, why is the author concerned about these? The line reference brings us right to the crux of the matter: "Further, sophisticated computer matching programs can produce intrusive personal profiles from information which, standing alone, does not threaten individual privacy." Extracting the general logical structure of this, we have a situation in which harmless individual elements, when combined, become harmful in some way. That's the situation we need to find among the choices, and (B) best approximates this situation: the species alone

aren't dangerous to the ecosystem, but put them together and look out!

It's helpful to restate exactly what we're looking for in order to eliminate the wrong choices: The logic of the original example in the passage states that things (bits of information) that individually don't have a certain effect (i.e., threaten privacy) DO have that effect when put together.

(A) Here, we have species that individually don't harm the ecosystem (so far so good) but when put together may harm *each other*. Not the same thing.

(C), like all of the wrong choices, starts out okay with individual species that by themselves don't harm the ecosystem, so we have to look to the end of the choice to see where it goes awry. In this case, the ecologist is chastised for asserting the safety of throwing the three species together into the ecosystem on the grounds that they may not allow other species to join later. Boo hoo. This result would not necessarily cause damage to the ecosystem.

(D) This time the ecologists' assertion is bashed on the grounds that the species in question may be happier somewhere else. Again, the "overlooked possibility" is not one that necessarily causes harm: The ecosystem might not be an optimal environment for the species, but that doesn't necessarily mean that the ecosystem itself will be damaged.

(E) Their *previous* ecosystems? What does that have to do with putting them together here in the ecosystem in question? This is far from the logic underlying the example in the passage.

Remember:

- Application questions ask you to "apply" something you've learned in the passage to another issue in a different context. If the question seems difficult, and you're having trouble making the connection, it might be a good one to save until the end of the passage—or to skip altogether.

- Questions with long answer choices may not be as difficult as they seem. Notice that every choice in this question starts with the same 29 words. Once you picked up on that, you should have had an easier time—in truth, you really only needed to read the last part of each choice to see how it differed from the others.

4. A

The mention of expenditures from 1980–1990 brings us squarely to paragraph 2, where the author informs us that expenditures increased significantly during that stretch and that "companies would not have made these efforts without prospects of success." Inference questions are not great candidates for prephrasing, so you probably moved on to the choices at this point. Hopefully, you saw that (A) is a reasonable inference based on this information. It stands to reason that companies spent more money on advertising because they expected to benefit from it (in accordance with the "laws of the market"). Therefore, the rise in direct marketing expenditures can be reasonably said to reflect their expectations regarding success.

(B), (C), and (D) The passage implies that companies benefited from direct marketing—meaning, they made greater profits—but we have no idea how much they benefited. Thus, a specific claim like (B)'s assertion that they made "more than double" the profit at the end than at the beginning of the period is not warranted. Similarly, we are told that expenditures increased from 1980 to 1990, but we don't know how much they increased in any given year. In fact, we can't be sure that expenditures increased every single year—we're only told that the 1990 figure was greater than the 1980 fig-

ure, so we don't have enough information to infer choice (C). The same is true of choice (D). We're only told that expenditures increased from 1980–90. We cannot infer anything about what companies might expect expenditures to be in the future.

(E) distorts information in the passage. The author tells us that "the laws of the market dictate" that companies would not have invested in direct marketing unless they expected it to be successful. But to say that the rise in expenditures "parallels" the laws of the market is a distortion of this concept. The rise in expenditures may be explained with reference to the laws of the economic market, but that's about it. (E)'s manner of combining these two elements of the passage is unwarranted.

Remember:

- Inference questions often refer to only a small part of the passage. Zero in on the relevant section using the specific words of the stem as your guide. Here, "expenditures" and "between 1980 and 1990" should lead you quickly to paragraph 2, and a quick rereading of the author's points regarding these matters should put you in an excellent position to evaluate the choices with confidence.

5. D

The words "according to the passage" clue us in that this is an Explicit Text question. The answer to a detail question like this will most likely not restate the passage's information directly, but will often be recognizable, nonetheless, as a close paraphrase. Since a number of parts of this passage deal with Americans' reaction to direct mail, perhaps the best method is to move right to the choices, seeing if any jump out. (D) is, in fact, a very close paraphrase of the author's main idea that emerges along the way and is summarized rather explicitly in the final paragraph.

(A) goes beyond the scope of the passage. The author does not discuss the "true dangers" of the enterprise (whatever these may be).

(B) This choice exaggerates material from the passage. The author states in paragraph 3 that Americans are willing to put up with the drawbacks of direct mail because they like its conveniences. We might interpret this as meaning that people are willing to overlook some problems in order to receive certain benefits. To say that people "consistently act against their deeply held convictions," however, is going too far. Besides, the dislike of direct mail probably doesn't qualify as a deeply held conviction in most people's books.

(C) This choice only gives us part of the author's view and is a distortion to boot. The author distinctly tells us that the public's reaction is mixed—it's not just negative, as this answer choice portrays it. In addition, the negative attitude of the American public revolves around both the privacy issue and the "annoyance" factor. It's a distortion to say that privacy is the primary issue.

(E) *Au contraire*. The author tells us that the industry has been very *successful* despite the public's negative attitudes. There is no indication that the industry will need to alter its practices.

Remember:

- The answers to Explicit Text questions will be drawn directly from material given in the passage. Rule out any answer choices that stray too far from the details in the passage and look for those that convey what the author has already stated.

6. D

This Logic question asks us to determine what function is served by the opinions expressed in the survey mentioned in the beginning of paragraph 2. These opinions are provided as evidence for the public's negative view of direct mail. But, later in paragraph 2, these opinions seem to contradict further findings of the same survey, which show that people who don't like direct mail buy from direct mail ads anyway! This function is captured in choice (D)—these opinions are brought up to form a contrast to the behavior of consumers described later in the paragraph, which in turn forms the basis of the author's main concern.

(A) goes beyond the scope of the passage. The negative attitudes revealed in this part of the survey would make it rather unlikely that the opinions were used by the author to justify increased direct mail spending.

(B) The author does not provide a "solution" to a paradoxical situation but rather an explanation for a seemingly contradictory phenomenon. If anything, the opinions cited contribute to a contradictory phenomenon, not to its explanation.

(C) The information about computer matching programs is presented in paragraph 1 and is unrelated to the author's discussion of the survey. The author develops his conclusion about the problem of the matching program without resorting to any opinion data.

(E) The opinions expressed in the survey *could* reasonably be used to argue that the direct marketing industry will fall on hard times; after all, the opinions expressed are quite negative. But that would be a different passage altogether—here, the author goes on to say that the industry seems to be booming *in spite of* these opinions.

Remember:

- A good road map can help you answer Logic questions more quickly by providing an outline of the entire argument and the author's main idea. Once you know the full argument and how each paragraph fits within it, you're in a better position to determine how any given part of the passage serves the whole.

7. B

This Inference question requires us to determine which statement could most likely be attributed to the author, based on the information presented in the passage. Again, our grasp of the author's purpose in writing the passage comes into play. This passage looks at the difference between Americans' attitudes about direct mail and their behaviors in response to it. Evidence for the public's attitudes is provided through opinion surveys, which suggests that the author believes that the attitudes revealed in surveys can help us understand public behavior, choice (B). Think of it this way: If the author didn't agree with (B), then there would be no contradiction to resolve, because the data from the opinion polls would be meaningless. The passage as is can exist only if the author believes that polls can provide insight as stated in choice (B).

(A) This choice exaggerates the author's conclusion. We are told that Americans respond to direct mail because they perceive its benefits, but it would be going too far to conclude from this that the author believes that direct mail has "an overall positive effect on American society."

(C) presents an unwarranted comparison that in no way can be attributed to the author. Nuisance and privacy invasion are two categories of responses from the poll of paragraph 2, with the former outranking the latter in the public's mind, but we can't infer from this that the author believes that presenting a nuisance is a greater offense than invading privacy when it comes to direct marketing, no less in the context of "commercial enterprises" as a whole.

(D) switches the terms of the second-to-last sentence of the passage. It also fails to take into account the qualified nature of the author's assertion indicated by the word "probably."

(E) Again, we are not given enough information to draw this inference. The author does not discuss the future growth of direct marketing, so it's too much of a stretch to infer how the author thinks the industry might increase or decrease. In addition, the passage states that the direct marketing industry has grown *despite* people's negative attitudes about it. Growth in the industry does not therefore seem directly proportional to negative attitudes, which is another reason why it is unwarranted to ascribe the belief in (E) to the author.

Remember:

- Watch out for answer choices to Inference questions that exaggerate the author's points or go beyond the scope of the passage. If a choice contains information about a subject that the author doesn't discuss, be wary of it. The correct answer to an Inference question will stick closely to the topic and scope of the passage.

PASSAGE 2—Continental Drift

Topic and Scope
Continental-drift theory; specifically, support for Wegener's continental-drift theory.

Purpose and Main Idea
The author's purpose is to demonstrate support for the theory of continental drift, first posed by Alfred Wegener. The main idea is that since Wegener's death, geologists have learned much that supports Wegener's revolutionary continental-drift hypothesis.

Paragraph Structure

Paragraph 1 introduces continental-drift theory. This theory was first posed by Alfred Wegener in 1912 as a way of explaining why the edges of South America and Africa seemed to "fit" with one another. There follows some technical description of the theory, but for our purposes, it's best to simply note at this point that Wegener's theory was at first rejected by scientists on the grounds that no causal mechanism had yet been discovered to explain how continents could "float" like icebergs on top of the denser basalt lying beneath them.

Things look up for Wegener in paragraph 2—or at least for his theory, since he didn't live to see its acceptance. The second clause of the paragraph's first sentence essentially outlines the direction of the remainder of the passage: The author states that "since his death in 1930, geologists have learned much that supports [Wegener's] revolutionary idea." Well, what have they learned? That alone is the subject of paragraphs 2 and 3. The support described in paragraph 2 concerns rock formations on the edges of South America and Africa. Scientists used continental-drift theory to trace rock formations on the African continent and predict the location of similar rock formations in South America. Empirical findings upheld the theory's predictions.

Paragraph 3, not surprisingly, provides further evidence for continental drift, this time in the form of fossils. Both Africa and South America contain fossils of identical animal species, despite the fact that these continents are separated by an ocean that today would prevent animals from migrating from one continent to the other. The final sentence returns to rock formation evidence that further enhances the plausibility of Wegener's theory.

The Big Picture

- Don't shy away from a passage just because it contains what appears to be technical scientific jargon! First check out the organizational structure of the passage to determine how difficult the passage might be. Some science passages, like this one, are well-organized and contain clear main idea statements. Their clarity makes them as good candidates as any to handle early in the section.

- Clear, well-organized passages like this one are easy to road map, which suggests that several question types (Global, Logic, etcetera) may be very manageable—even easier than you might expect for a technical science passage.

- Think ahead as you read; anticipate where the author is likely to go. When an author states that support has been found for a theory, expect to find out what it is. The details may be technical, even cumbersome (although these weren't so bad), but you're one step ahead of the game when you know what purpose such details are meant to serve.

The Questions

8. C

This Global question is a great one to get you off to a quick start. It lends itself well to prephrasing if you picked up on the huge importance of the first sentence of paragraph 2, as discussed above. The main idea of the passage appears in that sentence, namely that geologists have discovered support for Wegener's theory since his death. We know this is the main idea because everything in paragraph 1 serves as background for this notion, and everything in the rest of the passage serves to demonstrate it. Choice (C) captures this main point perfectly.

(A) Nowhere is it stated that Wegener's hypothesis is "more intriguing" than other theories, but even if this were implied, it still wouldn't constitute the passage's main point. What about all the *support* for Wegener's theory that makes up the bulk of the passage?

(B) *Au contraire*—the evidence discussed concerning fossils and rock dating clearly supports the continental-drift hypothesis.

(D) Too broad. The author is concerned specifically with continental-drift theory, not simply "geochronology."

(E) This may have been the main idea of Wegener's early critics, but even then it's possibly shot down by the end of the first paragraph by the mention of "convection," a factor that may bypass their objection. In any case, the author doesn't discuss "conclusive proof" of Wegener's theory, but rather evidence that makes that theory more likely to be valid.

Remember:

• Always strive to determine the purpose, main idea, and structure of each passage. If you do, you'll have an excellent shot at prephrasing an answer to Global questions that address these three issues.

9. A

This Inference question asks us about an issue that is developed in paragraph 2. The two-billion-year-old rock formations are mentioned as evidence to lend support to the continental-drift theory. The author tells us that this example lends proof to the idea that Africa and South America were once connected. If this is correct, the author must believe the statement in choice (A): The rocks would not be located where they are if the continents had not been connected.

(B) Nothing is suggested by the passage regarding rock formations on other continents; for all we know, the rock formations on Africa and South

America that are mentioned in the passage are unlike any formations anywhere else in the world.

(C) takes a rather large leap: We're never told how the rock formations were formed—what would make us believe that they were formed by the same force that drove them apart? We're merely told that scientists can use rock formations to accurately predict the location of similar rock formations.

(D) Fossil evidence doesn't come into the picture until paragraph 3, where the author maintains that in some places fossils of identical species are found on both sides of the Atlantic. The example given concerns formations in South Africa and Brazil. But the rock formations that are the focus of this question need not have any fossils in common, or even if they do, nothing says these formations need to contain fossils that are common to both continents.

(E) There is simply no evidence given to indicate that the two-billion-year-old rock formations resemble the basement rock in Ghana.

Remember:

• In Inference questions, beware of choices that attempt to link elements of the passage that have no logical connection. Sometimes, as in (D) here, facts from two different paragraphs are erroneously linked. Other times, facts from the same paragraph are tied together in a bogus way, such as (E)'s attempt to relate the two-billion-year-old rock formations to the basement rock of Ghana. Does the author even imply that these "resemble" each other? No. If the author doesn't explicitly make a connection, then neither should we.

10. D

The word *originally* in the stem of this Explicit Text question is a good indication of where this answer is likely to be found: Your mental road map should point you right to paragraph 1 where Wegener's theory and the original reception to it are introduced. Paragraph 1 tells us that the theory was developed through gravity measurements and observations and was originally rejected for lack of a propelling mechanism. We're then told in the first sentence of paragraph 2 that Wegener never found clear and convincing evidence for his theory while he was alive. It is certainly fair to say based on these pieces of evidence that Wegener's work was developed through observation but was not fully supported with evidence, choice (D).

(A) *Au contraire.* Wegener's theory didn't modify an early hypothesis; it was a "novel" approach to the problem it addressed.

(B) *Au contraire* again. The theory wasn't originally rejected because it was inconsistent with Bacon but rather because it provided insufficient evidence for its physical plausibility. Contrary to (B), Wegener's theory seems to have supported Bacon's suggestion that the "fit" between the continents was not merely a coincidence.

(C) and (E) distort the author's meaning in the passage. Wegener's theory attempted to explain why the edges of the two continents seemed to "fit together." Analysis of shared rock formations was one means of supporting Wegener's hypothesis; so was the evidence given regarding fossils on both sides of the South Atlantic. Wegener's theory wasn't used to explain these things—it was rather supported by them.

Remember:

• Beware of wrong answer choices that reverse the relationship between evidence and conclusion. In this case, rock formations and fossils are discussed as support for the continental-drift hypothesis, not the other way around.

11. E

To answer this Weaken question, we must first understand Wegener's theory and the support provided for it. The author describes two pieces of evidence that uphold Wegener's claims about continental drift: (1) Studying rock formations in Africa successfully helps predict the location of rock formations in South America; and (2) Fossils found on both continents suggest that the continents were once contiguous. These details are given as evidence that the continents were once locked together, but (E) weakens this argument significantly. If common rock formations and fossils exist on continents *without* interlocking coastlines, there is much less reason to believe that the existence of common rock formations and fossils points to a previous history of interlocked coastlines.

(A) Regardless of whether or not more fossils were uncovered in South Africa, the fact still remains that identical fossils were found on continents now separated by an ocean, so this statement does not weaken the argument at all.

(B) If a new explanation for the cause of continental drift were discovered, this could only strengthen Wegener's theory, not weaken it.

(C) and (D) Both of these choices are irrelevant to Wegener's argument. Even if Bacon's argument was based on speculation, this does not affect Wegener's views. Further, the relationship between age and composition of rock formations in general does nothing to cast doubt on evidence regarding the age, composition, and structure of rock formations in Africa and South America or what these factors portend for the validity of Wegener's theory.

Remember:

• To answer a Weaken question effectively, you must first have a good grasp on the argument to be weakened. Before answering, think about the conclusion and evidence of the argument or view in question. Then look for the choice that detracts from the author's reasoning by attacking the evidence, conclusion, or assumptions underlying the argument.

12. B

This Inference question relates to fossil evidence, an issue discussed only in paragraph 3. We're told that fossil evidence supports Wegener's theory of continental drift. In general, therefore, the author would be likely to believe (B)—that fossil evidence can contribute to the plausibility of a geological model. If the author didn't believe this, it would be hard to understand why he introduces the fossil evidence at all.

(A) offers a classic unwarranted comparison. The author presents rock formation evidence and fossil evidence, but he never compares the relative merits of one versus the other. We have no way of knowing which kind of evidence the author thinks is stronger.

(C) Australia is not mentioned or alluded to in the passage, nor does the author suggest that the fossil similarity described is unique to South America and Africa, so we have no way of knowing what the author would think about possible fossil links between South America and other continents.

(D) *Au contraire*. According to paragraph 3, fossil evidence suggests that certain species now greatly separated once lived in the same location. It is only *now* that those locations are separated because, according to the theory, the continents drifted apart. If you need another reason to reject (D), consider that the word "proves" is way too strong here—fossil evidence is used to merely support a hypothesis.

(E) Fossil evidence appears in the last paragraph, convention in the first. Nothing in between even remotely suggests any link between them, so (E) should have been a quick kill.

Remember:

- Be on the lookout for inferences that move from the specific to the general while still staying within the argument's scope. If an author uses a particular piece of evidence (fossils in Africa and South America) to uphold a claim (continental-drift theory), he or she is likely to believe that this category of evidence (fossils in general) is valid for supporting this sort of claim (geochronological hypotheses).

13. A

This straightforward Global question is found at the end of the question set, but good section management would recommend that you answer the question earlier rather than later. This might have been a great question to tackle second, after the first question on the author's main idea; after all, the answers to these two must be related. We've seen early on how the author's purpose here is to demonstrate support for continental-drift theory. Here we find this paraphrased in answer choice (A), which gives a more general depiction of the author's purpose.

(B) Too narrow. The author does discuss rock formations but only in one part of the passage. (B) is part of the author's support for the main idea, but it does not represent the author's full intention.

(C) Too extreme. This harks back to choice (D) of the previous question, where we discussed how the concept of "proof" is too strong for this passage. Here, the author doesn't set out to convince us that continental drift is beyond question, merely that it has strong support.

(D) The author doesn't *assess* evidence in this passage; rather, he *presents* evidence to support a theory.

(E) This tricky choice tests your eye for detail. The author *does* describe evidence for continental drift, but it's not *Wegener's* evidence. He tells us in paragraph 2 that this evidence wasn't discovered until after Wegener's death.

Remember:

• Read critically! Take out the creator of the theory in choice (E), and we're pretty much back to correct choice (A). If you blew past Wegener in (E), you'd surely have the darndest time choosing between the two.

• Not all questions in a Reading Comp set deal with strictly separate issues. If a question set contains both a Primary Purpose and a Main Idea question on a well-organized passage such as this one, you're in luck: The same concept is basically being tested twice. You may even wish to answer them consecutively, no matter where in the set they appear.

PASSAGE 3—Illegal Constitution

Topic and Scope

The Constitution; specifically, the legality and moral legitimacy of the Constitution.

Purpose and Main Idea

The author's purpose is to evaluate whether the Constitution is legal and morally legitimate. The main idea is that while the Constitution may not be legal (because its adoption by three-quarters ratification violated the sovereignty of nonratifying states), it nonetheless carries moral weight.

Paragraph Structure

The first paragraph tells us that although Congress authorized a group of commissioners to create the U.S. Constitution by revising the Articles of Confederation, Congress was surprised by the revolutionary nature of the Constitution that the commissioners submitted.

Paragraph 2 starts by explaining James Madison's argument that the commissioners were justified in submitting a revolutionary Constitution because the document served the goal of creating good government, a goal that was more important than adhering strictly to the Articles. Despite Madison's argument, the author questions the legality of the Constitution because it was ratified by only three-quarters of the states.

In the final paragraph, the author expands her argument from paragraph 2 by showing that the "three-quarters ratification" provision violated the rights of nonratifying states. At the same time, however, she claims that the Constitution's questionable legality does not cast doubt on its moral legitimacy and gives two reasons why this is so.

The Big Picture

• In some passages, the main idea will not be readily apparent early on. Here, paragraph 1 serves as background, but for what? The passage could go in many different directions, and you have to constantly ask the question, "Why was this thing written?" until you're satisfied that you've located the main idea. You may not get a full grasp of the main idea until the end of the passage.

• Taking note of contrast keywords help you to follow an author's twists and turns. One of the most popular and powerful contrast keywords is "however," a word that is used by authors to signal a change in direction. Note the strategically placed "howevers" in the middle of paragraphs 2 and 3; both are fundamentally related to the author's main idea. The first prefaces the notion

375

that despite Madison's justifications, the new Constitution may not be legal, while the second sets up the idea that despite its possible illegality, it nonetheless may carry moral weight.

The Questions

14. C

This Inference question asks us for a reason why Congress may have been surprised by how much the Constitution differed from the Articles of Confederation. What possibility might the Congress have overlooked? This topic is discussed in the very beginning of the passage, where we see that Congress authorized the commissioners to revise the Articles to create an "adequate" federal government. They asked for some alterations and got back something they deemed to be an illegal revolutionary document. To carry out Congress's wish, the commissioners felt they had to radically depart from the Articles, not just modify them. We can infer from its reaction that Congress did not foresee that mere modification of the Articles would not suffice to carry out its charge, choice (C).

(A) distorts information from the text. While the Constitution was adopted without unanimous ratification, this fact is not described by the author as an "inevitability" or as something that was bound to occur. Any lack of foresight on this issue cannot be blamed for Congress's surprise.

(B) Moral authority appears later in the passage and has no recognizable connection to Congress's surprise over the revolutionary Constitution. Congress certainly felt that the document submitted lacked legal authority, but the issue of moral authority is not raised at this point.

(D) *Au contraire:* Congress was presumably aware that the Constitution would differ from the Articles, because it specifically commissioned a revision of the Articles. What the Congress did not anticipate was the *extent* of this difference.

(E) The reaction of an individual such as Madison is irrelevant to Congress's surprise. The question concerns why Congress was surprised about the content of the Constitution, not how or why someone would later justify this content.

Remember:

- Since Inference questions are often not suited for prephrasing, the best tactic on such questions is to evaluate each answer choice and eliminate wisely. If you're having trouble spotting an attractive choice, ruling out two or three answer choices will still greatly improve your odds.

15. B

Next up is a question that asks us to draw an inference based upon Madison's views. In other words, given the discussion of Madison's perspective, which statement could he be expected to uphold? Since Madison's views are primarily discussed in paragraph 2, we can look to that paragraph to determine an answer. Madison based his argument about the legality of the Constitution on the principle that conflicts ought to be resolved in favor of more important goals, so choice (B) represents a statement he would be likely to agree with.

(A) Madison used the principle that conflicts should be resolved in favor of more important goals, but the author never stated or implied that Madison viewed "peace in the nation" to be an overriding national goal that should be used to resolve conflicts of interest.

(C) misrepresents the author's meaning in the passage. The author never specifies that unanimous approval is the most important objective in drafting a new constitution nor does he imply that Madison believed this. The issue of unanimous approval comes up later in a different context.

(D) *Au contraire.* The reason Madison raised his voice to justify the new Constitution in the first place was because it did *not* meet Congress's expectations.

(E), like (C), appeals to an issue that comes up later in the passage: moral obligation. The author states that the result of the Constitution was to forge a strong union of the states, but he does not indicate that Madison believed that the commissioners were *morally obligated* to create a Constitution that did so.

Remember:

- Some Inference questions can be answered by reference to one specific part of a passage. When this is the case, take advantage of it—keep your review limited to just the relevant portion, and dismiss choices like (C) and (E) here that attempt to bring irrelevant elements of the passage.

16. E

With this third Inference question, we are asked for a deduction based on the author's views. Where are we given the author's views about the legality of making changes to government? In paragraph 3, the author states flat out that "no government ought to have the power to entrench itself against amendment." So the author would be likely to support a group that rebelled against a state's decision to protect itself from changes.

(A) and (D) are *au contraire* choices that violate the spirit of the author's view on this matter. These choices can be eliminated at first glance, because we're looking for a positive or supportive attitude.

(B) Too extreme. First of all, it can be argued that "admiration" is too strongly positive; the author's views are more moderate than that, and "approval" matches her tone a little better.

Secondly, the author would certainly believe that opposition to the law in question would carry moral weight, but would she believe that "*any law* passed by such a government has no moral authority"? We can't tell—that's a different issue. We can speculate, but this is too extreme to be fully inferable here.

(C) The most we can infer here is how the author would react to the legitimacy of such an act of dissent. How she would feel about the reaction *to* the reaction against such a law is one step beyond the scope. While we can infer that she would support such dissent on moral grounds, there's no way to tell if she would be concerned about government reprisals or not.

Remember:

- Questions about author's attitudes lend themselves well to quick scanning of the main verb in each answer choice. Once you've determined whether the author's attitude is likely to be positive or negative, scan the choices looking for appropriate verbs. Here, you could have skipped over any negative verbs and focused on only the choices with positive verbs.

17. A

In order to choose the best weakener, we must first understand which argument the question is referring to. We are asked to determine which statement would best weaken the argument put forth in defense of the legality of the Constitution. Where is this argument made, and by whom? A quick reference to your road map should reveal that Madison argued in defense of the Constitution's legality, and this argument is presented at the beginning of paragraph 2. Here Madison claims that the Constitution is justified despite its radical nature because it upholds the overarching goal of creating a good government. Choice (A) serves as a good weakener: If one of the Constitution's provisions (nonunanimous ratification) prevented it from creating a good government, then Madison's argument would be far less convincing.

(B), (D), and (E) These choices are irrelevant to Madison's argument. The issue of "extensive debate" is not addressed in his justification. Neither are the issues of safeguarding the power of the ruling elite or the relative merits of oral versus written arguments. Since an argument can only be weakened on its own terms, these answer choices do not accomplish the task at hand.

(C) If anything, (C) supports the necessity for the radical nature of the Constitution handed in by the commissioners. However, it does not relate to Madison's specific reason for why he believed the Constitution to be legal. He viewed it as justified because it upheld the overriding goal of good government. If anything, (C) might strengthen Madison's *cause* (defending the Constitution), but since it does not address Madison's reasoning, we can say that it has no real effect on his particular argument.

Remember:

- LSAT Reading Comp arguments can only be weakened on their own terms. To choose a weakener, therefore, you must first understand the argument at stake. When a specific argument is referenced in a question stem, read back in the passage to make sure you understand the evidence and conclusion of that particular argument, and make sure the choice you select is directly relevant to them.

18. **A**

"According to the passage" lets us know that we're being asked for something that is found directly in the text. We need to find something that provided justification for the revolutionary nature of the new Constitution. Justification is given in two places:

Madison justifies the Constitution's legality, and the author justifies the Constitution's moral authority. Choice (A) relates to the final sentence of the passage in which the author justifies rebelling against the government under the Articles on the grounds that that government itself admitted it wasn't up to the task of dealing with the "exigencies"—that is, pressing needs—of the nation.

(B) The author uses this reason to argue against Madison's justification of the Constitution's legality.

(C) *Au contraire.* In paragraph 3, the author states that no government has the right to entrench itself against amendment.

(D) also presents the opposite of what we're looking for: If the commission followed Congress's recommendation, it would not have submitted such a radical document. Far from justifying the revolutionary Constitution, (D) describes a factor that would presumably guard against the creation of such a document.

(E) Madison does no such thing: His analysis attempted to justify the differences between the Articles and the Constitution. Nowhere does the author state that Madison questioned the extent of these differences.

Remember:

- In Explicit Text questions, be on the lookout for choices that describe the opposite of that stated in the passage.

19. **D**

Nowhere does the author directly relate legality to morality, but since we know about the author's attitude toward each independently, we must be able to infer a connection—otherwise, this question wouldn't exist. Briefly review what we learned about each: The author believes that the legality of the

Constitution is questionable but that its moral authority is not. It's a simple matter of putting these facts together: Inferably, the author believes that moral authority can exist without legality, choice (D).

The remaining choices are difficult insofar as they include all of the same terms as the correct choice, but each choice somehow fouls up the relationship between morality and legality:

(A) *Au contraire:* In stating that a document with questionable legal validity can nonetheless carry moral weight, the author evidently sees moral authority and legality as two separate issues.

(B) First of all, the author is concerned with the morality and legality of a written document, not a principle. But even if we overlook that fact, (B) reverses the situation in the passage, where there's something that could be illegal yet moral. Would the author think that something lacking morality can be legal? It's doubtful, since morality seems to carry lots of weight with this author. But still, there's no real way to tell.

(C), like (B), switches the scope from documents to "action." Still, had you overlooked that, you should have recognized that (C) runs counter to the author's beliefs: *Despite* its possible illegality, in the author's mind the new Constitution can still have moral authority.

(E) goes beyond the scope of the passage. The author's argument does not address court decisions but rather the country's governing documents.

Remember:

- In Inference questions, beware of choices that shift the scope from the focus of the passage.

20. E

The last question of this set is a straightforward Global question, showing that it pays to scan the question set before answering the questions! Your road map should have helped you to determine the author's purpose in writing the passage: to evaluate the legality and moral legitimacy of the Constitution. Answer choice (E) expresses this purpose in a more general manner to "assess the authority of a political event [i.e., the Constitution] on two grounds [i.e., legal and moral]."

(A) What two viewpoints are *reconciled*? The author argues against Madison's view, but that's about as close as we come in this passage to opposing viewpoints.

(B) The author does make an argument, but she isn't interested in illustrating the "argumentative power" of anything (except perhaps the evidence she provides).

(C) This choice misrepresents the author's purpose. She doesn't argue for a *re*consideration of the Constitution (after all, she states that "history has validated the wisdom of the change"), but apparently for an *initial* consideration of it. And besides, the Constitution can be considered a governing document, not a "doctrine" *per se.*

(D) The author's argument does not support the establishment of the Constitution over the Articles as much as it reviews some legal and moral considerations of the Constitution itself.

Remember:

- Because they lend themselves so well to prephrasing, Global questions are usually among the easier questions to answer in any Reading Comprehension question set. Don't let their positions in a question set lead you to answer them last! You can maximize your points on test day by scanning a passage's questions and answering the easiest ones first, no matter where they're located in the set. This strategy will allow you to accumulate points quickly at the outset of the passage, raising your confidence and giving you extra time to spend on the harder questions.

PASSAGE 4—Gerschenkron & Hough

Topic and Scope

The views of authors Gerschenkron and Hough; specifically, a comparison of these two authors' work on the former Soviet Union.

Purpose and Main Idea

The author's purpose is to compare how Gerschenkron and Hough approach the case of the former Soviet Union in their scholarly works. The main idea is that both authors share a similar theoretical approach in their works, and both are successful in their theoretical endeavors.

Paragraph Structure

Paragraph 1 introduces the passage by noting that both Gerschenkron and Hough view the former Soviet Union as an anomalous nation. Although they focus on different aspects of the former Soviet anomaly, they nonetheless share a similar approach in their research.

Paragraph 2 explains one aspect of similarity between the authors' approaches: Both develop ideas in reaction to existing theories in their fields. We are told first what Gerschenkron reacts to and then what Hough reacts to in his work.

Paragraph 3 provides a second aspect of similarity between the authors' approaches: Both attempt to supplement existing theories in their fields. Again, we are given a description of Gerschenkron's attempt, and then a description of Hough's.

The final paragraph summarizes the points made in paragraphs 2 and 3. It also draws a final conclusion: Not only are the authors' tasks similar, but they both succeed in these tasks.

The Big Picture

- A good road map doesn't include every detail of a passage. In a complex passage such as this one, your road map should recap the points of each paragraph and remind you where the evidence is to support these points. If you're asked a question regarding a specific detail from a paragraph, you can always go back to it.

- As you read, focus on isolating the author's purpose and main idea, along with significant pieces of evidence the author gives to uphold his or her conclusion. If you have a good grasp of the overall argument, you'll be able to answer several questions accurately and quickly—giving you more time to research detail questions if necessary.

The Questions

21. A

This question asks for the author's main point or the main idea of the passage. This question would be a good one to prephrase, since a careful focus on purpose and structure should make the main idea clear. In this case, the main idea has two parts and is summed up in paragraph 4: The theorists share similar tasks, and they succeed at these tasks as well. This is well stated in choice (A).

(B) and (C) These choices describe only parts of the author's claim; they are not broad enough to reflect the main idea. Choice (B) summarizes the point of paragraph 2, while choice (C) discusses a point raised in paragraph 1 about the anomalies of the former Soviet case.

(D) *Au contraire:* This choice contradicts the author's argument as laid out in paragraph 4. The author specifically states that the theorists use their anomalous cases to "enable the existing theories to more accurately explain the issues under investigation." In other words, their works supplement the existing theories.

This is a far cry from replacing the theories, as choice (D) suggests.

(E) Again, *au contraire*. The author tells us in paragraph 1 that Gerschenkron and Hough focus on different aspects of the Soviet experience—Gerschenkron on industrialization and Hough on bureaucratic organization. Their specific central tenets differ, but their overall theoretical *approach* is the same.

Remember:

• Be careful of answer choices that state the opposite of the author's claims in the passage or that focus on only part of the author's argument. The correct answer to a Main Idea question will reflect the author's argument accurately and will summarize the entire argument, not just one part.

22. C

This question begins with the words "according to the author," so we know that we're being asked for a detail from the text. How are the works of the two theorists similar? Maybe you were able to prephrase an answer here—after all, the first sentence tells us that both theorists view the Soviet Union as an anomalous case, and perhaps that stuck in your head. Or the fact that despite differences in their specific concerns, they share a similar overall theoretical approach. Either of these ideas would work. Unfortunately, however, the test makers decided to cull the answer to this one from paragraph 4, where it's stated that "Both authors also attempt to use the anomalies that they discover to enhance the explanatory value of the theories already existing in their fields." Choice (C) is a very close paraphrase of this.

(A) This answer choice contradicts the author's argument and is similar to incorrect answer choice (C) from the previous question. The author specifically tells us in paragraph 4 that the works of Gerschenkron and Hough enhance the explanatory power of existing theories—they do not invalidate these theories.

(B) Again, this goes against the grain: In paragraph 2 we're told that Gerschenkron and Hough react to existing theories in their fields and later that they expand upon them. Thus, it cannot be said that they adhere to these interpretations.

(D) Gerschenkron addresses industrialization, but Hough investigates bureaucratic organization. This is not a similarity in their works.

(E) misrepresents the author's meaning in the passage. She says that Gerschenkron and Hough use the former Soviet experience to draw attention to factors that expand existing theories. Nowhere are we told that their portrayals of the Soviet case are critical.

Remember:

• Don't be discouraged if you form a valid prephrase that's not reflected in a correct choice—it still may help you to eliminate wrong choices, and your attempt to prephrase answers is bound to pay off in the long run.

23. E

Here we're presented with another Explicit Text question, this time about Hough's work. Hough's work is discussed in detail in two places—paragraphs 2 and 3—so now is a good time to return to the passage and examine those in detail. The author states at the end of paragraph 3 that Hough believes that the Soviet experience shows that overlapping bureaucratic duties can promote organizational efficiency—a point reflected in choice (E).

(A) and (B) *Au contraire*. The author states in paragraph 3 that the former Soviet Union has an overlapping model of bureaucratic function that differs from the American monistic model. As we saw with correct choice (E), he also states here that the Soviet overlapping model may promote efficiency in certain cases.

(C) and (D) confuse Hough's work with that of Gerschenkron. England's industrial growth is part of Gerschenkron's work, and nowhere is this compared to the growth of Soviet bureaucracy (C). Similarly, the degree of economic backwardness is another element of the Gerschenkron discussion of paragraph 3, and nothing is stated about its effect on Soviet bureaucracy. Gerschenkron deals with industrialization, while Hough deals with bureaucratic organization. Choices (C) and (D) try to combine them, and thus must be tossed.

Remember:

• Beware of choices that combine elements of the passage in ways that are unwarranted. This is an especially common ploy in passages that deal with more than one view or theory. Keep the theories straight, and you won't fall for choices that attempt to mix them together like (C) and (D) here.

24. D

This Logic question asks you to determine the role played by one part of the passage in upholding the author's main idea. The paragraph focuses mainly on the way both theorists attempt to supplement existing theories in their fields. That's the specific gist of paragraph 3, but we're asked what this has to do with the passage as a whole. The best clue is the first word of the paragraph: "Second." This structural signal tells us that what's about to follow harks back to the earlier claim, back in paragraph 1, that their overall theoretical approaches were similar. Paragraph 2 presented the first similarity, and now in paragraph 3 we get the second. So this paragraph simply serves as additional support for the author's claim in the last

sentence of paragraph 1, and (D) captures the gist of this nicely.

(A) It is true that Gerschenkron and Hough study different aspects of Soviet development. This point is raised in paragraph 1 and may even be reinforced in paragraph 3, where again we see how Gerschenkron is concerned with industrialization while Hough is into bureaucratic structures. However, this is not related to the *function* of paragraph 3. These illustrations merely support the larger point that their overall goals are similar despite the fact that their specific subject matter differs.

(B) This answer choice distorts the author's argument. Nowhere does she state that Gerschenkron's and Hough's works can most effectively be compared by reviewing their research on the former Soviet Union.

(C) This choice captures part of what occurs in paragraph 3, but it does not describe the function of paragraph 3 in the entire argument. It merely describes one idea that is developed in that paragraph.

(E) *Au contraire*—the third paragraph supports the notion that Gerschenkron and Hough have similar approaches by showing that both theorists attempt to supplement existing theories in their fields. That's the overall point of the paragraph, differences in their specific topics notwithstanding.

Remember:

• A correct answer choice may not match your prephrase exactly. It may be more general, or more specific, than the prephrased answer you come up with. Still, a good prephrase will help you anticipate the correct answer and will help you recognize a broader or narrower variation when you see it.

25. D

This question begins with the words "the passage suggests," which lets us know that it is an Inference question. We are asked to choose a statement about which both Gerschenkron and Hough would likely agree. Rather than attempt to prephrase the answer (the possibilities could be very broad), we should scan the choices to determine the correct one. (D) provides the best summary of a statement that would align with both theorists' views, since paragraph 4 tells us that both men use research into anomalous cases to broaden the explanatory value of existing theories. Presumably, since both theorists use such cases to broaden such explanations, they would agree that using such research in this way is possible.

(A) The author doesn't suggest that studies of the former Soviet Union should be limited to any subjects, and neither does she imply that Gerschenkron and Hough believe this. All we know is that industrialization and bureaucracy are their respective areas of concern. We can't infer that they think that Soviet studies should be limited to their subjects.

(B) Gerschenkron would agree with this, but the passage does not indicate Hough's views on Rostow's model.

(C) Not even Gerschenkron would buy this one—the author states in paragraph 2 that Gerschenkron reacts against this notion. And of course, we don't know what Hough's views would be on the subject.

(E) *Au contraire*. Gerschenkron and Hough do not attempt to falsify the existing theories they deal with—they attempt to supplement them. They would therefore, if anything, probably *disagree* with the notion that empirical research should focus on falsification.

Remember:

- Inference questions often ask for the likely opinions of the characters, not the actual author, of the passage. When you answer a question pertaining to the views of two authors or theorists discussed in a passage, be sure to avoid choices that only relate to one author's views, such as (C) here.

26. E

This question asks again for a detail from the passage. We know this because we're asked for a statement that is "explicitly cited" in the text. Can't get much clearer than that! (E) generalizes the author's point in paragraph 3 regarding Gerschenkron, the references being to the discussion of Gerschenkron's incorporation of the "economic backwardness" factor into Rostow's industrialization model.

(A) *Au contraire*. Paragraph 2 tells us that Gerschenkron reacted to the notion that states *must* possess specific characteristics in order to industrialize.

(B) True, Gerschenkron may differ from Hough in the specific orientation of his work, but this statement is not explicitly cited as evidence of how Gerschenkron put his work to use.

(C) This description applies to neither Gerschenkron nor Hough's work. Gerschenkron addressed industrialization, not bureaucratic organization, and Hough's work showed that monism is not the only efficient method of bureaucratic organization.

(D) reverses the evidence in the text. Paragraph 3 tells us that Gerschenkron showed that economic backwardness affects the speed of industrialization, not vice versa.

Remember:

- The wrong answer choices to Explicit Text questions will attempt to throw you off course in many ways: by providing statements that contradict the text, by providing statements that reverse or confuse an idea given in the text, or by providing statements that were not explicitly laid out in the text at all, to name a few. If you are aware of these typical wrong answer pitfalls, you're more likely to avoid them on test day.

27. C

This Logic question asks us to determine what function is served by the introduction of the concept of monism in paragraph 2. Paragraph 2 demonstrates that both authors react in their works to existing theories. Without looking at the answer choices, we can prephrase that "monism is introduced to show that Hough's work reacted to an existing theory." Do we find such an answer with a scan of the choices? In fact, (C) conveys just this idea—albeit a bit more specifically than our prephrase.

(A) This choice refers to the subject discussed by Gerschenkron, not Hough.

(B) and (D) *Au contraire*. Hough reacts against the American system known as monism, and according to paragraph 3, Hough's examination of the former Soviet case results in an alternative conception of bureaucratic efficiency. In addition, the author tells us in paragraph 1 that Hough portrayed the former Soviet Union as anomalous, or different, in its bureaucratic structure. The mention of monism in paragraph 2 is in no way included to show otherwise.

(E) Again, the author states that Hough portrayed the former Soviet Union as *different* from the American monistic model.

Remember:

- *Au contraire* choices are ones that reflect the opposite of what the passage, author, or characters in the passage believe or suggest. They are quite common in passages that include a number of theorists and theories. The test makers are simply testing whether or not you're able to keep the various elements of the passage straight.

- If you find yourself frequently choosing *au contraire* choices, you may be prone to reversing the information in the passage, and you need to take better care in your initial reading of the passage to distinguish between the various characters and the views they espouse.

Section II: Logical Reasoning Explanations

1. C

The author explains that animals who get separated from their mothers early in life don't play and live well with the other animals. Specifically, they acquire aggression disorders, possibly leading to food fights and other unattractive behavior. The author's conclusion: These animals acquire aggressive disorders because they lack early, proper, parent-led socialization training. We're looking to strengthen this argument, which means that we want to reinforce the causal relationship between the lack of parent-led socialization training and aggressive disorders. (C) gets at this issue, and the fact that it approaches the issue from the other angle, saying that simulated parent-led socialization leads to less aggression, doesn't make it any less right. This choice strengthens the link between the two terms of the conclusion and therefore strengthens the argument by making us more likely to believe that the causal mechanism cited by the author is valid.

(A), if anything, weakens the hypothesis by linking aggressive disorders with animals *not* separated from their mothers. If separation and the resulting lack of parent-led socialization is the cause of aggression disorders, how would the hypothesis explain the excessive aggression of these nonseparated wildebeests?

(B) In order to make this answer choice work, you'd have to assume that a child who is put up for adoption inherently lacks access to parent-led socialization. If that were the case, then this would help support the hypothesis. But the assumption is unsupported; for all we know, adopted human babies receive plenty of parent-led socialization. (B), thus, has no direct bearing on the argument.

(D) Since we don't know whether these polar bears did or did not have early parent-led socialization, their aggressiveness does not strengthen (or weaken or do anything to) this argument. The argument discusses aggressive behavior in terms of socialization, so any information about aggression outside of that context doesn't affect the argument.

(E) This is the exact opposite of what we're looking for. The proposers of the hypothesis would feel better about their idea if these elephants were rude, ornery, stampeding aggressive beasts.

Remember:

- Always be prepared to see and eliminate an answer choice that would weaken an argument in a strengthen question and one that would strengthen an argument in a weaken question. They're often present to tempt less-focused test takers.

2. E

Since you'll need to find the one choice that isn't an inference, be prepared to keep track of the boundaries around the argument. That way you'll be better prepared to spot what isn't there. The author begins by noting that the Sarrin monks use Pran meditation only in cases of severe weather. The author then explains the differences between Pran meditation and ritual meditation. Understanding the difference will likely be key to getting this question right. Pran meditation is different than ritual meditation because it's more highly disciplined and uniquely involves isolation and fasting. Thus, there are three ways in which Pran meditation is different than ritual meditation. Let's go to the choices.

(A) The author states that Pran meditation is more disciplined than ritual meditation, so (A) must be true. Remember that "some" in the LSAT means "one or more." We have one example of less disciplined meditation, and that means that some practices are less disciplined. This is a valid inference, so it's not the answer.

(B) The monks only practice Pran meditation when there's severe weather, and since weather isn't precisely scheduled, then Pran meditation must not be precisely scheduled either. Sure, that's an inference.

(C) If Pran meditation involves the *unique* practice of isolation, then no other meditation, including ritual meditation, involves isolation.

(D) Again, "some" means "one or more," so since the monks practice Pran meditation in response to local weather threats, some types of meditation do in fact exist as a response to local threats.

(E) is correct because, even though the author implies that ritual meditation is *less* disciplined than Pran, that doesn't mean that it's *un*disciplined. (E) takes us beyond what the passage supports, so it's not a valid inference and is the correct answer here.

Remember:

- Get comfortable with the specifics of LSAT vocabulary well before test day so that you don't have to take time to think about what words like "some" or "unique" mean when you're taking the exam.

3. B

Following the lead of the question stem, our first task is to understand the discrepancy. The author tells us that a high volume of pirating sales causes studios to lose a great deal of money. However (a keyword that signals the discrepancy in the stimulus), a low volume of pirating sales generally indi-

cates a period of economic weakness in the movie industry. Why does a low level of pirating sales, which would seem to benefit the industry, actually signal a period of economic weakness in the industry? This is the question that we need to answer, so let's proceed to the answer choices.

(A) doesn't address the issues involved in the discrepancy, focusing as it does on whether these studios distribute smaller films.

(B) is correct because it creates a direct connection between pirating and the financial success of the entire industry. If pirating is related exclusively to big hits, then a low level of pirating signals a lack of blockbuster hits, in which case it's more understandable how a low level of pirating would correspond to periods of economic downturns in the industry.

(C) is off base, focusing as it does on the methods of pirated tape production and not on the connection between pirating and the economic health of the movie industry.

(D) is similarly off base, since it offers a comparative analysis between the largest and not so large studios, which isn't a comparison relevant to the original discrepancy.

(E) gives us information about the profitability of selling pirated movies, which may be interesting but doesn't explain why low pirating sales would signal an economic low point in the entire movie industry.

Remember:

- When dealing with complex discrepancy questions like this one, make sure to identify the primary issues involved, and then search for a choice that addresses those issues. Here, note how only (B) actually keeps focused on the issues at hand.

4. C

The author concludes that no beef has been available in Cebra for the past six months. The evidence is the first sentence: A blight wiped out all of the town's beef supply six months ago. With such a skimpy argument, we can anticipate that the correct inference will require us to have read it carefully. Since Inference questions are often tough to prephrase, there's not much else to do but to go to the answer choices.

(A) If we interpret this choice to mean that Cebra folks consume nothing but Cebra beef (i.e., no fruits, veggies, etcetera), then (A) is easy to dismiss—there's been no Cebra beef for six months, and these people must eat something. The more plausible reading of (A) is that the only type of beef Cebra residents consume is that raised by Cebra farmers. Still, this is going too far: Although for the past six months no non-Cebra beef has been brought into town (which is, incidentally, correct choice (C)), for all we know there was plenty of outside beef consumed in Cebra prior to the blight.

(B) makes an unsupported distinction between the categories of meat and discusses the issue of preferences. According to the author, lamb and poultry are available for consumption while beef is not. What's available is clear; what's *preferred* is not.

(C) must indeed be true if the conclusion and evidence are true. If the elimination of the town's beef supply means that no beef is available, then the town must have no external beef provider during the last six months.

(D) Technically, we don't even have enough information to infer that one resident is a meat eater, although since they do have meat available for consumption, it's likely that someone's eating it—otherwise, why would they have various kinds of meat available? However, we certainly can't infer that *most* people eat the stuff—that's just going too far.

(E) pushes us out of the stimulus' time frame. It provides no information about consumption patterns before the blight or even after. The argument concerns meat availability, not its consumption, so the comparison stated in (E) has no support in the passage.

Remember:

- What's the difference between an inference and an assumption? Both are unstated and must be true if the statements in the argument are true, but an assumption is central to the argument, connecting its evidence to its conclusion, while an inference can come from any part of the argument.

5. D

The author concludes that the food critic's review is flawed based on the following evidence: The critic criticized the soup for containing cilantro and sundried tomatoes but praised a chicken dish with those same ingredients. The author calls this an inconsistency that shows the critic to be unqualified. Thus, the critic's review is misguided because the critic is inconsistent. In order for the author's conclusion to be valid, one must assume that the two pieces of the comparison in the evidence are fully relevant to one another. Only if the two dishes are comparable can the critic's difference of opinion about the two be construed as an inconsistency. Therefore, the author must assume that cilantro and sun-dried tomatoes have the same culinary impact on strawberry soup and roasted chicken, which is what (D) says.

(A) is irrelevant because the author is concerned with the critic's inconsistent reviews, not with some customers' preferences.

(B) contradicts the argument. The critic clearly does like cilantro and sun-dried tomatoes in the chicken dish, so it's not the ingredients that he dislikes.

(C) would weaken the argument, showing how these particular ingredients are more appropriate to some dishes than others. If (C) were true, we'd be more likely to see the critic's supposed "inconsistency" as warranted and the author's criticism of the critic as off base. Nothing that would weaken an argument need be assumed by that argument.

(E) is entirely irrelevant to the argument, since the author never discusses nonroasted chicken. Information about that dish has no relationship to the author's conclusion.

Remember:

- Whenever an author uses one fact to prove the truth of another, make sure that the two objects of comparison really are fully comparable. If that comparability isn't demonstrated, then the author must assume it.

6. A

The author concludes that any astute literary critic will be able to correctly anticipate which underlying issues are addressed in Dovak's new book. The evidence comes earlier in the stimulus: Dovak's new novel will have the same form as his six previous works, all of which were philosophy novels in which the plot and characters demonstrated the author's own philosophical convictions. Thus, it seems clear that Dovak's new book will also demonstrate his philosophical convictions, but that will only yield the same underlying issues if the author assumes that Dovak's philosophical convictions have remained constant. The author's evidence provides information about the Dovak's motivations in writing, but they only support the conclusion's prediction about the content of Dovak's new book if those motivations, i.e., his philosophical convictions, have remained constant. (A) clearly states this assumption.

(B) The author says that the plot will "surely be different," but (B) makes that assertion even stronger by claiming that the plots have absolutely not one thing in common. (B) is wrong both because an assumption doesn't make the author's assertions more extreme, and because the plot of the text, unlike its underlying issues, is not the central concern in this argument.

(C) journeys outside of our scope as soon as it mentions the novels that Dovak wrote *before* the seven in which we're interested.

(D) The stimulus states that competent critics *can* make such predictions but doesn't suggest that their jobs involve such predictions on a regular basis. Also, the critics are less central to the conclusion than the underlying content of Dovak's new book, and that's what the correct assumption must address.

(E) ranks two elements in the stimulus—plot and underlying convictions—that aren't ranked by the author and that needn't be ranked for the author's conclusion to stand.

Remember:

- Be suspicious of comparisons and rankings that appear in the answer choices. The first thing you must ask yourself about such comparisons is, "Is this relevant?" The "irrelevant comparison" is a common wrong answer choice in Inference, Assumption, and Strengthen/ Weaken questions.

7. C

We get a lot of information before the author finally gets to the point, which is that the phony solicitation industry will likely "dwindle significantly" in the years to come. To support this opinion, the author explains that politicians are using phony solicitors less often and that's basically the extent of the evidence. In order for the loss of some politicians' business to so dramatically affect the phony solicitation industry, the author must assume that politicians represent a significant portion of that industry's clientele. Since this is a Weaken the Argument question, we can scan the answer choices to see if one might deny this central assumption. (C) fits the bill—it basically tells us that politicians are not the industry's major clients and suggests that the really major clients, the large retailers, are not following the politicians out the door. This weakens the argument because it downplays the importance of the politicians in this industry's survival; that is, it undercuts the author's central assumption.

(A) We already know that some politicians find public opinion polling useful enough to make them stop using the solicitors. Anything that further suggests the efficacy of public opinion polling could only strengthen the argument by suggesting that more than just politicians may begin to take advantage of it to the detriment of the phony solicitors.

(B), if true, wouldn't hurt or help the argument. The stimulus tells us that some people do share such information; whether or not *most* people share personal information isn't important in terms of this argument.

(D) Prosecution itself is not an issue central to the argument's conclusion or evidence, so (D) is just largely irrelevant.

(E) deals with the solicitors' techniques, when all we really care about in terms of the argument is whether the solicitors are going to go out of business due to the withdrawal of some politicians' business.

Remember:

- When evaluating the answer choices for Strengthen/Weaken questions, it's crucial that you be able to distinguish between choices that provide useless background information and

those that really have some impact on the argument. The easiest way to make this distinction is to evaluate each answer choice in terms of the author's conclusion and evidence. If a choice doesn't directly affect the way in which the evidence leads to the conclusion, then it cannot strengthen or weaken the argument.

8. B

This dialogue stimulus begins with Albert arguing that the CEO's proposal doesn't make business sense. His evidence: Teenagers can't afford luxury products. Bill disputes Albert's conclusion with the evidence that image enhancement boosts sales in the long run. The point at issue between them will be something that both men address and on which both men offer differing opinions. They use different evidence, so that's not the point of contention. They only explicitly disagree about whether the CEO's proposal will create sales. (B) captures that perfectly. Bill's would vote "yea" on (B), believing as he does that the CEO's proposal will financially benefit the company (albeit down the road), while that opinion is certainly one with which Albert, who's focusing only on immediate sales, disagrees.

(A) and (D) present views that neither person supports. Looking at (A), since neither man addresses any recent image problems, they certainly aren't disagreeing about that. Albert never discusses image at all, and Bill merely states a correlation between image enhancement and sales, which is not nearly strong enough to say that he feels the company's image is suffering. Sure, positive publicity can help image, but that doesn't mean that the company's image is bad as is. (D) directly contradicts Albert's evidence that teenagers would *not* be able to purchase the products, and it's an issue that Bill does not address.

(C) presents a view with which only one person, specifically Bill, would agree. This is a fundamental assumption in Bill's argument, but Albert never addresses the issue of publicity.

(E) distorts Bill's statement. He discusses the long-term financial benefits of a good public image but doesn't suggest that teenagers could buy the products. Furthermore, Albert never addresses the issue of publicity.

Remember:

- Dialogue stimuli are very similar to single stimuli that present different views: The second person in a dialogue never says "Yeah, you're 100 percent right! I have nothing to add." In both cases, you need to recognize what distinguishes the two views, as well as the scope of each view presented.

- The answer to a Point-at-Issue question has to revolve around an issue that's addressed by both people. If one of the parties has nothing to say regarding the subject of a particular choice, that choice must be wrong.

9. A

Next up is a Method of Argument question based on this same conversation between Albert and Bill, so you'll need to characterize the way in which Bill responds to Albert's argument. We already know that Bill disagrees with Albert's conclusion and that Bill offers supporting evidence for his claim. More specifically, Bill introduces the new issue of publicity and uses it to dispute Albert's conclusion. By adding a consideration of the long-term benefits of image enhancement, Bill certainly does "broaden the scope" of the argument in order to argue for the financial benefits of the CEO's proposal, as stated in (A).

(B) is tempting insofar as it mentions long-term gains. However, this answer choice is far too broad. Bill does not offer a general assessment of the values of short versus long-term gains but merely discusses one instance in which long-term considerations might benefit the company.

(C) First of all, Bill doesn't offer examples, or even one singular example. Second, he doesn't rank the issues of image and profit margins as competing factors in financial health; he suggests that a good image leads to higher sales, which leads to enhanced profit margins (returning to his first sentence).

(D) *Au contraire.* Bill does not argue that product sales do *not* lead to financial growth, but quite the opposite. Bill argues that a positive image leads to sales, which leads to financial growth. He introduces a new variable but maintains the direct relationship between sales and financial growth.

(E) Bill does not address Albert's concern with teenagers' disposable income. Bill immediately embarks on a different approach (the image enhancement theory of financial well-being), and neither argues against or supports Albert's contention that teenagers can't afford the company's products.

Remember:

- Method of Argument answer choices are sometimes difficult since they often depend on general terms like "presupposition," "scope," and "evidence." It's particularly easy to get lost in them if you aren't clear about what you're seeking. Tie the general terms back into the argument. In (A), for instance, consider what the scope really is, and then ask yourself if Bill has broadened it. Relate the general terms of the answer choices to the specific elements of the stimulus in order to assess them, and throw out any choice that deviates from the stimulus in even one respect.

10. D

The veterinary technician does not discuss the medical merits or weaknesses of Dr. Markey's recommendation but solely discusses Wisecrack's owner's financial situation. Because the Smiths cannot afford the procedure, the technician disagrees with the doctor's analysis concerning the horse's medical problem. The technician's flaw is her shift in the discussion—did you spot the scope shift? Just because the Smiths can't afford the surgery is no reason to disagree with the doctor's analysis; the fact that they can't pay for the surgery doesn't allow one to conclude that therefore the doctor was wrong in his diagnosis and subsequent recommendation. In other words, just because the Smiths can't act on Markey's recommendation doesn't mean that the analysis that prompted the recommendation is suspect. What's suspect here, as the stem puts it, is this form of logic—and (D) captures the technician's flaw perfectly.

(A) Indeed the technician is not quite the animal advocate that we might want our veterinary technician to be, but (A) doesn't characterize how her argument is flawed in this particular context. Her evidence is concerned only with the costs of treatment; she has no real obligation to take the costs of *not* treating Wisecrack into consideration.

(B) Who's to say what's in the "best interest" of the owners? As uncaring as it may sound, perhaps not spending money they can't afford is a higher priority for them than is treating the suffering horse. "Best interest" is too ambiguous here for (B) to be the flaw in this argument. And once again, one is obligated only to draw a logical conclusion—not one that's in the best interest of some party or another.

(C) Just in case this comes up in your own life, a disagreement is not necessarily a personal attack! The technician disagrees with the doctor's analysis, but she doesn't attack him personally.

(E) The technician's evidence concerns the inability of the Smiths to pay for the procedure. Certainly this can be independently verified.

Remember:

• Often among the wrong answer choices for an LR question, you'll see an answer choice that confuses what can be done for what should be done. For instance, if an argument argues for a certain course of action, it doesn't strengthen the argument to say that the course of action is actually achievable. By the same logic, it doesn't weaken an argument to assert that a course of action cannot be achieved. An argument that discusses what should happen is not weakened by a consideration of what can happen—they are entirely different arguments.

11. D

First things first: The recommendation is that the marrow in the shipment should not be used. What is the subsidiary conclusion justifying this recommendation? It's the conclusion that the marrow shipped is degenerative. The author presents two key pieces of evidence to support this: (1) The shipment comes from rats supplied by Cronin Labs which has a policy to supply rats that are four months old or older. Somewhat separated from this is key evidence number (2): Degenerative marrow comes from rats who are beyond their primary growth phase. If the rats provided by Cronin Labs do in fact provide degenerative marrow, then the author must assume a connection between the two pieces of evidence. Specifically, she must assume that rats four months old or older are past their primary growth phase. Since we're looking to strengthen this argument, we should look to see if any choice states this assumption. (D) is perfect because it informs us that four-month-old rats are indeed past their primary growth phase.

(A) contradicts part of the evidence, so it certainly doesn't strengthen the argument.

(B) doesn't help to justify the author's conclusion, which concerns a particular shipment of marrow derived from rats four months old *or* older. (B) just gives information on rats *more* than four months old. Assuming (B) were true, the shipment still could have come from rats exactly four months old, and we aren't given any information about whether their marrow is degenerative. Therefore, this doesn't support the argument because it only discusses part of the group of rats involved in it.

(C) wouldn't justify why this particular batch of marrow is degenerative because it doesn't link its information to the rats in the stimulus. Were those rats in their primary growth phase? Were they the ones with degenerative marrow? We don't know, so this information needn't underlie the argument.

(E) Even if you assume that the argument constitutes one of these rare instances, (E) would seem to weaken the argument, suggesting that the marrow may not have been degenerative because it might have come from younger rats in their primary growth phases.

Remember:

- When you have two pieces of disconnected evidence, often an assumption is necessary to tie them together, enabling them to lead to the conclusion as the author intended. Remain on the lookout for gaps in the argument, and don't neglect to prephrase assumptions in Strengthen/ Weaken questions when possible. Questions like this one reward you for that effort.

12. C

You can view this Inference/Conclusion question from a formal logic angle: If a client had pulled out, the company would have closed. The company did-

n't close, so you can continue along with the contrapositive to infer that no major client closed his or her account. You could pause at this point to scan the answer choices, and indeed you would see that (C) takes you exactly where you want to go. After all, the author tells us that a certain action would inevitably result in the company's closure. Since the company expanded, the death blow wasn't dealt—it must be the case that no major client pulled out.

(A) There's no information in the stimulus that would support this specific possibility. It could be true, but it might not be, so we really can't infer it.

(B) and (D) basically suggest ways in which Many Maids' business might have increased in the past year. But nothing in the stimulus suggests that business *must* have increased in these particular ways. (In fact, (B) mildly runs counter to the argument which states that Many Maids absolutely depends on the major clients to stay in business. Sure, it's possible that this dependence has been lessened by the acquisition of small accounts, but the fact remains that if one biggie pulls out, it's bye-bye cleaning company. So we can quibble over whether (B) is possible, possible but not probable, or what have you— but we can definitely say that it is not inferable.)

(E) Again, this might be true, and it seems reasonable that major clients provide this company with much of its revenue, but we have no information that would enable us to make such a precise statement as (E) offers.

Remember:

- When you see formal logic in the stimulus of an Inference question, you'll often see the statement's contrapositive among the answer choices as your correct answer. Consider that your reward for recognizing the formal logic and knowing how contrapositives work.

13. A

The author here begins by explaining a certain problem that the Fines Museum had: Its totem pole was too tall to fit into the storage vault. The author then concludes that the problem has been solved, and the totem pole can now be stored in that vault. The author's evidence is the ensuing explanation: The pole can now be separated into two pieces and then later reassembled without damaging the artifact. If you don't see the assumption, scan the answer choices while keeping the central issues of the conclusion and evidence in mind, which are size and storage. In order to work on a prephrase, consider the relationship between the pieces of the argument. The author argues that dividing the totem pole into two pieces will enable its storage in the vault, thereby overcoming the initial problem concerning the height of the pole. Size offered the only barrier to putting the pole in the vault, so if the pole can presently fit into the vault, it must have overcome the size problem. Accordingly, the author assumes that each piece of the separated pole can fit into the storage vault, as (A) states.

(B) is more precise than we need it to be. In order for the divided totem pole to fit into the storage vault, it just needs to be short enough to fit. That may not require that it be divided into equal pieces.

(C) focuses on the issue of expense, which the author never addresses as a relevant factor. The argument's only real issues are size and storage, so the correct assumption needs to maintain that focus.

(D) Again, this answer choice strays from the central issues of size and storage. The author really only cares about this particular totem pole. How its storage would affect the *other* pieces doesn't matter, so nothing about this need be assumed.

(E) Whereas the vault is temperature-controlled, the actual temperature of the vault isn't a crucial issue in the author's argument. We can't even presume that temperature is a motivation for putting the pole in the vault—it seems likely, sure, but we're not told one way or the other.

Remember:

- Prephrasing doesn't necessarily mean that you should have a full sentence in your head which you seek to more or less match with an answer choice. It means that you recognize the key issues that the right answer choice will likely address and understand the ways in which the choice should address them. If you identify the conclusion and evidence in this argument and recognize that the divided totem pole has to be short enough to fit into the vault, only (A) and (B) will have any appeal, and only (A) will survive a closer analysis.

14. E

The author concludes that psychologists who want their work to be nominated for the *Boatwright Psychology Review* award should only submit articles containing reviews on three or fewer books. The evidence: *Boatwright Psychology Review* basically will not publish any book review article that reviews more than three books. Look back over the conclusion and evidence, and you'll realize that they aren't really talking about the same thing. The conclusion is about what one should do in order to get his work nominated for the award, and the evidence is about what one should do in order to get his work published. That's a classic scope shift. The only way to make these two different subjects relate to one another is to assume that one must have a review article published in *Boatwright* in order to be eligible for the award. Otherwise the evidence about publication requirements would have no relevance to the conclusion about nomination requirements. (E) expresses this central assumption faithfully, tying the evidence concerning publishing to the conclusion concerning nominations.

 393

(A) Whereas the stimulus suggests that articles covering more books are longer, it nowhere suggests that this proportional relationship carries out to the extremes. What makes for the longest articles isn't central to the evidence and conclusion and hence need not be assumed in order for this argument to work.

(B) overstates the link between the two subjects. The argument in the stimulus assumes that publication is necessary for a book to be *nominated*, whereas (B) says that publication guarantees that a book will *win* the award.

(C) Too broad. The argument concerns book review articles, which do come with certain length restrictions. But (C) deals with *all* articles, and we don't know nor do we really care anything about articles besides book reviews that *Boatwright* may contain.

(D) makes an irrelevant distinction that doesn't directly pertain to the central issue: what must be done with an article before it can be nominated for the prestigious award. One book and two books are both on the acceptable side of the length restriction—no distinction between them need be assumed here.

Remember:

- A scope shift occurs when the nature of the evidence differs in some fundamental way from the nature of the conclusion, but the author treats them as if they were the same. The gap that results from this is often bridged by an assumption. In other cases, you'll be asked to recognize the discrepancy as a flaw in the logic.

15. A

The question asks you to determine the role played by a specific piece of information in the argument, so it stands to reason that we should begin by identifying the basic pieces of the argument. The author concludes that milk from organically raised cows is a necessary ingredient for the best-tasting ice cream. The evidence focuses on one factor: pesticides. Pesticide residues can make their way into the milk of non-organically raised cows and lower the quality of taste for ice cream made from that milk. Since you are asked to consider how the statement about taste and pesticides fits into the argument, you can see before you reach the answer choices that the statement is part of the author's evidence: It supports the author's conclusion that the best tasting ice cream must come from organically raised cows—answer choice (A).

(B) A logical consequence is something that follows from the author's conclusion or takes the author's conclusion one step further. The statement we're told to look at doesn't extend beyond the author's conclusion but rather serves to support that very conclusion as it is.

(C) The claim about taste and pesticides is stated in the argument, so by definition it cannot be an assumption, which, remember, is an *unstated* yet necessary component of the argument.

(D) This is a confusing answer choice, and the logic is a bit circuitous, but if you pick it apart you'll see why it's wrong: To the extent that the statement in question supports the author's argument, proving it false would, if anything, *strengthen* a viewpoint that opposes the one set forth by our author. To weaken an opposing viewpoint, we'd want to shore up, not falsify, the statement in the stem.

(E) The statement we're looking at explains the results of a taste test and thus present facts that contribute to the author's larger point, which is the conclusion in the first sentence.

Remember:

- To help identify the evidence and the conclusion in an argument, distinguish the facts from the opinions. Since an LSAT conclusion has evidence that supports it, that conclusion cannot be self-evident by itself; it cannot be presented as an uncontested fact or else it wouldn't need support. Surveys, statistics, and other facts usually support the opinion (a.k.a., the conclusion) and thus take the form of evidence.

16. B

The author begins with his conclusion that the increase in colloquialisms degrades the English language. For evidence, he then gives us an example of a colloquialism and states that imprecise word usage present on a large scale basically decreases the quality of the language, hence, the tie-in with the conclusion in the first sentence. The assumption resides in the gaps between these pieces of information; we were never told that these colloquialisms were rampant or imprecise. Indeed, the author states that imprecise words admitted on a large scale decrease a language's quality without showing that colloquialisms really fall into either category. For the author's conclusion to be valid based on this evidence, he must assume that the evidence is relevant to the conclusion and that colloquialisms are both imprecise and prevalent in English. The right answer choice, (B), picks up on both: Colloquialisms are both imprecise and appear on a large scale. Without this, the evidence simply doesn't lead all the way to the conclusion.

(A) focuses on the source of colloquialisms, which the author addresses but which plays a central role in neither the evidence nor the conclusion. This could or could not be true without impacting the conclusion.

(C) basically restates the evidence. If "no language" can permit such laxity, then these three lan-

guages would logically follow along, but since the stimulus already tells us this much, (C) is not a necessary assumption here.

(D), if anything, presents us with a flawed inference, which would only be accurate if the author assumed that the stated colloquialism were the *only* colloquialism in English, and that *only* colloquialisms degrade the English language. He assumes neither, so if this were an Inference question, (D) would be wrong on these counts. As far as being assumed—that is, being something that's *required* by the argument—(D) is even further off base.

(E) is too extreme. The author identifies one cause (proliferating colloquialisms), which leads to one effect (like degraded English). To make this argument, he does not need to assume that this cause is more or less serious than any other; even if colloquialisms were a minor part of this problem, the author's conclusion could still be valid.

Remember:

- When in doubt on an Assumption question, use the Kaplan Denial Test. If you denied, for example, (A) or (E), the conclusion might still be true. However, if (B) were false, then the conclusion would no longer be supported by the given evidence, and the argument would fall apart. Thus, (B) is necessary if the conclusion is to be true, which is why it's the assumption we seek.

17. E

Now we're asked to weaken the same argument. The right answer probably won't involve denying the argument's assumption because the first question for this stimulus already focused on that element. Therefore, we can go through the choices one by one, looking for a choice that will decrease the viability of the conclusion.

(A) discusses imprecise language "on a small scale" while the stimulus focuses on such language "on a large scale." Therefore, (A) is outside of the argument's scope.

(B) Because the author's argument relates colloquialisms to the quality of a language, information about their historical longevity does not impact the argument one way or the other. The real issue is the damage they do to the language while they're around.

(C) explains the media's role in determining the fate of a potential colloquialism and, since the argument itself does not concern the media or the mechanisms by which a colloquialism becomes a colloquialism, (C) has no effect on this argument.

(D) Like (C), (D) brings up the issue of the source of colloquialisms. The argument focuses on the *effect* of colloquialisms; their source plays no role in that focus.

(E) breaks apart the author's causal argument. The author asserts that colloquialisms lower the quality of a language, while (E) explains that they actually often contribute to the "highest quality" languages in the long run. (E) thus addresses a possibility that the author doesn't consider and that would weaken the author's argument.

Remember:

- The two most common ways of weakening an argument are by breaking down the argument's assumption and by locating alternative possibilities relevant to the argument. If you have a sense of what types of answers you might be looking for (even just knowing the common categories that they fall into), they'll be easier to find.

18. C

The author kindly identifies the relevant principle in the second sentence of the stimulus. Basically the principle is that a teacher should learn his or her subject matter as a student because that will enable the teacher to understand the subject matter well enough to then teach it. In other words, one should be on the receiving end of instruction before proceeding to train others in that same skill. The other parts of the stimulus provide additional information, but since the question instructs us to apply this specific principle to another situation, the principle is what we should focus on as we evaluate the answer choices.

(A) is off track because it emphasizes that dog trainers need to be licensed, not trained. Education and instruction are the key elements of the stimulus' principle, and this answer choice focuses on neither.

(B) starts off well but falls apart because the officers aren't going to use their psychological training to teach others about the same subject; they simply need to make sure they take the class. According to the stimulus, a group needs to learn a skill in order to then proceed to teach it to others.

(C) is entirely consistent with the original principle becasuse it explains that one must be taught how to treat a patient from the patient's perspective before teaching others the same skill. One must then receive another's instruction before instructing others to perform that same skill. This is therefore the situation that relates best to the principle in the passage.

(D) discusses the importance of training but is wrong. These students aren't using their training to teach others the same skill, but rather to prepare themselves to perform in competitions.

(E) again tells us why training is necessary to perform a job well but misses the element central to the stimulus where the trained individual then proceeds to train others.

Remember:

- When applying a principle to a new situation, bear in mind that the new situation must contain every important part of the original situation. Incomplete applications, like those in answer choices (D) and (E), are never correct, so develop a clear sense of the precise elements that need to be applied before looking through the answer choices.

19. A

The argument begins by explaining that fundraising specialists help foundations to raise much of their money, unlike financial planners who raise much less money but serve an important function as organizers. Before the blank, we see the ever-important keyword "therefore." That means that the right answer choice will provide a conclusion based on the information thus far provided. Remember that this is still an Inference question, so the right answer will need to be perfectly consistent with and supported by the information already provided in the stimulus. (A) is perfectly consistent with the argument and represents a logical conclusion for it. If fundraising specialists raise more funds, then it is certainly logical that a foundation seeking to raise funds should entrust such activities to those specialists.

(B) is too extreme. The stimulus discusses general trends but never states or supports the notion that companies lacking fundraising specialists can't still raise lots of money. It's not difficult to imagine how a huge company lacking financial planners may still raise as much if not more money than a tiny company with financial planners.

(C) ranks fund-raising specialists based on what knowledge they do or don't possess. The author never breaks the specialists into these groups or provides information about the specialists in terms of their knowledge of financial planning, so the stimulus as it stands provides no direct support for this conclusion.

(D) again takes us far beyond what we can reasonably infer from the stimulus. Financial specialists generally raise more money than financial planners, but whether or not that enables foundations who use specialists to meet their goals is more than we have the information to determine.

(E) isn't consistent with the passage, which states that financial planners serve a "key" role as organizers and advisors. Maybe they shouldn't be in charge of fund raising, but the stimulus does explain that financial planners serve important and useful functions for foundations. It doesn't follow that they therefore shouldn't be hired.

Remember:

- Fill-in-the-blank questions are always Inference questions, so they always follow the rules of Inference questions. This means that the right answer will make statements entirely consistent with the argument without unsupported innovation and that it won't stray beyond the scope of the argument.

20. B

In order to parallel the flaw, let's figure out what exactly that flaw is. The author argues that, since every individual in a group is unable to accomplish a certain task, the individuals working together must also be unable to accomplish that task. In general terms: An individual's deficiency must also imply a communal deficiency. Let's look for that in the choices:

(A) discusses only one individual without tying that individual to a group.

(B) Yes. Because something is true of individuals, it is therefore true of a group comprising those individuals. Flawed, parallel, and the correct choice here.

(C) says that if one person can't do something, then none of the others can either, but it doesn't mention whether they could do it working together. That's what we're after.

(D), like (A), has the wrong method of argument. (D) is a causal argument, arguing that one thing won't create a certain effect. The original argument doesn't argue against causation but makes a conclusion about a group based on the individual qualities of its members.

(E) mentions one person who *can* do something and others who cannot. In the stimulus, all individuals are equally incapable by themselves and as part of the group.

Remember:

- The key to Parallel Reasoning questions is characterizing the stimulus in such a way that you recognize the key elements that the right answer must contain while recognizing which elements are changeable. For instance, the order of the evidence and conclusion can change, but the relationship between them cannot. The subject matter can (and almost always will) change, but the method of argument cannot. Focus on what must remain the same, and quickly axe any choice that deviates in any fundamental way.

21. C

The author concludes that Leroy absolutely did not have the flu on Monday. His evidence is that Leroy had the flu on Tuesday and visited a friend with the flu on Sunday and that "there is no evidence that Leroy had the flu on Monday." Just because there's no evidence that Leroy had the flu on Monday doesn't mean that he definitely did not have it—we all know it's certainly possible to be sick the day before seeing a doctor and receiving official proof of the illness. Lack

of evidence to prove an event doesn't mean that the event itself didn't exist. (C) expresses this argument's error by pointing out that it is indeed possible that the diagnosis on Tuesday suggests that Leroy had the flu on Monday.

(A) gets the conclusion and evidence mixed up. Actually, the argument concludes that Leroy *didn't* have the flu based on the fact that there is no evidence to prove that he *did* have the flu.

(B) The author nowhere discusses how Leroy's co-worker got the flu, and there's no flaw in something that isn't part of the argument.

(D) isn't consistent with the argument, which suggests that Leroy's association with an ill person *isn't* entirely relevant to his own health status.

(E) is just strange. Leroy's professional ethics aren't discussed at all in the argument and certainly aren't central to the argument, as (E) suggests.

Remember:

- In every section of the LSAT, it is absolutely crucial that you maintain a structured approach. By breaking arguments like this one into conclusion and evidence, you can more easily ascertain whether the flaw comes up in one, the other, or both, and then proceed to define what that flaw is. If you don't take the time to understand the argument, you have terrible odds of getting the question right.

22. C

The author tells us that two school districts were running neck and neck until about 1990 as far as their junior high school students' reading scores were concerned. After 1990, district Y consistently took the lead, with its students demonstrating much higher average scores on the reading test. The superintendent of district Y proposes an explanation for this occurrence, attributing it to her district's reinstatement of a minimum reading require-ment in the junior high schools. This is an Inference question, so once we have a good grasp of the stimulus, we should move on to the answer choices.

(A) is more than we know because it deals with a non-relative increase in the average scores themselves. All we know is that district Y's aver-age score is higher than district X's, but we were given no information to suggest that the actual average score in district Y has been increasing.

(B) deals with minimum reading requirements in district X before 1990, which isn't a subject that the stimulus even addresses.

(C) is inferable. The superintendent attributes her district's successes to the reinstated reading requirement, and these successes began in 1990. This strongly suggests that the program must have been reinstated sometime around when the change in relative average scores occurred. Otherwise, it couldn't account for the district's post-1990 achievements. This leads to (C): If the requirement was reinstated around 1990 when district Y began to outpace district X, then it must be true that the requirement was not in effect at some point in district Y before 1990.

(D) is exactly the same as (B) except that it discuss-es the possibility that there was no reading requirement in district X at some point in time. But it's wrong for the same reason as (B): We know nothing about district X's history with the reading requirement, so we can't infer either answer choice.

(E) confuses averages with individual students. The stimulus states that the average score has increased in district Y relative to district X, but that certainly doesn't mean that each and every student in district Y is beating each and every student in district X.

Remember:

- Choices like (B) and (D) exist for those stu-dents who don't read answer choices carefully enough and miss the fact that both choices dis-cuss district X. Don't put your critical reading skills aside once you get to the answer choices; they need to be read at least as carefully as the stimulus.

23. E

This argument begins with a chain of causality: A crisis (step 1) can lead to a decrease in people's faith in their country's leaders (step 2), which can in turn lead to violence in unspecified segments of the pop-ulation (step 3). Propaganda limits the perception of the crisis, thereby keeping the first domino from falling and therefore favorably impacting at least the second step in the chain. This is the author's first explanation for violence, and the propaganda solu-tion refers only to it. The author then gives an entirely different explanation for violence, this time more specifically explaining youth violence: Youth violence is caused by boredom and lack of vision regarding a promising future. We have two paths explaining violence, and the answer to this Inference question will certainly test our ability to distinguish between them. Let's evaluate the answer choices, keeping the distinctions in mind.

(A) While the author offers us one potential anti-dote to the first type of violence without mak-ing any such reference in regards to the second, that doesn't mean that there is no solution for the second type. Because something isn't men-tioned, that doesn't mean it doesn't exist, so we have no way of inferring which type of violence is easier to quell.

(B) For all we know, propaganda alone may be enough to entirely diffuse dissent in some poor countries, possibly those without disaffected youth, or even those with disaffected youth who are not driven to dissent by such crises.

(C) is too extreme and distorts the argument. The author writes that economic and political crises lead to violence among "specific segments of the population," which may include youth; the author certainly doesn't rule out that possibility. Further, because boredom and lack of vision lead to habitual youth violence, that doesn't mean that *only* boredom and lack of vision lead to youth violence. The two explanations aren't mutually exclusive.

(D) also goes too far out on a limb. The author mentions two effects of the propaganda—it downplays the extent of the crisis and restores faith in the government. However, we don't know that an alteration in people's "fundamental beliefs" is inherent in either one of these cases; we simply know that the propaganda has an effect on their immediate actions at the time of the crisis.

(E) Yep. Since the author does not directly link habitual youth violence to economic or political crises, or to the decrease in faith which such crises create, propaganda probably doesn't decrease that violence by restoring faith in the country's leaders. The author says that habitual youth violence is not caused by a loss of such faith, so restoring the faith probably wouldn't help matters any. If propaganda helps to quell habitual youth violence, then it probably does it in some other way.

Remember:

- Beware of extreme answer choices in Inference questions. Notice all of the overly eager claims in answer choices (A) through (D): (A) mentions which revolt is "easier" to quell; (B) discusses the powers of "propaganda alone"; (C) affirms that crises don't lead to "any" instance of youth violence; and (D) discusses the "primary" effect of propaganda. All of these choices go farther than our author, who doesn't make such assertive claims. The right choice won't intensify the argument but, like choice (E), will more often discuss the possibilities that the argument leaves open.

24. A

The question stem directs us to locate a particular type of flaw in the stimulus; specifically, we're looking to find what the stimulus is wrong to neglect. The author states that Derek is good at everything he does and then predicts that Derek will be a good student president. We can immediately be suspicious of the word "everything," since the author's evidence shows that Derek is good at science, two sports, capitalistic ventures, and music. Is this a representative sample? Because Derek is good at these four things, does that mean that he'll be good at anything one asks him to do? We don't really know if being a good president necessarily follows from the fact that he's good at the activities mentioned—perhaps he's particularly interested in and suited for those things, and that's why he does them in the first place. This argument's flaw of omission is its failure to mention whether or not the four successes described accurately indicate that Derek will be good at anything he does. (A) captures the flaw: The author fails to consider that the causal mechanism may be the other way around; that is, Derek may only do those things he knows he's good at. If that's the case, the prediction of his presidential prowess may be a miscalculation.

(B) The author doesn't necessarily overlook this possibility. In painting Derek as a "Renaissance man" and making the bold prediction, the author evidently believes that any skill is within his grasp. His flaw lies there, not in overlooking the fact that the president's job will call on skills other than his musicianship.

(C) comes close because it would be a viable answer choice if those four skills weren't Derek's only skills. The author assumes that they are, so this answer choice states an assumption rather than identifying a flaw.

(D) is irrelevant because the conclusion only asserts that Derek would be a good president, not that nobody else would do the job as well. The argument is only about Derek, so the author's failure to mention other people isn't a flaw.

(E) isn't a flaw because the author isn't arguing that Derek can do the job; he's arguing that Derek would be good at it if he did.

Remember:

- When you have a question stem that's an incomplete sentence, like the one in the question above, make sure that you read each answer choice as an extension of that sentence, meaning you may want to reread the stem with each answer choice.

25. B

The first two sentences of this argument provide background information explaining why pediatric nurses were willing to take the difficult home-care assignments. The heart of the argument is the last two sentences. The author concludes that the nurses have clearly become cynical, and supports that conclusion by citing an increase in the number of nurses but a decrease in the number of home-care nursing assignments. The author argues that nurses have consciously rejected these home-care cases and assumes that no other factor might be responsible for this situation. Because we are asked to strengthen this argument, we'll look to support the author's argument that the decline in home-care nursing assignments truly is the result of growing cynicism among the nurses and not the result of other factors. (B) strengthens the argument precisely because it eliminates a possible alternative explanation. If there were simply fewer cases requiring at home pediatric nurses, we'd be able to argue that cynicism is not really the reason for the decrease in such assignments. The author assumes that this very plausible alternative (less demand) is not the case.

(B), by explicitly shoring up this assumption, strengthens the argument: If the demand for home-care pediatric nurses has remained constant, the author's explanation for the decline in accepted cases seems more reasonable.

(A) On the face of it, cases in a hospital setting may seem to fall outside the scope. The author is concerned with home-care cases, so our correct answer choice will most likely maintain that specific focus. On another reading, however, (A) may be seen to weaken the argument: If demand for hospital nurses in this area is way up, that could explain the steep decline in home care assignments—it may simply be a matter of prioritizing finite resources. If that were the case, then the author's cynicism theory would take one on the chin.

(C) This choice would provide a different reason for the nurses to take fewer home-assignments. Like (A), if anything, it would weaken the argument by providing an alternative explanation for the decline in accepted nursing home-care assignments.

(D) This comparison of compensation rates across communities doesn't strengthen this argument because it doesn't add anything new. The author states that the assignments pay poorly; the relative degree to which they pay poorly doesn't change the stated fact that money is not a strong incentive to take such cases. Since the information has no real impact, it doesn't strengthen the argument.

(E) The reason *why* the cynicism exists is irrelevant to this argument. We only care whether it's the cause of the decrease in nursing assignments to home-care cases.

Remember:

• In a Strengthen the Argument question in which an author constructs a causal relationship offering one way to explain a certain situation, you'll want to strengthen that link. The right answer choice will often do that directly. However, it may strengthen the argument indirectly by ruling out another possible cause, as (B) does here.

Section III: Logic Games Explanations

GAME 1—Stadium Ads

The Action

Six companies each advertise in one of two places—either the upper wall or the lower wall. So this is another Grouping game of distribution, but we'll also have to keep track of beverage and clothing companies. The *Key Issues* are:

- Which beverage companies can, must, and cannot be advertised on each wall?
- Which clothing companies can, must, and cannot be advertised on each wall?
- Which companies can, must, and cannot be advertised with which other companies?

The Initial Setup

A list of entities with two rows—one for the upper wall and one for the lower wall—will do just fine. We can distinguish beverage companies from clothing companies by writing the former in ALL CAPS:

The Rules

1) Now we see how the beverage/clothing distinction will play itself out. Each wall will have at least one of FGH and at least one of mnp. We can build this in directly by placing a "1+ in each" below the clothing ads and the beverage ads.

2) This one requires some translation. Remember, when an "only if" statement is translated into a standard if/then, the statement that follows the "only if" will follow the "then." So Rule 2 means that if M is on the lower wall, then the upper wall must have four ads, which in turn means that the lower wall must have two ads.

"M (lower) —> 4/2 upper/lower" is one way to capture this. Taking the contrapositive, we can deduce that if we don't have a 4/2 upper/lower distribution, then M cannot be on the lower wall, which in turn means that M must be on the upper wall.

3) This also requires some translation. Neither F nor N can be on a wall with exactly two ads. What does this mean in the context of this game? Let's turn to the *Key Deductions*.

Key Deductions

When you get a Grouping game, always pay attention to the numbers governing the game. Here, each deck gets at least one ad from each of two groups. In that case, the minimum number of ads on each wall is two, and the maximum number of ads on each wall is four. We can also expand on Rule 3. Since the minimum number of ads on a wall is two, and since neither F nor N will advertise on a wall containing exactly two ads, any wall with either F or N will have at least three ads.

The Final Visualization

F G H   m n p
1+ in each   1+ in each

upper
lower

M (lower) → 4/2 upper/lower
no 4/2 upper/lower → M (upper)
F or N on a wall → 3+ on that wall

The Big Picture

- This wasn't a bad place to start your Logic Games section. As it happens, the next game is probably easier, but a straightforward Grouping game is a good place to build some points and confidence.

- When you see a Grouping game, examine the numbers, looking for minimums and maximums. When you do, you'll probably discover that the game isn't as wide-open as it seemed initially.

- Treat "only if" statements with care! "X only if Y" means "If X then Y."

- Keep driving the abstract to the concrete, especially when forming contrapositives. Here, if M isn't on the lower wall, M must be on the upper wall, since those are the only two possibilities.

The Questions

1. D

First up is a straightforward hypothetical. If the upper wall has four ads, then the lower wall contains exactly two. In that case, neither F nor N can be on the lower wall (Rule 3) and so they must both be on the upper wall. F isn't among the choices, but N is choice (D). The other choices are possible only. (E) is tempting but does not answer the question. Remember that M is on the lower wall only if there are four on the upper wall, but just because there are four on the upper wall, doesn't mean that M has to be on the lower wall.

Remember:

- When you get a hypothetical, build in the new information, and see where it takes you. Don't look at the choices without looking for some deductions.

2. C

If G is one of only two companies that advertise on the upper wall, then Rule 2 comes into play. We don't have four companies on the upper wall, so M can't be on the lower wall, and therefore M is on the upper wall. That's (C).

Remember:

- You could have found this answer by deducing that the other companies must advertise on the lower wall; it just would have taken a little longer. That's okay, though. You can always find the correct answer by eliminating the other choices.

3. A

Here's a partial Acceptability question. We get only part of the setup, which means that some of the choices will likely be wrong because of their implications for the other deck. We can eliminate (C) and (E) fairly easily, since they contain pretty straightforward violations of Rules 3 and 1, respectively. Getting rid of (B) and (D) is a little harder. Rule 2 gets rid of (D) since (D) places M on the lower wall but places only three companies on the upper wall. Rule 3 gets rid of (B), which places only F and M on the lower wall, and we know that any wall with F must contain at least three ads. So (A) is correct.

Remember:

- When you get an Acceptability question that only gives you part of the arrangement, expect that you'll have to make deductions concerning the entities that aren't mentioned.

4. A

With N and P on the upper wall, M will have to go to the lower wall since M is the only clothing company left. That brings Rule 2 into play. Since M is on the lower wall, the upper wall will have four ads. Now Rule 3 comes into play. Since the lower wall has two ads, F must be on the upper wall. We can place every ad definitively except G and H. One of these two goes on each wall, but we can't tell which. So (A) must be true and is correct.

(B) and (C), and (D) are possible only because we don't know where G and H are.

(E) is impossible. P is on the upper wall, which has four ads.

Remember:

- To find deductions, look for the most relevant rule. Placing N and P on the upper wall should direct you to Rule 1. Once M is placed on the lower wall, Rule 2 comes into play, etcetera. Sometimes success in Logic Games is just a matter of knowing where to look.

5. E

In a different way, this question is asking what must be true if F is the only beverage company on the lower wall. In that case, G and H must be on the upper wall, and according to Rule 1, they must be joined by at least one clothing company. Now Rule 3 comes in. Since F is on the lower wall, the lower wall needs at least three ads. So the ads are split 3/3, which in turn means that M is on the upper wall (contrapositive of Rule 2). So N and P, the only ads left, must go on the lower wall. Here's what we've just deduced:

upper   G H m
lower   F n p

All the choices must be false except (E). N must be on the lower wall.

Remember:

- "X cannot be true unless Y" means "If X then Y."

6. E

This question is a little tougher since we don't know which wall has two of each ad type. So let's start by seeing what happens when the upper wall has two of each type. We know that F and N will have to be on the upper wall because they can't be on a wall with only two ads. Beyond that, there isn't much to deduce. Each wall will have one of G and H, and each wall will have one of M and P.

upper	F n	G/H	m/p	
lower	G/H	m/p		

From here, we can eliminate all the wrong choices. This scenario demonstrates that F and H could be together, (A); G and H could be apart, (B); G and N could be apart, (C); and M and N could be together, (D). So (E) must be true.

At this point, you don't have to explore what happens when the lower wall has two of each ad type, but if you did, here's what you might have found: F and N still have to be on the wall with four ads, and they still have to be joined by exactly one of G and H. However, we can make one extra deduction: Since the upper wall doesn't have four ads, M cannot be on the lower wall (contrapositive of Rule 2). So M is on the upper wall, which means P must be on the lower wall. Here's what we've deduced:

upper	G/H	m		
lower	F n	G/H	p	

In either scenario, M and P are on separate walls, so again, (E) must be true.

Remember:

- If a question breaks down into two distinct scenarios, work them both out. Then you'll know what must, could, and cannot be true.

GAME 2—Six Dives

The Action

Six dives are performed, one after the other in a row, so we're dealing with another Sequencing game. This one is a little different in that some divers will dive more than once, but otherwise this is business as usual. The *Key Issues* are:

- Which dives can, must, or cannot be performed by which people?
- Which dives can, must, or cannot be performed by the same person as which other dives?

The Initial Setup

Nothing fancy is required here. A list of the entities (X, Y, Z) and six slots will do just fine.

X Y Z

| __1__ | __2__ | __3__ | __4__ | __5__ | __6__ |

The Rules

1) So X performs three dives, and none in a row. At this point, you should be asking: how many different ways are there for this to happen? There aren't too many, and that leads to the *Key Deduction* below.
2) Y gets two dives, and we know we'll need to place at least one Y in one of the first two slots.
3) The meaning of this is clear enough: We can't have YZ.

Key Deductions

X gets three dives, but none consecutively. With only six slots, there aren't many ways to fit this in. So let's explore them. If X is first, then Y must be second (Rule 2). Now, if another X is third, where can the last X be? It can't be fourth or sixth, since

that would leave YZ together. So the last X would have to be fifth. Y and Z will split the fourth and sixth slots, in either order. Let's call this Option I.

Option I

X	Y	X	Y/Z	X	Y/Z
1	2	3	4	5	6

If X dives first and fourth, then X's third dive must be sixth. Now we have to split up YZ. The two Y's go second and third, and Z goes fifth. Let's call this Option II.

Option II

X	Y	Y	X	Z	X
1	2	3	4	5	6

Finally, if X dives second, then X's other dives must be fourth and sixth. Y then dives first (Rule 2), and Y and Z split the third and fifth slots. Let's call this Option III.

Option III

Y	X	Y/Z	X	Y/Z	X
1	2	3	4	5	6

That's it! There's no other way to spread out the three X's. So the entire game breaks down into three options. It takes a little time to find them, but once you do, the questions will drop like flies.

The Final Visualization

Option I

X	Y	X	Y/Z	X	Y/Z
1	2	3	4	5	6

KAPLAN

Option II

X	Y	Y	X	Z	X
1	2	3	4	5	6

Option III

Y	X	Y/Z	X	Y/Z	X
1	2	3	4	5	6

The Big Picture

- Knowing when to stop looking for deductions is an acquired skill. Early on, expect to stop looking too early in some instances and too late in others. That's okay, it's part of the learning process. In time, though, develop a sense for the "likely suspects," but move on when they aren't there.
- One of those "likely suspects" is Limited Options. If a game breaks down into only two or three scenarios, work out those scenarios. You'll fly through the questions.

The Questions

7. C

First up is a standard Acceptability question. Again, the Kaplan Method of using the rules to eliminate choices yields a quick point. Rule 1 kills (B) and (D). Rule 2 kills (E). Rule 3 kills (A). (C) remains and is correct.

Remember:

- When you get an acceptability question, use the rules to eliminate four choices, then pick the one that remains without checking it.

8. E

If Z is fifth, then we're either in Option II or Option III. In Option III, X dives neither first nor third, so (A) and (C) are wrong. In Option II, X doesn't dive second and Y doesn't dive first, so (B) and (D) are wrong. So (E) must be true. You don't have to check it, but Y is always third in Option II, and Y must be

third in Option III whenever Z is fifth, since Y and Z split the third and fifth positions.

Remember:

- When you have set out a game's options, use the stem to tell you which scenarios are in effect.

9. D

This one is a quick battle once you have the options. In Option I, X is first, Y can be fourth, Y can be sixth, and Z can be sixth. So (A), (B), (C), and (E) are all wrong. So (D) must be correct, and yes, Z can never be first.

Remember:

- When you've worked out all the possibilities up front, you always know what could, must, and cannot be true.

10. B

If X is third, then we're in Option I. (A) and (C) must be true. (D) and (E) could be true, but (B) must be false and is therefore correct. X can't be sixth since that wouldn't allow us to break up Y and Z.

Remember:

- If things are going well, don't second-guess yourself. Move swiftly and save time for harder games.

11. E

If Y performs two dives consecutively, then we're in Option II:

Option II

X	Y	Y	X	Z	X
1	2	3	4	5	6

All the choices must be true except (E). Boom.

Remember:

- Always read the question stem carefully! It can be easy to miss a word like "EXCEPT," even when it's in ALL CAPS.

12. **A**

Now the test makers have switched things around on us. Now X's dives must be consecutive. So how many ways can they be placed? X's dives cannot be first through third because we need a Y in the first two. If X's dives are second through fourth, then we can place Y first, but now we have YZ in fifth and sixth in violation of Rule 3. So can X's dives be third through fifth? Sure. Y's dives will be first and second, and Z will be sixth. That's one combination so far. Now can X's dives be fourth through sixth? No, since we wouldn't be able to split up Y and Z. So (A), one combination, is correct.

Remember:

- If a question involves a rule change, don't panic. You may have to rethink part of your understanding of the initial setup, but your experience working with the other rules will see you through.

GAME 3—Seven Instructors, Three Semesters

The Action

Seven instructors—J, K, L, M, N, P, and Q—each teach during exactly one of three semesters. In other words, we have to *distribute* the seven instructors among the three semesters. So, this is another Grouping game of distribution, and the *Key Issues* will be:

- Which instructors can, must, or cannot teach during which semesters?

- Which instructors can, must, or cannot teach during the same semester as which other instructors?
- How many instructors teach during each semester?

The Initial Setup

A list of the entities and three columns (one for each of the semesters) will allow us to keep track of the action here.

J   K   L   M   N   P   Q

Fall	Spring	Winter

The Rules

1) Here's a concrete rule: We can place K in the winter column permanently.

2) Rule 2 is a familiar enough Grouping rule. L and M are always together. "Always LM" captures this.

3) Rule 3 can be built in directly, with arrows pointing to the fall and spring semesters.

4) The winter semester gets twice as many as the fall semester. Okay, what does that mean in the context of this game? With seven instructors, there really aren't that many ways to split them up so that exactly twice as many wind up in the Winter semester. So how many combinations are there? If one instructor taught in the fall, then we'd need two in the winter, and the remaining four would teach during the spring semester. Or, we could have two in the fall, four in the winter, and one in the spring. That's it. It's either 1/4/2 or 2/1/4. We can't have three or more in the fall, since that would force us to have six or more in the winter, and that's no good because there are only seven instructors.

5) and 6) are familiar enough Grouping rules. We cannot have an NQ, and we cannot have a JP.

Key Deductions

The Big Deduction here was the 1/4/2 or 2/1/4 breakdown of the instructors. This essentially comes straight out of Rule 4, but if you noticed it at this point, that's okay, too. From here, you could have explored different scenarios, seeing if they set off any chains of inferences, but there wasn't anything else that qualifies as a major deduction. On to the questions!

The Final Visualization

1/4/2 or 2/1/4
Always LM
Never NQ
Never JP

The Big Picture

- This wasn't an easy game, but it was less complicated than Game 4. This game was probably best handled third, after Games 1 and 2.
- Get to know the usual suspects that appear in Logic Games. Grouping games are very common, and so you should get a feel for their mechanics. This will help should you encounter a similar game on test day.
- Always investigate the numbers behind Grouping games, and always turn abstract rules into concrete rules. Here, the game was pretty tough if you didn't make the numbers deduction early. But don't get down if you didn't make it. Instead, focus on the clues that will lead to similar deductions on test day.
- When a rule is abstract, think of concrete sce-

narios that would violate it, and see if there are a limited number of scenarios that don't violate it. Rule 4 is tough to deal with without paraphrasing, but once you see how it applies in context, you have the key to the game.

The Questions

13. D

This is a harder Acceptability question than most since we're only given part of the lineup. So you may have been forced to work out scenarios for each choice. Only (B) and (E) contain a straightforward violation of a rule. (According to Rule 6, we can't have J and P together, and according to Rule 1, K teaches during the winter). The rest of the choices require some work:

(A) With Q and M in the fall, we need L there as well (Rule 2). That's three in the fall, which is no good, since it would force us to place six in the winter.

(C) If L is in the fall, then so is M. Since the fall can hold no more, Q must go in the spring (Rule 3). That leaves K, J, P, and N for the winter. But we can't have J and P together, so (C) doesn't work. So (D) is correct by the process of elimination.

(D) For the record: Placing J, M, and N as the stem dictates means we must also place L in the winter. Since the winter now has three instructors, it will need a fourth to satisfy the 2/1/4 distribution. We also need to split up J and P. So we can place Q in the fall and P in the winter, and we have an acceptable arrangement.

Fall	Spring	Winter
J	N	K
Q		M
		L
		P

Remember:

- Acceptability questions are usually quick points, but they can be harder when you only see part of the arrangement. Often, the wrong choices in these questions don't contain obvious violations of the rules. Rather, they violate the rules by virtue of their implications for the other entities.

14. A

This one was quick if you worked out the scenario in (C) from the previous question. In that choice, we saw what happens when we put L in the fall: We need to put M there as well, and we're forced to place J and P together in the winter. So we can never put L (or M, for that matter) in the fall, and choice (A) is correct.

If you didn't see this, you still could have attacked this question strategically by postponing working on it until after you've built some acceptable scenarios from the other questions. (B) must be true in question 18, (E) could be true in question 18, and both (C) and (D) are true in the correct answer to the Acceptability question.

Remember:

- Postpone working on questions when your work in the other questions will eliminate some choices.
- Don't forget about the correct answer to the Acceptability question. It often eliminates a few wrong choices elsewhere.

15. C

If only one instructor teaches in the spring, then we have a 2/1/4 setup. We've seen we can't place L and M in the fall since that would force J and P together in the winter. So L and M teach in the winter, and (C) is correct.

(A), (D), and (E) are all possible only.

(B) is impossible. L teaches in the winter.

Remember:

- Sometimes a game's questions are similar to each other. So once you build some experience, you should be able to make inferences more quickly as the game goes on.

16. D

Here's another question that allows you to benefit from previous work. In the last question, we had K, L, and M together in the winter. They could be joined by either J or P without any violations. Once you know that we can have KLMJ or KLMP together, you can eliminate all four wrong choices because they all contain a subset of one of those groups. You also might have spotted correct choice (D) directly: K must be in the winter, and Q can never be in the winter. So (D) is correct.

Remember:

- Use your previous work whenever possible. It saves time.

17. D

Who doesn't teach in the winter semester? Since the winter semester has either 2 or 4 instructors, either three or five instructors don't teach during the winter semester. So (B) and (E) are wrong. Eliminating the other wrong choices was a little harder:

(A) splits up L and M, in violation of Rule 2.

(C) places J and P in the winter and thus violates Rule 6. So (D) is correct.

(D) For the record, we could place Q and P in the fall, N in the spring, and K, L, M, and J in the winter.

Remember:

- Numbers deductions are key in Grouping games. Always look for minimums and maximums, and then use that information to cut down on your work later on.

18. **B**

If more instructors teach during the spring semester, then we're dealing with the 1/4/2 setup. So where could L and M go? They can never go in the fall, and they can't go in the winter, since there are only two winter instructors and K is always there. So they must go in the spring. So (B) is correct. The wrong choices are possible only.

Remember:

- The challenge with this game was timing. Lots of people could find the right answers given unlimited time, but the real challenge is to find the right answers as quickly as possible. Take a second look at your work on these questions, and ask yourself how you could have used good test-taking strategies to save time. Then practice these strategies until you apply them automatically.

GAME 4—Doctors in Offices

The Action
Who's here? Doctors.

How many? Seven.

What are their names? a, b, c, d, e, f and g.

What do you want to know about them? The specialty (N, P, R, S or U) and the office (1, 2, 3, 4, and 5) in which they practice.

Rules and Deductions
All rules are not created equal. Which, if any, of the rules answers something you want to know directly? Right, Fred is in office 2. Moreover, he's alone. Here's how that might look:

Of course, you also want to know his specialty. It can't be N, since more doctors practice N than P and each specialty, P included, has at least one doctor. If Fred practiced N, he'd be the only one. So he must practice one of the others.

Now that you've realized that at least 2 doctors practice N, you might be tempted to think that b and g, who work in the same office, practice N. Don't jump to any conclusions until you've considered all the possibilities.

Although b and g MIGHT practice N, they don't have to. With 7 doctors and 5 offices, there might well be MORE than one office/specialty with more than one doctor. In fact, there would have to be two such office/specialties unless there were 3 doctors practicing N.

You're well on your way once you realize that the distribution of doctors among the office/specialties must be 3-1-1-1-1 or 2-2-1-1-1.

And since R = S, they must both have only one doctor, as does P, which has fewer doctors than N. Checking out the possibilities, only U can join N in having more than one doctor.

So perhaps b and g practice U, in which case two other doctors practice N. And maybe N and U are practiced in offices 4 and 5 (which have the same number of doctors):

and maybe they're not.

But maybe b and g and someone else all practice N, in which case they can't be in office 4 or 5 or 2.

But you shouldn't be worrying about what you don't know. Instead, you should be delighted at how much you've been able to figure out.

The Questions

19. D

What must be true is something you've been able to figure out so far. The deduction that specialty N has multiple doctors, whereas specialties P, R and S don't, steers you to answer (D).

Note that there is at least one possible scenario in which each of the other answers might not happen. But always remember that the best way to avoid wrong answers is having a sense of what you're looking for before diving into the answer choices.

20. C

Whenever a question gives you additional information, take it as far as you can. In this case, knowing that Fred practices U leads to the conclusion that 3 doctors (including b and g) must practice N. And, as we've already noted, they must do so in office 1 or 3.

You have no clue as to which of the two possible offices N is in, neither do you have any other hint as to where the other specialties may be located.

Since the question asks what must be false, you should be looking for a claim that N isn't where we know it is. That's answer (C). Once again, each of the wrong answers can be shown to be wrong because each could happen (in fact, answer (E) must happen).

21. B

You know that b and g are always together. Therefore, being told that b practices U in 1 tells you quite a bit. With 2 doctors practicing U, there must be 2 practicing N, and they must be in office 3. After all, lonesome Fred is in 2 and the same number must be in both 4 and 5.

Once again, taking the information to its logical extreme allows you to look for and find the right answer, however disguised, quickly and confidently. We knew that Fred was sandwiched between U and N, and that's exactly what it says in answer (B).

22. C

What could be true is anything consistent with (i.e. not in conflict with) the possibilities you outlined before you started answering questions. Since you'll have to try out answer choices, you might want to skip this one on your first pass through the questions, in favor of questions with additional concrete information.

It's actually pretty easy to "try out" these answers. Can b and c practice U? Nope; b and g go together and, since no more than 2 doctors can practice U, b, c and g would be too many. Can g practice R? Not without b at her side, and we know that there's only one R. Can a and e practice N? Well, that would force b and g into U, but there's certainly no rule against that. So the answer must be (C).

For the record, b can't practice S, (D), for the same reason that g couldn't practice R in the preceding paragraph. And c can't join g in P, (E), because there's only one P.

23. D

This seemingly innocuous "if" clause is LOADED with information. It tells us that b (and g) do not practice N, but are next door to the 2 doctors who do. So b and g practice U and 2 others practice N in offices 4 and 5, not necessarily respectively. Taking the information as far as you can is relatively easy.

The hard part is understanding this question. What does it mean to say, "all of the following could be true EXCEPT"? Except what? Except something that must be false.

So what must be false? N and U (which includes g and b) must be in 4 and 5, so putting them anywhere else must be false; and, sure enough, that is answer (D), which puts g next to f.

24. D

If g and e practice together, they must be joined by b, according to rule 4; they must practice N, as N is the only specialty that can possibly have three doctors; and they must do so either in office 1 or office 3, the only offices open to three doctors. We have it narrowed down to two offices, and the question requires that we go one step further: We need to find the piece of information that will allow us to precisely determine the office in which these three neurologists practice. Skimming the choices, the only one that mentions either relevant office (1 or 3) is (D): If as (D) says, we must assign urology to office 3, then clearly the only office available for g, e, and b is office 1. None of the other choices does anything to clear up the ambiguity.

Section IV: Logical Reasoning Explanations

1. B

The author's conclusion pops up at the end, where she states that Ed is likely to have ADD because he watches television a lot and is seven. The key piece of evidence is a recent study that the author cites which states that 85 percent of seven-year-olds with ADD watch more than five hours of television per day. The study thus only discusses the television-watching habits of seven-year-olds who have ADD. The author's conclusion is flawed because it makes a conclusion about a seven-year-old television watcher based on a study about seven-year-old television watchers with ADD. In other words, there's a scope shift between the evidence and the conclusion. The author errs in accepting the survey as relevant to Ed. (B) expresses this flaw most clearly: In order to make conclusions about Ed and whether he might have ADD, the author must come up with evidence that pertains to Ed since the original evidence does not. She needs a statistic that states the likelihood that a seven-year-old who watches more than five hours of TV a day would have ADD. The evidence provided sounds like that, but isn't, and (B) captures the gist of the author's mistake.

(A) is confusing, but the argument above isn't really about degrees of causation. The author doesn't suggest that age and television watching *cause* a child to contract ADD but that those factors generally appear with the disorder. (A) distorts the author's conclusion by suggesting that it says that Ed's television watching has caused him to contract ADD, but the author never suggests this.

(C) Yes it does, but that's not a problem. Perhaps some doctors might disagree with the author's definition, but its validity is not the issue at the heart of this argument. Rather, the argument's concerned with Ed's chances of having ADD based on a particular study.

(D) is easiest to remove for the fact that it contradicts the stimulus, where we learn that Ed *does* actually watch more than five hours of television per day. (You may have also noticed that the 15 percent figure is bogus—it's derived from the 85 percent figure in the stimulus, but that figure refers to the percentage of children with ADD who watch more than five hours of TV a day. Inferably, we can therefore say that 15 percent of children with ADD do not watch more than five hours of TV a day, but we can't turn this into 15 percent of children *in general* who don't watch more than five hours, as (D) attempts to do.)

(E) again distorts the argument, which never suggests that television watching causes ADD. Since no causality is mentioned, we can only assume that the data represents a correlation.

Remember:

- Scope shifts are often hard to spot, but the rewards are great when you find them. They often involve subtle distinctions between the evidence and the conclusion, so look carefully at the terms of each, especially in Logical Flaw questions, to determine whether the author shifts gears en route.

2. D

Even though the stem is skimpy, it does indicate that this is a Method of Argument question, so track the argument carefully. Basically, American and foreign Internet providers charge the same monthly fee, but foreign providers offer more services. Representatives for these foreign providers predict that their services will put the American providers out of business. The industry analyst clearly disagrees with this assertion in the sentence that begins with the contrast keyword "but." In that sentence, the analyst mentions two services offered by American providers that foreign providers may not be able to match. The analyst therefore disagrees with the representatives' conclusion and does so by introducing new factors into the equation. (D) perfectly captures this: The analyst's additional consideration (quality and customer service) does weaken the initial contention (that foreign providers will drive American providers out of the Internet industry).

(A) Too extreme. The analyst does suggest that foreign takeover may not be imminent, but he never suggests that American companies needn't have any fear of foreign competition.

(B) The analyst does not dispute the representatives' evidence that foreign providers offer two perks that most American providers do not. The analyst offers additional elements to consider but does not disagree with those that have been mentioned previously.

(C) starts off badly with the verb "reconciles" and doesn't get any better. The analyst disagrees with the representatives' prediction, neither offering his own nor harmonizing his view with that of the representatives. Also, the analyst doesn't refer to a "previous situation," so this choice is zero for three.

(E) Again, the analyst doesn't really make any proposals so we can be suspicious right off the bat. The analyst doesn't offer a plan by which American companies might ward off foreign competitors; he merely mentions an additional consideration that might make the representatives rethink their "bold" prediction.

Remember:

• Always be attuned to the presence of different views. This is more or less a dialogue stimulus without the dialogue formatting since it begins with the explanation of one view and offers a second opinion in response to the first.

Therefore, the analyst's method of argument is tied to the way in which he responds to the representatives' argument.

3. **C**

The author states that Travonia's suicide rate has increased, citing an increase in the number of overdoses following the recent release of certain brands of sleeping pills. Getting to the heart of the argument, the author then asserts that certain types of suicides have not increased in number, conceding that the percentage of elderly suicides has increased but noting that the percentage of teen suicides has decreased. The flaw is the author's blurred distinction between numbers and percentages. Just because the percentage represented by teen suicides has decreased, that doesn't mean that fewer teens are committing suicide. A decreased percentage needn't signify a decreased number of suicides, and the author's flaw comes in failing to recognize this, as (C) expresses.

(A) The argument doesn't explicitly discuss other groups (we don't really know where the sleeping pill poppers fall), but it certainly doesn't discount the possibility that other groups might exist.

(B) Not really, because the author doesn't link the sleeping pill takers to either demographic group, as mentioned in the explanation for (A).

(D) The total number of deaths in general is outside the scope of the argument, which deals exclusively with deaths from suicides and overdoses. The author need not consider the overall death figures in Travonia in order to make this argument.

(E) Too vague. The evidence about percentages doesn't contradict the author's conclusion; it just doesn't necessarily support it.

Remember:

- Whenever you see numbers and percentages discussed in a stimulus, look to see if the author is maintaining the distinction between them. You'll be rewarded for your effort in questions like this.

4. D

Re-evaluating the argument, we can see that the author presents one piece of evidence to support this assertion: Deaths resulting from sleeping pill overdoses have almost doubled since new nonprescription sleeping pills have been released. In order to use these overdoses to support the assertion that suicides have increased dramatically, the author must assume that the overdoses were indeed deliberate and hence qualify as suicides.

(A) brings up the same problem that we saw in the previous question's answer choices: the author makes no links between the people overdosing on the sleeping pills and the teens and elderly folk discussed later in the stimulus. The author needn't assume such a connection in order to assert that suicides have increased dramatically.

(B) Knowing what was the most pervasive suicide method ten years ago doesn't have any real bearing on the claim in the first sentence of the passage.

(C) is far outside the scope. Deaths from natural causes have no necessary relation to this argument about suicide.

(E)'s relative comparison of Travonia's suicide rate to the world's is not relevant to the assertion in question. The author only asserts that suicides in Travonia have increased; there is no mention of their relative increase or of the suicide rate in other countries.

Remember:

- Assumptions play a key role not just in Assumption questions, but in many other question types as well. You may have picked up on the central assumption that's tested in this question as soon as the author cited the evidence about the doubling of overdose deaths. Thinking ahead, you may have asked yourself right then and there, "But are these overdoses necessarily suicides?" Such proactive thinking is what allows you to prephrase answers and select choices with greater confidence.

5. B

Here's the paradox: Despite the fact that the rate of emphysema has declined 15 percent within the past 15 years in region A, the cost of caring for emphysema sufferers in the region is now roughly equal to what it was 15 years ago. In other words, the decline in the percentage of emphysema sufferers has not been accompanied by a corresponding decrease in the cost of treating such sufferers. Without trying to predict what might resolve this discrepancy, let's look to the answer choices for some sort of explanation:

(A) deals with the overall cost of health care in the region, which goes beyond our concern with one particular category of costs: the money spent on emphysema sufferers. Thus, knowing that the region's overall health care costs have increased doesn't help to explain what's going on with the cost of emphysema care in particular.

(B) addresses both parts of the paradox and does help to explain it. If improved technology has increased the cost of caring for emphysema sufferers, then a decline in sufferers wouldn't necessarily yield a decrease in costs since the cost per patient would increase. Also, if the technology worked, then there would be fewer sufferers. This technology would thus decrease the overall

KAPLAN

incidence of emphysema without necessarily decreasing the costs attending such care. Perfect.

(C) tells us that the region's overall health care costs haven't really increased in the past seven years, which, if anything, would only heighten the paradox. After all, the stimulus informs us that the costs of emphysema care *have* increased in the past eight years. After reading this choice, we still don't know what might account for that.

(D) doesn't connect the dots enough to really help. It only contributes to explaining the paradox if we assume that the research funds that have recently increased have actually been used and then assume that the "modest increase" in such funds would counteract the savings offered by the decline in the rate of emphysema sufferers. (D) doesn't tell us this much.

(E), like (C), would, if anything, only deepen the mystery: If the most expensive cases are becoming more rare, why hasn't the cost of caring for emphysema sufferers declined?

Remember:

- There are so many different ways to resolve any paradox that prephrasing one possible explanation usually won't help—you'll usually end up evaluating all of the choices anyway. Therefore, be careful not to fall into the common test-taker trap of losing track of the question by the time you get to choices (D) and (E); stay focused on what you're looking for.

6. E

The planner wants to broaden Maple Street, an action that he thinks will help the shops on that street. He supports this recommendation by noting that the shops on Maple Street aren't doing well, but the shops on two wider streets are doing quite well. This argument demonstrates a classic causal flaw. The author assumes that because the shops on Walnut and Crescent Streets are doing well and the

streets are wide, the width of the streets in some way *causes* the success of the shops. We're looking to strengthen this argument, and a good candidate would be one that supported this assumption and showed how wide streets really do help the businesses that reside on them. (E) works because it shows how wide streets will make it easier for people to shop, strengthening the connection between the two key elements of the argument.

(A) weakens the argument by explaining how wider streets *deter* shoppers. Wrong way.

(B) also heads in the other direction, explaining that the planner's recommendation will not bring more shoppers to the stores, only more congestion from drivers looking to get somewhere else.

(C) The comparison between the locations of Maple and Walnut seems relevant; if Maple is in a less populated area, perhaps widening the street won't help to attract business. In that case, this info would seem, if anything, to weaken the argument. But then we learn that Maple is *closer* to the city center than is Crescent, yet Crescent is prospering recently just like Walnut. All we can conclude, then, is that these relative distances from the city center have no apparent effect on the argument regarding the proposal to widen Maple.

(D) Oh good, street history. If anything, (D) might suggest why Walnut does so well, but it doesn't suggest that Maple would achieve the same success. Indeed, it doesn't draw any connection between or even discuss wide streets and shopping.

Remember:

- If you notice a logical flaw in the argument, it's tempting to weaken the argument by noting that flaw, which perhaps explains why many of the wrong choices here would, if anything, weaken the argument. Even if an argument is deeply flawed, if your task is to strengthen it, then you don't get to criticize it. Resist the temptation, and look instead for something that will bolster one of the argument's major assumptions.

7. D

The author concludes (though not explicitly) that the democratic principle of respecting basic individual rights can be ambiguous. As evidence, he discusses country Q, where minorities' basic rights were protected through the laws enacted by a non-elected dictator. According to the author, the dictator was able to enact such laws only because he didn't have to fear being ousted from office and could thus act contrary to public will. If country Q really does provide an accurate example of a situation where the principle of respecting individual rights is ambiguous (which it must for the author's argument to hold), then there needs to be some sort of confusion around the issue of individual rights in that country. The author says that the dictator "may" act against the public will in order to actually protect certain individuals' rights. The situation in country Q is only ambiguous if the dictator actually does act against the public will in order to bring about this particular democratic principle—otherwise he wouldn't need to be a dictator in order to enact his reforms. (D) states this assumption: The author's conclusion is only valid if it is assumed that the public would not have supported such reforms. Try the Denial Test: If popular will did support the protection of minorities' rights, then this example would not serve as an illustration of how establishing democratic principles leads to some "interesting scenarios." Everything would be harmonious—there would be no ambiguity and therefore no argument, for that matter.

(A) is outside of the argument's scope because it focuses on situations in democracies. Since the

author never discusses democracies, we have no way to accurately relate this information back to the stimulus. In any case, (A) certainly isn't necessary for the validity of the author's conclusion.

(B) If nonelected dictators can be ejected from office, then the dictator of country Q might have been taking a chance if he was acting against the popular will. But even so, it's still possible that the dictator's immunity to being voted out was the key factor. So (B) fails the Denial Test.

(C) The author never discusses democratic government. He only discusses one democratic principle, and even in that case, he doesn't suggest that it's incompatible with individual rights but that situations involving individual rights can sometimes become ambiguous.

(E) makes an irrelevant comparison regarding minority rights in dictator and nondictator-led countries. (E) doesn't seem particularly consistent with the argument as regards country Q, and its comparison clearly does not link the author's evidence to his conclusion.

Remember:

- This stimulus offers a clear example of a quite common argument structure, where the author will make a claim in his conclusion and will support it with an example in his evidence. The validity of such arguments rests on whether the example illustrates the claim(s) made in the conclusion. When answering Assumption questions for such arguments, look to fill any gaps between the example and the conclusion. The right answer will be the one that allows the example to actually illustrate the author's primary point.

8. B

The author's conclusion comes toward the end when she says that the plant should be built inside the city limits. Despite her acknowledgment that a plant built inside the city limits will disrupt more lives, she advo-

KAPLAN

cates this option because it will create jobs for the city residents and therefore offer economic benefits to the city. She's therefore deciding between two options. She concludes that one option is better than the other because it promises a certain benefit to the inhabitants of the city. In order for that conclusion to be valid, she must assume that the other option does not promise such a benefit. Thus, she must assume that only the inside city limits option would create jobs for the city's residents. (B) weakens the argument by denying this assumption, stating that either alternative will create jobs for the residents of the city.

(A) doesn't do a whole lot unless you assume more than the answer choice tells you (a sin for any LSAT test taker). Perhaps private-owned land is more expensive, in which case this choice would strengthen the argument, or perhaps it isn't. As it stands, there's no clear link between (A) and the central issues of the argument.

(C) shows how the location of the plant doesn't matter in terms of taxation. It's wrong because taxation isn't one of the criteria determining which option the author prefers. Choice (B) also notes a similarity between the options, but it's right because the similarity there pertains to job creation, which *is* central to the argument and which determines the option the author prefers.

(D) would, if anything, strengthen the argument by suggesting that the possible defect of the author's choice, disruption, isn't so bad.

(E) brings up taxes again, though this time the choice is about the workers' taxes and not the plant's. Still, the issue of taxation isn't even mentioned by the stimulus, and neither (C) nor (E) makes it relevant to the issues discussed in the argument.

Remember:

- When more than one choice addresses an issue that you don't remember encountering in the stimulus, it's tempting to reread the stimulus to see if you missed something. Resist that. If you've read carefully, you'll know what's important in the stimulus, and you can stay on track even when the answer choices might tempt you to question your understanding of the passage.

9. D

Four choices are going to weaken the argument? The argument's probably going to be pretty bad. The chancellor concludes that the lackluster school should be closed and the students redistributed so as to improve the performance of the whole district. His evidence is that firing a few people at that school won't help and that the school isn't meeting minimum achievement standards. There are lots of questionable assumptions tied into this argument, but it's not a good use of time to try to prephrase all four. Instead, evaluate the choices keeping the terms of the argument in mind and keeping in mind that the choice we seek will most likely be irrelevant to the argument.

(A) would indeed weaken the argument since it suggests that redistributing the students will not strengthen the overall educational performance of the entire district.

(B) would also weaken the argument by suggesting that the school may not need to close since it's actually improving.

(C) weakens the author's evidence where he indicates that the school employees' poor work habits are untreatable. (C) suggests otherwise.

(D) is entirely irrelevant to the argument since the school principal's previous successes don't have a clear relationship to the current problems at the school or the chancellor's "solution." Even if she's a "competent administrator" now (which we can't even be sure of), the fact remains that most of her teachers and administrators stink, so nothing's really changed. (D) is correct because it has no impact on the argument.

 419

(E), like (A), weakens the argument by indicating that the students' redistribution won't improve the educational performance of the entire district. In fact, both choices strongly suggest that if the plan is carried out, the neighboring schools will suffer.

Remember:

- In these sorts of questions, don't expect to find a choice that would strengthen the argument. It's possible, sure, but usually the right answer to a "weaken EXCEPT" or "strengthen EXCEPT" question will be the choice that just has no impact on the argument one way or the other.

10. E

That's a pretty user-friendly question stem because it tells us which part of the argument the inference will address. And with so many formal logic statements to choose from, it's a good thing we know where to start. The question stem gives us the first half of an if-then statement; the correct answer will likely be the second half. So, if the editors don't receive year-end bonuses, then what do we know? Scoping out the part of the stimulus that deals with bonuses, we come to sentences 2 and 3. Let's see if sentence 2 helps: If circulation has increased, then editors get their bonuses. We form the contrapositive of an if-then statement by reversing and negating the terms so the contrapositive of sentence 2 will read "if editors DO NOT get bonuses, then circulation has NOT increased." We're given the first part, the "if" clause in the stem; the second part, the "then" clause that must follow, is found in correct choice (E).

(A) deals with ad rates, about which we can make no inferences based on what we're told about bonuses.

(B) and (C) offer the two options regarding ad pages, but neither is right because, according to

what we know, ad pages might have increased or not. There's no accurate inference that we can draw on this subject based on the information we're given.

(D) *Au contraire.* As we saw above, forming the contrapositive allowed us to deduce that circulation has not increased. Be careful when constructing contrapositives to flip the statement and negate each part.

Remember:

- In detailed formal logic questions like this one, use the information in the question stem whenever possible to provide you with a starting point. Find the relevant statement in the stimulus and work backwards from there, employing the contrapositive whenever you can.

11. B

The two historians here offer two different views on the *metis,* a Canadian group derived from Native American and European heritage. The first historian thinks that the rejection of the *metis'* request for some autonomy was tragic since it led to their loss of a distinct identity and weakened Canada's cultural diversity. The second historian clearly expresses where she disagrees: She doesn't think that the rejection of the *metis'* request was tragic basically because the *metis* never constituted a culturally distinct group. They therefore disagree about whether the rejection of the *metis'* request was tragic and about whether the *metis* comprised a culturally distinct group. (B) picks up on that second difference: The first historian clearly believes that the *metis* were a distinct cultural group while the second historian clearly believes they weren't.

(A) is off track because it focuses on the denial of a "people's" request and not on the *metis* in particular. Both historians only express views on that one particular group without making generalizations from it. The fact that historian #2 believes that the denial of the *metis'* requests was not tragic doesn't mean that she necessarily believes that such a denial can *never* be considered tragic.

(C) is stated by the first historian and uncontested by the second. In fact, the second historian's argument suggests that she also believes the *metis* were a mixture of both cultures.

(D) The first historian certainly believes that the denial of a people's request for identity can be detrimental to a country's cultural diversity—he says this is the case with the *metis* and Canada. The second historian, however, doesn't venture an opinion on this issue of the *effect* of denying identity; she merely argues that the denial in this specific case was the right thing to do.

(E) is again something suggested by the first historian, but that's not discussed, much less disputed, by the second historian.

Remember:

- The correct answer to a Point-at-Issue question must relate to an issue taken up by both participants of the dialogue. It's common for wrong choices to focus on an issue that's addressed by only one speaker, so make sure when you evaluate a choice to check to see that both care about the issue it contains.

12. C

The author tells us that Betty's bad fortune was directly caused by Felix's salon and then proceeds to hold forth on the subject of competition in a free-market economy. Taking all of this to be true (accepting, for example, that Felix's store really did drive Betty's out of business), let's proceed to the answer choices to find a logical inference based on this information:

(A) might seem consistent with the author's attitude, but even then, it's a little too strong to be a view we can attribute to the author. Of course, that's not what we're looking for anyway—we simply want a statement that must be true based on the facts of the passage.

(B) might or might not be true. Since the author gives us no information about other salons, we can't make inferences on that topic.

(C) is valid. If Felix's store drove Betty's out of business, then he must have taken some customers from Betty. It's hard to imagine any other way that the appearance of Felix on the scene could "directly" cause Betty's store's demise.

(D) is too extreme. The author says that Felix's store caused the closure of Betty's store, but that doesn't necessarily mean that Betty's store would still be open were it not for Felix's. Perhaps someone or something else would have had the same effect; the author identifies one cause but doesn't suggest that it's the only possible cause.

(E) makes a generalization that would be more appropriate to a principle question. We're given information only about two specific stores; we don't know if their free-market experience is representative of all businesses everywhere.

Remember:

- One of the reasons why it's so important to start off with the question stem is that different question types have different sets of rules. If you were supposed to find a flaw in this question, you wouldn't want to assume that the conclusion were true, but since it's an Inference question, you do. The difference is entirely a result of the different question types, so it's a good idea to become very familiar with them and with what's expected of you in each.

13. E

A stimulus where logical reasoning meets Top Gun. In this argument, the general determines which of two types of aircraft would better the needs of the Air Force for an upcoming mission. While the commander of the Air Force prefers the G28 because it could perform the necessary task more efficiently, the general orders were that the D12 be used instead. He provides one piece of evidence to support this decision: Only the D12 can perform the task in time to meet the mission's deadline. We've seen this type of argument before. When an author argues for one option over another, the author must assume that the benefit provided by the preferred option can only be found in that option. In other words, the author must assume that the G28 would not fulfill the mission in the allotted period of time. The general says that it would take four days for the G28 to be ready for the mission, but he doesn't say that the G28 couldn't meet the deadline. Perhaps the plane's greater efficiency would enable it to still complete the mission in the allotted period of time. (E) expresses this assumption because, in order for the general's conclusion to be valid, he must assume that the G28 could not perform the mission by the immovable deadline. Thus, he assumes that the G28's efficiency would not save the time that it would take for the G28 to begin the mission.

(A) is unrelated to the argument. The stimulus doesn't state that one aircraft retrieves higher quality information than the other.

(B) goes too far. The author never states how long the mission would take, so there's no basis for stating that the D12 would be done before the G28 arrived. All the author needs to assume is that only the D12 could meet the mission's deadline, not that it would do so in the next four days.

(C) contradicts the stimulus, in which such an ability is a significant consideration to the commander. The general never contests the importance of the consideration; he just overrides it by making the deadline a *more* significant consideration.

(D) focuses on aircraft other than the G28. Aren't two enough to deal with? The author seems to think so because he only discusses two types of aircraft between which he has to choose. Any others aren't relevant.

Remember:

• This assumption might be difficult to prephrase since the author comes quite close to saying that the G28 couldn't meet the mission's deadline. Don't worry if you can't prephrase; just stay focused on the author's evidence and conclusion, and you'll find only one choice that links the two.

14. D

This Inference question is an exercise in keeping track of the many little pieces of information given to us through the stimulus. Everyone in the Rubberband Club lives in state A. Everyone in the Rubberband Club has bungee-jumped at least once in the past two years. The club's still chugging along, despite the fact that it's been illegal to bungee-jump in state A for the past 10 years. Even though it may seem like there's a possible contradiction in the stimulus, don't seek to resolve the seeming discrepancy; rather, remain faithful to the four primary pieces of information while searching for a proper inference.

(A) Too extreme. The stimulus doesn't tell us that they *can't* bungee-jump in state A but that it's illegal to do so. While each current member must have jumped in the last two years, some of them may have broken the law and jumped in state A anyway.

(B) and (E) take us too far also: It's quite possible that one or more of the current applicants or current members took the plunge legally in the state A 10 or more years ago before the ban was enacted.

(C) Too extreme. As mentioned above, while each must have jumped at least once in the last two years, they needn't have jumped in state A; perhaps they're getting all of their kicks in another state where jumping is legal.

(D) is perfect. If they didn't jump outside of state A, then they must have jumped within state A sometime in the last two years to fulfill the club's requirements. And if they did that, then they must have bungee-jumped illegally. There are no unsupported steps in this chain of reasoning, so it's a logical inference.

Remember:

- Sometimes Inference questions put you in the position of Goldilocks, looking for a choice that's not too narrow, not too broad, but just right. (D) is the best bowl of porridge here because, by explaining a possibility, it doesn't commit the flaw of the other four choices, i.e., making overly generalized claims.

15. A

The author concludes that Waters was not influenced by McTell in his formulation of the key elements of his psychosocial theory (although McTell may have aided in the theories' subsequent development). As evidence, she notes that Waters had already determined the basic components of his theory by 1947, years before Waters ever met McTell. The author gives you lots of other information about the two theorists and their relationship in the 1950s, but that's just extra information; the author's argument basically consists of the final two sentences. In order for the author's conclusion to be valid, she must assume that McTell could only influence Waters in person. Note that the author says that the two theorists had never "met" before the 1950s; she doesn't say that they had never communicated or that Waters knew nothing of McTell's ideas. Therefore, if she's correct in arguing that McTell didn't influence the formulation of Waters theory at all, she must assume that Waters was

not influenced by McTell in any way before they met. (A) gives a more concrete expression of this assumption: The author assumes that Waters hadn't read anything by McTell prior to their meeting and thus that Waters wasn't influenced by McTell in 1947. The Denial Test confirms this: What if Waters did know of and read McTell's work before he officially met him? Could the author then be so sure that the formulation in 1947 of Waters' theory was not influenced by the ideas of McTell? No, she couldn't, so (A) is necessary for this argument to work.

(B) Outside the scope. The author only discusses whether Waters got his ideas from one particular scholar, McTell. Waters could have completely plagiarized from someone else, and the conclusion might still be valid.

(C) Outside the scope. The author's claim isn't that Waters' ideas were completely original, in which case (B) and (C) would be relevant, but that he didn't get them from McTell. Other scholars, confidantes, and mentors just aren't relevant.

(D) goes against the grain—the author strongly suggests that McTell did influence Waters' ideas in the 1950s and helped him develop his theory. The only part the author feels McTell did not influence was the initial formulation.

(E) would be sad for McTell, but it's wrong because it deals with the 1950s. Technically, whether or not Waters benefited from his association with McTell in the 1950s has no impact on whether Waters' 1947 ideas were influenced by McTell. However, like (D), (E) seems to contradict the passage, which suggests that Waters *did* in fact benefit from his association with McTell in the 1950s.

Remember:

- Read proactively! Often, when we hear that something has "long been recognized . . . ," it will be followed up by opposition of some sort to the long-held theory. This is common in both Logical Reasoning and Reading Comp passages. Be on the lookout for this shift in sentiment. Here, the classic contrast keyword "however" in the second to last sentence signals the onset of the author's major point, which, not surprisingly, is a reworking of the academic community's long-held belief.

16. A

Too bad we don't get to weaken this one. The author states that there are fewer geniuses nowadays than there were, oddly, in the 17th century. The argument is pretty flimsy, based primarily on the assumption that it's legitimate to compare the two periods. To strengthen this argument, we'll want a choice to demonstrate that this comparison is more likely to be valid. This is where (A) comes in, stating a more specific element of this assumption. If people are indeed able to recognize geniuses while they're alive or soon after they die, then it's more valid to compare modern genius production to seventeenth century genius production. After all, in order to make a valid comparison about the number of geniuses by period, the author must assume that we can count them accurately, and if it took, say, a hundred years or more to recognize genius stature, then the comparison wouldn't allow the author to form the categorical conclusion in the first sentence; we'd just have to wait and see. Maybe in the year A.D. 2100, notables such as James Joyce and Howard Stern will grace the genius list, too.

(B) doesn't help the argument since the author concerns himself only with the geniuses of one certain (though undefined) stature. If anything, (B) might weaken the argument by suggesting the author's comparison is not valid. Maybe there's only one 20th century genius (Einstein) who's in the same category as the 17th century geniuses listed, but if there are other types of geniuses besides scientists and writers to consider, the author's conclusion may be a bit hasty.

(C) also does nothing to help the author's case because the author relies on a stable definition of the term genius in his argument. Throwing that definition into question would only weaken his argument.

(D) would only be relevant if it could be shown that extremes in educational attainment were somehow related to the development of geniuses. We have no support to make such a leap, so (D) can't assist our author here.

(E) At first glance, (E) would seem inconsistent with the author's argument: If scientific knowledge is increasing at an ever-greater pace, then why do we have so few geniuses? Still, this is all too vague. We can't be sure of the relationship between the expansion of scientific knowledge in general and the production of geniuses; maybe geniuses create themselves through the process of being forced to discover stuff on their own without simply looking it up on the Internet, for example. Besides, (E) is also too specific, focusing as it does only on science; Shakespeare was no scientist. All in all, no help here.

Remember:

- Arguments that rely on a central comparison are so common that it's useful to recognize them as a type. When they show up for Weaken questions, you can usually weaken the argument by undermining the comparison, and for Strengthen questions you can look for a choice that somehow validates the comparison. Be on the lookout for specific information that could serve those purposes.

17. E

According to Sylvia, the public's belief that Banner clothes dryers are particularly fire-prone is false since the number of such dryers that actually erupt into flames is small. She also compares this number to that of major manufacturers' dryers that catch on fire, stating that the number of Banner dryers fires (a rhyme which must plague their marketing department) is smaller. Alice does not offer an alternative argument but merely notes a flaw in Sylvia's evidence. Like a good LSAT student, Alice recognizes that Sylvia compares the number of Banner dryers and the number of major manufacturers' dryers that catch on fire rather than their rates of occurrence. Looking through the answer choices, we find (E): Alice does indeed note a flaw in Sylvia's argument and that flaw does involve a distorted use of numbers where percents would be more appropriate.

(A) Alice neither accepts nor rejects Sylvia's conclusion; rather, she identifies a problem in Sylvia's evidence. She certainly doesn't offer another path toward proving that the public is wrong to distrust Banner clothes dryers.

(B) is partially right because Alice does present new evidence, but that evidence doesn't contradict Sylvia's nor does it show how Sylvia's conclusion is wrong. Alice only criticizes the appropriateness of Sylvia's evidence in getting to where she's trying to go. She suggests that Sylvia's conclusion may be hasty, but she certainly doesn't "disprove" it.

(C) can be axed because Alice herself compares the same two groups of items (she simply compares them in a different and what she believes to be a more appropriate way).

(D) Too extreme. Alice doesn't refute Sylvia's evidence but merely demonstrates a flaw in using it to get to her conclusion. She never says or suggests that Sylvia's evidence (that Banner has fewer dryer fires than the major manufacturers) is incorrect.

Remember:

- Notice how frequently Method of Argument answer choices mention the conclusion and evidence of the initial argument. The prominence of those terms just underscores how important it is to identify the conclusion and evidence in the initial argument and to determine what precisely the respondent says in terms of them.

18. C

The first step in this stimulus is to recognize these assertions as formal logic statements and to translate them into if/then statements. The author first states that IF a building lacks sufficient ventilation and natural light, THEN it is not well designed (if A and B, then C). You can also form that statement's contrapositive: IF a building is well designed, THEN it has sufficient ventilation and natural light. Next: IF a building has many windows, THEN it has natural light (if D, then B). Finally, the author's conclusion is: IF a building has many windows, THEN it is well designed (if D, then C). Do you see the problem? The author first identifies two qualities necessary for a building to be considered well designed. The author then proceeds to discuss only one of those elements, completely neglecting to mention whether the building has sufficient ventilation. Instead of maintaining that a well designed building needs good ventilation and natural light, the author concludes that natural light itself (coming from many windows) can determine whether a building is well designed. The author fails to consider whether the building is also well ventilated, which is what (C) states. (You may have noticed that there's another major flaw here: Even if it were ascertained that a building had good ventilation and natural light, that would still not "ensure" that it is well designed; those factors are necessary, but not necessarily sufficient for well designed buildings. The stem asks for a flaw in the argument, most likely because here, there are two big ones.)

(A) is too extreme. The author needn't show that ventilation is *only* possible through windows but that windows provide adequate ventilation.

(B) is not established by the argument, but that's not a flaw. The author shows that windows provide natural light, which is sufficient for the author's conclusion in terms of the natural light issue. The author has no obligation here to switch the first clause of sentence 2 around.

(D) could be true, but it isn't really relevant to this argument, which concerns a building that does have many windows. Remember, windows are not part of the original rule, but come in later as one possible factor that ensures the presence of one of the elements (natural light) of the main rule. That's why the author need establish nothing about buildings *without* windows.

(E) points out a possibility that conflicts with the stimulus; failing to consider the impossible isn't a logical problem.

Remember:

- Since you will definitely see some Logical Reasoning questions involving formal logic on your exam, try to get comfortable with spotting formal logic statements, translating them, finding their contrapositives, and differentiating between necessity and sufficiency.

19. D

The author concludes that we should stop using certain products that harm the ozone layer despite the fact that their use is both legal and enjoyable. Rather, we should focus on our obligation to act in the best interests of future generations. Let's rephrase to make this sound more like a principle. The author argues against a course of action by stressing our obligation to consider the consequences of those actions on future generations. Thus, we shouldn't do something now because it'll hurt people later on. According to (D), the morali-

ty, or rightness, of an action depends on its future consequences, which is entirely in line with the logic underlying the author's argument.

(A) and (C) The author doesn't suggest what should determine the legality of one's actions. According to the stimulus, it's legal to use the mentioned products, so what determines legality isn't the issue.

(B) goes against the grain of the argument. It's legal to use the products, but the author argues that they still shouldn't be used, therefore arguing that the legality of an action does *not* necessarily determine its morality.

(E) discusses appropriate punishment, which the author never addresses. Also, the author never discusses any "illegal action." Out on two counts.

Remember:

- Try to generalize the stimulus before you get to the answer choice when dealing with Principle questions. The answer choices often sound so abstract, and sometimes even so similar to each other, that you can get lost in them without some sort of guide. Prephrase an answer by abstracting from the stimulus and putting the specifics of the situation into more general terms.

20. E

A Parallel Reasoning question with some formal logic thrown in—proceed carefully. The stimulus starts off by telling us that public service announcements try to advise teens but really just annoy them. Then comes the formal logic "only if" statement, which, when properly translated, means that IF teenagers follow advice, THEN they do not resent the delivery of that advice. (If you have any trouble translating "only if" statements into standard "if/then" statements, stop and work through this translation again until you see it.) The author then concludes that the announcements should be discontinued. Since this is a Parallel Reasoning question, we should get a better sense of the general structure of the passage. The author shows that a certain program has a goal and an unintended negative side effect. The author then explains that the goal can't be met if the side effect exists (which we know it does), and concludes therefore that the program doesn't work and should be scrapped. It's a pretty solid argument, and we can proceed to look for the same elements in the answer choices.

(A) identifies the goal of a certain program but never identifies an unintended negative side effect. You can stop there without having to delve too deeply into the touching patriotism in the remainder of the choice.

(B) never discusses the goal of zoning restrictions and so never survives past consideration of the very first element of the stimulus.

(C) again never explains the goal of the estate tax. Don't be fooled by the fact that it does include what could be called a side effect and a negative consequence of it—if every element is not present, then you have to move on.

(D) identifies the goal of a certain program and explains a negative side effect. But the second sentence the issue shifts away from the success of the conservation laws to their ability to get support. The original argument stays focused only on the program's potential for success.

(E) is correct because it outlines the goal of a program, discusses an unintended negative side effect, shows that the program can't succeed in the presence of that side effect, and concludes that the program should be eliminated. All the necessary elements are present.

Remember:

• Make a mental (or written) checklist for yourself when dealing with Parallel Reasoning. The

absence of one key element invalidates any choice.

21. C

This argument discusses the effects of a region-wide recession on two counties (X and Y). The comptroller of County X has stated that County X's depressed economy represents what will happen to all counties in the financially struggling region (the "inevitable" consequences). However, County Y is not currently suffering any financial difficulties, so the author concludes that County X's comptroller must be wrong. Our task is not to determine whether or not this conclusion is correct but explain the apparent contradiction presented in the stimulus. More specifically, we want an answer choice that will show how County X could be adversely affected by the recession while County Y is not. Keeping that in mind, let's look through the choices.

(A) doesn't explain the situation within the region, which is all the stimulus addresses. Comparing this region to any other doesn't shed light on the different situations occurring in Counties X and Y.

(B) compares the overall revenue generated by the two counties, which has no relationship to the issue at hand. Maybe X is ten times bigger than Y, accounting for the greater revenue. That wouldn't alter the fact that X is suffering compared to its usual economic state and that Y is robust.

(C) explains one important way in which County X is different than County Y, which certainly does help to explain the counties' different financial situations. If the region's recession decreased tourism, and County X depends on tourism for revenue more than County Y, then it makes sense for County X to be more affected by the recession than County Y.

(D) doesn't make this information relevant to the recession and its different impact on the two counties. Both (C) and (D) discuss one factor contributing to one county's revenue, but (D) is wrong because, unlike (C), it doesn't show how the issue relates to the recession's impact.

(E) doesn't do quite enough to explain the initial situation. Would the relocation of "a few retail businesses" hurt County X and stabilize County Y? We don't know; we can't even be sure that the businesses that relocated were successful. In (C), we were told that County X relied "almost entirely" on tourism that was "crippled" by the recession; the terms in that choice are far stronger. In contrast, (E)'s discussion of the relocation of a few businesses doesn't help to explain the larger differences in the financial situations of the two counties.

Remember:

• It's pretty common to see an argument in which an author discusses a difference existing between two apparently similar people or groups. The trap is to assume that because two groups are similar in one way, they're similar in all ways. That's seldom the case, and, as we see in this question, it's often important that you allow that dissimilarities might account for the differences between the groups.

22. A

For our second question relating to this stimulus, we're asked about the author's method of argument. Looking at the structure of the stimulus, we can see that the author begins by expressing the views of County X's comptroller, who makes a generalization about all of the counties in the state. The author then notes an exception to the comptroller's generalization and uses it to show that the comptroller must be wrong. Therefore, to make his argument, the author provides evidence that disproves a generalization. (A) best expresses this: The author counters the comptroller's claim with evidence about County Y that directly contradicts the comptroller's assertion that a depressed economy is the inevitable consequence for all counties in the region.

(B) The author doesn't dismiss any part of the comptroller's statement as irrelevant; he just says that the statement is wrong. Further, the comptroller doesn't provide any real evidence for his claim, so there's no evidence for the author to contest.

(C) starts off well but goes awry in the second half. The author clearly believes that the comptroller is wrong, but (C) misrepresents the way in which the author expresses his opinion. The author doesn't dispute the comptroller's statement by saying that it's *impossible* in this situation for all of the region's counties to be economically depressed. Rather, he provides opposing evidence (the booming economy of County Y) that proves that this is simply not the case.

(D) Who would be the authority appealed to in this scenario? There is no one in the stimulus who would fit this description, so (D)'s out.

(E) gets the argument all muddled up. The author doesn't make the generalization, the comptroller does. The author gives a specific example, and while it does counter the claim he opposes, a specific example is not a generalization.

Remember:

• In Method of Argument questions, test the general terms of the choices against the specifics of the stimulus. Here, ask yourself: "Is there an impossibility asserted? Is there an authority here?" Every aspect of the right choice must pan out.

23. A

Were you feeling unchallenged? Actually, this question type is one that you've seen many times before, but it has a little twist because you're directed not to determine the role played by just any piece of information, but by a certain assumption. The first task is therefore to see where the given assumption exists in the argument. The author begins by explaining a paradox: Kids who weren't vaccinated seemed to be immune to measles. This is the only place in the stimulus where the author discusses vaccination, so it must be where the stem's assumption comes in. Indeed, in this first sentence, the author does assume that vaccinations give kids immunity, or else the researchers wouldn't have been so surprised by this nonvaccination based immunity. How does this function in the argument? Well, it helps to set up the strange situation that the rest of the stimulus will strive to explain or, in other words, the problem that requires a solution provided in the argument. (A) captures this by noting that the first sentence (statement plus assumption) creates the confusion, which the researchers then worked to explain.

(B) would tie the assumption into the evidence regarding dihydron-X, but this assumption doesn't come from that part of the passage.

(C) contradicts the passage, which explains how the kids were able to achieve such an immunity. Therefore, such immunity is not impossible.

(D) This assumption is not what the researchers seek to prove; they seek to prove how the kids who *don't* receive the vaccination could get such immunity.

(E) Just because the kids became immune through their formulas, that doesn't overturn the assumption that vaccinations also create immunity. The researchers' conclusion does not contradict or undermine this particular assumption.

Remember:

- This isn't the way in which assumptions are normally tested on the LSAT, but that's foreseeable since if this were a regular assumption, you would already know what role it played in the argument without reading it. If you see something a little different on test day, just do what you would normally do with that question type. The first step on these "role in the passage" questions is to locate the information, and then to identify its function.

24. B

Next up is a "parallel the flaw" type of Parallel Reasoning question, so let's first find the flaw. This one is particularly amenable to an algebraic treatment. The author tells us that the Chief of Personnel claimed that no human resource employee was fired in the embezzlement scandal, but he ends up asserting that this claim must be false. So the author actually concludes that some human resource employees were fired in the embezzlement scandal. Let's find the evidence for this and begin our algebraic representation there (it's easier in a case like this to build the argument in order from evidence to conclusion). "Some human resource employees were fired in March" can be represented as "some X are Y." And "Some employees fired in March were fired in the embezzlement scandal" breaks down to "some Y are Z." The conclusion mentioned above would then be "some X are Z"—which we know is not necessarily true, because the group of human resource folks canned in March and the group of embezzlers who were tossed can be totally distinct groups. Searching the choices, we find that (B)'s logic is botched in the same way as the original: Some stars of *Icarus* starred in *Mrs. Jones* (some X are Y). Some *Mrs. Jones* folks went to Zeller (some Y are Z). Therefore, some *Icarus* actors went to Zeller (some X are Z). Same structure, and the same flaw: The stars of *Icarus* who were also in *Mrs. Jones* may not have been the same *Mrs. Jones* folks who attended Zeller.

(A) is out immediately because it doesn't commit any flaw. All members have good manners, and Candy is a member, so she must have good manners. That's fine, at least in terms of logic. No flaw, no good.

(C), like (A), commits no logical error. If the neighbors have young kids, and many people with kids stay home on weekend nights, then it's certainly reasonable to conclude that some of the neighbors *probably* stay home on weekend nights. The qualified nature of this argument—that is, the use of the word "probably"—makes this a very reasonable conclusion and differentiates it from the original argument in which the author claims that the Chief was wrong and that some human resource employee definitively *was* fired.

(D) Some X are Y. Some X are Z. Therefore, some X are both Y and Z. Flawed, but not parallel.

(E) contains no "some" terms to play with, so it's impossible for this choice to mimic the original. Kill it for that reason alone.

Remember:

- Algebraic representation is valuable in Parallel Reasoning questions made up of (or that can be translated into) formal logic terms. When you see words like *some, all, no, none, if,* and *then,* think of breaking down the terms in the original and in the choices into letters in order to find the one that matches.

25. E

The principal concludes that the Excellence Learning Services' promotional materials were "misleading" and supports this conclusion by discussing his own school's experience with the Service. Even though the school used the Excellence program to improve its students' reading and math scores, the students' performances on the tests were the same as they were 20 years ago. The principal uses this information to demonstrate that the Excellence program does not improve test scores, but there's an unwarranted assumption involved in his argument—did you spot it? Just because the students' scores equal those of the students 20 years ago, that doesn't necessarily mean that the Excellence program was wholly ineffective. Perhaps the students' scores would have been lower than those of the students 20 years earlier without the program. Perhaps equaling the scores of 20 years ago is a marked improvement over the score levels of recent years. The principal assumes that the Excellence program did not improve the students' scores, but that assumption is unwarranted because it's unsupported by the argument's evidence. (E) picks up on this flaw, noting that the principal does not demonstrate that the Excellence program did not improve student test scores.

(A) Since the author's conclusion solely concerns the accuracy of the Excellence program's advertisements, and thus solely intends to criticize the program, it needn't offer alternative solutions for support.

(B) is wholly irrelevant because the author never directly or indirectly discusses parents and their capacities. Parents are outside the scope here.

(C) criticizes the author's language, but it's hard to identify any language that might be called "emotionally charged" in the argument. "Misleading" certainly doesn't qualify, and that's the author's strongest term, so (C) identifies a flaw that the argument doesn't commit.

(D) is not directly relevant since the author's argument only concerns the program's claims to help students improve their math and reading scores. Other possible benefits aren't discussed or pertinent to the program's ability to specifically raise these test scores.

Remember:

- Many answer choices for Logical Flaw questions discuss issues that the author never addresses. Those choices only constitute correct flaws if the issues they introduce are directly relevant to the argument. Alternative solutions in choice (A), parents' capabilities in (B), and benefits in other areas in (D) do not fit this requirement.

GETTING INTO LAW SCHOOL

CHAPTER SEVEN

Introduction to Law School Admissions

HIGHLIGHTS -

- Prepare for all facets of the admissions process

I can still remember the day I received my LSAT score report in the mail. I was jubilant about my score, which put me in the top two percent of all test takers. This kind of LSAT performance, I thought—combined with my high college GPA—would surely get me into any law school I desired; all I had to do was decide which one I would deign to attend. I proceeded to apply to ten top law schools, fully confident that I would be accepted by all ten.

Well, it didn't turn out quite that way. By the following April, I had received a meager two acceptance letters, one wait-list letter, and an appalling seven rejection letters, including ones from Harvard and Stanford. As the rejection letters rolled in, one after the other, my original hubris slowly and painfully gave way to humility.

Two weeks after the last rejection, still reeling from the shock, I had the good fortune to bump into an admissions officer from a local law school at a party. I cornered her and began peppering her with questions about what could possibly have gone wrong. She mentioned several potential problems and suggested that I call a friend of hers at one of the law schools I had applied to and ask her to critique my application. What I found out was eye-opening: my application could not have been more inept. In fact, just about everything I'd done had contributed to pre-

Kaplan Rules

Being a strong, well-qualified candidate isn't enough to ensure admission to the law school of your choice. You have to *show* the admissions officers how strong and well-qualified you are—by conducting an effective, meticulously organized campaign for admission.

venting my admission to law school, including carelessly misspelling my name on the application (fortunately, the University of Michigan Law School saw fit to let me attend despite these blunders).

Today, after years of conversations with other lawyers, law students, and members of my Kaplan LSAT classes, I realize that my experience was hardly unique. An astonishing number of people apply to law school without a clue about the admissions process. That's why I've made something of a career out of ensuring that others don't make the same mistakes I did. In the last several years, I've spoken to admissions officers at more than 65 schools in all regions of the country, gleaning as much information from them as I could. And I've gathered together their combined wisdom in this book.

One cautionary note—admission officers are human beings; they don't all think alike. Attitudes and priorities vary from law school to law school. However, the suggestions that follow are the ones I've heard over and over again, straight from the most important source—the admissions officers themselves. Stick closely to these suggestions and you'll increase your chances of getting in the law school you want to attend.

CHAPTER EIGHT

Where to Apply

HIGHLIGHTS

- Learn how to evaluate criteria to select the right school for you
- Assess your chances of being admitted
- Create a profile of preferred, competitive, and "safe" schools

The question of where you should apply is usually a two-part question. What schools should you consider, regardless of your chances, and which of these schools can you actually get into? Let's begin with the first question.

What Schools Should You Consider?

A recent article about law school education published a remarkable statistic. Upon graduation, according to one study, 58 percent of all law students end up living and working within a one-hour drive of where they went to law school. That's nearly six out of every ten students!

There are many reasons for this surprising statistic. Obviously, a lot of people attend the local law school in the town where they have always lived and want to continue living. Also, since employers tend to interview and hire from nearby law schools, many recent grads stay put. Some students find that they just like the area and don't want to leave. Still others meet

Kaplan Rules

Deciding which law schools to apply to is an important decision. Treat it with the appropriate seriousness, which doesn't mean that you can't have a fun time researching schools.

and marry a local person during their three years. Whatever the explanation, a majority of all law students end up spending more than just the required three years in the city or region where they attend law school.

Despite the importance of law school selection, however, it's frightening how lightly many applicants treat the whole process, even students who spend a great deal of time studying for the LSAT or working on their applications. Horror stories abound—of distant relatives convincing someone to attend State University Law School just because they themselves did 40 years ago or of a student who decides not to apply to a school because his girlfriend's cousin heard that the social life was not so hot.

This point cannot be stressed enough. *Choosing a law school is a major decision in your life and should be treated as such.* There are several factors to consider when choosing where to apply, including reputation, location, and cost.

Reputation

How much does a law school's reputation matter? The short answer is that it matters very much in your first few years out of law school, when you're looking for your first job or two. Most employers evaluating you at this time will have little else to go on and so will tend to place a lot of weight on school reputation. After a few years, when you've established a reputation and a record of your own, the importance of your alma mater's rep will diminish.

The long answer to the question of academic reputation, however, is a little more complex. Each applicant must look at his or her situation and ask several questions:

Note

It's worth thinking about now: how important is it to you to get into a high-prestige school? Will you need the fancy credential for the kind of law you want to pursue?

- **Am I looking to work for a law firm or to do public service work?**
  Law firms tend to put more emphasis on the reputation of the school.
- **Do I want to stay in the area or have more mobility nationwide?**
  Some schools enjoy strong local reputations as well as strong alumni bases, whereas other schools have a nationwide appeal.
- **How competitive do I want my law school experience to be?**
  Although there are exceptions, as a general rule the schools with better reputations tend to be very competitive.
- **Do I want to consider teaching as an option?**
  Virtually all law school professors come from a handful of top-notch law schools. The same also applies for the most prestigious judicial clerkships.
- **To what extent am I willing to go into debt?**
  The schools with the biggest reputations also tend to have the biggest price tags.

How to Research Reputation

What's the best way to research reputation? Many publications rank law schools. How accurate these rankings are is anybody's guess, but they tend to become self-fulfilling. Once published, they're discussed over and over by students, lawyers, and faculty until they become fact. Although the methodology behind these rankings is often suspect, the results are frequently heeded by employers. Studies rank the top fifty schools, the top fifteen schools, or categorize all schools into four or five levels. (Most of these books can be found in the reference section of your local bookstore.) Many law firms rely heavily on such rankings in making their hiring decisions.

But there are other methods to determine a school's reputation. Speak to friends who are lawyers or law students. Lawyers have a habit of noting who their most formidable opponents are and where they went to law school. Look through law school catalogs and see what schools the professors attended. Finally, ask the placement offices how many firms interview on campus each year, and compare the numbers. Their answers can give you a strong indication of what the law-firm community thinks of a school.

Location

Location is of prime importance because of the distinct possibility that you'll end up spending a significant part of your life near your law school—three years at the very least. Even under the best of conditions, law school will be a difficult period in your life. You owe it to yourself to find a place where you'll be comfortable. Pick cities or areas you already know you like or would like to live. Pay particular attention to climate problems. Think about rural areas as opposed to urban centers.

How to Research Location

Visit as many law schools as possible, your top two or three choices at the very least. You may be surprised at what you find. For example, a recent student related that his dream was to get into the law school of one particular university because he'd visited its campus several years ago and loved it. But his dream was quickly crushed when told that the university's law school is not on the campus, but rather thirty minutes away in an area closer to downtown. Spend some time researching location by visiting *when school is in session*, which is when you'll get the most accurate picture. You should also:

- Buy a local newspaper and scan the real estate ads for prices near campus; check out campus housing to determine whether it's livable.
- Check out transportation options at the law school.
- Take the school's tour so you can hear about the area's good points.
- Look at bulletin boards for evidence of activities.

Kaplan Tip

Statistics show that you'll probably end up spending at least part of your working life in the area where you went to law school. So be sure to pick one in a location you can live with (and in).

Finally, don't be afraid to wander into the student lounge and just ask several law students what they think. Most are more than willing to provide an honest appraisal, but be sure to get more than one opinion.

Costs

Cost ranks at the bottom of many law students' list of criteria to consider, because law school financial aid works in much the same manner as a credit card—you get it now and pay for it later. Each year a number of students enter law school with the goal of doing some type of public service work, but then are forced to take higher-paying firm jobs in order to meet their loan payments. This is certainly understandable when you realize that many law students rack up debts of $50,000 to $100,000 over the course of three years.

Among the cost issues to consider are:

- **Low-Cost State Schools**
  State schools tend to have lower tuition, particularly for in-state residents.
- **Urban Versus Rural Living Costs**
  Schools in large urban areas will almost invariably have higher living costs than those in rural areas (although the larger cities also tend to have more part-time jobs for second- and third-year students, which can offset the extra cost).
- **Special Loan Programs**
  Many schools now offer special loan repayment or loan forgiveness programs for students who take low-paying public service jobs.
- **Special Scholarship Programs**
  Many law schools offer special scholarship programs that range from small grants to full three-year rides.

How to Research Cost
The law school application will tell you what the annual tuition was for the previous year. Many applications will even give you an estimate of living expenses. If you want to dig deeper, call the financial aid office and ask them to send you the breakdown of living expenses of the average law student. Also ask them to send information about any loan forgiveness programs and about scholarships offered by the law school.

Job Placement

With the legal job market shrinking, the proficiency of a law school's placement office is now a major factor to be considered. If interviews with law students can be believed, the competency of placement officers varies widely. Some see their job as simply setting up on-campus interviews and making sure they run smoothly. Others call and write letters on behalf of students and are constantly selling the school to employers. Some schools direct almost all of their efforts into placing students into private law firms. Other schools provide information on an entire range of opportunities. At some schools students are lucky if the placement office even provides them with a list of alumni in cities in which they'd like to live. At other schools the office calls alumni to hunt for leads.

How to Research the Job Placement Office

Ask the placement office for the percentage of graduates in the most recent class who had jobs upon graduation. Don't be fooled by statistics that show 98 percent of all graduates employed. Almost all law students are eventually employed, even if they drive taxis. The key is to determine how many are placed in law jobs *before* they leave law school.

Second, stop by the placement office on your visit and look around. Ask to see the placement library and check whether it's well organized and up-to-date. Note whether it carries materials on public interest or teaching jobs and how large this section is. Also ask whether a newsletter is published to keep alumni informed of any recent job openings.

Again, talk with law students. Most have very strong opinions about the performance of their placement office. Most students recognize and appreciate when the placement office is making an extra effort.

Course Selection

One of the nicest things about law schools today is their growing number of course selections and the new areas of law that are opening up. International trade, employment discrimination, sports and entertainment, and environmental law are all areas in which schools are providing more offerings. Many law students nowadays are becoming specialists, because of both personal preference and better marketability. If you're one of the many students who enter law school without a clue about what kind of law they want to practice, look for schools that offer a lot of different areas of study.

How to Research Course Selection

As a rule, schools with larger student populations offer not only more classes but also a greater variety. They need more professors to handle the standard course load, and most professors also like to teach and explore new areas of law as well.

Schools list the courses most recently taught in their recruiting brochure, which they will gladly send you. One note of caution: just because a class has been taught in the past and is listed in the brochure doesn't mean that it's taught every year or will be taught in the future. If

Kaplan Tip

Some placement offices are far better than others. It's a good idea to find out how effective the offices are at the schools you're considering.

Kaplan Tip

Some courses, particularly unusual ones, may not be taught regularly. If a particular course offering is important enough to you to affect your school selection, just make sure that the course will indeed be available should you go to that school.

you're interested in a particular class, call the registrar's department and find out how often the class has been taught in the past and whether it will be offered again in the future. Ask to speak with the professor who has taught the course in the past.

Social Life

Although it's an important part of the law school experience, social life should rank near the bottom of the list of factors to consider when choosing a law school. Why? Because your social life at any law school is what you make of it. Almost all law schools have monthly parties or weekly Thursday night get-togethers at local bars. And if you choose to expand that schedule, you can always find a willing accomplice. Furthermore, most schools now have a comparably full range of social organizations that cover race, religion, political affiliation, and sex.

How to Research Social Life

Examine the area surrounding the law school. During your first year, locale probably won't matter much. But as you get into your second and third years, you'll likely find that you do have some free time, particularly on weekends. Think about whether you want a quiet rural area where canoeing or skiing are readily available or whether you'd prefer a larger city with a vibrant restaurant and nightlife scene.

Additional Considerations

There are a few other factors that you may want to toss into the equation when deciding which law school is right for you.

Class Size

This factor is not as important as it is when choosing a college because, despite what you may read in a catalogue, virtually all first-year classes will be large. Nevertheless, there are some differences between a school such as Georgetown, with more than 2,000 students, and a school such as Stanford, with fewer than 800. In the second and third years, the larger schools tend to have more course offerings, whereas the smaller schools focus on smaller class size and more contact between professors and students. Smaller schools also tend to encourage a greater sense of camaraderie and less competition. Larger schools, on the other hand, produce more alumni and thus more contacts when it comes time for your job search.

Attrition Rates

Law schools generally try to keep their attrition rate below 10 percent. There are exceptions, however, and if the school you're interested in has an attrition rate above 10 percent, you should ask an admissions officer why. There may be a reasonable explanation, but you should probably approach the school with some caution.

Joint-Degree Programs

Joint-degree programs are designed to help students pursue two degrees jointly in less time than it would take to earn them separately. The most common examples are the Master of Public Policy (M.P.P.) or the Master of Business Administration (M.B.A.) combined with the law degree. These programs generally take four to five years to complete. Most schools are becoming more daring in this field—indeed, some are now encouraging students to create their own joint-degree program in any area that they choose, as long as it meets both departments' approval. It's not uncommon now to see joint degrees in law and foreign languages, music, or sociology. Check with the schools to see what joint-degree programs are routinely offered, but don't be limited by them. If you have a specialized program in mind, call the registrar's office and see how flexible they are.

Clinical Programs

Every law school in the country now offers one or more clinical programs. A clinic is a unique, hands-on opportunity that allows law students to see how the legal system works by handling actual civil cases for people who can't afford an attorney (and getting credit for it at the same time). Not only are these clinics a tremendous learning tool, but they are also the highlight of many law students' three years of study.

Usually the workload is heavy on landlord/tenant disputes or other debt-collection cases. However, many schools are branching out and offering specialized clinics in such areas as child abuse, domestic violence, and immigration. One word of caution: Clinics tend to be popular with students. In many cases, it's very difficult to get a spot in the class, and admission usually depends on the luck of the draw. As a general rule, the schools in large cities have bigger and more clinics because they tend to have more clients.

Internships

Like clinical programs, internships are becoming more popular and varied. Internship programs vary widely from school to school, and may include anything from working for an international trade organization in Europe for an entire year to getting three hours credit for part-time work at the

Note

At many colleges, you can create your own joint-degree program, combining a law degree with just about anything imaginable. If that kind of flexibility is important to you, make sure you choose schools that are willing to accommodate you.

Kaplan Tip

If clinical work is important to you, find out now how many clinics are offered by the schools you're considering—and how hard it is to get into these clinics.

local prosecutor's office. Internships are often overlooked by students who are afraid to veer from the traditional path. Yet they can be a welcome break from regular law studies and may also help in the later job search.

Computer Facilities and Law Library
Legal research is a big part of your three years in law school. Nothing will frustrate you more than to have a brief due the next day only to find that your library lacks essential volumes on the subject or that the few computers they have are either occupied or not working. If you make a visit to the law schools, check out their facilities. Again, don't be afraid to ask students for their opinions.

Where Can You Get In?

Let's turn to the second major question in the selection process: "Where do you have a chance of being accepted?"

Anyone who tells you that he can predict where you'll be accepted is fooling himself and, worse, fooling you. Stories of students accepted by a Harvard, Stanford, or Michigan only to be turned down by schools with far less glamorous reputations are common. Yet what is often overlooked is how well the process does work, considering the volume of applications and the amount of discretion exercised by admissions officers.

One reason the admissions process runs smoothly is that all law schools use the combined LSAT score and GPA as the most important determinant in making the decision. This provides a degree of consistency to the admissions process and gives the applicants some direction in deciding where to apply.

Those Legendary Law School Grids
Each year, Law Services publishes the *Official Guide to U.S. Law Schools* (the LSAT application booklet tells you how to order it). This guide includes a wealth of information on all the accredited law schools in the United States. The schools themselves provide most of the information for the book, including the LSAT scores and GPAs of the most recently admitted class. These are generally presented in grid form and are the single most valuable tool in determining your chances of being accepted at any particular law school. The grid shown here is a hypothetical grid, similar to the ones found in the *Guide.*

STATE UNIVERSITY LAW SCHOOL

LSAT Percentile Rank

GPA	< 40%	41–50%	51–60%	61–70%	71–80%	81–90%	91–99%
4–3.75	11/1	21/3	29/5	41/12	62/33	68/55	48/47
3.74–3.5	16/0	14/0	8/2	38/16	84/38	115/64	102/81
3.49–3.25	18/0	9/1	12/0	24/8	73/28	96/38	76/48
3.24–3.0	13/0	13/0	22/2	25/6	55/15	71/28	53/27
2.99–2.75	3/0	5/0	8/0	19/2	38/6	49/10	31/9
2.74–2.5	1/0	0/0	3/1	18/3	41/2	32/4	11/5
<2.5	1/0	1/0	3/0	9/1	9/0	6/2	3/1

Take a close look at the hypothetical grid above. Note that GPAs are divided into categories that drop .25 every line. Also note that LSAT scores are listed by percentile rank rather than by score. This is done because the scoring system for the LSAT was changed in 1991, and law schools still receive applications from students with scores under the old system. In order to use the grid, first find the line where your GPA fits in. Then read across until you find the percentage category of your existing or anticipated LSAT score. There you'll find two numbers, divided by a slash. The first number indicates the number of people in that range of LSAT scores and GPAs who applied to that school. The second number is the number accepted.

Most students apply to too few schools. According to Law Services, the average applicant applies to only about five schools. Admittedly, the cost of applications is rising, and sending out ten or more applications can result in an outlay of $500 or more. But keep in mind that if the cost of application presents a real hardship, most schools will waive the application fee—provided you give them a good, credible reason.

Kaplan Rules

Don't skimp on the number of applications you make. Yes, it's expensive, but this is one of the most important decisions you're likely to make in life. It pays to give yourself as much of a choice as possible.

Assembling a List of Schools

Using the grid numbers as a guide for determining your chances of acceptance, you should create a list of schools to apply to, dividing the list into three categories: preferred schools, competitive, and safe schools.

Preferred Schools

These are schools you'd *love* to attend, but your numbers indicate a less than 40 percent chance of admission. Apply to two or three schools in this group. Long-shots rarely pay off, but daydreaming about them is always nice.

Competitive Schools

Competitive (or "good fit") schools are those where your grid numbers are in the ballpark and where, depending on the rest of your application, you have a decent chance of getting admitted. These are schools where your numbers give you a 40–80 percent chance of admission. These are the schools on which you should focus most of your attention. Applying to four to seven schools in this group is reasonable and increases your odds of getting into at least one school where you are competitive.

"Safe" Schools

These schools are not high on your preference list, but your odds of admission are excellent there. Look at the grids and determine two or three schools where your chances of getting in appear to be 80 percent or better. One suggestion for this list would be to pick schools in locations that you particularly like.

Note: Students with low numbers may need to be a little more flexible and work a little harder. Be willing to travel a little farther to go to school. Also, look at schools in areas that aren't quite as popular or that tend to draw mostly local students. Sometimes the more expensive schools are applied to by fewer applicants and can be easier to get into.

Drawbacks to Using the Law School Grids

Although the grid system is very helpful, it does have its problems. Remember that the law schools provide the grids. Some schools take the opportunity to enhance their reputation by making their numbers seem higher than they really are. This is not done by lying, but rather by the schools' selectively using pertinent information to artificially enhance the numbers. If a school's numbers don't jibe with its reputation, be skeptical.

Second, because each category in a grid covers a fairly wide range of numbers (i.e., 10 LSAT percentile points or .25 GPA points), don't be fooled into thinking that your 3.51 and 71 percent put you on the same level as the student with the 3.74 and 79 percent, even though you fall in the same place on the grids. There are wide gaps in every category.

Third, many law schools—including some of the very best—do not provide Law Services with grids. However, these schools generally will tell you the average GPA and LSAT score for the previous year's entering class. If you want to get a picture of your chances at these schools, try determining which schools are similar in reputation. You can do so using the published ranking lists discussed earlier. Then determine which one of these schools comes closest in number of applications and size of the entering class to the school in question and use that grid.

Use the application list on the following page to plot out your law school application campaign.

APPLICATION LIST

Note: You should apply to at least eight schools.

Preferred Schools
Chances of admission 40 percent or less. Choose two or three.

1. _____

2. _____

3. _____

Competitive Schools
Chances of admission 40–80 percent. Choose four to seven.

1. _____

2. _____

3. _____

4. _____

5. _____

6. _____

7. _____

"Safe" Schools
Chances of admission 80 percent or greater. Choose two or three.

1. _____

2. _____

3. _____

CHAPTER NINE

When to Apply

- Find out why applying early is advantageous
- Set up an application schedule
- Complete the LSDAS checklist

With the explosion in the number of law school applications in the 1980s, law schools have had to make a number of adjustments. Foremost among them has been the lengthening of the application season and the move towards rolling admissions. Now let's see how these changes affect you.

Admission Schedules

Prior to the 1980s, the typical law school application season began in October or November with the mailing of the brochures and application forms. The schools would begin accepting applications in December or January and set a deadline for all applications to be completed by around March. Once all applications were received, the schools would begin the decision-making process, usually sending out acceptances or rejections in April, May, or June.

Kaplan Tip

Does it really pay to go to a lot of trouble to apply early? Yes, particularly in this era of rolling admissions. Start your campaign 18 months before you intend to step into your first law class.

Today, the scenario is quite different. Schools send out application forms in August and September, begin accepting applications in October, and start sending out acceptance letters by November. (As proof that they have a heart, most law schools will not begin sending out rejection letters until after the holiday season.) Application deadlines may still be in February or March, but because the schools have begun filling their classes in the fall, it is not unusual for more than 75 percent of the anticipated acceptance letters to have been sent by the spring deadline date. This is what's known as rolling admissions, which creates the scenario of unaware applicants who proudly deliver their applications on the deadline date only to find that they have put themselves at a distinct disadvantage.

The Advantages of Early Application

Does applying early really provide you with an advantage? The answer is a definitive yes! Here are the major reasons why.

Rising Index Numbers

The first reason has to do with index numbers. Your index number is based on the combination of your LSAT score and your GPA. At the beginning of the application process, most schools set an automatic admittance index number. Applicants whose index numbers surpass that figure are admitted quickly with only a cursory look at their application to confirm that they are not serial killers. At the beginning of the process, law schools are always afraid that they'll have too few applicants accepting their offers, which would mean less tuition money and almost certainly some complaints from the school's administrative office. Thus, they usually begin the application process by setting the automatic admittance index number on the low side. Then they gradually increase it as the admission season wears on and they discover that, their fears are unfounded.

Fewer Available Places

Because schools have a tendency to be a little more lenient early in the process, they begin reaching their admission goals fairly quickly. By February, the school may well have sent out more than 75 percent or more of all the acceptance letters it plans to send. Yet, at this point, all of the earlier applicants haven't been rejected. Instead many people are left hanging, just in case better applicants don't start coming through the system. This means that if you apply in March, you're now shooting for fewer possible positions, yet you're still competing against a fairly substantial pool of applicants.

At a Glance

LSAT Registration
- Online registration: www.lsac.org. Phone registration: (215) 968-1001. For a free copy of the *LSAT/LSDAS Registration and Information Book* or for more information, call the above number, or email: lsacinfo@lsac.org.
- Cost of exam (at press time): $96. Fee waivers available; contact LSAC for free copy of Fee Waiver Packet.
- Walk-in (day-of-test) registration is not permitted.
- You may register for no more than three LSATs in two years. Be aware that even cancellations count towards this limit.
- Register early to secure a particular testing site. Many sites are very popular and have limited seating.

The "Jading" Effect

If they are candid, admissions officers will admit that by the time they get to the two thousandth essay on "Why I want to go to law school," they're burned out, and more than a little jaded. Essays or applications that might have seemed noteworthy in the beginning now strike the reader as routine.

The Nay-Sayers

A handful of prelaw advisors and admissions officers dispute the importance of early applications, and at a few schools, there may indeed be no special advantage. Law schools are almost always open to exceptional applicants, and will sometimes admit someone well after the deadline if the student can give a good reason for the late application. Furthermore, a few schools routinely accept applications up until a week or two before classes start.

But these are exceptions. We became convinced of the importance of early applications while working with a student a few years ago. She hadn't taken the LSAT until December and was running late on her applications, barely making the deadline at the eight law schools to which she applied. Eventually she was rejected by seven of the schools and accepted by one. She decided to sit out a year and try again. The next time, she applied in November to the same eight schools, changed almost nothing on her application, and was accepted at five of the schools and wait-listed at two others. The only logical explanation was the timing of the application.

How Early Is Early?

For the most part, a pre-Halloween application is overdoing it. When schools are just gearing up, you run the risk of documents being misplaced. Pre-Thanksgiving is the preferable choice and assures that you'll be among the early entries. Shortly before Christmas is not as desirable, but should still hold you in good stead. After Christmas and the holidays, however, you're on the downside and may well find yourself among the last 30 percent of all applications received. And if you go with a post-Valentine's Day application—well, you'd better have strong numbers.

Remember that this discussion applies to the date on which your application is *complete*, not just the date on which the school receives your application forms. Applications are not considered complete until the LSAT score, LSDAS (Law School Data Assembly Service) reports, transcripts, and all recommendations have been received. Even though other people are sending these pieces, it's your responsibility to see that they arrive at the law school promptly. This does *not* mean calling the law school three times a week to see if they've arrived. It means prodding your recommenders or your college to send in the necessary documentation. Explain to them the importance of early applications.

At a Glance

LSDAS organizes, analyzes, and summarizes biographical and academic information about school applicants, to provide a single, standard format for schools to compare candidates directly to one another. LSDAS provides member law schools with a single standard report with LSAT scores (including average), a normalized GPA, copies of college transcripts, and LSAT writing sample. The LSDAS service is mandatory.

- Cost (at press time): $95 for a twelve-month subscription to LSDAS.
- You sign up for LSDAS at the same time that you register for the LSAT. You will need to have your college transcripts forwarded to LSDAS.
- LSDAS sends your application, scores, transcripts, and writing sample to each school you apply to. You do not have to specify the number of schools you will be applying to when you sign up for the LSDAS, but if you do you will save some money.
- Check your college transcripts and your LSDAS files for accuracy.
- LSDAS sends you monthly updates on which schools have received your records.

Kaplan Tip

Use the application schedule/checklist at the end of this chapter to keep yourself on track. Check it often to make sure you're not letting an important deadline pass.

When to Start

If you want to have a complete application at the law schools by, say, late November, you can't start planning just a few weeks in advance. Your campaign for admission should begin five or six months before that deadline—i.e., eighteen months before your first day as a law student. We've included, at the end of this section, a schedule that you can use to organize your campaign. As you'll see, you should plan to devote plenty of time to your applications the summer before they're due.

Here are some of the important things to do each season. For convenience, let's assume that you want to go to law school the fall after you graduate from college.

Spring of Junior Year

Your first step should be to register for the June LSAT. You won't need your LSAT score for a while yet, but if you take the June test and bomb out, you'll be able to retake the test in October. Get a copy of the *LSAT/LSDAS Registration and Information Book* at any local college or law school admissions office or at any Kaplan Center. The registration booklet will tell you not only about the LSAT but also about the LSDAS. The LSDAS is the organization that will be sending your LSAT scores and transcripts to the law schools you apply to. You'll want LSDAS to open a file on you as early as possible. The book will explain exactly how to do this and how much it will cost (yes, they charge for their mandatory services).

It's a good idea to buy the *Official Guide to U.S. Law Schools*, which contains those grids we talked about, as well as other information about American law schools. If you can't find it in your local bookstore, you can order it from LSDAS.

The Summer Before Senior Year

Start thinking about a "theme" for your application, which can serve as a way to stand out from the crowd and as an organizing principle for personal statements, recommendations, and everything else in your file. Think about how you'd like to be identified. As the environmentalist who plays oboe recitals for the local recycling center? Of course, you don't *have* to have a theme, but any kind of "high concept" will help your application stick in the minds of admissions officers. You should also be assembling your list of schools at this point. Visit as many of them as you can. Send for their catalogues and applications.

Early Fall of Senior Year

This is when the action really starts. Applications will start arriving. (In filling them out, follow the procedures outlined in the "How to Apply" chapter.) Line up your recommenders. Make sure they have everything they need to write you a great letter. (More on how to do so in the "How to Apply" chapter.) Take the October LSAT, if you've decided to do so. Revise your personal statement. Revise it again. And again.

Late Fall of Senior Year

Complete and submit your applications. Prod recommenders so that your applications are complete before Thanksgiving.

Applying to law school is a time-consuming process that tests your organizational skills and your attention to detail. Students who believe that they can simply plot out four hours on a weekend to complete this ordeal are kidding themselves. Plan to set aside some big blocks of time well in advance to work intensively on this important step in achieving your admission goals.

An Ideal Law School Application Schedule

Your campaign for law school admission should start up to eighteen months before you step into your first law classroom. Here's a schedule of what you should be doing when:

Spring of Junior Year

❑ Get the *Official Guide to U.S. Law Schools*.
❑ Register for the June LSAT (you can retake it in October if you blow it).
❑ Prepare for the LSAT.
❑ Subscribe to LSDAS (they take care of sending your transcript and LSAT scores to each school you apply to).

Summer Before Senior Year

❑ Take the June LSAT.
❑ Start drafting your personal statement.
❑ Think about whom you'll be asking for recommendations.
❑ Make a list of schools you'll be applying to, using the grids from the *Official Guide* as an aid.
❑ Send away for applications, and start visiting as many schools as you can.
❑ Register for the October LSAT if you're not satisfied with your June score.

Early Fall of Senior Year

❑ Familiarize yourself with the applications as they roll in.
❑ Make a checklist and schedule for each application, and photocopy all forms.
❑ Send transcript request forms to all undergraduate and graduate schools you've attended.
❑ Line up your recommendation writers. Give them the specific info they need to write an outstanding recommendation of you.
❑ Revise your personal statement. Tailor it to specific essay topics, if any, on individual applications.

Midfall of Senior Year

❑ Finalize your personal statements.
❑ Transfer application information from the photocopies to the actual application forms.
❑ Make sure your recommendation writers are on board.
❑ Take the October LSAT (if necessary).
❑ Send in your applications. (Make sure you don't mix up the mailings!)

Late Fall of Senior Year

❑ Remind your recommendation writers to send in recommendations ASAP.
❑ Get Master Law School Report from LSDAS, summarizing transcripts, etcetera.

Winter and Spring/Summer after Senior Year

❑ Receive monthly updates from LSDAS, telling you which schools your records have been sent to.
❑ Cross your fingers while you wait for the acceptances to roll in.
❑ Decide which offer to accept.
❑ Send in acceptance.
❑ Apply for financial aid.

Fall after Graduation

❑ Start your first semester at the law school of your choice.

LSDAS CHECKLIST

❑ Get the *LSAT/LSDAS Registration and Information Book*.
To order a free copy, call LSAC at (215) 968-1001, or email your request to lsacinfo@lsac.org.
The book is also available at law school admission offices and prelaw adviser offices.

❑ Subscribe to LSDAS by completing the registration form in the *Registration and Information Booklet*.
Parts A, C, and D apply to LSDAS.
You can subscribe to LSDAS on the same form you use to register for the LSAT.
Again, don't forget to sign the form and send payment!

❑ Use transcript request forms (they're in the *Information Book*) to request transcripts from all undergraduate and graduate institutions you've attended.
They will send transcripts directly to LSDAS.

❑ Receive LSDAS Subscription Confirmation.

❑ Receive Master Law School Report—summarizing your academic information.
They get sent shortly after LSDAS receives your transcripts.
Check it carefully; report any inaccuracies to Law Services.

❑ If you've decided to apply to more schools than you originally planned to, order extra reports from LSDAS and pay an additional fee.

❑ Receive monthly reports from LSDAS.
Check them for accuracy or discrepancies.

❑ If necessary, renew your LSDAS subscription after twelve months.

CHAPTER TEN

How to Apply

HIGHLIGHTS

- Learn how to create a winning application package
- Review the do's and don'ts of personal statements
- Know the characteristics of a good recommendation
- Complete the application checklist

After you've made the decision to apply to law school and have decided where and when to apply, you need to order the application forms from the various schools you've chosen. This can be done by mail, but the quickest way is just to call the admissions offices around July and get put on their mailing lists. Once the applications begin arriving (usually around Labor Day) you'll notice one thing quickly: *no two applications are exactly alike.* Some require one recommendation, others two or three. Some ask you to write one essay or personal statement, while others may ask for two or even three. Some have very detailed forms requiring extensive background information; others are satisfied with your name and address and very little else.

Despite these differences, most applications follow a general pattern with variations on the same kinds of questions. So although not all of this section is relevant to all parts of every application, these guidelines will be valuable for just about any law school application you'll encounter.

Note

No two law school applications are exactly alike, but most ask for the same kind of information and look for the same qualities in the applicant. You won't be writing ten different applications so much as ten variations on a single application.

Kaplan Tip

Start thinking early about what theme you want your application to convey. Decide what your real purpose is in applying to law school, and make sure that this sense of purpose comes through in all aspects of your application.

For instance, is it your goal to pursue environmental law? If so, give your entire application an environmental theme. Do some volunteer work for a local recycling organization (and make sure to list that activity on your application form); ask the head of the same organization to write a recommendation for you; use the personal statement to discuss your involvement in the organization's various causes. All of these efforts will give your application coherence and a sense of purpose—and help it stick in the minds of the admissions officers.

Kaplan Rules

You control how you are perceived by the admissions committee—through your application. You can't afford to miss a single opportunity in the application process to make yourself seem desirable as a law student. And the first step is *getting organized.*

The Application as Marketing Tool

The most important thing to keep in mind about your law school application is that it is, above all else, a sales pitch. The application is your single best opportunity to sell yourself. Remember, every person who applies will have strengths and weaknesses. It's how you *present* those strengths and weaknesses that counts. *You* are in control of what that admissions committee sees on your application and how they see it.

So what's the best way to sell yourself? We all know that some people are natural-born sellers in person, but the application process is written, not spoken. The key here is not natural talent but rather organization—carefully planning a coherent presentation from beginning to end and paying attention to every detail in between. But be careful not to focus so much on the overall theme that you neglect the details. That can be disastrous.

Getting Organized

You must first put together a checklist of the forms that each of your chosen schools requires, double-checking to make sure you don't overlook anything. Some schools may require you to fill out residency forms or financial aid forms in addition to the regular application forms. Don't ignore these and put them off until last. Schools may require proof of residency or income verifications that you might not have readily available.

Next, make photocopies of all forms before you complete them. Changes and corrections will have to be made no matter how careful you are. These changes should not be made on the original form, which will go to the school. Almost every admissions officer we have spoken with explicitly prizes neatness. The feeling is that if the application is sloppily prepared, the student is not very serious about attending that law school. Work on your photocopied rough draft until you are sure you are ready to transfer to the original application.

The Application Form

For the most part, filling out the application form requires simply putting down factual information. But even in something so apparently mindless, you can still make sure you present yourself as a thorough, organized person who can follow directions.

The key to filling out the application form can be summed up in a single sentence: *Don't make the admissions officers do more work than they have to.* Make sure that they have all of the information they need at their fingertips. If they have to hunt down your statistics, if your application is full of unexplained blanks, if they can't read what you've written—all of these things will just serve to annoy the very people you want to impress.

One key to not annoying the admissions people is to make sure you answer *all* of the questions asked on the application form. If some questions don't seem to apply to you, type in "not applicable"; leave nothing blank. If the admissions officers see blank spaces, they don't know whether you found the question not applicable, just didn't want to answer it, or overlooked it. Many schools will return the application if even a single question is left blank. This can be a real problem, because it may be a month or more before the application is looked at and returned and then filled in and looked at again. That kind of delay can easily turn an early application into a late one.

Along these same lines, don't answer questions by saying *see above* or *see line 22*. Most applications will ask you for things like your address or phone number more than once. Go ahead and fill them in again. Remember that law schools are flooded with documentation and may separate parts of the application. They don't appreciate having to find what you wrote back on line 22 if they've asked you for that information again on line 55.

As long as we're talking about practices that annoy the decision makers, another is the failure to follow directions on the forms. If the form says, "Don't write below this line," then don't write below the line. You are not an exception to this rule. If they ask for an explanation in 150 words or less, then don't give them 300 words. One admissions officer remarked that the comment, "He couldn't even follow directions," is heard several times a year in committee meetings.

Addendums

An important part of the application form will not be in the package sent from the law school. These are your addendums. Addendums (or *addenda*, if you want to be fancy) are the additional page or pages that you staple onto the forms when the space they give you to answer a question is too small.

This is where an addendum comes in. Simply write "continued on addendum" on the application form after you've used their space up, and then clearly mark what you are listing at the top of the addendum. Staple this addendum at the back, and you've solved a tricky problem. Law schools appreciate addendums because they're much neater than attempts to cram things into a limited space—*and* they show careful organization. But don't overdo it. One or two addendums should be sufficient for any application.

Kaplan Tip

A sloppy application says more about you than you may think. Law schools want people who display organization and care in *all* of their endeavors. So put in the extra time to make sure your application is neat and free of typos.

Kaplan Rules

Admissions officers are human beings. They're overworked. They've got piles of applications on their desks. Many of them will be looking for any little excuse to reject yours and get on to the next one. Don't give them that excuse. Make sure that nothing about your application is annoying to them.

Addendums can be used to preserve neatness when the application blanks are of insufficient length. But they can also be helpful if an answer requires further explanation. For example, if you won the Grant R. Humphrey Science award, it's not enough just to list it. You need to explain what it is, what it's given for, and possibly how many others were competing for it or how prestigious it is.

Honesty

One final topic about the application form that needs to be discussed is honesty. If you think you can get by with a lie or two on your application—well, you may be right. Law schools as a rule don't have the resources to verify all aspects of every application. But before you go overboard and decide to put down that you were once the Prince of Wales, you should realize that you're taking a big chance.

First of all, many schools are beginning to devote more time to checking up on applicants' claims. Recently, the president of an undergraduate prelaw society told us that she regularly gets calls from law schools verifying membership of applicants. Secondly, there's always the chance that, if you lie, some other part of your application will contradict the lie and get you booted.

Finally, even if you fool the law school, get in, and graduate with honors, you'll find that any state in which you apply to take the bar exam will do a much more extensive background check than that done by the law school. This check very well might include looking for contradictions in your law school application. Lying on your law school application, in fact, is considered grounds for refusing admittance to a state bar.

Additional Points

Here are a few more things to take note of when filling out the application form:

Be sure to type the application from start to finish. A surprising number of applicants still handwrite the application—something that, according to admissions officers, costs you dearly.

Don't use application forms from previous years. Most applications change from year to year, often substantially. Also, don't use other school's forms because you lost the form of the school you're applying to (yes, people have done that, believe it or not).

Staple extra sheets to the forms. Don't use paper clips unless told to do so. Paper clips—and the pages they attach—tend to get lost.

Always double- and triple-check your application for spelling errors. You lose a certain amount of credibility if you write that you were a "Roads Scholar."

Check for accidental contradictions. Make sure that your application doesn't say you worked for a law firm in 1997 when your financial aid forms say you were driving a cab that year.

Prioritize all lists. When a question asks you to list your honors or awards, don't begin with fraternity social chairman and end with Phi Beta Kappa. Let the admissions committee know that you realize what's important—that is, always list significant scholastic accomplishments first.

Craft your list of extracurricular activities. Don't list every event or every activity you ever participated in. Select the most significant and, if necessary, explain them.

Don't mention high school activities or honors. Unless there's something very unusual or spectacular about your high school background, don't mention it, even if it means you don't take note of the fact that you were senior class president.

Clear up any ambiguities. On questions concerning employment, for instance, make sure to specify whether you held a job during the school year or only during the summer. Many applications ask about this, and it may be an important point to the admissions officer.

The Personal Statement

There are about as many theories on what constitutes a winning personal statement as there are theories on the Kennedy assassination—and, unfortunately, many of them have about the same validity. To begin with, how can you tell 85,000 annual applicants with 85,000 different personalities and backgrounds that there is one correct way to write a personal statement? Furthermore, if even a small percentage of those applicants read and come to believe that a certain way is the correct way, it automatically becomes incorrect, because law schools despise getting personal statements that are familiar—that are, in other words, *im*personal.

For that reason, this section on personal statements has been broken down into two parts. First, we'll look at the procedure of putting together a personal statement. Then we'll look at a list of DOs and DON'Ts that admission officers most frequently mention.

Kaplan Rules

When juggling several applications at once, it's easy to make careless mistakes. Double-check yourself at every step.

Note

Next to your numbers, your personal statement is probably the most important part of your application, particularly at the top schools (where so many applicants have great numbers).

Putting Together an Outstanding Personal Statement

Next to your LSAT score and GPA, the personal statement is probably the most important part of your application. If your numbers are excellent or very poor, the essay may get only a cursory glance. But if your numbers place you on the borderline at a school, then it may very well make the difference between acceptance and rejection.

What Kind of Essay to Write

The personal statement is exactly what its name implies—a statement by you that is meant to show something about your personality and character. But that doesn't mean you are to create a lengthy essay detailing every aspect of your life since birth. Nor is the personal statement intended to be a psychological profile describing all of your character attributes and flaws. Several admissions officers have said that the best essays are often only remotely related to the applicant. The point is that you need not write an in-depth personality profile baring your innermost soul. Admissions officers are adept at learning what they want to know about you from your essay, even if it doesn't contain the words *me, myself,* and *I* in every sentence.

One exception, however, should be noted. Although most schools still provide wide latitude in their directions about what the personal statement should be about, some schools are becoming more specific. The problem with specific requirements like these is that you may well have to write a separate essay for that school alone. Be sure to check the instructions carefully and follow them closely. If a law school asks for a specific type of essay and you provide them with a more general one, they'll likely feel that you're not very interested in attending that particular school.

But take heart. Most schools provide few restrictions on what you can write about, so unless you're very unlucky, you should be able to limit the number of essays you must write to two or three.

How Long an Essay to Write

How long should the personal statement be? Some schools place a word limit on the essay; others specify one or two typed pages. Always follow the specific directions, but you should be in good shape with virtually all schools if your essay is one and a half to two pages in length.

Writing the Essay

The personal statement shouldn't be done overnight. A strong personal statement may take shape over the course of months and require several different drafts. One practice that many have found particularly effective is to write a draft and then let it sit for four to six weeks. If you leave it

Kaplan Tip

Your reader might not find your life quite as fascinating as you do, so be careful not to go on at length. A boring personal statement is a good excuse to toss an application onto the "No" pile.

Kaplan Tip

Start drafting your personal statement now, so that you'll be able to put it aside for a few weeks or even months. You'll be amazed at how different it will look when you go back to it.

alone for a significant period of time, you may find that your first instincts were good ones. On the other hand, you may shudder at how you could ever have considered submitting such a piece of garbage. Either way, time lends a valuable perspective.

Try to start the essay sometime during the summer before you apply. Allow at least three months to write it, and don't be afraid to take it through numerous drafts or overhaul it completely if you're not satisfied. Get several different perspectives. Ask close friends or relatives to scrutinize it to see if it really captures what you want to convey. Be sure to ask them about their initial reaction as well as their feelings after studying it more carefully. Once you've achieved a draft that you feel comfortable with, try to have it read by some people who barely know you or who don't know you at all. If certain criticisms are consistently made, then they're probably legitimate. But don't be carried away by every suggestion every reader makes. Stick to your basic instincts because, after all, this is *your* personal statement, no one else's.

Proofreading is of critical importance. Again, don't be afraid to enlist the aid of others. If possible, let an English teacher review the essay solely for spelling and grammar mistakes.

Essay Content

As stated earlier, there's no one correct way to write an essay, but admissions officers do provide some helpful tips about what they like and don't like to see in a personal statement. Let's begin with a list of the things that officers most often mentioned they disliked seeing.

Personal Statement DON'Ts

Don't turn your personal statement into a résumé. This is the personal statement that begins at birth and simply recites every major (and sometimes minor) event of the person's life. Most of this information is repetitive since it's included on other parts of the application. But worse than that, it's just a boring format.

Avoid the "why I want to go to law school" essay. Although this can be a *part* of any law school essay, too many people make it the entire focus of their statement. The problem is that there are not many new variations on this theme, and the admissions officers have likely heard them all before, probably many times.

Avoid talking about your negatives. The personal statement is not the place to call attention to your flaws. Don't forget that you're selling yourself, and the personal statement is your most prominent sales tool.

Don't be too personal. Stories of abuse or trauma are often very moving and can be particularly effective if tied into a person's reason for

Kaplan Tip

Try to let as many people as possible read and comment on your personal statement. But don't be swayed by everything that every person says. Listen to all comments, but only take them to heart if you really think they're valid.

Kaplan Tip

Admissions officers read about a lot of noble intentions in personal statements. Naturally, they're skeptical of such claims, especially if the rest of your application demonstrates no such selfless impulse. So be careful with protestations of high ideals. If you can't back them up with hard evidence, they're bound to come off sounding empty and insincere.

wanting to practice law. Several admissions officers, however, have noted a trend towards describing such problems in graphic detail in personal statements. This kind of confessional essay can easily cross the line and become too personal.

Don't discuss legal concepts. Along those same lines, don't try to impress the reader with how much you already know about the law. The school assumes that they can teach you what you need to know, regardless of the level at which you start. By discussing a legal concept, you also run the risk of showing a certain amount of ignorance about the subject while at the same time appearing arrogant enough to have tried to discuss it.

Don't put down lawyers or the legal profession. Although it may seem that spewing cynicism about the legal profession is a clever device, trust us when we tell you that it isn't. Once you become a member of the legal profession, you can make as many lawyer jokes as you want. Until then, watch your step.

Don't try to cover too many subjects. Focus on one or two areas you really want to talk about. One of the worst mistakes applicants make is writing essays that ramble from one subject to another and back again. Fight the desire to talk about every highlight of your life.

Now that you've got a sense of what not to do in your personal statement, let's turn to a list of suggestions for things that you *should* do.

Personal Statement DOs

Tell stories. Readers respond much better to a concrete story or illustrative anecdote than to an abstract list of your attributes. Instead of just writing how determined you are, for instance, tell a story that demonstrates it. Stories stick in people's memories. The same holds true when you're trying to make sure the admissions officers remember you.

Be funny—if you can pull it off. Humor, particularly self-deprecating humor, is a very effective device. Admissions officers appreciate occasional flashes of irony. However, be careful in your use of humor. Don't overdo it—a couple of funny lines or a funny story can be great, but include too many jokes and you start to sound flippant. Finally, think about using *self-deprecating* humor. Law schools often complain about the lack of humility among students and appreciate those who show some.

Be unique. The term *unique* has been overused. Even some applications now ask you to describe what is unique about you. Applicants rack their brains trying to figure out how they're different from the other 5,000 people applying to that law school. Or worse, some interpret *unique* to mean disadvantaged and rack their brains trying to think how they have suffered more than others. But what the admissions officers want to know is what qualities or experiences in your life would make you a particularly valuable member of a law school class.

Start strong. In private moments, admissions officers will often admit that they don't read every essay carefully. They may just glance at an essay to get a general impression. That's why it's important to grab them from the beginning. Tell the ending of a story first and make them want to read on, to see how it all started, for example.

The above points are as much general advice as one can responsibly give about the personal statement in a book such as this. We hope that they'll provide you with some ideas or keep you from making some costly mistakes. In the end, however, it *is* a personal statement, and it must come from you.

Recommendations

During the last ten years, as law school applications have increased dramatically and the odds against being accepted at any particular school have increased, applicants have taken various approaches to stand out from the crowd. Too often overlooked in this mad pursuit, however, is one of the very best ways for an applicant to stand out—that is, by getting terrific, vividly written recommendations.

Because so many recommendations tend to be blasé, an outstanding recommendation that goes beyond the standard language can really make an applicant stand out. Not only does such a recommendation serve the purpose of pointing out an applicant's strengths, it also shows that the recommender thought enough of the person to put time and effort into carefully writing it.

What Makes a Recommendation Outstanding?
Outstanding recommendations can vary in format, but there are several qualities they all tend to have in common.

An Outstanding Recommendation Must Be Personal
By far the most common mistake made by applicants is believing that the prestige or position of the recommender is more important than what that person writes. Admissions officers tend to treat recommendations

from senators, governors, and chief executive officers of major corporations with a great deal of skepticism, because very few applicants have a truly personal relationship with such people. To make matters worse, these officials tend to respond with very standard recommendations that rarely offer any real insight into the applicant's character; in a worst-case scenario, they may even be computer-generated.

Find people who truly know you and are able to make an honest assessment of your capabilities. This means that it may be better to have the teaching assistant with whom you had daily contact write the recommendation, rather than the prestigious professor you spoke to once during the year.

An Outstanding Recommendation Compares You to Others

When an admissions officer reads a recommendation, he or she often has to put into perspective the meaning of overused phrases—such as *hardworking* and *quick mind*—as they relate to the applicant. A much better format, and one that admissions officers appreciate, is the comparison recommendation, one that compares the applicant to other people that the recommendation writer previously knew in the same position, or (in a best-case scenario) to people he or she has known who are alumnae of that particular law school.

An Outstanding Recommendation Tells Stories

A concrete and specific recommendation stands out. Rather than merely listing attributes, a good recommendation engages the reader by telling an insightful story about the applicant. Recently, a professor of political science chose not to submit the standard phrase about what a quick study a student was. Instead, he related a story about the student in class. It seems the professor introduced a new and difficult concept in class that the student discussed intelligently and actually took further than the professor was prepared to do. That kind of story sticks in a reader's mind.

An Outstanding Recommendation Focuses on Scholastic Abilities

Although recommendations often cover a lot of ground, from the applicant's attitudes about school to his or her personality traits, admissions officers focus on comments about a person's scholastic ability. Obviously, this means that a strong recommendation from a professor carries a great deal of weight. However, a lot of people are in a position to observe a person's intellectual aptitude. Employers, friends, clergy, and workers at volunteer agencies are all usually able to discuss an applicant's scholastic abilities—and should.

Kaplan Rules

Beware of the impersonal recommendation. It's a definite red flag to the admissions officer. Better to have a recommendation written by a lab assistant who knows you well rather than the Nobel-winning professor who doesn't remember your name.

An Outstanding Recommendation Will Contain Some Negative Comments
In many ways, this is the trickiest area of writing a recommendation, yet it can also prove to be a vital component. A recommendation that is only laudatory, failing to mention a single negative thing about an applicant, may lose credibility. By pointing out a small character flaw or a potential weakness, the recommender gains credibility with the admissions officers and tends to make them less skeptical about the preceding positive comments.

One word of caution, though: Admissions officers universally hate "fake" negatives—for example, "If Suzy has one fault, it is that she works just too darn hard." Much more appreciated are such comments as, "Joe can afford to improve his attention to detail." Combined with effusive praise for the applicant's strong points, this sort of comment impresses admissions officers as being straightforward and helpful.

How to Ensure You Receive Outstanding Recommendations
Now that you know what makes for an outstanding recommendation, all you have to do is ensure that each of your recommenders produces one. While you can't actually write the recommendations yourself, you *can* have a great deal of influence over how accurate and persuasive they are.

Choose the Right People to Recommend You
What are the qualities of a good recommender? Obviously, you should choose someone who likes you and who thinks you're good at what you do. This doesn't mean that you have to be intimate pals, but sworn enemies don't often write good recommendations. It helps if the person is a good writer so that he or she can clearly express an opinion about you.

Most, if not all, of your recommendations for academic programs should come from professors or other academic faculty. If you've been out of school for a few years and haven't kept in touch with your professors, call or write the admissions offices of the schools to which you're applying. Don't assume that it's okay to send fewer letters than required or to substitute other kinds of information for recommendation letters. Most likely, schools will allow you to submit recommendations from employers or from other nonacademic people with knowledge about your background, skills, and goals.

Balance Your List of Recommendation Writers
Three professors from your undergrad major department probably will have similar things to say about you, so why not include someone from another field who can speak to your thinking and writing skills?

Kaplan Rules

Discrepancies between your personal statement and a recommendation can undermine the credibility of your entire application. Make sure your recommendation writers know who you are and what you're about.

Kaplan Rules

When asked whether you want to see what your recommendation writers have written about you, *say no!* If admissions officers know that you'll be seeing your recommendations, they'll discount much of what is said in them.

Kaplan Tip

Try to set up an appointment with each of your recommenders—to make sure they're up to speed on who you are and what you're all about.

Kaplan Rules

Be diplomatic. Make sure you let your recommendation writers know what *kind* of things you'd love their recommendations to contain. But be careful not to create the impression that you're manipulating them. It could easily backfire.

Be Considerate of Your Recommendation Writers

As soon as you decide to go to law school, you should start sizing up potential recommenders and letting them know that you may ask them for a letter. This will give each plenty of time to get to know you better and to think about what to say in the letter. Once they've agreed, let them know about deadlines with plenty of lead time to avoid potential scheduling conflicts. The more time they have, the better the job they'll do recommending you.

Make Sure Your Recommendation Writers Know What They Need to Know

Once someone has agreed to consider writing a letter for you, you should arrange an appointment to discuss your background and goals for your future. If you live thousands of miles away from your recommender, arrange a telephone appointment.

Bring to the appointment copies of appropriate documentation such as your transcript, papers you've written, your résumé or curriculum vitae, your personal statement, and a sheet of bullet points that you plan to feature in your application and essay. Supply the appropriate form or forms, as well as stamped, addressed envelopes and a copy of your home address and phone number.

Keep the appointment relatively brief—you're already taking up enough of their time. Give your recommenders a good idea of why you want to go to law school. Play up your good points, of course, but be reasonably humble. If you have a very specific "marketing" image that you're trying to project, let your recommenders in on it—they may want to focus on some of the same points you're trying to stress. But don't tell your recommenders what to write—don't even give them the impression that you're doing so! Recommenders tend to resent any attempts at manipulation, and may, as a consequence, refuse to write your letter. What recommenders *do* appreciate, however, is some direction as to what you'd like to see.

Keep Your Recommendation Writers on Schedule

Finally, make sure your recommenders know how important it is to complete the letters as early as possible. If they procrastinate, gently remind them that their deadline is approaching and be sure to remind them of the importance of early applications.

Common Questions About Recommendations

Here are other points about recommendations that should be considered.

How Long Should a Recommendation Be?

Like the personal statement, the recommendation should be short and concise. A one-page recommendation is usually sufficient. In any case, it should be no longer than two to two and a half pages.

Should I Request to Look at the Recommendation?

Easy answer—NO! Almost all schools have a box you check to indicate whether or not you would like to be able to see the recommendation once it's provided to the school. Just say no! If the school believes that the recommender cannot be completely honest for fear of offending the applicant, the school will heavily discount what is written, no matter how laudatory.

Can I Send More Recommendations Than the School Requests?

Be careful. Law schools may request anywhere from one to four recommendations from an applicant (the recent trend is towards fewer recommendations). Invariably, the situation arises in which a student has three good recommendations, but the school only asks for two. Some schools are very specific in their instructions that they will not accept more than the exact number requested. If the application doesn't spell out how the school handles it, call the school and ask to make sure.

Should I Use the Letter of Recommendation Service?

The Letter of Recommendation Service is set up by Law Services as a convenience. Basically, the service allows your recommenders to send letters to LSAC, who then forwards them to the law schools. Note that the same letter is sent to each school, and so school-specific letters should not be sent through this service. For more information, check out the latest *LSAT/LSDAS Information Book*, or contact your target schools to see if they prefer that you use the service.

A Final Check

After you've completed everything and are getting ready to place it in a manila envelope and mail it, make sure you go through one more time and check each document. Law schools frequently receive documents that were intended to go to another law school. With all of this paperwork, it's easy to see how that can happen, and the law schools expect a certain amount of it. However, it can be embarrassing if you've written in your personal statement that ABC Law School is the one and only place for you—and then you accidentally send it to XYZ Law School instead.

Kaplan Rules

Don't send videos or pictures of yourself with the application (unless you're specifically asked to). The admissions officers usually aren't terribly interested in what you look and sound like.

APPLICATION CHECKLIST

The three major parts of your law school application:

1. The application form
2. The personal statement
3. Recommendations

The Application Form
❑ Working photocopies of applications made
❑ Information/addresses/other data gathered
❑ Addendums (if any) written
❑ Information transferred to actual application
❑ Application proofread
❑ Final check done

The Personal Statement
❑ Theme finalized
❑ Readers selected and notified
❑ First draft written
❑ Self-evaluation made
❑ Second draft written
❑ Comments from readers received
❑ Final draft written
❑ Final statement proofread

Recommendations
❑ Recommendation writers chosen
❑ Recommendation writers on board
❑ Informational meeting with recommendation writers conducted
❑ Reminders to all recommendation writers sent

❑ Notice of complete application received

How Did We Do? Grade Us.

Thank you for choosing a Kaplan book. Your comments and suggestions are very useful to us. Please answer the following questions to assist us in our continued development of high-quality resources to meet your needs.

The title of the Kaplan book I read was: _____

My name is: _____

My address is: _____

_____

My e-mail address is: _____

What overall grade would you give this book?   (A)   (B)   (C)   (D)   (F)

How relevant was the information to your goals?   (A)   (B)   (C)   (D)   (F)

How comprehensive was the information in this book?   (A)   (B)   (C)   (D)   (F)

How accurate was the information in this book?   (A)   (B)   (C)   (D)   (F)

How easy was the book to use?   (A)   (B)   (C)   (D)   (F)

How appealing was the book's design?   (A)   (B)   (C)   (D)   (F)

What were the book's strong points? _____

How could this book be improved? _____

Is there anything that we left out that you wanted to know more about?

Would you recommend this book to others?   ☐ YES   ☐ NO

Other comments: _____

_____

_____

Do we have permission to quote you?   ☐ YES   ☐ NO

Thank you for your help.
Please tear out this page and mail it to:

Managing Editor
Kaplan, Inc.
1440 Broadway, 8th floor
New York, NY 10018

KAPLAN®

Thanks!

You've prepared for the LSAT...
NOW
prepare for
Law School

CD-ROM Installation and Technical Support

Congratulations! You've purchased the best test-prep software on the market, the software that's more fun than an abacus and more educational than an overhead projector. Kaplan's CD-ROM is the most comprehensive, instructive, and entertaining software product in the field of test prep to arrive since . . . well, since the dawn of humankind!

In this software, you get:

- Interactive lessons detailing the famed Kaplan approaches to each question type
- Full-Length and Practice Tests, so that you can try out your new skills as you move through the sessions (remember, Practice Test One appears both in the book and on the CD—your choice!)
- Your own personalized study plan based on your needs
- A writing sample area
- Invaluable admissions information and more!

This CD provides the tools that will help you devise your own personal test-taking plan. Each test you take is closely analyzed, with detailed feedback on your strategic performance. Naturally, every question comes with a complete explanation. And our detailed scoring charts will track your progress on every type of question. Only Kaplan offers this range of features essential for successful test performance.

Installation Instructions

1. Start your PC and Windows.
2. Insert the *Higher Score* CD into the CD-ROM drive.
3. From the Start menu, choose RUN and type d:\lstsetup.exe (where d: is your CD-ROM drive).

Please note: This CD-ROM is Windows-compatible only.

Tech Support

For additional technical assistance, please visit the "Customer Service" area of our website at *www.kaptest.com*.

Copyright and Permission Notices

Most reading passages in these tests, as on the actual LSAT, are condensed and adapted from published material. The ideas contained in them do not necessarily represent the opinions of Kaplan, Inc. To make the text suitable for testing purposes, we may in some cases have altered the style or emphases of the original.

Kaplan, Inc. wishes to thank the following for permission to reprint excerpts from published material used with test questions appearing herein:

"Adaptive Management: Learning from the Columbia River Basin Fish and Wildlife Program," by Kai N. Lee and Jody Lawrence, *Environmental Law*, vol. 16, no. 3, Spring 1986. Reprinted with permission of *Environmental Law*.

"The Evolutionary Tradition in Jurisprudence," by E. Donald Elliot. *Columbia Law Review* 38 (1985). Copyright © 1985. Reprinted with permission of *Columbia Law Review*.

"Black Power and the Transformation from Protest to Politics," by Robert C. Smith. Reprinted with permission of *Political Science Quarterly*, 96 (Fall 1981), pp. 431–443.

"Extremist Speech and the Paradox of Tolerance—a Review of Lee C. Bollinger's 'The Tolerant Society: Freedom of Speech and Extremist Speech in America'," by Michael Rosenfeld, *Harvard Law Review*, Vol. 100, no. 6, June 1987. Reprinted with permission of the President and Fellows of Harvard College, 1988.

"Law and the Innovative Process: Preliminary Reflections," by Aryeh S. Friedman. Reprinted by permission of the author and *Columbia Business Law Review*, volume 1986, number 1.

"Licensure of Health Care Professionals: The Consumer's Case for Abolition," by Charles H. Baron. Reprinted with permission from *American Journal of Law and Medicine*, vol. 9, no. 3. Copyright © 1983 by American Society of Law and Medicine, Boston, Massachusetts.

"Must Virtue Be Taught?" by Thomas D. Eissele, originally printed in *The Journal of Legal Education*, vol. 37, December 1987. Copyright © 1987.

"Reforming Environmental Regulation: Three Modest Proposals," by Paul R. Portney, *Columbia Journal of Environmental Law*, vol. 13: 201–215 (1988). Reprinted with permission of *Columbia Journal of Environmental Law*.

"The Republic Reborn by Steven Watts, " by Fred Anderson, *American Historical Review*, vol. 94, no. 2 (April 1989), p. 516. Reprinted with permission of *American Historical Review*.

"Social Policy and the Welfare of Black Americans: From Rights to Resources," by Charles V. Hamilton, *Political Science Quarterly*, vol. 101, no. 2, 1986. Reprinted with permission of *Political Science Quarterly*.

Excerpt from *Sacred Groves and Ravaged Gardens*, by Louise Westling, The University of Georgia Press, 1985.

"The Wages of Sex: The Uses and Limits of Comparable Worth," by Paul Weiler, *Harvard Law Review*, Vol. 99: 1728 (1986). Reprinted with permission of *Harvard Law Review* and Paul Weiler.

Sound Effects provided courtesy of Dominion Entertainment, Inc.

Photo Credits:
© Archive Photos/Edwin Levick/PNI
© Culver Pictures/PNI
© Hulton Deutsch/PNI
© Magnum/Chris Steele-Perkins/PNI

LSAT is a registered trademark of the Law School Admission Council, which does not endorse or sponsor this product.

Minimum System Requirements

Operating System:	Windows® 98, 98SE, NT 4.0, 2000, ME, XP
CPU Type and Speed:	Pentium® 266 MHz
Hard Drive Space:	15 MB
Memory:	8 MB
Graphics:	640 x 480 thousands of colors (millions recommended)
CD-ROM Speed:	4X or higher

Note: Internet connection required for the web features of the program

Software License/Disclaimer of Warranties

1. ACCEPTANCE. By using this compact disc you hereby accept the terms and provisions of this license and agree to be bound hereby.

2. OWNERSHIP. The software contained on this compact disc, all content, related documentation and fonts (collectively, the "Software") are all proprietary copyrighted materials owned by Kaplan, Inc. ("Kaplan") or its licensors.

3. LICENSE. You are granted a limited license to use the Software. This License allows you to use the Software on a single computer only. You may not copy, distribute, modify, network, rent, lease, loan or create derivative works based upon the Software in whole or in part. The Software is intended for personal usage only. Your rights to use the Software and this License shall terminate immediately without notice upon your failure to comply with any of the terms hereof.

4. ADDITIONAL RESTRICTIONS. The Software contains copyrighted material, trade secrets, and other proprietary material. In order to protect them, and except as permitted by applicable legislation, you may not decompile, reverse engineer, disassemble or otherwise reduce the Software to human-perceivable form.

5. LIMITED WARRANTY; DISCLAIMER. Kaplan warrants the compact disc on which the Software is recorded to be free from defects in materials and workmanship under normal use for a period of ninety (90) days from the date of purchase as evidenced by a copy of the receipt. Kaplan's entire liability and your exclusive remedy will be replacement of the diskette or compact disc not meeting this warranty. The Software is provided "AS IS" and without warranty of any kind, and Kaplan and Kaplan's licensors EXPRESSLY DISCLAIM ALL WARRANTIES, EXPRESS OR IMPLIED, INCLUDING THE IMPLIED WARRANTIES OF MERCHANTABILITY OR FITNESS FOR A PARTICULAR PURPOSE. FURTHERMORE, KAPLAN DOES NOT WARRANT THAT THE FUNCTIONS CONTAINED IN THE SOFTWARE WILL MEET YOUR REQUIREMENTS, OR THAT THE OPERATION OF THE SOFTWARE WILL BE UNINTERRUPTED OR ERROR-FREE, OR THAT DEFECTS IN THE SOFTWARE WILL BE CORRECTED. KAPLAN DOES NOT WARRANT OR MAKE ANY REPRESENTATIONS REGARDING THE USE OR THE RESULTS OF THE USE OF THE SOFTWARE IN TERMS OF THEIR CORRECTNESS, ACCURACY, RELIABILITY OR OTHERWISE. UNDER NO CIRCUMSTANCES, INCLUDING NEGLIGENCE, SHALL KAPLAN BE LIABLE FOR ANY DIRECT, INDIRECT, PUNITIVE, INCIDENTAL, SPECIAL OR CONSEQUENTIAL DAMAGES, INCLUDING, BUT NOT LIMITED TO, LOST PROFITS OR WAGES, IN CONNECTION WITH THE SOFTWARE EVEN IF KAPLAN HAS BEEN ADVISED OF THE POSSIBILITY OF SUCH DAMAGES. CERTAIN LIMITATIONS HEREIN PROVIDED MAY BE PRECLUDED BY LAW.

6. EXPORT LAW ASSURANCES. You agree and certify that you will not export the Software outside of the United States except as authorized and as permitted by the laws and regulations of the United States. If the Software has been rightfully obtained by you outside of the United States, you agree that you will not re-export the Software except as permitted by the laws and regulations of the United States and the laws and regulations of the jurisdiction in which you obtained the Software.

7. MISCELLANEOUS. This license represents the entire understanding of the parties, may only be modified in writing and shall be governed by the laws of the State of New York.

KAPLAN